CORPORATE FINANCE

Theory & Practice

For Dash and Dino
(who waited impatiently for their walk)

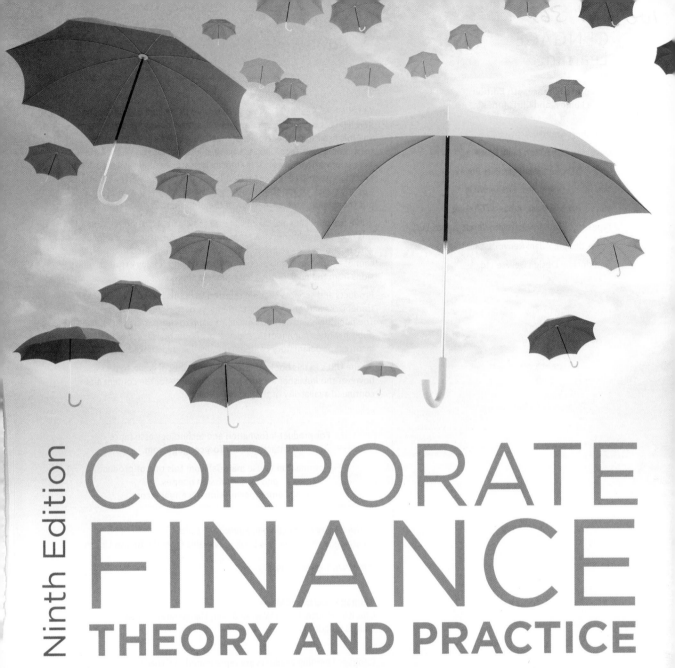

CORPORATE FINANCE
THEORY AND PRACTICE

Ninth Edition

Steve Lumby
Chris Jones

CENGAGE
Learning®

Australia • Brazil • Mexico • Singapore • United Kingdom • United States

CENGAGE
Learning·

Corporate Finance, 9th Edition
Steve Lumby, and Chris Jones

Publisher: Andrew Ashwin

Development Editor: Felix Rowe

Content Project Manager: Sue Povey

Manufacturing Buyer: Elaine Willis

Marketing Manager: Amanda Cheung

Typesetter: Integra Software Services Pvt. Ltd.

Cover design: Adam Renvoize Creative

Text design: Design Deluxe Ltd

For product information and technology assistance,
contact **emea.info@cengage.com.**

For permission to use material from this text or product,
and for permission queries,
email **emea.permissions@cengage.com.**

British Library Cataloguing-in-Publication Data
A catalogue record for this book is available from the British Library.

ISBN: 978-1-4080-7989-8

Cengage Learning EMEA
Cheriton House, North Way, Andover, Hampshire, SP10 5BE
United Kingdom

Cengage Learning products are represented in Canada by Nelson Education, Ltd.

For your lifelong learning solutions, visit
www.cengage.co.uk

Purchase your next print book, e-book or e-chapter at
www.cengagebrain.com

Printed in China by RR Donnelley
Print Number 01 Print Year 2015

BRIEF CONTENTS

PART
4

PART 4: FINANCING DECISIONS

PART
5

PART 5: INTERNATIONAL ISSUES

CONTENTS

PART		
2	**INVESTMENT DECISIONS**	27

ABOUT THE AUTHORS

Steve Lumby has been involved with teaching corporate finance over many years, in both universities and business schools. He is a former Managing Director of the LCA Business School. After 5 years in industry with the H.J. Heinz Company, he spent several years lecturing and researching in corporate finance at the London School of Economics. He has also held teaching posts at both King's College (University of London) and at Brunel University, and was a specialist advisor on finance to the Parliamentary Select Committee on Energy. He currently teaches a course in financial management at University College, London and also lectures in several international locations, on an executive MBA course for the London School of Commerce.

Chris Jones has lectured in accounting and finance for over 30 years since leaving Arthur Young, and recently retired from his position as Principal Lecturer in Accounting and Finance at Sheffield Hallam University.

PREFACE

There is a popular feeling that 'theory' is opposed to practice and the merits lie with 'practice'. This is a false conclusion, based on a false supposition. If practice has long been successful and does not conform to theory, the theory is bad and in need of revision.... The distinction should not be between theory and practice; it should be between good theory and bad theory, between good practice and bad practice.... Practice is brick; theory is mortar. Both are essential and both must be good if we are to erect a worthy structure.

D. PAARLBERG, GREAT MYTHS OF ECONOMICS

The description in plain language will be a criterion of the degree of understanding that has been reached.

W. HEISENBERG, PHYSICS AND PHILOSOPHY

This book takes these two quotations as its starting point. Its subject matter covers some of the financial decisions that face companies: investment, financing, the dividend decision and the management of risk. These are areas of vital importance to companies because they represent the main ways by which firms can enhance the worth of the owners. This importance is reflected in the fact that corporate finance is a standard element of most undergraduate and post graduate degree courses that are concerned with business and management, as well as being a prominent element in professional accountancy examinations.

It is with all these groups of people in mind that this book has been written. However, it is hoped that practising financial managers will also find its contents of interest, in that it may help to provoke thoughtful reflection on how financial decisions should be and are actually made.

The book's origins lie in the courses taught at various universities and business schools around the world at both undergraduate and postgraduate level and in the courses taught to students studying for professional accountancy qualifications. In many ways this is not *our* book but our *students'* book. Their searching questions have often prompted us to think through the subject matter in greater depth and to seek out alternative ways of providing clear and full explanations of the subject matter. This is not an easy book, but patience and application will be richly rewarded with understanding.

This new edition has been fully updated and a number of amendments, revisions and deletions have been made. The purpose of these changes has been to re-focus the contents to be more in line with the original objective of the book, which was to provide a clear, simple and highly structured analysis of the key elements of corporate finance theory.

It is all too easy for authors to lose sight of just how difficult some topics can be to the new reader. Familiarity, if not exactly breeding contempt, can sometimes lead to an over-concise exposition of the subject being discussed. Hopefully this pitfall has been avoided, so that the changes made further enhances the book's clarity of presentation of, what is, quite challenging subject matter.

The purpose of the Learning Objectives is to provide the reader with a 'road map' of what is to come in each chapter; while the summaries are designed to give an overview of the key areas that have been discussed in each chapter and to provide a snapshot of the main points. The suggested further reading has been compiled with particular emphasis on providing articles that are, in the main, accessible to those readers who do not possess a higher degree in mathematics! The quiz questions are to test both recall and understanding and to give the reader essential feedback – the quiz answers are tucked away at the back of the book, in order to reduce the temptation to cheat! Finally, the end-of-chapter exam-style questions have been selected to try and cover the major elements of each chapter's subject matter. The answers to many of these questions are available to students on the accompanying online platform. However, some are only available to course lecturers.

'Real World Views' feature boxes have also been introduced and these are interspersed throughout the text to help put theories and concepts into context, to present differing views from economies around the world and to invoke group debate.

As before, it should be made clear that this is not a 'how-to-do-it' book of corporate financial management. Such a book is not really a possibility in the complex, practical and ever-changing area of corporate finance. Instead, it is an attempt at a fairly detailed, reasoned discussion of the *normative* theory of corporate finance. Where examples have used real-world data, they are there for the purposes of exposition, rather than to encourage unthinking application of the theory to practical decision-making. It is not the aim to put forward theoretical solutions to practical problems, but to promote thought and reflection on how decisions are actually made and, perhaps, how they can be improved.

As far as possible, the presentation has been argued in descriptive and graphical terms rather than using a strict mathematical analysis. The reasons for this are two-fold. First, a mathematical treatment often excludes a great many potential enquirers and reduces the subject matter to a degree of terseness that makes unrealistic demands upon the concentration of the reader. Second, a mathematical treatment, although often rather elegant, can sometimes fail to make clear the full significance of important conclusions. However, it has been impossible to exclude mathematics completely – indeed it would have been counterproductive to do so in some areas – but its complexity has been kept to an absolute minimum. The derivation of formulae and relationships just for the sake of it has been resisted and only occurs where the mathematical derivation leads to a greater understanding for the reader.

All that remains is to thank the people at Cengage Learning, in particular Annabel Ainscow as Commissioning Editor, Felix Rowe, the Development Editor, and Sue Povey, the Project Editor for all their help, understanding and general prodding to get the new edition finished and onto the bookshelves. Most of all our thanks go to our students who make writing and teaching so enjoyable!

Steve Lumby
Chris Jones
2015

PUBLISHER'S ACKNOWLEDGEMENTS

The publisher would like to thank the following reviewers for their invaluable feedback in developing this new edition:

- Aaron Toogood, Leicester Business School, De Montfort University (UK)
- Per Bjarte Solibakke, Molde University College (Norway)

In addition, we wish to thank Dr Carl-Gustaf Malmström (Professor of Finance at SBS Swiss Business School) for his advice and assistance in sourcing ideas and composing the *Real World View* features, which have been written specifically for this edition.

WALK-THROUGH TOUR

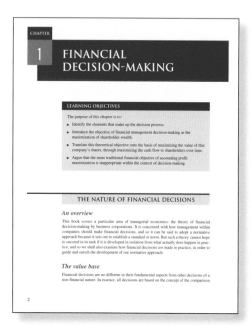

Learning Objectives – Listed at the start of each chapter, these provide the reader with a 'road map' of what is to come in each chapter.

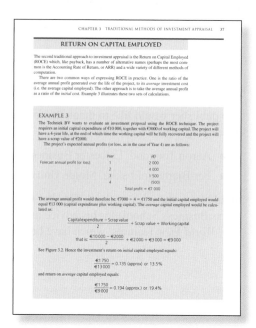

Examples and Scenarios – Examples and scenarios are dispersed throughout the text to illustrate practical application.

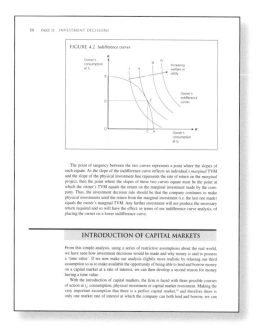

Numbered Figures and Tables – Clearly set out on the page, to aid the reader with quick conceptualization.

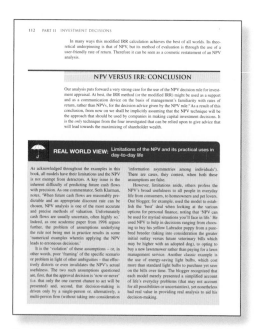

Real World Views – Boxes throughout help to provide context of application in practice and relevant developments in the real world.

Summary – The end of each chapter has a summary designed to give an overview of the key areas that have been discussed, and to provide a snapshot of the main points.

Appendix – Some chapters have an appendix, containing additional useful information.

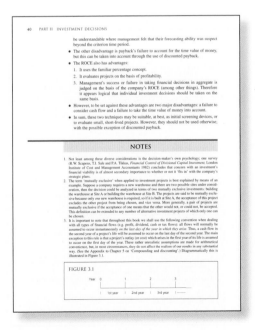

Notes – Useful end-of-chapter notes provide helpful additional information and clarification.

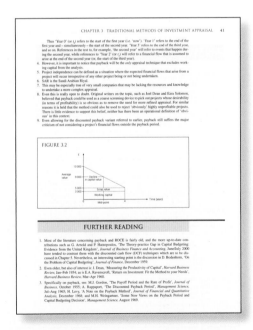

Further Reading – Provide helpful directions to further sources of information, compiled with particular emphasis on providing articles that are, in the main, accessible to those readers who do not possess a higher degree in mathematics.

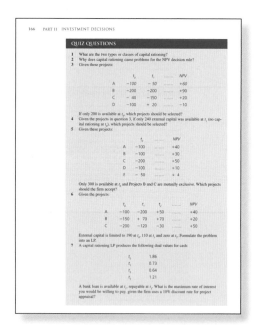

Quiz Questions – Included at the end of every chapter, these test both recall and understanding and give the reader essential feedback.

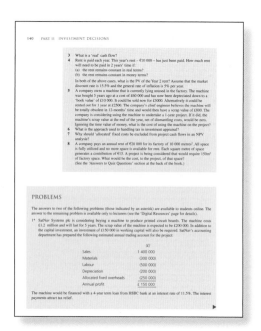

Problems – Exam-style questions which cover the major elements of each chapter's subject matter – some answers are included on the students' online platform, whilst others go on the lecturers' side only.

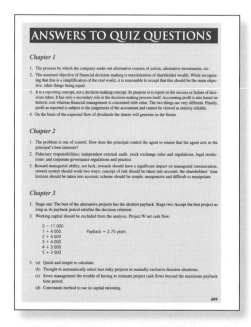

Answers to Quiz Questions – Helpfully provided at the back of the book to enable students to easily test themselves.

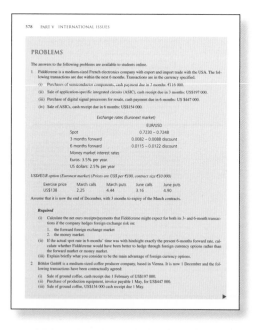

Answers to Problems – The majority of answers to the exam question-style problems are available to students online, though some lecturer-only answers are on the lecturers' password protected website.

INTRODUCTION

1. **Financial decision-making**

2. **Decision objectives**

FINANCIAL DECISION-MAKING

THE NATURE OF FINANCIAL DECISIONS

An overview

This book covers a particular area of managerial economics: the theory of financial decision-making by business corporations. It is concerned with how management within companies should make financial decisions, and so it can be said to adopt a normative approach because it sets out to establish a standard or norm. But such a theory cannot hope to succeed in its task if it is developed in isolation from what actually does happen in practice, and so we shall also examine how financial decisions *are* made in practice, in order to guide and enrich the development of our normative approach.

The value base

Financial decisions are no different in their fundamental aspects from other decisions of a non-financial nature. In essence, all decisions are based on the concept of the comparison of alternatives, and it is in this sense that the theory of financial decisions really has its roots in valuation theory, because all the alternatives in any decision-making situation have to be valued in order to be compared. Therefore, although we can say that all types of decisions involve the same fundamental process, each is given its own unique characteristics by the valuation base that it employs.

The financial decision theory developed in this book is founded on the valuation bases that come from the idea of a competitive market economy. However, many parts of our financial theory will be applicable to other types of economic organization, and you may wish to consider and reflect upon the implications of our theory for more social value bases, such as those that might be appropriate to the public sector.

The 'model' approach and the structure of the text

This book is structured in five parts:

1. Introduction to the context of financial decisions – Chapters 1 and 2.
2. The capital investment decision – Chapters 3 to 8.
3. The impact of uncertainty on financial decisions – Chapters 9 to 14.
4. Financing decisions – Chapters 15 to 21.
5. Financial decisions in an international context – Chapters 22 to 24.

In the course of our development of a normative approach to financial decisions, a considerable number of abstractions from and simplifications of the 'real world' will be made, in order to distil the difficulties and focus attention on areas of major importance.

Adopting this type of 'modelling' approach is normal in the study of economics and related areas. However it brings with it a danger that it is seen as fully describing a 'real' world and providing simple solutions to real-world problems. It is important to remember that we are developing a normative theory and are therefore attempting to give advice on how financial decisions *should* be taken. In general we will work with simplified models and if the theory were to be followed in practice, without recognizing the full range of possible complicating factors, the quality of financial decisions made in business might deteriorate rather than improve.

The difficulties caused by taxation, inflation and capital scarcity will all be taken into account, as will the concept of risk and the fact that the future is uncertain. These real-world complexities will be added layer by layer to the simplified model with which we start. Even though that model might be a poor reflection of the real world, it provides a logically sound framework upon which to build.

A warning

As a final point, the reader should be constantly aware that the theory of financial decisions presented here is neither in a state of general detailed agreement, nor does it yet provide complete solutions to many of the important problems of financial decision-making. In order to reflect this state of affairs, we shall examine the causes and evidence of these controversies and point out the irrationalities, ambiguities and inconsistencies that necessarily accompany the development of any theory that aspires to real-world application.

THE DECISION PROCESS

In order to examine the decision process and to answer the question, 'How do we make a decision?', we have first to discuss the circumstances in which a decision needs to be made. We can specify two necessary conditions for a decision situation: the existence of alternatives and the existence of an objective or goal.

The first necessary condition

The existence of alternatives is necessary because, if there are no alternatives from which to choose, then there is no need for a decision. This condition can be specified further in that not only must alternatives exist, but they must be seen to exist by the potential decision-maker. There are two points of interest here.

First, notice that we talk of a decision *situation* and of a *potential* decision-maker. This is because the mere existence of perceived alternatives does not necessarily mean that a decision will be made. For instance, the potential decision-maker may well procrastinate, and therefore the passage of time takes him (or her) out of a decision situation and into a situation where there is only one possible course of action and no alternatives are available. (Death is the ultimate example of the passage of time removing a decision situation from an individual.)

The second point of interest is that we are *not* specifying that all possible alternatives are perceived; if they were, we could call this an optimal decision situation. We are, rather, examining how decisions are made, given that a particular decision situation exists. Whether the decision is truly optimal or non-optimal is of no concern at present.

The second necessary condition

The second necessary condition for a decision situation arises from the fact that the actual process of 'making a decision' is liable to cause the decision-maker to expend both time and effort. Rationally decision-makers will be unwilling to do so unless they expect that some of the perceived alternatives will be preferred to others in relation to attaining the desired objective. Thus, the existence of an objective is the second necessary condition: without it, there will be no purpose in making a decision.[1]

Valuation of alternatives

Together, these two necessary conditions provide the rationale for making decisions: if the decision-maker does not perceive alternatives, or sees no reason to choose between the alternatives if they are perceived, then no decision will be made (except one of a totally arbitrary kind, as in note 1). But once these conditions do exist, a decision cannot actually be made until values are placed upon the alternatives. In fact, we can assert that the only reason why any alternative course of action is ever evaluated is in order to make a decision about it; therefore, the valuation method used must be related to the objective involved in making the decision and the way in which that objective is expressed.

For example, if our objective were to drive from A to B in the shortest possible time, then we should value the alternative routes from A to B by a common value criterion that was related to our objective of time, and choose whichever route took the shortest time.

Suppose there were three alternative routes: one we valued by time, one by distance and one by scenic beauty. We obviously could not make a decision because the alternatives have different measures or yardsticks of value and so cannot be compared. Alternatively, if all three routes were measured in terms of scenic beauty, we should again be unable to make a decision, even though we could compare the routes, because the basis of the comparison is not the one that gives the rationale for the decision: the value base of the objective, which in this example is 'time'.[2]

Therefore, any decision-making process consists of these three components: a series of perceived alternatives, an expectation that these alternatives are not all equally desirable in terms of attaining an objective held by the decision-maker, and a common value base related to the decision objective. So it is with all financial decisions made in business.

FINANCIAL DECISION-MAKING

This book focuses attention on only two of the three components that we have identified in the decision process and examines how they relate to the making of financial decisions: the expectation that the perceived alternatives are not all equally desirable in terms of attaining a specific objective, and the common value base that is related to this objective and is used to compare the alternatives.

The remaining component of the decision process is the series of perceived alternatives. We shall not be examining it in the main body of the text as it is primarily a condition for the decision *situation*, and we are concentrating on the actual decision-making, assuming that the decision situation already exists. However, this omission does not mean that the 'search process' (as it is called) for alternatives is unimportant. It is in fact extremely important. If this search process is not efficient in seeking out alternatives, then there is a grave danger that the decision itself will not be optimal because the 'most preferred' alternative may go unperceived.

The decision objective

Turning to the two decision process components that we shall examine in detail, we immediately become involved in a value judgement, because the objective we use for financial decision-making, and the consequent value base, will determine the decision reached as to which alternative is selected. Therefore, what objective are we going to use and what valuation base are we going to set up for our theory of financial decisions?

We stated earlier that the fundamental value judgement upon which our approach is based on is the concept of a market economy. In such economies, it is reasonable to assume that companies exist for one overriding purpose: in order to benefit their owners.[3] While companies provide income for their employees and the wider local community, supply the needs of a particular market, and provide other benefits such as technological advance, the fact remains that the fundamental rationale for their existence must be to bring benefit to their owners.

This rationale for existence undoubtedly holds true for the great majority of privately owned companies and so management's objective in making financial decisions should be to further the very reason for the company's existence, of benefiting the owners, i.e. the shareholders. We shall see that there might be other managerial objectives but, in essence, we will treat those as deviating from what they should be (this is consistent with the idea of adopting a normative approach). So if the decision objective is to benefit the owners, what is the value base to be used for the comparison of alternatives?

To answer this question, we have to examine the decision objective more closely. It is obvious from what we have already said that not only should company managements make financial decisions so as to benefit the shareholders but they should also strive to maximize that benefit, otherwise shareholders will be interested in replacing them with a set of decision-makers who will do this. Therefore, what is meant by the term 'maximizing owners' or shareholders' benefit'?

Maximizing shareholder wealth

We are going to assume that maximizing benefit means maximizing wealth. Although there is nothing surprising about this, we have to be careful here because we are going to assume that maximizing the increase in the owners' wealth is the *only* way in which management decisions can benefit owners.

This is a slight simplification of the real world, because it is quite possible for shareholders to gain benefit from a company other than by increases in wealth. For example, shareholders of a company such as the UK property development company, Land Securities plc, may gain benefit from ownership in terms of pride in the fact that the company has a proactive stance towards protecting the environment for which it has won awards. This is also reflected in various ethical mutual funds, which emphasize the ethical, rather than wealth-generating, properties of their investments.. However, despite the growing interest in environmental issues, we shall proceed on the assumption that increase in wealth is the main, if not the sole source of benefit from company ownership.

Should we be concerned about companies selling military arms to countries that have repugnant policies, or firms causing pollution to land, air or water resources? Do these types of activity enter into consideration of our decision objective? On the basis of our underlying assumption about the nature of the economy, our answer must be that they should not, because if these activities were thought to be truly undesirable, governments would legislate or regulate to constrain companies' decision-choice alternatives so as to exclude them (as in many cases they do). Company decision-makers should only need to perceive and analyze the decision alternatives in terms of maximizing the owners' wealth. From this viewpoint we can treat financial decisions as not being anything to do with morality. Morality, the law and other things might act as constraints on what a company does but they are entirely different issues and are generally assessed using different criteria.

In market economies, we can develop a theory of financial decisions for privately owned firms in this way because of the workings of the market system for company capital. Share capital, the substance of ownership, is normally provided through supply and demand markets (e.g. stock exchanges), which means that potential shareholders can buy shares in companies that they expect will provide them with the greatest possible increase in wealth (i.e. shareholders have to make financial decisions in much the same way as management, choosing between alternative ownership opportunities), and existing shareholders can sell their shares if they see other companies providing greater increases to their owners' wealth than they are receiving. (An important concept here, and one we have yet to deal with, is that the future is uncertain and so any decision amongst alternatives usually has a risk attached to it: the risk that the alternative chosen may not turn out as expected. Some alternatives are riskier than others and so shareholders will really want to own companies that they expect will give them the greatest possible increase in wealth, for a given level of risk. This concept will be considered much more fully later.) Therefore, if a company were to make its decisions on a basis other than that of maximizing shareholder wealth, the whole rationale for the company's existence – so far as shareholders are concerned – would be in doubt and they would be likely to take their investment funds elsewhere. In the extreme case, company law provides the opportunity for shareholders to replace a company's decision-makers if enough of them believe that decisions are not being taken in their best interests.

REAL WORLD VIEW: The Rise of Shareholder Revolts

Shareholder 'revolts' have become much more common in recent years, particularly when there is a feeling that the senior managers are rewarding themselves too generously, at the expense of shareholders. But shareholders also revolt over what they see as poor management decisions that are likely to lead to a reduction in share values. Examples of such actions include:

Exxon – the world's largest oil company – faced a significant shareholder revolt in 2008 over the company's reluctance to invest in 'green' energy technologies which many shareholders thought would prove to be a bad business decision and allow rival companies to gain a competitive advantage.

Inmarsat – the satellite company – was the subject of one of the biggest shareholder revolts of 2013 when over one-third of shareholders voted against the proposed salary and remuneration package for its chairman for the second consecutive year, as well as voting against the proposed remuneration package for the chief executive, following an 11% fall in revenues. However, the vote was not so large as to be able to overturn the remuneration proposals.

GSW Immobilien is a German property investment fund. Both its executive chairman and the chairman of its supervisory board resigned in June 2013 following shareholder pressure and a 'no confidence vote' by around two-thirds of shareholders. The point at issue was that both directors had been involved in another property company which had run into severe difficulties and shareholders feared the same thing might happen to GSW with these two people in control. Following the resignations, the GSW share price rose by 5%.

Both Apple and Microsoft have also been subject to significant amounts of shareholder action, with investors being unhappy about the way each company was being run and the subsequent impact on share values.

At Glencore Xstrata, the giant international mining firm, several directors lost their positions in 2013 following an 80% vote by shareholders over what were seen as financially excessive 'executive retention packages' following on from the recent merger of the two companies.

Another oil and gas company with strong interests in Russia and the Ukraine – JKX Oil and Gas – faced a shareholder revolt in June 2013 concerning the re-election of its CEO, who was accused of 'poor management' that had resulted in an 88% decrease in the share price over the previous 5 years. However, this was seen as an attempt by two large investors to gain greater control of the company and the subsequent vote backed the incumbent CEO.

As a final example, of many possible examples, there is the US Hess Corporation – a company which is involved in both the retail petroleum market and oil exploration. A group of unhappy shareholders attempted to change the direction of the company's management, saying: 'Hess needs to be run for the 90% of shareholders who hold Hess stock for economic returns, rather than the 10% who want to head a global dynasty.'

Defining wealth

However, we still cannot determine the value base for financial decision-making until we have defined 'wealth', because the purpose of the value base is to act as a common denominator with which to make the alternative courses of action directly comparable and to see which one leads furthest towards the decision objective. As the objective of financial decisions is assumed to be to 'maximize the increase in owners' wealth', let us define 'wealth' and so determine the value base.

Wealth can be defined as the capacity to consume, or, to put it in more straightforward terms, money or cash.[4] Thus, the objective of management becomes the maximization of shareholders' purchasing power, which can be achieved by maximizing the amount of cash paid out to shareholders in the form of dividends. But which dividends should a company's management try to maximize: this year's, next year's or what?

The point here is that it would be a relatively easy task for a company to maximize a single year's dividend, simply by selling up all the assets and paying a final liquidation dividend! Obviously this is not what is meant by our decision objective of maximizing dividends, and the trouble arises through the omission of the time dimension. When fully defined, including the time dimension, the objective of a company's financial decision-makers becomes the maximizing of the *flow* of dividends to shareholders *over or through time.*

The role of accounting profit

There are two points of fundamental importance that arise from the development of this decision objective. First, the word 'profit' has not been mentioned and the emphasis has been laid on wealth defined as cash. Second, the introduction of time means that decisions must be analyzed not only in terms of immediate cash gains and losses, but also in terms of *future* gains and losses.

These two points are interlinked. Profit, when used in a business sense, is a concept developed by financial accountants in order to assist them with their reporting functions, performed on behalf of shareholders.

Accounting has developed over hundreds of years from a base called 'stewardship'. It was really designed to provide evidence that people holding responsibility for other people's assets could account for them (i.e. demonstrate where the resources went). In many ways this still lies at the heart of financial accounting. Although financial reports are produced each year and contain the figure 'profit' it should not be interpreted as being the same thing as the increase in the value of the company during the year. Annual financial reports are produced using a number of conventions and rules, the most important of which is that the figures are expressed in terms of historic cost (with one or two possible exceptions). There is also a certain amount of judgement exercised in the production of the statement and it has been said that profit is 'the invention rather than the discovery' of the accountant. The International Accounting Standards Board (IASB), the European body that defines many of the rules used by accountants within Europe and beyond, has expressed the view that accounting should not be seen as being concerned with value or worth apart from very specific circumstances. As we will see, wealth, worth and value are all concepts related to the future (and cash flows in the future) but accounting profit is related to the past.

Financial decisions are basically economic or resource allocation decisions. Management have to decide whether they should allocate the firm's scarce resources (land, labour, machinery, etc.) to a particular project. The economic 'unit of account' is cash, not accounting profit, because it is cash which gives power to command resources (i.e. resources are purchased with cash, not profit). Thus, to use the accounting profit concept in financial decision-making would be to use an entirely inappropriate concept – a concept specially developed for reporting the outcome of decisions and not developed for helping to take the actual decision itself.

However, we cannot discard the accounting profit concept completely. To do so would be rather like a sports team whose policy is that they do not mind whether they win or lose, so long as in playing they give maximum entertainment to their supporters. This is fine, and it is probably the correct attitude, but often it is on the winning or losing that the success of the team is ultimately judged and therefore that part of the game cannot be ignored. So it is with accounting profit. The company's financial decision-makers should have as their major concern the maximization of the flow of cash through time to the shareholders, but they should always do so with an eye to reported profit. Profitability, as expressed in annual financial reports, forms a major criterion by which shareholders and prospective shareholders judge a company's success and, as we shall see later, it is important that people do form correct judgements about a company's performance.

Therefore, with the exception of this proviso, we can say that the financial decision theory developed here is built on an analytical framework that is largely devoid of the accounting profit concept, although it would be correct to assume that, in the longer run, good company cash flows will result in good reported profits.

The time dimension

Turning to the second point of importance in our decision objective, we have to return to our discussion on value.

An asset (such as a machine or a share in a company) is valued on the basis of the gains, or losses, that the owner receives. Furthermore, these gains and losses do not refer to just a single time period, but to the whole period of future time for which the asset will exist. (This concept is sometimes referred to as the asset's earning power.)

Let us consider an asset of company ownership: a single share. Shares are traded (i.e. bought and sold) in supply and demand markets (stock markets), and so a share's market valuation represents an equilibrium value, a value at which demand for the share by people who wish to buy it equates with the supply of the share by people who wish to sell it. But what process actually gives a share its equilibrium price, what makes prospective purchasers wish to buy it at that price and what makes prospective sellers willing to sell it at that price? Let us examine the prospective purchaser's reasons.

Suppose a share of Jeddah Company has a stock market price of €25. Prospective owners of that share would only be willing to buy it if they thought it was worth €25. In other words, they would expect that the gains to be received from ownership would have a value of at least €25.

These gains of ownership consist of two elements: the stream of dividends received for as long as the share is owned, and the selling price received when the share is sold (and so ownership relinquished) at some future point in time. However, it is important to note that this future selling price of the Jeddah share is itself based on the value the succeeding owner in turn puts on the benefits expected to be received from ownership – the dividend flow received and the selling price that will be received upon selling the share at some future point in time. So the process goes on ad infinitum. Therefore, although there are two benefits of ownership, the dividends received and the future selling price, this latter benefit is itself determined by the flow of dividends expected to be generated by the share subsequent to its sale.

Given this argument, our theory will assume that shares derive their stock market price on the basis of the sum of the future dividend flow that they will produce through time. (As the future is uncertain, it is more correct to talk of valuation based on the *expected* dividend flow, but we shall return to this later.) Thus, the greater the future dividend flow, the more highly are the shares valued. Therefore, if our financial decision-makers are taking decisions so as to maximize dividend flow through time, then, via the direct link between dividend flow and a share's market price, this action will result in the *maximization of the market value of the company's shares*. It is this that we shall take as being the operational objective of financial management decision-making.[5]

The objective hierarchy

So let us summarize our assumed hierarchy of decision objectives:

1. Decisions are taken by companies so as to maximize owners' wealth.
2. Owners' wealth can be maximized through maximizing owners' purchasing power.
3. Purchasing power can be maximized through maximizing the amount of cash the company pays out to shareholders in the form of dividends.
4. With the introduction of the time dimension the objective becomes the maximizing of the value of the dividend flow through time to the shareholders.
5. The maximization of the value of the dividend flow through time maximizes the stock market's valuation of the company's share capital.

However, it is important to realize that although it is this 'fifth level' of objective we shall use in developing the theory of financial decision-making, it is really only a surrogate objective for the fundamental, underlying objective of maximizing shareholders' wealth.

A fundamental assumption

As a final point, let us state the assumptions about the shareholder that have been implied in the analysis. It was earlier argued that the maximization of shareholders' wealth had to be the fundamental decision objective, because of the nature of the capital markets. However, the validity of this assertion depends entirely upon the assumption that shareholders perceive wealth in the way we have postulated and that in this perception they are rational. In essence this means that we have assumed that shareholders see wealth as the receipt of cash flows through time and that they will always prefer a greater to a lesser cash flow. These appear reasonably safe assumptions, but we shall consider situations where they may not hold when we look later at dividend policies.

SUMMARY

The decision process consists of three elements:

1. A series of perceived alternatives.
2. An expectation that these alternatives are not all equally desirable in terms of attaining an objective held by the decision-maker.
3. A common value base, related to the objective, by which the alternatives may be compared.

   - As far as financial management is concerned, it is assumed that the objective of financial management decision-making is the maximization of shareholder wealth. This is normally translated to mean maximizing the current worth of the company's shares.

- Given that shareholder wealth is seen in terms of an ability to consume goods and services and that it is cash that provides consumption power, so share value can be maximized by maximizing the sum of the expected stream of dividends through time generated by the share.

- Accounting profit is essentially an inappropriate concept within the context of financial management decision-making because it is a *reporting* device, not a decision-making device. Finance decisions are economic or resource allocation decisions and the economic unit of account is cash; hence decisions are evaluated in terms of their cash flow impact. However, the reported profit impact of financial decisions remains an important consideration in terms of the correct communication of management's actions to shareholders and others.

NOTES

1. In a way, in specifying this second necessary condition, we are ignoring the situation where a decision *has* to be made, even though this second condition does not exist. For instance, if you are out for a walk with no particular destination in mind and you come to a crossroads, a decision *has* to be taken on which direction to take, even though the second necessary condition is really unfulfilled. Such situations are of little interest as far as the decision *process* is concerned; we could call them indifference decisions.
2. For the present, we shall ignore the possibility of multiple objectives, although we shall touch upon it later. However we may observe that, where multiple objectives exist in real life, one objective is often regarded (either implicitly or explicitly) as being of overriding importance, with the other objectives acting as constraining factors or considerations.
3. In abstract terms we can define a company as a collection of assets. The owners of the company have therefore pooled their funds to assemble such a collection and are logically only likely to do so in order to bring benefit (either directly or indirectly) to themselves.
4. We shall be ignoring the effects of inflation until later.
5. Of course, if the company's shares are not quoted on a stock exchange, then the objective simply reduces to the maximization of the value of the company's shares. This, however, still leaves the problem of how the shares are to be valued. In fact they should be valued on exactly the same basis as quoted shares: the future expected dividend flow. It is one of the great advantages of a stock market quotation that this value is 'automatically' and continuously provided for use both by management and by investors.

QUIZ QUESTIONS

1   What is the search process?
2   What is the fundamental objective of financial management decision-making?
3   Why is accounting profit an inappropriate criterion for financial decision-making?
4   On what basis are company shares valued?
    (See the 'Answers to the Quiz Questions' section at the back of the book.)

DECISION OBJECTIVES

The purpose of this chapter is to:

- Introduce the idea of principal–agent relationships where the principal is represented by the owners of the firm (the shareholders), and the management team are their agents.

- Highlight that the key problem in such relationships is control: how can owners control the actions of managers to ensure that managers are acting in the shareholders' best interests?

- Demonstrate that the response to the problem has been the development of a range of management monitoring devices and incentive schemes.

- Explain that whilst shareholder wealth maximization is the theoretical objective of companies, in reality, the relationship between investors (the principals) and managers (the agents) often compromises this objective.

- Explain the responsibilities of managers and, more specifically, directors, and the various mechanisms designed to ensure these are carried out appropriately.

WEALTH MAXIMIZATION AND THE COMPANY

In Chapter 1 we concluded that maximization of shareholder wealth (the maximization of the value of the company's shares) was a fundamental objective of financial decision-making. Therefore the company can be seen as a mechanism for transferring resources from the shareholder into 'real' investments (factories, equipment, machinery, etc.) and back again to the shareholder in the form of profits, or more correctly, cash. See Figure 2.1.

In one sense, the company only exists for the purpose of facilitating these cash flows and it is needed because the individual shareholder is not otherwise in a position to make the investment in large real investments, such as a factory. However, the company is not a passive vehicle in this transfer process because it contains decision-makers (managers) who have their own, personal, objectives, as well as that of maximizing shareholder wealth.

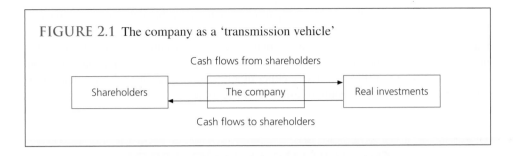

FIGURE 2.1 The company as a 'transmission vehicle'

In the situation where the shareholders are not the same people as the managers, this has the potential to result in conflicts of interests and may well mean that not all decisions are made in order to maximize shareholder wealth. In the chapters that follow we will generally be assuming that the techniques we develop are intended to maximize shareholder wealth. However, in this chapter we discuss how this potential 'conflict of interest' may be, to some extent, overcome.

Maximizing versus satisficing

A company's management (or, more strictly speaking, its directors) are in what is termed a 'principal–agent' relationship with the shareholders. The shareholders are the principals – the owners of the company's assets – and the managers are employed as their agents to manage those assets on their behalf.

As we have just been discussing, the major problem facing any principal (owner) is that of control: how to control the agent (manager) to ensure that the agent always acts in the best interests of the principal (and not simply in the best interests of the agent). The problem arises out of the fact that there may well be this conflict between the personal objectives of the agents and the objectives that their principal wishes them to pursue.

Shareholders will want their managers to take decisions so as to maximize the worth of the company's shares. However, management will have their own personal objectives. These objectives will be mainly concerned with three things: their pay (including bonuses and the value of share option schemes), their perks (non-monetary rewards such as holiday entitlements, working conditions, company cars, etc.) and their job security.[1] As we saw in Chapter 1, there are many examples of managers who appear to have rewarded themselves with over-generous remuneration packages. (Keep in mind that the money paid out to managers in excessive salaries is money taken away from the company's shareholders.)

In such circumstances, it is sometimes argued that managers will become shareholder wealth *satisficers* rather than maximizers. This implies that managers will do just enough to keep shareholders reasonably satisfied in terms of increasing their wealth and, at the same time, put their remaining efforts into the pursuit of their own personal objectives. Thus, a satisficing management may be thought more likely to pursue a specific target, which, if achieved, would be felt to be sufficient to keep shareholders satisfied, rather than to pursue a more general target of maximization. For example, management might pursue a target of increasing the value of the company's shares by, say, 10% per year, rather than having as their objective trying to achieve the maximum possible annual growth rate in the share price.

In addition, satisficing behaviour implies that the management team will not organize the search process for alternative courses of action so as to seek out the very best maximizing course of action. Instead, they will terminate the search process as soon as a satisfactory (but not necessarily the best) course of action is identified.

'Agency theory' postulates that principals respond to the problem they face in two ways. First, they develop monitoring devices to try to ensure that managers are attempting to maximize the company's share price. Second, they create incentive schemes for management so that it is in the manager's *own* best interest to pursue share price maximization. In practice it is very difficult to devise either monitoring or incentive schemes that can be relied upon to produce the required results for shareholders.

OWNERSHIP AND CONTROL

There are many ways in which the actions of a company's managers are monitored and controlled so as to try and ensure that they act in their shareholders' best interests rather than their own. However, before we briefly examine these it is important to make one clarifying observation. This is that a principal–agent problem only really arises when there is a significant divorce between ownership and control.

For example, in an owner-managed business there is no such problem whatsoever, as the owners are the managers, and so the objectives of one group are also the objectives of the other. If we move on to a larger, family-owned business, where the owners are not necessarily the managers, there is still likely to be very little problem. This is because, in these circumstances, the owners will still be able to exercise close *personal* control over their managers. Even though the shareholders may not be the managers, the shareholders in such a company are likely to know who the senior managers are, and are able to monitor their actions directly.

It is only when a company's development reaches the point where there is a clear-cut division between owners and managers – when the company is too large and the owners are too widespread for them to be able to exercise effective personal control – that the principal–agent problem of control starts to manifest itself. For many companies this point is reached when they decide to stop being a private company and instead become a public company, quoted on a stock exchange.

For the vast majority of private companies – especially, small private companies – the principal–agent problem does not exist in any meaningful sense. Thus, in discussing the problem, we must view it in relation to the larger company, and, in particular, to the stock exchange quoted company.

REGULATION OF THE RELATIONSHIP BETWEEN DIRECTORS AND SHAREHOLDERS

Within the UK, for example, we can identify seven main mechanisms by which the actions of directors are regulated and constrained, so that they act solely in their shareholders' interest, and not in their own; and similar constraints are found in all other developed economies, and in many developing economies as well. Thus, in the UK, directors' actions are regulated and constrained by:

1. The fiduciary responsibility that is imposed on directors by company law.
2. The legal requirement for an annual financial report and an independent external audit of the company.

3. The 'listing rules' of the Stock Exchange.

4. The Stock Exchange's 'Model Code' on directors' share dealings.

5. Company law regulations on directors' transactions.

6. The 'City Code' on takeovers and mergers.

7. The UK Corporate Governance Code.

Fiduciary responsibilities

A fiduciary responsibility arises whenever assets (either tangible or intangible) are entrusted by one party to the care of another party. Thus, it can be said that fiduciary responsibilities arise directly out of principal–agent relationships. In essence, the directors of companies have a fiduciary responsibility to their shareholders to act in their best interests. Furthermore, they must be prepared to demonstrate that they have discharged their responsibilities correctly if challenged to do so in the law courts.

The scope of these responsibilities is not clear-cut; nor are the responsibilities unchanging. However, they are underpinned by three basic principles that have the force of law behind them:

1. Directors should not place themselves in a position where their own personal interests conflict with the interests of shareholders.

2. They should not profit from their position at the expense of shareholders.

3. They cannot use information that is obtained in confidence from the company for their own benefit, or for the benefit of any other persons except the shareholders.

Annual reports and independent external audit

Another important element in the array of devices set up to monitor and control the actions of boards of directors is the annual audit requirement of the company's annual financial reports.

Legally, all limited companies (with the exception of very small companies) are required to have an annual audit of their financial affairs, conducted by independent, external auditors. The prime purpose of this audit is to report to the shareholders on the conduct of the management's stewardship of the company's assets by certifying that the financial statements prepared by the company can be relied upon and provide a 'true and fair' view of the position and performance of the company. As such, this independent external audit can be seen as the bedrock control mechanism of the principal–agent relationship between shareholders and their managers. Indeed, it is interesting to note that although such an audit is now a legal requirement, independent external audits existed long before they were enforced by law. The audit not only certifies the annual report of the company but also examines the company's financial systems to ensure that proper control is being exercised. There has been some discussion in the literature relating to the effectiveness of audit. Clearly users of financial reports feel more confident when the reports have been audited by reputable audit practices. However, there have been significant audit failures. Perhaps most notable of these, in terms of size and impact, were the audits of the financial accounts of Enron Corporation, WorldCom and Lehman Brothers – all US-based companies, but each with a global reach; and more recently there are the cases of the Sino-Forest Corporation in Canada and China, Olympus in Japan and Autonomy in the UK.

REAL WORLD VIEW: The Failure of External Auditors

The list of examples of where external auditors have seemingly failed to pick up (often massive) management wrongdoing is a long one and it does little to support the claim that the process of an independent external audit is an effective mechanism for safeguarding the interests of shareholders.

In the examples that follow, the senior management were not simply satisficing rather than maximizing; instead the senior management were manipulating the accounting data in a totally fraudulent manner – often to enhance their bonuses which were linked to the stock market price of their company's shares. Furthermore, when the true picture of their fraudulent actions did emerge – it was not through the external audit process, but through either an internal management 'whistleblower' or by the company subsequently running into financial difficulties.

Enron Corporation

There were two massive cases of management fraud in the early 2000s that went undetected by the external audit function, the first of which was Enron Corporation.

Enron was a US-based multinational that was primarily engaged in the wholesale energy market. It could trace its origins back to a corporate merger in the mid-1980s, and within 17 years became one of the largest and most powerful companies in the USA, with 21 000 employees and activities in over 40 countries around the world. By the end of 2000 Enron's share price was over $83 per share and it had a total market worth of $60 billion.

Enron's trouble can be put down to its excessive, rewards-based management culture, where managers were awarded large bonuses for achieving high levels of business growth. The senior management team, in particular, became fixated with meeting or exceeding stock market expectations about both revenue and profit growth. When, in the late 1990s, the business became unable to meet these expectations in reality, the management started to manipulate the accounting data to exaggerate revenues and profits

and to hide borrowings in order to present a picture of ongoing financial strength and vitality.

By 2000 there was some significant concern within the financial community about the complexity of the company's financial accounts – and hence a difficulty in truly understanding the story that they were telling; and this concern about the company's accounting practices continued to grow strongly throughout 2001, with the result that the share price began to fall rapidly as the market started to realize that the published financial statements did not tell the true story with regards to either the company's financial position or financial performance.

A senior Enron manager sent a letter to the chairman in August 2001, warning about the fraudulent nature of the company's accounting practices which, she claimed, could only lead to embroiling the company in an accounting scandal. The chairman contacted the external auditors to help to counter the whistleblower's criticism and the auditors' effective response was that not only did they approve the company's accounting practices, but there was nothing financially amiss. (It was later alleged that the huge size of the fees received by the external auditors from Enron – over $50 million in 2000 alone – compromised the integrity of the auditors' position and opinion.) By 2001 year-end Enron's share price had fallen from $83 to just $1 until finally, in early December 2001, Enron Corporate became the largest corporate bankruptcy in US history … and this eventually led to the collapse of the auditing firm and lengthy jail sentences for some of the key executives involved in the scandal.

WorldCom

The company started life in1983 and grew rapidly to become the largest long-distance telephone operator in the USA by 2000. However, from 1999 onwards, the company hit difficult business conditions and began using fraudulent accounting practices to inflate both revenues and profits in order to keep up the share price (and maintain management bonuses).

During the early part of 2002, a small team of the company's own *internal* auditors worked in secret to uncover $3.8 billion of fraudulent accounting transaction and informed the board of directors of their findings. This resulted in the company going into bankruptcy in July 2002. WorldCom became the new record holder for the largest ever US bankruptcy, and the resultant analysis showed that the company had exaggerated profits by $3.2 billion in 2000 alone and had fraudulently inflated the value of the company's assets by around $11 billion.

Where were the external auditors in all this? Unfortunately, WorldCom's external auditors were the same auditors as used by Enron's auditors, but although this question was asked by investigators, the auditors' response – that could not be disproven – was that WorldCom's senior financial controller had withheld vital information from them and they were not complicit in the fraud. Although the auditors were not specifically blamed for the company's demise, it represents yet another example of a failure of the external audit system to protect shareholders.

Lehman Brothers

Our third example occurred in 2008 and ultimately lead to the worldwide financial crisis which is, to some extent, still ongoing at the time of writing in 2014.

Lehman Brothers went bankrupt in September 2008 (and so gained the new record for the largest US corporate bankruptcy!). Before that they had been a very large and successful global financial services firm. They were the fourth-largest investment bank in the USA and in 2007 had recorded both record revenues and record profits. Their success was down to a very high level of risk-taking at a time when markets were booming. They had borrowed very large amounts of money and had become heavily involved in lending in the US 'sub-prime' housing mortgage market which consisted of dealings in very high risk or 'toxic' assets. When this market began to hit problems, the company started to find itself with an extreme level of risk exposure – not a good situation for a bank to be in – and in an attempt to disguise the seriousness of the situation, Lehman sold $50 billion of these high risk/toxic assets to 'friendly' banks in the Cayman Islands, on the understanding that Lehman would then buy them all back at a later date. As a result, they created the illusion in their financial accounts that they had $50 billion more cash and $50 billion less of toxic assets than was the reality: a clear case of accounting manipulation. The bankruptcy court-appointed investigator reported that the board of directors had issued misleading statements and had used financial 'gimmicks' (many similar to those used by Enron) to hide the truth. Furthermore, the investigator alleged that the external auditors knew of these potential accounting irregularities, but had failed to raise the issue with the directors. The bank's auditors were subsequently sued for assisting a massive accounting fraud, but this allegation went unproven in the courts. However, at the very least, the Lehman Brothers scandal is yet another example of large-scale accounting fraud that had gone undetected by the external auditors who are supposed to be one of the key components in the array of mechanisms designed to protect the interests of shareholders.

Stock exchange rules

The London Stock Exchange regulates the UK stock exchange in accordance with European Union directives. These regulations are contained in what is referred to as the 'Yellow Book', which stipulates that the directors of a quoted company have both an individual and a collective responsibility to ensure that the company complies with obligations under the regulations.

For the purposes of the current discussion, a key obligation of directors imposed by the Yellow Book rules is to release share price-sensitive information to the market as a whole so as to avoid a 'false market' in the valuation of a company's shares. The implications of this requirement, in terms of the principal–agent problem, is fairly obvious. If directors should fail to disclose information to the stock market, such that the share price is kept artificially high or low, then this could result in misleading investors into share buying and selling actions that would be damaging to their wealth. Shareholders might find themselves buying shares which, in reality, were overvalued; or they might sell their shares when they were undervalued.

Directors' transactions

Closely related to the foregoing is the London Stock Exchange's 'Model Code' on directors' share dealings and the Companies Act regulations on directors' transactions.

To buy or sell shares on the basis of information that has not been publicly disclosed is known as 'insider dealing' and is illegal. This ruling applies to directors as well as to all other potential investors. However, it causes particular problems for directors for they will, almost inevitably, be in possession of some price-sensitive information concerning the company which has not yet been disclosed to the stock market, but which would alter the market's valuation of the company's shares.

Therefore, at certain times (for example, just before the company announces its annual results), the directors may have information that indicates that the shares are currently being overvalued or undervalued by the stock market. If directors were allowed to deal in the shares at such times, it would clearly not be in the interests of their shareholders.

As a result, the London Stock Exchange specifically requires companies to stipulate a code of practice for their directors based on the exchange's own 'Model Code'. Although the provisions of the Code are quite lengthy, the principal elements are:

1. Directors must not deal in their company's shares on a short-term basis (i.e. buying and subsequently selling over a short period over time).
2. Directors are not allowed to deal in the shares of their company prior to the disclosure of regularly recurring information (such as the annual results), or an announcement of an exceptional nature (such as a takeover bid).

Company law also regulates transactions between directors and their companies and stipulates that if a director has either a direct or indirect interest in a proposed contract with the company (for example, a director may own an asset that he intends to sell to the company), then that interest must be declared at a board meeting, and there may also be a duty to disclose the information in the company's accounts and often will need the prior approval of shareholders.

The 'City Code' on takeovers and mergers

Although this is a specialized area, it is worth noting, within the context of the present discussion, that directors' actions are particularly constrained when the company is subject to a takeover bid.

It is easy to conceive of a situation in which a takeover bid for a company may be unwelcome to its directors – who might fear that they will lose their jobs and/or independence as a result – but which may be in the best interests of shareholders in that the price offered values the shares at a premium to their current market value. (Or, alternatively, the directors may wish the bid to succeed although it is not in the best interests of the shareholders.) Under such circumstances, the directors may be in a position to defeat the bid through the actions that they take. In such a situation, the directors are subject to a code of best practice, known as the City Code.

The City Code is based on a number of principles of best practice codified into a complex set of rules. Among these principles are a number that are of direct relevance to the current discussion:

1. All shareholders must be made the same offer.
2. Relevant information must be disclosed to all shareholders so as to allow them to make a properly informed decision.
3. All information supplied to shareholders must be prepared with the highest standards of care and accuracy.
4. The directors must take no action, without the consent of their shareholders, which is specifically designed to 'frustrate' (i.e. defeat) the bid.

In this way, the City Code ensures that at one of the most important times in a company's life – when it is subject to a takeover bid – its directors are required to act in their shareholders' best interests.

The UK Corporate Governance Code

A number of reports were undertaken in the UK in the 1990s following concerns about:

1. An increasing use of 'creative accounting'.
2. A number of high profile business failures.
3. High levels of pay for directors.
4. Short-termism (i.e. actions by managers driven by personal, short-term objectives such as bonuses rather than long-term shareholder value).

This resulted in what is now called the UK Corporate Governance Code, which was implemented in order to establish and regulate 'best practice' standards in corporate business. To ensure they adhere to this both appropriately and comprehensively, all public companies listed on the stock exchange must present a report detailing their practices in compliance with the Corporate Governance Code, or explain why, where and how the criteria have not been met. Regulated by the Financial Reporting Council, the UK Corporate Governance Code consists of Sections A–E, which in turn address: leadership, effectiveness, accountability, remuneration, and relations with shareholders.

Section A on *leadership* necessitates that every company quoted on the stock exchange must have an effective board in place, which assumes collective responsibility and is committed to driving the company's success in the long term. In emphasizing this collective responsibility, the Code also demands that decision-making should be dispersed among all on the board, with responsibilities clearly divided and defined, without bestowing unchecked powers on any one individual.

Section B addresses *effectiveness*. According to the Code, the board should possess the necessary capabilities and traits to carry out their duties effectively, including relevant company knowledge, sufficient experience and independence. They must also have the necessary time to devote to the role. The process by which new members are elected to the board must be formally conducted, rigorous and transparent. It emphasizes the need for continuous reappraisal of performance, skill sets and knowledge to remain effective as directors, in addition to receiving appropriate induction upon initial election.

Section C details the Code's best practice with regard to *accountability*. A key issue in this is risk, and the systems and procedures in place to ensure this is approached responsibly and relatively to the company's strategic objectives. It also upholds the requirement for company assessment that is both balanced and clear.

Section D concerns the role that *remuneration* plays in furnishing the company with a board of directors of sufficient quality to bring the company success. The Code recognizes the importance of remuneration in attracting and retaining talent, but equally that it must be capped appropriately, closely regulated and transparent, and independently issued.

Section E concludes the Code by detailing its stance on *relations with shareholders*. The board has a responsibility for ensuring an environment of open communication with shareholders, mutual respect and understanding. Investors should be encouraged to participate in dialogue through the annual general meeting (AGM).

INCENTIVE SCHEME CRITERIA

Earlier, in our general discussion about principal–agent relationships, we stated that principals have two responses to the problem that they face: the first is the development of regulatory devices, as we have just seen; and the second is the creation of management incentive schemes to try to ensure that there is much greater congruence between management's own personal objectives and the shareholders' objective of wealth (or share price) maximization. To be successful, an incentive scheme must fulfill a number of criteria:

1. It should reward management effort and ability, not luck.
2. Its rewards should be potentially large enough to have a significant impact on management's total remuneration.
3. The incentive reward system must work each way by rewarding good performance and penalizing poor performance.
4. The incentive scheme must take the concept of risk into account.
5. Reward should be related to performance over a time horizon that matches that of the shareholders.
6. The scheme should be simple and inexpensive to operate and be difficult to manipulate or exploit.

Let us expand a little on each of these points in turn. Shareholders are interested in wealth maximization, which, as we know, translates through into the maximization of the value of the company's shares. The first criterion in the list above relates to the fact that the performance of all companies is, to a greater or lesser extent, dependent on general economic conditions within both the domestic and international economy. Therefore management should not be rewarded for a rise in the company's share price that has simply occurred through an improvement in general economic conditions. Nor should they be penalized for a share price fall resulting from depressed economic conditions. This implies the need for an incentive scheme based on relative share price performance. In other words, management should be rewarded when the movement in the company's shares (either up or down) is more favourable than their competitors' share price movements: they should be rewarded for a greater rise in the share price, or a smaller fall.

The second criterion is required because, rationally, a manager will always have in mind the trade-off that exists between his incentive scheme gain from trying to maximize the worth of the shares and the likely gain from directly pursuing personal objectives through satisficing activities. Therefore, if the incentive reward is relatively small it is unlikely that the scheme will result in the desired modification of managerial behaviour.

The third criterion is necessary if the incentive scheme is to be proactive in affecting managerial behaviour. In other words, satisficing activity must be seen to have a negative rather than just a neutral impact on managerial rewards. A one-way incentive scheme rewards good performance, but does not penalize poor performance.

The danger with a 'one-way' scheme is that it encourages management to take risks, without them suffering as a result from a potential adverse outcome: management might be tempted to undertake a risky venture on the basis that if it turns out to be successful there will be a favourable impact on their remuneration. But, if the outcome is unsuccessful only the shareholders – and not management – bear the resulting costs.

This is therefore the reasoning that lies behind the fourth criterion. Any incentive scheme must force management to look at both possible outcomes (i.e. good and bad) of a risky investment.

The fifth criterion relates to the problem that shareholders wish management to maximize the value of their shares over the time period that they intend to hold them. Therefore it becomes necessary to avoid any incentive scheme that might encourage management to make decisions that have a favourable short-term impact on the share price, but an adverse longer term impact.

Finally, the need for the last criterion is fairly self-evident. If the incentive scheme is complex and expensive to operate, it may well be that the benefits that it brings are outweighed by the monitoring costs. Furthermore, if the incentive scheme is capable of being manipulated, then shareholders may find themselves rewarding management for illusory gains to themselves.

Types of scheme

Fundamentally, there are two types of managerial incentive scheme, with many potential variations. One is based on accounting numbers – typically profitability (although it may be on sales growth) – and the other is based directly on share price performance.

A typical incentive scheme based on accounting numbers would reward management with a bonus based on either the growth rate of profitability or the absolute level of profitability (usually in excess of some minimum level), where 'profitability' may be defined either pre- or post-tax and interest charges.

Out of our six specified criteria, such a scheme is likely to be satisfactory on only one count: it is likely to be simple and cheap to operate. In all other respects (with the possible exception of criterion two) such a scheme is unlikely to bring about the desired effects from the shareholders' point of view.

Incentive schemes based on share price performance are usually option-based. In such a system, key decision-makers in the senior management team are allocated share options. These give the individual the right (but not the obligation) to buy a specific number of the company's shares at a fixed price per share at any time over a specific future time period (typically, between 3 and 10 years).

Having stated earlier that there are basically two types of managerial incentive scheme, they do of course both have the same objective of trying to ensure that managers take decisions that are in their shareholders' best interests. The great advantage of this second type of scheme is that it is directly related to shareholder wealth through the market value of the company's shares. Incentive schemes based on accounting profit only have, at best, an indirect relationship to shareholder wealth.

The key point about share option schemes is that management has the right to buy shares in the company at a fixed price. Therefore, the higher the actual share price, the greater is the worth or value of the option. Consequently, management has a very direct interest in maximizing the value of the company's shares.

Share option incentive schemes are likely to be more effective than profit-related bonus schemes, in that they will satisfy more of the criteria that we specified. However, they are likely to be far from ideal. The main problems with share option schemes are:

1. They represent a type of 'one-way' incentive.

2. They can reward management for share price movements that arise out of general economic conditions, rather than superior managerial performance.

3. They fail to deal adequately with the question of risk in decision-making.

4. As we have seen with some of the real-world examples discussed earlier, an incentive scheme in which management bonuses are linked to share price performance can, in extreme cases, lead to attempts by management to mislead financial markets through fraudulent actions.

Can a 'perfect' incentive scheme be devised that satisfies our six criteria and results in a congruence of managers' and shareholders' objectives? The answer is probably not.

There are two main reasons for this assertion. The first is that a really effective scheme is likely to be complex and expensive to administer. Therefore, the sixth criterion is unlikely to be satisfied. The second reason relates to the fact that – particularly with respect to the first criterion specified – what is really required is a scheme that rewards *relative* share price performance. The problem here is one of being able to identify a genuinely similar company for comparison purposes.

We mentioned earlier that, although the financial performance of *all* companies is affected, to some extent, by general economic conditions, they are not all affected to the *same* extent. Therefore, when comparing the share price performance of different companies, we can only compare those companies which are similarly affected by general economic conditions. Such genuinely comparable companies may, in practice, be difficult to identify.

CONCLUSION

What conclusion can be drawn from this discussion? We began by assuming that the objective behind financial management decision-making was the maximization of shareholder wealth, which is 'operationalized' in terms of maximizing the value of the company's shares.

We then asked the question: are managers really maximizers, or are they more likely to be shareholder wealth satisficers? This point is important because, as was mentioned earlier, if management really has as their objective the satisficing rather than the maximizing of shareholders' wealth, then our normative theory of financial decision-making would change. It is clear from the discussion above that some managers have been criticized for taking more out of companies than would seem appropriate. However, it is very difficult to judge the value of top managers to companies. We are of the view that although satisficing behaviour may well exist in the short term, it is unlikely to persist in the medium to long term – particularly in stock exchange quoted companies. There are two principal reasons for this argument:

1. The competitive market for the shareholders' funds.
2. The competitive market for management jobs.

In a stock exchange quoted company, shareholders can monitor their management's performance through their company's share price performance **relative** to that of similar companies. If one set of management is only satisficing, while the management of a similar company is striving to maximize shareholder wealth, then this fact can be expected to be reflected in the respective share price performance of the two companies over the longer term (because of the resulting lower flow of dividends). Under such circumstances the satisficing company's management are likely to suffer adverse criticism in the financial press and their shareholders are likely to 'vote with their feet' – selling their shares and buying into the maximizing company. The resulting selling pressure on the first company's shares is likely to depress their market price and, unless the situation is corrected fairly rapidly, market forces – perhaps in the form of an 'unwelcome' takeover bid – will lead to a change in management.[2] Thus, the competitive market for shareholders' funds can help to ensure adherence to the maximizing objective. So, a manager might be paid a very large amount of money but the shareholders of the company can make up their own minds as to whether or not he or she is worth it.

In addition, one way for managers to pursue their own objectives in terms of pay and perks is through job promotion. Given that most managers perceive that promotion can be gained through doing a job well, then it follows that in a competitive market for managerial jobs – as exists within a company – *individual* maximizing managers will look to advance their own personal objectives by replacing satisficing managers. Thus, a satisficing manager runs the risk of being displaced by an ambitious maximizing manager.

It is never going to be possible to ensure that all actions by the executives of companies are in the best interests of their shareholders. As we have pointed out, there is significant evidence that company executives often do behave in their own interests and not in the interests of their shareholders. It is thus not possible to argue that all decisions made in companies will necessarily follow the **theories** and 'good practices' we will be describing throughout this book. However, this does not mean that we should simply throw up our hands and surrender to management self-interest. Indeed, one measure of management performance that might be used by shareholders is how far decisions do follow the good practices we describe.

SUMMARY

This chapter has covered the following major points:

- Shareholders and managers are in a principal–agent relationship where the principal is faced with the problem of controlling the agent's actions to ensure that the agent works in the best interests of the principal.

- The principal's response to the problem is to develop monitoring devices and create incentive schemes.

- Managerial (and especially directors') performance is monitored and controlled by a range of different legal and quasi-legal devices, which include fiduciary responsibilities, external audits, Yellow Book rules, the 'Model Code' on directors' share dealings, Companies Act regulations on directors' transactions and the Combined Code of best corporate governance practice. These will never be able to stop completely deliberate manipulation of information, but they do at least spell out what is expected.

- Incentive schemes are a useful way to bring about goal congruence between directors and shareholders. However the design of such schemes is fraught with problems and they are, in reality, unlikely to provide really effective control.

- Financial managers are unlikely to be able to sustain satisficing rather than maximizing behaviour for more than the short run. This is because of the competitive market for shareholders' funds causing the shareholders of satisficing companies to switch to maximizing companies; and because of the competitive market for management jobs both within the firm and between firms.

NOTES

1. Job security refers here to the risky nature of a company's business. The more risky the company, the more likely it is to go bankrupt, so causing the management to lose their jobs. Hence management may be concerned to reduce the company's exposure to risk and such action may not be in the shareholders' best interests. This point will be explored further at a later stage.
2. Changes in management, and hence changes in objectives, may come about in several ways. Shareholders, either behind the scenes or in the open at the company's AGM, might force a change or, alternatively, a company's non-executive directors may be the catalyst responsible for action.

FURTHER READING

1. Three classic articles that give an interesting overview of finance are: J.F. Weston, 'Developments in Finance Theory', *Financial Management,* Spring 1981; S.C. Myers, 'Finance Theory and Financial Strategy', *Midland Corporate Finance Journal,* Spring 1987; and W. Beranek, 'Research Directions in Finance', *Quarterly Review of Economics and Business,* Spring 1981.

2. Pike reports survey data on managers' perceived objectives (among other things) in R.H. Pike, 'An Empirical Study of the Adoption of Sophisticated Capital Budgeting Practices and Decision-Making Effectiveness', *Accounting and Business Research,* Autumn 1988, and R.H. Pike, *Capital Budgeting Survey: An Update,* Bradford University Discussion Paper, 1992. In addition, two interesting earlier articles on objectives are R.N. Anthony, 'The Trouble with Profit Maximization', *Harvard Business Review,* November–December 1960 and B. Branch, 'Corporate Objectives and Market Performance', *Financial Management,* Summer 1973; J.S. Wallace, 'Value Maximization and Stakeholder Theory: Compatible or Not?', *Journal of Applied Corporate Finance*, Spring, 2003.

3. For a discussion on conflicts between managers' and shareholders' objectives, see: G. Donaldson, 'Financial Goals: Management vs. Stockholders', *Harvard Business Review,* May–June 1963; C.M. Findley and G.A. Whitmore, 'Beyond Shareholder Wealth Maximization', *Financial Management,* Winter 1974; N. Seitz, 'Shareholders' Goals, Firm Goals and Firm Financing Decisions', *Financial Management,* Autumn 1982; J.R. Grinyer, 'Alternatives to Maximization of Shareholder Wealth', *Accounting and Business Research,* Autumn 1986, McKinsey and Company: T. Koller,

M. Goedhart, and D. Wessels *Valuation*, 4th ed., John Wiley, New York 2005 and J.S. Wallace, 'Value Maximization and Stakeholder Theory: Compatible or Not?', *Journal of Applied Corporate Finance*, Spring 2003.

4. The ideas of satisficing and of the principal–agent problem can be found in: H.A. Simon, 'Theories of Decision Making in Economics and Behavioural Science', *American Economic Review,* June 1959; M.C. Jensen and W.H. Meckling, 'Theory of the Firm: Managerial Behaviour, Agency Costs and Ownership Structure', *Journal of Financial Economics,* October 1976; and E.F. Fama, 'Agency Problems and the Theory of the Firm', *Journal of Political Economy*, Spring 1980; K. Zhao, C. Baum and W. Ford, 'The CEO Share of Earnings: A New Approach to Evaluating Executive Compensation', *Business Economics,* April 2009 provide evidence that CEO rewards have not increased as much as the popular press suggests; R. Masulis, C. Wang and F. Xie, 'Agency Problems at Dual-Class Companies', *Journal of Finance*, Vol. 64, No. 4, 2009 concludes that when management have more control, they pursue own personal objectives, rather than the corporate objectives; Finally, see an interesting discussion in B. McSweeney, 'The Pursuit of Maximum Shareholder Value: Vampire or Viagra?', *Accounting Forum*, Vol. 31, No. 4, 2007.

5. The UK Corporate Governance Code, 2012, published by the Financial Reporting Council, provides a very clear and comprehensive account of the purpose and application of the principles of corporate governance.

6. For more detailed coverage of the issues relating to corporate governance and ethics see: J. Solomon, *Corporate Governance and Accountability*, 2nd ed., Wiley 2007; K. Hopt *et al.*, *Corporate Governance in Context*, Oxford University Press 2005; C. Mallin, *Corporate Governance*, Oxford University Press 2004; J. Brickley, J.C. Smith and L. Zimmerman, 'Corporate Governance, Ethics and Organizational Architecture', *Applied Corporate Finance*, Spring 2003; L. Bebchuk, A. Cohen and A. Ferrell, 'What Matters in Corporate Governance?', *Review of Financial Studies*, Vol. 22, No. 2, 2009, which examines which particular corporate governance factors impact on the value of the firm. Finally, K. John, L. Litov and B. Yeung, 'Corporate Governance and Risk-taking', *Journal of Finance* Vol. 64, No. 4, 2008 postulates that better corporate governance reduces management's natural risk aversion.

7. The Takeover Code published by the Panel on Takeovers and Mergers, 11th ed., London 2013, is a long and complex document – its contents index alone runs for 28 pages and it is essentially a document for financial practitioners. However, Sections A to C covering the Introduction, General Principles and Definitions, make interesting reading.

8. The background to the Enron scandal is discussed by Gary M. Brown in K. Hopt *et al., Corporate Governance in Context,* Oxford University Press 2005. The more interested reader is referred to *The Watchdogs Didn't Bark: Enron and the Wall Street Analysts: Hearing Before the Senate Committee on Governmental Affairs.* Congressional 2nd Session, 27 February 2002.

9. For a clear account of the chronology of the WorldCom scandal, see the CRS Report for Congress: WorldCom – the Accounting Scandal, Bob Lyke and Mark Jickling, Congressional Research Service, Library of Congress, 2002.

10. For a brief but informative discussion on the accounting scandal behind the Lehman Brothers collapse, see The Lehman Brothers Case, Arturo Bris, 2010, IMD Business School, Switzerland.

11. For a really different view of the relationship of managers to their company and shareholders, see B. Burough and J. Helyar, *Barbarians at the Gate*, Arrow Books 1990.

QUIZ QUESTIONS

1 What is the principal–agent problem?

2 List the main ways in which directors' actions might be monitored and controlled.

3 What are the main criteria for an effective managerial incentive scheme? (See the 'Answers to Quiz Questions' at the back of the book.)

PROBLEMS

The answers to three of the following problems (those indicated by an asterisk) are contained in the 'Answers to Problems' section on the students' companion website. Answers to the remaining two problems are available only to lecturers via the website (see the 'Digital Resources' page for details).

1* How might you go about devising an incentive scheme for top management?

2* What is meant by the term 'a risky investment'? What makes some investments more or less risky than others?

3* What might be the financial management objectives of government-owned industries?

4 Discuss the means by which management's actions are monitored and controlled by shareholders.

5 Discuss the implications of the Enron and WorldCom affairs for institutional and private investors.

INVESTMENT DECISIONS

TRADITIONAL METHODS OF INVESTMENT APPRAISAL

LEARNING OBJECTIVES

The purpose of this chapter is to:

- Introduce the two 'traditional' methods by which companies make capital investment decisions: Payback and Return on Capital Employed (ROCE).

- Examine and explain how these two techniques are used to provide investment decision advice.

- Discuss the advantages and disadvantage of Payback and ROCE as decision tools.

INTRODUCTION

In its simplest form, an investment decision can be defined as one that involves the firm making a cash outlay *now*, with the aim of receiving, in return, *future* cash inflows. (Numerous variations on this definition are possible, such as a cash outlay with the aim of reducing or saving further cash outlays, but these can all generally adapt to the initial definition with little trouble.)

Decisions about buying a new machine, building a factory, extending a warehouse, improving a delivery service, instituting a staff training scheme or launching a new product line are all examples of the investment decisions that may be made in practice. In order to help in making such decisions, and to ensure that they are consistent with each other, a common method of evaluation is required which can be applied equally to the whole spectrum of investment decisions and which should, in terms of the decision structure so far outlined, help to decide whether any particular investment will assist the company in maximizing shareholder wealth (via share price maximization).

A warning

In looking for such an investment appraisal method we shall begin by examining two methods – payback and return on capital employed – that have been used by industry and commerce for many years – to see how well they fit in with our financial decision objective and value base. However, before doing so we should be clear about two points.

The first is that these two 'traditional' methods of investment appraisal are not underpinned by economic rationale, but are more akin to 'rule of thumb' techniques. In other words, they appear logical at the superficial level, but do not withstand more rigorous evaluation.

The second point is that neither of these two methods, nor any other method of investment appraisal, can give a *definitive* decision. They cannot tell a company's financial decision-maker to 'invest' or 'not invest', but can only act as a decision *guide*. This extremely important point will become obvious as we develop our theory, but it is all too easy to slip into the erroneous (and sometimes comforting) belief that the techniques that we shall develop here will make investment decisions. They will not. All they will do is help to communicate information to the decision-maker, but when the actual decision is finally made, it is based on a whole range of very diverse considerations which are beyond our present capabilities to capture in a simple decision-making technique.[1]

There has sometimes been a considerable amount of resistance on the part of financial managers, to the introduction of any new investment appraisal technique, based partially on the belief that with such methods their decision-making function would be reduced to a simple mechanistic operation. Such a belief is ill-founded, not only for the reason already given, but also because investment is all about the future. Almost all investment decisions will involve making forecasts/estimates/guesses about the investment's future performance, and appraisal techniques are applied to the numbers that emerge from that process. The future is, almost without exception, *uncertain* and so any investment appraisal technique can only produce *advice* based on these forecasts and not a decision that is guaranteed to turn out to be optimal. Therefore, investment appraisal techniques can never replace managerial judgement, but they can help to make that judgement more analytical and consistent.

 REAL WORLD VIEW: The Importance of CFOs

The role of the chief financial officer (CFO) in any company is an extremely important one, in being a key decision-maker: managing the balance sheets and purse strings, overseeing performance in real terms, coordinating investment decisions, and in helping to steer a company's strategy, whether in times of growth or turbulence.

As former CFO of Nestlé, the largest food company in the world, Jim Singh is in a good position to talk about what being a CFO means. Speaking in 2011 (whilst still CFO), he reasoned that 'The mission of the finance function is to provide information derived from sound analyses of the business conditions and performance so that management can have good, relevant information on time to make decisions to run the company.' For Singh, the CFO was co-pilot to the CEO's captain.

Bruce Besanko, CFO of OfficeMax, extends this view, going so far as to say: 'As CFO, I'm in a unique position within the organization, at the absolute centre of the universe. The only other executive besides me that has that same presence at the centre is the CEO.'

Meanwhile, an article on *the-financedirector.com* suggests that many CEOs feel the same way. CFOs were asked to describe their jobs in one word. The words ranged from 'co-pilot' to 'leader', and CFOs admitted they saw themselves as 'visionaries', 'wizards' and 'oracles'; as well as 'navigators', 'architects' and 'strategists'.

It is clear that the role of CFO is a crucial one to a company, whether this is in terms of guiding business partners by giving risk assessment and management; or in terms of generating their own ideas based on financial research. Throughout the book, we address many scenarios that a CFO may face day-to-day, and look at various theoretical models that may be applied in approaching these effectively. As Singh notes, having 'the right policies, procedures and guidelines in place' is essential, in both maintaining a healthy organization and being prepared for the many uncertainties of today's business environment.

THE PAYBACK METHOD

Let us start by looking at the first of these two traditional methods of investment appraisal: the payback method. This is one of the most tried and trusted of all the investment appraisal techniques and its name neatly describes its operation, referring to *how quickly* the incremental benefits that accrue to a company from an investment, 'pay back' the initial capital invested – the benefits being defined in terms of the after-tax cash flows generated by the investment.

The payback method can be used as a guide to investment decision-making in two ways. First, when faced with a straight accept-or-reject decision, it can provide a rule where projects are only accepted if they pay back the initial investment outlay within a certain predetermined time. Second, the payback method can provide a rule when a comparison is required of the relative desirability of several *mutually exclusive* investments.[2] In such cases projects can be ranked in terms of 'speed of payback', with the fastest paying-back project being the most favoured and the slowest paying-back project the least favoured. Thus, the project that pays back quickest would be chosen for investment.

Given below are examples of the payback method operating in both decision-making situations. With Project A, assuming that the criterion for project acceptance is a 4-year (maximum) payback, then we can see that it should be accepted because it pays back the initial outlay of £4000 in only 3 years:

Project A Year	Cash flow (£)
0	−4 000
1	+1 000
2	+1 000
3	+2 000 payback period
4	+3 000
5	+1 000

Projects B and C are mutually exclusive. Project B pays back in 2⅗ years (i.e. 2 years: years 1 and 2 cash flow plus three-fifths of the year 3 cash flow); whereas Project C pays back in 2 years exactly. As Project C has the faster 'speed of payback', it is the preferred investment.

Project B Year	Cash flow (£)	Project C Year	Cash flow (£)
0	−10 000	0	−12 500
1	+3 000	1	+5 000
2	+4 000	2	+7 500
3	+5 000	3	+1 000
4	+6 000	4	+1 000
		5	+1 000

Working capital

Most projects involve expenditure not only on capital equipment but also on working capital. For example, suppose a company was considering investing in a sausage-making machine. Not only would the company have to incur the capital expenditure on the machine itself, but it would also have to invest in 'working capital': raw material inventories, inventories of finished goods and trade debtors (accounts receivables). The point here is that, at the end of the project's life, although the capital equipment will only have (at best) a scrap value, the working capital should be recovered in full. This is because, at the end of the project's life, the firm can run down its inventories of raw materials and finished goods to zero and, hopefully, all outstanding monies from customers will be received.

The following question then arises: should working capital be included as part of the project's outlay and so be included in the payback calculation? Example 1 illustrates such a situation.

EXAMPLE 1

Aqua Liquide SA is considering the purchase of a water bottling production line. The production line would cost €12 000 000, have an expected life of 5 years and a zero scrap value (net of disposal costs) at the end of that time. In addition, an expenditure of €8 000 000 on working capital will be required throughout its life. The firm's management accountants have estimated the net, after-tax, operating cash flows of the project as follows:

Year	Operating cash flow (€)
1	+6 000
2	+6 000
3	+6 000
4	+4 000
5	+3 000

Aqua Liquide evaluates investment opportunities using a maximum payback criterion of 3 years.

The problem here is what set of cash flows should be evaluated using payback – Alternative 1 or 2?

▶

▶

	Alternative 1				Alternative 2	
Year	Capital expenditure (€)	Working capital (€)	Operating cash flow (€)	Year	Capital expenditure (€)	Operating cash flow (€)
0	−12 000	−8 000		0	−12 000	
1			+6 000	1		+6 000
2			+6 000	2		+6 000
3			+6 000	3		+6 000
4			+4 000	4		+4 000
5		+8 000	+3 000	5		+3 000

If working capital is taken into account, the project should be rejected, as it takes 3½ years to recover the total initial outlay of €20 000 000 (€12 000 000 + €8 000 000). But if working capital is excluded from the analysis, the project is acceptable as it has just a 2-year payback.

We would argue that the correct approach to use would be 'Alternative 2' which excludes the working capital.[4] The logic behind this conclusion is as follows. Payback is concerned with how long it will take the project to reach its breakeven point where the investment cost has been recovered. Management is interested in this point because they recognize the uncertainties that surround any estimate of a project's future cash flow and the fact that estimates *further ahead* in time become even more uncertain. Thus, they view an investment project as being of lower risk, the more quickly it achieves the break even point. As a project's working capital is likely to be recovered *whenever* the project comes to the end of its life (i.e. working capital is automatically paid back with the inventory levels being run down to zero and all outstanding sales receipts collected), it should be excluded from the analysis of the breakeven point.

Advantages of payback

As can be seen from the two initial illustrations of Project A and Projects B and C, payback is quick and simple to calculate (once the project's cash flow forecasts have been made) and the concept is likely to be readily understood by management. This is one of its greatest advantages as an appraisal technique, but it has other advantages in addition.

A second advantage is that it is often thought that the use of payback will lead to the automatic selection of the *less risky* project in mutually exclusive decision situations. The point has already been alluded to in our discussion of Example 1. One of the most difficult tasks in investment appraisal is the forecasting of future project cash flows. In this respect, generally speaking, the further ahead in time is the cash flow estimate, the less reliable is that estimate. Therefore by emphasizing 'speed of return' and selecting the project, from a series of alternatives, that pays back quickest, the payback appraisal method is – almost by definition – choosing the least risky project, in that it chooses the one that reaches breakeven most quickly. However, this is a complex point and we shall return to it later when the problem of risk in investment decision-making is more fully discussed.

A further advantage of payback is that it saves management the trouble of having to forecast cash flows over *the whole* of a project's life. Given that the forecasting process is difficult, and the further ahead in time the forecast has to be made the greater the difficulty, the fact that project cash flows need not be forecasted beyond the maximum payback criterion (by which time the project either is or is not acceptable) is an obvious advantage. For instance, in Example 1, although the bottling line investment was thought to have had a 5-year life, there really was no need to forecast its cash flows beyond 3 years (the decision criterion) in order to evaluate it.

A final advantage of payback that is seen by many managers is that it is a logical method to use in 'capital rationing' situations. Capital rationing is a subject we shall return to later. However, it basically refers to a situation where a company does not have unlimited investment funds. (Perhaps the limit has been imposed by the company itself in the form of an annual capital expenditure budget.) Example 2 illustrates the situation and demonstrates how the capital rationing problem can be helped by ranking the investment projects in terms of their *speed of payback*. In addition, the approach can also claim to have yet another advantage in that, in such a situation, it appears to select the most appropriate investments in a situation where investment expenditure is limited. If finance is in short supply, it could be argued that the best projects to accept would be those that returned the expenditure rapidly – which is exactly what the payback method does.

EXAMPLE 2

Al Khalim Cement is a Saudi Arabian company which has identified five independent[5] investment opportunities and wishes to evaluate their desirability. The company normally uses payback with a 3-year criterion and has specified a maximum capital expenditure budget for the year of SAR200 000 000.[6] The project's net after-tax cash flows are estimated as follows:

Project	A	B	C (all cash flows in SAR000 000s)	D	E
Year					
0	−100	−300	−100	−200	−250
1	+50	+100	+80	+50	+50
2	+50	+100	+40	+100	+100
3	+50	+100	+50	+100	+80
4		+80	+30	+100	+80

Using payback, Projects A to D are all acceptable as they each payback within the 3-year criterion. Project E is unacceptable. However, the company has a problem. To undertake all four acceptable projects will require total expenditure of SAR700 000 000 and only SAR200 000 000 has been budgeted. How is the firm to 'ration out' the available cash among the competing projects?

The solution is to order the projects in terms of their speed of payback and to then accept the projects in that order until all the investment funds have been utilized:

Project	Cost	Payback	Rank	Decision
A	100	2 years	2nd	Accept
B	300	3 years	4th	Reject
C	100	1.5 years	1st	Accept
D	200	2.5 years	3rd	Reject
E	250	3.25 years	5th	Reject

The decision criterion

Nothing has so far been said about how the payback decision criterion is set. There are a number of possible methods that management might utilize. One would simply be to base the criterion on past experience; for example, if the firm's experience is that most success-ful projects have paid back within 4 years, then that time period might be set as a criterion. Alternatively, general 'industry practice' might be taken as the guideline.

One obvious, and very sensible, basis for setting the decision criterion would be fore-casting ability. For example, if a firm believed that, realistically, it could not forecast pro-ject cash flows with sufficient accuracy beyond 5 years ahead, then 5 years might be set as the criterion. Here management would be recognizing their forecasting limitations and would be sensibly deciding not to evaluate a project on cash flow forecasts that might be seen more as guesses than estimates.

Disadvantages of payback

Having looked at the advantages – valid or otherwise – we now turn to the disadvantages. The first is the problem of what is meant by the term 'investment outlay'. If we look at Projects D and E below, just how should the investment outlay be defined in each case?

Project D Year	Cash flow (£)	Project E Year	Cash flow (£)
0	−10 000	0	−5 000
1	+5 000	1	+1 000
2	+5 000	2	−5 000
3	+5 000	3	+3 000
4	−2 000	4	+3 000
		5	+4 000

Is Project D's outlay £10 000 or £12 000? Is Project E's outlay £10 000 or £9000? The point is that in each case we can come to an arbitrary decision – say, Project D's outlay is £10 000 and E's is £9000 – but the situation is too ambiguous to conclusively justify the decision made.

The problem of ambiguity can also be seen in the definition of *the start* of the payback time period. In other words, from what point do we begin counting? Suppose that Project E will be accepted only if it pays back within 3 years. If this means that E must pay back its outlay by Year 3 – that is, 3 years after its commencement – clearly, it should not be accepted. On the other hand, if the payback criterion means that it should pay back within 3 years of the completion of its outlays – that is, by Year 5 – then it is acceptable. Once again, as it stands, the decision rule is too ambiguous to give a definitive ruling.

This ambiguity is an important problem. When any technique, designed as a decision-making aid, is open to ambiguity in interpretation, then it is likely to be manipulated so as to lend backing to the *desired* decision, rather than the *correct* decision. Any decision rule open to such manipulation is potentially dangerous and must only be used with great care.

A further problem, and probably the most important one, arises from the fact that the decision is concentrated purely on the cash flows that arise within the payback period, and flows that arise outside this period are ignored. Projects F and G illustrate the problem that this can cause:

Project F Year	Cash flow (£)	Project G Year	Cash flow (£)
0	−100 000	0	−100 000
1	+10 000	1	+50 000
2	+20 000	2	+50 000
3	+40 000	3	+10 000
4	+80 000		
5	+160 000		
6	+320 000		

According to the payback rule, if the two projects are mutually exclusive, Project G is preferred because it pays back the outlay more quickly. If the two projects are independent (i.e. either one or both could be accepted or rejected) and the company has a 3-year payback period criterion, again Project G would be accepted and F rejected. In both situations, looking at the cash flows over the *whole life* of each project, we can see that the wisdom of the decision advice given by the payback method is open to some doubt.

The time value of money

A final problem with the payback method is that, in the format used above, it suffers from the fundamental drawback of failing to allow for the 'time value of money'. However, this difficulty can easily be overcome by applying the decision technique – not to ordinary cash flows but to 'present value' cash flows. In such circumstances, the technique is usually referred to as 'discounted' payback.

The concept of *the time value of money* has a central place within financial decision theory and will be developed formally in subsequent chapters. Nevertheless, it will be useful to introduce the idea briefly at this point.

Essentially what is meant by the term 'the time value of money' is that a given sum of money has a different value depending upon when it occurs in time. The idea is not directly concerned with inflation or deflation (let us assume that neither exists, so that price levels are stable through time) but really concerns the fact that money can be invested so as to earn a rate of interest.

Suppose you were owed £100 and were given the choice of having your £100 returned to you either now or in 1 year's time (assume that, if you choose £100 in a year's time, the event is 'certain' – i.e. you are certain to be paid the money). Most people would instinctively take the £100 now – even if they did not need the money – and this would be the correct decision in terms of the time value of money.

The reason why £100 in a year's time has a lesser value than £100 now is because if you took the £100 now, the money could be placed on deposit at (say) a 6% interest rate and so turn into £106 in 1 year's time (£100 deposit + £6 interest). Therefore if the person who was in debt to you offered the choice of £100 now or £106 in 1 year's time (again both events are certain to occur), you would have *no preference* for either alternative. Thus we could say that the *present value* of £106 received in a year's time is £100, or that the *future value* of £100 now is £106 in one year's time (assuming a 6% interest rate).

This concept of the time value of money will be much more fully discussed when the discounted cash flow methods of investment appraisal are discussed in Chapter 5, but the point to be made here is that the payback method does not make any allowance for the *timing* of a project's cash flows and the time value of money, its emphasis on the speed of return being purely a consideration of project risk. For example, the payback method would be indifferent between Projects I and J whereas, as the reader may well discern, if allowance is made for the time value of money, Project J is preferable to Project I, as money received *nearer* in time is more valuable than money received later in time.

Project I Year	Cash flow (£)	Project J Year	Cash flow (£)
0	−4 000	0	−4 000
1	+500	1	+3 000
2	+500	2	+500
3	+3 000	3	+500
4	+500	4	+500

A worked example of discounted payback will be examined when the time value of money concept is more fully explored in Chapter 5.

In conclusion

Despite these criticisms, payback has a robust ability to survive, because surveys reveal it to be among the most widely used of all appraisal methods. This popularity stems mainly from two of the reasons that we have already stated, that of its simplicity of application and its apparent bias towards less risky projects. Indeed it can be strongly argued that the payback method does provide a very useful 'rule of thumb' check mechanism for the very many minor investment decisions that companies have to make, which are financially too small (either in relative or absolute terms) to justify the time and expense that would necessarily be incurred in using a complex, but more theoretically correct appraisal method.[7] Furthermore, as shall be seen at the end of Chapter 5, a particularly persuasive case can be made for the discounted payback technique.

The real problem does not stem from the payback concept itself, but more from the way the method is used in the decision-making process. Except in the case of very minor investment decisions, it should not really be used to give decision advice at all, but only to give information on the speed of return of the initial outlay, which may or may not be of relevance (depending upon the firm's liquidity) in the decision process. It cannot really be considered as an investment appraisal technique because of its major defect: its inability to evaluate an investment project over its *whole* life because it fails to take into account the investment's post-payback period flows. Using the payback method to choose between alternative investments or to set a minimum criterion for investment acceptance is really applying it to a task that is well beyond its ability to handle. At best, for large investments, it can act successfully only as an initial screening device before more powerful methods of appraisal are applied.[8]

RETURN ON CAPITAL EMPLOYED

The second traditional approach to investment appraisal is the Return on Capital Employed (ROCE) which, like payback, has a number of alternative names (perhaps the most common is the Accounting Rate of Return, or ARR) and a wide variety of different methods of computation.

There are two common ways of expressing ROCE in practice. One is the ratio of the average annual profit generated over the life of the project, to its *average* investment cost (i.e. the average capital employed). The other approach is to take the average annual profit as a ratio of the *initial* cost. Example 3 illustrates these two sets of calculations.

EXAMPLE 3

The Techniek BV wants to evaluate an investment proposal using the ROCE technique. The project requires an initial capital expenditure of €10 000, together with €3000 of working capital. The project will have a 4-year life, at the end of which time the working capital will be fully recovered and the project will have a scrap value of €2000.

The project's expected annual profits (or loss, as in the case of Year 4) are as follows:

	Year	(€)
Forecast annual profit (or loss):	1	2 000
	2	4 000
	3	1 500
	4	(500)
	Total profit =	€7 000

The average annual profit would therefore be: €7000 ÷ 4 = €1750 and the initial capital employed would equal €13 000 (capital expenditure plus working capital). The *average* capital employed would be calculated as:

$$\frac{\text{Capital expenditure} - \text{Scrap value}}{2} + \text{Scrap value} + \text{Working capital}$$

$$\text{that is: } \frac{€10\,000 - €2000}{2} + €2\,000 + €3\,000 = €9\,000$$

See Figure 3.2. Hence the investment's return on *initial* capital employed equals:

$$\frac{€1\,750}{€13\,000} = 0.135 \text{ (approx) or } 13.5\%$$

and return on *average* capital employed equals:

$$\frac{€1\,750}{€9\,000} = 0.194 \text{ (approx.) or } 19.4\%$$

ROCE can be employed in the investment appraisal of both individual, independent projects and mutually exclusive projects. First, a decision criterion is set in terms of the company's *minimum* acceptable level of ROCE. (The figure used for this often reflects the company's *overall* return on capital.) Then, for an independent project to be acceptable, its ROCE must at least equal the criterion return specified. In a situation of mutually exclusive projects, the best of the alternative investments is the project with the highest ROCE. However, this 'best' project will only be accepted by the firm if it too meets the set criterion.

Advantages of ROCE

The ROCE investment appraisal technique is quite widely used in practice, although it is probably declining in popularity. It has three main advantages. The first is that by evaluating the project on the basis of a *percentage* rate of return it is using the concept of a 'percentage rate of return', that all managements are familiar. For example, being told that a project has 'a 4-year payback' would not immediately convey whether that was good or bad; but being told that a project is expected to produce 'a 35% ROCE' would be immediately much more meaningful.

The second advantage is connected to the first. It is the fact that the method evaluates the project on the basis of its *profitability*. Again, profitability is a familiar concept to all managers and one with which they feel comfortable.

Finally, a third advantage is that of logic. Managers' own performance is often evaluated by shareholders in terms of the company's overall ROCE. Therefore it does seem to be logical to evaluate individual capital investments on a similar basis. (This line of thinking then often leads to the specification of the ROCE criterion being set equal to the company's targeted overall return on capital.)

Disadvantages of ROCE

To set against these advantages, there are a number of major disadvantages, the first of which is the ambiguous nature of the ROCE concept. There are so many variants that no general agreement exists on how capital employed should be calculated, on whether initial or average capital employed should be used or on how profit should be defined, (e.g. before or after tax). As a result, the method lays itself open to abuse as a technique of investment appraisal by allowing the decision-maker to select a definition of ROCE that best suits their preconception of a project's desirability.

Second, because the method measures a potential investment's worth in percentage terms it is unable to take into account the financial size of a project when alternatives are compared. For example, suppose a company was considering whether to build a large factory at a cost of £10 million, or a small factory at a cost of £3 million. If the large factory turned out to have an ROCE of 20% while the small factory's ROCE was 24%, then the latter investment would be the one chosen (assuming 24% exceeded the ROCE criterion). However, it is not at all certain that the small factory would be a wise choice. While the small factory would result in an aggregate profit of £720 000 (24% of £3 million), the large factory would produce a profit of £2 million for the firm.

However, these two criticisms are relatively insignificant when compared to two further difficulties. The first concerns the fact that *accounting profit* rather than *cash flow* is used as the basis of evaluation. As our earlier discussion in Chapter 1 showed, this is an entirely *incorrect* concept to use in a decision-making context. Accounting profit is a reporting concept; not a decision-making concept. A capital investment decision is an *economic* or *resource allocation* decision and the economic unit of account is cash, because it is cash that gives power over resources. Therefore such decisions should correctly be made on the basis of cash and the flow of cash through time.

The other major criticism of ROCE is that it also ignores the time value of money. Furthermore, unlike payback, where discounted payback can be used to allow for the time value of money, there is *no way* that ROCE can be modified to take the time value of money into account.

However, despite these criticisms, the method is still widely applied to investment decisions in industry and it may be fair to say that, like payback, although there are many problems associated with its application, it may give acceptable decision advice when applied to relatively minor, short-run investment projects. Nevertheless, there is survey evidence that does indicate a decline in the technique's popularity.

CONCLUSIONS

Comparing these two 'traditional' investment appraisal techniques, each has its own advantages and disadvantages and it is not clear whether either is superior. Each has its own group of advocates and it is quite common to find *both* used in conjunction so as to produce a 'two-tier' decision rule – e.g. projects may be accepted only if (say) they pay back within 5 years *and* have a minimum ROCE of 12%.

In the final analysis, our conclusion must be that, apart from the possible exception of the evaluation of relatively small, short-lived investments, neither method has sufficient advantages to offset its disadvantages, and particularly the failure of both techniques normally to allow for the time value of money.[9] In the next chapter we shall start to examine investment appraisal methods that do attempt to make such an allowance.

SUMMARY

This chapter has covered the following major points:

- The two 'traditional' methods of capital investment appraisal – payback and ROCE – were examined to see how they are calculated and how they are applied, both to individual project evaluation and to situations involving mutually exclusive projects.

- As far as payback is concerned, the technique is usually applied to a project's after-tax cash flows, but working capital is excluded entirely from the evaluation.

- Basically there are four advantages to payback:
    1. Quick and simple.
    2. Seen as automatically selecting the less 'risky' project from amongst alternatives.
    3. Seen as helpful in capital rationing situations.
    4. Management need only to forecast project cash flows up to the payback point and not over the whole of the project's life.

- Payback's main disadvantage is its failure to consider project cash flows *after* the point of payback. However, it was argued that, to some extent, this omission might be understandable where management felt that their forecasting ability was suspect beyond the criterion time period.

- The other disadvantage is payback's failure to account for the time value of money, but this can be taken into account through the use of discounted payback.

- The ROCE also has advantages:

   1. It uses the familiar percentage concept.

   2. It evaluates projects on the basis of profitability.

   3. Management's success or failure in taking financial decisions in aggregate is judged on the basis of the company's ROCE (among other things). Therefore it appears logical that individual investment decisions should be taken on the same basis.

- However, to be set against these advantages are two major disadvantages: a failure to consider cash flow and a failure to take the time value of money into account.

- In sum, these two techniques may be suitable, at best, as initial screening devices, or to evaluate small, short-lived projects. However, they should not be used otherwise; with the possible exception of discounted payback.

NOTES

1. Not least among these diverse considerations is the decision-maker's own psychology; one survey (R.W. Scapens, T.J. Sale and P.A. Tikkas, *Financial Control of Divisional Capital Investment,* London Institute of Cost and Management Accountants 1982) concludes that concern with an investment's financial viability is of almost secondary importance to whether or not it 'fits in' with the company's strategic plans.

2. The term 'mutually exclusive' when applied to investment projects is best explained by means of an example. Suppose a company requires a new warehouse and there are two possible sites under consideration, then the decision could be analyzed in terms of two mutually exclusive investments: building the warehouse at Site A or building the warehouse at Site B. The projects are said to be mutually exclusive because only *one* new warehouse is required, so if it is built at Site A, the acceptance of this project excludes the other project from being chosen, and vice versa. More generally, a pair of projects are mutually exclusive if the acceptance of one means that the other would not, or could not, be accepted. This definition can be extended to any number of alternative investment projects of which only one can be chosen.

3. It is important to note that throughout this book we shall use the following convention when dealing with all types of financial flows (e.g. profit, dividend, cash or tax flows): all flows will normally be assumed to occur instantaneously *on the last day of the year in which they arise.* Thus, a cash flow in the second year of a project's life will be assumed to occur on the last day of the second year. The main exception to this rule is that a project's outlay (or cost) which arises in the first year of its life is assumed to occur on the first day of the year. These rather unrealistic assumptions are made for arithmetical convenience, but, in most circumstances, they do not affect the realism of our results in any substantial way. (See the Appendix to Chapter 5 on 'Compounding and discounting'.) Diagrammatically this is illustrated in Figure 3.1.

FIGURE 3.1

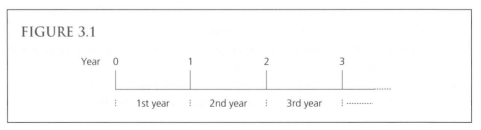

Thus 'Year 0' (or t_0) refers to the start of the first year (i.e. 'now'). 'Year 1' refers to the end of the first year and – simultaneously – the start of the second year. 'Year 3' refers to the end of the third year, and so on. References in the text to, for example, 'the second year' will refer to events that happen during the second year, while references to 'Year 2' (or t_2) will refer to a financial flow that is assumed to arise at the end of the second year (or, the start of the third year).

4. However, it is important to notice that payback will be the *only* appraisal technique that excludes working capital from the analysis.

5. Project independence can be defined as a situation where the expected financial flows that arise from a project will occur irrespective of any other project being or not being undertaken.

6. SAR is the Saudi Arabian Riyal.

7. This may be especially true of very small companies that may be lacking the resources and knowledge to undertake a more complex appraisal.

8. Even this is really open to doubt. Original writers on the topic, such as Joel Dean and Ezra Solomon, believed that payback could be used as a coarse screening device to pick out projects whose desirability (in terms of profitability) is so obvious as to remove the need for more refined appraisal. For similar reasons it is held that the method could also be used to reject 'obviously' highly unprofitable projects. There is little evidence to support this belief, neither has there been an operational definition of 'obvious' in this context.

9. Even allowing for the discounted payback variant referred to earlier, payback still suffers the major criticism of not considering a project's financial flows outside the payback period.

FIGURE 3.2

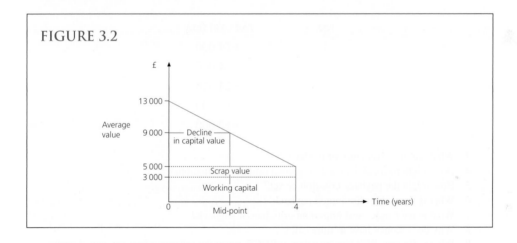

FURTHER READING

1. Most of the literature concerning payback and ROCE is fairly old, and the more up-to-date contributions such as G. Arnold and P. Hatzopoulos, 'The Theory-practice Gap in Capital Budgeting: Evidence from the United Kingdom', *Journal of Business Finance and Accounting*, June/July 2000 have tended to contrast them with the discounted cash flow (DCF) techniques which are to be discussed in Chapter 5. Nevertheless, an interesting starting point is the discussion in D. Bodenhorn, 'On the Problem of Capital Budgeting', *Journal of Finance*, December 1959.

2. Even older, but also of interest is: J. Dean, 'Measuring the Productivity of Capital', *Harvard Business Review*, Jan–Feb 1954; as is E.A. Ravenscroft, 'Return on Investment: Fit the Method to your Needs', *Harvard Business Review*, Mar–Apr 1960.

3. Specifically on payback, see: M.J. Gordon, 'The Payoff Period and the Rate of Profit', *Journal of Business*, October 1955; A. Rappaport, 'The Discounted Payback Period', *Management Science*, Jul–Aug 1965; H. Levy, 'A Note on the Payback Method', *Journal of Financial and Quantitative Analysis*, December 1968; and M.H. Weingartner, 'Some New Views on the Payback Period and Capital Budgeting Decision', *Management Science*, August 1969.

4. Two interesting articles that discuss reasons for the continuing popularity of payback are: M. Statman, 'The Persistence of the Payback Method: A Principal–Agent Perspective', *Engineering Economist,* Winter 1982; and R.H. Pike, 'Owner Manager Conflict and the Role of the Payback Method', *Accounting and Business Research,* Winter 1985.

5. The ROCE method is generally recognized as being inadequate, but see: M.J. Mepham, 'A Reinstatement of the Accounting Rate of Return', *Accounting and Business Research,* Summer 1968; and C.G. Hoskins and G.A. Mumey, 'Payback: A Maligned Method of Asset Ranking?', *Engineering Economist*, Autumn 1979.

QUIZ QUESTIONS

1 What is the payback decision rule for mutually exclusive projects?

2 What is the payback of the following project?
Project 'W' requires the purchase of a machine costing £11 000 plus an investment of £4000 in working capital. At the end of the machine's 5-year working life, it can be sold for £1000 as scrap. Project W's net cash flows (excluding any of the above information) are forecasted as follows:

Year	Net cash flow
1	+£4 000
2	+£4 000
3	+£4 000
4	+£3 000
5	+£2 000

3 What are the advantages of payback?
4 How might payback be used in 'capital rationing' situations?
5 How might the payback criterion be set?
6 What is meant by 'discounted payback'?
7 What is the single most important criticism of payback?
8 Why does money have a 'time value'?
9 What is Project 'W''s (see question 2) ROCE, given the following forecast annual profits:

Year	Annual profit
1	£2 000
2	£2 000
3	£2 000
4	£1 000
5	zero

10 What are the main advantages of ROCE?
11 What are the two most serious disadvantages of ROCE?
(See the 'Answers to the Quiz Questions' section at the back of the book.)

PROBLEMS

The answers to problems indicated by an asterisk are available to students online. Answers to the other problems are available only to lecturers (see the 'Digital Resources' page for details).

1* Grupo Ribeirinho is a diversified industrial conglomerate based in Portugal. Its head office staff are currently evaluating investment proposals put up by different divisions for approval.

The telecoms division has put forward a proposal to produce a cell phone which, because of rapid technological change, can only be expected to have a 4-year life, once the production facilities have been set up during the first 12 months.

The industrial property division propose taking a 4-year lease on a building that already has a tenant paying an annual rent.

The mining division propose to spend €1.5 million extracting a small copper deposit. The deposit would be fully depleted after 3 years. At the end of that time, the environmental damage the company had caused would need to be rectified at a cost of €0.75 million.

The net cash flows of all three projects (excluding working capital) are as follows (€000s):

Year	Telecoms	Property	Mining
0	−1 000	−1 000	−1500
1	−1 000	+200	+500
2	+800	+400	+1000
3	+800	+400	+800
4	+800	+400	−750
5	+800		

Grupo Ribeirinho normally uses payback to evaluate projects with a decision criterion of 3 years.

Required:

(a) Calculate the payback of all three projects and determine the decision advice.

(b) If the Telecoms and Property division projects were mutually exclusive, which project would you advise the company to accept? Think carefully before reaching a decision and then justify your decision.

(c) If the Property and Mining division projects were mutually exclusive, which project would you advise the company to accept? Again, think carefully and justify your decision.

(d) Comment on the company's use of the same decision criterion for projects from all three divisions. Would you think this wise?

2* De Rosa Basso is an Italian manufacturer and distributor of ice cream. The management are currently considering a project that will require capital expenditure of €200 000, together with €50 000 of working capital. The capital equipment is expected to have a scrap value of €80 000 at the end of its 4-year life and 80% of the working capital will also be recovered. (The remaining 20% of unrecovered working capital will consist of out-of-date inventory.) The project's annual revenues and operating cash costs are estimated as follows (€000s):

Year	Revenues	Operating costs
1	200	150
2	260	200
3	400	290
4	100	80

▶

The company calculates depreciation on a straight-line basis. Normally projects are evaluated using both payback and the ROCE. The criterion used is 3 years for payback and 13% for ROCE.

Required:

(a) Evaluate the project using the company's normal decision criteria. What advice would you give?

(b) Natalia Basso, the chairman of the company, is puzzled over your treatment of working capital in the payback calculation. Explain to her your reasonings.

(c) The chairman also wondered whether the return on *average* capital employed should be used instead of initial capital. What would your advice be and would the decision advice change? Think carefully before giving your answer; your promotion depends upon it!

(d) If De Rosa Basso decides to use only one appraisal technique, which would you advise – payback or ROCE – and why?

INVESTMENT–CONSUMPTION DECISION MODEL

The purpose of this chapter is to:

- Develop a simple graphical investment–consumption decision model for decision-making within a single owner company.

- Introduce the concept of a financial market which leads to a 'separation theorem' between investment and consumption decisions.

- Further develop the model through the introduction of a multi-owner company.

- Explain the concept of indifference curves.

INTRODUCTION TO THE MODEL

In the previous chapter two longstanding and widely used investment appraisal decision rules, payback and ROCE, were examined. One criticism of payback was that it ignored the time value of money – unless discounted payback was used. A similar criticism was made of the ROCE approach but, in addition, that was also criticized for evaluating projects on the basis of profit, not cash flow.

The other two main methods of capital investment appraisal are net present value (NPV) and the internal rate of return (IRR). These will be examined in detail in Chapters 5 and 6. However, in this chapter we take the opportunity to expand upon our initial discussion about the time value of money, and then look at how, in theory, capital investment decisions should be taken. This will enable a judgement to be made as to how closely the four alternative investment appraisal techniques accord with the theoretically correct approach.

In order to look at the theory of investment decision-making, we are going to develop a simple graphical analysis.[1] In no way does this analysis purport to represent the real world, but it allows conclusions to be reached that do have real-world validity.

The basic assumptions

So as to simplify the analysis and to lay bare the problem of investment decision-making, we shall specify six assumptions about the real-world environment within which investment decisions are made.

Assumption 1

The decision-maker is only concerned with making investment decisions over a *single-period* time horizon, which we will treat as *one year* for the sake of simplicity. Given this time horizon, there are only two points of time that concern us – the start of the year or now (i.e. t_0 or Year 0) and the end of the year (i.e. t_1 or Year 1). Therefore all the available investment opportunities possess the general characteristic of requiring a cash outlay *now* in return for a cash inflow at *the end* of the year. No investment cash flows extend beyond t_1.[2] (We will show later that this analysis can be easily expanded to cash flows that extend over many years.)

Assumption 2

The size and timing of any investment's cash outflow and subsequent cash inflow is known *with certainty* by the decision-maker and so *no risk* is involved in the investment decision.

Assumption 3

Only 'physical' investment opportunities are available – i.e. investments involving the use of factors of production (land, labour and machinery) to produce a future return. This means that there are no 'capital market' investments available, where money can be lent or borrowed at a rate of interest.

Assumption 4

All investment projects are infinitely divisible; therefore fractions of projects may be undertaken, and they exhibit decreasing returns to scale.

Assumption 5

All investment project cash flows are entirely independent of each other. Therefore the cash inflow produced at the end of the year from any investment now is unaffected by any other investment decision.

Assumption 6

The person in receipt of the cash flow from investment decisions is rational, in that 'more cash' is always preferred to 'less cash' in any time period.

These are the six major assumptions that we are going to make initially (although there are several other assumptions that we shall specify later as we develop the analysis), and obviously many of them are very unrealistic and in no way reflect the real world: investors are almost invariably faced with making decisions where the effects stretch over many periods; the future is largely unknown and so future cash flows cannot be certain; non-physical/capital market investments, such as placing money on deposit at a bank, are usually available to investors; investment projects are often *indivisible* and so must either be undertaken completely or not at all; many investment project cash flows depend upon what other investment decisions have or have not been made. However, such simplifying assumptions do provide a starting point for our analysis; we shall examine later the effect of replacing them with more realistic descriptions of the real world, but for the moment let us accept them.

THE TIME VALUE OF MONEY

We have already defined an investment decision by a company as one that involves the company making cash outlay (now) with the aim of receiving a (future) cash inflow in return. If we also make the simplistic but basically correct assumption that a company can do either of two things with its cash resources – it can pay it out to shareholders as a dividend or retain it within the company and invest it – then if a company makes a decision to invest, it is in fact deciding *not* to pay that cash to shareholders now, but instead to put it into an investment with the aim of obtaining an increased amount of cash in the future, which can then be paid out as a dividend.

Therefore, when a company makes an investment decision, this means that, as a result, shareholders are having to forgo the opportunity of consumption now (i.e. having the cash invested as a dividend now) with the aim of increasing future consumption (i.e. an enlarged cash dividend later).[3] In other words, investment decisions are about the delaying of *current consumption* in order to increase *future consumption*. (Or in non-economic terms, not spending money on consuming goods and services now, but investing the money instead so as to produce more money later which can then be spent on an increased quantity of goods and services.)

To look more closely at the investment decision, let us first consider the case of the single-owner firm (i.e. one in which the company has only one shareholder, who owns all the shares, and whose entire wealth is represented by the company) in which the owner is also the decision-maker. In deciding to invest, the owner is forgoing some present consumption in order to increase future consumption and, in taking such action, the owner must also have decided that the future consumption so gained is of greater value than the present consumption sacrificed in making the investment.

To make such investment decisions in a consistent manner,[4] the owner requires a specific criterion that will enable him or her[5] to judge whether or not any particular investment opportunity will produce sufficient compensation, in terms of increased future consumption, for having to reduce current consumption in order to make the investment.

Suppose our owner-manager requires a minimum of €1.20 back at the end of the year in order to persuade him to invest €1 now. Thus he requires compensation of 20 cents for every €1 of current consumption he forgoes. This requirement – which is a type of *exchange rate* of money between points in time and is, in fact, the owner's *time value of money* (TVM) – can be expressed as a percentage:

$$\frac{€1.20}{€1.00} - 1 = 0.20 \text{ or } 20\%$$

On this basis an investment appraisal decision rule could be formulated in which an investment project is only undertaken if it produces at least a 20% return on capital (i.e. the project produces at least €1.20 for every €1 invested). The owner-manager would not be willing to invest in a project that produced *less than* a 20% return, because 20% represents his time value of money.

It is important to realize that this TVM is unlikely to remain a constant but will probably increase as more and more present consumption is given up for investment. That is to say, with each successive reduction in current consumption, the owner is likely to demand a higher and higher minimum future return in order to persuade him to invest, because each additional €1 of current consumption forgone is likely to be of increasing value (in terms of the benefits received from consumption), and each additional €1 of future consumption gained is likely to be of decreasing value. This is an example of the economic concept of diminishing marginal utility.

THE BASIC GRAPHICAL ANALYSIS

The single-owner firm case

The one-period graphical analysis, made under our six assumptions, is shown in Figure 4.1. The curve AB is called the physical investment line[6] (PIL) and is composed of all the physical investment opportunities available to the company at t_0, arranged in order of decreasing return.[7] Thus the most 'profitable' investments – in terms of greatest return – would be undertaken first by the firm.

The physical investment line represents the complete range of maximum consumption combinations that the owner can obtain between the two points in time[8] by applying varying amounts of the company's existing resources to physical investment opportunities. Therefore, as the owner gives up increasing amounts of current consumption in order to make physical investments, the company locates further and further up and around the

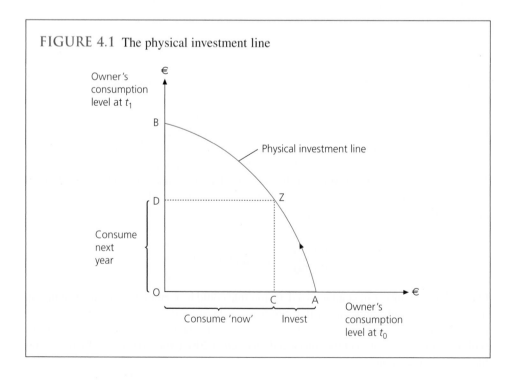

FIGURE 4.1 The physical investment line

physical investment line. (For instance if it locates at point A, no investment is undertaken and if it locates at point B, all possible physical investments are undertaken.)

Using Figure 4.1, OA represents the owner's total wealth now (i.e. at t_0) and can be regarded as the liquidation value of the company. If all this wealth is consumed now and none is invested, then there will be zero wealth available for consumption next year (i.e. t_1). If only part of this year's wealth is consumed, say OC, and the rest, CA, is invested, then the company locates itself at point Z on the physical investment line and this level of investment will produce OD available for consumption next year.

The return received by the company from the last (i.e. marginal) €1 of investment made at t_0 – the final piece of investment that brings the company to locate at point Z – can be found from the *slope* of the physical investment line at that point.[9] But besides being the return on the marginal investment, this slope represents something else. The company has located at point Z because the owner must feel that any *further* investment is not worthwhile. In other words, the gain in next year's consumption generated by a marginal increase in investment now, does *not* provide sufficient compensation for the additional reduction in present consumption that would be necessary to finance the increased investment. Therefore the marginal return on investment being obtained at Z must be equal to the owner's TVM.

If the marginal return at Z was *greater than* the owner's TVM, the company would continue to invest, and if it were *less than* the TVM, the company would have stopped investing *before* reaching point Z, because the return gained from a move along the PIL from *below* Z to point Z, would not have been sufficient compensation for the present consumption that would have had to be forgone in order to make the investment.

Introduction of indifference curves

We can derive this result more precisely by asking the question: given that the physical investment line represents a whole series of infinitely divisible and independent opportunities for investment projects, arranged in decreasing order of rate of return, so that the investment with the greatest return is ranked (and undertaken) first and the one with the smallest return last, how does the company know when to stop investing? In order to answer this question fully, we have to make use of another economic concept: *indifference curves*.

It is assumed that the reader is familiar with the derivation and meaning of the concept of indifference curves – it is explained in most introductory economic textbooks. In brief, indifference curves are curves of *constant* 'utility' or 'well-offness', and when mapped on to the graph of consumption 'now' and consumption 'next year', an individual indifference curve indicates all possible combinations of consumption, at the two points in time, which give the same level of utility. The curves are convex to the origin, indicating that there is diminishing marginal utility attached to consumption at any single point of time, and each indifference curve, moving from left to right, gives the individual a *higher* overall level of utility.

Their place here concerns the fact that the set of indifference curves belonging to the company's owner can be mapped on Figure 4.1 graph, as shown in Figure 4.2, and can be used to indicate at what point the company should stop investing: it is that point on the physical investment line which enables the owner to achieve his *highest possible* indifference curve – that is, his highest level of utility. This is found at the point of tangency between an indifference curve and the physical investment line. In terms of Figure 4.2, the company invests CA 'now' because the two time-point pattern of consumption that results for the owner – OC 'now' and OD 'next year' – places him on his highest possible indifference curve and so maximizes his welfare.

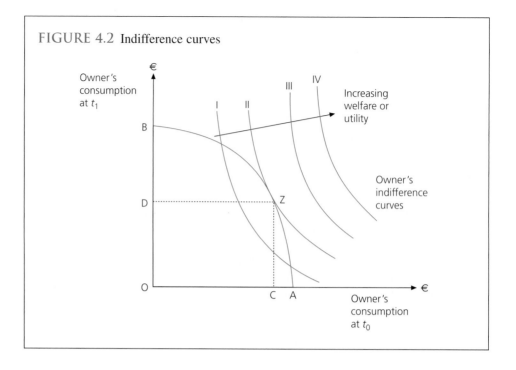

FIGURE 4.2 Indifference curves

The point of tangency between the two curves represents a point where the slopes of each equate. As the slope of the indifference curve reflects an individual's *marginal* TVM and the slope of the physical investment line represents the rate of return on the *marginal* project, then the point where the slopes of these two curves equate must be the point at which the owner's TVM equals the return on the marginal investment made by the company. Thus, the investment decision rule should be that the company continues to make physical investments until the return from the marginal investment (i.e. the last one made) equals the owner's marginal TVM. Any further investment will not produce the necessary return required and so will have the effect, in terms of our indifference curve analysis, of placing the owner on a lower indifference curve.

INTRODUCTION OF CAPITAL MARKETS

From this simple analysis, using a series of restrictive assumptions about the real world, we have seen how investment decisions would be made and why money is said to possess a 'time value'. If we now make our analysis slightly more realistic by relaxing our third assumption so as to make available the opportunity of being able to lend and borrow money on a capital market at a rate of interest, we can then develop a second reason for money having a time value.

With the introduction of capital markets, the firm is faced with three possible courses of action at t_0: consumption, physical investment or capital market investment. Making the very important assumption that there is a perfect capital market,[10] and therefore there is only one market rate of interest at which the company can both lend and borrow, we can use the one-period graphical analysis to illustrate how the company makes investment decisions so as to allow the owner of the company to distribute his consumption between the two points in time in such a way that he maximizes his welfare.

The financial market line

In terms of Figure 4.3, suppose the single-owner firm has amount OG available for consumption at t_0 and OH available at t_1. The capital market can be represented by a straight line, AE, which passes through point F, the coordinate of the existing consumption distribution. The slope of this line[11] is given by $(1 + r)$, where r is the market rate of interest, and the line is termed the financial investment line (FIL).

This line shows the range of capital market transactions available to the firm, given the existing distribution of cash resources of OG now (i.e. t_0) and OH next year (i.e. t_1). A move *down* the financial investment line from F to (say) point L means that the firm *borrows* GM on the capital market now – so increasing consumption at t_0 from OG to OM – and repays (capital plus interest) HN next year, so reducing consumption at t_1 from OH to ON. Notice that the maximum that can be borrowed now is amount GA; if the firm attempts to borrow more than this, there will not be sufficient resources available next year to repay the capital and accrued interest.

A move *up* the financial investment line to (say) point I means that the firm is *lending* JG on the capital market so as to reduce consumption now (to OJ) and to increase consumption next year (to OK). Again notice that a maximum of OG can be lent now – reducing current consumption to zero – and which results in having OE available for consumption next year.

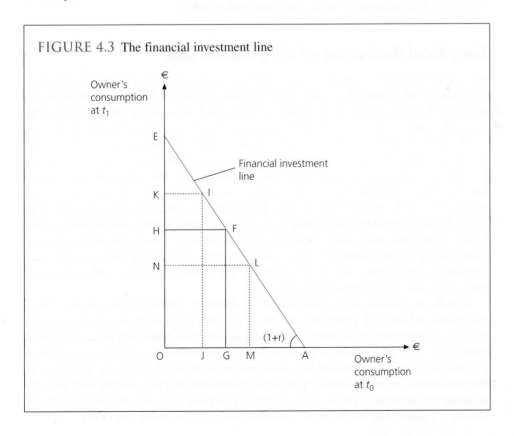

FIGURE 4.3 The financial investment line

THE SEPARATION THEOREM

Having seen how the FIL works, we can now combine the *physical* and *financial* investment lines on a single graph. This allows us to examine how both physical investment decisions and capital market borrowing or lending decisions are made in conjunction with each other, in order to allow the owner to achieve his highest possible indifference curve and so optimize his consumption spread over the year and maximize his utility.

However, up to this point we have taken as our decision-making entity the single-owner firm, where the investment decision-maker and the owner are one and the same person. Introducing the possibility of using the capital market allows us to analyze the investment decision process not only in the single-owner case, but also in the much more important situation where there are *many* owners (i.e. shareholders) and they are *separate* from the investment decision-makers (i.e. management). This is the so-called Separation Theorem.[12]

Under the separation theorem the capital investment decision rule now becomes: the company (i.e. the managers) undertakes *physical* investments until the return from the marginal physical investment equates with the perfect capital market interest rate. This amount of physical investment results in some particular dividend flow, at t_0 and t_1, to the shareholders. The shareholders then make *financial* investment decisions (by either borrowing or lending on the capital market) until their *individual* marginal time values of money equate with the capital market rate of interest. Such action will result in them achieving their highest possible indifference curves by producing a distribution of consumption over the period, which maximizes their individual levels of utility.

Graphical derivation of the decision rule

We can see how these separation theorem decision rules are derived and why they help to maximize the shareholder's utility by examining Figure 4.4. Here the financial investment line is superimposed on the Figure 4.1 situation. Let us assume for the moment that although ownership is separate from management, the company has only one shareholder.

The current liquidation value of the company is OA. In the absence of a capital market we know that the company management will invest amount AC, and so make physical investments up to point Z on the physical investment line. This represents the point of tangency between the physical investment line and the owner's indifference curve (UT$_1$), and therefore at this point the return from the marginal investment (derived from the slope of the physical investment line) equates with the shareholder's time value of money (given by the slope of the indifference curve tangential to point Z). Thus in our one time-period world, the shareholder would receive a 'dividend' of OC now and OD next year. This distribution of consumption over the period places him on his highest attainable indifference curve, UT$_1$, and so maximizes his utility.

With the introduction of a capital market, the company's management now invest more than before, amount AQ, rather than AC, so as to undertake physical investments up to the point where the return on the marginal physical investment equates with the capital market interest rate (derived from the slope of the financial investment line). This occurs at point P where the financial investment line is tangent to the physical investment line. Thus the shareholder now receives a different dividend distribution: OQ now and OR next year. The company has undertaken physical investments up to point P because this has the effect of placing the shareholder on the highest possible financial investment line (VW).

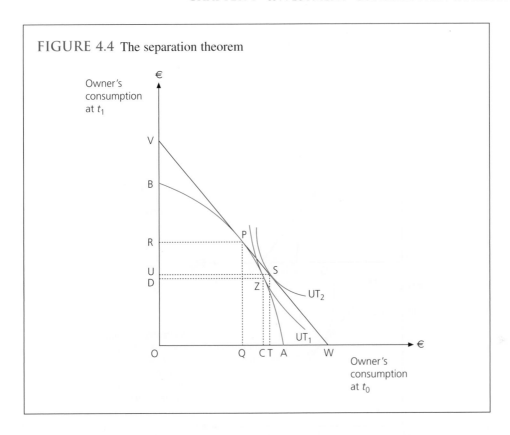

FIGURE 4.4 The separation theorem

Unlike the situation where capital market opportunities did not exist, the shareholder now does not have to accept the pattern of dividend distribution given by the company for consumption. Instead, he can borrow or lend on the capital market (i.e. move down or up VW from point P) so as to adjust his received dividend flow to suit whatever consumption pattern is preferred.

This preferred pattern is given by the point on the financial investment line that is tangent to one of his indifference curves, because this indifference curve will be the highest attainable. Thus the shareholder either lends or borrows on the capital market until his marginal time value of money (derived from the slope of the indifference curve) equates with the perfect capital market rate of interest. In Figure 4.4 the shareholder achieves this point, S (and so lands on a higher utility curve – UT_2), by moving down the financial investment line and borrowing an amount QT to make a total of OT available for consumption 'now' and OU available for consumption 'next year'. (A dividend of RO is received from the company next year, but part of this, RU, is used to repay the borrowed capital and accrued interest.)

Whether the shareholder lends or borrows or even omits to use the capital market at all depends solely upon the location of the point of tangency between the financial investment line and the shareholder's indifference curve, as Figure 4.5 shows. What Figure 4.4 illustrates is how, by taking advantage of both physical *and* financial investment opportunities, the shareholder can attain a higher indifference curve, UT_2 (and so increase his utility), than would have been possible from making physical investments alone. (In fact this can unambiguously be seen occurring in Figure 4.4, because the shareholder has managed to increase his consumption in *both* t_0 and t_1 through using the capital market: by amount

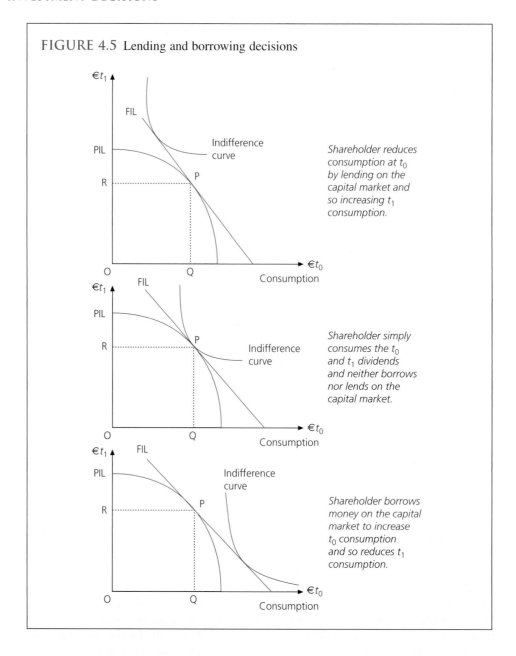

FIGURE 4.5 Lending and borrowing decisions

Shareholder reduces consumption at t_0 by lending on the capital market and so increasing t_1 consumption.

Shareholder simply consumes the t_0 and t_1 dividends and neither borrows nor lends on the capital market.

Shareholder borrows money on the capital market to increase t_0 consumption and so reduces t_1 consumption.

CT 'now' and UD 'next year'. Such a result is likely to be the exception, rather than the rule. More generally, increasing one time period's consumption will result in reducing consumption in the other time period.[13])

The multi-owner firm

The development of this separation theorem is extremely important. It results in a company's management making only *physical* investment decisions and leaving individual shareholders to adjust their received dividend pattern to fit their particular consumption requirements by either lending or borrowing money on the capital market. In the owner-manager firm, it makes no difference to the analysis whether the individual owner uses the capital market or the company uses the capital market on the owner's behalf (as long as, in the case where owner and management are separate, the managers are aware of the owner's marginal time value of money).

However, the crucial importance of the separation theorem comes when ownership is separated from management *and* there is *more than one* owner. Quite simply, different individuals have different time values of money, and so a company would be able to undertake the physical investment decisions but not the financial investment decisions, because there would be more than one marginal time value of money. The use of the separation theorem avoids this problem by leaving the financial investment decisions to the individual shareholders.

Figure 4.6 shows a situation where a company is owned by *two* shareholders: one with 75% of the equity (Shareholder 1) and the other with 25% of the equity (Shareholder 2). The firm continues to make physical investments until the marginal return on investment equates with the market rate of interest, and then pays out the resulting dividends to each shareholder in proportion to their shareholdings. In so doing, the company would still be ensuring that each individual shareholder is placed on the highest possible financial investment line. It is then up to the individual shareholder to make whatever decision is best, in the knowledge of his own set of indifference curves and time value of money, with regard to using the capital market in order to adjust his received dividends to a more preferred split of consumption between t_0 and t_1.

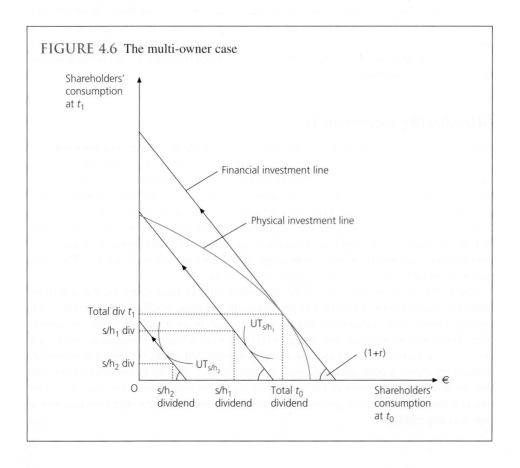

FIGURE 4.6 The multi-owner case

In the example shown in Figure 4.6, Shareholder 1 (75% holding) will use the capital market to borrow and so increases consumption t_0, at the expense of a reduced consumption level at t_1, by moving down the FIL. Shareholder 2 will use the capital market to lend and so move up the FIL, thereby reducing consumption at t_0 but, in return, having an increased level of consumption at t_1.

THE CONCLUSIONS OF THE BASIC MODEL

This development of the single-period investment–consumption model, as it is called, is important not only for illustrating how and why money has a time value, but also as acting as an introduction to financial decision-making in general. In this respect, we stated that management's objective must be to try to maximize shareholders' wealth and this would be achieved through the maximization of the dividend flow through time. The separation theorem places this latter statement in a clearer light.

Management must make investment decisions so as to maximize the dividend flow to shareholders. But this is only the first stage of a two-stage process, because the individual shareholder then uses the capital market to adjust the timing of this dividend flow so that it accords with his desired pattern of consumption.

The conclusions of our one-period investment–consumption model, and the assumptions upon which it is based, are important and wide-ranging (as we shall see later). The model implies that we require a technique of investment appraisal that will ensure that companies undertake physical investment until the return from the marginal investment equates with the capital market rate of return. In other words, companies should undertake capital investment projects as long as the return generated (from each one) is *not less than* the market rate of interest.

Introducing uncertainty

At this point it should also be noted that, just as individuals have their own personal time value of money – which represents an opportunity cost in terms of the alternative investment returns foregone – so the capital market interest rate represents the *economy's* average time value of money. Therefore the capital investment decision rule for companies could be restated as: undertake capital investment projects as long as the rate of return generated from each one is not less than the market's time value of money. However, it should also be noted that this decision rule, as it stands, is set in a world of *certainty*. In an *uncertain* world, as we shall see, there is a whole range of different market interest rates. Therefore this decision rule will require some slight modification.

The problem of uncertainty will be developed fully in later chapters, but it will be helpful to introduce the basic idea at this stage. In a certain world, an investment's outcome is known with certainty by the decision-maker. In an uncertain world, an investment's outcome is uncertain and hence is referred to as a 'risky' investment. With such investments, decision-makers are not entirely uninformed about the possible outcome, in that they *expect* a particular outcome (or cash inflow) from an investment, but realize that the actual outcome may differ from what was expected. (Notice too, therefore, that risk is a two-way street. An investment's actual outcome may be either better or worse than was expected.)

Generally speaking, investors dislike uncertainty of outcome – they are said to be 'risk averse'. This does not mean that they are unwilling to take on a risky investment. Instead it means that they require a *reward* for doing so and this reward is a higher level of *expected* return. Therefore, in an uncertain world, there is not just a single capital market interest rate/rate of return, but a whole series of different rates of return – one for each level of risk: the higher the risk, the higher the capital market rate of return.

As a result, in an uncertain world, our capital investment decision rule for companies now has to be modified. Projects should only be undertaken as long as they generate a rate of return which is not less than the capital market's rate of return *for a risk level equivalent to that of the project*.

PAYBACK AND ROCE

Clearly, the payback investment appraisal method does not meet the requirements of our decision rule that has been derived through this graphical analysis. This is because – even allowing for the fact that it can be adapted to allow for the time value of money – it uses *speed of return*, rather than *rate* of return, as its criterion of project desirability.

Equally unsuitable is the return on capital employed technique because, although it is a rate-of-return concept, it ignores the time value of money. In the next chapter we shall turn to the discounted cash flow methods of investment appraisal and examine the extent to which they meet the requirements of our model.[14]

SUMMARY

This chapter has developed the Hirshliefer single-period investment–consumption model to examine what is required of a capital investment appraisal decision rule. The following were the main points covered:

- The model was developed initially under six basic assumptions:
    1. Single time period horizon.
    2. Certainty of investment outcome.
    3. Only physical investment opportunities.
    4. Investments exhibit infinite divisibility and diminishing returns to scale.
    5. Investments are all independent.
    6. Investors are rational.
- The concept of the investor's marginal time value of money was introduced, which would be likely to be an increasing function of the amount invested.
- The firm's physical investment line was introduced and it was seen that the slope of the function represents the marginal rate of return on investment projects at any point.
- As a result, firms would locate on the physical investment line at the point where the slope of the line (the marginal project rate of return) equates with the investor's own marginal time value of money.

- In terms of indifference curves, this optimal investment point occurs at the point of tangency between the PIL and the investor's indifference curve set: the slope of the indifference curve reflecting the investor's marginal time value of money.

- With the introduction of capital markets and the financial market line, the graphical analysis can now handle cases other than the single-owner firm. The decision rule now changes so that the firm should invest in projects as long as their return is not less than the *market* rate of return – given by the slope of the FIL, which reflects society's average time value of money.

- This capital investment decision rule then allows each individual shareholder to adjust the received pattern of dividends/cash flow by using the capital market to locate on their highest possible indifference curve.

- This analysis is known as the Hirshliefer separation theorem in that the capital investment decision (made by managers) is *separated* from the capital market decision (made by owners/investors/shareholders).

- Finally, the concept of risk was briefly increased. It was argued that, in an uncertain world, the investment decision rule that arises out of the Hirshliefer analysis has to be modified: the firm should accept projects as long as they are expected to produce a return that is not less than the capital market rate of return for that level of risk.

NOTES

1. This approach was first used by the US economist Irving Fisher (and hence has become known as Fisherian Analysis) in *The Theory of Interest* (New York, Macmillan 1930). Its use was revived specifically in terms of financial decision theory by Jack Hirshliefer, 'On the Theory of Optimal Investment Decisions', *Journal of Political Economy,* August 1958.
2. Alternatively we could say that all investment opportunities have a life span of just one period of time, t_0 to t_1.
3. At this stage we will ignore the complications caused by the possibility of selling shares and the linkage of their value to investment decisions.
4. We can define a consistent criterion for investment decisions as one that would produce the following decision: if Project A is preferred to Project B and Project B is preferred to Project C, then the decision criterion should result in Project A being preferred to Project C. If not, the criterion is not producing consistent decisions. Technically, the decision-making must exhibit 'transitivity'.
5. From now on, for the sake of convenience, wherever the text refers to the decision-maker as being of male gender, we will assume that it refers to a decision-maker of *either* gender.
6. The literature gives this curve a variety of names, such as investment opportunity line, productive opportunity line or time-exchange function.
7. As a result of this arrangement and of our assumption that all physical investment opportunities are infinitely divisible and display decreasing returns to scale, the PIL is likely to be generally smooth and concave to the origin. In the real world of investments that are not infinitely divisible, it is anything but smooth.
8. The term 'maximum consumption combinations' is meant in the sense that with any given amount of current consumption, no higher consumption next year is possible with the company's existing resources and similarly, with any given amount of consumption next year, no higher level of current consumption is possible.
9. The return on the marginal investment – the marginal return – can properly be found from the first derivative of the function of the PIL. For illustration purposes it can be very roughly approximated by Figure 4.7:

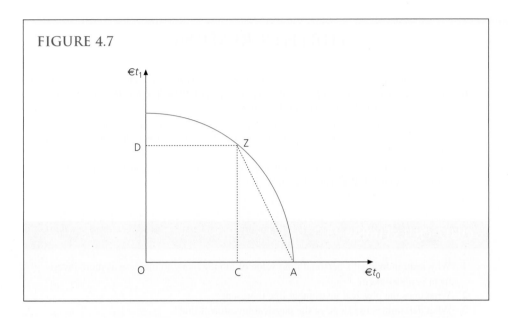

FIGURE 4.7

$$\frac{OD - CA}{CA} = \frac{OD}{CA} - \frac{CA}{CA} = \frac{OD}{CA} - 1$$

Therefore, if the company has a total value now of €1000 (OA) of which the owner consumes €600 (OC) and invests the remainder, €400 (CA) in order to produce €480 (OD) next year, we can obtain a rough approximation of the return on the marginal project (point Z) as:

$$\frac{480}{400} - 1 = 0.20 = 20\%$$

Graphically, we are finding the slope of the dotted line ZA. In fact this calculation of 20% does not provide the return on the *marginal* investment, but the *average* return on the *total* investment. However, it serves to illustrate the general point.

10. The concept of a perfect capital market will prove extremely important to us in later developments of the theory. For the time being we shall define it – under the assumption of a world of certainty – as a market where everyone can borrow or lend as much money as they wish (within their ability to repay) at a single rate of interest which is applicable to all, whether borrowing or lending. Additionally there are no transaction costs involved in using the market, no single investor or group of investors dominate the market and all information is freely available.

11. To be precise, this term is actually negative, that is −(1 + r) because the line AE has a negative slope – it slopes downwards from left to right.

12. This is often referred to as the *Hirshliefer* separation theorem after its original exponent.

13. The reader must be careful not to be misled here. The test of being 'better off' or increasing utility is whether or not a higher indifference curve is reached. So we could just as easily get a situation where the shareholder achieves a higher indifference curve through using the capital markets but this results (say) in a decrease in consumption 'now' and an increase 'next year'. As a higher indifference curve has been reached the reduction in consumption 'now' must be more than offset (in the shareholder's mind) by the gain in consumption 'next year'.

14. It may be wise to correct here a mistaken impression that the reader could possibly gain from this presentation and development of the theory. Historically, payback and ROCE were derived (largely) in ignorance of the single-period investment–consumption model. It is therefore not surprising that neither method meets the model's requirement for an investment appraisal technique. However, the two major discounted cash flow methods, which are to be discussed in the next chapter, were *not* developed in isolation from the model but arise out of the logic that lies behind the model's construction. The reader should not believe that it is just fortuitous that these latter two methods of investment appraisal accord (as we shall see) with the model.

FURTHER READING

1. The basic reading for the ideas discussed in this chapter is: J. Hirshliefer, 'On the Theory of Optimal Investment Decisions', *Journal of Political Economy*, August 1958. The article is not easy reading, especially the second half, but is very much worthwhile.

2. Although the idea of risk has only been introduced very briefly at this stage, an accessible article to read would be: J. Hirshliefer, 'Risk, the Discount Rate and Investment Decision', *American Economic Review*, May 1961.

3. Students wishing to examine this topic further are referred to H. Bierman and S. Smidt, *The Capital Budgeting Decision*. 9/E Routledge, December 2006.

QUIZ QUESTIONS

1 Why is an individual's personal time value of money likely to increase as more investment is undertaken?

2 What does the physical investment line represent?

3 What determines the slope of the physical investment line?

4 What is an indifference curve?

5 Given a single owner-manager firm, how does the firm decide on its level of capital investment?

6 If an owner wants to lend money at t_0, does he move up or down the financial investment line?

7 What is the two-part decision rule that arises out of the Hirshliefer separation theorem?

8 Define a risky capital investment.

9 Taking risk into consideration, what is the capital investment decision rule that managers should follow if they wish to maximize shareholder wealth?

10 What are the four main assumptions (remember, two were dropped at later stages in the analysis) of the single-period investment–consumption model?

11 What is the generally assumed attitude of investors to risk?

12 If an investor's personal marginal time value of money was less than the market interest rate, would they want to lend or borrow money?
(See the 'Answers to Quiz Questions' section at the back of the book.)

PROBLEMS

The answer to this problem is available to students online (see the 'Digital Resources' page for details).

1 Hellenic Evga is a Greek company that has €500 million of cash resources available at t_0. It has identified three investment projects, as follows (all values in € millions):

Project	I	II	III
Outlay at t_0	100	200	200
Inflow at t_1	120	300	210

▶

▶

Assume that all projects exhibit *constant* returns to scale.

Required:

(a) Draw, to scale, the physical investment line facing the firm.

(b) Given that the market interest rate in Greece is 8%, show graphically Hellenic Evga's investment decisions and the resulting t_0 and t_1 cash flow to the company's owners.

(c) How might the investment decisions of the firm change if the Greek interest rate moved:

   (i)   to 4%?

   (ii) to 25%?

   (iii) to 20%?

(d) Given the market interest rate of 8%, before the firm can implement the investment plan given in your answer to part (b) an extra project is identified:

Project	IV (€ millions)
Outlay at t_0	250
Inflow at t_1	330

Show the new situation graphically. What is your revised investment decision advice to the company's management?

5 THE DISCOUNTED CASH FLOW APPROACH

LEARNING OBJECTIVES

The purpose of this chapter is to:

- Explain the mathematics of compounding and discounting including particular patterns of cash flows such as perpetuities and annuities.

- Formally introduce the concept of the time value of money (TVM).

- Develop the net present value (NPV) and internal rate of return (IRR) investment appraisal techniques.

- Demonstrate how the NPV and IRR techniques can be integrated into the investment consumption model developed in Chapter 4.

- Examine how the Payback technique can be modified to allow it to take into account the time value of money.

NET PRESENT VALUE

Having examined the two 'traditional' methods of capital investment appraisal, it is now time to turn to the other two main appraisal techniques. These are NPV and IRR, both of which are described as discounted cash flow (DCF) methods. However, this initial look will just focus on the basic analysis and then the following two chapters will add in some 'real world' complications. We start by first examining the NPV technique.

The NPV investment appraisal method works on the simple, but fundamental, principle that an investment is worthwhile undertaking if the money generated by the investment is greater than the investment's cost. On this very commonsense principle, Project A is worth investing in. For an outlay of €500, it produces a total cash inflow of €600. We can say that the investment has a net value of +€100.

Project A	
Year	Cash flow (€)
0	−500
1	+200
2	+200
3	+200
	+100 net value

It is clear that with such a straightforward approach the decision rule would be: accept all investments with a positive, or even zero, net value (as they produce a return either greater than, or equal to, their cost), and reject all those with a negative net value.

However, let us take a totally different situation. Suppose you were made the following offer: if you pay €500 now, you will immediately receive 200 pounds, 200 Japanese yen and 200 US dollars. How would you go about deciding whether the offer was worthwhile? What you certainly would *not* do is to think: 'I have to give up 500 pieces of paper and, in return, I'll get 200 + 200 + 200 = 600 pieces of paper. As I end up with 100 more pieces of paper, the deal is worthwhile!' Instead, you would recognize that in order to evaluate the offer, you have to convert all the different *currencies* to a *common* currency, and then undertake the comparison.

Although it does not look as foolish as initially suggested with the currency offer, our suggested approach to evaluating Project A is just as foolish. In the same way that money in different *currencies* cannot be compared directly, but first has to be converted to a *common* currency, cash flows in the same currency (as in Project A), but occurring at *different points in time*, cannot be compared directly, but must first be converted to a *common* point of time. This is because of the time value of money.

It is with this reasoning in mind that the net present value investment appraisal decision rule basically takes the same approach as that used with Project A, but with one vital difference. That difference is that the TVM is taken into account in assessing whether the investment has a positive or negative net value.

 REAL WORLD VIEW: Dilemma for Pensioners – Annuity or Lump Sum?

With rising standards of living and the resultant increase in life expectancy, we all have to make our earnings go a little bit further and think about how we'll support ourselves in retirement. Unsurprisingly, then, pensions continue to be a hot topic in the news. In 2014, an automatic pension-enrolment policy was implemented in the UK to all qualifying workers, while the government announced plans to enable lump sums of the state pension to be drawn upon retirement, allowing greater flexibility of the money pot and opening up potential for investment. At one extreme, some ministers have even called for the public to be informed of when they are most likely to die (based on their socioeconomic group and health records, amongst other factors).

All these developments are part of a wider call to encourage the workforce to think more actively about their retirement and to support themselves accordingly, through carrying out more rigorous financial planning at an earlier stage in their lives. However, as the following example highlights, there are many considerations to think about when trying to maximize your retirement fund, not least when taking into account the TVM.

Increasingly, companies are giving their retiring employees the option to take their pensions either as an annuity payout or as a lump sum distribution (for more on annuities see the Appendix at the end of this chapter). Hassan, for instance, who is 65 years old, retires shortly after working for a multinational corporation for many years. With a life expectancy of 20 years, he must now decide what to do with the money in his pension account.

Upon retirement he has €387 655 in his account and is offered the following alternatives:

- Take an annuity payout: Hassan will receive €2259 per month for as long as he lives.

- Take the lump-sum distribution: Hassan will receive €387 655. He can now choose to invest these funds as he wishes.

If Hassan opts for the lump sum distribution, he can do whatever he pleases with the money. If managed carefully he could generate a return while retaining control of the principal. In reality, however, generating a good return typically relies on following a long-term investment strategy, yet he has no guarantee of success.

If he manages to secure a regular annual return of 5% on his investment, he will receive €19 383 annually, which is €1615 per month. This is €644 less than the monthly payout, but he will maintain the principal.

This is the dilemma that many new pensioners will face: managing the asset (and associated risk) whilst retaining the principal, or keeping the money locked up in the pension plan for a guaranteed monthly pay out for life.

The discounting process

The TVM is taken into account through the discounting process. The arithmetic of discounting is dealt with in the Appendix to this chapter and the reader is advised to become familiar with its contents. However, it will help in explaining the NPV technique, if the basic concepts of discounting are developed here.

We have already seen from our initial discussion on the TVM in Chapter 3 that, given the choice between €100 now, and €100 in 12-months' time, most people would intuitively take the €100 now. This is because the €100 received now could be placed on deposit for the next 12-months at (say) 6% interest and so turn itself into €106 in 1 year's time. (And, being rational investors, €106 in 12-months' time will always be preferred to only €100 in 12-months' time.) Therefore, in this case, 6% – the interest rate – represents the time value of money.

The mathematics of this process works through the compound interest formula:

$$A(1 + r)^n$$

where A is the initial amount invested or placed on deposit, r is the (annual) rate of interest and n is the number of years for which A is left on deposit.

In the example used above, these three variables have the respective values of €100, 0.06 (6% expressed in decimal terms) and 1. So, €100 left on deposit for 12 months is turned into:

$$£100(1 + 0.06)^1 = £100 + £6 = £106$$

Using this compound interest formula, but switching it around, we can also calculate that to receive €106 in 12-months' time, the amount to be invested now is:

$$\frac{£106}{(1 + 0.06)^1} = £106 \times \frac{1}{(1 + 0.06)^1} = £100$$

Therefore €100 is the 'present value' (PV) of €106 received in 12-months' time and €106 the 'future' (or 'terminal') value of €100 deposited 12 months earlier, assuming the rate of interest is 6%.

Similarly, €100 invested for 2 years at a 6% compound interest rate would, in 2-years' time, produce:

$$£100 \times (1 + 0.06) \times (1 + 0.06) = £100 \times (1 + 0.06)^2 = £112.36$$

Similarly, €112.36 received in 2-years' time is equal to:

$$\frac{£112.36}{(1 + 0.06)^2} = £112.36 \times \frac{1}{(1 + 0.06)^2} = £100 \text{ now}$$

Thus, *future* value of €100 invested now is €112.36 in 2-years' time; while the *present* value of €112.36 received in 2-years' time is €100. (In each case we are assuming an annual interest rate of 6%.)

In general terms, $A(1 + r)^n$ is the future value of an amount A that has been placed on deposit for n years at an annual compound interest rate of r. Similarly: $A \times \dfrac{1}{(1 + r)^n}$ is the present value of an amount A received in n-years' time, where r is the annual compound rate of interest.

In the calculation of the future value, an amount of money is being 'compounded' *forwards* through time, whereas in the calculation of the present value, an amount of money is being 'discounted' *backwards* through time. To distinguish between these two processes, it is usual to refer to the interest rate, when used in the discounting process, as the 'discount rate'. Also, usually a slightly easier notation is used for the present value expression: $A(1 + r)^{-n}$. Thus, in the previous example, the present value of €112.36 received in 2-years' time, when the annual rate of discount is 6%, is given by:

$$\frac{£112.36}{(1 + 0.06)^2} = £112.36(1 + 0.06)^{-2} = £112.36 \times 0.8900 = £100$$

A discounting example

The NPV method makes use of the idea of present values by expressing all the investment's *future* cash flows in terms of their *present* values, and then calculating the *net* present value of the investment's cash flows.

To see how the NPV method works, let us return to Project A, but this time, instead of just netting out the cash inflows and outflows to produce a net value of +€100, we first of all convert (or 'discount') the investment's future cash flows to present value cash flows, in order to allow for the TVM, and then net out the inflows and outflows. Thus, with a discount rate of (say) 8%, the NPV of Project A is +€15.40:

Project A

Year	Cash flow (€)	×	Discounting factor	=		=	Present value cash flow (€)
0	−500	×	$(1 + 0.08)^0$	=	− 500 × 1	=	−500.00
1	+200	×	$(1 + 0.08)^{-1}$	=	+200 × 0.9259	=	+185.18
2	+200	×	$(1 + 0.08)^{-2}$	=	+200 × 0.8573	=	+171.46
3	+200	×	$(1 + 0.08)^{-3}$	=	+200 × 0.7938		+158.76
						NPV	+€15.40

From this analysis we can see that Project A *is* worth undertaking, because its cost is less than the sum of its future cash inflows, expressed in present value terms. The time value of money has been taken into account by the fact that all the cash flows of the project, for the purposes of comparison, are converted to values at a single point in time: the present time/now.

To emphasize this important point further, it is vital to understand that once the fact is accepted that money has a time value, then it follows that money at *different* points in time is not directly comparable: €1 now cannot be directly compared with €1 next year, and so the cash flows of a project that arise at different points through time all have to be converted to a value at one particular point in time. By convention, and because it has many practical advantages, the point in time normally chosen is the present time/now.

Thus our original netting procedure with Project A which produced a net value of +€100 was nonsensical, because we were not comparing like with like, but were trying to net out the money flows arising at different points in time without first converting them to a common point in time. The NPV approach tells us that in terms of present values (i.e. converting all the cash flows to money values now) Project A produces a return that is €15.40 in excess of the investment outlay (i.e. in *present value* terms its cost is €500 and the total cash inflow the project generates is €515.40) and is therefore a worthwhile investment.

Project B

Year	Cash flow(€)	×	Discounting factor	=	Present value cash flow (€)
0	−1 000	×	$(1 + 0.08)^0$	=	−1 000.00
1	+100	×	$(1 + 0.08)^{-1}$	=	+92.59
2	+200	×	$(1 + 0.08)^{-2}$	=	+171.46
3	+200	×	$(1 + 0.08)^{-3}$	=	+158.76
4	+550	×	$(1 + 0.08)^{-4}$	NPV	+404.25
Net value	+50				−172.94

As another example, evaluating Project B without taking into account the time value of money, the cash inflows exceed the cash outflows by €50 and so the project appears to be a worthwhile investment. However, if we do take into account the time value of money by discounting the cash flows into present values at an 8% discount rate, then we can see that Project B is *not* a worthwhile investment, because the project's cost (€1000), is greater than the present value of the cash inflows produced, resulting in a *negative* NPV.

Calculating present values

The discounting factors, such as $(1 + 0.08)^{-3}$, can be calculated quite easily on any basic calculator or app that has a 'powers' function, i.e. x^y or '^'. In addition, a complete set of discounting factors for a variety of values of n and i is included in the Appendix of tables at the end of this book (Table B). These tables can be used to find that $(1 + 0.08)^{-3}$ equals 0.7938. In other words, the present value of €1 in 3-years' time at an 8% rate of discount is 79.38 pence. Therefore, €200 in 3-years' time has a present value of: €200 $\times$ 0.7938 = €158.76.

The NPV decision rule

In general terms, we can express the NPV of an investment project as the sum of its net discounted future cash flows:

$$\sum_{t=0}^{n} \frac{A_t}{(1 + r)^t}$$

where A_t is the project's cash flow (either positive or negative) at time t (t takes on values from Year 0 to Year n, where n represents the point in time when the project comes to the end of its life) and r is the annual rate of discount or the time value of money (which is here assumed to remain a constant over the life of the project). If the expression has a positive, or even zero, value, the company should invest in the project. If it has a negative value, it should not invest. (This general mathematical expression for the NPV of an investment project is more fully explained in the Appendix to this chapter on 'Compounding and Discounting'.)

Let us take a closer look at Project B to see why the NPV method tells us not to invest. Project B requires an outlay of €1000 and is expected to produce cash inflows for the 4 following years. However, if we did not invest €1000 in B we could, presumably, put the money on deposit (i.e. lend the money on the capital market) at the going rate of interest of (in this example) 8%. At the end of 4 years this would produce €1000 $\times$ $(1 + 0.08)^4$ = €1360.50.

Suppose we *did* invest in Project B and as the generated cash inflows arose we placed them on deposit (at 8% interest). How much cash would we be able to accumulate by the end of 4 years (i.e. by the time the life of the project was completed)? This is shown below, where the €100 Project B produces in 12-months' time can be invested for 3 years, the €200 it produces in 24-months' time can be invested for 2 years, and so on:

Project B

Year	Project's cash inflow (€)	×	Compounding factor	=	Terminal value (end of Year 4) (€)
1	+100	×	$(1 + 0.08)^3$	=	+125.97
2	+200	×	$(1 + 0.08)^2$	=	+233.28
3	+200	×	$(1 + 0.08)^1$	=	+216.00
4	+550	×	$(1 + 0.08)^0$	=	+550.00
			Total terminal value		+€1 125.25

As we saw before, placing the €1000 on deposit for 4 years produces €1360.50 at the end of 4 years, whereas if we invest our €1000 in Project B and place on deposit any cash flows that arise, at the end of 4 years this will produce only €1125.25.

Therefore, looking at the two alternatives, the project is not the most desirable investment: we should be better off placing the €1000 on deposit in the capital market. This is the basis of the advice given by the NPV appraisal method. The capital market investment of €1000 would produce €1360.50 at Year 4, but the Project B investment would only produce €1125.25 at Year 4, which is (€1360.50 − €1125.25) €235.25 shortfall, in Year 4 terms.

The *present* value of this €235.25 shortfall from Project B is €172.94, which is the calculated amount of Project B's negative NPV.

So we can see that the NPV method of investment appraisal evaluates projects by looking at a capital market investment as an *alternative* to an investment in the project. It automatically carries out this comparison of alternatives through the decision rule: only invest in projects that produce positive, or zero, NPVs. (A project with a *zero* NPV is simply one which produces the *same return* as would a capital market investment. A project with a *positive* NPV produces a *better return* than a capital market investment.) As we have seen, the *value* of a project's NPV represents the increase or decrease (depending upon whether the NPV is positive or negative) in return that would arise from investing in the project rather than lending the money on the capital market at the market rate of interest, and it is this rate that is used as the discount rate.

ALTERNATIVE INTERPRETATIONS OF NPV

There are some equally valid, alternative interpretations of the meaning behind a project's NPV that it might be helpful to examine in order to gain a deeper understanding. We will take another project as an example. Project C is expected to produce the following net cash flows:

Year	Cash flow (€)
0	−100
1	+30
2	+40
3	+50
4	+20

Referring back to our brief discussion at the end of the previous chapter about risk, suppose that the capital market rate of return available from an investment of *similar risk* to Project C is 10%. Thus, 10% is the relevant time value of money and so is the appropriate discount rate to use in an NPV analysis.

Project C's NPV is calculated as:

Year	Cash flow (€)		Discount factor		PV cash flow (€)
0	−100	×	$(1 + 0.10)^0$	=	−100.00
1	+30	×	$(1 + 0.10)^{-1}$	=	+27.27
2	+40	×	$(1 + 0.10)^{-2}$	=	+33.06
3	+50	×	$(1 + 0.10)^{-3}$	=	+37.57
4	+20	×	$(1 + 0.10)^{-4}$	=	+13.66
				NPV	+€11.56

Project C has a positive NPV and therefore, according to the decision rule, is a good investment. There are three obvious interpretations that can be made of this result:

1. An investment of €100 in Project C produces €11.56 more, in t_0 terms, than investing on the capital market. In this sense, the €11.56 is an *excess* return or a measure of 'economic profit'. (Notice, **not** *accounting* profit, which is a different concept entirely.)

2. As Project C produces a positive NPV, it is generating a return which is *greater than* 10%, the discount rate used.

3. If €100 were borrowed at 10% interest, in order to undertake Project C, then the project would generate a sufficient cash flow to pay the interest, repay the loan *and* leave a surplus of €11.56 in present value terms.

Given these three interpretations, the logic of the NPV decision rule becomes even more obvious:

1. A negative NPV project is unacceptable because it indicates that the project makes a *loss* relative to a capital market investment (i.e. an opportunity loss).

2. A negative NPV project is unacceptable because it is producing a return *less than* that available for a similar level of risk on the capital market.

3. A negative NPV project is unacceptable as it would *not generate* sufficient cash flow to repay the financial cost of undertaking it.

Also notice, given these interpretations, that a zero NPV project would be acceptable – but we would not be overjoyed with such an investment.

Finally, there is a fourth interpretation of a project's NPV that can be made. In many ways, this is the most important interpretation and how it arises will be seen in the next section when we return to the Hirshliefer analysis. Quite simply, a project's NPV indicates the increase in shareholders' wealth that it will generate if it is undertaken. Hence, the technique links directly into our fundamental objective of financial management decision-making.

NPV and the investment–consumption model

When looking at our single-period investment–consumption model, we saw that in order to act in the best interests of its owners, a company should move along the physical investment line until the return from the marginal investment becomes equal to the return given by the capital market (i.e. the market rate of interest). How does the NPV method of invest-ment appraisal help us achieve that point?

Returning to Project A, we saw that using an 8% discount rate the project had an NPV of +€15.40, while Project B had an NPV of −€172.94. On the basis of what we already understand about the NPV, we can also say – using the two examples above – that as Project A has a positive NPV when discounted at 8%, it must be producing a rate of return *greater* than 8%, and similarly, as Project B has a negative NPV when discounted at 8%, then it must be producing a rate of return of *less than* 8%.

Just what the *exact* rate of return is in each case we shall consider later, but looking at Project D, since it gives a *zero* NPV when discounted at 8%, we can conclude that it has a rate of return exactly *equal* to 8%:

Project D

Year	Cash flow (€)		Present value factor		Present value cash flow (€)
0	−400	×	$(1 + 0.08)^0$	=	−400.00
1	+200	×	$(1 + 0.08)^{-1}$	=	+185.18
2	+100	×	$(1 + 0.08)^{-2}$	=	+85.73
3	+162.62	×	$(1 + 0.08)^{-3}$	=	+129.09
				NPV	€0

Therefore, if a company follows the NPV rule and invests in all physical investment opportunities available to it that possess either zero or positive NPVs, using the market rate of interest as the discount rate, it will automatically move along the physical investment line until a point of tangency is reached with the financial investment line.

If a company makes physical investments beyond this optimal point, these projects will have a rate of return which is *less than* the market rate of interest and therefore *negative* NPVs. As long as investment decision-makers within companies follow the NPV decision rule and only invest in projects with zero or positive NPVs, then the company is ensured of optimally locating on the physical investment line.

The graphical interpretation

In Figure 5.1, if management assess the company's total resources (i.e. the full, liquidated value of the company at time t_0) as OA and they have sought out all the investment alterna-tives available to them, expressed by the Physical investment line AB, then using the NPV method of investment appraisal, they will invest in all projects with positive or zero NPVs when discounted at the market rate of interest.

This simple decision rule will lead to DA of the company's resources being put into productive investments at t_0 and the remainder, OD, being paid out to shareholders as dividends. This investment will result in a total dividend of OC being paid out at t_1. Shareholders can then adjust their individual dividend receipts to fit their desired con-sumption pattern by lending or borrowing on the capital market (line EF). This two-stage

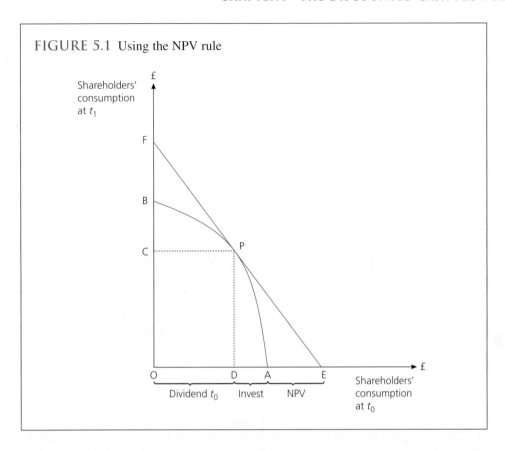

FIGURE 5.1 Using the NPV rule

process, with the company first making *physical* investment decisions and then the individual shareholder making *financial* investment decisions, will ensure that individual shareholders will achieve their highest possible indifference curves and hence maximize their level of utility.

We should also note that if the company does invest up to the optimal point P in Figure 5.1 (i.e. the point of tangency between the physical and financial investment lines), then the present value of the cash inflows generated by all the company's investment project undertakings is given by DE, the cash expenditure made on these investments is given by DA and so, by difference, AE represents the total NPV of the investment projects undertaken by the firm. (Alternatively, OE can be said to represent the present value of the sum of dividend OD at t_0 and dividend OC at t_1.)

From this we can see the derivation of that important *fourth interpretation* of the idea of NPV. Notice that with no investment undertaken, the total worth of the company's resources (in t_0 terms) is given by AO. If amount DA is invested to yield OC at t_1, then the worth of the company (again, in t_0 terms) increases to amount OE. Thus undertaking the investments required to locate at point P on the PIL has resulted in an *increase* in the current worth of the company – in other words, in shareholders' wealth – of AE, which of course represents the total NPV of the investments undertaken. Therefore, the NPV of a project represents the amount by which shareholders' wealth (measured in t_0 terms) will change as a result of accepting the project. (It thus becomes obvious why management should not accept negative NPV projects – they will cause shareholders' wealth to be reduced.)

FIGURE 5.2 Under-investing and over-investing

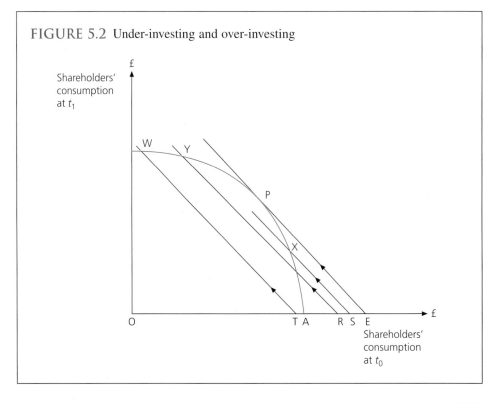

In general, the single-period investment–consumption diagram can measure the NPV of a company's total physical investments as the distance between the point at which the physical investment line cuts the horizontal axis and where the financial investment line, passing through the point at which the firm has located on the physical investment line, also cuts the horizontal axis. As can be seen from Figure 5.2, if a company either *under-invests* and locates at (say) point X, or *over-invests* and locates at (say) point Y, or *optimally* invests and locates at point Z on the physical investment line; in each case the total NPV earned by the company's investment decisions is given by the distance on the horizontal axis between the physical investment line and the financial investment line passing through the location point: respectively AS, AR and AE.[1] Locating at the optimal point on the physical investment line (at the point of tangency with the market line) also maximizes NPV and so here is yet another surrogate for the financial decision-making objective of maximizing shareholder wealth, that of maximizing total NPV.

One final point of interest from this graphical analysis is to use it to look at the effect of a change in the market rate of interest. A fall in the market rate of interest will cause the financial investment line to pivot *anticlockwise* and become flatter. This would then have the effect of moving the point of tangency (and hence the optimal physical investment point) higher up the physical investment line, thus increasing the amount of investment that a company must undertake to reach its point of optimality. This is just as we would expect, as is the case where the market rate of interest *rises* and the *reverse* effect is observed.

(The reader no doubt has noticed how the analysis has slipped in and out of the assumption of a single-period time horizon. This assumption was made in the Hirshliefer analysis in order to allow a graphical/two-dimensional presentation. However, the conclusions drawn can be quite simply applied to a multi-time period example, such as that of Project D.)

INTERNAL RATE OF RETURN

Before looking more carefully at this analysis and specifically at the implicit and explicit assumptions that lie behind the NPV method, let us turn to the second major discounted cash flow investment appraisal technique, the internal rate of return or IRR. (As we shall see later on in the discussion, the IRR has some significant theoretical and practical difficulties as a method of investment appraisal, and indeed it may be questioned whether it is truly a method of appraisal at all, or just an arithmetic result.)

The IRR model

To discover what the IRR is, let us return briefly to our discussion of NPV. We stated that if a project had a *positive* NPV at a certain discount rate, say 10%, this meant, amongst other things, that the project's return was *greater* than 10%, whilst if the project had a *negative* NPV then its return was *less than* the discount rate, and if it had a *zero* NPV, then its return was *equal to* the discount rate.

The IRR of a project can be defined as the rate of discount which, when applied to the project's cash flows, produces a *zero* NPV (hence the method could be seen as just an arithmetic result of the NPV method). In general terms, the IRR is the value for *r* that satisfies the expression:

$$\sum_{t=0}^{n} \frac{A_t}{(1 + r)^t} = 0$$

For a very simple project, with cash flows that extend over only 1 or 2 years in the future, the IRR can be calculated by using simple algebra. However, to calculate the IRR of more realistic investments, whose cash flows extend over several future time periods, we have to use an estimation procedure called *linear interpolation*. This estimation process is illustrated by means of the very simple example involving Project F.

Estimating the IRR via linear interpolation

Suppose Project F has the following expected cash flow:

Project F	
Year	Cash flow (€)
0	−100
1	+60
2	+50

If a whole series of *different* discount rates were applied to Project F's cash flow and the resulting NPVs were then calculated, these could then be plotted out on a graph against the discount rate used. Figure 5.3 illustrates the result that might occur, termed the 'NPV profile', where the various discount rates used to calculate the NPV are plotted along the horizontal

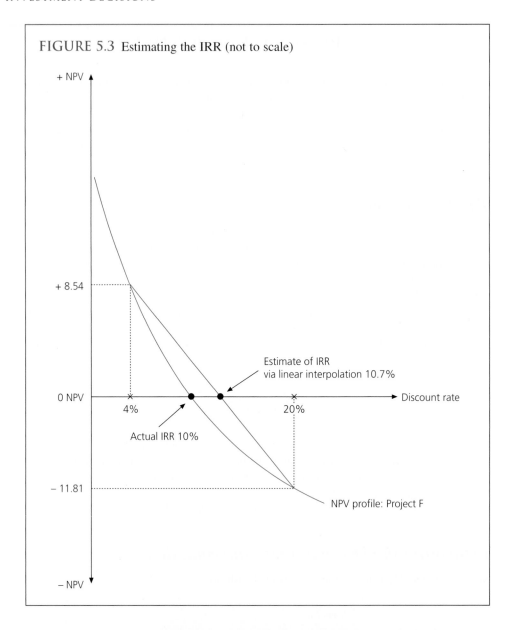

FIGURE 5.3 Estimating the IRR (not to scale)

axis and the resulting NPVs plotted on the vertical axis. The project's IRR is given by the point where the NPV profile cuts the horizontal axis. Linear interpolation is a 'shortcut' technique which can be used to give a reasonable approximation of an investment's precise IRR.

We will first deal with the mechanics of linear interpolation, and then examine its rationale. The mechanics are as follows. A pair of discount rates is selected so that one of them, when applied to the project's cash flow, produces a *positive* NPV and the other produces a *negative* NPV for the project. From observing Figure 5.3, it can be seen that as the discount rate (the TVM) gets larger, the positive NPV gets progressively smaller, passes through zero, and then becomes an increasingly large negative value. (This result is, of course, not surprising, knowing as much as we do about the time value of money concept.) Therefore a low and a high discount rate need to be selected to provide the required positive and negative NPVs.

Using 4% and 20% discount rates (the extreme discount rate values given in the Appendix of tables at the end of the book), the NPV of Project F can be calculated as:

4% Discount rate			20% Discount rate		
$0 - 100 (1.04)^0$	$=$	-100.00	$0 - 100 (1.20)^0$	$=$	-100.00
$1 + 60 (1.04)^{-1}$	$=$	$+57.69$	$1 + 60 (1.20)^{-1}$	$=$	$+50.00$
$2 + 55 (1.04)^{-2}$	$=$	$+50.85$	$2 + 55 (1.20)^{-2}$	$=$	$+38.19$
	NPV	$+8.54$		NPV	-11.81

The investment's IRR is estimated on the basis of proportions. Given that the project has a +NPV at a 4% discount rate and a −NPV at a 20% discount rate, the discount rate that gives a zero NPV must lie somewhere between the two values.

The difference between the two NPVs is: $+8.54 - (-11.81) = 20.35$. The project's NPV at a 4% discount rate $(+8.54)$ represents: $8.54/20.35 = 0.42$ or 42% of this difference. Therefore the discount rate at which the project has got a zero NPV can be estimated as equal to the lower of the two discount rates used, plus 42% of the difference between the two discount rates used: $20\% - 4\% = 16\% \times 0.42 = 6.7\%$. Thus the investment's IRR can be estimated as: $4\% + 6.7\% = 10.7\%$.

This linear interpolation calculation can be more formally presented as:

$$IRR = 4\% + \left[\frac{+8.54}{+8.54 - (-11.81)} \times (20\% - 4\%) \right]$$

$$IRR = 4\% + [0.42 \times 16\%] = 10.7\%$$

Figure 5.3 shows the linear interpolation method diagrammatically. The IRR is only estimated because the NPV profile is being approximated by a straight line. This 'bracketing' of discount rates around the true IRR so as to produce a positive and negative NPV is not strictly necessary, but it does make the approximation calculation easier. Furthermore, the narrower the bracketing around the actual IRR, the more accurate the estimate of the IRR. For example, using 8% and 12% discount rates, linear interpolation estimates Project F's IRR as:

At 8% discount rate: $+2.70$ NPV

At 12% discount rate: -2.58 NPV

$$IRR = 8\% + \left[\frac{+2.70}{+2.70 - (-2.58)} \times (12\% - 8\%) \right] = 10.04\%$$

This gives a much closer result to the actual IRR (which is actually 10%). However, for most investment appraisal purposes, a highly accurate estimate of the IRR is not justified and an estimate with the accuracy of our initial calculation is usually more than sufficient.

Finally, notice that the arithmetic of linear interpolation can still be used, even if the two discount rates used do *not* produce one positive and one negative NPV, as they have done in the examples used so far.

The general rule for using linear interpolation is as follows. Select any two discount rates, a lower rate and a higher rate. Calculate the project's NPV at each discount rate. Given that:

LRNPV	=	NPV of the project when calculated at the lower discount rate
HRNPV	=	NPV of the project when calculated at the higher discount rate
LDR	=	Lower discount rate, and
HDR	=	Higher discount rate, then:

$$IRR = LDR + \left[\frac{LRNPV}{LRNPV - HRNPV} \times (HDR - LDR) \right]$$

This is illustrated in Example 1.

EXAMPLE 1

Cintra Automotive wish to estimate the IRR of a project that is under evaluation. Its expected cash flows are as follows:

Year	Cash flow (€)
0	−10 000
1	+5 000
2	+8 000
3	+3 000

Again using 4% and 20% as the two discount rates, the NPV of the project is as follows:[2]

At a 4% discount rate, the NPV is +€4871

At a 20% discount rate, the NPV is +€1458

Therefore the project's IRR can be estimated as:

$$IRR = 4\% + \left[\frac{4871}{4871 - 1458} \times (20\% - 4\%) \right] = 26.8\%$$

The IRR decision rule

Having seen how to calculate a project's IRR, how are we to use it for investment appraisal purposes? The decision rule is as follows: only projects with an IRR greater than or equal to some predetermined 'cut-off' rate should be accepted. This cut-off rate is usually the market rate of interest (i.e. the discount rate that would have been used if an NPV analysis were undertaken instead). All other investment project opportunities should be rejected. Therefore Project F would be acceptable if the market interest rate was 10% or less. However, if the decision criterion was 15%, then the investment advice would be to reject.

Likewise, Cintra Automotive's investment would be acceptable as long as the market inter-est rate/decision criterion was less than 26.8%.

The reasoning behind the IRR decision rule is similar to that behind NPV. The market interest rate reflects the *opportunity cost* of the capital involved. Thus, to be acceptable, a project must generate a return at least equal to the return available elsewhere on the capital market.

IRR and the investment–consumption model

Again, just as the NPV method fitted into our single-period investment–consumption model, so too does the IRR method. We originally described the physical investment line as representing the whole series of infinitely divisible physical investment projects that were available to the company, arranged in order of decreasing rate of return. This rate of return can be viewed as the individual project's IRR and can be derived (as we have already seen) from the slope of the physical investment lines.[3]

In Figure 5.4 therefore, moving progressively along the line from point A to B, the slope gets less and less steep, indicating that the company initially invests in projects with high IRRs and then works its way through to projects with much lower IRRs. Thus, the slope of the physical investment line at point C can be derived from the IRR of the marginal physi-cal investment represented by that point.

The IRR decision rule tells a company to invest in all projects with IRR greater than or equal to the market rate of interest. Thus a company will move up and around its physical investment line until it reaches the point of tangency with the financial investment line.

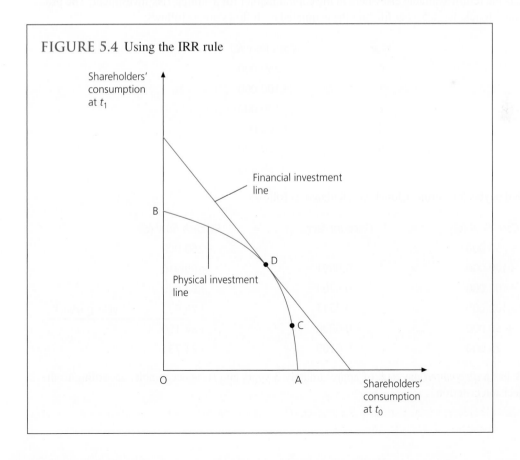

FIGURE 5.4 Using the IRR rule

Up to this point, all investment projects that the company has undertaken will have IRR greater than the market rate of interest. At point D on Figure 5.4, the marginal project will have an IRR *equal* to the market interest rate, and it is at this point that the company will cease further investment, because the remaining investment opportunities will all have an IRR that is less than the market interest rate. Therefore, the IRR investment appraisal rule, like the NPV rule, will ensure that a company locates at the optimal point on its physical investment line.

DISCOUNTED PAYBACK

Having examined the basic application of the two discounted cash flow techniques of capital investment appraisal, it is appropriate to return briefly to look at the discounted payback technique, which was referred to in Chapter 3. There it was stated that a major limitation of payback was that it did not take the time value of money into account. However, this criticism could be overcome through the use of discounted payback.

EXAMPLE 2

Janssen NV wishes to evaluate an investment opportunity using discounted payback, for which it uses a 4-year decision criterion. For discounting purposes, the company uses a 10% discount rate, which, it is judged, reflects the return available elsewhere in the capital market for a similar risk investment. The project, code-named Jonck, has a 5-year life and the estimated cash flows are as follows:

Year	Cash flow (€)
0	−250 000
1	+100 000
2	+100 000
3	+102 000
4	+ 50 000
5	+ 35 000

The discounted payback of Project Jonck is calculated as follows:

Year	Cash flow (€)	×	Discount factor	=	PV cash flow (€)	
0	−250 000	×	1	=	−250 000	
1	+100 000	×	0.9091	=	+90 910	
2	+100 000	×	0.8264	=	+82 640	
3	+102 000	×	0.7513	=	+76 633	3-year payback
4	+ 50 000	×	0.6830	=	+34 150	
5	+ 35 000	×	0.6209	=	+21 731	

Project Jonck has a *discounted* payback of approximately 3 years and so is acceptable, according to the company's decision criterion.

All that discounted payback does is to see how quickly a project takes to pay back its outlay in *present value* (rather than *undiscounted*) cash flow terms. Example 2 illustrates the approach.

TRUNCATED NPV

Discounted payback can be looked upon as a variation of the basic payback technique. However it is perhaps instructive to see it more as a variation on the NPV method.

In Example 2 the decision rule used by the company implied: accept the project as long as its NPV is at least zero (if not positive) at the end of 4 years. If a project complies with this requirement then it does pay back within the criterion period. Thus discounted payback is no more than a truncated version of NPV. Instead of calculating the project's NPV over the whole of its life, the NPV is effectively calculated up to some specified cut-off point which, in this example, happened to be 4 years.

Discounted payback still suffers from the criticism made of standard payback – that of ignoring project cash flows that lie outside the payback time period.

However, as before, the point should be made that setting this artificial time horizon on a project's life may be no more than making a realistic allowance for management's limited forecasting abilities.

Finally, despite the foregoing, it should be pointed out that the use of discounted payback will not necessarily lead to the firm's optimal physical investment line location. This is because some positive NPV projects may well be rejected because they do not generate that positive NPV sufficiently quickly. A further criticism will be made of discounted payback in Chapter 6.

SUMMARY

This chapter has looked at the basic application of the two DCF methods of investment appraisal. The main points covered were as follows:

- The fact that money has a time value (i.e. an opportunity cost in terms of a rate of interest) means that cash flows that arise at different points in time cannot be compared directly but must first be converted to a common point of time (usually t_0, the present time).

- The NPV decision rule states: accept a project if its NPV ≥ 0 (i.e. positive or zero); reject a project if its NPV < 0 (i.e. negative).

- Although a number of different (but correct) interpretations can be made about the meaning of NPV, the most important is that the magnitude of a project's NPV represents the increase in shareholder wealth that can be expected to come about through the project's acceptance.

- It was seen that the NPV decision rule (see above) would lead the company to locate at the optimal point on the physical investment line of the Hirshliefer analysis. It is from this analysis that the connection between NPV and shareholder wealth can be seen.

- The IRR of a project is that discount rate which, when applied to a project's cash flow, produces a zero NPV. It is therefore a simple arithmetic result.

- The IRR decision rule is: accept a project if its IRR ≥ decision criterion (which is usually the market interest rate); reject if its IRR < decision criterion.
- Like NPV, use of the IRR decision rule will also lead to the company optimally locating on its physical investment line.
- Discounted payback, in which the speed of payback is computed in present value cash flow terms, was seen to be simply a version of NPV with an artificially truncated project life.

APPENDIX: COMPOUNDING AND DISCOUNTING

Tables A to D can be found in the Appendix of tables at the end of this book.

1. Compounding Cash Flows

Pushing money *forward* through time to calculate its *future* value is called the compounding process.

The future of $1 which is placed on deposit for N years at a constant annual rate of interest of i is given by:

$$\$1 \times (1 + i)^N$$

Where $(1 + i)^N$ is known as the *compounding factor*. Thus, $500 placed on deposit for 6 years at an annual rate of interest of 12%, has a future value of:

$$\$500 \times (1 + 0.12)^6 = \$500 \times 1.9738 = \$986.90$$

Similarly, if $200 is placed on deposit for 3 years at 10% and 2 years at 8%, then the accumulated sum at the end of 5 years is:

$$\$200 \times (1 + 0.10)^3 \times (1 + 0.08)^2 = \$200 \times 1.3310 \times 1.1664 = \$310.50$$

Table A provides *compound factors* for a range of values of N and i.

2. Discounting Cash Flows

Pulling *future* amounts of money *back* through time to calculate their present value is referred to as the *discounting* process.

The present value (i.e. the value now) of €1 arising in N-years' time when the rate of discount (interest) is i, is given by:

$$€1 \div (1 + i)^N \text{ or } €1 \times (1 + i)^{-N}$$

Where $(1 + i)^{-N}$ is known as the *present value* or *discounting factor*.

Thus, €500 arising in 6 years' time, when the annual rate of discount is 12%, has a present value of:

$$€500 \times (1 + 0.12)^{-6} = €500 \times 0.5066 = €253.30$$

Similarly, €200 arising in 5 years, where the annual rate of discount is 10% for 3 years and 8% for 2 years, has a present value of:

$$€200 \times (1 + 0.10)^{-3} \times (1 + 0.08)^{-2} = €200 \times 0.7513 \times 0.8573 = €128.82$$

Table B provides present value factors for various values of N and *i*.

3. Annuities

An annuity can be defined as a constant annual cash flow that arises for a specific number of consecutive years. Three main types of annuity can be defined:

1. An annuity *due*, where the first cash flow arises now, at t_0.
2. An *immediate* annuity, where the first cash flow arises in 1 year's time, at t_1. (This is the *usual* type of annuity that we will use in developing our theory of financial decision-making.)
3. A *deferred* annuity, where the first cash flow arises in 2 or more years' time.

    Examples of the cash flows of 4-year $100 annuities of each type are given below:

Year	0	1	2	3	4	5
Annuity due	$100	$100	$100	$100		
Immediate annuity		$100	$100	$100	$100	
1-year deferred annuity			$100	$100	$100	$100

The present value of an immediate annuity lasting for N years, at a discount rate of '*i*' can be calculated using:

$$\frac{1 - (1 + i)^{-N}}{i}, \text{ denoted as: } A_{N, i}$$

where $A_{N, i}$ is known as the *annuity discounting factor*. Thus, the present value of an immediate annuity of $1 a year for N years at a discount rate of '*i*' would be calculated as: $1 \times A_{N, i}$. Table C provides the $A_{N, i}$ annuity discounting factors for the present values of $1 *immediate* annuities for various values of N and *i*.

How the annuity discounting factor is applied is illustrated in the following examples:

1. The present value of a 4-year $100 *immediate* annuity, where the rate of discount is 16%, can be calculated as:

$$\$100 \times \frac{1 - (1 + 0.16)^{-4}}{0.16} = \$100 \times A_{4, 0.16} = \$100 \times 2.7982 = \$279.82$$

2. The present value of a 4-year $100 annuity *due*, where the rate of discount is 16%, is:

$$\$100 + (\$100 \times A_{3, 0.16}) = \$100 + (\$100 \times 2.2459) = \$324.59$$

3. Finally, the present value of a 4-year $100 annuity, *deferred* for (say) 1 year (so that the first cash flow arises at Year 2), at a rate of discount of 16%, is:

$$\$100 \times A_{4,\,0.16} \times (1 + 0.16)^{-1} = \$100 \times 2.7982 \times 0.8621 = \$241.23$$

Notice the precise function of the $A_{N,i}$ factor. It gathers the annuity together and brings it to a point in time that is one year earlier than the point of time when the first cash flow occurs. For an immediate annuity, one year earlier than when the annuity cash flow starts is t_0. Thus $A_{N,i}$ will *automatically* provide the present value of an *immediate* annuity; but for a *deferred* annuity the $A_{N,i}$ factor will have to be applied with an additional discount factor – as in the example above – to get it back to present value.

4. Perpetuities

A *perpetuity* is simply an annuity that continues forever. In the real world perpetuities are rare, but not unknown. Historically, some governments and financial institutions have borrowed money on a permanent basis and so will pay a constant rate of interest on the loan forever. However, in terms of our analysis of financial decision-making, the concept of a perpetuity cash flow is useful as the calculation of a perpetuity's present value is very simple.

The present value of a perpetuity cash flow of $1 per year, where the first of the cash flows occurs at Year 1, is: $\dfrac{\$1}{i}$ where 'i' is the market rate of interest/time value of money. Therefore the present value of a perpetuity of €1000 per year:

Year:	0	1	2	3	4	5	∞
	$1000	$1000	$1000	$1000	$1000		....

where the TVM is 10% is simply:

$$\frac{\$1000}{0.10} = \$10\,000$$

Notice that what this simple piece of arithmetic is doing is gathering all the perpetuity cash flows together and discounting them back to a point in time that is one year *before* the cash flow starts. In this case the cash flow starts at Year 1 and so the perpetuity arithmetic discounts the entire cash flow back to Year 0 – i.e. present value.

As a result, where a perpetuity cash flow starts later than Year 1 an additional discounting procedure has to be carried out to bring its value back to present value. For example, if we have a perpetuity of €100 per year, starting at Year 3, where the discount rate is 10%:

Year:	0	1	2	3	4	5	6..........∞
Cash flow:				€100	€100	€100	€100.........

Then: $\dfrac{£100}{0.10} = £1000$ brings the value of the perpetuity back to one year before it starts – i.e. Year 2 – and so this has now got to be discounted back a *further* 2 years to bring it to its *present value*: $€1000 \times (1 + 0.10)^{-2} = €826.40$ present value.

5. *Annual equivalent factors*

The annual cash flow of an *immediate* annuity that lasts for N years, where the rate of discount is i, and which has a present value of €1, is given by:

$$\$1 \times \frac{i}{1 - (1 + i)^{-N}} \text{ , denoted as } \$1 \times A_{N, i}^{-1}$$

where $A_{N, i}^{-1}$ is known as the *annual equivalent factor*. Table D gives annual equivalent factors for a variety of values of N and i.

Therefore the annual cash flow of an immediate annuity that lasts for 5 years, where the rate of discount is 8%, and which has a present value of €2000, is:

$$£2000 \times \frac{0.08}{1 - (1 + 0.08)^{-5}} = £2000 \times A_{5, 0.08}^{-1} = £2000 \times 0.2505 = £501 \text{ per year}$$

NOTES

1. Notice that if the company were to over-invest up to point W, the *total* NPV of its investment decision would be negative. In other words, the shareholders would have been better off if management had undertaken no investment at all, rather than over-investing to such an extent. This analysis does serve to support management's general inclination to invest conservatively (i.e. a tendency to under-invest, or to invest less than the optimal amount). Under-optimal investment must always lead to an increase in shareholders' wealth, relative to their wealth if management undertook zero investment, as long as negative NPV projects are not undertaken. However, with over-investment, a situation like point W is possible where shareholders are actually worse off as a result of the company's investment decisions. In the real world, a management with poor appraisal ability may well do right to err on the side of conservatism, rather than taking a very sanguine or cavalier attitude to investment decisions.
2. Remember, any two discounts could be used although of course, they will give a slightly different result because the linear interpolation method is only *estimating* the IRR. Thus, using a different pair of discount rates will produce a different estimate.
3. Strictly speaking, this is not correct. The IRR of a project is its *average* rate of return, whilst under our assumptions of infinite project divisibility and diminishing returns, the IRR of each incremental piece of a project will be slightly lower than that of the previous increment. Hence the physical investment line is composed of the IRRs of each incremental investment in the projects that are available, rather than of the IRRs of each complete project that is available.

FURTHER READING

It is fair to say that the theoretical supremacy of NPV was established many years ago and has never really been undermined. However, there is a significant body of literature that has examined its practical application.

1. At this stage we are only midway through our evaluation of the two discounted cash flow investment appraisal techniques. Therefore many relevant articles will not yet be appropriate. However, a very interesting starting point is two articles that question the whole basis of the investment decision-making developed here: P.F. King, 'Is the Emphasis of Capital Budgeting Theory Misplaced?', *Journal of Business Finance and Accounting,* Spring 1975; and D. Cooper, 'Rationality and Investment Appraisal', *Accounting and Business Research,* Summer 1975.

2. In addition, a further article which is of interest at this stage is: E.M. Lerner and A. Rappaport, 'Limit DCF in Capital Budgeting', *Harvard Business Review,* September–October 1968.

3. Finally, it is perhaps a good idea to introduce a dose of realism at this early stage and an interesting arti-
    cle to pursue is T. Crick and S.H. Kim, 'Do Executives Practice what Academics Teach?', *Management
    Accounting,* November 1986.

QUIZ QUESTIONS

1   Using a 14% discount rate, what is the NPV of the following project?

Year	Cash flow
0	−€1000
1	+€500
2	+€600
3	+€400

2   If a project costing €1000 has an NPV of +€120 at a 10% discount rate, how would you
        interpret the NPV figure and what should be the investment advice?

3   Estimate the IRR of the following project:

Year	Cash flow
0	−$500
1	+$200
2	+$300
3	+$200

4   Using the project in question 3, what is its discounted payback given a 10% discount
        rate?

5   In the real world where the outcomes of investment projects are uncertain, what should
        the NPV discount rate represent?

6   What is the connection between the NPV discount rate and the IRR hurdle rate/decision
        criterion?

7   Given a 10% discount rate, calculate the NPV of the following project that costs
        CHF1000 (CHF = Swiss Francs) and which generates an *annuity* cash flow as
        follows:

Year	Cash flow (CHF)
0	−1000
1	+350
2	+350
3	+350
4	+350

8   What are the three main types of annuity?

9   A project costs €1000 and produces a cash inflow of €100 per year forever. What is
        its IRR?

10   Using annuity factors, what is the NPV of the following project at a 16% discount rate?

Year	Cash flow
0	−¥1000
1	+¥200
2	+¥200
3	+¥500
4	+¥500
5	+¥500

(See the 'Answers to the Quiz Questions' in the section at the back of the book.)

PROBLEMS

The answers to two of the following problems (those indicated by an asterisk) are available to students online. The answer to the remaining problem is available only to lecturers (see the 'Digital Resources' page for details).

1*   Majeelah Trading Company is based in Dubai and it has recently merged with a Kuwaiti-based company, Wataniya Logistic Controls. For some weeks, the finance departments in the two companies have been discussing investment appraisal techniques. Majeelah traditionally uses payback and the return on average capital employed, while Wataniya has used NPVs.

   The discussion on appraisal techniques has now reached a crisis as a decision is required on a proposal to invest 1.8 million Kuwaiti dinars (KWD) on a new satellite tracking logistics system. The financial details are as follows:

Outlay:	KWD1.8 million at t_0
Life:	10 years
Net cash flow:	Years 1−6 + KWD500 000/year
	Years 7−10 + KWD300 000/year
Scrap value:	KWD0.5 million

The merged company uses straight-line depreciation and has a target rate of return, for both ROCE and NPV, of 18%, and a payback criterion of 5 years.

   Required:

   (a)   Calculate the NPV of the proposed investment.

   (b)   Calculate the ROCE in line with company practice.

   (c)   Calculate the investment's payback.

   (d)   On the basis of your calculations, formulate your investment decision advice. Write a report to the chairman – Yusuf Tarek – that justifies your decision and mention any reservations that you might have.

▶

(e) In order to try and resolve the conflict between the two managements you suggest that the company uses discounted payback as a compromise. Estimate the project's discounted payback and write a memo to the chairman outlining its advantages and disadvantages.

(f) Comment critically on the company's existing decision criteria.

2* Illovo Pharma Holdings is a South African-based healthcare company, based in Johannesburg, specializing in the production of generic medicines. The company is currently considering the selection of one of a pair of mutually exclusive investments. Both would involve purchasing production machinery with a life of 5 years.

Project 1 would generate annual cash flows (receipts less payments) of SAR200 000; the machinery would cost SAR556 000 and have a scrap value of SAR56 000.
Project 2 would generate annual cash flows of SAR500 000; the machinery would cost SAR1 616 000 and have a scrap value of SAR301 000.
Illovo uses the straight-line method of providing for depreciation. Its cost of capital is 14% per annum. ('SAR' is the South African Rand.)

Required:

(a) Calculate for each investment project:

(i) the ARR (ratio over project life of average accounting profit to average book value of investment) to the nearest 1%

(ii) the NPV

(iii) the IRR to the nearest 1%

(iv) the payback period, to one decimal place.

(b) State which investment project you would select for acceptance, if either, giving reasons for your choice of criterion to guide the decision.

3. Gallarado is an ambitious young executive who has recently been appointed to the position of financial director of Festina Aspes, a small exploration company, listed on the Spanish stock exchange. Gallarado regards this appointment as a temporary one, enabling him to gain experience before moving to a larger organization. His intention is to leave Festina Aspes in 3 years, with its share price standing high. As a consequence, he is particularly concerned that the reported profits of the company should be as high as possible in his third and final year with the company.

Festina Aspes has recently raised €350 000 from shareholders, and the directors are considering three ways of using these funds. Three different investments (A, B and C) are being considered, each involving the immediate purchase of equipment costing €350 000. Only one investment can be undertaken and the equipment for each one will have a zero scrap value at the end of the project. Gallarado favours Investment Project C because it is expected to show the highest accounting profit in the third year. However, he does not wish to reveal his real reasons for favouring Project C and so, in his report to the company's chief executive officer, he recommends Project C because it shows the highest IRR. The following summary is taken from his report:

Net cash flows (€000s)

Project	0	1	2	3	4	5	6	7	IRR %
A	−350	100	110	104	112	138	160	180	27.5
B	−350	40	100	210	260	160	—	—	26.4
C	−350	200	150	240	40	—	—	—	33.0

▶

The CEO of Festina Aspes, Cristina Alvares, is accustomed to projects being appraised in terms of payback and ROCE, and she is consequently suspicious of the use of IRR as a method of project selection. As a result, she has asked for an independent report on the choice of project. The company's cost of capital is 20% and a policy of straight-line depreciation is used to write off the cost of equipment in the financial statements.

Required:

(a) Calculate the payback period for each project.

(b) Calculate the ROCE for each project.

(c) Prepare a report for the CEO, with supporting calculations, indicating which project should be preferred by the ordinary shareholders of Festina Aspes.

(d) Discuss the assumptions about the reactions of the stock market that are implicit in Gallarado's choice of Project C.

NET PRESENT VALUE AND INTERNAL RATE OF RETURN

LEARNING OBJECTIVES

The purpose of this chapter is to:

- Explain the use of NPV in choosing between mutually exclusive and linked projects.

- Explain the use of IRR for mutually exclusive and linked projects.

- Explain the relative strengths and weaknesses of NPV and IRR.

- Apply the NPV and IRR investment appraisal methods to the situation of 'mutually exclusive' investments.

- Examine the problems that result from the IRR decision method.

- Discuss how some of these problems may be overcome through the use of a modified version of the IRR technique.

- Illustrate how the NPV technique can be adapted to cope with a situation involving a continuous replacement cycle.

NPV AND PROJECT INTERDEPENDENCE

In Chapter 3, when examining the payback and ROCE techniques, two investment decisions were dealt with:

1. Decisions involving *single*, independent projects where a straightforward 'accept' or 'reject' decision was required.

2. Decisions involving *mutually exclusive* projects, where a decision on the single best project from a series of alternative projects was required.

In Chapter 5 when examining the two discounted cash flow techniques of NPV and IRR, the discussion only covered the decision rule for single independent project decisions. In this chapter, we start by looking at the NPV and IRR decision rules when faced with mutually exclusive projects and other forms of project decision interdependence.

NPV and mutually exclusive projects

We have already seen from the single-period investment–consumption model that, in terms of NPV, the higher the aggregate NPV of a firm's investments, the higher will be the level of wealth achieved by its shareholders. Therefore, as far as deciding between mutually exclusive investment alternatives is concerned, the decision rule would appear to be quite straightforward in terms of using NPV: accept whichever alternative projects result in the greatest positive NPV, because this will produce the greatest addition to the shareholders' wealth.[1]

As an example, suppose a company has to make an investment decision concerning two mutually exclusive projects, A and B, the cash flows and NPV calculations for which are set out as follows:

Project A

Year	Cash flow (€)	×	10% discount factor	=	Present value cash flow (€)
0	−1500	×	1	=	−1 500
1	+500	×	0.9091	=	+ 454.55
2	+800	×	0.8264	=	+ 661.12
3	+1000	×	0.7513	=	+ 751.30
				NPV	+ 366.97

Project B

Year	Cash flow (€)	×	10% discount factor	=	Present value cash flow (€)
0	−1 900	×	1	=	−1900
1	+500	×	0.9091	=	+ 454.55
2	+800	×	0.8264	=	+ 661.12
3	+1000	×	0.7513	=	+ 751.30
4	+700	×	0.6830	=	+ 478.10
				NPV	+ 445.07

Assuming that the appropriate discount rate is 10%, when the project cash flows are converted to present values, Project B is preferred to A because it has the larger positive NPV. It is important to realize that the appraisal method in such circumstances is entirely unaffected by the fact that these two projects have differing costs and different life spans. The whole decision is based purely on the *absolute size* of the positive NPV.

The mutually exclusive investment decision can be made in this way because of two important assumptions underlying the analysis. When developing the single-period investment–consumption model, a number of simplifying assumptions about the real world were specified. However, when we then moved on to examine the two DCF invest-ment appraisal techniques, many of these assumptions (such as a single time period and a world of certainty) were either implicitly or explicitly dropped. Nevertheless, there are two important assumptions that underlie the use of both DCF techniques. They are:

1. The existence of a perfect capital market. Reference has already been made to this concept, when the existence of a capital market was introduced in the Hirshleifer analysis in Chapter 4. A perfect capital market describes a market where investors can lend and borrow money and which has a number of particular characteristics. We will examine the concept in greater detail at a later stage but, for the present, all that is required is to specify that characteristic which is of particular importance as far as the DCF techniques are concerned. It is that investors/companies will always be able to raise finance to undertake any project that they identify as having a non-negative NPV (or with an IRR that meets the decision criterion hurdle rate). Therefore, decision-makers will never find themselves in a position where they are unable to take on a positive NPV project because of lack of finance. In addition, we should add to this condition the assumption that the cost of the finance raised will always be at the going rate of return for investments of that particular risk level.

2. The discount rate used in an NPV analysis, or the hurdle rate used in an IRR analysis, correctly reflects the degree of risk involved in the project. This refers to the fact that the discount rate should represent the return available elsewhere in the (perfect) capital market on a similar risk investment. Therefore notice how this assumption is, itself, dependent upon the first assumption.

As a result of these two assumptions the choice between Projects A and B can be made on the basis used. The fact that B is a more costly project than A is irrelevant, given the first assumption. Project B is preferred to A simply because it is capable of generating a cash flow that will pay back its outlay and its financing costs and leave an economic profit, in present value terms (a rise in shareholder wealth), of €445.07. Project A will also repay its outlay and its financing costs, but will only cause shareholder wealth to rise by €366.97.

Also, the fact that B is more expensive than A, and has a longer life than A, might suggest that it is more risky. (Neither fact will *necessarily* make B more risky than A.) However, these differences can also be ignored in the decision analysis because of our second assumption. In other words, the whole problem of riskiness is taken account of in the discount rate. The fact that both projects are being discounted at 10% implies that a judgement has been made that they are equally risky.

In this respect, if it were felt that two mutually exclusive projects were of different risk levels, then different discount rates should be used to evaluate each one. However, the decision – with its focus on maximizing the increase in shareholder wealth – would remain unchanged. Example 1 illustrates such a situation.

The point to notice about Example 1 is that the decision has been taken on the basis of what would be the resulting increase in shareholder wealth. The fact that the quad-bike adventure park development produces a return in excess of 18% (in fact its IRR is approximately 18.6%), whilst the private housing development only produces a return in excess of 10% (its IRR is approximately 12.5%), is irrelevant. Rates of return cannot be compared in isolation, but must be looked at *relative to the risk involved*. In this example, given the risk involved, the private housing development is the better project from the viewpoint of shareholder wealth.

Finally, the operation of this modified NPV rule for mutually exclusive projects requires an additional assumption in the face of unequal project lives (but not unequal investment outlays). This is that the mutually exclusive projects are 'isolated' investments in the sense that they do not form part of a replacement chain. In other words, it is assumed that the nature of the mutually exclusive projects is such that, whichever project is chosen, it will not be replaced when it reaches the end of its life. If this assumption does not hold, then we are involved with a different type of project interdependence that requires a more complex decision rule. (This issue is examined separately when the *replacement decision* is discussed.)

EXAMPLE 1

Al Gharafa is a Qatari company, based in Doha, engaged in house-building. The company is currently considering whether to purchase a piece of land that has come up for sale at a cost of 10 million riyals. Two suggestions have been made for the use of the land. One is to construct a number of private houses for sale and the other is to construct and operate a quad-bike adventure park.

The company's finance staff have made the following estimates of both projects' net cash flows (including the cost of the land):

Year	Private house development (QARm)	Adventure Park (QARm)
0	−10	−10
1	− 5	− 8
2	+ 7	+ 4
3	+ 9	+ 6
4	+ 4	+ 8
5		+ 7
6		+ 9

The company uses NPV to evaluate projects and normally takes 10% as a discount rate, as this reflects the return available elsewhere on house-building investments. In the present situation this appears to be a suitable rate for the private housing development, but not for the adventure park. After much research, the company has decided that the minimum required rate of return that they should expect on this more risky project is 18%.

On this basis, the project's NPVs were calculated:

Private housing development: +QAR 733 000
Amusement park development: +QAR 264 000

Therefore the company's decision was to purchase the land and undertake a private housing development.

Interlinked projects

Another type of project interdependence can arise when a project's cash flows are affected by investment decisions taken elsewhere. It would be highly unusual to find any project which had truly independent cash flows, as almost certainly the magnitude and timing of a project's cash flows will be affected to some extent by other investment decisions. This problem really arises out of uncertainty about the future, and will be examined later in that context.

The case of interdependence to be examined here is the simpler case in which the cash flows of an investment opportunity are directly affected by the company's decision regarding another investment project. For example, Projects C and D are two non-mutually exclusive projects. Project C involves building a car park in a town centre location and Project D consists of building an adjacent supermarket. Project C has the following cash flows, which are independent of any other investment decisions made by the company:

Project C – car park project

Year	Cash flow (£000s)	×	10% discount factor	=	Present value (£000s)
0	−1 000	×	1	=	−1 000
1	+400	×	0.9091	=	+ 363.64
2	+500	×	0.8264	=	+ 413.20
3	+200	×	0.7513	=	+ 150.26
				NPV	− £72.90

When discounted by 10% (assumed to be the appropriate rate), Project C has a negative NPV of £72 900. Viewed in isolation, and following the NPV rule for independent projects, it would be rejected as an unsuitable investment.

However, suppose Project D, which is also under consideration, has two alternative sets of cash flows and NPVs, depending upon whether Project C – the car park project – is accepted by the company (cash flow 1) or rejected (cash flow 2):

Project D – supermarket project

Year	Cash flow 1 (£000s)	×	10% discount factor	=	Present value (£000s)
0	−2 000	×	1	=	−2 000
1	+ 500	×	0.9091	=	+ 454.55
2	+ 800	×	0.8264	=	+ 661.12
3	+1 000	×	0.7513	=	+ 751.30
4	+1 000	×	0.6830	=	+ 683.00
				NPV	+ 549.97

Year	Cash flow 2 (£000s)	×	10% discount factor	=	Present value (£000s)
0	− 2 000	×	1	=	−2 000
1	+ 500	×	0.9091	=	+ 454.55
2	+ 800	×	0.8264	=	+ 661.12
3	+ 1200	×	0.7513	=	+ 901.56
4	+ 600	×	0.6830	=	+ 409.80
				NPV	+ 427.03

The correct way to analyze this situation, within the assumptions made, is to treat the problem as *three* mutually exclusive investments: Project C alone, Project D alone and Projects C + D combined. The alternative which produces the largest positive NPV should be accepted. In this example:

Project C − car park only   = − £72 900
Project D − supermarket only   = + £427 030
Projects C + D − car park + supermarket = − £72 900 + £549 970 = + £477 070

Thus the correct investment decision, in terms of maximizing shareholder wealth, is to accept Projects C and D jointly and build both the supermarket and adjoining car park, because it is this alternative that produces the largest positive NPV.

IRR RULE AND INTERDEPENDENT PROJECTS

Introduction

We have seen that in the face of these two types of non-independent cash flow, the NPV investment decision rule can be fairly easily modified so as to produce the correct decision advice. In terms of the single-period investment–consumption model, these modified decision rules would ensure a company's attainment of the optimal point on the physical investment line and the consequent maximization of shareholder wealth. But what modifications would have to be made to the IRR decision rule?

In a situation of mutually exclusive investment projects, a modification, apparently similar to that made to the NPV rule, is traditionally advocated: accept whichever project has the greatest IRR, as long as it exceeds the decision criterion/hurdle rate. Such an approach is *incorrect*, but it has been widely advocated because of a misunderstanding concerning the process involved in using both NPV and IRR as criteria for investment decisions.

We have already seen that when an individual project is evaluated by NPV, an 'automatic' comparison is made between the cash flows produced by the project and the cash flows that would have been produced (but were forgone, and so represent an opportunity cost under the assumption of a perfect capital market), if the project's outlay had been invested on the capital market for the period of the project's life span. Therefore, the decision whether to accept or reject the project is not an absolute decision, but a *relative* one – relative to what the forgone alternative would have yielded. As a result, when faced with mutually exclusive investments, the choice between projects is carried out on the basis of this automatic comparison with the capital market. Whichever project performs best, *relative to the capital market*, is chosen – given that the chosen alternative outperforms the capital market alternative, i.e. has a positive NPV.

Incremental cash flows

We can approach this idea another way. Suppose we have a pair of mutually exclusive projects, E and F, which have the following cash flows, lives and present values when discounted at the appropriate market rate of return of 10%:

Project E

Year	Cash flow ($)	×	10% discount factor	=	Present value ($)
0	−1 500	×	1	=	−1 500
1	+ 550	×	0.9091	=	+ 500.00
2	+1 400	×	0.8264	=	+1 156.96
				NPV	+ 156.96

Project F

Year	Cash flow ($)	×	10% discount factor	=	Present value ($)
0	−1 900	×	1	=	−1 900
1	+ 400	×	0.9091	=	+ 363.64
2	+ 800	×	0.8264	=	+ 661.12
3	+ 800	×	0.7513	=	+ 601.04
4	+ 700	×	0.6830	=	+ 478.10
				NPV	± 203.90

Project F would be preferred to Project E, as it has the larger, positive NPV.

Now, let us look at the present value of the extra, or incremental, cash flows that the firm would obtain from investing in Project E, rather than Project F and vice versa:

Year	Project E cash flow	−	Project F cash flow	=	Incremental cash flow (E−F)	×	x10% present value factor	=	Present value cash flow
0	(−1 500)	−	(−1 900)	=	+400	×	1	=	+400
1	(+ 550)	−	(+ 400)	=	+150	×	0.9091	=	+136.36
2	(+1 400)	−	(+ 800)	=	+600	×	0.8264	=	+495.84
3		−	(+ 800)	=	−800	×	0.7513	=	−601.04
4		−	(+ 700)	=	−700	×	0.6830	=	−478.10
								NPV	− 46.94

Year	Incremental F–E cash flow	×	10% present value factor	=	Present value cash flow
0	−400	×	1	=	−400
1	−150	×	0.9091	=	−136.36
2	−600	×	0.8264	=	−495.84
3	+800	×	0.7513	=	+601.04
4	+700	×	0.6830	=	+478.10
				NPV	± 46.94

In our initial analysis of this decision problem, Project F was preferred to Project E. The incremental analysis shown above helps to explain further the reason for the decision: if F is chosen in preference to E, this will produce an NPV which will be $46.94 greater than if E was preferred to F. (Notice the NPV of Project F, less that of Project E, is: $203.90 – $156.96 = $46.94.) Therefore, F is chosen.

Use of the IRR

In the case of mutually exclusive investments, use of the IRR decision rule causes problems. Unlike the NPV calculation which automatically compares the project with the alternative capital market investment forgone, the IRR method makes the comparison on a somewhat different basis by using the decision rule: does the project yield a greater or lesser return than the capital market? In doing so, however, it does not give a consistently reliable indication of *how much* better or worse the project is relative to the capital market investment alternative.

Thus, the IRR decision rule is safe to apply to single, independent decision situations (when all that is required is an answer to the question: does the project produce a return better or worse than that of the capital market?), but it cannot reliably be used to judge *between* alternative projects. This is a rather subtle, but important, point and it requires some further explanation.

Using linear interpolation, the IRRs of the two projects E and F can be estimated. For E the IRR is estimated at 17%, and for F at 15%. As E has the larger of the two IRRs and this is greater than the decision criterion hurdle rate (10%), the IRR decision rule would suggest that Project E is accepted and Project F rejected. However, to formulate decision advice on this basis is to forget that the IRR method only compares a project with the capital market alternative in the operation of the accept/reject decision rule. (Indeed the fact that this standard IRR decision rule gives unreliable decision advice is made obvious in this example, because the decision reached is the *opposite* of that reached by NPV.)

The IRR method can correctly advise in this case that both projects are worthwhile: Project E is worthwhile as it produces a return that is greater than that of the capital market; likewise with Project F. But it does not necessarily follow that E is *better* than F because it has an IRR of 17% as opposed to 15%. Indeed we know from operating the NPV decision rule that the advice is incorrect: F is a better investment than E; and selecting E will result in a $46.94 loss of NPV.

IRR and incremental cash flows

The correct approach to evaluating mutually exclusive investments using the IRR is to examine the *incremental* cash flows that arise between the alternatives. In order to clarify the problem and derive the correct IRR decision rule in such circumstances, we shall make use of a device that was used earlier to examine the IRR concept: the *net present value profile*.

Figure 6.1 graphs the NPV profiles of Projects E and F and both the differential cash flows (E–F, F–E). This demonstrates one of the real problems of using the IRR as a decision criterion when choice between alternatives is involved.

Project E always has a higher IRR than Project F, whatever the rate of discount, and therefore, basing the choice between mutually exclusive investments on size of IRR, the decision is independent of the capital market rate of interest. In contrast to this, when the decision is based on the NPV rule, the choice of project *changes* as the discount rate/market rate of interest *changes*. It can be seen from Figure 6.1 that at rates of discount below 12.4%, Project F is preferred because it has the higher NPV; but at discount rates above 12.4%, Project E is preferred.

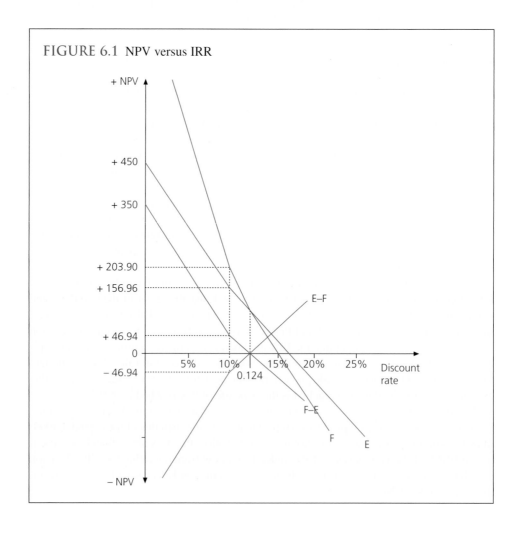

FIGURE 6.1 NPV versus IRR

The intersection point of the two *differential* cash flow profiles is at a discount rate of 12.4% and so, at this rate, the decision would be indifferent between the two projects because they both produce the same NPV. Also notice that, as we would expect at that discount rate, the NPV of both differential cash flows is zero: both projects are equally acceptable, and the differential cash flows reflect this indifference.

On the basis of Figure 6.1, a number of firm conclusions can be made about the use of both methods in appraising mutually exclusive projects. The NPV can be used to give the correct decision advice with just a small (and commonsense) modification to the basic rule: accept whichever alternative has the highest positive NPV when discounted at the appropriate capital market rate of interest. The use of the IRR involves a more complex decision rule. This complexity arises both from the fact that the IRRs of the differential cash flows have to be computed and (as can be seen from Figure 6.1) from the fact that the IRRs of both incremental cash flows are identical. The complete modified decision rule is as follows.

Calculate the IRRs of the two projects and the IRR of *either* of the differential cash flows, then:

1. If the differential cash flow IRR is *greater* than the cut-off rate, and

    (a) less than both project IRRs, then accept the project with the *smallest* IRR

    (b) greater than both project IRRs, then accept the project with *highest* IRR.

2. If the differential cash flow IRR is *less* than the cut-off rate, and

    (a) the IRRs of one or both projects are higher than the cut-off rate, then accept the project with the *highest* IRR

    (b) if neither project's IRR is greater than the cut-off rate, reject both.

In the example, therefore, using the NPV decision rule, Project F should be accepted because it has the highest positive NPV when discounted at 10% – the perfect capital market interest rate. The modified IRR decision rule also leads to the acceptance of F because the IRR of the differential cash flow (12.4%) is greater than the cut-off rate (10%) and less than the IRR of both projects (15% and 17%). Therefore, the project with the smallest IRR, Project F, is chosen.

A less complex, but somewhat incomplete decision rule can also be used in most cases:

1. If the IRR of the differential cash flow is less than the cut-off rate, accept the project with the *largest* IRR.

2. If the IRR of the differential cash flow is greater than the cut-off rate, accept the project with the *smallest* IRR.

In the example used above, as the IRR of the differential cash flow, at 12.4%, is greater than the 10% cut-off rate, then Project F should be accepted as it has the smallest IRR; 15% as against 17% for Project E.

The conclusion that can be drawn from this example is that the IRR decision rule is excessively complex and unwieldy when compared against the NPV decision rule. What is more, the example used only two mutually exclusive projects. If faced with a choice between (say) a dozen alternatives, the NPV rule simply requires the calculation of each project's NPV and the project with the largest positive NPV is selected. With the IRR rule, the IRRs *of pairs* of projects and their differential cash flow have to be calculated, making a choice between each pair of projects in turn, until an outright 'winner' is found – an extremely tedious operation.

A further example

Example 2 may help to clarify this approach to resolving the conflict that can occur between the advice given by the NPV decision rule and the advice given by the standard IRR decision rule for mutually exclusive decision situations.

EXAMPLE 2

Fiocchi Momo manufactures machine parts in Milano, Italy. It is currently involved in making a decision concerning the acquisition of a new machining tool. Two different versions of the tool are available: X and Y. The cash flows of the two alternatives are as follows:

Year	Tool X (€000s)	Tool Y (€000s)
0	−1 000	−450
1	+ 400	+300
2	+ 600	+150
3	+ 187	+106

Given the risk involved, it is judged that 6% would be an appropriate NPV discount rate and IRR hurdle rate.

NPV calculation of Tool X

Year	Cash flow (€)		Discount factor		
0	−1 000	×	1	=	−1 000
1	+ 400	×	0.9434	=	+ 377.36
2	+ 600	×	0.8900	=	+ 534.00
3	+ 187	×	0.8396	=	+ 157.00
					+ 68.36 NPV

NPV calculation of Tool Y

Year	Cash flow (€)		Discount factor		
0	−450	×	1	=	− 450
1	+300	×	0.9434	=	+ 283.02
2	+150	×	0.8900	=	+ 133.50
3	+106	×	0.8396	=	+ 89.00
					+ 55.52 NPV

Using the NPV decision rule for mutually exclusive projects, Tool X is preferred to Tool Y as it has the largest positive NPV and so will give the greatest increase in shareholder wealth.

▶

IRR calculation of Tool X

At 6% it has an NPV of +68.36 NPV

At 20%:	−1 000	×	1	=	−1 000
	+ 400	×	0.8333	=	+ 333.32
	+ 600	×	0.6944	=	+ 416.64
	+ 187	×	0.5787	=	+ 108.22
					− 141.82 NPV

IRR calculation of Tool Y

At 6% it has an NPV of +55.52 NPV

At 20%:	− 450	×	1	=	− 450
	+ 300	×	0.8333	=	+ 249.99
	+ 150	×	0.6944	=	+ 104.16
	+ 106	×	0.5787	=	+ 61.34
					− 34.51 NPV

Linear interpolation can now be used to estimate the IRR of both projects:

$$\text{Tool X: } 6\% \times \left[\frac{68.36}{68.36 - (-141.82)} \times (20\% - 6\%) \right] = 10.5\%$$

$$\text{Tool Y: } 6\% \times \left[\frac{55.52}{55.52 - (-34.51)} \times (20\% - 6\%) \right] = 14.6\%$$

Given that the IRR for Tool X is 10.5% and the IRR for Tool Y is 14.6%, then using the standard IRR decision rule for mutually exclusive projects, Tool Y is the better project as it has the higher IRR and should be accepted because its IRR exceeds the hurdle rate of return of 6%.

Therefore, in this case, we are getting a *conflict* between the advice given by NPV – which says 'Accept X' – and the advice given by the IRR decision rule – which says 'Accept Y'. However, if the *modified* IRR decision rule is used, we need also to calculate the IRR of the *differential* cash flow:

Tool X cash flow minus Tool Y cash flow.

Year	Cash flow X (€)	−	Cash flow Y (€)	=	Differential cash flow
0	−1 000	−	(− 450)	=	− 550
1	+ 400	−	(+ 300)	=	+ 100
2	+ 600	−	(+ 150)	=	+ 450
3	+ 187	−	(+ 106)	=	+ 81

NPV at a 4% discount rate:

− 550	×	1	=	− 550
+ 100	×	0.9615	=	+ 96.15
+ 450	×	0.9246	=	+ 416.07
+ 81	×	0.8890	=	+ 72.01
				+ 34.23 NPV

NPV at a 20% discount rate:

− 550	×	1	=	− 550
+ 100	×	0.8333	=	+ 83.33
+ 450	×	0.6944	=	+ 312.48
+ 81	×	0.5787	=	+ 46.87
				− 107.32 NPV

Again, using linear interpolation:

Differential cash flow IRR:

$$4\% + \left[\frac{34.23}{34.23 - (-107.32)} \times (20\% - 4\%) \right] = 7.9\%$$

Given the IRR of the differential cash flow is 7.9%, and that is greater than the IRR 'hurdle rate' of 6%, then the modified IRR decision rule states that the project with the *smallest* IRR – Tool X – should be accepted. This now agrees with the (correct) decision given by NPV.

Given Example 2, it should be made clear that it is very unlikely that any company actually uses this modified IRR decision rule in practice. To use it in this way implies a belief in the correctness of the NPV decision rule – because the modified IRR rule is designed always to give the same advice as NPV. But in that case it is both simpler and easier to use the NPV rule itself. Example 2 illustrates how it would be possible to use the IRR decision rule in mutually exclusive project situations so as to provide correct (i.e. shareholder wealth-maximizing) decision advice.

The 'opportunity cost of cash' assumption

The fact that, in a decision choice involving mutually exclusive projects, selecting the project with the highest positive NPV will give a correct decision but selecting the project with the highest IRR will, only by chance, also give the correct decision, has been explained on the basis that the IRR ranks projects in an order of preference that is independent of the capital market rate of return. But we have not really answered the question of why, in the example used, the NPV rule accepts Project F and rejects Project E. After all, Project E produces a higher return (17%) than Project F (15%). The reason lies in what is (somewhat misleadingly) called the 'reinvestment assumption' of each decision rule. Perhaps a more apt description would be the 'opportunity cost of capital' assumption.

The NPV decision rule assumes that project-generated cash flows are reinvested to earn a rate of return equal to *the discount rate* used in the NPV analysis. (More strictly, remember, it is not so much a reinvestment rate of return, but an opportunity cost or benefit.) In contrast, the IRR method assumes project-generated cash flows are reinvested to earn a rate of return equal to *the IRR of the project* that generated those cash flows. Therefore, using Project E as an example:

Project E	Year	Cash flow ($)	
	0	− $1 500	NPV at a 10% discount
	1	+ $ 550	rate = + $156.96
	2	+ $1 400	The IRR is approximately 17%.

The NPV decision rule assumes that the $550 and $1400 cash flows generated at Years 1 and 2 respectively can be reinvested to earn a 10% rate of return. The IRR method assumes they can be reinvested to earn a 17% rate of return.

This difference can be seen in the general forms of the two models. With the NPV model, the discount rate used is the market rate of interest:

$$\sum_{t=0}^{N} \frac{A_t}{(1 + i)^t} = \text{NPV}$$

where: A_t = project cash flow at time t
   i = market discount rate
   N = number of years of the project's life.

However, with the IRR model, the discount rate used is the project's own internal rate of return:

$$\sum_{t=0}^{N} \frac{A}{(1 + i)^t} = 0, \text{ where: } r = \text{project's IRR}$$

A simple example will help to illustrate the point. Suppose that the following project, G, is available, where the market rate of discount is 5%. The project has an NPV of +£12.39 and an IRR of 10%. What these results mean is shown in Example 3, where the reinvestment assumptions can actually be seen to be in operation.

EXAMPLE 3

Both the NPV discount rate and the IRR hurdle rate are 5%.

Project G:	Year	Cash flow (£)	
	0	− 173.55	NPV = + £12.39
	1	+ 100	
	2	+ 100	
			IRR = 10%

▶

The project's NPV can be found by calculating the amount of money that can be generated from the project by the *end* of its life (where intermediate cash flows are reinvested at 5%), and then comparing this with the amount of money that could be generated by placing the project's outlay in a similar-risk capital market investment. On this basis, Figure 6.2 shows that a total of £205 can be generated from the project by the end of its life at Year 2. Whereas, if the project's outlay of £173.55 was placed on deposit for 2 years at 5% interest, it would only produce £191.34 at the end of Year 2. The difference between the two amounts is £13.66 in Year 2 terms, and has a *present value* of £12.39: the project's NPV.

FIGURE 6.2

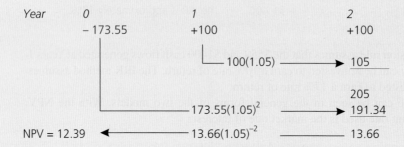

The project has an IRR of 10%. If it truly does produce a 10% return it must be capable of generating the same amount of cash by the end of its life that would be generated from investing the project's outlay to yield a 10% return. Investing £173.55 for 2 years at 10% generates £210. The only way that Project G could generate £210 by the end of its life is to assume that the intermediate cash flow (£100 at Year 1) can be reinvested to earn 10%, as Figure 6.3 demonstrates.

FIGURE 6.3

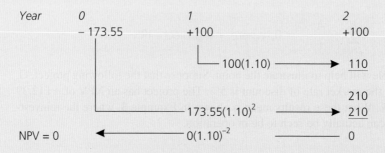

The IRR approach assumes that the project cash flows can be reinvested to give a return equal to the IRR of the project that generated those cash flows. Now the important point is that investments yielding such returns may well be available to the company but the flaw in the IRR's assumption is that these investments will be available *independently* of whether or not the company accepts the particular project under consideration. The NPV model accepts this argument, taking the market rate of interest as the opportunity cost of the project cash flows.

The market rate of interest is viewed as the opportunity cost because, even if a project's cash flow is used by a company to undertake an investment with a very high yield, if that cash flow were not available, the high yielding investment could *still* be undertaken by using money borrowed from the capital market, at the market rate of interest. What the IRR model does is to credit some of the assumed profitability of those other investments to the project being appraised, by assuming that the opportunity cost of the project-generated cash flows is equal to the project's own IRR or yield.

Therefore, we can conclude that, given the presence of a perfect capital market, it is the NPV model, not the IRR model, that makes the *correct* assumption about the opportunity cost of a project's cash flow. Hence it is the NPV decision rule that gives the correct decision advice. As a result, if we are to use the IRR, then we have to make use of the type of complex *modified* decision rule that was derived earlier. However there is no real logic to that type of rule – it simply ensures that the same decision is produced as that given by the (much simpler) NPV decision rule.

Finally, there is also a logical inconsistency in the IRR's reinvestment assumption. As an example of this, take Projects H and I.

Project H	Year	Cash flow (€)	Project I	Year	Cash flow (€)
	0	− 100		0	− 150
	1	+ 30		1	+ 70
	2	+ 70		2	+ 70
	3	+ 19.80		3	+ 74.41

Project H has an IRR of 10%, while Project I has an IRR of 20%. Therefore the implicit assumption is that Project I's cash flows can be reinvested to earn 20%, but Project H's cash flows can only be reinvested to earn 10%. This raises the question, why, for example, can the €70 generated at Year 2 by Project I be reinvested at twice the rate as the same amount of cash, generated at precisely the same point in time, by Project H? There is a fault in the logic of the assumption. There is no logical reason why cash flows that arise at the same time from two different sources should be reinvested at different rates (i.e. have different opportunity benefits).

EXTENDING THE TIME HORIZON

Introduction

Having examined the case of mutually exclusive projects, let us now turn to another issue. This concerns the fact that the Hirshleifer single-period graphical analysis was undertaken under the assumption of a single-period investment time horizon. Certainly, since starting to examine the DCF methods of investment appraisal, examples have been used of projects which involve cash flows extending over more than one period. But what we must now ask is whether the assumption of a single-period time horizon is simply an assumption of convenience which allows the model to be developed graphically.

In short, the answer to the question is that it is not. In a single-period world we have seen that both the NPV and IRR decision rules will give the same, correct decision advice (even if some fairly complex adjustments sometimes have to be made to the IRR rule). Both methods should enable a company to locate optimally on its physical investment line. However, problems can occur for the IRR decision rule once this two-dimensional world is left behind.

Average and marginal rates of return

As soon as the assumption of a single time period $(t_0$-$t_1)$ is explicitly relaxed, we get new support for the rationale of the NPV approach (to the detriment of IRR) and a new perspective from which to view the 'reinvestment' assumption. So far, in all the examples used, we have implicitly assumed that the capital market interest rate remains fixed over time. However, suppose a company is evaluating Project J, the cash flows for which are given below. In this case, the annual market interest/discount rate is expected to be 10% over the next year and 15% over the year after. Project J's NPV can be calculated as follows:

Project J						
Year	Cash flow (SAR)		Discount factor			
0	− 100	×	1		=	− 100
1	+ 60	×	$(1.10)^{-1}$		=	+ 54.55
2	+ 60	×	$(1.10)^{-1} \times (1.15)^{-1}$		=	+ 47.43
				NPV		+ 1.98

The IRR of Project J is approximately 13%.

As far as the NPV decision rule is concerned, known fluctuations in the discount rate do not cause any problems. Project J has a positive NPV after its cash flows have been discounted by the appropriate market discount rate for each time period.

But what of the IRR decision rule? Project J should be accepted if its IRR is greater than the decision criterion/hurdle rate, but, in this example, the IRR of J is *greater* than the market interest rate in one time period, and *less* than the rate in the other time period. In such circumstances, a single-figure IRR is just not valid for decision-making purposes.

This is a very real problem with the IRR decision rule. Unless future market interest rates can be assumed to be at least approximately constant, the rule breaks down. What we are seeing in this example is that, although both DCF methods recognize that money has a time value and so cash flows that occur at different points of time cannot be directly compared, but first have to be converted to values at just one common point of time via a weighting mechanism,[2] the IRR uses the *average*, or long-run, rate of return for weighting, whilst the NPV uses the *marginal*, or period-by-period, rate of return.

MULTIPLE IRRS

Another problem for the IRR decision rule, which arises out of the mathematics of its computation, also becomes apparent when the investment time horizon is extended. The IRR of a project's cash flow is the root of a polynomial equation, the mathematics of which is explained in a note.[3] The problem is that any particular investment project may have more than one IRR (i.e. there may be more than one rate of discount that will reduce the project's cash flow to a zero NPV), or it may not have any IRR at all. This important (and not uncommon) phenomenon can be examined in terms of the NPV profiles of projects on the basis that the IRR is given by the point at which the profile line cuts the graph's horizontal axis (along which the discount rate is measured).

To start with, we must define what have become known as 'conventional' and 'non-conventional' cash flows.[4] A *conventional* project cash flow is one where a cash outflow (or a series of cash outflows) is followed by a cash inflow (or series of cash inflows). The essence of the definition is that in a conventional cash flow, there is only one *change in sign* (from + to −, or vice versa) between the time periods. All three cash flows given below are therefore conventional:

			Year		
Project	0	1	2	3	4
K	− 1 000	+ 400	+ 500	+ 800	+ 50
L	− 1 000	− 500	− 600	+ 1 500	+ 2 000
M	− 500	− 600	+ 2 000		

The one change of sign for Project K comes between Year 0 and Year 1, for Project L it comes between Year 2 and Year 3, and for Project M it comes between Year 1 and Year 2. In each project cash flow there is only one sign change. Such projects will only have *one* IRR each (there is an exception to this, to which we shall return), and so no problems arise for the IRR decision rule.

Non-conventional cash flows can therefore be defined as those that involve *more than one* change in sign, such as shown below:

			Year			
Project	0	1	2	3	4	
N	− 100	+ 20	− 50	+ 80	+ 170	3 changes of sign
P	− 100	+ 60	+ 80	− 20		2 changes of sign

Such projects are likely to have more than one IRR and, as a general rule of thumb, a project will have as many IRRs as its cash flow has changes in sign. The problem this causes is illustrated in Example 4.

EXAMPLE 4

Infogrames SA has been given permission to undertake an exploratory shale oil extraction project in western France. It will require an investment of €1 050 000 to undertake the initial drilling and is then expected to produce annual cash flows of €800 000 for 5 years. At the end of the 5 years, Infogrames will have to spend €3 000 000 to landscape the area, which is a requirement of the extraction permission. The company normally uses IRR for investment appraisal, with a minimum IRR of 10% required to make an investment acceptable.

The cash flows produce two IRRs (that is, two discount rates, when applied to the project's cash flows, will produce a *zero* NPV). These two IRRs are 2% and 43% and the NPV profile is graphed in Figure 6.4. The company's problem is obvious: which IRR should it use to make a decision? Which IRR is 'correct'? Is *either* IRR correct?

FIGURE 6.4 Multiple IRRs

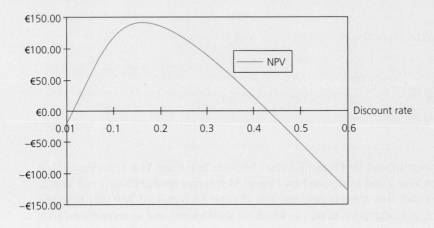

Non-conventional cash flows can make life very difficult for the IRR decision rule. For example, suppose that Project Q's NPV profile is illustrated in Figure 6.5. This project has three IRRs: 10%, 15% and 18%. In itself, this is not too disturbing if the cut-off rate is either less than 10% or greater than 18%, because the IRR rule still manages to give unambiguous (and operationally correct) decision advice. But if the cut-off rate is (say) 12%, the IRR decision can only give – at best – highly ambiguous advice (which may be incorrect). In such circumstances, the NPV rule would have no difficulty in giving the correct advice: to reject the project because it has a negative NPV.

However, it can be shown that with most project cash flows that are likely to occur in practice and, where multiple IRRs occur, the variations in the project's NPV between the IRRs are usually very small, and the value of the NPV itself is likely to be close to zero. Therefore it follows that with a simple accept-or-reject decision the problem of multiple IRRs is not too serious. If a project is accepted on the basis of (say) the majority of its IRRs being greater than the cut-off/discount rate, whereas when evaluated using NPV it turns out to have a negative NPV, then the IRR-based decision would not be disastrous as the magnitude of the negative NPV would likely be relatively small. Nevertheless, the problem of multiple IRRs does remain to cause difficulties in the case of mutually exclusive investment decisions. In such circumstances, the differential cash flow may well have multiple IRRs, which causes the decision rule to become non-operational.

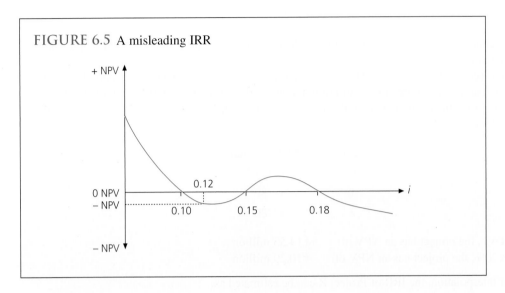

FIGURE 6.5 A misleading IRR

Despite the foregoing argument concerning the practical unimportance of multiple IRRs, the conclusion reached must still be that the possible presence of multiple IRRs is yet one more factor to count against the use of that particular DCF technique. The argument that, while the IRR rule may give the wrong decision, it will not be *very* wrong, is not a persuasive one.

EXTENDED YIELD METHOD

One approach that is often suggested, and sometimes used in practice, to handle the problem of multiple IRRs, is the 'extended yield' method. The extended yield method solves the problem of multiple IRRs by eliminating the offending second change in sign. This is achieved by discounting the unwanted cash flow back to present value at the hurdle rate, and then netting the figure off against the Year 0 outlay. Example 5 illustrates the approach.

EXAMPLE 5

Soudal Bruxelles is a Belgium company involved in copper mining. The company wishes to evaluate a short-term investment to extract a small copper deposit which is located in a scenic tourist area of Luxembourg. Because of the environmental issues concerned, the company will have to remove all adverse environmental damage at the end of the extraction project. The company uses IRR decision rule to make investment decisions, with a 10% hurdle rate. The project's expected cash flows are as follows:

Year	Cash flow (€m)
0	− 100
1	+ 50
2	+ 80
3	− 10

▶

▶

As this project has a non-conventional cash flow, the company uses the 'extended yield' approach to avoid the problem of multiple IRRs.

To do this, the Year 3 cash flow, the cost of repairing the environmental damage (i.e. where the second *change of sign* occurs), is discounted back to present value at the hurdle rate of 10%: $-10 \times (1.10)^{-3} = -7.51$ and this figure is then netted off with the Year 0 project cost to provide a *revised* cash flow for the project of:

Year	Cash flow (€m)
0	− 107.51
1	+ 50
2	+ 80

At 4%, the project has an NPV of: +€14.53 million
At 20%, the project has an NPV of: −€10.29 million

Using linear interpolation, the IRR of Project R can be estimated as:

$$4\% + \left[\frac{14.53}{14.53 - (-10.29)} \times (20\% - 4\%) \right] = 13.4\% \text{ IRR}$$

The company's copper mining project has now got a single IRR of 13.4% and as this is greater than the 10% hurdle rate, it indicates that the investment is acceptable.

However, it should be noted that the extended yield method only *gets around* the problem of multiple IRRs – it does not solve the problem.

Although a single IRR has been calculated for Soudal Bruxelles' copper mining project, the point remains that in reality the project has two IRRs (and neither will be the 13.4% estimated by the extended yield method).

OTHER PROBLEMS WITH THE IRR RULE

If we return to the example of Infogrames SA and their shale oil project (Example 4), but we slightly modify the project's cash flows, then we find another problem with IRR. This is illustrated in Example 6.

EXAMPLE 6

As before it will cost €1 050 000 for Infogrames to undertake the initial drilling for the shale oil project. The project is then expected to produce annual cash flows of €800 000 for 5 years. However, at the end of the 5 years, it will now cost €3 *090 000* (a €90 000 cost increase) to landscape the area and so remove the environmental damage caused by the project. The company wish to assess the investment using IRR, and will accept it if it produces an IRR of at least 10%, which is equal to the capital market interest rate.

The NPV profile of the Infogrames shale oil project, with this modified cash flow, is illustrated in Figure 6.6 and it demonstrates another potential problem for the IRR decision rule. Now the oil shale project only has a *single* IRR – despite having a non-conventional cash flow – but at **no** rate of discount does the project yield a *positive* NPV. At a 10% rate of discount – the capital market rate of interest – the project would have a negative NPV and the NPV rule would correctly reject the project. However, the IRR rule would accept it because its IRR (20%) is greater than the hurdle rate.

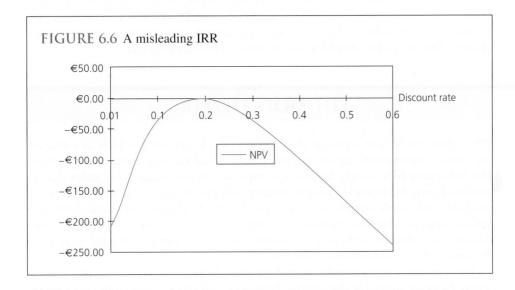

FIGURE 6.6 A misleading IRR

Figure 6.7 illustrates another NPV profile that, this time, causes the IRR decision rule to break down *completely*. Here we assume that all the cash flows for the Infogrames shale oil project remain the same, except for the fact that the landscaping will now cost €3 200 000. As a result the investment appears to have no IRR at all![5]

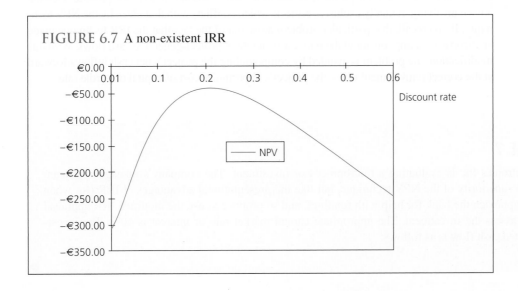

FIGURE 6.7 A non-existent IRR

Finally, a further difficulty that arises out of the IRR approach is caused by the fact that it evaluates projects on the basis of a *percentage* rate of return. In other words, it examines a project's return relative to its outlay, rather than in absolute terms as with NPV.

For example, suppose a company is evaluating a pair of mutually exclusive projects: a large factory or a small factory. The large factory has an outlay of €100 million, the small factory has an outlay of €20 million. Suppose the large factory has an IRR of 18% and the small factory 24%, and the hurdle rate is 15%. Therefore both alternatives are acceptable in their own right, but the standard IRR decision rule would accept the small factory, as it produces the higher IRR. The problem is that the company would end up with a significantly better *incremental* cash flow from an 18% return on €100 million than from a 24% return on only €20 million. This is, of course, yet another reason for the possible existence of conflicting advice between NPV and the standard IRR decision rule.

THE MODIFIED IRR

Whilst there can be little argument about the theoretical superiority of NPV as a decision rule, surveys of managers suggest that many of them feel that they understand the idea of IRR better than NPV, simply because it is expressed in *percentage terms* rather than an absolute figure. Managers are used to dealing with percentages – e.g. return on capital, dividend yields, profit margins, etc. This has led to the development of *modified IRR*. It is thus an attempt to overcome the theoretical difficulties of the normal IRR technique, whilst retaining an evaluation of the project based on a percentage rate of return and so avoiding the perceived 'user-unfriendliness' of NPV.

The approach is really founded on an NPV analysis that is then converted into a rate of return. However, instead of discounting the project cash flows – at the appropriate opportunity cost of capital – to present value, the cash flows (with the exception of the project's outlay) are compounded forward to a total terminal value. On the basis of these two cash flows – the project's outlay and the terminal value of its net cash inflows – the IRR is then calculated. This is illustrated in Example 7.

This particular modification to the IRR technique has two great technical advantages. First, it eliminates any potential problem of multiple IRRs. Second, it will not provide decision advice involving mutually exclusive projects which conflicts with that given by the NPV technique. If you recall, that particular problem arose out of the fact that the IRR technique made an incorrect assumption about the reinvestment rate of project-generated cash flows. With this modification, the problem is avoided by compounding the project's net cash inflows forward at the correct reinvestment rate – the project's opportunity cost of capital or hurdle rate.

EXAMPLE 7

Phoenix Electronics Inc is evaluating a microprocessor investment. The company's management team recognize the superiority of the NPV technique, but like the presentational advantages of IRR (for when they have to approach the bank for help with funding), and so propose to use the modified IRR appraisal technique to assess the investment. The appropriate capital market rate of interest is 10%. The investment's expected cash flow is as follows:

▶

▶

Year	$m
0	(100)
1	50
2	40
3	50

The terminal value of the project's net cash inflows (i.e. their accumulated value at Year 3 when the project finishes), can be calculated as:

Year	$m		
1	$50(1.10)^2$	=	60.5
2	$40(1.10)^1$	=	44.0
3	$50(1.10)^0$	=	50.0
Total terminal value		=	$154.5m

The project now has a modified cash flow of:

Year	$m
0	(100)
3	154.5

The IRR can now be estimated, as usual, using linear interpolation:

NPV at 4%   :   +$37.50 million
NPV at 20%   :   −$10.59 million

$$IRR\,4\% + \left[\frac{37.50}{37.50 - (-10.59)} \times (20\% - 4\%) \right] = 16.5\%\ IRR$$

As the investment has an estimated (modified) IRR of 16.5%, which is greater than the capital market interest rate/hurdle rate of 10%, this indicates the investment should be accepted. (The project actually has an NPV of about +$16 million.)

In Example 7, the project is shown to have an estimated *modified* IRR of 16.5%. For the purposes of this discussion, it is necessary to remember that the linear interpolation technique only *estimates* a project's IRR. In fact the modified *actual* IRR of Phoenix's microprocessor project is 15.6%. What we have to ask is: does the project genuinely produce a rate of return of 15.6%? The answer is that it does *if* the project-generated cash flows can accumulate at the end of the project's life to the same amount as could be accumulated by investing the project's outlay to earn an annual rate of return of 15.6%.

Investing $100m for 3 years at an annual rate of return of 15.6% yields a terminal value of:

$$\$100m \times (1 + 0.156)^3 = \$154.5\ million$$

This is *precisely* the terminal value of the project's net cash inflows calculated in Example 7. In other words, the project **does** genuinely earn a rate of return of 15.6%.

In many ways this modified IRR calculation achieves the best of all worlds. Its theoretical underpinning is that of NPV, but its method of evaluation is through the use of a user-friendly rate of return. Therefore it can be seen as a cosmetic restatement of an NPV analysis.

NPV VERSUS IRR: CONCLUSION

Our analysis puts forward a very strong case for the use of the NPV decision rule for investment appraisal. At best, the IRR method (or the modified IRR) might be used as a support and as a communication device on the basis of management's familiarity with rates of return, rather than NPVs, for the decision advice given by the NPV rule.[6] As a result of this conclusion, from now on we shall be implicitly assuming that the NPV technique will be the approach that should be used by companies in making capital investment decisions. It is the *only* technique from the four investigated that can be relied upon to give advice that will lead towards the maximizing of shareholder wealth.

REAL WORLD VIEW: Limitations of the NPV and its practical uses in day-to-day life

As acknowledged throughout the examples in this book, all models have their limitations and the NPV is not exempt from detractors. A key issue is the inherent difficulty of predicting future cash flows with precision. As one commentator, Seth Klarman, notes, 'When future cash flows are reasonably predictable and an appropriate discount rate can be chosen, NPV analysis is one of the most accurate and precise methods of valuation. Unfortunately cash flows are usually uncertain, often highly so.' Indeed, as one academic paper from 1998 argues further, the problem of assumptions underlying the rule not being met in practice results in some 'numerical examples wherein applying the NPV leads to erroneous decisions.'

It is the 'violation' of these assumptions – or, in other words, poor 'framing' of the specific scenario or problem in light of other ambiguities – that effectively distorts or even invalidates the NPV's actual usefulness. The two such assumptions questioned are, first, that the approval decision is 'now-or-never' (i.e. that only the one current chance to act will be presented) and, second, that decision-making is driven only by a single-person or, alternatively, a multi-person firm (without taking into consideration

'information asymmetries among individuals'). There are cases, they contest, when both these assumptions are false.

However, limitations aside, others profess the NPV's broad usefulness to all people in everyday life from consumers, to homeowners and pet lovers. One blogger, for example, used the model to establish the 'best' deal when looking at the various options for personal finance, noting that 'NPV can be used for myriad situations you'll face in life.' He used NPV to help in decisions ranging from choosing to buy his yellow Labrador puppy from a purebred breeder (taking into consideration the greater initial outlay versus future veterinary bills which may be higher with an adopted dog), to opting to buy a new lawnmower rather than paying for a lawn management service. Another classic example is the use of energy-saving light bulbs, which cost more than standard light bulbs to purchase yet save on the bills over time. The blogger recognized that each model merely presented a simplified account of life's everyday problems (that may not account for all possibilities or uncertainties), yet nonetheless had real value in providing real analysis to aid his decision-making.

THE REPLACEMENT CYCLE PROBLEM

Optimal replacement cycle

It was noted earlier that, when faced with a mutually exclusive investment decision, the NPV decision rule was to accept whichever project had the largest positive NPV. This decision rule was based on the assumption of a perfect capital market *and* on the assumption that the projects involved were 'one-offs'. In other words, they did not form part of a *continuous replacement cycle*.

However, where a project does form part of a continuous replacement cycle, the NPV decision rule needs to be modified. This situation is referred to as the 'replacement cycle problem', and Example 8 illustrates the approach.

EXAMPLE 8

Groupa Zaklad is a Polish sausage manufacturer, based in Krakow. It evaluates all capital investments using an NPV analysis. Currently the management is evaluating the purchase of a new sausage production line which, when it comes to the end of its economic life, is expected to be replaced by an identical production line and so on, continually. It is thought that 10% is the correct capital market interest rate to evaluate such an investment. Because of its very high rate of usage (the production line is expected to be running 24 hours a day, 7 days a week), it has a maximum working life of 3 years but, as its productivity declines with age (producing fewer sausages and higher operating costs), it could be replaced after either just 1 or 2 years. The financial details (in Zloty) are as follows (all figures in Z000s):

Year	0	1	2	3
Outlay	−1 000			
Revenues		+900	+800	+700
Costs		−400	−350	−350
Scrap value		+650	+400	+150

The decision as when to replace the production line can be seen as a choice between three mutually exclusive alternatives, the cash flows and NPVs of which are as follows:

		Cash flows	
Dispose of machine at end of:		0	1
First year	Outlay	−1 000	
	Revenue		+ 900
	Costs		− 400
	Scrap		+ 650
	Net cash flow	−1 000	+ 1 150

▶

Second year	Outlay	−1 000		
	Revenue		+900	+800
	Costs		−400	−350
	Scrap			+400
	Net cash flow	−1 000	+500	+850
Third year	Outlay	−1 000		
	Revenue		+900	+800	+700
	Costs		−400	−350	−350
	Scrap				+150
	Net cash flow	−1 000	+500	+450	+500

Disposal point		*NPV (Z000s)*
Year 1	$-1\ 000 + 1\ 150\ (1.10)^{-1}$	$= +Z45\ 460$
Year 2	$-1\ 000 + 500\ (1.10)^{-1} + 850(1.10)^{-2}$	$= +Z156\ 990$
Year 3	$-1\ 000 + 500\ (1.10)^{-1} + 450(1.10)^{-2} + 500(1.10)^{-3}$	$= +Z202\ 080$

If these were straightforward mutually exclusive projects, then the decision could be based on whichever alternative has the largest positive NPV. However, the production line – whenever the decision is taken to replace it – will be replaced by an identical production line which will itself be replaced by another identical production line and so on. Therefore, purely on the basis of the NPVs alone, 'like is not being compared with like' as each NPV is generated over a different span of time: 1, 2 or 3 years.

In order to place the three alternatives on a comparable basis, the equivalent *annual* cash flow[7] of each has to be computed as follows (remember, the $A_{n,i}$ annual equivalent factors can be found in Table D in the Appendix):

Disposal point	*NPV (Z000s)*	÷	$A_{N,10\%}$		*Equivalent annual cash flow*
Year 1	+ Z45 460	÷	$A_{1,10\%}$	=	+Z50 000
Year 2	+Z156 990	÷	$A_{2,10\%}$	=	+Z90 460
Year 3	+Z202 080	÷	$A_{3,10\%}$	=	+Z81 260

In order to understand the meaning of the 'equivalent annual cash flow' figures, let us take the 2-year replacement option as an example. Quite simply, the cash flow of the production line over a 2-year life has an NPV that is equal to the NPV of a 2-year (immediate) annuity of Z90 460 per year:

Year 0	*Year 1*	*Year 2*		
−1 000	+ 500	+ 850	=	+156.99 NPV
	+ 90.46	+ 90.46	=	+156.99 NPV

As a result, replacing the production line every 2 years is equivalent to a cash flow of Z90 460 at the end of every year:

Year	0	1	2	3	4	5	6 → ∞
1st line	−1 000	+ 500	+ 850				
2nd line			−1 000	+500	+ 850		
3rd line					−1 000	+500	+ 850
etc., etc.							−1 000
Equivalent c/f		+ 90.46	+ 90.46	+ 90.46	+ 90.46	+ 90.46	+ 90.46

Therefore, the optimal replacement cycle of the production line can be decided on the basis of which replacement cycle gives the most favourable equivalent annual cash flow. In this example it is two-year replacement, which produces an annual equivalent cash flow of €90 460. Both one- and three-year replacement will result in a *lower* equivalent annual cash flow. If the production line is replaced every year, this produces an annual cash flow equivalent to only €50 000; while replacing the production line every 3 years produces a cash flow equivalent to €81 260 per year.

Repair versus replace

The *repair versus replace* decision is very common. How long should a company continue to spend money on keeping an existing machine working, and when should it be replaced with a new machine?

With this type of situation, it is important to realize that *two* decisions are involved:

1. When should the existing machine be replaced?
2. What is the optimal replacement cycle of the new machine?

Furthermore, decision 2 must be made before decision 1 can be made. Example 9 continues on from Example 8 to illustrate the procedure.

EXAMPLE 9

Groupa Zaklad, referred to in Example 8, already have an existing sausage production line that is doing the job that will be done by the new production line analyzed as having an optimal replacement cycle of every 2 years. Therefore, the only remaining decision is: when should the company's existing production line be scrapped? The financial details are as follows (all figures in Z000s):

Existing production line	Year Z000s		
	0	1	2
Scrap value	+250	+200	+ 50
Repair cost	−100	−250	
Revenue		+600	+600
Costs		−300	−340

On the basis of this information, the existing sausage production line could be kept operational for a maximum of 2 more years. If it is to be kept operational for the next 12 months, it would require Z100 000 of repairs to be carried out now. To extend the production line's life for a further year – up to the end of Year 2 – would require an additional Z50 000 to be spent on repairs in 12-months' time. However, the repair costs in any particular year could be avoided by scrapping the production line in that year. (For example, the Z250 000 of repair costs at Year 1 would not be spent if the production line were to be scrapped at the end of Year 1.) The cash flows of the different options are as follows, based on the assumption that, when scrapped, the existing production line will be replaced by the new production line (analyzed in Example 8) which is itself replaced every 2 years and so locks the company into an equivalent annual cash flow of + Z90 460 in perpetuity.

Scrap the existing line at:	*Year*	*0*	*1*	*2*	*3 → ∞*
Year 0	Scrap value	+250			
	New line		+ 90.46	+ 90.46	+90.46
	Net cash flow	+250	+ 90.46	+ 90.46	+90.46
Year 1	Scrap value		+200.00		
	Repair cost	−100			
	Revenue		+600.00		
	Cost		−300.00		
	New line			+ 90.46	+90.46
	Net cash flow	−100	+500.00	+ 90.46	+90.46
Year 2	Scrap value			+ 50.00	
	Repair cost	−100	−250.00		
	Revenue		+600.00	+600.00	
	Cost		−300.00	−340.00	
	New line				+90.46
	Net cash flow	−100	+ 50.00	+310.00	+90.46

The NPV of each of these perpetuity cash flows is:[8]

Scrap at Year 0: + 250 + (90.46 ÷ 0.10) = + Z1 154 600 NPV
Scrap at Year 1: − 100 + 500 × (1.10)$^{-1}$ + [90.46 ÷ 0.10] × (1.10)$^{-1}$ = +Z1 176 920 NPV
Scrap at Year 2: − 100 + 50 × (1.10)$^{-1}$ + 310 × (1.10)$^{-2}$ + [90.46 ÷ 0.10] × (1.10)$^{-2}$ = +Z949 200 NPV

Therefore the best option for the company is to scrap the existing sausage production line in 12-months' time (the largest NPV option) and replace it with the new production line, which itself will then be replaced every 2 years thereafter (see Example 8).

Finally, a major drawback of the repair or replace decision procedure should be pointed out. The drawback is the implicit assumption of unchanging technology. In other words, the assumption in the optimal replacement cycle that the new production line will be replaced by an identical production line, with the same technology and same cash flows, ad infinitum, is clearly unrealistic. Thus, the technique's real-world usefulness should be seen with this limitation in mind.

SUMMARY

This chapter has looked at the application of the two DCF investment appraisal methods in the context of decisions between mutually exclusive projects. Arising out of this are a number of difficulties with the IRR decision rule. The main points made are:

- The NPV decision rule for mutually exclusive decisions is: accept whichever project has the largest positive NPV. The logic behind this is obvious, given the objective of shareholder wealth maximization and the meaning of NPV.

- The decision rule holds even when the alternative investments are of unequal magnitude, duration or risk, assuming a perfect capital market and that the discount rate used properly reflects the return available elsewhere on the capital market from a similar-risk investment.

- The standard IRR decision rule for mutually exclusive investments is: the 'best' project has the highest IRR; accept the best project if its IRR > hurdle rate.

- This standard IRR decision rule gives unreliable investment decision advice in situations of mutually exclusive projects: the problem arises from the arithmetic of the IRR and the fact that it assumes project-generated cash flows will be reinvested to earn a rate of return equal to the IRR of the project generating those cash flows.

- The reinvestment assumption is, strictly speaking, an assumption about the opportunity cost of project-generated cash flows: given a perfect capital market, the assumption made by the IRR is incorrect – their opportunity cost equates with the capital market rate of return for the risk level involved. The NPV method makes this, correct, assumption.

- The problem of the IRR can be resolved, in an artificial way, by a modified decision rule which, in its simplest form, states:

  (a) if IRR of the differential cash flow is > hurdle rate, accept the project with the smallest IRR

  (b) if IRR of the differential cash flow is < hurdle rate, accept the project with the largest IRR.

- A further problem for the IRR arises out of the possible existence of multiple IRRs, when the decision rule then breaks down completely.

- The problem of multiple IRRs can be resolved, again in a purely artificial way, through the use of the *extended yield* technique. However, this was shown not to deal with the problem, merely to avoid it.

- The theoretical objections to the IRR can be overcome by the use of the 'modified' IRR technique, but in reality it is more akin to a cosmetic restatement of NPV.

- The strong conclusion to the chapter is that, for many reasons, the IRR investment appraisal technique is – just like payback and ROCE – unsatisfactory. Therefore only NPV remains as an investment appraisal technique that will give consistently reliable advice, leading to shareholder wealth maximization.

- Finally, a related area was examined: the optimal replacement cycle and the repair-or-replace decision. This was seen to be a special case of mutually exclusive projects involving the use of the annuity discounting factors.

NOTES

1. This, of course, would be the decision rule for revenue-generating projects. For purely cost-generating projects (such as the installation of air conditioning equipment in a factory), the best project would be that which produces the smallest negative NPV.
2. The processes of discounting and compounding can be viewed simply as a method of assigning weights to cash flows.
3. The IRR calculation simply involves finding the roots of a polynomial equation of n terms (where n = the number of periods of the project's life). In general, the IRR equation of a project which lasts for n years will have n roots or solutions or IRRs. However, with a conventional type of cash flow, only one of these solutions is a real number and the rest will be imaginary (e.g. $\sqrt{-2}$), with mathematical, but no economic importance. However, a non-conventional project cash flow can produce a polynomial equation of a type that may have several real number roots, each one of which is an equally valid IRR. (Conventional and non-conventional cash flows are defined in the following paragraph in the main text.)
4. The use of these terms should not lead the reader into the all-too-easy substitution of 'usual' and 'unusual'. Non-conventional cash flows can be extremely common in practice, as we shall discover when we examine the impact of taxation on investment appraisal.
5. The IRR is said not to exist only as a 'real' number in such cases. It will exist, and so there will be roots to the polynomial, in terms of imaginary numbers. This mathematical result, however, has little relevance for our purposes.
6. Even this may be a disadvantage in that management may falsely believe that the IRR is essentially the same as ROCE, when in fact the two measures are totally distinct.
7. See the Appendix to Chapter 5.
8. The reader might like to refer back to the section on perpetuities in Chapter 5.

FURTHER READING

1. On the problems with the IRR technique, see R. Dorfman, 'The Meaning of Internal Rates of Return', *Journal of Finance,* December 1981; A. Herbst, 'The Unique, Real Internal Rate of Return: Caveat Emptor!', *Journal of Financial and Quantitative Analysis,* June 1978; S.M. Keane, 'The Internal Rate of Return and the Reinvestment Fallacy', *Journal of Accounting and Business Research,* June 1979; and C.R. Beidleman, 'DCF Reinvestment Rates Assumptions', *Engineering Economist,* Winter 1984. M.J. Osborne 'A Resolution to the NPV–IRR Debate', *The Quarterly Review of Economics and Finance,* November 2010 provides an up-to-date summary of the debate and a proposal for resolving the differences.
2. For a description of the modified IRR technique, see W.R. McDaniel, D.E. McCarty and K.A. Jessell, 'DCF with Explicit Reinvestment Rates: Tutorial and Extension', *The Financial Review,* August 1988.
3. There are many articles reporting the results of surveys on capital budgeting practice. Amongst these, the following are of particular interest: M. Ross, 'Capital Budgeting Practice in Twelve Large Manufacturers', *Financial Management,* Winter 1986; R.H. Pike and T.S. Ooi, 'The Impact of Corporate Investment Objectives and Constraints on Capital Budgeting Practices', *British Accounting Review,* August 1989; S.H. Kim and L. Guin, 'A Summary of Empirical Studies on Capital Budgeting Practices', *Business and Public Affairs,* Autumn 1986; and S.C. Weaver *et al.,* 'Capital Budgeting: Panel Discussions on Corporate Investments', *Financial Management,* Spring 1989; J. Graham and C. Harvey. 'How CFOs Make Capital Budgeting and Capital Structure Decisions', *Journal of Finance,* Spring 2002.
4. F. Alkaraan and D. Northcott, 'Strategic Capital Investment Decision Making: A Role for Emergent Analysis tools?', *British Accounting Review,* June 2006; surveys what investment appraisal techniques are used by large UK manufacturing companies, plus a discussion of the alternative techniques. I. Ekanem, 'Bootstrapping: The Investment Decision-making Process in Small Firms', *British Accounting Review,* December 2005 concludes that small companies do not follow what investment appraisal theory recommends and J.R. Graham and C.R. Harvey, 'The Theory and Practice of Corporate Finance: Evidence from the Field', *Journal of Financial Economics,* May 2001 is a straightforward discussion and survey of investment appraisal practice in a range of US companies.
5. Finally, two rather thoughtful articles are: S.C. Myers, 'Notes on an Expert System for Capital Budgeting', *Financial Management,* Autumn 1988; and M. Bromwich and A. Bhimani, 'Strategic Investment Appraisal', *Management Accounting,* March 1991.

QUIZ QUESTIONS

1   Project A has an outlay of $1 million and when using a discount rate of 10%, to reflect its risk, it has an NPV of + $20 000. Project B has an outlay of $10 million and when discounted at 20%, to reflect its risk, has an NPV of + $15 000. If A and B are mutually exclusive, which project should the firm accept?

2   In question 1, what assumptions are you making in giving your answer?

3   What are the reinvestment assumptions of NPV and IRR, which is correct, and under what circumstances?

4   Under what circumstances can multiple IRRs occur, and what can be done to avoid the problem?

5   Project C has the following cash flows:

	€000s
0	−100
1	+60
2	+80
3	−20

Using the 'extended yield technique', what is its IRR, given a 10% hurdle rate?

6   Sketch out a diagram showing how the conflict between NPV and IRR can occur.

7   What is the simple modification to the IRR decision rule?

8   Project D has the following cash flows:

	£000s
0	−80
1	+40
2	+80
3	−30

Given that the minimum required rate of return is 10%, what is its modified IRR? (See the 'Answers to Quiz Questions' section at the back of the book.)

PROBLEMS

The answers to three of the following problems (those indicated by an asterisk) are available to students online. The answer to the remaining problem is available only to lecturers (see the 'Digital Resources' page for details).

1*   Danske Haldor is a Danish boatbuilder, based in Stockholm. The company is currently evaluating a proposal to invest in producing a new type of inshore rescue boat. Two possible boat designs, Type A and Type B, have now been developed, each of which is expected to have a 5-year sales life, before a radical redesign would be required. The Type A design would require an investment of 1 million krones (DKK), while the Type B design would require an investment of 2 million krones. The expected cash flows of the two boat types are as follows:

▶

Year	Type A (K000s)	Type B (K000s)
0	−1 000	−2 000
1	+ 350	+ 640
2	+ 350	+ 640
3	+ 350	+ 640
4	+ 350	+ 640
5	+ 350	+ 640

The appropriate discount rate is 10% per annum. Both alternatives can be considered marginal investments and acceptance of either one would leave the company's risk unchanged. The company operates in a perfect capital market. Ignore taxation and inflation.

Required:

(a)   The managing director of Danske Haldor insists that the investment alternatives should be appraised using the IRR. You are therefore required to appraise these projects on that basis alone. State the decision rule you use, making sure that it will produce the correct investment decision advice in terms of maximizing shareholders' wealth.

(b)   Present a careful and detailed outline of the argument you might put forward to the managing director for using the NPV appraisal technique, rather than the IRR, given the present conditions surrounding Danske Haldor.

Note that your answer to part (b) should *not* be confined to a discussion of the two investment opportunities under consideration in part (a). Assume that all cash flows arise on the last day of the year to which they relate, with the exception of the project outlays, which occur at the start of the first year.

2*   August Horvat runs a small technology consultancy company – Prva Voda – in Zagreb, Croatia. He is presently considering opening up an additional office in Split and is evaluating two alternative locations. Property A is in the centre of town, while property B is larger, but is slightly further out from the centre. Each property would involve an immediate cash outlay of 100 000 kuna to convert them into suitable premises. Mr Horvat estimates that the net cash inflows from each alternative property will be as follows:

Net cash inflow at end of:	Project A (€n)	Project B (€n)
Year 1	60 000	10 000
Year 2	40 000	20 000
Year 3	30 000	110 000

Required:

(a)   Prepare a graph to show the functional relationship between NPV and the discount rate for the two property investments (label the vertical axis 'NPV' and the horizontal axis 'discount rate').

(b)   Use the graph to estimate the IRR of each project.

(c)   On the basis of the information given, advise Mr Horvat which project to accept if his discount rate is (i) 6%, (ii) 12%.

(d)   Describe briefly any additional information you think would be useful to Mr Horvat in choosing between the two properties.

(e)   Discuss the relative merits of NPV and IRR as methods of investment appraisal.

Ignore taxation.

3* Aventis Zebre is an aerospace company based in southern France. The company is considering which, if any, of four independent projects to undertake. The forecast cash flows for each project are listed below; receipts arise at the end of each year.

			Net cash flows (€000s)	
Project	Year 0	Year 1	Year 2	Year 3
1	−2 500	+1 000	+1 000	+ 1 000
2	−1 000	+ 100	+1 400	0
3	−1 000	+ 800	+ 600	0
4	−4 000	0	0	+ 5 000

The company faces a perfect capital market, in which the interest rate for the projects' risk level is 10%.

Required:

(a) Using the NPV decision rule, indicate which projects the company should accept. State clearly the reasons for your decisions.

(b) How would your conclusions in (a) differ if the projects were mutually exclusive?

(c) Estimate the IRRs of Projects 2 and 3. Would it be valid to choose between Projects 2 and 3 on the basis of their expected IRRs? If not, present revised calculations so that the IRR method, and the method you have used in (a), lead to the same, unambiguous conclusions.

(d) In practice, the IRR method has been observed to be far more widely used than NPV. Suggest reasons for this relative popularity. Why might the supposed superiority of NPV be an illusion or an irrelevance, in reality?

4 Verdet Maritime owns and operates a car ferry – called the Marcel Olar – which could be in use for a maximum of 2 more years. The ferry originally cost €45 million 5 years ago. Its realizable value is currently €8 million (because a special opportunity for sale has arisen), but it would be virtually zero at all subsequent times. If the ferry were to be used for 2 more years, it would require a major overhaul at a cost of €9 million in 1 year's time. A new purpose-built car ferry is now available. It costs €40 million and has a maximum life of 10 years, provided that special maintenance is undertaken at a cost of €10 million after 5 years, and at a cost of €20 million after 8 years. The new ferry is unlikely to have any realizable value at any time. Assume that no other new car ferries are likely to be built in the foreseeable future, and that no changes are expected in costs or demand on the ferry's proposed route. Verdet Maritime uses a discount rate of 15% to evaluate new investments.

Required:

Prepare calculations to show whether Verdet Maritime's existing car ferry should be replaced now, or after 1 or 2 years.

PROJECT CASH FLOWS

INVESTMENT APPRAISAL AND INFLATION

Up to this stage in the analysis we have implicitly assumed, within our world of managerial investment decision-making, that prices have been stable. That is not to say that we have excluded the possibility of any price changes, but that we have assumed that there are no general price movements within the economy, either upwards (inflation) or downwards (deflation). Indeed it was made clear when dealing with the concept of the time value of money that the concept, fundamentally, has nothing to do with inflation, and so inflation was assumed not to exist.

In this section we will now drop this assumption and examine how the existence of general price movements within an economy affect investment appraisal and decision-making; and how appraisal techniques can be adapted, if need be, to cope with such circumstances. The impact of general price movements will be examined by analyzing the inflation case, but the approach used and conclusions drawn will also apply, by analogy, to the case of deflation.

The problem of inflation

Inflation can be simply defined as a situation where prices in an economy are, in general, rising over time. Its expected (or unexpected) presence is likely to cause problems for the appraisal of investment opportunities in two main ways.

The first problem is that it will make the estimation of a project's expected future cash flow more difficult. When a project is being appraised, management will have to provide estimates of its inputs and outputs. With inflation, the future prices of these inputs and outputs are likely to change, and management will hence have to estimate the magnitude of these changes. In other words, management will have to estimate the expected future rates of inflation. Thus there is a *forecasting problem* caused by the presence of inflation.

The second problem is, in one sense, an extension of the first. Market interest rates, or rates of return, can be viewed as representing the *price of money*, and so interest rates – like other prices – can be expected to rise when there is general inflation within the economy. Therefore management has the additional task of estimating the effects of inflation on the project appraisal discount rate.

'Real' and 'money' rates of interest

The effects of inflation on market interest rates can most easily be seen by way of an example.

EXAMPLE 1

No inflation

For the moment, suppose that within the economy there is no inflation. An investor, M. Badoit, is willing to lend you €100 for 1 year in return for receiving €110 back in 12-months' time. In other words, he is willing to give up €100 worth of consumption now, as long as he is rewarded with an extra 10% consumption in 12-months' time. Thus, the 10% interest rate that he is demanding can be seen both in *money* terms – he wants an extra ten €1 coins – and in terms of consumption or *purchasing power* – M. Badoit wants to be able to buy/consume 10% extra goods or services. However, it is this latter interpretation that is of fundamental concern to the investor – how much *additional consumption* he is to receive in the future for giving up current consumption. (Euro coins by themselves are of little use. What makes them desirable is that they give the power to consume; consumption and consumption power – or purchasing power – is the point of importance.)

5% inflation

Now let us take a slightly different situation, with inflation expected to raise the *general* level of prices in the economy by 5% over the next 12 months. (We will go on to develop the idea of general and *specific* rates of inflation. The *general* rate of inflation relates to the *average* rate of price increases in the economy. *Specific* inflation rates refer to the rate of price increase for *specific* goods and services – such as the rate of wage inflation or the rate of inflation of raw material prices. For the moment, whenever reference is made to the 'inflation rate', this relates to the **general** rate of inflation in the economy.)

We know that M. Badoit would be willing to give up €100 worth of current consumption as long as he is rewarded with an extra 10% of consumption in 12-months' time. However, an extra €10 at t_1 will **not** now be sufficient cash to buy this additional consumption, because of the presence of inflation.

In order to consume, in 12-months' time, the *same* amount of consumption as that given up now, M. Badoit will need €100 × (1 + 0.05) = €105, because of the rise in prices. But our investor wants to be able to consume 10% *extra* in order to be persuaded to give up current consumption and so, in *money* terms, he will require €105 × (1 + 0.10) = €115.50 at t_1 in order to have 10% extra *purchasing* power.

What this illustrates is that *two* rates of interest (two time values of money) can be identified. One is the interest rate that is expressed in terms of *money* – in this example 15.5% – our investor receives 15.5% extra money at t_1 in exchange for giving up €100 at t_0. The other is the interest rate that is expressed in terms of the *purchasing power* of the extra money – in this example 10% – the 15.5% extra money our investor receives allows him to buy only 10% extra goods and services at t_1 because prices have risen by 5% over the intervening 12 months.

We know from the discussion about the concept of the time value of money that suppliers of investment capital make a trade-off between consumption now and consumption at some future point in time. Generally speaking, current consumption is preferred to future consumption and so, in order to be persuaded to forgo consumption now (and invest instead), investors need to be rewarded with the promise of *increased* consumption at a later point in time. Market interest rates reflect this time 'exchange rate' of consumption. As has been seen from the analysis in Example 1, in inflationary conditions, two interest rates can be identified – a *money* (or nominal) interest rate and a consumption (or purchasing power) interest rate. In Example 1 these were 15.5% and 10% respectively.

We shall refer to the former rate as the '*money*' interest rate (as it is the interest rate in terms of money) and to the latter as the '*real*' interest rate. (It is real in the sense that it represents the market interest rate, in terms of its *purchasing power*, rather than in simple *cash* terms. Putting this another way, the real interest rate is the market rate that has been *deflated* to take out the effect of *inflation*.)

The general relationship between inflation and money and real interest rates which is often referred to as the Fisher Effect, after the US economist who first developed it, is shown below:

$$\left(\begin{array}{c} \text{Real} \\ 1 + \text{interest} \\ \text{rate} \end{array} \right) \times \left(\begin{array}{c} \text{General} \\ 1 + \text{rate of} \\ \text{inflation} \end{array} \right) = \left(\begin{array}{c} \text{Money} \\ 1 + \text{interest} \\ \text{rate} \end{array} \right)$$

Notice that the Fisher Effect equation contains *three* items of data: the real interest rate, the inflation rate and the money interest rate. Therefore, if we have *any two* of these items of data, the Fisher Effect can be used to find the third item. For example:

$$[(1 + \text{Real interest rate}) \times (1 + \text{Inflation rate})] - 1 = \text{Money interest rate}$$

$$\left[\frac{1 + \text{Money interest rate}}{1 + \text{Inflation rate}} \right] - 1 = \text{Real interest rate}$$

and even: $$\left[\frac{1 + \text{Money interest rate}}{1 + \text{Real interest rate}} \right] - 1 = \text{Inflation rate}$$

The application of these Fisher Effect relationships can be illustrated by using the data from Example 1:

$$\text{Money interest rate} = [(1 + 0.10) \times (1 + 0.05)] - 1 = 0.155 \text{ or } 15.5\%$$

$$\text{Real interest rate} = \left[\frac{1 + 0.155}{1 + 0.05} \right] - 1 = 0.10 \text{ or } 10\%$$

$$\text{Inflation rate} = \left[\frac{1 + 0.155}{1 + 0.10} \right] - 1 = 0.05 \text{ or } 5\%$$

Two possible approaches

Example 1 showed that under inflationary conditions we can identify two possible interest or discount rates: the *money*/market interest rate and the *real*/purchasing power interest rate. The question that now arises is: which one should be used in an NPV investment appraisal analysis? The answer to this question is that *either* rate can be used, but they must each *only* be applied to an appropriate definition of the project cash flow. Specifically, we can state either:

1. *money* cash flows of the project can be discounted by the *money* interest rate to give the present value cash flows, or

2. *money* cash flows of the project can be discounted by the rate of *general* inflation to give the 'current general purchasing power' cash flows, and then these current general purchasing power cash flows can be discounted by the *real* interest rate to give the present value cash flows.

Either approach will generate exactly the same NPV for the project.

In these statements the term 'money' cash flow can be defined as the physical quantity of money that the project will generate at any particular point in time, and the term 'current general purchasing power' (CGPP) cash flow refers to the money cash flow, deflated by the *general* rate of inflation, so as to reflect the *current* general purchasing power of that future money cash flow. Example 2 can clarify these definitions and can also be used to show that these two alternative discounting approaches are entirely consistent with each other.

EXAMPLE 2

Ludza Baltic is based in Riga and is a wholesale coffee supplier to Latvia and Estonia. The company's management is evaluating an investment in a new coffee roasting machine. The company has taken great care to estimate how future rates of inflation will affect the prices charged for the roasted coffee beans that the machine will produce (and hence its revenue), and how inflation will also affect the key input cost of raw coffee beans, as well as energy, labour and distribution costs. As a result, the money cash flows of the coffee roaster project have been estimated as follows:

Year	Cash flow (Lats 000s)
0	−1000
1	+ 800
2	+ 600

The company believes that a 15.5% return is available elsewhere on the capital market for a similar risk project (i.e. the market rate of return). The Latvian general inflation index is expected to increase by 5% per year over the next 2 years.

Therefore the money discount rate is 15.5% and the general inflation rate is 5%. The real discount rate can be found from using the Fisher Effect:

$$\left[\frac{1 + 0.155}{1 + 0.05}\right] - 1 = 0.10 \text{ or } 10\%$$

▶

▶

Approach 1: Take the project's money cash flows and discount by the money discount rate (15.5%) to NPV.

Year	Cash flow Lats (000s)	×	15.5% Discount rate	=	Present value cash flow
0	−1 000	×	1	=	−1 000
1	+ 800	×	0.8658	=	+ 692.64
2	+ 600	×	0.7496	=	+ 449.76
					+ 142.40 NPV

Approach 2: Stage 1: Take the project's money cash flows and discount by the general rate of inflation (5%) to a CGPP cash flow. Stage 2: Discount the CGPP cash flow by the real discount rate (10%) to NPV.

Stage 1

Year	Cash flow Lats (000s)	×	5% discount rate	=	CGPP Cash flow
0	−1 000	×	1	=	−1 000
1	+ 800	×	0.9524	=	+ 761.92
2	+ 600	×	0.9070	=	+ 544.20

Stage 2

Year	CGPP cash flow	×	10% discount rate	=	Present value cash flow
0	−1 000	×	1	=	−1 000
1	+ 761.92	×	0.9091	=	+ 692.66
2	+ 544.20	×	0.8264	=	+ 449.73
					+ 142.39 NPV

Notice that the two NPVs are (virtually) identical. (The fact that they are not identical simply arises from rounding errors because only four-figure discount factors were used.) Given that the project has a positive NPV of approximately 142 400 Lats, it should be undertaken.

In Example 2 we should have expected the net present values to be exactly the same for obvious reasons: in the first approach, the cash flow is being discounted by 15.5%, whereas in the second approach the cash flow is being discounted by 10% and 5%. Thus in each alternative the cash flow is being discounted by the same amount because:

$$(1 + 0.155) = (1 + 0.10) \times (1 + 0.05)$$

Therefore it is for this reason that it was stated earlier that either the money discount rate, or the real discount rate could be used in an investment appraisal analysis, as long as each was applied to an appropriate definition of cash flow.

The money discount rate is an interest rate expressed in money terms and so it is applied to the actual money cash flows that the project is expected to produce. The real discount rate is an interest rate expressed in consumption or purchasing power terms, and so it should be applied to the project cash flows that are similarly expressed; in other words it is applied to the money cash flows after they have had the inflationary element taken out.

There are two further points to be noticed about this example. The first is that discounting the money cash flow by the general rate of inflation has nothing to do with the idea of the time value of money. It is simply a calculation to express the project cash flow, not in money terms, but in consumption/purchasing power terms. The idea of the time value of money is not taken into account until the discounting of these deflated cash flows by the *real* discount rate.

The second point to notice is that the project money cash flows are deflated (or discounted) by the general rate of inflation, *not* by the specific rate of inflation that applies to a particular cash flow. For example, suppose that although the general rate of inflation (as given by changes in the Latvian general inflation index) is 5%, the rate of raw coffee bean price inflation is 8%. The actual money cash flow paid out in raw coffee bean costs would be discounted by 5% and not by 8%. This is because we wish to express the money cash flows of a project in terms of their ability to purchase a *general range* or collection of goods, not their ability to purchase any one particular good.

The above analysis shows that the two possible approaches to project appraisal are exactly equivalent. Both start with the actual 'money' cash flows that the project is expected to produce, and both result in an identical set of present value cash flows from which the NPV can be found.

Given this equivalence, it does not much matter which approach is used, although discounting the money cash flows by the money (or market), interest rate would appear more straightforward because it only involves a *single set* of discounting calculations and so is the recommended approach to use.

INFLATION AND THE IRR TECHNIQUE

This discussion about allowing for inflation in investment appraisal has been conducted within the context of an NPV analysis. Nevertheless it is simple to transfer the conclusions into the context of an IRR analysis. Either the IRR of the *money* cash flows of the project can be compared against the hurdle rate of the *money* interest rate or, alternatively, the IRR of the project's *current general purchasing power* cash flows can be matched against the *real* interest rate. However, in order to be able to use the IRR successfully, it is important to remember that it is necessary to assume that either the money interest rate or the real interest rate will remain constant over the project's life.

INVESTMENT APPRAISAL AND TAXATION

Introduction

Taxation has an important role to play in investment appraisal, as it can have a substantial impact on the desirability, or otherwise, of an investment opportunity. Furthermore, taxation considerations affect virtually every area of financial decision-making both in a practical and in a theoretical context. Indeed, the complexity of the tax system found in most countries and the fact that its application to individual financial decision-making situations can sometimes be difficult to generalize, mean that it causes problems for the development of a realistic theory of financial decision-making. In this section we shall deal briefly with only the relatively general aspects of taxation, in order to examine its impact on investment project cash flows and their subsequent evaluation.

The impact of tax

The theory of financial decision-making is developed on the basis of the important underlying assumption that the company's management is taking decisions so as to maximize the wealth of the shareholders. It therefore follows that in the appraisal of an investment project, what is of importance is the cash flows that will be generated by the project, and *that are available for shareholders*. In other words, as far as investment appraisal is concerned, we would wish to evaluate the *after-tax cash flows* of a project.

In this analysis of the impact of tax on project appraisal, only a very generalized version of a typical corporate tax system will be used. Furthermore, it is assumed that the reader is aware – in outline – of the tax system that applies to their own particular country and can adjust aspects of the following analysis where necessary. (However, for those who lack knowledge in this area, a brief Appendix at the end of the chapter outlines the very basic elements of a typical corporate tax system.) It should also be remembered that tax rates are set by governments each year. Thus it is important to note that any tax rates used in this book are for the purposes of illustration only.

There are three ways in which a typical tax regime impacts upon a company's project appraisal:

1. *Impact 1.*
   Expenditure on capital investments is a 'tax allowable expense' and is usually spread over the assumed life of the investment. Thus a capital investment costing €1000 and with a life of 4 years, would have its cost – for tax calculation purposes – spread evenly over those 4 years of its life – €250 per year.

2. *Impact 2.*
   A tax liability will arise on any 'taxable profit', generated by the project.

3. *Impact 3.*
   There may also be a tax impact caused by how the project is financed. If it is financed with the help of debt capital, then there will be tax relief available on the interest payments.

With these three factors in mind, the approach taken to project appraisal is to evaluate the 'after-tax project cash flows' of the investment, using the 'after-tax discount rate'. The *after-tax project cash flows* take into account impacts 1 and 2 above; and the *after-tax discount rate* takes into account impact 3.

Financing cash flows

Up to this stage of our analysis of investment appraisal, very little has been said about how a project should be financed and the effect of the financing method on the project appraisal. This is how the position will remain until the capital structure/financing decision is discussed in detail in later chapters.

However, the basic philosophy of the approach of investment appraisal – and the NPV technique in particular – will be outlined now. This approach is that the financing method, and hence *all* the cash flows associated with the financing method, including interest payments, divided payments and loan repayments, can be ignored. This is because, in effect, they are implicitly taken into account in the *discount rate* used in the NPV analysis. Example 3 attempts to show the underlying rationale to this advice using a very simple situation.

EXAMPLE 3

Lisboa Santo is evaluating the acquisition of a new container tractor that it will rent out to shipping companies. The tractor costs €100 000 and will have a 3-year operating life. It is expected to generate a net revenue (i.e. revenues less cash *operating* costs – not *financing* costs) of €45 000 per year.

The company has approached its bank for a €100 000 3-year term loan in order to buy the tractor. The bank agrees to the loan, after examining the riskiness of the proposed investment, and requires a loan interest rate of 10%. (We will assume that this interest rate, like any rate of return, reflects the risk of the investment involved.)

Normally the company would then evaluate the NPV of the tractor investment, *ignoring* how it was to be financed and the cash flows (i.e. ignoring the interest payments and the eventual loan repayment) associated with the financing method.

Using a 10% discount rate (as this reflects the project's risk) the NPV is:

$$€100\ 000 + [€45\ 000 \times A_{3,\ 10\%}] = +€11\ 910\ NPV$$

However, it could be argued that this NPV analysis does not represent the true ***company*** cash flow, as effectively *the bank*, not the company, buys the machine. Thus, from the *company's* standpoint the true cash flows associated with the project are:

Year	0	1	2	3
Interest		−10 000	−10 000	− 10 000
Loan repayment				−1 00000
Net revenue		+45 000	+45 000	+ 45 000
Net cash flow[1]	0	+35 000	+35 000	− 65 000

However, when this cash flow is discounted to NPV at 10%, the result is ***exactly*** as before:

$$[+€35\ 000 \times A_{2,\ 10\%}] - [€65\ 000 \times (1 + 0.10)^{-3}] = €11\ 910\ NPV^{[2]}$$

The reason for this is important: it is that the present value of the financing cash flow ***always equals*** the amount of the finance. Hence the present value of the bank loan cash flow equals the amount of the bank loan:

$$€100\ 000 = [€10\ 000 \times A_{3,\ 10\%}] + [€100\ 000 \times (1 + 0.10)^{-3}]$$

Therefore, in the original NPV analysis of the project, the financing method is not really being ignored, because the project's outlay represents the present value of the financing cash flows.

Finally, care should be taken in not being misled by this simple example. The NPV analysis would have been undertaken in exactly the same way (with exactly the same +€11 910 NPV) if the project had been financed with (say) a €60 000 bank loan and €40 000 of the company's retained earnings. The €100 000 outlay in the NPV analysis would implicitly represent the present value of *all* the financing cash flows, *however* the project was financed.

Example 3 shows why an NPV analysis can (apparently) ignore how a project is financed. The costs of finance are taken into account within the discount rate used. In a similar way – although this will not be explained in detail until Chapter 16, where the 'cost of capital' is examined more fully – using an *after-tax* discount rate also takes into account the fact that the company will receive 'tax relief' on the loan's interest payments.

Tax relief on capital expenditure

If a company spends money on a capital investment (that is, an investment which would be classed as a 'non-current asset' in financial accounting terms), the tax authorities in most countries do not usually allow that *whole* expense to be used to affect the tax liability in the year in which it is incurred. Instead, the expense – and so the tax relief – has to be *spread* over the project's life in accordance with a specific schedule. Typically that schedule is one where the investment's cost is spread *equally* over the asset's expected life, although sometimes this spreading is forward-loaded as a way of encouraging a greater amount of investment. Example 4 illustrates the general approach.

EXAMPLE 4

Simba Veterinary Ltd produces a range of vaccines for farm animals in southern-Sahara Africa and is based in Johannesburg in South Africa. The company's management is currently evaluating the purchase of an item of production machinery which would cost R12 000 000 (South African rand). The machinery would have a 4-year life, at the end of which time it would be sold for scrap metal for R400 000. The machinery will generate the following costs and revenues:

Year	Revenues	Operating costs
	R000s	R000s
1	6 500	1 500
2	9 000	2 200
3	8 000	1 800
4	5 000	1 200

The corporation tax rate in South Africa is 28%, payable at the end of each year. Simba Veterinary use an *after-tax* discount rate of 10% to appraise new capital investments*.

The company will pay tax on the revenues generated each year over the life of the project, but will receive tax relief on the operating costs each year and on the capital expenditure, which would be spread over the life of the investment and which would be calculated as follows:

Tax relief on capital expenditure

Capital cost	R12 000 000
Disposal value	−R400 000
Reduction in value	R11 600 000 ÷ 4 years = R2 900 000
Tax relief	R2 900 000 × 0.28 = R812 000 per year

* Remember the *after-tax* discount rate is applied to the *after-tax* cash flows of the project. The after-tax project discount rate automatically takes into account any tax impact on the investment's financing method.

▶

Therefore the investment cost will be spread over the investment's 4-year life at the rate of R2 900 000 per year of tax-allowable capital cost, which reduces the companies tax charge by R812 000 per year.

After-tax project cash flows: (R000s)

For clarity, the tax impact of the investment will be split into two components: the tax charge on the revenues, less the operating costs, and the tax relief on the capital expenditure.

Year	0	1	2	3	4
Revenues		6 500	9 000	8 000	5 000
Operating costs		(1 500)	(2 200)	(1 800)	(1 200)
Taxable net revenues		5 000	6 800	6 200	3 800
28% tax charge		(1 400)	(1 904)	(1 736)	(1 064)
Tax relief on investment		812	812	812	812
Initial investment	(12 000)				
Scrap value					400
After-tax cash flow	(12 000)	4 412	5 708	5 276	3 948
	×	×	×	×	×
10% discount factor		0.9091	0.8264	0.7513	0.6830
Present value cash flow	(12 000)	4 011	4 717	3 964	2 696

Net Present Value: + R3 388 000

Finally, Example 5 illustrates a slightly more complex situation to further illustrate many of the points discussed.

EXAMPLE 5

Oostmeyer NV is an import–export company, based in Amsterdam. It is considering investing in a new logistics scheduling system that will require a capital expenditure outlay of €500 000. Because of the rapid pace of technological change, the logistics system is expected to only have a 4-year life and, at the end of that time, the system used will be sold off for €20 000.

In addition to the capital expenditure, €40 000 of working capital[3] will be required from the start of the project – this consists of an inventory of spare components and other supplies, and this will have to be *increased* to €50 000 at the end of the second year. All the working capital investment will be recovered at the end of the project's life.

The project is expected to increase the company's annual revenues by €400 000 and to incur annual cash operating costs of €160 000. The company believes that an after-tax discount rate of 10% would be appropriate. The logistics system would be financed with a 4-year bank loan of €500 000 at 6% interest. The working capital would be financed out of Oostmeyer's own retained profits. Corporation tax rate is 20% in the Netherlands and is paid at the end of each year. Capital expenditure, less scrap value, attracts tax relief and is spread evenly over an investment's expected life. There is no tax relief on working capital investment.

▶

Tax relief on capital expenditure

Capital cost	€500 000
Disposal value	−€20 000
Reduction in value	€480 000 ÷ 4 years = €120 000
Tax relief	€120 000 × 0.20 = €24 000 per year

Tax charge on project's profits (€000s)

Annual revenues	400
Less annual costs	160
Taxable 'profit'	240
Tax at 20%	€48

NPV calculation (€000s)

Year	0	1	2	3	4
Capital expenditure	(500)				
Scrap value					20
Tax relief		24	24	24	24
Working capital	(40)		(10^4)		50
Revenues		400	400	400	400
Costs		(160)	(160)	(160)	(160)
Corporation tax		(48)	(48)	(48)	(48)
Net cash flow	(540)	216	206	216	286
10% discount factor	× 1	×.9091	×.8264	×.7513	×.6830
Present value cash flow	(540)	196.4	170.2	162.3	195.3

NPV: +€184 200

Notice that all the financing cash flows have been ignored for the reasons outlined earlier in this section.

THE RELEVANT CASH FLOWS

In an earlier chapter it was stated that in order to properly appraise an investment opportunity, we have to evaluate *all* the cash flows that arise either directly or indirectly, as a result of the project. These cash flows are the *incremental* cash flows of the project – i.e. those cash flows that *only arise* if the investment is undertaken. Many of these cash flows that only arise as a result of undertaking a project are both obvious and easy to identify. For example, if a project consists of buying a machine, operating it and selling its output, there are some 'obvious' cash flows involved, such as the cost of the machine and the revenue generated from the sale of the output. However, the identification of all the incremental cash flows that are relevant to a project's appraisal are not always so obvious.

Guiding rules

A set of 'guiding rules' will be used to outline the most important points and then a comprehensive example will be used to illustrate their application.

Rule 1: All costs incurred (and revenues generated) *prior* to the investment appraisal decision being made should be excluded from the analysis. These are known as 'sunk costs' in that they are unaffected by the investment decision under appraisal and will be incurred whatever investment decision is made – they are non-incremental cash flows. Example 6 illustrates this logic.

EXAMPLE 6

London Waste Management plc is a UK company. It has spent £800 000 undertaking the development of a new product. They have now reached the stage where a decision needs to be taken on whether to invest in manufacturing facilities for the new product. In this investment appraisal, the £800 000 spent on R&D is a *sunk cost* and so is irrelevant to the decision to be made.

To see how misleading it could be to *include* the development expenditure, suppose the manufacturing equipment costs £5 000 000 and the product is expected to produce net revenues of £5 500 000. (For this simple example, we will ignore any discounting.) If the sunk costs were ignored, the decision would be to accept, but if the sunk costs were included in the analysis, the decision would be to reject:

Sunk cost excluded (£)		Sunk cost included (£)	
Cost	− £5 000 000	Cost	−£5 000 000
Net revenues	+ £5 500 000	R&D expenses	−£ 800 000
'Profit'	+ £ 500 000	Net revenues	+£5 500 000
		'Loss'	−£ 30 000
Decision	Accept	Decision	Reject

The point here is that if the company *accepts* the project, at least they have the £500 000 'profit' to offset the £800 000 spent on the development work, leaving a net cost of only £300 000. If they *reject* the project, they are simply left with an £800 000 development cost.

Rule 2: Ignore depreciation charges. Depreciation is a *non-cash* flow and so does not enter into the NPV cash flow analysis.

Rule 3: Ignore all financing cash flows (e.g. interest charges, loan repayments, dividends, etc.) and all their tax effects (e.g. interest tax relief). This is because, as was seen in the previous section, these are all implicitly taken into account through the discounting process.[5]

Rule 4: Ignore all non-incremental cash flows. This is the more general case of Rule 1. Only those cash flows that arise because of the project should be included in an NPV analysis. Any cash flow that would arise whether or not the project was undertaken should be excluded.

(An example of Rule 4's application would be 'allocated' fixed costs. If a company normally allocated a particular proportion of its fixed head office costs to any new project, as part of its budgeting/costing process, these should be *excluded* from the investment appraisal. They would be cash flows that are non-incremental to the investment decision, in that the head office costs would still be incurred whether or not the project was accepted.)

Rule 5: This concerns the cost, to the project, of using resources (usually raw materials) that the firm already holds in stock. Here there are three possible 'costs':

1. original purchase price/historic cost
2. current replacement cost
3. resale value or disposal cost.

The first of these is never relevant – the historic cost of the raw material stock is a *sunk* cost. However, which of the other two costs is relevant depends upon the particular circumstances.

Where the resources held in stock are used elsewhere in the company, then the cost to the project of using them is their *replacement* cost. This is because if the resources are used on the project, then those stocks will have to be replaced. Hence the current replacement cost is the opportunity cost[6] of their use.

If the resources already held in stock have no other use in the company than their use on the project, then they will not be replaced. (Such a situation might arise through, say, the company using those particular resources in the past but no longer doing so, although some surplus stocks still remain.) Under these circumstances, if the stocks have a resale value then their *resale* value would be the (opportunity) cost to the project of their use. (The company, in using them on the project, forgoes the opportunity to sell them off.) If they only have a disposal cost, then their use on the project would *save* these costs. Hence the project would be credited with a benefit – or cash inflow – the saved *disposal* cost.

Rule 6: This concerns the use, by the project, of resources already in use with the company and where the company cannot obtain further supplies of those resources. In other words, this is the situation where the project utilizes 'scarce' or limited resources. The rule is that the cost of their use on the project is their total opportunity cost. Example 7 illustrates this situation.

EXAMPLE 7

There is a shortage of well-qualified mining engineers in Kazakhstan. Astana Minerals is based in the city of Shymkent in southern Kazakhstan and presently employs 100 mining engineers who are all fully utilized undertaking various projects. The company is now considering the development of a small uranium mine which would require five mining engineers. Because of the shortage of such staff, they cannot recruit any more, and so, if they undertook the new mining project, the engineers would have to be taken away from their existing tasks elsewhere in the company.

Suppose that each engineer is currently *contributing* 20 million tenge (the Kazakhstan currency), per year to the company's profits (i.e. revenue generated, less the engineer's salary, less the material and incremental costs incurred, equals T20 million). This will be lost if the company redeploys the engineer onto the new project: it would be the *internal* opportunity cost of using each engineer on the new project.

Thus the *total* cost of each engineer used on the new mining project would be the forgone contribution (the *internal* opportunity cost), plus the engineer's salary (the external opportunity cost – or *market price* of the scarce resource).

These rules are now used in combination in Example 8.

EXAMPLE 8

Zhongfeng Electronics is based in Shanghai. It has been offered a contract to produce six special communication systems for the Chinese government. Construction would take a total of 3 years at a rate of two systems per year. Payment would be in two instalments: 350 million yuan at the start of construction and another ¥350 million upon completion.

The company is now evaluating the contract to see if it is worthwhile undertaking, and its contracting department has produced the following estimates about the resources required to produce the special communication systems:

1. Materials

Type of material	Quantity per system (tonnes)	Amount in stock now (tonnes)	Original cost of stock per tonne (¥)	Current purchase price per tonne (¥)	Current realizable value per tonne (¥)
Copper	2 000	6 000	7 000	10 000	8 000
Radium	1 000	2 000	5 000	7 500	See below

Copper is used regularly by the company on many contracts. Radium is used rarely, and if the existing stock is not applied to this contract it will have to be disposed of *immediately* at a net cost of ¥1000 per tonne. Materials required for the contract must be purchased and paid for annually *in advance*. Replacement costs of copper and radium and the realizable value of copper are expected to increase at an annual compound rate of 20%.

2. Labour

Each of the six systems will require 200 000 hours of skilled electronic engineering and 100 000 hours of unskilled labour. Current wage rates are ¥100 per hour for skilled electronic engineers and ¥45 per hour for unskilled labour.

Zhongfeng expects to suffer a shortage of skilled electronic engineers during the first year, as a result acceptance of the contract would make it necessary for the firm to give up other work on which a contribution of ¥65 per skilled labour hour would be earned. (The 'other work' would require no unskilled labour.) Again, in the contract's first year only, the company expects to have 250 000 surplus unskilled labour hours. Zhongfeng has an agreement with its workers, committee whereby it 'lays off' employees for whom there is no work and pays them two-thirds of their normal wages during the lay-off period.

All wage rates are expected to increase at an annual compound rate of 15%.

3. Overheads
Overhead costs are currently allocated to contracts at a rate of ¥150 per skilled electronic engineer, calculated as follows:

Fixed overheads (including equipment depreciation of ¥50)	¥110.00
Variable overheads	40.00
	¥150.00

Special equipment will be required to undertake this contract, and will be purchased at a cost of ¥20 million payable immediately. It will be sold once the contract is completed for ¥5 million. Both fixed and variable

▶

overheads are expected to increase in line with the Chinese general inflation index (CGI). The special equipment will be financed with the first contract instalment paid by the government.

Zhongfeng has considerable experience in constructing communication systems and believe that a return of 20% would be available elsewhere for a similar risk investment. The CGI index is expected to increase by 15% per year over the life of the contract.

It can be assumed that all current prices will hold for the next 12 months, before increasing in line with inflation. Therefore, for example, the material costs incurred for the second year's production will be 20% higher than the current market prices. Also it can be assumed that all cash flows arise on the last day of the year to which they relate, unless otherwise stated. Taxation should be ignored for the purposes of this evaluation (to simplify the analysis).

Project cash flows (¥ millions)

Year	0	1	2	3
Revenues	+350			+ 350
Equipment cost	−200			
Scrap value				+ 5
Copper cost	− 40	− 48	− 57.6	
Radium cost	+ 2		− 18	− 21.6
Elec. engin. cost		− 66	− 46	− 52.9
Unskilled labour		− 3	− 10.4	− 11.9
Variable overheads		− 16	− 18.4	− 21.2
Net cash flow	+112	− 133	− 150.4	+ 247.4
20% discount factor	× 1	× .8333	× .6944	× .5787
Present value cash flow	+112	− 110.8	− 104.4	+ 143.2

Contract's NPV: +¥40 million. Therefore the contract is worth undertaking.

Data calculations

1. Materials:

Copper   Year 1: Use 4000 tonnes from stock. As this will have to be replaced, its cost is the current purchase price of ¥10 000 per tonne.

Year 2: Buy in 4000 tonnes at ¥10 000 (1.20) = ¥12 000 per tonne.

Year 3: Buy in 4000 tonnes at ¥10 000 $(1.20)^2$ = ¥14 400 per tonne.

Radium   Year 1: Use 2000 tonnes from stock. This will save a disposal cost of ¥1000 per tonne (opportunity benefit), payable immediately.

Year 2: Buy in 2000 tonnes at ¥7500 (1.20) = ¥9000 per tonne.

Year 3: Buy in 2000 tonnes at ¥7500 $(1.20)^2$ = ¥10 800 per tonne.

▶

2. *Labour:* 400 000 hours of skilled engineers required per year.

100 000 hours of unskilled labour required per year.

Skilled Year 1: 400 000 hours taken from elsewhere in the company. Cost is wage rate plus lost contribution: ¥100 + ¥65 = ¥165 per hour.

Year 2: Hire 400 000 hours at ¥100 (1.15) = ¥115 per hour.

Year 3: Hire 400 000 hours at ¥100 $(1.15)^2$ = ¥132.3 per hour.

Unskilled Year 1: Utilize 2 200 000 hours of surplus labour. Cost is the *incremental wages paid: ¥15 per hour.*

Year 2: Hire 200 000 hours at ¥45 (1.15) = ¥51.8 per hour.

Year 3: Hire 200 000 hours at ¥45 $(1.15)^2$ = ¥59.5 per hour.

3. Overheads:

Fixed Excluded as non-incremental.

Depreciation Excluded as non-cash flow.

Variable Year 1: ¥40 per skilled labour hour.

Year 2: ¥40 (1.15) = ¥46 per skilled labour hour.

Year 3: ¥40 $(1.15)^2$ = ¥52.90 per skilled labour hour.

SUMMARY

Having concluded in the previous chapter that of the four basic investment appraisal techniques, only one – the NPV technique – is satisfactory, this chapter then turned to examine some of the possible problems that may be encountered with the application of NPV to investment appraisal: inflation, taxation and relevant project cash flows. The main points made are as follows:

- Inflation is not the *cause* of the time value of money, but it does affect its value through the Fisher Effect relationship.

- The simplest approach to take in an investment appraisal in an inflationary environment is to discount a project's actual *money* cash flows by the market (or *money*) discount rate to NPV.

- 'Real' cash flows should not be confused with cash flows in current terms. 'Real' refers to expressing an actual money cash flow in current general purchasing power terms. This will only be the same as a cash flow in current terms if the latter is expected to inflate at the general rate of inflation.[7]

- With taxation, there are three impacts on project appraisal:

  (a) tax relief on capital expenditure

  (b) tax charge on the project's profit

  (c) tax effects on the project's financing method: tax relief on debt interest.

- The approach to use is to evaluate the after-tax project cash flows with the after-tax discount rate. The after-tax project cash flows take account of the capital expenditure tax relief and the tax charge on the project's profit. The third tax impact is taken into account through the after-tax discount rate.

● As far as the relevant project cash flows are concerned, an investment appraisal should only include the *incremental* cash flows. This is the key concept. Any cash flows that have already occurred prior to the investment decision, or any subsequent cash flows that will occur whether or not the project is undertaken, are irrelevant.

● In addition, use has to be made of the opportunity cost concept to ensure that the full costs and benefits of undertaking the project are captured in the investment appraisal.

APPENDIX: A TYPICAL CORPORATE TAX SYSTEM

This appendix briefly outlines the basics of a typical corporate tax system as it affects investment appraisal. In no way does it purport to represent a complete analysis. However, some familiarity with the tax regime is necessary in order to be able to appreciate how it is likely to impact on project appraisal.

1. Company 'profits' are subject to a rate of tax – which can vary depending upon the situation – and the tax is generally paid shortly after year-end.

2. Profit can be defined as revenues less allowable costs. Within these costs, depreciation is not an allowable cost, nor are dividend payments or working capital expenses. However, interest payments are an allowable cost. Most normal business expenses such as labour, materials and overhead costs are allowable against tax.

3. As a substitute for depreciation, companies will be allowed to spread out capital expenditure costs over the expected life of the investment, less the expected scrap value, as a tax allowable expense. (Notice in the calculation of the tax allowable capital cost expense in Example 4 that the tax relief at 28% was taken into account separately. It could have been incorporated into the 'taxable profit' calculations.)

4. Companies normally receive tax relief on loan interest costs. They do not receive tax relief on either loan repayments or on dividend payments.

NOTES

1. Alternatively, the cash flows could be shown as:

Year	0	1	2	3
Loan from bank	+1 000			
Interest		−100	−100	− 100
Loan repayment				−1 000
Capital expenditure	−1 000			
Net revenue		+450	+450	+ 450
Net cash flow	0	+350	+350	− 650

but the net effect is the same.

2. Actually, using four-figure discount tables the NPV is +€11 908, but the difference between the two NPVs is solely brought about through rounding error.

3. 'Working capital' consists of an investment in *current* assets – such as inventories and receivables. With any capital investment which also requires additional investment in working capital, that working capital investment must be taken into account in the project appraisal, but it attracts neither a *tax charge*, nor *tax relief* and so has **no** tax impact.

4. The required investment in working capital increases by €10 000 from €40 000 to €50 000.

5. There are two important possible exceptions to this rule. One is in a special investment appraisal situation: the lease versus purchase decision. The other is in the case of overseas project appraisal. Both topics will be covered at a later stage.

6. The concept of 'opportunity cost' is important in all forms of economic analysis. See the suggested reading.

7. An example might help to make this statement clear. Suppose the current wage rate is $20 per hour and we require 100 hours of labour at Year 2. Therefore the Year 2 labour cost in current terms is $2000. This may or may not equal the Year 2 labour cost in real terms, depending upon the inflation rate of labour costs. If labour costs inflate at 10% per year and the *average* rate of inflation in the economy is also inflating at 10% per year, the current labour cost *will* equal the real cost. But if labour costs inflate up at a different rate from the *average* rate of inflation in the economy, then the two things are *not* equal:

(a) Labour inflates up at 10% per year.

RPI inflates up at 10% per year.

Actual Year 2 cash flow: $2000 $(1.10)^2 = 2420.

Real Year 2 cash flow: $2420 \times (1.10)^{-2} = 2000.

Current Year 2 labour cost = $2000.

(b) Labour inflates up at 15% per year.

RPI inflates up at 10% per year.

Actual Year 2 cash flow: $2000 \times (1.15)^2 = 2645.

Real Year 2 cash flow: $2645 \times (1.10)^{-2} = 2185.83.

Current Year 2 labour cost = $2,000.

FURTHER READING

1. A good overview article on the problem of inflation and capital investment appraisal is: N.J. Coulthurst, 'Accounting for Inflation in Capital Investment: State of the Art and Science', *Accounting and Business Research,* Winter 1986.

2. Other interesting studies include: B. Carsberg and A. Hope, *Business Investment Decisions Under Inflation: Theory and Practice,* ICAEW 1976; A. Rappaport and R.A. Taggart, 'Evaluation of Capital Expenditure Proposals Under Inflation', *Financial Management,* Spring 1982; M.K. Kim, 'Inflationary Effects in the Capital Investment Process', *Journal of Finance,* September 1979; and S.N. Chan, 'Capital Budgeting and Uncertain Inflation', *Journal of Economics and Business,* August 1984. J. Thomas and F. Zhang, 'Understanding Two Remarkable Findings about Stock Yields and Growth', *Journal of Portfolio Management,* Summer 2009 provides an interesting insight into the distinction between nominal and real rates of return.

3. Finally, on the whole area of relevant cash flows and opportunity costs see: L. Amey, 'On Opportunity Costs and Decision Making', *Accountancy*, July 1961; J.R. Gould, 'Opportunity Costs: The London Tradition', in *Debits, Credits, Finance and Profits,* H.C. Edey and B.S. Yamey (eds), Sweet and Maxwell 1974; and N.J. Coulthurst, 'The Application of the Incremental Principle in Capital Investment Project Evaluation', *Accounting and Business Research,* Autumn 1986.

QUIZ QUESTIONS

1   If the market interest rate is 13% and the general rate of inflation is 4%, what is the real interest rate?

2   What approaches can be taken to an NPV investment appraisal in inflationary conditions?

3   What is a 'real' cash flow?

4   Rent is paid each year. This year's rent – €10 000 – has just been paid. How much rent will need to be paid in 2 years' time if:
   (a) the rent remains constant in real terms?
   (b) the rent remains constant in money terms?

   In both of the above cases, what is the PV of the Year 2 rent? Assume that the market discount rate is 15.5% and the general rate of inflation is 5% per year.

5   A company owns a machine that is currently lying unused in the factory. The machine was bought 5 years ago at a cost of £60 000 and has now been depreciated down to a 'book value' of £10 000. It could be sold now for £3000. Alternatively it could be rented out for 1 year at £2500. The company's chief engineer believes the machine will be totally obsolete in 12-months' time and would then have a scrap value of £800. The company is considering using the machine to undertake a 1-year project. If it did, the machine's scrap value at the end of the year, net of dismantling costs, would be zero. Ignoring the time value of money, what is the cost of using the machine on the project?

6   What is the approach used to handling tax in investment appraisal?

7   Why should 'allocated' fixed costs be excluded from project cash flows in an NPV analysis?

8   A company pays an annual rent of €20 000 for its factory of 10 000 metres^2. All space is fully utilized and no more space is available for rent. Each square metre of space generates a contribution of €15. A project is being considered that would require 150m^2 of factory space. What would be the cost, to the project, of that space?
   (See the 'Answers to Quiz Questions' section at the back of the book.)

PROBLEMS

The answers to two of the following problems (those indicated by an asterisk) are available to students online. The answer to the remaining problem is available only to lecturers (see the 'Digital Resources' page for details).

1* SatNav Systems plc is considering buying a machine to produce printed circuit boards. The machine costs £1.2 million and will last for 5 years. The scrap value of the machine is expected to be £200 000. In addition to the capital investment, an investment of £150 000 in working capital will also be required. SatNav's accounting department has prepared the following estimated annual trading account for the project:

	(£)
Sales	1 400 000
Materials	(300 000)
Labour	(500 000)
Depreciation	(200 000)
Allocated fixed overheads	(250 000)
Annual profit	£ 150 000

The machine would be financed with a 4-year term loan from HSBC bank at an interest rate of 11.5%. The interest payments attract tax relief.

The company believes that 10% would be the minimum after-tax return acceptable from a project with this level of risk and, if that return is achieved, then they will be able to increase dividends to shareholders by £50 000 a year over each of the next 5 years. The corporate tax rate is 25%.

Required:

Calculate the project's NPV.

2* Helvestic Geosystems AG is a geothermal imaging company, based in Geneva. It is owned by two partners, Henrik Blom and Max Bauer, who each hold 50% of the company's shares. The company's latest accounts show a balance sheet value for share capital and reserves of CHF 250 000 (Swiss francs) and an annual turnover of CHF 1.25 million. The company has recently been offered two contracts, both of which would commence almost immediately and last for 2 years. Neither contract can be delayed. The prices offered are CHF 700 000 for Contract 1 and CHF 680 000 for Contract 2, payable in each case at the contract's completion. The skilled labour force of Helvestic is committed during the coming year to the extent that sufficient skilled labour will be available to support only *one* of the two contracts. Due to a labour shortage in Switzerland, the company will not be able to expand its skilled labour force in the foreseeable future. If necessary, Helvestic could subcontract one entire contract, but not both, to a nearby company, Odier Technology, which is of a similar size to Helvestic. If one contract were subcontracted, all work would be undertaken by Odier, subject to regular checks of progress and quality by Henrik Blom. Odier has quoted prices of CHF 490 000 for undertaking Contract 1 and CHF 530 000 for Contract 2, payable in either case by two equal instalments, half at the start of the contract and the remainder at the end of the first year.

Helvestic uses a standard costing system and normally prices contracts on a 'cost-plus' basis. Total cost is calculated by adding 60% to direct costs for overheads, this percentage being based on previous experience. A target price is then calculated by adding a 25% profit mark-up to total cost. Max Bauer has calculated the following target prices for the two contracts under consideration:

	Contract 1 (CHF)	Contract 2 (CHF)
Materials: Special equipment (at original cost)	50 000	—
Other supplies (at standard cost)	200 000	24 000
Labour: Skilled (at standard cost)	80 000	80 000
Unskilled (at standard cost)	1 12 000	1 26 000
Direct costs	42 000	46 000
Overheads: 60% of direct costs	65 200	67 600
Total cost	07 200	13 600
Profit mark-up: 25% of total cost	76 800	78 400
Target price	84 000	92 000

The following additional information is available:

Materials: Contract 1 would require the immediate use of special imaging equipment that was purchased 1 year ago at a cost of CHF 50 000 for a contract that was not completed because the customer went into liquidation. This special equipment has a current purchase cost of CHF 60 000 and a current realizable value of CHF 30 000. The company foresees no alternative use for this special equipment. Usage of the other supplies would be spread evenly between the 2 years of each contract's duration. These other supplies are all used regularly by the company. Their standard costs reflect current purchase prices which are expected to continue at their present level for the next 12 months. In the following year, prices are expected to rise by 10%.

Labour: Skilled labour costs for each contract represent 4000 hours each year for 2 years at a standard cost of CHF 10 per hour. Unskilled labour hours required are 8000 hours per annum for Contract 1 and 9000 hours per annum for Contract 2, in each case at a standard cost of CHF 7 per hour. Standard costs are based on current wage rates. Hourly wage costs for both skilled and unskilled labour are expected to increase by 5% in the current year and then by a further 10% in the following year.

Overheads: An analysis of Helvestic's most recent accounts shows that total overheads may be categorized as follows:

Fixed administrative and office costs	60%
Depreciation of plant and equipment	30%
Costs which vary directly with direct costs	10%
	100%

Fixed administrative and office costs are expected to increase as a result of inflation by 5% in the current year, and by a further 10% in the following year.

Helvestic has a money cost of capital of 10% per annum in the current year. Henrik Blom expects this to increase to 15% per annum in the second year of the contract.

Assume that all payments will arise on the last day of the year to which they relate, except where otherwise stated.

Required:

Provide calculations, on the basis of the estimates given, showing whether Helvestic Geosystems should accept either or both contracts, and which one, if any, should be subcontracted to Odier Technology.

3   Tramontana SA is based in Granada, in southern Spain. The company is developing a new product, the 'Caja' folding beach chair, to replace an established product, the 'Alpha' leisure seat, which the company has marketed successfully for a number of years. Production of the Alpha will cease in 1 year, whether or not the Caja is manufactured. Tramontana has recently spent €75 000 on research and development relating to the Caja. Production of the new product can start in 1 year's time. Demand is expected to be 5000 units per annum for the first 3 years of production and 2500 units per annum for the last 2 years of its expected life.

Estimated unit revenues and costs for the Caja, at current prices, are as follows:

	(€)	*(€)*
Selling price per unit		140.00
less costs per unit:		
Materials and other consumables	32	
Labour (see (a) below)	24	
Machine depreciation and overhaul (see (b) below)	50	
Other overheads (see (c) below)	36	142
Loss per unit		2

(a) Each Caja requires 2 hours of labour, paid at €12 per hour at current prices. The labour force required to produce Caja comprises six employees, who are at present employed to produce Alphas. If the Caja is not produced, these employees will be made redundant when production of the Alpha ceases. If the Caja is produced, three of the employees will be made redundant at the end of the third year of its life, when demand halves, but the company expects to be able to find work for the remaining three employees at the end of the Caja's 5-year life. Any employee who is made redundant will receive a redundancy payment equivalent to 1000 hours' wages, based on the most recent wage at the time of the redundancy.

(b)   A special machine will be required to produce the Caja. It will be purchased in 1 year's time (just before pro-duction begins). The current price of the machine is €760 000. It is expected to last for 5 years and to have no scrap or resale value at the end of that time. A major overhaul of the machine will be necessary at the end of the second year of its life. At current prices, the overhaul will cost €240 000. As the machine will produce the same quality of Cajas each year, the directors of Tramontana have decided to spread its original cost and the cost of the overhaul equally between all Cajas expected to be produced (i.e. 20 000 units). Hence the combined charge per unit for depreciation and overhaul is €50 ([€760 000 + €240 000]/20 000 units).

(c)   Other overheads at current prices comprise variable overheads of €16 per unit and head office fixed costs of €20 per unit, allotted on the basis of labour time.

All wage rates are expected to increase at an annual compound rate of 15%. Selling price per unit and all costs other than labour are expected to increase in line with the Eurozone inflation index, which is expected to increase in the future at an annual compound rate of 10%. Corporation tax in Spain is 30% on net cash income and is payable in full at the end of each year. Capital expenditure is tax allowable but must be spread evenly over the productive life of the investment. Tramontana uses an after-tax money discount of 20% to evaluate capital investments.

Assume that all receipts and payments will arise on the last day of the year to which they relate. Assume also that all 'current prices' given above have been operative for 1 year and are due to change shortly. Subsequently all prices will change annually.

Required:

(a)   Prepare calculations, with explanations, showing whether Tramontana should undertake production of the new Caja folding beach chair.

(b)   Discuss the particular investment appraisal problems created by the existence of high rates of inflation.

CAPITAL RATIONING

LEARNING OBJECTIVES

The purpose of this chapter is to:

- Explain the concept of 'capital rationing' and the problems that it causes for the investment decision process.
- Investigate how the investment decision procedures may be adapted to cope with the existence of capital rationing.

INTRODUCTION

In Chapter 4 we developed a single-period investment–consumption model to use as a guide to effective financial investment appraisal. The model was a crude and unrealistic simplification of the real world, but it was used so that the underlying principles of investment decisions could be examined, without becoming embroiled in elaborate complications (such as the existence of taxation, inflation and an uncertain future). In addition, a time horizon of only one time period was used so that the conclusions could be presented graphically rather than algebraically.

We saw that neither payback nor ROCE were satisfactory investment appraisal rules in terms of the Hirshleifer analysis, as they did not lead to the firm optimally locating on the physical investment line. In contrast, both the DCF techniques – NPV and IRR – did lead the firm to locate optimally. However, a closer examination of the IRR method uncovered a number of problems with its use and so, at the end of Chapter 6, we were able to conclude that the NPV decision rule was the only one of the four investment appraisal techniques which would *consistently* lead to investment decisions being taken that would help to maximize shareholder wealth. Even so, the NPV decision rule required the assumption of a perfect capital market.

In this chapter we are going to examine what happens to the NPV decision rule in the absence of a perfect capital market. In particular, we are going to examine the case where the company may *not* be able to undertake *all* the positive NPV projects it has discovered, because of a shortage of capital investment funds. This particular capital market imperfection is known as '*capital rationing*'.

Capital market borrowing

A great deal of attention, in both the applied and theoretical literature, has been paid to the problem of capital rationing but, even so, there is no general agreement on what precisely is meant by the term, and this has resulted in a certain amount of confusion. In an effort to avoid adding to this, it is important that we state from the outset what we shall take to be the meaning of capital rationing.

From the viewpoint of the making of investment decisions by financial management within companies, capital rationing is a *managerial* problem. It is, most certainly, a theoretical problem for our decision-making model but, more importantly, it is also a practical problem.

Up to this point, we have followed the NPV investment appraisal rule because it is most likely to indicate (in a practical sense) consistently good investment decisions. In its basic form the NPV decision rule says: accept all projects with cash flows which, when discounted by the market interest rate and then summated, have a positive or zero NPV. Such projects are acceptable because they yield a return that is either *greater than* (+ NPV), or at least *equal to* (zero NPV) the return that is available on the capital market for a similar-risk investment (which is defined by the rate of discount used).

Therefore, in terms of opportunity cost, the discount rule can be viewed as the minimum return that management must earn from investing investors' money in physical investment opportunities. It represents the minimum acceptable rate of return because it is the return that investors themselves can earn by placing their money in financial investment opportunities (i.e. investing on the capital market). Hence management should not invest investors' money to earn a lower rate of return than can be obtained on the capital market.

Implicit in the NPV decision rule is the idea that as long as a company's management can find investment opportunities that yield at least the capital market return (i.e. they satisfy the NPV decision rule), then money will be available to finance them. This is because investing funds in projects with *non-negative* NPVs ensures that the project will yield a return that will *at least* be sufficient to repay the capital, plus its required return. In terms of the single-period investment–consumption diagram, this implies that if a company identifies so many acceptable projects (i.e. + or 0 NPV) that the company's existing resources at t_0 provide insufficient investment capital to undertake them all, then additional finance can be raised from the capital market.

In Figure 8.1, OA represents the company's existing resources at t_0 and AB represents the physical investment line. The point of tangency between the physical and financial investment lines is at point C. Therefore the company has identified acceptable projects that require a total investment outlay at t_0 of AD. As the company's existing resources only amount to OA, amount OD will have to be borrowed from the capital market.

The investment AD undertaken at t_0 will produce a cash inflow at t_1 of OE. The amount required to repay the loan, plus interest, is given by EF, leaving an amount OF for shareholders. Notice what the net result has been of the borrowing on the capital market by the company. Without borrowing, the maximum amount of cash that could have been generated at t_1 would have been OG; but with borrowing (and hence undertaking additional physical investment), the company has been able to increase the t_1 cash flow available to the owner by the amount FG.

The term 'capital rationing' refers to the situation where the implicit assumption within the NPV decision rule, that capital will always be available to finance acceptable projects, does **not** hold. For example, using the situation as found in Figure 8.1, suppose that the company was unable to borrow OD on the capital market, then a situation of capital rationing would exist: acceptable projects requiring a total outlay of AD had

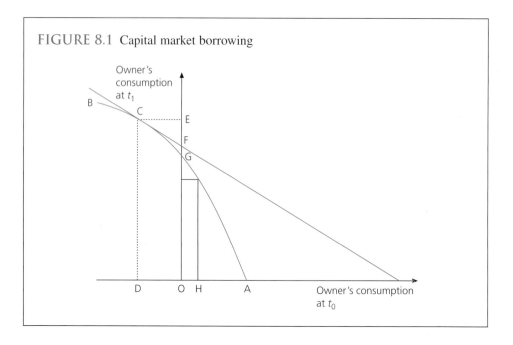

FIGURE 8.1 Capital market borrowing

been identified, but they cannot all be accepted because only OA of finance is available. Management has therefore to 'ration out' this limited amount of investment capital between the available projects.

The existence of capital rationing need not only apply to externally raised funds. For example, not only may the company be unable to raise any capital market finance, but the shareholders (in the example used in Figure 8.1) may be unwilling to allow the company to invest the whole of OA. Suppose that for some reason the maximum that shareholders will allow to be applied to physical investments is AH. Then the company has an even tighter capital constraint than before: only AH of capital available, although it has identified acceptable projects that require a total of AD of capital.

It should be clear from the above that the existence of capital rationing represents a *capital market imperfection*: investment funds are no longer freely available at the market rate of return. The reasons why such capital rationing may occur in practice are many and varied, but in the context of our analysis they are only of passing interest. The point that we wish to examine is, given a situation of capital rationing, how does it affect the efficiency of the investment decision advice given by the NPV appraisal technique, and can NPV be adapted to operate successfully in such situations?

HARD AND SOFT CAPITAL RATIONING

Two types or classes of capital rationing are usually specified: 'hard' capital rationing (which has received the lion's share of attention in the literature but which is probably of little importance in practice, as far as investment decisions in companies are concerned), and 'soft' capital rationing.

Hard capital rationing describes the situation where forces *external* to the company, usually either the capital market itself or the government (which may or may not act through the capital market), will not supply unlimited amounts of investment capital to a company, even though the company has identified investment opportunities that would be able to produce the required return.

Soft capital rationing arises from forces *internal* to a company, such as a capital budget, which limits the amount of capital available for investment. In certain situations and in certain cases, the distinction between hard and soft capital rationing and between the various different causes of hard rationing may be important for the analysis. Where they are, such a distinction shall be made, but for the moment we shall concentrate simply on the problems that capital rationing creates for investment appraisal, rather than the *cause* of the capital rationing situation itself.

An example

In a situation where capital rationing is non-existent (and hence we are assuming a perfect capital market), investment decision-making involves a comparison between the investment funds being applied to the particular investment under consideration and the alternative of being applied to a similar-risk capital market investment, because this latter alternative reflects the *opportunity cost* of undertaking the investment. With the introduction of capital rationing, choice is still involved, but the alternative to the application of capital to a proposed investment project is not *necessarily* the capital market investment, but may instead be another of the firm's investment projects.

In other words, the opportunity cost of undertaking a particular investment is now not necessarily reflected in the capital market rate of return, but may be a higher value, represented by the return yielded by *another* project, which could not be undertaken by the company because the supply of capital is limited. An example can help to illustrate the point.

Suppose a company has discovered two independent projects, A and B. Each requires $50 000 of investment capital, and Project A produces a return[1] of 12%, whereas B generates a return of 15%. If the company's cost of capital was 10% and funds were unlimited, *both* projects would be accepted because both would have positive NPVs. The acceptance procedure, using the NPV method, would involve the comparison of the return given by each project *in turn*, with the return available on the capital market.

However, if capital rationing exists, and the company's investment funds are limited to a total of $50 000 then a different decision process is required. The company must now choose, not between each project and the capital market return, but first between the two projects themselves and then, once it has decided which is the better of the two projects, must compare its return with the alternative given by the capital market. Thus, in a non-rationing situation the company would be making *two decisions*: accept/reject Project A, accept/reject Project B; whilst in a rationing situation they would be making *one, two-stage decision*: select Project A or B, then accept/reject the selected project.

SINGLE-PERIOD CAPITAL RATIONING

It appears at first sight that capital rationing involves little more than another type of the 'mutually exclusive projects' decision, which we dealt with earlier. In fact, as we shall see, the existence of capital rationing produces a much more difficult decision problem.

Most readers will be familiar with the idea of a budget as a means of planning and control[2] and so, for the sake of presenting a clear argument, we shall assume that for each decision period (say, 1 year), management have a *capital budget* within which to keep, i.e. total capital expenditure must not exceed some stated upper limit: the capital budget or (to avoid terminology confusion) the capital *constraint*. Therefore we shall be assuming a *soft* rationing situation, but the conclusions we derive will be equally applicable to *hard* rationing.

Let us begin with the most simple and straightforward capital rationing problem: a situation where capital is rationed at present (i.e. t_0) but will be freely available in the future – a rather unlikely situation in practice – or one where the collection of investment projects the company wishes to appraise involve capital outlays *only* in the current period (i.e. the capital outlay required for the project does not extend over more than one point in time). In addition, it is assumed that projects are *infinitely divisible*, so that *fractions* of projects may be undertaken, and that they exhibit *constant* returns to scale (i.e. we could undertake 25% of the project and it would produce 25% of the expected cash flows and generate 25% of the expected NPV).

In such a situation, only a slight modification to the standard NPV decision rule is required. Each investment opportunity should have its expected future cash flows discounted to net present value by the appropriate market discount rate. This NPV is then expressed as *a ratio* of the capital outlay which the project requires in the rationed time period, and is often termed the 'benefit–cost ratio' (or 'profitability ratio/PI'). Therefore if an investment cost $50 000 and it had an NPV of +$10 000 its benefit–cost ratio would be: $10 000 / $50 000 = 0.20. In other words, for every $1 invested, it produces 20 cents of positive NPV.

All projects that have a positive or zero *benefit–cost ratio* would normally be accepted in a non-rationed situation. However, because capital rationing exists and a choice has to be made between the alternative projects, they should be ranked in order of decreasing benefit–cost ratio. Starting with the project with the largest (positive) ratio, and working down the rankings, as many projects as possible (with positive or zero ratios) should be accepted, until all the available capital is allocated.

Examples of benefit–cost ratios

Example 1 shows this decision method in operation. It assumes that capital rationing will only exist in the current time period (Year 0), all the projects are independent and divisible, and exhibit constant returns to scale and none can be delayed.

EXAMPLE 1

The Emirates Construction Company has identified five possible investment projects (none are mutually exclusive and so could be accepted or rejected in any combination). Their expected cash flows are set out in the table below. In a non-rationing situation all the projects in the table would be accepted as they have a positive NPV when discounted at the 10% market interest rate. In order to undertake all five of these projects, the company would require a total of 450 million dirhams of capital *now* (Year 0) and this would produce a total amount of positive NPV of Dhs283.4 million. Therefore acceptance of Projects A to E would cause shareholders' wealth to rise by Dhs283.4 million.

▶

Project	0	1	2	3	4	NPV when discounted at 10%	NPV
A	−100	+20	+ 40	+ 60	+ 80	⇒	+50.96
B	−150	−50	+100	+100	+140	⇒	+57.94
C	− 50	+20	+ 40	+ 27	—	⇒	+21.60
D	−100	+60	+ 60	+100	—	⇒	+79.26
E	− 50	+20	+ 40	+ 60	+ 40	⇒	+73.64

All cash flows in Dhs million

Suppose that capital rationing exists at Year 0 (but not in Years 1 to 4) and as a result the company has only Dhs300 million of investment capital available. It therefore cannot undertake all of the five positive NPV projects. Which projects should be selected to be undertaken? The second table ranks all the projects in *decreasing order* of benefit–cost ratio. (Note, in particular, how Project B's benefit–cost ratio is calculated. Although B requires two capital outlays, at Year 0 and Year 1, the ratio concerns the NPV and the outlay in the rationed time period *only*. Hence the denominator of the ratio is simply B's Year 0 outlay.)

Project	NPV / Year 0 outlay	=	Benefit–cost Ratio	Ranking
A	50.96/100	=	+0.51	3
B	57.94/150	=	+0.39	5
C	21.60/50	=	+0.43	4
D	79.26/100	=	+0.79	2
E	73.64/50	=	+1.47	1

Project	Ranking	Year 0 outlay
E	1	50
D	2	100
A	3	100
C	4	50
B	5	150

The investment decision can then be made as follows:

Available finance	Dhs300
Accept Project E costing	(Dhs50)
Available finance	Dhs250
Accept Project D costing	(Dhs100)
Available finance	Dhs150
Accept Project A costing	(Dhs100)
Available finance	Dhs50
Accept Project C costing	(Dhs50)
Available finance	—

The table shows that the Dhs300 million of available capital should be applied to Projects E, D, A and C. Project B should be rejected. This gives the company, for its Dhs300 million capital outlay, a total positive NPV of:

$$Dhs73.64 + Dhs79.26 + Dhs50.96 + Dhs21.60 = Dhs225.46 \text{ million}$$

which is the *maximum possible* total NPV, given the capital expenditure constraint.

Therefore, because investment capital is limited to just Dhs300 million, shareholder wealth will only rise by Dhs225.46 million as a result of the investment decisions made, rather than by the possible total of Dhs283.4 million. Thus, we can see that, as far as shareholders are concerned, there is a definite cost to capital rationing. In this case, because of the presence of capital rationing, shareholders' wealth will be approximately Dhs57.94 million *below* the value it would have otherwise attained.

However, given the situation specified, the process of selecting projects on the basis of their benefit–cost ratios ensures that the company will maximize the total amount of positive NPV gained from the available projects, assuming limited investment capital. This is because the terms in which the benefit–cost ratio focuses attention on the size of a project's NPV are not absolute, but relative to the scarce resources required to undertake it. In other words, projects are ranked in order of preference, in terms of the NPV they produce, for every unit (i.e. 1 dirham) of the limited investment capital which they require. In the example used above, Project A is preferred to Project B (even though B has the larger total NPV) because it produces 51 fils (100 fils = 1 dirham) of (positive) NPV for every Dhs1 of the scarce investment capital applied to its undertaking in Year 0, whereas Project B only produces 39 fils of NPV per Dhs1 of investment outlay.

Example 2 is divided up into two separate single-period capital rationing situations. In the first situation there is straightforward Year 0 rationing. However, in the second situation a further element is added to the analysis. This shows that the standard NPV decision rule for independent projects – accept all non-negative NPV projects – breaks down in capital rationing situations. This means that not only will some positive NPV projects (like Project C in Example 1) not be accepted, but there may also be circumstances where it is advantageous to accept a *negative* NPV project.

EXAMPLE 2

The management accounting department of Port Elizabeth Holdings (PEH) Ltd has identified six independent investment opportunities, codenamed G to L. The Year 0 and Year 1 cash flows of these projects, together with their NPVs, are as follows:

	(Year)			
Project	*0*	*1*		*NPV*
G	−100	−500	....	+25
H	−200	− 90	....	+36
I	−150	−220	....	+44
J	−300	−100	....	+30
K	− 50	+100	....	+10
L	−100	+ 80	....	−12

Under normal circumstances, PEH would accept Projects G to K, as they all have positive NPVs, and Project L would be rejected. However, to undertake Projects G to K, a total of 800 000 South African rand would be required at Year 0, and an additional R910 000 at Year 1. (Notice that Project K does not require a further cash outlay at Year 1.)

Situation 1

In the first situation, PEH's board of directors has stipulated that, although there will be no capital expenditure constraint at Year 1, the company is only willing to undertake R275 000 of capital expenditure at Year 0. Thus the company faces a single time-period capital rationing situation.

In order to solve the problem, benefit–cost ratio rankings are used:

Project	NPV	÷	Year 0 outlay	=	Benefit–cost ratio	Rank
G	+25	÷	100	=	+0.25	2
H	+36	÷	200	=	+0.18	4
I	+44	÷	150	=	+0.293	1
J	+30	÷	300	=	+0.10	5
K	+10	÷	50	=	+0.20	3
L	−12	÷	100	=	−0.12	—

			NPV
Investment decision:	275	available	
	(150)	invested in I, producing	+44
	125	balance	
	(100)	invested in G, producing	+25
	25	balance	
	(25)	invested in 50% of K, producing	+ 5
	—	all funds invested	
			+74

Thus the company should undertake Projects I and G, and 50% of K. This will generate a total positive NPV of R74 000, which will be the maximum possible, given the expenditure constraint.

Situation 2

The second situation is somewhat contrived, but serves to show an important point. Suppose that, instead of constraining capital expenditure at Year 0, the board of directors decided that there is **no** constraint on expenditure at Year 0, but at Year 1 there is only R290 000 of *external* finance available. However, this figure can be added to by any *internally* generated funds that arise from projects at Year 1.

Once again, the management are faced with capital rationing and, although there is no constraint at Year 0, they must be careful at that time only to undertake projects for which there will be sufficient finance available at Year 1 for them to be continued. (It would be no good accepting every non-negative NPV project available at Year 0, only to find that many would subsequently have to be abandoned at Year 1 through insufficient finance.)

The revised set of benefit–cost ratios is now:

Project	NPV	÷	Year 1 outlay	=	Benefit–cost ratio	Rank
G	+25	÷	500	=	0.05	4
H	+36	÷	90	=	0.40	1
I	+44	÷	220	=	0.20	3
J	+30	÷	100	=	0.30	2
K	+10	÷	—			
L	−12	÷	—			

Obviously PEH will undertake Project K: it has a positive NPV and does not require any outlay in the rationed time-period. Furthermore, because it actually generates a cash *inflow* of £100 000 at Year 1, this amount can be added to the external funds available for capital expenditure. Thus the investment decision is:

			NPV
	290	Available	
plus	100	from investment in K, producing	+ 10
	390	balance	
	90	invested in H, producing	+ 36
	300	balance	
	100	invested in J, producing balance	+ 30
	200	balance	
	200	invested in 91% of I, producing	+ 40
	—	all funds invested	
		Total NPV	+116

However, this is not the end of the decision. Although the R390 000 of funds has been fully utilized, it is possible to obtain additional funds at Year 1 by investing in Project L. The question is: does the *additional* positive NPV generated from investing Project L's Year 1 cash inflow compensate for the negative NPV arising from Project L directly? The answer lies in examining Project L's cost–benefit (rather than benefit–cost) ratio and comparing it with the benefit–cost ratio of the 'marginal' project.

Project L has a cost–benefit ratio of $-12/+80 = -0.15$. In other words, every R1 generated at Year 1 from investing in Project L has a cost of 15 cents of negative NPV.

The 'marginal' project in PEH's investment decision is Project I, because it was into Project I that the last one rand of the available expenditure was spent. Project I can have a total of R220 000 invested in it at Year 1. So far, only R200 000 has been invested and so, if any further investment funds are available – up to a maximum of R20 000 – they too would be invested in Project I. The benefit gain from a further investment in I is given by its benefit–cost ratio of 0.20. In other words, every one rand extra invested in I generates an additional 20 cents of positive NPV. From this comparison of Projects I and L, it can be seen that the benefit generated from a further investment in I *does* exceed the cost arising from the investment in L (i.e. $0.2 > 0.15$). Investing in the whole of L will produce R80 000 at Year 1, but as only a further R20 000 can be invested in I, for the moment, the decision will be to undertake just 25% of project L to produce the required cash flow:

	NPV
Invest in 25% L to yield R20, costing	−3
Invest R20 in 9% of I, yielding	+4
Net gain	+1

PEH has now undertaken the whole of Projects K, H, J and I, as well as 25% of L. On the benefit–cost ratio rankings, if any more investment funds were available, the next best project is G. Therefore is it worthwhile undertaking the remaining 75% of L – which would produce an extra R60 000 of funds at Year 1 – in order to invest in 12% of Project G (60 ÷ 500)? Again comparison of the ratios provides the answer: every R1 generated from L costs 15 cents of negative NPV; every R1 invested in Project G produces 5 cents of positive NPV. Therefore further investment in L in order to invest in Project G is **not** worthwhile. The gain of 5 cents for every rand invested is less than the 15-cent cost of generating each additional investment rand. Thus the optimal investment decision is: undertake Projects K, H, J, I and 25% of L. This will yield a maximum total of positive NPV of: 10 + 36 + 30 + 44 − 3 = +R117 000 NPV.

Divisibility assumption

The benefit–cost ranking approach to the situation of single-period capital rationing depends heavily on the assumption that investment projects are divisible (i.e. that fractions of projects can be undertaken, such as 25% of Project L in Example 2). When this assumption does not hold, benefit–cost ratios do not work and instead, the investment selection decision has to be undertaken by examining the total NPVs of *all possible alternative combinations* of whole projects, to see which combination gives the greatest amount of total NPV. Example 3 illustrates this approach.

EXAMPLE 3

Tunisie Mabrouk is an import–export company operating along the North African coast and is based in Tunis. The company has recently identified six new shipping routes which are all expected to produce a future Tunisian dinar (DT) cash flow generating a positive NPV. The cost of developing each new route, together with its expected NPV, is given below:

Route	Development cost	NPV
(000's dinars)	(000's dinars)	
1	100	+20
2	200	+35
3	50	+10
4	50	+15
5	100	+28
6	100	+30

The problem faced by the company is that to develop all six routes would require a total investment of DT600 000 and it has only DT300 000 of investment funds available. Naturally, all six projects are indivisible (given that each project represents the development of a new shipping route), and so the company must decide which to accept and which to reject.

Given there are limited funds available and only whole projects can be accepted, the DT300 000 can be invested in the following whole project combinations:

▶

Investments	NPVs	Total NPV
1 + 2	20 + 35	+55
1 + 3 + 4 + 5	20 + 10 + 15 + 28	+73
1 + 3 + 4 + 6	20 + 10 + 15 + 30	+75
1 + 5 + 6	20 + 28 + 30	+78
3 + 4 + 5 + 6	10 + 15 + 28 + 30	+83
2 + 5	35 + 28	+63
2 + 6	35 + 30	+65
2 + 3 + 4	35 + 10 + 15	+60

And on this analysis, the company should invest in routes 3, 4, 5 and 6 and reject routes 1 and 2, in order to gain the maximum amount of total NPV, at DT83 000.

Mutually exclusive investments

A variation on the infringement of the divisibility assumption occurs when projects are mutually exclusive. Suppose the data from Example 1 is used again, but now it is assumed that Projects A and E are mutually exclusive. Therefore either one or the other, or neither, can be accepted, but both cannot be accepted. In order to obtain the optimum selection of projects we would proceed as we did originally, going down the list of projects ranked by their benefit–cost ratios until all the capital is utilized, but now this process has to be undertaken twice – once *excluding* Project A from the list and then again, now *excluding* Project E from the list. Example 4 demonstrates the analysis.

EXAMPLE 4

Using the data from Example 1, the Emirates Construction Company had identified five divisible investment opportunities. All five projects had positive NPVs but required a total investment of Dhs450 million and the company only had Dhs300 million of available funds. The projects are:

Project	Year 0 cost	NPV	Rank
(Dhs millions)	(Dhs millions)		
A	100	+79.29	3rd
B	150	+57.94	5th
C	50	+21.60	4th
D	100	+79.29	2nd
E	50	73.64	1st

The company is now faced with a further complication: Projects A and E are mutually exclusive.

▶

▶

Investment decision excluding Project A

		NPV
Available:	300	
1st accept E	(50)	+73.64
Available	250	
2nd accept D	(100)	+79.29
Available	150	
4th accept C	(50)	+21.60
Available	100	
5th accept ⅔ B	(100)	+38.63
	-	+Dhs213.16 total NPV

Investment decision excluding Project E

		NPV
Available:	300	
2nd accept D	(100)	+79.29
Available	200	
3rd accept A	(100)	+50.96
Available	100	
4th accept C	(50)	+21.60
Available	50	
5th accept ⅓ B	(50)	+19.32
	—	+Dhs171.17 total NPV

As a result of this analysis the company's investment decision is clear – they should undertake projects E, D, C and ⅔ B. Project A should be rejected. This will lead to the greatest amount of NPV being generated, given the limited funds available and the fact that projects A and E are mutually exclusive.

Single-period rationing and the IRR

Before leaving the single-period rationing case, it is worth noting that the IRR investment appraisal technique cannot cope adequately with capital rationing. Ranking projects in terms of their IRRs is not the same as ranking via benefit–cost ratios. The reason why the IRR technique fails to adapt to capital rationing is because of the fact that the IRR is simply an *absolute* percentage rate of return, whereas what is required is a measure of project performance *relative* to the rationed investment outlay. Hence this is just one more example of the limitations of the IRR technique.

MULTI-PERIOD CAPITAL RATIONING

Introduction

The problem of investment decision-making in the face of capital rationing that extends over more than one period is both complex and, at present, not completely resolved. The complexity of the problem has not been helped by general confusion and differences in the literature over what precisely is meant by capital rationing and by the range of differing assumptions that have been made, both explicitly and implicitly. The main source of confusion over capital rationing, as far as the theory of corporate investment decision-making is concerned, has occurred through a failure to isolate the problem from general capital market theory. As a result, a number of paradoxical problems have arisen.

In attempting to outline a normative theory of investment decision-making, we shall try to be both as practical and realistic as possible. In doing so, we will assume that hard (or external) capital rationing, both for individuals and companies, is likely to be only a relatively short-run phenomenon which may well arise, in practice, out of poor forward planning.[3] It is certainly true to say that unlimited amounts of investment capital are not immediately available to companies, because capital-raising operations can take some time to arrange. Thus there can be a definite limit to capital supplies in the very short run. However, as long as a company plans its future operations carefully and well ahead of time, and its management appears competent, it is unlikely that it will be unable to raise the capital it requires for any planned project which is expected to be 'profitable', i.e. it is unlikely that it will run into any serious, externally imposed capital rationing. We are not assuming that hard capital rationing never occurs but that, in the majority of cases, for most of the time, it is an unlikely phenomenon.

Soft capital rationing

If we make the assumption that externally imposed constraints on the supply of capital to a company are unlikely to be anything but relatively short-term phenomena, we are left with the task of examining the effects of internally imposed or soft capital rationing on the investment decision-making process. We can define soft capital rationing as a capital expenditure constraint which is imposed on a company by its own internal management, rather than by external capital markets, and which limits the amount of capital investment funds available in any particular time period.

This capital limit will normally be imposed by a capital expenditure budget, of which, in a well-managed company, there are likely to be two: a short-term capital budget for the immediate 12 months ahead and a medium-term capital budget which covers the next 3 to 5 years ahead.[4] Both budgets are likely to impose relatively inflexible capital constraints upon management.

When looking at how the NPV appraisal method could be adapted to deal with the single-period rationing problem, we saw that when the capital constraint was binding (i.e. there was insufficient capital available to invest in all projects with positive NPVs), companies would have to forgo undertaking some projects which they would have otherwise undertaken. Such a situation is understandable when imposed from outside the company, but it seems ludicrous when imposed from within the company. Why should a company wish to constrain itself in this way?

The reason is that companies are required to plan for the future and to monitor, control and evaluate the implementation of these plans, so that future planning and control can be further improved upon. A capital budget is just one part of these plans and of the *controlling* process. It requires the imposition of a ceiling on capital expenditure, because capital investment is not a simple operation, but one which takes time and a range of resources.

For example, the decision to invest in a particular project does not consist simply of the evaluation and appraisal process. Finance may have to be raised for the project (an operation that cannot be carried out instantaneously), the company must have the trained manpower available to implement the project and monitor its performance (again, not an instantaneous process), and even the evaluation and decision procedure itself is likely to have its own manpower and resource constraints, as is the whole of the company's organizational structure. Thus, in order to plan carefully and to control efficiently, limits may quite properly have to be imposed – in the short and medium terms – on the level of capital investment expenditure that a company allows itself to undertake.[5]

The existence of capital budgets within companies is likely to mean that management are faced with the problem of decision-making in a situation of multi-period capital rationing (i.e. where capital rationing extends over a number of future periods). In such circumstances, the simple benefit–cost ratio technique cannot be used to place investment opportunities in an order of preference. This is because, in the single-period rationing case, the problem was to allocate investment capital amongst competing projects in the face of a single constraint, in order to maximize the total amount of positive NPV gained. In the multi-period case, this allocation procedure has to be carried out *simultaneously* under more than one constraint, as each period's rationing forms a separate constraint. To assist in this simultaneous allocation problem, we have to employ mathematical programming optimizing techniques, such as linear programming. (It is assumed that the reader is familiar with the basic mechanics of this technique, which can be found in most introductory books on business mathematics.)

The opportunity cost of capital dilemma

The presence of multi-period capital rationing does not alter the objective of financial management decision-making: the maximization of shareholder wealth. This, we know, can be achieved through making investment decisions so as to maximize the total amount of positive NPV generated. The NPV figure gains its significance from the fact that it represents the result of netting out project cash flows and comparing this net cash flow with the opportunity cost, which is embodied in the perfect capital market discount rate.

In examining how investment resources can be allocated to projects in a situation of multi-period capital rationing, we will assume that the suppliers of capital to a company do not themselves impose any form of capital rationing. It is self-imposed, rather than market-imposed capital rationing. This assumption releases the analysis from one of the major difficulties of the multi-period rationing problem: the choice of discount rate.

We know that the discount rate used in the NPV calculation represents the opportunity cost of cash which, in a perfect capital market, is reflected in the market rate of interest. Once a perfect capital market no longer exists, then the market interest rate no longer necessarily reflects the opportunity cost of capital. In such circumstances, as we saw when looking at the single-period rationing problem, the opportunity cost of investment capital is represented by the return gained from the marginal project in the rationed period. Therefore, in a multi-period rationing situation, the appropriate discount rate for any period is given by the return on the marginal project in that particular period. This is the dilemma.

The company needs to know the opportunity cost of cash in each period to use as the discount rate, in order to make the correct selection. Each period's opportunity cost of cash is represented by the return on the marginal project in that particular period, but this marginal project can only be identified *after* the correct project selection has been made. In other words, in order to make the correct investment project selection, the opportunity cost of capital in each rationed period needs to be known, but this can only be known once the correct selection of projects has been made. Thus, we are firmly on the horns of a dilemma, unless we assume that the company faces a perfect capital market and it is the company alone that imposes capital rationing. In such circumstances, the market interest rate still represents the opportunity cost of capital and so can be used as the discount rate to aid project selection. Hence, the need to assume soft capital rationing.

REAL WORLD VIEW: Interest rates go nuclear

At the beginning of this chapter we addressed the limitations of a single-period investment–consumption model in its simplification of a complex world. The following example highlights just some of unknowns and variables that can affect a typical venture in reality over a period of time.

Darlington Nuclear Generating Station is a nuclear power station in Ontario, Canada. Being an incredibly advanced nuclear generating station, it is a significant producer of energy, providing up to 20% of Ontario's electricity.

However, what this station is arguably most well-known for is its vast cost overruns. Initially the station was estimated to cost \$3.9 billion CAD (Canadian dollars) to build in the late 1970s. By 1981, however, this had almost doubled, increasing to \$7.4 billion. The final cost of the station was \$14.4 billion – over three times the original estimate.

Various delays in a project of this scale had caused interest charges on its debt. These ended up being 70% of the cost overruns. Simultaneously, inflation during the late 1970s to early -80s was at 46%, and interest rates at 20%. On top of this was the loss of production and projected earnings all the while the station remained closed.

An overhaul at Darlington is due to be finished by 2025, with the work estimated to cost \$2 million a day (plus losses of \$1 million a day for every day the reactors are off-line). \$35 million has been spent on a mock-up station to ensure that the overhauls, once begun, go as quickly and as smoothly as possible.

The linear programming solution to capital rationing

Example 5 illustrates how, in multi-period capital rationing, linear programming can help to allocate scarce investment capital to projects so as to maximize the total amount of positive NPV.

EXAMPLE 5

Oxford Technical Solutions is a young UK-based company involved in bio-engineering sciences. The company's Research and Development division has identified six new independent investment opportunities. These new projects have been codenamed A to F and their expected cash flow projections are as follows (all figures in £000s):

	Year					
Project	*0*	*1*	*2*	*3*	*4*	*5*
A	−100	− 50	− 25	+100	+100	+100
B	− 50	− 70	+100	+100		
C		−100	− 30	+150	+200	
D	− 10	− 20	+ 50	−100	+100	+100
E	−100	−100	+200	+100	+ 50	
F			−200	+300	+100	+100

For a variety of reasons, none of these projects can have the timing of its cash flow brought forward or delayed (and none can be undertaken more than once), and all six projects exhibit *constant* returns to scale.

Finally, the perfect capital market rate of interest is 10% for investments of this risk level and this is expected to remain unchanged over the next 5 years.

Calculating the NPVs of the projects, using a 10% discount rate, we can see that the company would wish to undertake them all, because each has a positive NPV:

Project	NPV (£000s)
A	+ 39.4
B	+ 44.1
C	+133.6
D	+ 68.4
E	+ 83.6
F	+190.5

In order to do so, however, the company would require the expenditure of £260 000, £340 000, £255 000 and £100 000 of investment capital in the next four time periods (Years 0–3) respectively.

However, because the company is at the early stages of its development, and the directors are relatively inexperienced, they are cautious about allowing the company to expand over-quickly and so have imposed an *absolute* annual capital expenditure constraint of £150 000. Clearly, in these circumstances, the company cannot undertake all six projects, and so a decision is required as to which projects should be selected to be undertaken and which should be rejected.

There are several ways in which this problem could be formulated into a linear programme, but each alternative formulation would produce a solution giving exactly the same selection of investment projects to undertake. One approach, which fits directly into our NPV approach, is to take as the linear programming's (LP's) *objective function* the maximization of the total amount of NPV which the company can generate over the next 5 years, given the imposed constraints. Thus, taking $a, b, c \ldots f$ to represent the proportion of Projects A, B, C … F undertaken:

Objective function:

$$39.4a + 44.1b + 133.6c + 68.4d + 83.6e + 190.5f \text{ Max}$$

Constraints:

$$
\begin{aligned}
100a + 50b + 10d + 100e &\leq 150 \text{ (Year 0)} \\
50a + 70b + 100c + 20d + 100e &\leq 150 \text{ (Year 1)} \\
25a + 30c + 200f &\leq 150 \text{ (Year 2)} \\
100d &\leq 150 \text{ (Year 3)} \\
a, b, c, d, e, f &\leq 1 \\
a, b, c, d, e, f &\geq 0
\end{aligned}
$$

Solving this linear programme (using a standard optimization software package – for example, see **www.sourceforge.net/projects/lipside/**) gave the following investment decision advice: the whole of both Projects C and D should be undertaken, together with 30% of Project E and 60% of Project F; Projects A and B should not undertaken.[6] This selection results in a total NPV of +£341 400 being generated, which is the *maximum possible* total NPV, given the circumstances specified.[7]

The assumptions behind LP

In using LP to solve this type of capital rationing problem, a number of assumptions and limitations are involved, one of which we have already touched upon: the specification of the rate of discount to be used. In addition, the technique assumes that all the relationships expressed in the model are linear (for example, all the projects are assumed to exhibit *constant* returns to scale) and that the variables are *divi*sible. There is also an assumption that the project cash flows are known with certainty because, as yet, no way has been found of satisfactorily adjusting the technique to take account of risk.

The first of these three assumptions does not necessarily cause too much trouble because, where non-linear relationships are involved, they can often be adequately described in the LP formulation as a number of linear approximations. Similarly, the second assumption also may not be too troublesome, especially if the LP is being applied to the solution of the capital rationing problem within a company operating in a process industry (e.g. oil or chemicals), because the output is (approximately) infinitely divisible. (*Integer programming* – another type of allocation optimization technique – avoids this assumption, but in doing so involves a number of new, and often more difficult, problems.) However, what really is a serious practical drawback to the use of LP in capital rationing situations is the inability of the technique to handle uncertainty. There have been some attempts to allow for uncertainty,[8] but by and large they represent mathematical solutions to mathematical, rather than practical, problems.

The dual values

In Example 5, where the objective was to maximize the total amount of positive NPV generated, the solution involved the company undertaking the whole of Projects C and D, together with 30% of Project E and 60% of Project F. The reader will be able to confirm from the project cash flow information that this solution results in the utilization of only £40 000 of the £150 000 available for investment in Year 0, and of only £100 000 of the £150 000 available in Year 3. Therefore, although the company's capital expenditure is constrained in these two periods, the constraints are '*non-binding*', i.e. they do not bind or constrain the company in its efforts to achieve its objective. For this reason, there is no *additional* opportunity cost of the cash used for capital expenditure in these two periods (i.e. there is no opportunity cost incurred in addition to that opportunity cost already allowed for in the discounting process used to convert the project cash flows to NPVs), because the company does not forgo any of its investment project opportunities as a result of these two constraints.

The situation is different in respect of the Year 1 and Year 2 capital expenditure constraints. In these periods, the linear programme's project selection results in the £150 000 available (in both Years 1 and 2) being *fully utilized* and therefore the constraints are said to be '*binding*': their existence limits the company's freedom of action in pursuit of its objective of NPV maximization because it limits the amount of investment the company can undertake. As a result, there is an additional opportunity cost attached to the use of investment cash in each of these two periods.

These additional opportunity costs are represented by the '*dual*' values produced by the linear programme. In Example 5, the LP solution produced the following dual values for the four capital expenditure constraints:

Year	Dual value (£)
0	0
1	0.837
2	0.952
3	0

The dual values that are produced from LP with a maximizing objective function represent the increase (decrease) in the total value of the objective function that would arise if a binding constraint were marginally – i.e. by one unit – slackened (tightened). Thus, in this example, the investment capital constraints result in the company achieving a total NPV (i.e. the objective function's value) of £341 400. If £150 001 were available for investment in Year 1 – i.e. an extra £1 of finance is available (keeping the £150 000 limit in force in each of the three other periods), then the value of the objective function would rise by £0.837 to £341 400.837.

In this very simple example this increase in the value of the objective function would be achieved by increasing the level of investment in Project E (the marginal project in Year 1) from 30% of E to 30.001%.[9] Also, because the use of LP assumes linear relationships, a *reduction* in the amount of capital available in Year 1 to £149 999 would result in the value of the objective function *falling* by £0.837.

A similar analysis can be made in terms of the Year 2 capital constraint dual value of £0.952 which is caused by a 0.0005% change in the level of investment in Project F. Because the capital constraints in Years 0 and 3 are non-binding their dual values are both zero: a marginal change in either constraint will leave both the original project selection and the value of the objective function unaltered.

There are a number of points to be made here. The first is that the example used is a highly simplified one and the practical application of the use of LP to solve capital rationing problems is far more complex and problematical. We have only outlined the approach and specified the main theoretical difficulties.

Second, if we accept that Projects E and F are the marginal projects in Years 1 and 2 respectively (i.e. investment levels in these two projects change in response to marginal changes in available investment capital in these 2 years), it is important to realize that the relative IRRs of these two projects do not produce their dual values, because the IRR represents a project's *average* return over the whole of its life, whilst the dual value refers to a project's *marginal* return in just the period specified.

A third point of importance is that dual values apply only to incremental/marginal changes in binding constraint values. To identify the effect of any non-marginal change – i.e. a substantial change – the LP has to be reformulated accordingly and resolved. Finally, dual values apply only to individual marginal changes in binding constraints, i.e. they operate under a *ceteris paribus* assumption that all other variables in the formulation remain unchanged. Thus, in the example used, if an extra £1 of investment capital is available in both Years 1 *and* 2, the resulting change in the value of the objective function is not necessarily the sum of the two individual dual values. Therefore we can see that dual values can be informative in that they represent part of the opportunity cost of investment capital, but their usefulness is relatively limited because of their marginal nature.

Two applications of dual values

Two examples (Example 6 and Example 7) of possible applications of dual values will serve to indicate their potential usefulness and will also help to demonstrate the different procedures required. The first example concerns the evaluation of an additional investment, and the second shows how to determine the value of additional sources of cash.

In order to do so, use will be made of our original multi-period Example 5 in this section, involving six independent projects (A to F), where the LP's solution to the multi-period capital rationing problem was:

Investment plan:	Project A: reject
	Project B: reject
	Project C: undertake 100%
	Project D: undertake 100%
	Project E: undertake 30%
	Project F: undertake 60%
Dual values:	Cash at Year 0: 0
	Cash at Year 1: £0.837
	Cash at Year 2: £0.952
	Cash at Year 3: 0

EXAMPLE 6

Suppose that, before the investment plan can be undertaken, the R&D department at Oxford Technical Solutions identifies a new project: Project Windsor. This project involves the following cash flows (all figures in £000s):

Year	Cash flow
0	−100
1	+ 20
2	+ 90

The dual values produced by the LP can be used to indicate either that this new project is *not* worth considering or that it *is* worth considering and so the LP should be reformulated to include Project Windsor's cash flows, and then re-solved.

If the original LP formulation dual values are to be used, the project's NPV has first to be determined, and then the opportunity cost of its cash flows calculated. If the *net* effect is positive, the project is worth considering and the LP should be reformulated and re-solved. If the net effect is negative, the project can be discarded without further analysis. The calculations are as follows:

Year	Cash flow		10% discount rate		PV cash flows
0	−100	×	1	=	−100
1	+ 20	×	0.9091	=	+ 18.18
2	+ 90	×	0.8264	=	+ 74.38
			NPV	=	£− 7.44

▶

Year	Cash flow		Dual value		Opportunity cost cash flows
0	−100	×	0	=	0
1	+ 20	×	0.837	=	+ 16.74
2	+ 90	×	0.952	=	+ 85.68
			Opportunity benefit		+102.42

Net effect of project: NPV + opportunity benefit = − £7.44 + £102.42 = + £94.98.

As the overall net effect of the project is *positive*, this indicates that the project is worth considering further and the LP should be reformulated (now including Project Windsor's cash flows) and re-solved.

This analysis is in fact very similar to the analysis made in Chapter 7 when looking at relevant cash flows. There we saw that the cost of utilizing a scarce resource was equal to its total opportunity cost: the internal opportunity cost, plus the external opportunity cost – the market price of the resource. That is exactly the approach used to evaluate Project Windsor. The NPV analysis evaluates the project's use of cash in terms of the market 'price' of cash (the discount rate); and then the subsequent analysis evaluates the project in terms of its impact on the firm's capital rationing problem – the internal opportunity cost, or in this case, opportunity benefit.

On this basis, therefore, Project Windsor could have been evaluated directly on the total opportunity costs involved:

	10% discount rate	+	Dual value of cash	=	Total opportunity cost of cash
Year 0	1	+	0	=	1
Year 1	0.9091	+	0.837	=	1.7461
Year 2	0.8264	+	0.952	=	1.7784
Year 3	0.7513	+	0	=	0.7513

Project Windsor

Year	Cash flow		Opportunity cost		
0	−100	×	1	=	−100
1	+ 20	×	1.7461	=	+ 34.92
2	+ 90	×	1.7784	=	+160.06
					+ 94.98

Thus, if Project Windsor is accepted, it should enable the total NPV generated by the projects under consideration to be increased.

EXAMPLE 7

Oxford Technical Solutions, having formulated its production plan from the original six available projects, is now offered an opportunity to borrow additional cash at Year 2 as long as it is repaid (with interest) at Year 3. What is the maximum interest rate that the company would be willing to pay to take out such a loan?

▶

The maximum interest rate represents the point of indifference or 'equality' between what would be gained (in terms of the objective function) by borrowing (say) £1 at Year 2 and what would be lost from the resulting repayment of capital plus interest at Year 3. Using the total opportunity cost figures calculated in Example 6 makes for a simple solution to the problem:

$$£1 \times \text{opportunity cost of cash at Year 2} = [£1 \times (1 + i)] \times \text{opportunity cost of cash at Year 3}$$
$$£1 \times 1.7784 = [£1 \times (1 + i)] \times 0.7513$$
$$1.7784 = 0.7513 + 0.7513i$$
$$[1.7784 - 0.7513] \div 0.7513 = i = 1.367 \text{ or } 136.7\%$$

This very high rate of interest should not come as a surprise. The firm should be willing to pay such a rate of interest (at a maximum) for the sake of gaining extra cash in a time period when cash is in short supply, and repaying in a time period when there is surplus cash.

SUMMARY

This chapter has covered the capital rationing problem. The main points made were as follows:

- Capital rationing refers to a situation where a company cannot undertake all positive NPV projects it has identified, because of a shortage of capital.

- Two different types of capital rationing situation can be identified, distinguished by the source of the capital expenditure constraint. Hard capital rationing occurs when the constraint is externally imposed on the firm by the capital market. Soft capital rationing occurs when the constraint is internally imposed on the firm, by its own management.

- In a situation of capital rationing the standard NPV decision rule for independent projects no longer holds and so has to be modified.

- In the single-period capital rationing situation, the NPV decision rule is replaced with a benefit–cost ratio analysis that evaluates the project's NPV relative to the required outlay in the rationed time period.

- In multi-period capital rationing, the optimal investment solution can only be obtained through solving the individual capital rationing constraints simultaneously via linear programming.

- The solution to a multi-period capital rationing LP not only provides advice on the capital investment decision (the LP's primal solution), but it also provides a dual solution. The dual solution indicates the (internal) opportunity cost of the scarce resources which, in this type of situation, is principally cash.

- The usefulness of the dual values is limited because of their marginal nature. However, they can be used to help evaluate some decisions that arise after the capital rationing LP has been solved.

NOTES

1. This return would be the project's IRR. For simplicity, we are abstracting from the problems that may arise in calculating or using an IRR.
2. If not, any book on management accounting will outline the basic principles. For example, see Colin Drury, *Management and Cost Accounting,* 8th ed., Cengage Learning EMEA.
3. We will shortly discuss the reason for making this assumption.
4. In addition, there may be a very much longer-term capital budget that might stretch as far as 20–25 years ahead, depending upon the company and the industry in which it operates and upon the gestation period of its major capital investment projects.
5. It could be argued that even this internally imposed capital rationing is, in reality, produced by external (but not exclusively financial) market inefficiencies, in that there is a time-lag between demand signals and the subsequent supply.
6. The primal solution reads: $a = 0, b = 0, c = 1, d = 1, e = 0.3, f = 0.6$.
7. If it *were* possible to relieve the capital expenditure constraint through the use of internally generated funds (from projects), then the LP formulation would have to be revised and a different solution would result:

$$39.4a + 44.1b + 133.6c + 68.4d + 83.6e + 190.5f \text{ Max.}$$
$$100a + 50b + 10d + 100e \leq 150$$
$$50a + 70b + 100c + 20d + 100e \leq 150$$
$$25a + 30c + 200f \leq 150 + 100b + 50d + 200e$$
$$100d \leq 150 + 100a + 100b + 150c + 100e + 300f$$
$$a, b, c, d, e, f \leq 1$$
$$a, b, c, d, e, f \leq 0$$

8. By including 'chance' constraints into the LP formulation, whereby some level of cash flow must be provided by the solution, with a given level of probability.
9. Project E produces a total NPV of + £83 700, and 0.001% of this amount is £0.837, the dual value for Year 1. This information on how the dual value arises is supplied by the software solution to the problem. In a more complex example the source of the dual value is likely to involve more than merely an adjustment to the level of investment in a *single* project.

FURTHER READING

1. For a good starting point on the literature of capital rationing, see J.H. Lorie and L.J. Savage, 'Three Problems in Rationing Capital', *Journal of Business,* October 1955, and H.R. Fogler, 'Ranking Techniques and Capital Budgeting', *Accounting Review,* January 1972.

2. For an approach equating with the Hirshleifer analysis, see F.D. Arditti, R.C. Grinold and H. Levy, 'The Investment–Consumption Decision under Capital Rationing', *Review of Economic Studies,* July 1973.

3. For application of LP to multi-period capital rationing, see two articles by K.N. Bhaskar, 'Linear Programming and Capital Budgeting: A Reappraisal', *Journal of Business Finance and Accounting,* Autumn 1976, and 'Linear Programming in Capital Budgeting: The Financing Problem', *Journal of Business Finance and Accounting,* Spring 1983.

4. Perhaps the most thoughtful article of all on the subject is H.M. Weingartner, 'Capital Rationing: *n* Authors in Search of a Plot', *Journal of Finance,* December 1977; whilst also of interest is G.W. Trivol and W.R. McDaniel, 'Uncertainty, Capital Immobility and Capital Rationing in Investment Decision', *Journal of Business Finance and Accounting,* Summer 1987.

5. For empirical evidence of the effects of capital rationing, see R. Pike, 'The Capital Budgeting Behaviour of Capital-Constrained Firms', *Journal of Business Finance and Accounting*, Winter 1983.

QUIZ QUESTIONS

1   What are the two types or classes of capital rationing?

2   Why does capital rationing cause problems for the NPV decision rule?

3   Given these projects:

	t_0	t_1	....	NPV
A	−100	− 50	....	+60
B	−200	−200	....	+90
C	− 40	−150	....	+20
D	−100	+ 20	....	−10

If only 200 is available at t_0, which projects should be selected?

4   Given the projects in question 3, if only 240 external capital was available at t_1 (no capital rationing at t_0), which projects should be selected?

5   Given these projects:

	t_0	....	NPV
A	−100	....	+40
B	−100	....	+30
C	−200	....	+50
D	−100	....	+10
E	− 50	....	+ 4

Only 300 is available at t_0 and Projects B and C are mutually exclusive. Which projects should the firm accept?

6   Given the projects:

	t_0	t_1	t_2	....	NPV
A	−100	−200	+50	....	+40
B	−150	+ 70	+70	....	+20
C	−200	−120	−30	....	+50

External capital is limited to 190 at t_0, 110 at t_1 and zero at t_2. Formulate the problem into an LP.

7   A capital rationing LP produces the following dual values for cash:

t_0	1.86
t_1	0.73
t_2	0.64
t_3	1.21

A bank loan is available at t_1, repayable at t_2. What is the maximum rate of interest you would be willing to pay, given the firm uses a 10% discount rate for project appraisal?

8 Given the dual values in question 7, the firm now discovers an additional project:

Year	Cash flow
0	−100
1	+ 40
2	+ 90

What action should be taken?
(See the 'Answers to the Quiz Questions' section at the back of the book.)

PROBLEMS

The answers to two of the following problems (those indicated by an asterisk) are available to students online. The answer to the remaining problem is available only to lecturers (see the 'Digital Resources' page for details).

1* Lijn-Libeco NV is a privately owned Belgium bakery company with other interests including ice-cream manufacture and specialized catering. For investment appraisal purposes, it uses a 15% rate of discount. The management are considering the company's capital investment plans for the coming year. One project under consideration is the purchase of a fleet of delivery vans. Two alternative proposals have been put forward. One is to purchase a fleet of petrol-engined vans; the other is to purchase more eco-friendly electric-hybrid vans.

Investment in the petrol-engined fleet would yield an IRR of 25% whilst the electric-hybrid fleet would only yield a return of 20%. However, when the two alternatives are evaluated using NPV, the electric-hybrid fleet has the larger positive NPV.

In addition to the above, the company has identified four other projects (all independent). Their outlays and NPVs are shown below:

Project	Outlay (t_0) (€000)	NPV (€000)
A	50	+ 60
B	80	+ 40
C	140	+ 84
D	80	+ 32
Petrol fleet	100	+ 80
Electric fleet	170	+110.5

All projects require only a single outlay at t_0, except Project A which requires a further €70 000 1 year later at t_1. The company has only €290 000 available for capital investment projects at t_0. Capital is expected to be freely available from t_1 onwards. None of the above projects can have their starts delayed. All projects are divisible, exhibit constant returns to scale and have the same level of risk, which is the same as that of the projects already being undertaken by the company.

Required:

(a) Carefully explain the reasons for the conflict in the investment advice about the fleet of delivery vans. In the absence of capital rationing, which vehicle fleet should be purchased and why?

(b) When faced with capital rationing, which projects should the company undertake at t_0? Explain the reasons for your decision.

(c) How would your advice in (b) above be modified if the start of the delivery fleet project could be delayed until t_1? What would be the resulting gain in shareholder wealth?

2* Plovidba Grupa is based in Zagreb. It is involved in the tourism business in Croatia and has built and operates several small hotels and guest-houses. The company has identified five potential investments – codenamed A to F – comprising two hotel developments in popular tourist resorts (Projects A and B), and three small complexes of holiday villas. Projected cash flows are as follows:

Project	t_0 Immediate outlay (kn000s)	t_1 Year 1 (kn000s)	t_2 Year 2 (kn000s)
A	−100	−100	+302
B	− 50	−100	+218
C	−200	+100	+107
D	−100	− 50	+308
E	−200	− 50	+344

Required:

(a) Plovidba faces a perfect capital market, where the appropriate discount rate is 10%. All projects are independent and divisible. Which projects should the firm accept?

(b) The company faces capital rationing at t_0. There is only 225 000 kuna of finance available. None of the projects can be delayed. Which projects should the firm accept?

(c) The situation is as in (b) above, except that you are now informed that Projects A and B are mutually exclusive. Which projects should now be accepted?

(d) All projects are now independent but indivisible. Which projects should be accepted? What will be the maximum NPV available to the company?

(e) All projects are independent and divisible. There is capital rationing at t_1 only. No project can be delayed or brought forward. There is only 150 000 kuna of external finance available at t_1. Which projects should be accepted?

(f) Given the information as in (e) above, except that there is capital rationing at both t_0 (225 000 kuna available) and t_1 (150 000 kuna available), formulate the linear programme to solve the problem, so as to maximize the total NPV generated.

(g) Suppose that the solution to the above linear programme produces the following dual values for cash:

t_0 0.92

t_1 0.84

t_2 0

If money can be transferred from t_0 to t_1, via a deposit account, under what circumstances would it be worthwhile?

(h) Given the circumstances in (g) above, what minimum rate of interest would be required to make the linear programme transfer cash from t_1 to t_2?

In all the above questions, none of the projects can be accepted more than once.

3 Hellenic Leptos is a privately owned housebuilding company in Limassol, Cyprus. The company is financed entirely by its two owners and for project appraisal purposes they use a discount rate of 10%.

The two owners are considering the company's capital investment programme for the next 2 years, and have reduced their initial list of projects to four. Details of the projects are as follows:

Project	Immediately (€000s)	After 1 year (€000s)	After 2 years (€000s)	After 3 years (€000s)	NPV (at 10%) (€000s)	IRR (to nearest 1%)
A	−400	+ 50	+300	+350	+157.00	26%
B	−300	−200	+400	+400	+ 150.0	25%
C	−300	+150	+150	+150	+ 73.5	23%
D	0	−300	+250	+300	+ 159.5	50%

None of the projects can be delayed. All projects are divisible; outlays may be reduced by any proportion and net inflows will then be reduced in the same proportion. No project can be undertaken more than once. Hellenic Leptos is able to invest surplus funds in a bank deposit account yielding a return of 7% per annum.

Required:

(a) Prepare calculations showing which projects Hellenic Leptos should undertake if capital for immediate investment is limited to €500 000, but is expected to be available without limit at a cost of 10% per annum thereafter.

(b) Provide a LP formulation to assist the two owners in choosing investment projects if capital available immediately is limited to €500 000, capital available after 1 year is limited to €300 000 and capital is available thereafter without limit at a cost of 10% per annum.

(c) Outline the limitations of the formulation you have provided in (b).

(d) Comment briefly on the view that in practice capital is rarely limited absolutely, provided that the borrower is willing to pay a sufficiently high price, and in consequence a technique for selecting investment projects which assumes that capital is limited absolutely, is of no use.

RISK ANALYSIS

9

SIMPLE RISK TECHNIQUES

LEARNING OBJECTIVES

The purpose of this chapter is to:

- Introduce the concept of investment risk.

- Discuss three practical approaches to dealing with risk in investment appraisal: expected NPV analysis; sensitivity analysis; risk-adjusted discount rates.

- Identify the problems and limitations with these simple approaches to investment risk.

- Analyze the special case of the 'abandonment' decision.

RISK AND RETURN

We live in a world where the outcome of virtually all investments is *uncertain*. This statement would apply equally to individuals investing in say, shares, and also to companies investing in projects. These investments are said to be 'risky': thus a *risky investment* can be said to be one where the investment's future financial performance is uncertain. However, before we go on to explore this issue further, we need to clarify the distinction that can be made between the terms 'risk' and 'uncertainty'.

If a future cash flow is described as 'risky', this implies that *a probability* can be assigned to the cash flow – based on knowledge from past observations and experience – that indicates its likelihood. For example, we *expect* an investment will produce a cash flow of €1000 in 12-months' time, but we are not sure. However, based on our experience of similar investments undertaken in the past, we estimate that there is an 80% chance – an 80% *probability* – of that €1000 cash flow actually occurring. In such circumstances, the €1000 cash flow is said to be *risky*.

On the other hand, if a probability *cannot* be assigned to the likelihood of that future cash flow forecast, because we have no past observations to base it on, then the future cash flow is said to be '*uncertain*', rather than risky.

For our purposes, this precise distinction between these two terms is not particularly helpful and we shall tend to use them interchangeably – as was done in the initial paragraph of this chapter – and in general we shall assume that it **is** possible to assign probabilities to these future cash flow forecasts. So let us now turn to a closer examination of these risky investments and how the presence of risk affects the decision-making process.

Risky investments and risk-aversion

When an investor buys shares, he or she expects to gain a return on that investment. This return arises in two forms. One is in the form of the *dividends* that are expected to be paid to shareholders by the company. The other is in the form of the expectation of being able to sell the shares at some point in the future, at a higher price than that at which they were originally bought, and so generating a *capital gain*. However, the amount of dividends that a company will pay and the future selling price of the shares are both uncertain: hence the actual level of return received by the investor will be uncertain.

Similarly, if a company buys a sausage machine, the return (or profit) that it will receive on that investment is also uncertain. This is because there is likely to be some uncertainty over virtually every aspect of the investment: the life of the machine; its repair and maintenance costs; its output of sausages; the selling price of those sausages; and the production costs of the sausages. Obviously the company makes its investment decision on the basis of forecasts about these various factors – but such forecasts are really just 'intelligent guesses' as to the expected levels of these uncertain values. Hence the investment's expected return is uncertain.

This uncertainty that surrounds an investment's outcome is referred to as its 'risk'. The greater the degree of uncertainty, the greater is the risk and vice versa. Both individual investors and companies, not unnaturally, dislike this uncertain nature of an investment's outcome: they are said to be *risk-averse*. This risk aversion does *not* mean that investors will be unwilling to undertake a risky investment; but what it does mean is that they will require a *reward* for taking on a risky investment. This reward will be in terms of an increase in the level of the investment's expected return. The *greater* the risk, then the greater will be the expected return required to make the investment acceptable.

This relationship between risk and return, and the issues that it raises – how to measure risk, how to determine what expected return is required for a given amount of risk, etc. – is of central importance to corporate financial decision-making. It is to these issues that we now start to turn.

EXPECTED NET PRESENT VALUE

In an uncertain world, even assuming the presence of perfect capital markets, use of the NPV method of investment appraisal cannot be said necessarily to lead to optimal investment decisions or to the maximization of shareholder wealth. All it can lead to is the *expected* maximization of wealth. Hindsight, that is knowledge about the actual outcome of past events, may suggest different advice from that given by the NPV appraisal rule, because the latter is based only upon estimates of the future.

When we examined the rationale and operation of the NPV appraisal method, we paid very little attention to how the estimates of a project's future net cash flows were derived. In practice, management is unlikely to produce a series of 'point' (i.e. single figure) estimates of each future year's net cash flow but instead is likely to construct a *range* of estimates.

For example, a project may have an initial cost of £1000 and a life of 3 years, but the level of the net cash flows may be uncertain, depending, say, on the general state of the industry in which the company operates. Example 1 shows a simple illustration of the estimated annual net cash flows based on three economic states: boom, normal and depressed conditions. From these estimates the project's NPV is calculated in each state and a figure is attached expressing the probability, or likelihood, of each state actually occurring. These NPVs are combined to produce the arithmetic mean (i.e. *average*) NPV of the project – what is called the *expected* **NPV** of the project, given the different estimates and their probabilities of occurrence. It is upon the value (and more importantly, the sign) of this expected net present value (ENPV) that the normal investment appraisal decision rule is then applied.

EXAMPLE 1

Hoy Bikes manufactures gear mechanisms for racing bikes. It is evaluating an investment proposal to produce a radical type of cast metal-fibre cyclo-cross bike from its factory in Manchester, England. The investment will cost £1 000 000 and is expected to have a market life of 3 years before the technology used changes and improves. However, the estimate of the annual net revenue from the investment is uncertain and depends on the state of the UK economy. The company's management has produced the following estimates (£000s):

State of UK economy	0	1	2	3
(I) Rapid growth	−1 000	+500	+700	+980
(II) Slow growth	−1 000	+500	+600	+700
(III) No growth	−1 000	+300	+300	+250

Hoy Bikes intends to use a 10% discount rate in project appraisal, believing that this correctly reflects the risk of the project.

On this basis, the NPV of the cyclo-cross bike investment project has been calculated as follows:

State	NPV (£000s)
Rapid growth	+769
Slow growth	+477
No growth	−291

Latest forecasts from the International Monetary Fund (IMF) suggest the following probabilities for the UK's future economic growth prospects:

State	Probability
Rapid growth	20%
Slow growth	60%
No growth	20%

On this basis, Hoy Bikes estimates the investment's *expected* (i.e. arithmetic mean or average) NPV will be:

▶

▶

State	Probability		NPV		
Rapid growth	0.20	×	+769	=	+153.8
Slow growth	0.60	×	+477	=	+286.2
No growth	0.20	×	−291	=	− 52.2
					+387.8 ENPV

As the project has a positive *expected* NPV, it should be accepted. The investment is expected – on average – to produce a positive NPV of £387 800.

It is important to notice that, as this example shows, management not only have the task of estimating the project's annual net cash flow in each of the different states of the national economy, but must also estimate the probability of the occurrence of each state. (Strictly, these are subjective probabilities, because they are based upon management's subjective judgement, rather than on past observations of similar events.)

In addition, it is also assumed in Example 1 that, whichever state of the economy occurs, the UK will remain fixed in that economic state for the duration of the project. If this assumption is unrealistic, further adjustments will need to be made to the ENPV calculation. Example 2 illustrates this more complex type of situation.

EXAMPLE 2

Maravista SA is a Portuguese company that designs and manufactures clothes for the 13–15 years segment of the fashion industry. The success or otherwise of its products depends upon whether they are in fashion in any particular year.

The company's management is considering investing €40 000 to produce a range of dresses which, they believe, will have a 2-year fashion life. However, the outcome of the project is dependent upon whether the dress design turns out to be in fashion and hence successful (State I), or out of fashion and so a relative failure (State II), or a marketing disaster (State III).

Maravista's marketing analysts have studied the situation carefully and have estimated the following net revenue figures for the project (€000s):

Year 1 State	Prob.	Net revenue	Year 2 State	Prob.	Net revenue
			I	0.6	+100
I	0.5	+80	II	0.3	+ 80
			III	0.1	+ 20
			I	0.4	+ 80
II	0.3	+30	II	0.3	+ 40
			III	0.3	+ 10
			I	0.1	+ 70
III	0.2	+10	II	0.4	+ 40
			III	0.5	+ 5

▶

For example, as Maravista's marketing analyst explained to the chief executive, we believe that in the first year of the product's life it has a 50% chance of being 'in fashion' and, hence, a success. Given it is successful in the first year, then there is a 60% chance of being similarly successful in its second year, a 30% chance of it then being a relative failure and, finally, a 10% chance of it turning into a marketing disaster.

On this basis, the analysis can be simplified by estimating the expected (i.e. arithmetic mean) revenue in the second year, for each possible first year state:

Year 1 State	Year 2 revenue		Prob.			
	+100	×	0.6	=	+60	
I	+ 80	×	0.3	=	+24	
	+ 20	×	0.1	=	+ 2	
					+86	Expected Year 2 net revenue
	+ 80	×	0.4	=	+32	
II	+ 40	×	0.3	=	+12	
	+ 10	×	0.3	=	+ 3	
					+47	Expected Year 2 net revenue
	+ 70	×	0.1	=	+ 7	
III	+ 40	×	0.4	=	+16	
	+ 5	×	0.5	=	+ 2.5	
					+25.5	Expected Year 2 net revenue

Now, the project's expected cash flows have been simplified to:

Year 1 State	Probability	Year 0 outlay	Year 1 net revenue	Year 2 expected revenue
I	0.5	−40	+80	+86
II	0.3	−40	+30	+47
III	0.2	−40	+10	+25.5

Maravista usually uses a 20% discount rate to reflect the high-risk nature of the fashion industry and, on this basis, the project's expected NPV in *each individual state* can be calculated:

State (€000s)	Project NPV
I	+86.4
II	+17.6
III	−14.0

And now, the project's *overall* expected NPV can be calculated:

▶

Year 1

State	Probability		NPV		
I	0.5	×	+86.4	=	+43.2
II	0.3	×	+17.6	=	+5.3
III	0.2	×	−14.0	=	−2.8
					+45.7 ENPV

As the project has a positive ENPV of approximately €45 700, Maravista decides to proceed with production of the new fashion line.

Limitations of ENPV

The concept of expected NPV (indeed an expected IRR could be similarly calculated), has been found by management to be useful for project appraisal in an uncertain world because it provides an *average* value of the proposed project's performance. However, it is important to realize that it cannot be said to take account of risk, because all that the ENPV calculation provides is a measure of the investment's *expected* performance, whereas risk is concerned with the likelihood that the *actual* performance may diverge from what is expected.

Example 3 illustrates this point very simply. Two mutually exclusive projects have identical expected NPVs. Therefore, on the basis of the ENPV decision rule, the management should be indifferent between them – they are both expected to make a positive NPV of $8.5 million. However, almost certainly, the management of Stateside Holdings Inc. will not be indifferent, but instead will strongly prefer the *silicon chip* project. The reason for this is that this project is likely to be viewed as being less risky than the semi-conductor project.

EXAMPLE 3

Stateside Holdings Inc. wants to enter the electronics industry and is considering two possible projects. Both projects require the same outlay of $10 million and both have the same ENPV. However, because this is a venture into a new area of business, Stateside only wants to undertake *one* of the projects. The figures are as follows ($ millions):

State of world economy	Probability	Semi-conductor project NPV	Silicon chip project NPV
Strong growth	0.20	+30.6	+13.0
Slow growth	0.60	+ 8.5	+ 8.5
Recession	0.20	−13.6	+ 4.0

▶

▶

Semi-conductor project:	0.2	×	+30.6	=	+6.12	
	0.6	×	+ 8.5	=	+5.10	
	0.2	×	−13.6	=	−2.72	
					+8.5	ENPV
Silicon chip project:	0.2	×	+13.0	=	+2.6	
	0.6	×	+ 8.5	=	+5.1	
	0.2	×	+ 4.0	=	+0.8	
					+8.5	ENPV

Risk is to do with the fact that the project's actual outcome can vary from what is expected. In this respect the actual outcome can either be better (the *upside potential*) or worse (the *downside risk*) than the expected outcome. A 'gambling' investor will focus most of his attention on the upside potential, but a 'risk-averse' investor will be more concerned with looking at the expected outcome and the downside risk.

Given the assumption (which is generally correct) that investors dislike risk – they are *risk-averse* – the managers of Stateside are likely to view the silicon chip project as less risky because, even in the 'recession' state of the world, it is still expected to produce a small positive NPV. In contrast, the semi-conductor project will produce a large negative NPV of $13.6 million if the economy moves into recession.

There is however one set of circumstances in which the ENPV approach does 'allow' for risk. That is to say, there is one set of circumstances when, if faced by the two alternative projects in Example 3, it would be correct to conclude that the company would be indifferent between them because they produce the same ENPV.

Those circumstances would be where the company intended to undertake a large number of similar or identical projects. In that case the ENPV indicates (quite correctly) the average outcome of each individual investment. Thus, if the company were to undertake (say) 100 semi-conductor projects, then 20 of them would produce an NPV of +$30.6 million, 60 would produce an NPV of +$8.5 million and the remaining 20 would produce negative NPVs of $13.6 million. Thus the average outcome per project would be a positive NPV of $8.5 million.

Similarly, the average outcome of 100 silicon chip projects would be a +$8.5 million NPV per project. Of these projects, 20 would produce an NPV of +$13 million, and so on. Therefore, in these circumstances, the company would be indifferent between the two projects, given they have the same ENPV.

Unfortunately, most capital investment projects are not undertaken a great number of times, but are unique, one-off investments. It therefore follows that the idea of ENPV remains as an inadequate way of taking risk into account in project appraisal.

Value of additional information

One interesting use of the ENPV technique is that it can help to indicate the value of *additional* information. Example 4 illustrates such a situation.

EXAMPLE 4

Budryk Polska is a mining technology company, based in Warsaw. The company has developed a new diamond drill head, using laser guided production technology, and has now reached the stage of making a decision whether or not to undertake manufacture. The manufacturing equipment would cost 900 000 zloty (Z) and the drill is expected to have a market life of 6 years. However, the performance of the product in the market place is dependent on the future level of international metal prices.

Budryk's marketing director has indicated that there are four possible outcomes for the diamond drill project (States I, II, III or IV): very successful, moderately successful, disappointing and complete failure. On this basis, the company's finance department have estimated the possible NPVs and the project's overall expected NPV (Z000s):

State	Probability		NPV		
I	0.2	×	+110	=	+22
II	0.5	×	+ 70	=	+35
III	0.2	×	+ 50	=	+10
IV	0.1	×	− 65	=	− 6.5
				ENPV	+60.5

As the ENPV is positive, the company decides to go ahead with production but, just before this decision is implemented, Centertel Intelligence, an economic forecasting company, offers to undertake a review of future metal prices which will indicate, *in advance of production* of the new drill head, what outcome is likely to occur. The cost of the survey would be Z5 000 and the management of Budryk are now trying to decide if they should commission the review.

The approach to take is to examine what action the company would take in response to the various possible outcomes of the survey. Clearly, if the research survey indicated that States I, II or III would occur, the company would undertake production, as to do so would generate a positive NPV. However, if the market research indicated that State IV would occur, the company would not proceed with manufacture, as manufacture would lead to a negative NPV of Z65 000.

Survey indicates: State	Company's investment decision	Probability of survey result		NPV outcome of decision		
I	Accept	0.2	×	+110	=	+22
II	Accept	0.5	×	+ 70	=	+35
III	Accept	0.2	×	+ 50	=	+10
IV	Reject	0.1	×	0	=	0
					ENPV	+67

Therefore:

▶

	(Z)
ENPV of project *with* market research survey	67 000
ENPV of project *without* market research survey	60 500
Maximum worth of survey	6 500
Cost of survey	5 000
Net benefit of survey to Budryk	+Z1 500

On the basis of this analysis, the research survey is worthwhile. The company should commission the survey *prior* to production of the diamond drill bit and *only* proceed to manufacture if the research indicates that States I, II or III will occur.

In Example 4 the additional information was always correct. A more complex analysis involving the opportunity cost concept is required if the additional information may be *incorrect*. This situation is illustrated in Example 5.

EXAMPLE 5

Pretoria Construction Ltd is considering building a new shopping mall on the outskirts of Bloemfontein, in South Africa, costing 60 million rand to construct. The outcome of the project is uncertain because it is difficult to predict how popular it will be with both shops and their customers. It is thought to have a 60% chance of being successful and, if so, it will generate a R100 million *positive* NPV for the company. However, there is a 40% chance that it will fail to attract both shops and customers and would result in a R40 million *negative* NPV. On this basis, the project's expected NPV is positive as follows:

Outcome	Probability		NPV Rmillion		
Success	0.6	×	+100	=	+60
Failure	0.4	×	− 40	=	−16
ENPV					+44

A market research survey will indicate, *with 90% accuracy*, which outcome will actually occur. The maximum worth of the market research survey can be estimated as follows:

There are four possible states of the world:

State
   A: Survey indicates 'success' and is correct.
   B: Survey indicates 'success' and is wrong.
   C: Survey indicates 'failure' and is correct.
   D: Survey indicates 'failure' and is wrong.

▶

There is a 60% chance the survey will indicate 'success' and a 40% chance that it will indicate 'failure'. There is a 90% chance that the survey result will be correct and a 10% chance that it will be wrong. The probabilities of each of the four 'states of the world' will be given by the product of the individual probabilities:

State					Probability
A	0.6	×	0.9	=	0.54
B	0.6	×	0.1	=	0.06
C	0.4	×	0.9	=	0.36
D	0.4	×	0.1	=	0.04

State	Decision	Probability		Outcome		
A	Accept	0.54	×	+100 NPV	=	+54.0
B	Accept	0.06	×	− 40 NPV	=	− 2.4
C	Reject	0.36	×	0 NPV	=	0
D	Reject	0.04	×	−100 NPV*	=	− 4.0
				ENPV	=	+47.6

ENPV with survey	:	+R47.6 million
ENPV without survey	:	+R44.0 million
Max worth of survey	:	+R3.6 million

*Note that this is an opportunity cost. If the survey incorrectly forecasts 'failure' and we act on the survey's advice, we forgo the opportunity of gaining an NPV of +100.

THE ABANDONMENT DECISION

Another 'special case' of the ENPV decision is the evaluation of an option to *abandon* a project before it reaches the end of its life. Such an analysis is illustrated in Example 6.

However, the limitations of the abandonment analysis should be noted. The first is that when multiple abandonment points are available – such as at the end of Years 1, 2 and 3 of a project with a life of 4 years – there is a real-world information problem as to how reliable future abandonment values are to be estimated. The second problem is that the analysis of a multiple abandonment point decision is much more complex than that of Example 6. A 'dynamic programming' analysis is required. The problem here is that the more complex the analysis required, the more reluctant management often are to accept its advice, as they lack an understanding as to how the advice was generated.

EXAMPLE 6

ItalBenelli SpA operates a series of copying and scanning service shops in which customers can walk in off the street and have their copying requirements undertaken immediately. The company normally keeps its copying and scanning equipment for 2 years before disposing of it on the second-hand market and replacing it with more modern technology.

It has recently been approached by a manufacturer of scanning equipment who is trying to break into the Italian market and has offered to sell ItalBenelli its latest scanners – the IXI – for €10 000 each.

ItalBenelli believe that the crucial factor is the reliability of the new scanners. On past experience it believes that there is only a 60% chance that they will prove to be reliable.

On this basis they have estimated the following net cash flows (in euros), produced by an individual IXI scanner:

Scanner	Year 1	Year 2	Scrap
Reliable	+8 000	+6 000	+400
Unreliable	+4 000	+3 000	+200

A 15% discount rate is used to reflect the risk of the scanning business and, on this basis, the project's possible NPVs and ENPV are calculated:

Reliable scanner $-10\ 000 + [8000 \times 1.15^{-1}] + [6400 \times 1.15^{-2}] = +1796$ NPV $\times 0.60 = +1078$

Unreliable scanner $-10\ 000 + [4000 \times 1.15^{-1}] + [3200 \times 1.15^{-2}] = -4102$ NPV $\times 0.40 = \underline{-1641}$

ENPV: $-€536$

As a result of this analysis ItalBenelli decides not to buy the IXI scanners. However, in order to try to get IntelBenelli to change its mind, the scanner manufacturer offers to buy them back at the end of the first year for 50% of their purchase cost. In other words, IntelBenelli are being offered an *abandonment* option. How this new situation is analyzed is shown below.

First, assuming that the company purchases a photocopy machine and then, at the end of the first year, decides **not** to abandon, the resulting NPVs of the decision are as follows:

Scanner	Year 1	Year 2		NPV
Reliable	$-5\ 000 \times (1.15)^{-1}$	$+6\ 400 \times (1.15)^{-2}$	=	$+\ 491$
Unreliable	$-5\ 000 \times (1.15)^{-1}$	$+3\ 200 \times (1.15)^{-2}$	=	$-1\ 928$

In each case, the *negative* cash outflow at Year 1 is an *opportunity cost*. If the photocopier is *not* abandoned, the company forgoes the opportunity to sell it back to the manufacturer for €5000.

This analysis demonstrates that if the scanner turns out to be *reliable*, the correct decision to take at the end of Year 1 is *not* to abandon as this results in a positive NPV (+€491). However, if the scanner turns out to be *unreliable*, the scanner *should be* abandoned at Year 1, because *not* abandoning the scanner will result in a negative NPV (−€1928).

Second, having decided what Year 1 action to take, the initial (Year 0) investment decision can be re-analyzed:

▶

Scanner reliable:

Outlay	−10 000					
Net revenues		+8 000		+6 000		
Scrap				+ 400		
Net cash flow	−10 000	+8 000	$(1.15)^{-1}$	+6 400	$(1.15)^{-2}$ =	+1 796 NPV

Scanner unreliable:

Outlay	−10 000				
Net revenues		+4 000			
Abandon value		+5 000		=	−2174 NPV
Net cash flow	−10 000	+9 000	$(1.15)^{-1}$		

Photocopier	*Probability*		*NPV*		
Reliable	*0.6*	×	*+1 796*	=	+1078
Unreliable	0.4	×	−2 174	=	− 870
				ENPV	+ 208

This analysis results in the new IXI scanners now having a positive ENPV (of €208 per machine), and so ItalBenelli should go ahead and purchase the IXI scanners, but should abandon the project by selling them back to the manufacturer at the end of the first year if they prove to be unreliable.

REAL WORLD VIEW: When to Abandon a Project? – Fail to Plan = Plan to Fail

In financial planning and forecasting, calculating the costs of failures, unsatisfactory results and worst-case scenarios whilst actively preparing for these eventualities is just as important as planning for success. In reality, many ventures have such large set-up costs that they may be crippled before even going into operation, and even those fortunate enough to become operational may yet be strangled by unsustainable running costs or servicing charges. This highlights the importance of building in an opt-out policy, or exit strategy, at the earliest stages of development.

Far from being a sign of weaknesses or lack of confidence in a project, many would contest it's better to be prepared and aware of the potential implications of early withdrawal than to continue to pour money into a project that is clearly logistically or financially unviable to maintain. Furthermore, organized withdrawal or hastening of a venture on the business's own terms – or, indeed, rejecting the proposal at the planning stage – is preferable to having it forced upon them under conditions which may be decidedly less favourable.

There are many potential practical applications of ENPV in order to reach an abandonment decision. It has been used in considering the viability of ventures as diverse as the development of new drugs and clinical trials, opening and closure of mines, pipeline management, project evaluation of SMEs (small and medium-sized enterprises) – particularly in time of recession, building of large commercial or combat aircraft, and in other military scenarios, such as in assessing the costs associated with pulling out of foreign operations. Used appropriately, it can be an effective tool in decision-making.

Nevertheless, as the following example shows, there can be many complex issues – political, moral and otherwise – in making the tough decision to abandon a project, not least when many stakeholders and environmental factors are involved. A common pitfall is the reluctance to admit defeat coupled with a dogged determination to see it through (sometimes at any cost), particularly when considerable funds, resources and often goodwill will have already been committed to the development. This can be inflamed further by the threat of ramifications and responsibility for the failed or shortened enterprise.

A particularly significant and embarrassing abandonment decision in recent years concerned a new IT system implemented by the UK's National Health Service. Originally heralded as a forward-thinking 'technical revolution', a state-of-the-art system for sharing, nationalizing and standardizing patient records was proposed and developed, promising huge benefits in data transparency between hospitals, surgeries and practices. However, in reality it was thwarted by technological failures, contract disputes and spiralling legal bills, costing the UK taxpayer in excess of £10 billion (with the final figure set to rise, despite the original estimate set at only £6.4 billion). The ensuing pandemonium saw the various stakeholders embroiled in a near decade-long political 'blame game' which at the time of writing is still ongoing. One critic labelled it 'One of the worst and most expensive contracting fiascos in the history of the public sector.' Whilst they may not agree on who or what is to blame, all parties would surely concede that important lessons could be learnt from the episode.

SENSITIVITY ANALYSIS

The appraisal of almost any investment project in the real world will involve the making of a large number of estimates. For example, the outlay required to undertake the project, its life, the annual cash inflows and outflows it will generate, the scrap value it will have, and even the correct rate of discount to reduce the cash flows to PVs. Estimates will be made for all these factors and the project will then be appraised by calculating an ENPV.

If this NPV is positive then the appraisal is in favour of acceptance. But, in terms of downside risk, the decision-maker is also interested in how *sensitive* the decision advice is to changes in the estimates made about the project. In other words, the decision-maker is likely to be interested in the 'margin of error' that there can be in the estimates made about the individual components of the project (i.e. outlay, life, etc.) *before* the advice that the appraisal gives (in this case to accept) becomes incorrect.

The decision pivot point

The decision whether to accept or reject a particular project 'pivots' around the point of a zero NPV. If the NPV is greater than zero (i.e. positive), then the advice is to accept. On the other hand, if the NPV is less than zero (i.e. negative), then the advice is to reject. Thus a *zero NPV* becomes the decision *pivot point*.

Sensitivity analysis is the term used to describe the process where each estimated element of a project's cash flow is taken in turn (with a *ceteris paribus* assumption holding all other estimates constant) to see the extent to which it can vary before the project's positive NPV is reduced to a zero value. Therefore, if the estimated element varies by *more than* this amount, then the decision advice given by the original estimate of the project's NPV will be incorrect. These sensitivity calculations are illustrated in Example 7.

EXAMPLE 7

Deutsche Meindl manufactures components for the European automotive industry. The company's finance department have made the following estimates about an investment proposal concerning a new laser-guided machine tool (all data in €000s):

Outlay	€1 000
Life	3 years
Annual revenues	€2 000
Annual costs	€1 500
Appropriate discount rate	10%

On the basis of these estimates, the investment's NPV can be calculated as follows:

	Year			
	0	*1*	*2*	*3*
Capital outlay	−1 000			
Revenues		+2 000	+2 000	+2 000
Costs		−1 500	−1 500	−1 500
Net expected cash flows	−1 000	+ 500	+ 500	+ 500

$$\text{NPV} = -1000 + [500 \times A_{3,\,10\%}] = +\text{€243 or } +\text{€243 000 NPV}$$

Taking each of the five estimated factors in turn (and holding all the others constant at their initial estimated values), we shall examine the degree of variation necessary to reduce the +€243 000 NPV to zero.

1. *Outlay:*

Let the cost of the investment be x. Therefore:

$$-x + [500 \times A_{3,\,10\%}] = 0 \text{ NPV}$$

$$x = 500 \times A_{3,\,10\%}$$

$$x = 500 \times 2.4869 = 1243$$

The cost of the investment can be as high as €1 243 000 before the appraisal advice to invest (i.e. + NPV) becomes incorrect; in other words the *original* estimated cost of the investment can increase by up to €243 000 or by (243/1000 =) 0.243 or 24.3%, before the original decision advice – to accept – is incorrect.

▶

2. *Life:*

Let the life be x years.

$$-1\,000 + [500 \times A_{3,\,10\%}]_0 = 0 \text{ NPV}$$

Using *linear interpolation*, we know that when $x = 3$ the NPV equals $+ £243$. Trying $x = 2$:

$$-1\,000 + [500 \times A_{2,\,10\%}] = -132 \text{NPV}$$

Thus the value for x that produces a zero NPV lies between 2 and 3:

$$x = 2 + \left[\frac{-132}{-132 - (243)} \times (3 - 2) \right] = 2.35 \text{ years}$$

Therefore the project's life can be as short as 2.35 years before the advice of the original investment appraisal is incorrect; i.e. the original estimate can decrease by 0.65 year or by $0.65/3 = 0.217$ or 21.7%.

3. *Revenues:*

Let the annual revenue be x.

$$-1000 + [x \times A_{3,\,10\%}] - [1500 \times A_{3,\,10\%}] = 0 \text{ NPV}$$

$$x = \frac{1000 + [1500 \times A_{3,\,10\%}]}{A_{3,\,10\%}} = 1902$$

Thus the annual revenues can be as low as €1902, over the 3 years, before the original advice is incorrect; i.e. the original annual revenues estimate can decrease by up to €98 per year or $98/2\,000 = 0.049$ or 4.9%.

4. *Costs:*

Let the annual costs be x.

$$-1\,000 + [2000 \times A_{3,\,10\%}] - [x \times A_{3,\,10\%}] = 0 \text{ NPV}$$

$$x = \frac{1000 + [2500 \times A_{3,\,10\%}]}{A_{3,\,10\%}} = 1598$$

The annual costs can be as high as €1598 in each of the 3 years before the original investment advice is incorrect, i.e. the original annual costs estimate can increase by €98 per year or $98/1500 = 0.065$ or 6.5%.

5. *Discount rate:*

Let the discount rate be x (i.e. the project's IRR).

$$-1000 + [500 \times A_{3,\,10\%}]_x = 0 \text{ NPV}$$

$$A_{3,10\%} = \frac{1000}{500} = 2$$

▶

Using linear interpolation, $A_{3,\,10\%} = 2.11$ and $A_{3,\,10\%} = 1.95$

$$x = 0.20 + \left[\frac{2.11 - 2.0}{2.11 - 1.95}(0.25 - 0.20) \right] = 0.234$$

Thus the estimate for the discount rate can be as high as 23.4% before the original investment advice is incorrect; i.e. the original estimate can be increased by 13.4% or 0.134/0.10 = 134%.

Sensitivity table

Variable	Original estimate	Maximum change	Allowable change	% Allowable change
1. Outlay	1 000	1 243	+243	24.3%
2. Life	3	2.35	−0.65	21.7%
3. Revenues	2 000	1 902	−98	4.9%
4. Costs	1 500	1 598	+98	6.5%
5. Discount rate	10%	23.4%	+13.4%	134%

The sensitivity table in Example 7 shows that the decision to invest is *most sensitive* to the estimates of annual revenues (where an actual outcome of only 4.9% below estimate would cause the NPV decision advice to be incorrect) and the annual costs (a decision sensitivity of 6.5%). The decision advice is fairly insensitive to all the other estimates. We would conclude from this that management of Deutsche Meindl should review both of these decision-sensitive estimates to ensure that they are as accurate as possible.

Example 7 outlines the general approach of the sensitivity analysis technique, which is a good *working tool* in that it makes the decision-makers more aware of the possible effects of uncertainty on investment decisions. In addition, it can also help to direct attention to those particular estimates that require a special forecasting effort on account of their effect on the decision's sensitivity.

Limitations of sensitivity analysis

The technique suffers, in particular, from an obvious and important drawback: the fact that each estimated component is varied *in turn*, whilst all the others are held *constant*. Thus, in Example 7, the discount rate can be as high as 23.4% (approximately) before the NPV calculation advises rejection of the project, but this degree of sensitivity only holds if all the *other* estimates turn out to be accurate. In other words, the technique ignores the possible effects on the decision of two or more of the estimated components varying simultaneously.[1]

Even if this problem with sensitivity analysis is set to one side, it can also be criticized on the basis that it makes no attempt to analyze risk in any formal way. Nor does it give any indication as to what the decision-maker's *reaction* should be to the data presented in a sensitivity table.

In the example set out above, the original NPV calculations indicated a decision to accept. Sensitivity analysis provides no rules to guide the decision-maker as to whether the initial appraisal advice should or should not be amended in the light of the sensitivity data. With these limitations in mind, let us now look at another approach that may be used to deal with the problem of uncertainty in investment appraisal.

THE RISK-ADJUSTED DISCOUNT RATE

Risk and return

The risk-adjusted discount rate approach attempts to handle the problem of risk in a more direct and thoughtful way. As we know, investors are risk-averse and so require a reward for undertaking a risky investment in the form of the rate of return that it is expected to produce. The more risky the investment, the greater must be its expected return if investors are going to be persuaded to undertake it.

It is this idea – the relationship between risk and return – that the risk-adjusted discount rate approach picks up on. We have seen from our analysis of the NPV decision rule that a positive NPV means that the project produces a return greater than the discount rate – which itself represents the minimum acceptable rate of return. Thus the risk-adjusted discount rate idea takes the commonsense approach to handling risk in investment appraisal by adjusting the *level* of the minimum acceptable return to reflect the project's level of risk.

The approach taken is usually to add a risk 'premium' to the 'risk-free' rate of return. The greater the project's perceived level of risk, the greater is the risk premium. The risk-free rate of return is usually taken to be the going rate of return on government bonds (on the basis that such bonds have little or no risk of default).

For example, suppose that the current rate of return on government bonds is 8%. Management may decide to classify investment proposals into three broad categories, low, medium and high-risk, and assign risk premiums of 3%, 5% and 9% respectively. Therefore, the cash flows of low-risk projects would be discounted to present value using a discount rate of 8% + 3% = 11%, whilst projects of medium- or high-risk would be evaluated by discounting their cash flows to present value using 13%, (8% + 5%) and 17% discount rates respectively.

In one very important way, the risk-adjusted discount rate approach to the problem of uncertainty is much more useful to the decision-maker than sensitivity analysis, in that it does actually produce *decision advice*, in the form of a *risk-adjusted* NPV. In addition, the method is easily understandable and appears to be intuitively correct: investors *do* require a higher expected return on riskier investments. However, we can identify several drawbacks in this essentially correct (but too casual) analysis.

The problems

The two main problems are the allocation of projects into risk classes and the identification of the risk premiums. In addition there is a technical problem with this approach to allowing for risk, in that it implicitly implies that risk increases over time (which may or may not be the case).

The problems of the allocation of projects to a particular risk class and the risk premiums simply arise from the casual nature of the analysis. Thus the allocation of a project to a particular risk class and the premium assigned to each class will be based on the manager's own personal attitude towards risk, and on the manager's personal perception as to the nature of risk and the reward required for accepting risk. Our earlier discussion on objectives is sufficient for us to realize that the manager's view of risk – and the required rewards – may not be the same as those of the shareholders. (This whole area will be examined much more closely in the chapters that follow.)

Certainty-equivalents[2]

The 'technical' problem is easy to illustrate, as is shown in Example 8. The problem is that a constant risk premium implies increasing risk over time. In Example 8 a risk-adjusted discount rate of 8% implies that a project's cash flows become more risky over time. It is debatable whether the riskiness of a project's cash flows do correspond with this assumption.

EXAMPLE 8

An investment produces an uncertain cash flow at Year 1, which is expected to be £100. If you would be willing to accept £90 for certain at Year 1, instead of the uncertain £100, then £90 is said to be the 'certainty-equivalent'.

Given that you are indifferent between the two amounts, the certainty-equivalent factor at Year 1 – a_1 – can be identified by:

$$£90 = a_1 \times £100$$

$$a_1 = \frac{£90}{£100} = 0.90$$

What this certainty-equivalent factor of 0.90 means is that, at Year 1, every £100 of uncertain cash flow is valued as being equivalent to £90 of certain cash flow. Therefore the smaller the certainty-equivalent factor, the *more risky* is the uncertain cash flow and the less valuable it is. For example, if the certainty-equivalent factor was 0.70 this implies that investors would be willing to accept £70 for certain for every uncertain £100: the less you are willing to accept for certain, the more risky is your perception of the equivalent uncertain cash flow.

Furthermore, given that these two amounts are seen as equivalents – or equal – their present values should also be the same. Therefore the present value of the certain £90, discounted at the risk-free interest rate, should be the same as the present value of the uncertain £100, discounted at a rate which has been adjusted to reflect the risk involved.

If we let the risk-free interest rate be r_F and the risk-adjusted discount rate be r, then, in our example:

$$\frac{£90}{(1 + r_F)^1} = \frac{£100}{(1 + r)^1}$$

and given that £90 = $a_1 \times$ £100, then:

$$a_1 \times \frac{£100}{(1 + r_F)^1} = \frac{£100}{(1 + r)^1}$$

▶

▶

This can be rearranged to give:

$$a_1 \times \frac{(1 + r_F)^1}{(1 + r)^1}$$

More generally, the certainty-equivalent factor at any time period *t* is:

$$a_1 \times \frac{(1 + r_F)^t}{(1 + r)^t}$$

To see what this implies, let's put in some numbers. Suppose the risk-free interest rate is 5% and you judge that a satisfactory risk-adjusted discount rate is 8% (i.e. there is a 3% risk premium being added to the risk-free rate of return).

The certainty-equivalent factors will be as follows:

Year 1	$(1.05/1.08)^1$	=	0.9722
Year 2	$(1.05/1.08)^2$	=	0.9452
Year 3	$(1.05/1.08)^3$	=	0.9190
	etc.		etc.

As can be seen, over time the certainty-equivalent factor is getting *smaller*. In other words, the implicit assumption is that, over time, a project's cash flows are becoming *more risky* and so, *less valuable*.

SUMMARY

This chapter has looked at some of the approaches used to cope with the problem of risk in capital investment appraisal. None of these can be said really to tackle the issue except in a rather intuitive, rule-of-thumb way. However, it could be argued that their use in practice is better than ignoring the presence of risk completely. The major points made were as follows:

● The ENPV approach examines the *average* outcome of a project. However, because of this it fails to capture what is the essence of risk, by ignoring *variability* of outcome.

● However, the analysis can be useful for examining the value of additional information to a company.

● The abandonment decision analysis can help to evaluate investment appraisal situations where an option is available to abandon the project before it reaches the end of its life.

● The abandonment decision analysis suffers from the difficulty of obtaining reliable abandonment value data and requires a complex mathematical analysis in all but the simplest problems.

● Sensitivity analysis examines the degree to which the various estimates made about a project can change before the decision advice given by NPV is overturned.

- There are two main advantages of sensitivity analysis. The first is that it highlights those estimates to which the decision advice is most sensitive. Management can then go back and take more time and trouble to ensure those particular estimates are as accurate as possible. The second advantage is that it gives the decision-maker more information to use in deciding whether or not to accept the advice of the original NPV analysis.

- There are two disadvantages of sensitivity analysis. The first is the more serious: it only looks at the effect of changing one estimate at a time. It doesn't examine the effects of simultaneous changes in two or more estimates. The second disadvantage is that it gives no indication as to how the decision-maker should evaluate and make use of the sensitivity data.

- The risk-adjusted discount rate approach described in this chapter represents an intuitive attempt to recognize the relationship between risk and return.

- It can be faulted on a number of grounds. First, on the basis of how the risk premiums are derived and the project's risk category is determined. Second, we saw that using a risk-adjusted discount rate makes an assumption about implicit project risk that may not be justified.

NOTES

1. In theory this problem can be overcome by use of the statistical technique of simulation; in practice, however, this does little to enhance or clarify the decision-maker's view of the effects of uncertainty on a project's desirability.
2. These are discussed further in Chapter 10.

FURTHER READING

1. The articles in this general area of the more traditional approaches to handling risk are not particularly rewarding. However, two interesting pieces are: G.J. Grayson, 'The Use of Statistical Techniques in Capital Budgeting', in *Financial Research and Management Decisions,* A.A. Robicheck (ed.), John Wiley 1967, which looks at the use of sensitivity analysis; and A.A. Robicheck and S.C. Myers, 'Conceptual Problems in the Use of the Risk Adjusted Discount Rate', *Journal of Finance,* December 1966.

2. Other articles of interest are: D.B. Hertz, 'Risk Analysis in Capital Investment', *Harvard Business Review,* January–February 1964; J.F. Magee, 'How to Use Decision Trees in Capital Investment', *Harvard Business Review,* September–October 1964; A. Rappaport, 'Sensitivity Analysis in Decision Making', *Accounting Review,* July 1967; and E.F. Brigham, D.F. Shone and S.R. Vinson, 'The Risk Premium Approach to Measuring a Utility's Cost of Equity', *Financial Management,* Spring 1985.

3. On the abandonment decision, see J.E. Jarrett, 'An Abandonment Decision Model', *Engineering Economist,* Autumn 1973.

4. X. Li and Z. Wu, 'Corporate Risk Management and Investment Decisions', *Journal of Risk Finance,* Vol. 10 2009 discusses the significance of downside risk and the concept of 'value at risk'.

5. Finally, on certainty-equivalents, see: A.A. Robicheck and S.C. Myers, 'Conceptual Problems with the Use of Risk-adjusted Discount Rates', *Journal of Finance,* December 1966; and G.A. Sick, 'A Certainty-Equivalent Approach to Capital Budgeting', *Financial Management,* Winter 1986.

QUIZ QUESTIONS

1   A machine costs €1000 and has a life of 3 years. It can either be a success or a failure. If it is successful – and it has a probability of 45% – then it will produce an annual net cash flow of €500. If it is a failure, the annual net cash flow will be only €350. The discount rate is 10%. What is its ENPV?

2   What is the maximum worth of a survey that would tell you, in advance of the decision, whether the machine in question 1 would be a success or failure?

3   What would be the maximum worth of the survey in question 2 if it was only 75% accurate?

4   Given the following information:

State	Probability	NPV $000s
I	0.3	+ 100
II	0.5	+ 50
III	0.2	− 300

What would be the maximum worth of a survey that could tell you, in advance, which state of the world would occur?

5   A machine costs R14 000. It has a 2-year life and a 15% discount rate correctly reflects its risk. Its performance depends upon the state of the world:

State	Year 1	Year 2	Probability
I	+10, 000	+10 000	0.70
II	+ 6 000	+ 6 000	0.10
III	+ 4 000	+ 4 000	0.20

The company can sell the machine at the end of Year 1 for R6000. At the end of Year 2 the machine will be worthless. Advise the company.

6   Given the following information about a project:

Outlay:	£1000
Life:	5 years
Net cash flow:	+£280 per year
Discount rate:	10%

How sensitive is the decision advice to changes in the estimate of the life and the annual net cash flow?

(See the 'Answers to Quiz Questions' section at the back of the book.)

PROBLEMS

The answers to three of the following problems (those indicated by an asterisk) are available to students online. The answer to the remaining problem is available only to lecturers (see the 'Digital Resources' page for details).

▶

1* The directors of Caucasus Oil are based in Tbilisi. The company is considering whether to make an immediate payment of 60 million lari for a licence to drill oil in a particular geographical area in the south of Georgia. Having acquired the licence, the company would commission a seismic survey to determine whether the area is a suitable prospect, i.e. whether there are any geological structures present which could contain oil. If the area is a suitable prospect, exploration wells would be drilled to discover if oil is in fact present. If oil is present, appraisal wells would be drilled to ascertain the size and characteristics of the potential field.

The company's development expert has produced the following data about the licence area, based upon the results from adjoining areas. If oil is discovered by the exploration wells, the appraisal wells will indicate one of the three following types of oilfield:

Type	Probability of occurrence	Millions of barrels	Expected life (years)
I	60%	negligible	0
II	32%	42	4
III	8%	2 250	10

The annual oil production will decline over the life of the field. To approximate the decline, the expert argues that a sensible approach would be to assume that the annual production of the field during the first half of its life is twice the annual production during the second half. For example, for a type II field the first 2-years' annual production rate would be 14 million barrels per annum and the second 2-years' annual production rate would be 7 million barrels per annum.

During the entire life of the field, a barrel of oil is expected to sell for 66 lari. The annual operating cash surplus is expected to be 45% of sales revenue. The combined tax costs for the company are usually 77% of the operating cash surplus and these tax cash flows can be assumed to be payable at the end of each year. Production of oil would start in 1 year's time and the first annual net revenues would arise at the end of the first year of production.

The cost of drilling the appraisal well will be L300 million and drilling the exploration well will cost L30 million. Both costs will be paid in 1 year's time. The seismic survey costs of L6 million will be paid immediately. All three of the costs, together with the cost of the licence to drill oil, will give rise to tax relief equal to 50% of the cost.

It is expected that there will be a 50% chance that the seismic survey will indicate the prospect of oil and a 30% chance that the exploration drilling will find oil. The company's after-tax cost of capital for this type of project is 15% per annum.

Required:

(a) Calculate the ENPV of the venture.

(b) Calculate the maximum price the company should pay for an alternative type of seismic survey that will reduce the probability of indicating a positive prospect from 50% to 30% and so increase from 30% to 50% the chance that the exploration drilling will find oil.

2* Saudi Juffalli is investigating the introduction of a new fruit drink, to be called Quraya. Extensive market research by an outside agency, at a cost of 80 000 riyals, has suggested that a price of 40 riyals per bottle to the retail trade would be acceptable.

Production of Quraya will require specialized purifying and flavouring equipment which, it is estimated, would cost R1.6 million. As with most purifying equipment, this installation is likely to have a long production life but, due to its rather specialized nature, when production of Quraya ceases it will only be able to be sold for scrap for about R16 000 (net of dismantling costs). Variable costs of production are estimated at R24 per bottle and overheads are estimated at R200 000 per year, avoidable only if production ceases.

At the proposed selling price, the beverage trade is expected to demand 50 000 bottles per year, well within the capacity of the production equipment, but after 4 years interest is expected to decline and so production will cease. However, the company believes that it may well be able to extend product life for a further 2 years by either running a small trade advertising campaign at the start of Years 5 and 6 at a cost of R80 000 per year, or alternatively by reducing the price per bottle by R3 in these 2 years. The market research company believes that the two alternatives would achieve similar sales results, but just what these sales would be is uncertain. If the campaign is successful in Year 5 then sales of 35 000 bottles could be expected in that year, with sales of 28 000 or only 9000 bottles being equally likely in Year 6, or alternatively the Year 5 promotion may be relatively unsuccessful with sales of only 7000 bottles in that year and an equal likelihood of either 12 000 or 5000 bottles in the following year. The market research agency believes that the campaign has only a 60% chance of being successful in Year 5.

All expenses and revenues will be paid or received in cash at the end of the year in which they arise, with the exception of the production equipment, for which payment is due at the start of the first year of manufacture and the advertising expenditure which must be paid for at the start of each year in which a campaign is mounted. Saudi Jaffalli normally uses a 10% discount rate for project evaluation purposes.

Required:

(a)   Evaluate the financial feasibility of the proposed new fruit drink in respect of its normal expected life of 4 years, including in your presentation details about the sensitivity of the decision advice to changes in all the estimates made, except the scrap value and discount rate.

(b)   Briefly, advise management on the results of the sensitivity analysis.

(c)   Evaluate which of the two alternative methods (if any) should be used to extend the product life.

3*   Goodbuild is a small housebuilding company operating in Ghana. The company has 201 000 cedi in cash that is surplus to current requirements. The cash will eventually be used to help finance the construction of a small housing development. The housing development depends upon obtaining permission to build the houses from the local government planning department in Accra. It is believed that this permission will be given in 2-years' time.

The GH¢201 000 can be invested in the money market to yield a return of 10% per year.

Alternatively, an opportunity exists for the funds to be invested on a temporary basis in GoGhana, a family-owned car hire business which wishes to expand its car hire fleet by 30 cars costing GH¢6700 each. GoGhana is temporarily short of funds because of recent tax payments. If the funds are invested with GoGhana they will produce an annual net cash inflow to GoodBuild , but the size of this cash flow is now known with certainty, and the cash flow at the end of the second year is dependent upon the cash flow at the end of the first year. Estimates of the net cash inflows to GoodBuild are detailed below.

	End of Year 1		End of Year 2
Probability	Cash inflow (GH¢)	Probability	Cash inflow (GH¢)
0.6	80 000	0.6	80 000
		0.4	90 000
0.4	100 000	0.6	100 000
		0.4	110 000

In addition GoGhana will make a payment to GoodBuild at the end of the first year of GH¢141 000, or at the end of the second year of GH¢81 000. GoodBuild has to choose at the end of the first year whether to receive payment of GH¢141 000 then or GH¢81 000 a year later. If the payment of GH¢141 000 is received by GoodBuild at the end of the first year, then the investment will be terminated and there will be no further cash flows to GoodBuild from GoGhana.

GoodBuild considers 18% per year to be an appropriate discount rate for investments in the car hire business.

Required:

(a) Prepare a report recommending whether GoodBuild should invest in the car hire business or in the money market. All relevant calculations must be included in your report. Ignore taxation. State clearly any assumptions that you make.

(b) Discuss the practical problems of incorporating abandonment opportunities into the capital investment decision-making process. Suggest possible reasons why a company might decide to abandon an investment project part way through its expected economic life.

4   Piraeus Technology is a small technology development partnership located outside Athens. The partners of Piraeus are planning the launch of a new tablet computer, the SQ, using a revolutionary processing system. The market for tablet computers is very competitive and the anticipated product life of the SQ is only 3 years. The marketing partner of Piraeus has produced the following data showing three different estimates of likely demand for the SQ during each year of its life.

Demand predictions	Probability	Year 1 Units	Year 2 Units	Year 3 Units
Most optimistic	0.2	32 000	16 000	12 000
Best guess	0.5	16 000	8 000	6 000
Most pessimistic	0.3	4 000	2 000	1 500

The above estimates assume a constant selling price of €500 over the 3 years. The variable production cost per unit of an SQ is €400.

The partner in charge of production has stated that their small manufacturing facility is in a position to produce 32 000, 16 000 or 4 000 units per annum, but, once decided, the chosen production level could not be increased until the start of the following year. The total cost of setting up the production line would consist of fixed costs of €1 million, and variable costs of €50 for each unit of production capacity. These costs would be paid at the start of the year's production.

A market research firm has offered, for a fee of €300 000, to carry out a detailed survey which would determine precisely the future level of demand for the SQ. The partners of Piraeus Technology wish to know whether the market survey is likely to be worthwhile.

In order to assess whether the survey is worth undertaking the following simplifying assumptions are made:

(i)   cash flows relating both to sales and variable production costs are to be deemed to arise at the end of the year in which they are incurred

(ii) demand can be represented by only one of the three sets of probabilities envisaged by the marketing partner

(iii) the level of the demand in the first year will determine the levels demanded in the second and third years

(iv) the appropriate discount rate for the venture is 10% per annum.

Required:

(a) Determine the initial production capacity that Piraeus Technology should choose, and compute the resulting ENPV of producing and selling at that level.

(b) Calculate whether the market survey should be commissioned, and comment on any reservations you might have relating to the use of expected values as an aid in decision-making.

(c) Discuss the advantages to the company of conducting a market survey of this kind.

10

RISK AND RETURN

LEARNING OBJECTIVES

The purpose of this chapter is to:

- Offer a more detailed development of the concept of risk through the introduction of the 'expected utility model'.
- Examine the key financial management relationship between risk and return.
- Discuss the limitations of the concept of 'expected utility' for practical investment decision-making.

INTRODUCTION TO UNCERTAINTY

Having looked at some of the less theoretically sound approaches that are used in the handling of risk in investment appraisal, we now begin to take a much more analytical and structured approach to the problem.

We will begin by examining how investment appraisal can cope with the fact that the future is largely unknown and that decision-making has to be carried out on the basis of expectations. That is, in an uncertain world, capital investment decisions have to be taken on the basis of *expected* project cash flows, which may or may not turn out to be the same as the cash flows that *actually* arise.

In our analysis of the handling of uncertainty in financial decision-making we shall use the two terms 'risk' and 'uncertainty' interchangeably. As we have already seen, although it is possible to distinguish between the two terms, there is little purpose in doing so for our present needs. Thus when reference is made to a *risky* investment decision, we are concerned with a situation where we are *uncertain* about that investment's actual future outcome.

REAL WORLD VIEW: Are You a Risk Taker?

In February 2013, Monster.com and Millennial Branding released results from a survey conducted worldwide across generations of professionals.

This survey looked into risk taking, and discovered that 40% of Gen X employees (between the ages of 30–49 years) and 43% of Boomers (between the ages of 50–69 years) identified with being high risk. In a significant step lower, Gen Y (those aged 18–29) were much more risk adverse, with only 28% defining themselves as high risk.

Why does the youngest generation seem to be the most risk adverse? Is it to do with age, or (possibly more likely) to do with where people are in their careers? Do you think that you would be more likely to take risks towards the end of your career in business or at the beginning of it?

Taking risks does not necessarily mean that certain employees are more 'business-minded' than others. This survey also found that younger employees were more likely to be interested in 'riskier' small or start-up companies, where they have more freedom to be creative and make decisions.

Employees were also asked whether they defined themselves as having the resources to be an intrapreneur: someone who 'takes direct responsibility for turning an idea into a profitable finished product through assertive risk-taking and innovation'. Respondents replied almost evenly to this question, with 32% of Gen Y, 30% of Gen X and 30% of Boomers all defining themselves as intrapeneurs.

With this in mind, do you think that high risk is reflective of certain generations? Would you take risks?

A simple approach

Our original approach to the problem of investment decision-making in an uncertain world was to assert that investors are averse to uncertainty – in other words they dislike risk. Therefore, in order to be persuaded to take on an investment for which the outcome is uncertain, they have to be offered the expectation of a higher return[1] from the investment as a reward, or as compensation for taking on the risk involved. Further, it followed that the greater the degree of uncertainty surrounding an investment's outcome, the greater would have to be the level of expected return in order to make the investment attractive to investors.

In such a world as outlined above, the perfect capital market would not display just a *single* rate of interest, but a whole range of interest rates, one for each level of risk: the higher the risk, the higher the interest rate. We could therefore adapt the NPV appraisal technique by using as the discount rate for any particular project's appraisal, the perfect capital market discount rate which related to *that particular project's level of risk.*

In such a way the discount rate would still correctly reflect the opportunity cost of undertaking the investment: the investment should only be undertaken if it produces a return that is at least equal to the return that could be obtained on the capital market, *for a similar level of risk.* (The IRR appraisal technique could be similarly adapted. The perfect capital market interest rate appropriate for the project's level of risk would be used at the hurdle/cut-off rate.)

However, this simple analysis – although fundamentally and conceptually correct – does generate two rather problematic questions: how are we to identify the degree of risk associated with a particular investment project and, given that we can measure a project's risk level, how are we then to identify the corresponding perfect capital market interest rate? These two questions will form the basis for much of the following discussion.

A caution

The impact of uncertainty has a fundamental and pervasive impact on the whole of financial decision-making. It is often useful to assume away its existence in order to clarify the basic analysis of investment decision-making; however, if our theory is to have any real-world validity then we must come to grips with the problems it poses.

In Chapter 1 it was pointed out that the theory of financial decision-making is still evolving, and many areas of the theory contain considerable controversy. In fact, there is still much to find out about how financial decisions *should* be made, or indeed, how they *are* made and there are probably more unanswered questions than answered questions.

However, when we look at the research work that is currently being undertaken, we find that a very substantial proportion of it is concerned with the presence of risk in decision-making, because it is our lack of understanding about risk – its nature, measurement and investors' attitudes towards it – that causes the greatest number of problems and unanswered questions. The more traditional approaches to risk are not seen as providing satisfactory solutions and so recent years have seen the development of different approaches such as chaos theory.

Given the situation as outlined above, we must treat our analysis of uncertainty with considerable caution. Generally speaking, it is believed that the analysis we shall develop does move in the right direction – it is relatively sound – but the conclusions reached can only be tentative, and can be expected to alter over time as our understanding improves.

THE EXPECTED UTILITY MODEL

We are concerned with the construction of a theory of financial decision-making by a company's management on behalf of its shareholders. Given the fact that management will have to take decisions about investment proposals the outcomes of which are uncertain, it is important that we should be aware of how the individual shareholders would themselves come to a decision in such circumstances. Therefore we require a model that adequately reflects the risk attitudes of shareholders: how they perceive risk and how they react to its presence. Unlike our theory of financial decisions, which is a normative theory outlining how management *should* make financial decisions, the model of shareholders' risk attitudes needs to be a *positive* model – it should try to reflect their *actual* attitudes, rather than what *should be* their attitudes. Only in this way will we be able to construct a normative theory of managerial financial decision-making based on shareholders' actual desires. To this end we have to make some carefully specified assumptions about shareholders and investors generally.

Investors' behaviour axioms

Stated succinctly, we shall assume that when faced with making risky financial decisions, individual shareholders or investors act rationally and consistently. More specifically, we can formulate four basic axioms[2] regarding the behaviour of investors when making decisions:

1. Investors are able to choose between alternatives by ranking them in some order of merit, i.e. they are capable of actually coming to a decision.

2. Any such ranking of alternatives is 'transitive', i.e. if alternative A is preferred to B and alternative B is preferred to C, then alternative A *must* be preferred to C.

3. Investors do not differentiate between alternatives that have the same degree of risk, i.e. their choice is dispassionate in that it is based solely upon consideration of the risk involved, rather than on the *nature* of alternatives available.

4. Investors are able to specify for any investment whose returns are uncertain, an exactly equivalent alternative which would be equally preferred but which would involve a certain return, i.e. for any gamble, investors are able to specify a certainty-equivalent.[3]

These four axioms of investors' decision-making behaviour can be used to construct an expression or function of utility. This utility function[4] can then be used as the basis of a model of investors' risk attitudes that will enable us to explore the way in which individuals make decisions about risky alternatives, on the assumption that they do so in order to maximize their own expected utility index.

Example 1 goes through the process by which an individual's utility function may be derived. Although this process may appear rather unrealistic, it is perfectly practical as long as the individual's decisions are both consistent and rational, in line with the four axioms stated above.

EXAMPLE 1

Suppose that we tell an individual investor that an investment will be made available to him and that we wish to know the maximum amount he would be willing to pay to be allowed to undertake it. There are just two possible outcomes from this project: one is a gain of $5000 (+$5000) and the other is a loss of $2000 (−$2000).[5]

In order to construct the utility function we need a measure or index of utility. This measure is completely arbitrary, but for convenience we shall assign the utility index number '1' to the +$5000 outcome and '0' to the −$2000 outcome:[6]

Outcome	Utility function index
+$5 000	1
−$2 000	0

Alternatively this could be written as:

$$U(+\$5000) = 1 \qquad U(-\$2000) = 0$$

If the probability of an outcome of +$5000 is p and of –$2000 is $(1 - p)$, then the *expected* utility of the project will be:

$$p \times U(+\$5000) + (1 - p) \times U(-\$2000)$$

As $U(+\$5000) = 1$ and $U(-\$2000) = 0$, then the expected utility of the project reduces to:

$$p \times 1 + (1 - p) \times 0 = p$$

▶

▶

From axiom 4 we assume that for any project with a risky outcome, an investor can specify an equivalent certain alternative: the certainty-equivalent or $(C-E)$. This represents the maximum sum an investor would be willing to pay to undertake the risky project. In this case, the utility of the certainty-equivalent can be specified:

$$U(C-E) = p \times U(+\$5000) + (1 + p) \times U(-\$2000)$$
$$U(C-E) = (p \times 1) + (1 + p) \times 0 = p$$

We are now in a position to construct a utility function for a specific individual investor. However, before doing so, it is important to emphasize that the utility function we shall construct will be *unique* to this particular (hypothetical) investor – we will call him 'Marcel'. Different investors are likely to have different utility functions because they are based on each individual's personal attitude to risk.

The approach that we shall use is to ask Marcel to state the maximum (certain) price he would be willing to pay to be allowed to undertake the investment, for a whole range of different probabilities attached to the two outcomes. For example, if we said that the probability of the investment producing +$5000 is 0.80 and the probability of producing −$2000 is $(1 − 0.80) = 0.20$, then suppose that Marcel states that he would be willing to pay a maximum of (say) $2000. This is the investment's certainty-equivalent, and its utility index can be calculated as:

$$U(C-E) = p \times U(+\$5000) + (1 - p) \times U(-\$2000)$$
$$U(+\$2000) = (0.80 \times 1) + (0.20 \times 0) = 0.80$$

Again we might specify that the probability of the investment producing +$5000 was 0.40, and suppose Marcel now allocates this investment a certainty-equivalent of (say) – $500. In other words, with probabilities of 0.40 and 0.60 attached to the investment's two possible outcomes of +$5000 and −$2000 respectively, Marcel would have to be *paid* $500 to induce him to undertake the project. The utility index of this certainty-equivalent would be:

$$U(-\$500) = (0.40 \times 1) + (0.60 \times 0) = 0.40$$

This procedure could be continued indefinitely, with a variety of different probabilities.

Utility function construction

The process shown in Example 1 could be carried on indefinitely, because there is an unlimited number of different pairs of probabilities (each adding up to 100%) which can be attached to the project's two outcomes. Eventually we shall have gathered sufficient utility indices of certainty-equivalents to enable us to plot Marcel's personal utility index. This is illustrated in Figure 10.1.

The shape of the utility function

The general shape of this utility function is of interest. Let us return to the first pair of probabilities attached to the investment's outcome in Example 1, where there was an 80% chance of an outcome of +$5000 and a 20% chance of an outcome of −$2000.

FIGURE 10.1 Marcel's utility function

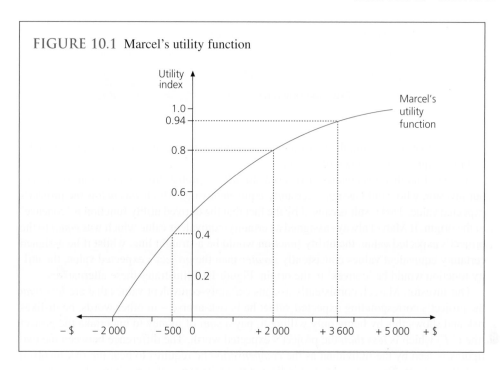

Project outcome	×	Probability		
+$5 000	×	0.80	=	+$4 000
−$2 000	×	0.20	=	−$ 400
Expected outcome			=	+$3 600

The investment's *expected* outcome has a value of +$3600, whereas Marcel assigned it a certainty-equivalent of only +$2000. That is, the expected utility of the project to Marcel is *less than* the utility of the project's expected outcome or value. This can be written using the following notation:

$$E[U(\text{PROJ})] < U[\$(\text{PROJ})]$$

In this particular case, the expected utility of the investment is the utility of the certainty-equivalent value assigned by Marcel of +$2000, and the utility of the investment's expected value is the utility of +$3600. Using the utility function in Figure 10.1 we can read off the following utility index values for these amounts:

$$\left.\begin{array}{l} E[U(+\$2000)] = 0.80 \\ U[E(+\$3600)] = 0.94 \end{array}\right\} 0.80 < 0.94$$

The second pair of probabilities, where our investor, Marcel, assigned a certainty-equivalent of −$500, also has this characteristic:

Project outcome	×	Probability		
+$5 000	×	0.40	=	+$2 000
−$2 000	×	0.60	=	−$1 200
		Expected outcome	=	+$ 800

We see that once again, the investment's expected outcome of +$800 is higher than the certainty-equivalent assigned of –$500.

We will find that this characteristic holds for *all* the probability combinations offered to our investor, who would assign a certainty-equivalent value which was *below* the project's expected value. This result is caused by the fact that the derived utility function is 'concave' to the origin. If Marcel always assigned a certainty-equivalent value which was *equal* to the project's expected value, the utility function would be a straight line, whilst if he assigned certainty-equivalent values consistently *greater* than the project's expected value, the utility function would be 'convex' to the origin. Figure 10.2 illustrates these alternatives.

Our investor, Marcel, consistently assigns certainty-equivalent values that are *less than* the project's corresponding expected value; he is risk-averse – in other words, he dislikes risk and shows this by being only willing to pay a sum of money to undertake the project (the *C-E*) which is *less than* the project's expected worth. The difference between the two figures is seen by the individual as the *compensation* he requires to bear the risk involved with the project. Thus when Marcel indicated that $2000 was the maximum he would pay to undertake a project with an expected value of +$3600, the difference of $1600 is the expected compensation required because of the risk involved.

Similarly, if Marcel assigns certainty-equivalents equal to the project's expected value, he is termed 'risk-neutral' in that he requires no compensation for undertaking a risky project. If the assigned certainty-equivalents are greater than the project's expected value,

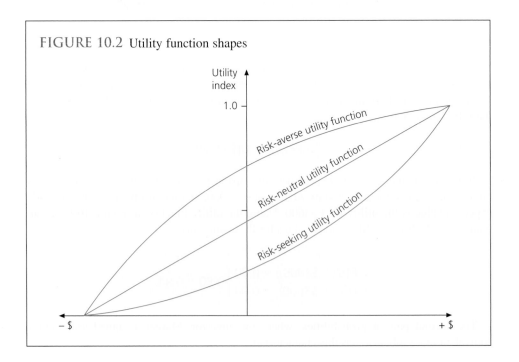

FIGURE 10.2 Utility function shapes

the investor is termed a 'risk-seeker', because he is willing to pay a premium in order to be allowed to bear a risk.

Figure 10.2 illustrates the possible utility functions for the three categories of attitudes to risk. It follows that the greater the aversion or attraction to risk, the more pronounced will be the concavity and convexity respectively of the utility functions, and vice versa.

Individual choice amongst risky investments

Once an individual's utility function has been constructed in this way, it can be used to indicate how he would choose between alternative risky investments, on the assumption that he will attempt to achieve the greatest possible amount of utility, i.e. the individual selects whichever alternative is expected to produce the highest utility index value. This process is illustrated in Example 2.

EXAMPLE 2

Suppose that Marcel, whose utility function is displayed in Figure 10.1, must decide between two alternative investments: A and B. Once again, we shall assume that the returns produced by both investments occur almost immediately after their required outlays, so as to avoid the need for discounting.

The possible net returns from these two investments and their relevant probabilities are set out below, together with the calculation of the utility that Marcel would expect to derive from each:

Investment A Possible net return	×	Probability			Investment B Possible net return	×	Probability		
−$1 000	×	0.3	=	−$ 300	+$ 500	×	0.2	=	+$ 100
+$2 000	×	0.4	=	+$ 800	+$1 500	×	0.6	=	+$ 900
+$5 000	×	0.3	=	+$1 500	+$2 500	×	0.2	=	+$ 500
Expected return:				+$2 000	Expected return:				+$1 500

$$E[U(Inv:A)] = 0.3 \times U(-\$1000) + 0.4 \times U(+\$2000) + 0.3 \times U(+\$5000)$$

$$E[U(Inv:B)] = 0.2 \times U(+\$500) + 0.6 \times U(+\$1500) + 0.2 \times U(+\$2500)$$

Using the utility function in Figure 10.1 to determine the utility index value:[7]

$$E[U(Inv:A)] = (0.3 \times 0.28) + (0.4 \times 0.8) + (0.3 \times 1) = 0.704$$

$$E[U(Inv:B)] = (0.2 \times 0.59) + (0.6 \times 0.74) + (0.2 \times 0.85) = 0.732$$

As $E[U(Inv.B)] > E[U(Inv.A)]$, Marcel will select investment B in order to maximize his utility.

From the above, it can be seen that although investment A has the largest *expected return*, Marcel would actually select investment B because it produces a higher level of *expected utility*: a utility index of 0.732 as opposed to 0.704. In other words, investment B is preferred because our risk-averse investor judges that it possesses a superior risk-expected return combination than does investment A.

The problem with this expected utility model of investment decision-making is that its practical usefulness is virtually zero because of its elaborate procedure. To derive an accurate representation of an individual's utility function is both difficult and time-consuming. In fact, it could be argued that it is virtually impossible to measure it in a real-world way. Deriving the function from answers to questions when real money is not at stake might be very different from the real risk attitude of the individual. In addition, an individual's attitude to risk can be expected to change over time as his or her personal attitudes and circumstances change, thus necessitating a periodic re-estimation of the function.

In addition, in terms of our normative theory of managerial financial decision-making, the model presents another problem. Assuming that a company has several shareholders, the company's management would need to be aware of *each* shareholder's utility function. Even assuming that this was possible, the utility functions of these individuals are likely to be different, and there is no way in which they can sensibly be aggregated to assist managerial decision-making. However, the expected utility model *does* provide a starting point for a more analytical approach to the problem of handling risk. In particular, of greatest interest is the fact that risk-averse investors generally are likely to have 'concave to the origin' utility functions in the forms of a quadratic equation:

$$U(x) = a + bx - cx^2$$

as shown in Figure 10.1.

THE APPROACH TO PORTFOLIO THEORY

Introduction

Accepting the fact that the operational usefulness of the expected utility model is severely limited, we must look elsewhere for a means of measuring an investment's risk. One particularly fruitful approach that can be seen as having its foundations in the expected utility model is that of portfolio theory. This theory was originally developed within the context of a risk-averse individual investor who was concerned with how to combine shareholdings in several different (stock exchange) quoted companies in order to build an investment portfolio that would maximize the amount of expected return, given a specified level of risk. (Such a portfolio is termed 'efficient', and could also be defined as one that minimizes risk for a given level of expected return.)

Initially we outline the main characteristics of portfolio theory within the context of an investor constructing a share portfolio, but later we will turn to examine the implications and validity of the theory for managerial financial decision-making.

However, to start, we need to define two terms: the 'return' and the 'risk' on an investment in the shares of a company.

Return on investment

We shall continue to avoid the problems that can arise through the discounting process by considering the return on a share over just a *single* time period. Therefore the return on an investment in the shares of a company takes on a very simple definition:

$$\text{Return} = \frac{(\text{Selling price}[8] - \text{Purchase price} + \text{Dividends received})}{\text{Purchase price}}$$

Thus the return is simply the amount of the capital gain (or capital loss), in other words the difference between the buying and selling price, plus the dividends received while the share was held, expressed as a proportion of the original purchase price. For example, if a share was bought for 100 cents and was sold for 114 cents and during the time it was held a 3 cent dividend was received, then the return on the share was:

$$\frac{(114\,\text{cents} - 100\,\text{cents}) + 3\,\text{cents}}{100\,\text{cents}} = \frac{14\,\text{cents} + 3\,\text{cents}}{100\,\text{cents}} = \frac{17}{100} = 0.17 \text{ or } 17\% \text{ return}$$

There are two things to note about this example. The first is that although the return is defined as a single-period return, it can be applied to *any* single time period – a week, a month, a year or whatever – because it is determined solely by the period of time between when the share was bought and when it was sold. However, because we are used to dealing with *annual* rates of return, we will assume from now on that the period of time under consideration is that of a year.

The second point to note is that the example tells us a piece of history: what *has been* the return that *was* received on this share. However, we are interested in decision-making and so, although the actual achieved return on an investment is of interest in assessing decision-making performance, we are really concerned with what *will be* the *future return* on an investment.

Expected returns

If we are trying to calculate the *future* return that we should expect from investing in a company's shares, we need to estimate the future selling price and the dividends expected to be received while holding the share. In such an exercise it is unlikely that just a single estimate would be made, but instead a range of estimates, which might be determined by (say) general economic conditions. Example 3 illustrates such a situation for a company called Maribor Roto.

EXAMPLE 3

If the current price of a share of Maribor Roto, a company quoted on the Slovenian stock market, is €5 and the following estimates are made about what will happen over the next 12 months:

Prevailing economic conditions	Estimated selling price	Estimated dividends received
Strong growth	€6.50	40 cents
Slow growth	€5.80	30 cents
No growth	€5.25	5 cents

then we estimate that the return will be 38% (30% capital gain + 8% dividend), if the economy grows strongly, 22% if it exhibits slow growth and only 6% if there is no economic growth. Although this

▶

▶

information is of interest, it is of limited use for decision-making purposes unless we have some idea about *how likely* each possible set of economic conditions is, and hence how likely is each possible investment outcome. In other words, we need to apply some (subjective) probabilities to each outcome in order to produce a probability distribution of possible returns.

Suppose the following probability estimates are made:

Economic conditions	Probability	Return on investment
Strong growth	0.30	38%
Slow growth	0.40	22%
No growth	0.30	6%

This is obviously a very crude representation of a probability distribution as it only allows for three possible returns on the investment (38% , 21% and 6%) and ignores the possibility of some intermediate return such as 18%. However such a degree of simplification is acceptable for our present purposes.

The probability distribution illustrated in Example 3 is *symmetrical* in its range of possible returns and if constructed with greater complexity could be represented graphically as in Figure 10.3.

The returns are symmetric, in that they are evenly or regularly distributed around the most likely outcome. Such a distribution is termed a 'Normal' probability distribution and it can be fully described in terms of just two attributes: a measure of *central tendency* of the returns and a measure of the *dispersion* of the returns around the central tendency.

If the returns are not distributed symmetrically around the central tendency, as for example in Figure 10.4, then the distribution is said to be *asymmetrical* or *skewed* and so a third attribute is required: a *measure of skew*. For the moment, we shall assume that the returns on the investment are *symmetrically* distributed, but we shall return to the point at a later stage.

The measure of central tendency of returns we shall use is the *arithmetic mean* return (usually referred to as the **expected** return[9]) and the measure of dispersion, the *variance* (or the square root of the variance, the **standard deviation**).

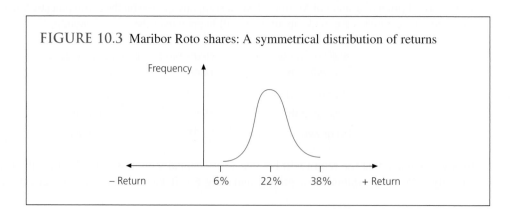

FIGURE 10.3 Maribor Roto shares: A symmetrical distribution of returns

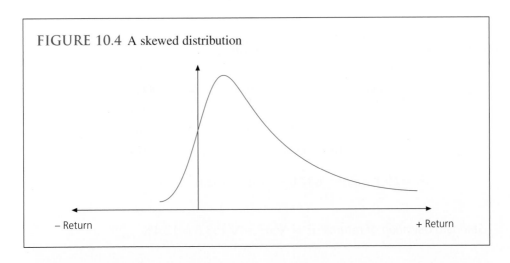

FIGURE 10.4 A skewed distribution

− Return

+ Return

The expected return, variance and standard deviation of returns are calculated in Example 4, using the data from Example 3.

EXAMPLE 4

The expected return is given by:

$$E(r) = \sum r_i \rho_i$$

The variance is given by:

$$\sigma^2 = E(r^2) - E(r)^2$$

$$= \sum r^2 \rho_i - \left(\sum r_i \rho_i \right)^2$$

The standard deviation is given by:

$$\sigma = \sqrt{\sigma^2}$$

For the example of Maribor Roto shares, these values can be calculated as follows:

Expected return:

Return		Probability	
r_i		ρ_i	
38%	×	0.30	= 11.4%
22%	×	0.40	= 8.8%
6%	×	0.30	= 1.8%
$E(r) = \sum r_i \rho_i$			= 22.0%

▶

Variance of returns:	(Return)²		Probability		
	r_i^2		ρ_i		$r_i^2\rho_i$
	1 444	×	0.30	=	433.2
	484	×	0.40	=	193.6
	36	×	0.30	=	10.8
	$E(r^2) = Er_i^2\rho_i$			=	637.6

$$\sigma^2 = E(r^2) - E(r)^2 = 637.6 - 22.0^2 = 153.6$$

Standard deviation of returns: $\sigma = \sqrt{\sigma^2} = \sqrt{153.6} = 12.4\%$

Summary:[10]

$$E(r) = \text{Expected return} = 22\%$$
$$\sigma^2 = \text{Variance} = 153.6$$
$$\sigma = \text{Standard deviation} = 12.4\%$$

Risk

In Example 4, the investment under consideration is 'expected' to produce a return of 22%. That is, 22% represents the average or arithmetic mean return, but the *actual* return may turn out to be considerably better (up to 38%) or considerably worse (down to 6%) than the 22% expected. Thus the investment is *risky*: it involves some uncertainty, meaning that it is possible for the actual return to be somewhat different from what is expected. We really require a method by which the risk of the investment can be *measured* or quantified, to be able to answer: how risky is the investment?

If risk is defined as being concerned with the probability that the actual outcome may be something other than expected, then one way of obtaining a measure of risk would be to use the *range* of possible outcomes. Thus, in the example used above, the possible return ranged from 6% to 38%, and this 32% difference could be used as a measure of the risk involved. However, such a measure is rather crude and simplistic, as Example 5 shows.

EXAMPLE 5

Suppose a choice has to be made between two alternative investments, A and B, whose probability distribution of return is given below:

R_A	Probability	R_B	Probability
20%	0.30	20%	0.20
8%	0.40	8%	0.60
−4%	0.30	−4%	0.20

Both investments have the same expected return of 8% and both have the same range of outcomes of 24%, but are they equally risky? Having defined risk as being concerned with the fact that the actual outcome may differ from the expected outcome, it would – quite correctly – appear that, in reality, they are *not* of equal risk and that investment A was the *more risky* of the two alternatives as the extreme outcomes of A (20% and –4%) have a *greater chance* of occurring than the extreme outcomes of B. Conversely, the expected outcome of B has a greater probability of occurrence (60%) than with A (40%).

What we are looking for in a measure of risk is not the simple range of outcome, but how this range is *dispersed* (or distributed) around the expected outcome. Both the variance and the standard deviation provide acceptable measures of this dispersion, with the **standard deviation** being especially useful as it provides a measure in the same units as the expected return.[11]

Thus we can conclude that the risk of an investment can be measured by the variance or standard deviation of possible returns around the expected return: the greater the dispersion, the greater the risk and the greater the variance or standard deviation and vice versa; and where there is no dispersion of possible returns, then the expected return is a *certain* return, there is no risk and both variance and standard deviation give a measure of zero.

Therefore, returning to the data used in Example 4, the return expected from the investment in the shares of Maribor Roto is 22% and its risk can be measured by the standard deviation of 12.4% (or by the variance of 153.6). In Example 5, which considered two investments, A and B, we concluded that A intuitively appeared to be more risky than B. The standard deviation of returns for A is 9.3% and for B is 7.6%, which confirms A as the more risky investment as it has the larger standard deviation.

Further, if we continue to assume that the possible returns on an investment are symmetrically distributed around the expected return, then measuring the risk of an investment by means of its standard deviation can be converted into an intuitively more meaningful measure by using the properties of the area under the normal curve.[12]

For example, if an investment has an expected return of 10% and a standard deviation of returns of 7%, then it can be said that:

1. There is a 65% chance (approximately) that the *actual* return will lie somewhere between 17% and 3% (i.e. 10% ± 7%).

2. There is a 95% chance (approximately) that the *actual* return will be somewhere between 24% and −4% (i.e. 10% ± (2 × 7%)).

Therefore, the greater the standard deviation, the greater the dispersion of *possible* returns around what is the *expected* return.

Downside risk

One factor in the above discussion that may strike the reader as rather strange is that investment risk is defined as both the probability of the investment doing worse than expected *and* the probability of it doing better than expected. This does not seem to fit in precisely with our initial assertion that investors are risk-averse – that they dislike risk and require a reward or compensation for taking it on. This would tend to suggest that risk is really concerned with the chance that the investment's outcome will be *worse* than expected. In one sense, this is quite correct. A risk-averse investor *is* concerned with the chance of the investment performing below expectation, often referred to as the '*downside risk*' of the

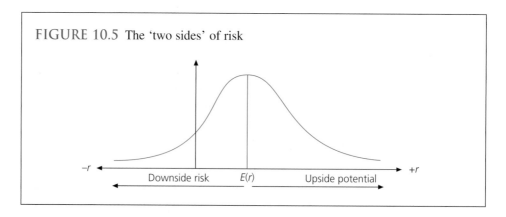

FIGURE 10.5 The 'two sides' of risk

investment. However, part of the reward for holding this risk is the chance that the invest-ment's performance might *exceed* expectation: the '*upside potential*' of the investment; therefore *both* elements are of interest to the investor and are illustrated in Figure 10.5.

The distinction between these two elements of investment performance variability is important if the distribution of returns is *asymmetrical*. With a symmetrical distribution, the expected return divides the probability distribution into two identical halves. Thus standard deviation (or variance) measures both upside potential and downside risk equally well.

Where the distribution is skewed, the standard deviation measure describes neither type of investment risk adequately, but produces a measure of dispersion which is an unhelpful average of the two risk types.

Example 6 illustrates the problem caused by asymmetric distributions.

EXAMPLE 6

Nederlandse Software NV is evaluating a pair of mutually exclusive investment opportunities and is inter-ested in identifying which investment has the best risk and return combination. The two investments are code-named AJAX and BANCO and their forecasted returns, together with the estimated probabilities, are shown below.

	AJAX		BANCO	
R_{AJAX}	Probability	R_{BANCO}	Probability
−10%	0.10	10%	0.60
10%	0.10	20%	0.10
20%	0.40	30%	0.20
30%	0.30	60%	0.10
40%	0.10		

When the expected returns and standard deviation of returns are calculated for these two investments, we find:

Project	Expected return	Standard deviation
AJAX	21%	13%
BANCO	17%	15.8%

On this basis it would appear that the AJAX project is best as it has both a higher expected return (21% > 17%), and a lower standard deviation (13% < 15.8%), than the BANCO project.

However, if we look at the situation more closely, the decision is not so straightforward. Project AJAX certainly does have a higher expected return and lower standard deviation than BANCO, but, on the other hand, AJAX has a 10% chance of producing a **negative** return (of 10%), while the BANCO project *always* produces **positive** returns. In addition, the AJAX project's maximum possible return is only 40%, while the BANCO project can produce a return of up to 60%. Therefore, it is not really possible to say which alternative investment is the correct choice in terms of risk and return because the skewedness of the distribution of investment returns makes the standard deviation (and the variance) an inadequate measure of investment risk.

One possible solution to this problem would be to use a specific measure of the dispersion of each risk type. This can be provided by a statistic called the 'semi-variance', which measures the dispersion of each half of the distribution individually. However, use of the semi-variance tends to complicate several of the calculations involved, and therefore for the sake of convenience – if nothing else – we will assume symmetrically distributed returns and so continue to make use of the standard deviation and variance.

Risk and expected utility

The above analysis contained what could be called a casual justification for measuring investment risk by the standard deviation or variance of returns. However, it is possible to give a more analytical justification for these risk measures.

Our analysis of the expected utility model allowed us to conclude that risk-averse investors would be expected to have a utility function of the general form:

$$U(x) = a + bx - cx^2$$

and, therefore, in terms of the utility an investor could expect to obtain from the return on an investment in the shares of a company, we can express the utility function as:

$$E[U(r)] = a + bE(r) - cE(r^2)$$

In other words, the expected utility of the investment is determined by the distribution of the possible returns (which produce values for $E(r)$ and $E(r^2)$) and by the investor's personal attitude towards risk (which determines the values for the constants a, b, c[13]). Given the definition for variance that we have used:

$$\sigma^2 = E(r^2) - E(r)^2$$

then the third term of our general utility function can be re-expressed as:

$$-cE(r^2) = -c[\sigma^2 + E(r)^2]$$

and multiplying this out, the general utility function can be re-expressed as:

$$E[U(r)] = a + bE(r) - c\sigma^2 + cE(r)^2$$

The advantage of undertaking this bit of algebraic manipulation is that we can now see that the expected utility produced by an investment's return is determined by the three risk-attitude constants *(a, b, c)*, and two of the characteristics of the probability distribution of the investment's return: the expected return [$E(r)$ and $E(r)^2$] and the variance of returns (σ^2).

We know that if an investment's return is *certain*, then the variance has a value of *zero*, whereas if the investment's actual return is *uncertain*, the variance will have a *positive* value. However, because the constant attached to the measure of variance (*c*) in the utility function is negative for the risk-averse investor (it is this that causes the utility function to be concave to the origin), a *positive* variance results in a *reduction* in the value of the utility expected from the investment.

Thus the more *uncertain* the actual return on the investment, the greater will be the value of the variance and the *less* will be the utility expected from the investment by the investor.

This is exactly what we would expect for a risk-averse investor: the more risky the investment, the less attractive is the investment, and hence the lower is the utility it is expected to provide.

Required assumptions

This analysis provides us with a much more carefully reasoned justification for using variance or standard deviation as a measure of investment risk. However, at least one of two alternative conditions must hold true for this analysis to be seen to have real-world validity.

The first is that the variance is acceptable as a measure of risk so long as the probability distribution of possible returns is symmetrical. If it is *strongly* asymmetrical then we know that the arithmetic mean and variance no longer provide a complete description, as a measure of skew would also be required. Furthermore, neither the standard deviation nor variance would then provide an adequate measure of downside risk.

Alternatively, the conclusion only holds if investors' utility functions do follow the quadratic form that was developed earlier and are therefore solely determined by the expected return and variance of return variables. If investor utility functions have a more complex form than that of a simple quadratic (and assuming returns are asymmetrically distributed), it follows that any measure of risk is also likely to be more complex.

The practical validity of these two alternative assumptions is troublesome. For example, there is evidence to suggest that investors' utility curves may exhibit both convexity and concavity – i.e. they may be risk-seekers or risk-averse, depending upon the size of the investment under consideration. They might also be prepared to take greater risks if they feel that it is the only way to achieve targets. However, perhaps the question of skew in investment returns poses the greater problems.

Intuition tells us that investment returns *must* be skewed: the maximum downside risk on an investment in a 'limited liability' company is –100%, but the upside potential return can quite easily exceed that percentage. Further, there is some evidence to suggest that investors *are* interested in skew and do recognize that skewed returns can exist.

However, we shall continue our analysis on the assumption that variance (or standard deviation) of return is an adequate measure of risk, based on the reasoning that even if returns are skewed, the amount of skew is likely to be relatively small, and so will not be too much at odds with the assumption of symmetry.

Limitation of the analysis

Our analysis up to this point remains extremely limited as far as investment decision-making is concerned. Assuming an investor is interested in maximizing expected utility and is risk-averse, then if a choice has to be made between two investments with identical expected returns, we can state that the alternative with the smaller amount of risk (either standard deviation or variance) will be preferred. Alternatively, given a choice between two investments with an identical amount of risk, the investor will prefer whichever has the highest expected return. Thus A is preferred to B and C is preferred to D:

$$\text{Choice 1:} \begin{cases} E(r_A) = E(r_B) \\ \sigma_A < \sigma_B \end{cases}$$

$$\text{Choice 2:} \begin{cases} E(r_C) = E(r_D) \\ \sigma_C < \sigma_D \end{cases}$$

However, the decision here is extremely limited. Certainly, we can conclude that A should be preferred to B, but we cannot say whether or not the investor will actually choose to *invest* in A, i.e. we cannot tell whether A gives a sufficiently large expected return to provide adequate compensation for the risk involved.

Furthermore, once we move away from this rather special choice situation, we cannot even make a preference statement: we cannot reach any conclusion as to which of the following pair of alternatives would be preferred:

$$\text{Choice 3:} \begin{cases} E(r_E) > E(r_F) \\ \sigma_E > \sigma_F \end{cases}$$

For a possible solution to these decision problems, we now have to look at **Portfolio Theory**. In addition, thinking back to the two questions that were posed at the start of this chapter: 'How are we to identify the degree of risk associated with a particular capital investment project?', and 'How can we identify the corresponding capital market interest rate that is appropriate for that level of risk?', it would appear that the analysis outlined above goes some way to providing an answer to the former, but not to the latter. We shall not comment further on these two questions at this stage, but wait until our understanding of the risk and expected return relationship has been further developed.

SUMMARY

This chapter has taken a closer look at the relationship between risk and return in investment decision-making. In particular, it considers how the risk and expected return of an investment might be measured. The main points covered are as follows:

- Four axioms of investor behaviour are specified:
  - (a) choice is possible
  - (b) choice is transitive
  - (c) choice is dispassionate
  - (d) certainty-equivalents can be specified for any gamble situation.

- Given these axioms, it is possible to construct a utility function for a risk-averse investor, of the general form: $U(x) = a + bx - cx^2$, where the constants a, b and c reflect the investor's own personal risk attitude.

- With such a utility function, when faced with an investment the following relationship holds: the expected utility of the investment will be less than the utility of the investment's expected outcome. The difference is the required reward for risk-taking.

- As far as stock exchange investment is concerned, the expected return on a share can be measured as its arithmetic mean return and the risk of the share can be measured either as its variance or – more conveniently – its standard deviation of returns.

- However, standard deviation (or variance), whilst fitting in with the utility function concept of risk, is only a satisfactory measure of risk if either investment returns are symmetrically distributed around the expected return, or if investors' utility functions actually follow the quadratic form specified;

$$E[U(r)] = a + bE(r) - cr^2 + cE(r)^2$$

- Finally, the analysis developed so far is highly limited. It can allow a choice to be made either between projects of equal risk, or between projects of equal expected return. It does not allow a choice between projects where there is neither equal risk nor equal expected return (unless of course one alternative enjoys both a higher return and lower risk). Nor does it allow decision-making on any investment's *absolute* desirability (i.e. accept or reject), but just on *relative* desirability (when compared with another project).

NOTES

1. 'Higher', that is, than what they would have received if the investment's outcome was known for certain. They would get a higher return as a reward for taking on the risk involved.
2. An axiom can be defined as a statement that is generally accepted without any need for proof or verification.

3. We have come across the idea of certainty-equivalents in the previous chapter. For example, suppose an investor is offered an investment that has a 60% chance of producing €5000 and a 40% chance of producing only €1000. We are assuming that the investor will be able to specify a certain sum of money which would be equally acceptable to this uncertain investment. This sum might be €3000. Thus €3000 is said to be the certainty-equivalent of the uncertain investment: the investor would be indifferent between receiving €3000 *for certain*, or receiving €5000 with a 60% probability and €1000 with a 40% probability.

4. We have already come across the idea of utility or indifference curves in the development and use of the single-period investment–consumption model.

5. We will assume that the investment's outcome will occur almost immediately and so avoid – at this stage – the need to consider discounting.

6. Quite literally any utility index numbers could be used; for instance we could give +$5000 an index of 75 and −$2000 an index of 36 if we wished. The advantage of assigning index numbers of 1 and 0 to these two outcome extremes is simply that it eases the arithmetic.

7. Figure 10.1 is not sufficiently detailed for the reader to obtain these values. However, they were obtained from the utility index as shown.

8. To calculate the return on a share, you do not need to have actually *sold* the share. You may continue to hold the share and simply wish to know what return you *could have* made to date. In such circumstances the 'selling price' would be replaced by the 'current market price'.

9. Note that the word 'expected' is now being used in a technical sense, meaning the arithmetic mean.

10. Notice that the standard deviation can be expressed as a percentage, just as can the expected return. However the variance involves a 'squaring-up' of the data and so cannot be viewed as a percentage, but simply as an uncategorized measure of dispersion.

11. The standard deviation is stated in rates of return whilst the variance represents 'rates of return squared'. Because it is easier to discuss risk as a *percentage rate of return*, rather than a *rate of return squared*, the standard deviation is now commonly used to measure risk. However, it is sometimes mathematically more convenient to measure risk by variance. Either definition of risk is conceptually valid, since they are mathematically equivalent. The two measures cannot be used interchangeably, but they do give consistent rankings of risk.

12. Any introductory textbook on inferential statistics will discuss these properties in detail, but see the Appendix to Chapter 13.

13. The *c* constant is negative to ensure that the utility function is that of a risk-averse individual and hence concave to the origin.

FURTHER READING

1. Utility theory is not a simple area, but for an easy introduction see: R.O. Swalm, 'Utility Theory – Insights into Risk Taking', *Harvard Business Review,* November–December 1966.

2. For an example of an actual attempt to construct utility functions, see: C.J. Grayson, 'The Use of Statistical Techniques in Capital Budgeting', in *Financial Research and Management Decisions,* A. Robicheck (ed.), John Wiley 1967.

3. Finally, for a more complete discussion on utility functions, see Chapter 11 of J.C. Francis and S.H. Archer, *Portfolio Analysis,* 3rd ed., Prentice-Hall 1986.

QUIZ QUESTIONS

1   If the NPV discount rate should reflect the return available elsewhere in the capital market for an investment of similar risk to the project being appraised, what two practical problems arise?

2   What is meant by the term 'transitive' with regards to ranking alternatives?

3   What is a certainty-equivalent?

4   If an investment has two outcomes: +€10 000 and −€5000 and an investor indicates that €3500 is the certainty-equivalent of a 60% chance of a +€10 000 outcome, what is the utility measure of €3500 on a 0 to 1 scale?

5   If a utility function is concave to the origin, what risk attitude does this indicate?

6   What would the utility function of a risk-neutral investor look like?

7   For a risk-averse investor what is the relationship between an investment's expected outcome and its certainty-equivalent?

8   Define the return on a share.

9   Given the following information, what is the expected return and risk of an investment in the following shares?

Economic conditions	Probability	Investment return
Strong growth	0.20	+40%
Weak growth	0.60	+15%
Economic decline	0.20	−10%

10   What is downside risk?

11   Why is it a potential problem in terms of choice if returns are not distributed symmetrically about the mean?
(See the 'Answers to Quiz Questions' section at the back of the book.)

PROBLEMS

The answer to this problem is available to students online.

1*   An investor carefully considers a number of gambles and decides that he is indifferent between a certain income of R2500 p.a. and each of the following probabilities:

(i)   A 60% chance of receiving R4500 p.a. and a 40% chance of receiving R500 p.a.

(ii) A 75% chance of receiving R1600 p.a. and a 25% chance of receiving R4500 p.a.

(iii) A 55% chance of receiving R1600 p.a. and a 45% chance of receiving R3500 p.a.

(iv) A 75% chance of receiving R2000 p.a. and a 25% chance of receiving R3500 p.a.

(v)   A 50% chance of receiving R2000 p.a. and a 50% chance of receiving R3000 p.a.

(vi) An 85% chance of receiving R2000 p.a. and a 15% chance of receiving R4000 p.a.

The investor has an occupation which gives him an income of R1000 p.a. which he regards as certain. He is now considering which of the two alternative additional activities he should undertake:

(1)   Offers a 50% chance each of an annual income of R1500 and of R2000.

(2)   Offers a 50% chance each of an annual income of R1000 and of R2500.

▶

Required:

(a)   Sketch a utility function for the investor. What does this function indicate about his attitude towards risk?

(b)   Use utility analysis to indicate which new opportunity he should accept.

(c)   Calculate the variance of each possible income stream available to the investor.

(d)   Comment briefly on the implications for the usefulness of variance calculations in analyzing decisions subject to uncertainty.

PORTFOLIO THEORY

LEARNING OBJECTIVES

The purpose of this chapter is to:

- Introduce 'portfolio theory' and the risk-reduction effect of diversification.
- Introduce the concept of a risk-free investment.
- Develop the concepts of the 'market portfolio' and the 'market price of risk'.
- Demonstrate how these concepts combine to enable investment decisions to be taken without reference to the indifferences curve set of any particular investor.

The 19th-century Scottish/American millionaire philanthropist, Andrew Carnegie, is reported to have said: 'The way to make a fortune is to put all your eggs into one basket and then watch the basket very carefully.' In fact, as we shall see, this is a high-risk strategy. Choosing the right basket might indeed lead to the making of a fortune but choosing the wrong basket could turn out to be the way to lose one! As we will demonstrate, a more logical approach to investment is to diversify and thus spread our risk.

TWO-ASSET PORTFOLIOS

Portfolio theory – as its name implies – is concerned with the construction of *investment portfolios* – a combination of several investments. Essentially it is based on the application of fairly simple mathematics that shows that if we know the means and variances of multiple, individual probability distributions, together with the degree to which their returns *covary*, then the mean and variance of the *combined* probability distribution can be specified.

Thus, if the shares of several different companies are combined into an investment portfolio and the expected returns, variances of returns and *covariances of returns* are known for each company's shares, then the expected return and variance of the investment portfolio can be determined.

However, the importance of portfolio theory does not lie so much in this statistical result, but in what arises out of it. Although the expected return of the investment portfolio is simply a weighted average of the expected returns on the individual investments that go to make up the portfolio, the *risk* of the portfolio (measured by its standard deviation of returns) is *less than* the weighted average risk of the individual constituent investments.[1] In other words, the statistical result upon which portfolio theory is founded supports the wisdom of the old proverb of **not** keeping 'all your (investment) eggs in one basket'. Risk can be reduced through diversification without an associated reduction in returns.

Risk and expected return

Suppose that an individual investor – let's call her Shada – has a sum of money with which she wishes to construct an investment portfolio by buying the shares of different companies. In order to keep the arithmetic simple, we shall initially assume that Shada is going to purchase the shares of just two companies – therefore she is constructing what can be termed a '*two-asset risky portfolio*'. Later on we will see how the approach used can be directly expanded to involve portfolios that consist of shareholdings in many companies.

Shada's investment portfolio consists of holding shares in Agrip Corporation – AC – and Baja Holdings – BH. Shada uses a proportion of her investment funds – x – to buy shares in company AC, and the remainder of her money – $(1 - x)$ – is used to buy shares in company BH. The statistical result, that is the foundation of portfolio theory, allows us to determine the expected return, $E(r_{port})$, and variance of return, σ_{port}, of the resulting investment portfolio:

$$E(r_{port}) = xE(r_{AC}) + (1 - x)E(r_{BH})$$
$$\sigma^2_{port} = x^2\sigma^2_{AC} + (1 - x)^2\sigma^2_{BH} + 2x(1 - x)\text{Cov}(r_{AC,}r_{BH})$$

For the moment it will be more convenient for us to deal with portfolio risk in terms of the *standard deviation* of returns, σ, and so the second expression becomes:

$$\sigma_{port} = \sqrt{[\,x^2\sigma^2_{AC} + (1 - x)^2\sigma^2_{BH} + 2x(1 - x)\text{Cov}(r_{AC,}r_{BH})]}$$

The covariance

We are familiar with all the notation used in these expressions, except for $\text{Cov}(r_{AC,}r_{BH})$. This notation represents the measure of the *covariance* between the returns on the shares in Agrip Corporation and in Baja Holdings. In other words, the covariance examines the degree to which the returns on the shares of both companies vary in relation to each other.

This covariance can either be positive or negative and can also be weaker or stronger. *Positive* covariability indicates that the returns on the two shares will tend to move in the *same* direction as each other (i.e. if, in a particular period, the return produced by the shares in Agrip is above what was expected, then there will be a tendency to find that the return on the shares in Baja is similarly above expectations – and *vice versa*), whereas *negative* covariability indicates that the returns will tend to move in opposite directions.

In addition, the greater the strength of covariability (say, positive covariability) then the stronger will be the tendency for the variability in returns between the two companies to move in the same direction.. It helps to explain the meaning of the covariance if its components are examined. We can express the covariability of returns (Cov), as follows:

$$Cov(r_{AC}, r_{BH}) = \sigma_{AC} \times \sigma_{BH} \times \rho_{AC,BH}$$

In other words, the covariance of returns in Agrip and Baja represents the product of the risks of the shares in the two companies (measured by the standard deviation of returns), and the *'correlation coefficient'* – $\rho_{AC,BH}$ – between the returns in Agrip and in Baja.[2]

The correlation coefficient expresses the strength of the linear relationship between the two variables – in this case the returns of the shares of Agrip and Baja – and can take on any value between +1 and −1. A correlation coefficient of +1 indicates *perfect positive* correlation, such that the returns of the two shares will move in perfect lock-step (i.e. a 10% rise in the return from one company will be precisely matched by a 10% rise in the return from the other company); whereas a correlation coefficient of −1 indicates *perfect negative* correlation. In this case the returns on the two shares will move in perfect *negative* lock-step (i.e. a 10% *rise* in the return from one company will be precisely matched with a 10% *fall* in the return from the other company). A positive correlation coefficient, but one which is less than +1, indicates that there is a tendency for the returns on the two shares to move together in the *same* direction; and a negative correlation coefficient, one which is less than 0 but greater than −1, indicates that there is a tendency for the returns to move in *opposite* directions. Given the relationship above, the sign attached to the correlation coefficient determines the sign of the covariance.

The further away the correlation coefficient is from +1 or −1 (and hence the closer it is to zero) the weaker is the general tendency indicated by the sign of the correlation – or the greater is the tendency for movements in returns to be unrelated, or 'uncorrelated'. A correlation coefficient of 0 indicates that there is *no* relationship between the two shares in terms of the variability of their returns.

In practice, almost all shares are positively correlated with each other (but **not** *perfect* positive correlation).

The covariance calculation

This may be a good stage at which to provide a simple example of the calculations required to determine the covariance, as illustrated in Example 1.

EXAMPLE 1

Suppose the shares of two companies, Cordella and Dwyka, have the following probability distributions:

State of economy	Probability	Returns on Cordella	Returns on Dwyka
Strong growth	0.2	24%	5%
Slow growth	0.6	12%	30%
No growth	0.2	0%	−5%

Then their expected returns and standard deviation of returns can be calculated as:

$$E(r_C) = 12\% \qquad E(r_D) = 18\%$$
$$\sigma_C = 7.59\% \qquad \sigma_D = 15.03\%$$

▶

and the covariance of returns is given by:

$$\Sigma[r_C - E(r_C)] \times [r_D - E(r_D)] \times \text{Probability}$$

That is:

$$
\begin{array}{rcr}
(24\% - 12\%) \times (5\% - 18\%) \times 0.2 & = & -31.2 \\
(12\% - 12\%) \times (30\% - 18\%) \times 0.6 & = & 0 \\
(0\% - 12\%) \times (-5\% - 18\%) \times 0.2 & = & +55.2 \\
\text{Cov}(r_C, r_D) & = & +24.0
\end{array}
$$

Given that $\text{Cov}(r_C, r_D) = \sigma_C \times \sigma_D \times \rho_{C,D}$ then:

$$\rho_{C,D} = \frac{\text{Cov}\left(r_C r_D\right)}{\sigma_C \sigma_D} = \frac{+24}{7.59 \times 15.03} = +0.21$$

This is a relatively low, positive correlation. It indicates that although the returns on the shares in the two companies *tend* to vary in the *same* direction, the tendency is rather weak.

Given the above information, if Shada were to construct a two-asset portfolio consisting of shares in Cordella and Dwyka, such that 75% of her funds were placed in the shares of Cordella (i.e. $x = 0.75$), and the remainder of her funds placed in Dwyka (i.e. $(1 - x) = 0.25$), then the resulting portfolio would have an expected return $(E(r_{port}))$ and risk (σ_{port}) as follows:

$$E(r_{port}) = (0.75 \times 12\%) + (0.25 \times 18\%) = 13.5\%$$

$$\sigma_{port} = \sqrt{[(0.75^2 \times 7{:}59\%^2) + (0.25^2 \times 15.03\%^2) + (2 \times 0.75 \times 0.25 \times 24.0)}$$

$$\sigma_{port} = \sqrt{(32.40 + 14.12 + 9.0)} = \sqrt{55.52} = 7.45\%$$

The risk-reduction effect

Returning to the expression for the risk and expected return of a two-asset portfolio, but now expanding the covariance term in the risk expression, we can examine the *cause* of the *risk-reduction effect* of investment diversification:

$$E(r_p) = x.E(r_A) + (1 - x)E(r_B)$$

$$\sigma_p = \sqrt{[x^2\sigma^2_A + (1 - x)^2\sigma^2_B + 2x(1 - x)\, \sigma_A\sigma_B\rho_{AB}]}$$

The first of these two expressions does not give cause for much excitement. It simply shows that the portfolio's expected return is an *average* of the expected returns on the two component investments $(E(r_A)$ and $E(r_B))$, weighted by their respective importance (by value) in the overall portfolio. This is just as we would have thought; however, the second expression is of considerably greater interest. This interest is caused by the last element in the expression – the correlation coefficient of returns which can take on any value between $+1$ and -1 (including zero).

The third term in the expression for portfolio risk: $2x(1 - x)\, \sigma_A\sigma_B\rho_{AB}$ is at its largest value when the correlation coefficient is $+1$. The further away the correlation coefficient is from $+1$, the smaller is the value of this third term and hence the smaller is its contribution to the portfolio's risk. (In fact when the correlation coefficient becomes negative, the term actually makes a *negative* contribution to portfolio risk, which reaches a maximum when the returns are perfectly negatively correlated, i.e. -1.)

It is this third term (and in particular the correlation coefficient that it contains) that is the cause of the risk-reduction effect of investment diversification. Measuring portfolio risk as the standard deviation of returns, we can say that the portfolio risk is a weighted average of the risk of the component investments (just as with the expected return), **but only** if the returns on the shares in the two companies are *perfectly positively* correlated (i.e. $\rho_{AB} = +1$). If the correlation coefficient is less than $+1$ (as will normally be the case) then the risk of the portfolio is *less than* a weighted average of the risk of the individual investment components. The further away the correlation coefficient is from $+1$, the greater will be the risk reduction effect.

Example 2 will help to clarify matters at this point.

EXAMPLE 2

An investor – Jan Meerling – wishes to construct a portfolio that consists of placing 60% of his available funds into the shares of Slotten Construction (SC) and the other 40% into the shares of Heerlen Logistics (HL). The two companies have the following expected returns and risk:

$$E(r_{SC}) \quad = \quad 30\% \quad E(r_{HL}) \quad = \quad 10\%$$
$$\sigma_{SC} \quad = \quad 12\% \quad \sigma_{HL} \quad = \quad 3\%$$

The expected return on Jan Meerling's portfolio will be a weighted average of the expected returns on the portfolio's two investments:

$$E(r_{port}) = (0.60 \times 30\%) + (0.40 \times 10\%) = 22\%$$

But what of the portfolio's *risk?* That will depend upon the correlation coefficient between the returns on the shares of the two companies. If the correlation coefficient is: $+1$ then there will be no risk-reduction effect and the portfolio's risk:

$$\sigma_{port} = \sqrt{[(0.60^2 \times 12\%^2) + (0.40^2 \times 3\%^2) + (2 \times 060 \times 0.40 \times 12\% \times 3\% \times +1)]} = 8.4\%$$

This is simply a weighted average of the risk of the portfolio's components:

$$\sigma_{port} = (0.60 \times 12\%) + (0.40 \times 3\%) = 8.4\%$$

However, the further away the correlation coefficient is from $+1$, the greater will be the amount of risk eliminated through the diversification effect. To illustrate this effect, three examples will be used:

(i)   If $\rho_{SC,HL} = +0.5$, then $\sigma_{port} = 7.9\%$

(ii) If $\rho_{SC,HL} = 0$ then $\sigma_{port} = 7.3\%$

(iii) If $\rho_{SC,HL} = -1$, then $\sigma_{port} = 6.0\%$

From Example 2 it can be seen how portfolio risk, but not portfolio expected return, is progressively *reduced* as the correlation coefficient moves further and further away from perfect positive correlation (i.e. $\rho = +1$).

Example 3 is designed to illustrate graphically the points made above and to show how the portfolio risk and return can also be varied by changing the proportions of the investment funds placed in each risky asset.

EXAMPLE 3

Georg Linhof wants to invest in the shares of two German companies: Gebröder (G) and Henkelwerke (H). The two companies have the following risk – as measured by the standard deviation – and expected return:

	Gebröder			Henkelwerke	
$E(r_G)$	=	25%	$E(r_H)$	=	18%
σ_G	=	8%	σ_H	=	4%

From the foregoing analysis, we know that the expected return and risk of any portfolio made up of the shares in these two companies depends not only on the above information, but also on the proportions of the available funds invested in each company's shares (i.e. x and $(1-x)$) and on the correlation coefficient of the returns from each company's shares (i.e. $\rho_{G,H}$).

Figure 11.1 illustrates the range of possible portfolio risk and expected returns that Georg Linhof could obtain by varying the proportions of his funds between the two companies, in three particular cases: when the correlation coefficient of returns has a value of $+1, 0$ and -1. For example, if Georg chose to construct a portfolio that consisted of splitting his investment funds equally between the shares of Gebröder and Henkelwerke (i.e. $x = 0.50$ and $(1-x) = 0.50$), then the expected return of the portfolio would be:

$$E(r_{port}) = (0.50 \times 25\%) + (0.50 \times 18\%) = 21.5\%:$$

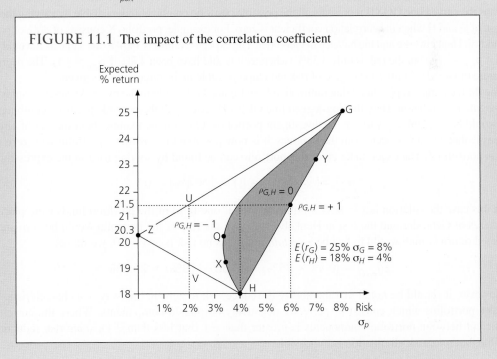

FIGURE 11.1 The impact of the correlation coefficient

However, the risk of this portfolio varies, depending upon the value of the correlation coefficient:[3]

$\rho_{G,H}$	σ_{port}
+1	6%
0	4%
−1	2%

Once again we see that portfolio risk is maximized where the two components are perfectly positively correlated (+1), and minimized where they are perfectly negatively correlated (−1). For correlation coefficients between these two extremes, then portfolio risk will be less than 6%, but more than 2% (e.g. when $\rho_{G,H} = 0$, $\sigma_{port} = 4\%$).

Both portfolio risk and expected return can also be varied by varying the proportions of *investment funds* placed in the two shares. Assuming that $\rho_{G,H} = +1$, then we know that splitting the investment funds evenly between Gebröder and Henkelwerke produces a risk of 6% and an expected return of 21.5%; but any of the risk-expected return combinations that lie along the straight line GYH in Figure 11.1 could be obtained, simply by varying the proportions of money invested in Gebröder and Henkelwerke shares.

At one extreme the portfolio would consist only of shares in Gebröder, then $E(r_{port}) = E(r_G) = 25\%$ and $\sigma_{port} = \sigma_G = 8\%$. At the other extreme the portfolio could consist solely of Henkelwerke shares, when the risk and expected return would be 4% and 18% respectively. Alternatively any *intermediate* portfolio could be constructed such as Y (on Figure 11.1), which consists of 75% of funds being placed in Gebröder and the remainder in Henkelwerke. This portfolio has a risk and expected return of 7% and 23.25%, respectively.

Notice that where Gebröder and Henkelwerke are perfectly positively correlated, all the possible portfolio risk-expected return combinations that are available – through varying x and $(1-x)$ − lie along a straight line. In other words, both the expected return *and* the risk of the portfolios constructed are simple weighted averages.

In contrast, the risk-expected return portfolio combinations for all other correlation coefficient values (i.e. except for $\rho = -1$) lie along non-linear lines, with the non-linearity becoming more pronounced as the correlation coefficient moves further away from +1. Indeed this non-linearity is a graphical representation of the risk-elimination effect.

Thus the curved line GQXH represents all the possible portfolio combinations available by varying the proportion of G and H when the correlation coefficient is zero. For example, portfolio X consists of 80% of portfolio funds in Henkelwerke and the balance in Gebröder. The expected return is 19.4% (the same as it would have been if $\rho_{G,H} = +1$) but the risk is only 3.58% (whereas it would have been 4.8% if $\rho_{G,H} = +1$). The degree of curvature of GQXH signifies the degree of risk reduction possible in the circumstances given.

The third example represented diagrammatically in Figure 11.1 is where the two risky assets display perfect *negative* correlation. Here the dog-legged line GUZVH reflects all the possible portfolio combinations that would be available by varying the investment portfolios. One unique feature about this set of circumstances is that, as can be seen from the diagram, it is now possible to construct a portfolio with **zero risk**. This is portfolio Z. The exact make-up of this portfolio can be found by solving for x in the expression:[4]

$$\sigma_{port} = [\, x \times 8\% \,] - [(1-x) \times 4\%] = 0$$

In this case the solution is $x = 0.33$. In other words, if one-third of the portfolio funds were placed in the shares of Gebröder and the rest in Henkelwerke, then the risk of the portfolio would be zero and the expected return (which would in fact be a *certain* return, as no risk is involved), would be:

$$E(r_{port}) = (0.33 \times 25\%) + (0.66 \times 18\%) = 20.3\%$$

However, it should be noted that the ability to reduce risk to zero in this way is a characteristic *only* of risky portfolios which consist of perfectly negatively correlated components. Where the correlation coefficient between portfolio components is greater than −1 (but less than +1), *some* risk reduction is possible, but *total* risk elimination is impossible.

In practice, the shares of most companies exhibit correlation coefficients (with shares in other companies) with values greater than zero but less than $+1$, thereby limiting the degree of risk reduction possible through portfolio manipulation. The shaded area on Figure 11.1 therefore gives the likely risk-return combinations that might be possible in practice with a two-component portfolio consisting of ordinary shares in Gebröder and Henkelwerke.

Dominance and portfolio efficiency

Continuing with the example where the two portfolio components are perfectly negatively correlated, we can use it to illustrate the fact that, under some circumstances, there would be portfolios available to investors that will be seen as being unambiguously *better* than other portfolios, in that some portfolios can be said to *dominate* other portfolios, either by giving a higher return for the same risk, or by involving less risk for the same return. This is demonstrated in Example 4.

EXAMPLE 4

Georg Linhof now wants to construct an investment portfolio consisting of shares in a computer games company – Infintek – and Jenbräu – a gold exploration company (represented by I and J in Figure 11.2). We will assume that the two companies are perfectly negatively correlated. (Remember, in practice, this would be highly unlikely.) In Figure 11.2 the line IKLMJ can be termed the *portfolio boundary*, because it represents all possible portfolios constructed with the shares of the two companies, given the correlation coefficient.

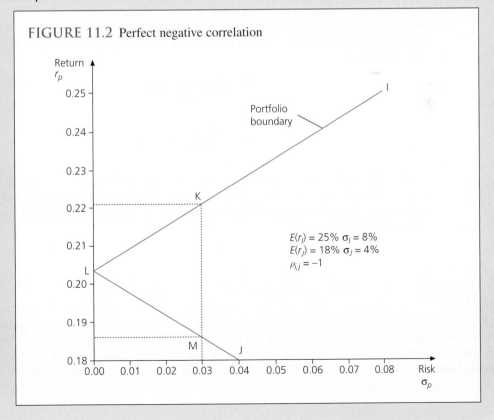

FIGURE 11.2 Perfect negative correlation

$E(r_I) = 25\%$ $\sigma_I = 8\%$
$E(r_J) = 18\%$ $\sigma_J = 4\%$
$\rho_{i,j} = -1$

▶

From Figure 11.2 we can see that a rational risk-averse investor would not choose *any* portfolio lying along the *lower part* of the IKLMJ dog-leg, i.e. between L and J. The reason for this is that there will always be a *better* portfolio lying along the upper part of IKLMJ (where 'better' is defined in terms of a portfolio giving a *higher* expected return for the *same* amount of risk).

For example, Georg Linhof is always going to prefer portfolio K to portfolio M. Both involve the same amount of risk, but K is expected to produce a substantially higher return: portfolio K is said to '*dominate*' portfolio M. In fact all the portfolios lying along the lower part of the dog-leg are dominated by portfolios lying along the upper part. The portfolios that lie along the boundary between points I and L are therefore termed '*efficient*', in that each represents the maximum possible expected return for a given level of risk.

Returning to the previous figure (Figure 11.1) along the portfolio boundary for which the correlation coefficient is *zero*, portfolios lying between points G and Q are similarly *efficient* and those lying between points Q and H, *inefficient*.

MULTI-ASSET PORTFOLIOS

A three-asset portfolio

So far, we have considered two-asset portfolios only. However, the analysis can be quite easily extended to portfolios containing many assets (e.g. investments in many different companies), although the calculations become much more lengthy. The risk (measured here by *variance*) and the expected return of a portfolio consisting of '*N*' different investments (or 'assets'), can be calculated from the expressions given below, where *x* represents the proportion of funds invested in a particular investment, going from shares in company 1 to company N.

$$E(r_p) = \sum_{i=1}^{N} x_i E(r_i)$$

$$\sigma_p^2 = \sum_{i=1}^{N} \sum_{j=1}^{N} x_i x_j \sigma_i \sigma_j \rho_{i,j}$$

It is the calculation of the *portfolio variance* that is particularly time-consuming, because it is calculated as the sum of the weighted variance of all possible combinations of pairs of investments. Example 5 illustrates the computations necessary for a simple three-company investment portfolio.

EXAMPLE 5

Maartje Graaf has an investment portfolio that consists of share holdings in three companies: Nagemeyer, Pakuis NV and Quadroon – N, P and Q. Maartje has invested 20% of her money in Nagemeyer, 70% in Pakuis and the remaining 10% in Quadroon. As a result, her investment portfolio, termed Portfolio Z, has an *expected return* of 26.2% and a *standard deviation* of return of 8.04%, calculated as shown:

▶

Company	Portfolio proportion	$E(r_i)$	σ_i	$\rho_{i,j}$
N	0.20	20%	6%	N, N = +1
				N, P = +0.7
				N, Q = +0.4
P	0.70	30%	10%	P, N = +0.7
				P, P = +1
				P, Q = +0.8
Q	0.10	12%	2%	Q, N = +0.4
				Q, P = +0.8
				Q, Q = +1

$$E(r_p) = \sum_{i=N}^{Q} x_i E(r_i)$$

$$= (0.20 \times 20\%) + (0.70 \times 30\%) + (0.10 \times 12\%) = \mathbf{26.2\%}$$

$$\sigma_p^2 = \sum_{i=N}^{Q} \sum_{j=N}^{Q} x_i x_j \sigma_i \sigma_j \rho_{i,j}$$

$$
\begin{aligned}
= \quad & 0.20 \times 0.20 \times 6\% \times 6\% \times 1 & = 1.44 \\
& 0.20 \times 0.70 \times 6\% \times 10\% \times 0{:}7 & = 5.88 \\
& 0.20 \times 0.10 \times 6\% \times 2\% \times 0{:}4 & = 0.096 \\
& 0.70 \times 0.20 \times 10\% \times 6\% \times 0{:}7 & = 5.88 \\
& 0.70 \times 0.70 \times 10\% \times 10\% \times 1 & = 49.0 \\
& 0.70 \times 0.10 \times 10\% \times 2\% \times 0{:}8 & = 1.12 \\
& 0.10 \times 0.20 \times 2\% \times 6\% \times 0{:}4 & = 0.096 \\
& 0.10 \times 0.70 \times 2\% \times 10\% \times 0{:}8 & = 1.12 \\
& 0.10 \times 0.10 \times 2\% \times 2\% \times 1 & = 0.04
\end{aligned}
\quad \Bigg\} \quad +
$$

$$\sigma_{port}^2 = 64.672$$

$$\sigma_{port} = \sqrt{\sigma_{port}^2} = \sqrt{64.672} = \mathbf{8.04\%}$$

Therefore Maartje Graaf's portfolio Z, consisting of a 20% investment in Nagemeyer shares, a 70% investment in Pakuis and a 10% investment in Quadroon has the following characteristics:

Expected return = 26.2%   Risk = 8.04%

If this risk is then compared to the portfolio's *weighted average* risk:

$$[0.20 \times 6\%] + [0.70 \times 10\%] + [0.10 \times 2\%] = 8.4\%$$

It can be seen that the 'diversification effect' of portfolio theory has resulted in eliminating: 8.4% − 8.04% = 0.36% of the investment risk.

A graphical representation

Whereas all possible portfolios that can be constructed from just two assets (with a specified correlation coefficient) can be illustrated graphically as lying along a *line* (as in Figure 11.1 and Figure 11.2), when dealing with multi-asset portfolios all possible combinations are represented by an '*area*'.

Figure 11.3 illustrates the *area* of possible portfolios that may be obtained from combining the shares of companies involved in Example 5: Nagemeyer, Pakuis NV and Quadroon (N, P and Q). Point Z represents the location of Maartje Graaf's portfolio that was used in Example 5.

However, we know from our previous discussion of *dominance* that, for risk-averse investors, the only portfolios of interest will be those lying along the *north–west boundary* of the portfolio area, PXYQ: the 'efficiency boundary' or 'efficient frontier'. The portfolios that lie along that north–west boundary provide the greatest possible expected return for a given level of risk. Therefore, a risk-averse investor – like Maartje Graak – would not actually be interested in holding portfolio Z because, for example, *portfolio X* would give her a higher expected return than Z for the same level of risk; whilst portfolio Y would give her the same return as Z, but for a lower level of risk. Indeed, *all* the portfolios lying along that part of the efficiency boundary between X and Y would be preferred by Maartje to portfolio Z.[5]

Therefore, any investor – like Maartje Graaf – who is faced with holding a portfolio consisting of shares in Nagemeyer, Pakius NV and Quadroon would *only* consider the portfolios lying along the efficiency boundary and would select the portfolio that maximized their utility, given their own particular attitude to risk and return. In terms of indifference curves, Maartje Graaf would select that portfolio which allowed her to obtain her highest possible indifference curve, which is portfolio W in Figure 11.4.

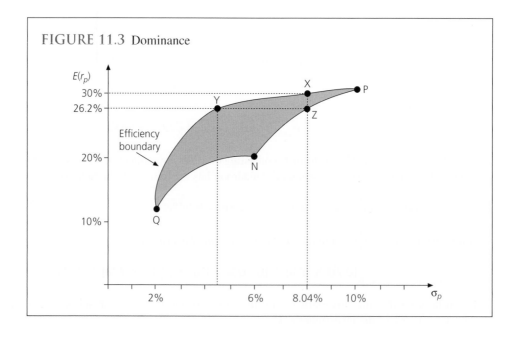

FIGURE 11.3 Dominance

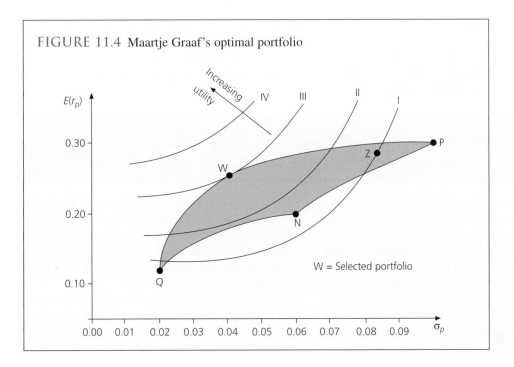

FIGURE 11.4 Maartje Graaf's optimal portfolio

Considerations of practicality

Up to this point, although the analysis has been useful in identifying that it is the risk and expected return characteristics of *combinations* of investments that are of importance, rather than the risk and expected return characteristics of *single* investments, the practical usefulness of the analysis is limited.

Individual investors themselves, never mind others who may be taking decisions on their behalf, are unlikely to be aware of the nature of their set of indifference curves. Thus in Figure 11.4, in the circumstances given, portfolio W would be optimal for Maartje Graaf, if that was her set of indifference curves as shown. However, in practice investors will not really know what their set of indifference curves looks like and so can do little more than follow their own rather poorly formed 'judgement' as to what combination of the three investments will produce the 'best' risk-return combination.

The main stumbling block to the practical application of the ideas we have developed so far is the vast numbers of calculations that would be needed to identify the efficiency boundary in practice. The example used above involved the consideration of just three risky assets – and only looked at one possible portfolio – but we still saw that a substantial number of calculations were required as each possible combination of pairs of investments had to be considered. In the real world the investor faces a vast number of risky assets and so the data and computations necessary to identify the efficiency boundary become astronomical in number and, to all intents and purposes, totally impractical.

For example, the total amount of data required – in terms of expected returns, variances and covariances – is given by $N(N+3)/2$, where N is the number of different companies' shares. An investor dealing with the London Stock Exchange alone (the London Stock Exchange is the biggest European stock exchange, but is only the fourth largest in the world) has a choice of almost 3000 different companies' shares from which to choose. In terms of portfolio theory, this would require over 4 million calculations! Thus, even if an investor were knowledgeable about his own set of indifference curves, it is unlikely that he would be able to identify the efficiency boundary, let alone the optimal portfolio lying along that boundary.

REAL WORLD VIEW: Is diversification the 'best bet'?

Andrew Carnegie may well have profited from 'putting all his eggs in one basket' but, as the opening section of this chapter noted, his case is not necessarily the norm and diversification is arguably the more savvy option for would-be investors looking to protect and grow their assets. A study conducted at the beginning of 2014 looking back at the previous year highlighted trends that point towards the adoption of diversification strategies amongst investors. Looking at the top five most popular funds, a wide variety of asset classes was covered, with small-to-medium-sized businesses featuring relatively prominently.

Other commentators have noted that whilst a diversification strategy may not seem the most exciting one, unlikely to create 'clicktastic headlines', it can actually be a very effective policy that

reaps long-term returns. As Jeff Reeves in *The Wall Street Journal's Market Watch* noted, current 'hot' investments can soon turn cold, and having a diversified portfolio helps curb reliance upon accurate predictions and the need to move money from one investment to another.

These claims are backed up by a study conducted by J.P. Morgan Asset Management which also recognized the reduced volatility that diversification brings. J.P. Morgan considered a hypothetical situation comparing two opposing investment strategies. The diversified portfolio was the clear winner, returning 118% over a 10-year period, in comparison to only 99% with the Standard & Poor's 500. It would seem that often, and where possible, diversification is the best bet.

INTRODUCTION OF A RISK-FREE INVESTMENT

A two-asset portfolio

A move towards greater practical usefulness can be made if a '*risk-free*' investment is introduced into the analysis. With such an investment, the return is known for certain and exhibits *no variability*. Short-term government bonds (stocks) held to maturity are usually considered such an investment.[6]

To see the effect of introducing a risk-free investment we will start by examining the characteristics of a *two-asset* portfolio where one asset is a *risk-free* investment (e.g. a government bond) and the other is a *risky* investment (e.g. the shares of company A). The risk-free return will be designated as r_F (it is no longer an *expected* return, but is now certain), and because its return is certain, its risk – measured by either the Standard deviation (σ_F) or the variance (σ_F) – is *zero*.

The resulting portfolio has the following characteristics:

$$E(r_{port}) = xE(r_A) + (1-x)r_F$$

$$\sigma^2_{port} = [x^2\sigma^2_A] + [(1-x)^2\sigma^2_F] + [2x(1-x)\sigma_A\sigma_F\rho_{AF}]$$

As the risk-free investment has a zero variance and standard deviation, the expression for portfolio risk reduces to:

$$\sigma^2_{port} = x^2\sigma^2_A \ \text{or} \ \sigma_{port} = x\sigma_A$$

The risky–riskless boundary

Figure 11.5 illustrates the range of portfolio risks and expected returns that are possible from combining risky investment A, with an expected return of 18% and a standard deviation of 5%, with a risk-free investment producing a certain 8% return. The different portfolios that are available from combining the two investments lie along a straight line because, as the above expression for portfolio risk shows, when combining a risk-free and a risky investment, portfolio risk becomes a simple weighted average of the risk of the components.

To identify this particular type of portfolio boundary, we will term it the '*risky–riskless*' boundary. Portfolio P on this boundary consists of 75% of risky investment A and 25% of the risk-free investment. In other words, portfolio P is three-quarters of the way up the boundary line between the risk-free asset (government bonds) and the risky asset (shares in company A). It produces the following characteristics:

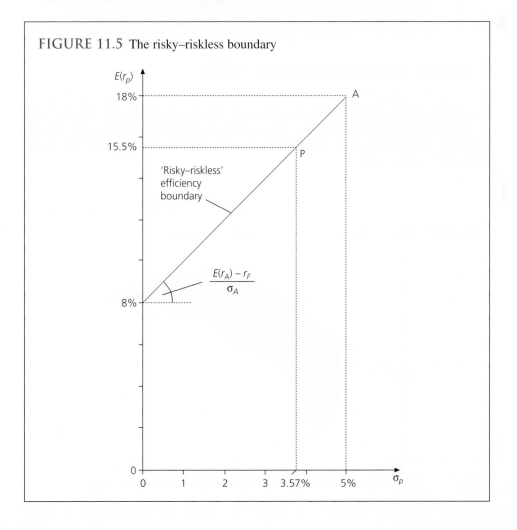

FIGURE 11.5 The risky–riskless boundary

$$E(r_{port}) = [\,0.75 \times 18\%] + [0.25 \times 8\%] = \mathbf{15.5\%}$$

$$\sigma_{port} = 0.75 \times 5\% = \mathbf{3.75\%}$$

The slope of this boundary is particularly interesting. It is calculated as $[E(r_A) - r_F]/\sigma_A$ and gives the *additional* amount of expected return produced by the portfolio for each unit increase in its risk. Therefore, in this example, every 1% increase in portfolio risk (σ_{port}), produces an extra $(18\% - 8\%)/5 = 2\%$ of expected return.

For example, if we wished to undertake a portfolio investment that involved taking on a risk of 4.75% (measured by standard deviation), then this should provide an expected return of $4.75 \times 2\% = 9.5\%$ *in excess* of the risk-free return of 8%. Thus the total expected return from the portfolio would be $9.5\% + 8\% = 17.5\%$.

This can be seen to fit in with the portfolio risk and expected return expressions. If the portfolio is to display risk of 4.75%, then:

$$\sigma_{port} = x \times 5\% = 4.75\%$$

$$\text{this gives: } x = 4.75\% \div 5\% = 0.95$$

$$\text{and so: } (1 - x) = 0.05$$

$$\text{therefore: } E(r_{port}) = [0.95 \times 18\%] + [0.05 \times 8\%] = 17.5\%$$

A riskless asset plus a risky portfolio

Extending this approach further, suppose that an investor — let's call him Tom Scott – is faced with a choice amongst many alternative risky investments (such as the London Stock Exchange or the Euronext Exchange). The shaded area in Figure 11.6 represents all possible risky investment portfolios available to him, and AB represents the boundary of *efficient*[7] portfolios available.

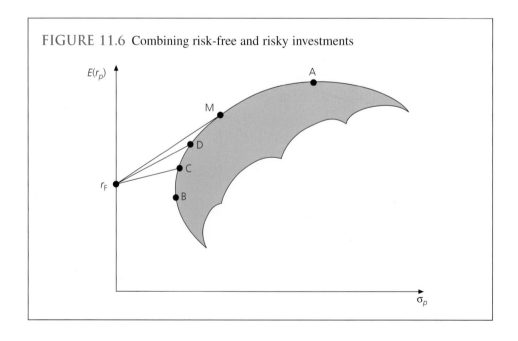

FIGURE 11.6 Combining risk-free and risky investments

If the possibility of undertaking a risk-free investment is introduced, he can now consider constructing another two-asset portfolio where one asset is risk-free and the other is risky. The difference between the situation here and that in the previous example is that now the risky asset is not a *single* investment (i.e. shares in a single company), but an investment in an efficient *portfolio* of company shares.

Suppose such an investment was efficient risky portfolio C in Figure 11.6, then the two-asset portfolios available to Tom Scott would lie along the line r_F, C. The point of interest to us here is that the introduction of this two-asset portfolio dominates *part* of the original efficiency boundary AB. Those portfolios lying along BC of the efficiency boundary are dominated by those lying along r_F, C. Figure 11.7 shows this situation in more 'close-up' detail.

Returning to Figure 11.6, it can be seen that combining government bonds (r_F) with efficient risky portfolio C is not the *best possible* two-asset combination available to Tom Scott. For example, government bonds and portfolio D dominate all the 'r_F, C' portfolios, as well as all those portfolios from B to D on the original risky portfolio efficiency boundary.

Another way of looking at this analysis is in terms of the *slope* of the risky–riskless efficiency boundary. We saw in the previous section that the slope of this boundary gave the additional amount of expected return (in excess of the risk-free return), for each unit increase in risk taken on. It therefore follows that it is in the investor's best interests to combine government stock with that efficient risky portfolio that creates the *steepest* possible risky–riskless boundary slope. This portfolio is found at the point of tangency of a line drawn from the risk-free return to the risky portfolio efficiency boundary: portfolio M in Figure 11.6.

Under these circumstances the original efficiency boundary AB has now been radically modified to 'AM, r_F'. If Tom Scott wishes to locate somewhere along A to M, he has to specifically identify the particular portfolio of risky investments. However, if he wishes to locate along M to r_F he will simply place a proportion of his investment funds in government bonds and the remainder in risky portfolio M. Tom Scott will no longer be interested in any portfolio lying along M to B as these are all dominated by portfolios lying along the risky–riskless boundary of M, r_F.

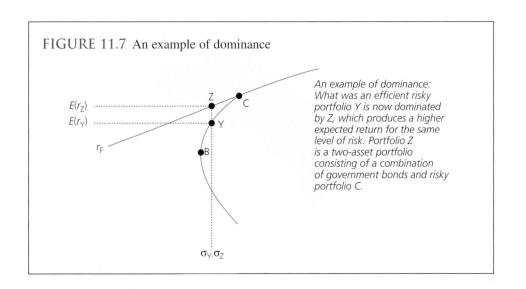

FIGURE 11.7 An example of dominance

An example of dominance: What was an efficient risky portfolio Y is now dominated by Z, which produces a higher expected return for the same level of risk. Portfolio Z is a two-asset portfolio consisting of a combination of government bonds and risky portfolio C.

The possibility of borrowing

Buying government bonds can be viewed as simply *lending money* to the government, and therefore the return on government bonds – r_F – is the risk-free *lending* interest rate. In the previous section we saw how the original efficiency boundary was modified and extended by the introduction of a risk-free investment: lending at the risk-free interest rate. A complementary extension and modification can also be achieved by the introduction of the possibility that our investor Tom Scott can add to his investment funds by *borrowing* some additional money.

Assuming Tom Scott can borrow any amount of money (given his ability to repay) at an interest rate of r_B, and assuming that both the interest payments and loan repayments are certain, then Figure 11.8 illustrates the modification and extension possible to the *original* boundary of efficient risky portfolios: the line AB. The revised efficiency boundary now becomes BNX, where X extends without limit (i.e. unlimited borrowing capacity).

For reasons similar to those of the previous analysis, portfolios lying along that part of the original efficiency boundary of A to N are no longer desirable, as they are dominated by portfolios lying along NX. However the composition of the portfolios lying along NX are somewhat different to those lying along r_F, M in Figure 11.6.

In Figure 11.6 the portfolios on the risky–riskless boundary were composed of investments split between risky portfolio M and risk-free government bonds. In Figure 11.8, the investments lying along NX are constructed by Tom Scott placing *all* his own investment funds into risky portfolio N, borrowing some extra money and investing this *also* in risky portfolio N. The greater the amount of money Tom borrows, relative to his own money, the further up the line NX, towards (and beyond) X will his resulting investment portfolio be located.

An illustration of a portfolio lying along NX is shown in Example 6 in conjunction with Figure 11.8.

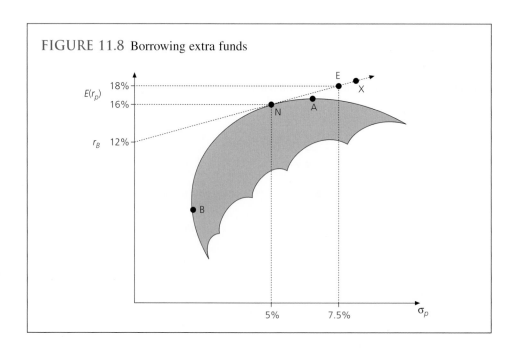

FIGURE 11.8 Borrowing extra funds

EXAMPLE 6

In conjunction with Figure 11.8, suppose the expected return on risky share portfolio 'N' is 16% and its risk/standard deviation is 5%. Our investor, Tom Scott, can borrow any amount of money at an interest rate of 12%. Because we assume that Tom's loan is risk free, it has a standard deviation of zero:

$$E(r_N) = 16\% \qquad r_B = 12\%$$
$$\sigma_N = 5\% \qquad \sigma_B = 0\%$$

Tom Scott has £1000 available for investment, and he wants to increase his investment funds by 50% (0.50), by borrowing £500, then the risk and expected return of the resulting portfolio 'E' will be given by:

$$x = \mathbf{1.50} \qquad (1 - x) = (1 - 1.50) = \mathbf{-0.50}$$

In other words, Tom invests 150% of his money – 100% of his own money plus 50% extra in portfolio 'N'...and so:

$$E(r_E) = [1.50 \times E(r_N)] + [(-0.5) \times r_B]$$
$$\sigma_E = 1.50 \times \sigma_N$$
$$E(r_E) = [1.50 \times 16\%] - [0.5 \times 12\%] = \mathbf{18\%}$$
$$\sigma_E = 1.50 \times 5\% = \mathbf{7.5\%}$$

An *alternative* way of calculating the *expected return* would be as follows:

£1500 invested in N at 16%	= £240 expected annual return
less £500 borrowed at 12%	= £ 60 annual interest
	= £180 net expected annual return

An annual return of £180 on an outlay of £1000 of the investor's own cash represents a percentage return of **18%** = $E(r_p)$.

Combined borrowing and lending possibilities

Figure 11.9 combines the opportunity of *borrowing* money at an interest rate of r_B and the opportunity of *lending* money at an interest rate of r_F, by buying government bonds, where $r_B \neq r_F$. The resulting efficiency boundary is now r_F, M, N, X.

Up to this point we have not advanced the *practicality* of portfolio theory to any great extent, because we still have to rely on knowledge of the investor's set of indifference curves to identify which portfolio of risky assets is to be held and we still have the problem of identifying the composition of that risky portfolio. For example, Figure 11.9 shows the points of tangency between the indifference curves and efficiency boundary for three different investors: I, II and III.

Investor I will hold portfolio W, which involves her placing a proportion of her investment funds in government bonds and the balance in risky portfolio M. Investor II holds portfolio Y, which simply consists of placing all his investment funds in the collection of

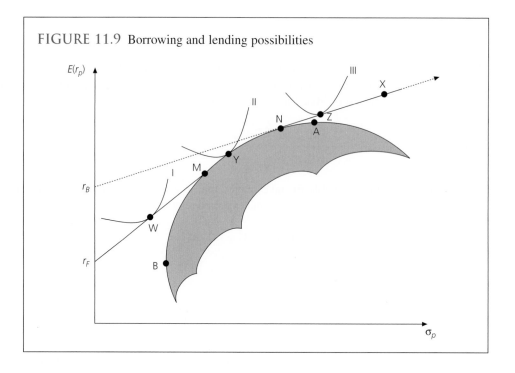

FIGURE 11.9 Borrowing and lending possibilities

risky assets of which portfolio Y is composed. Finally, investor III holds portfolio Z, which consists of placing all her own investment funds in risky portfolio N, plus borrowing *additional* funds at a rate of interest of r_B and placing these funds also in portfolio N.

The situation displayed in this example is a slight improvement (in practical terms) when compared to the original situation, where neither borrowing nor lending took place. We no longer have to identify the composition of the *complete* risky portfolio efficiency boundary of AB, but we still have to be able to identify a considerable proportion of this boundary. In terms of Figure 11.9, we still have to identify the set of risky portfolios lying between M and N.

THE CAPITAL MARKET LINE

From the above analysis, and from Figure 11.9, we can see that the only efficient portfolios that are composed solely of risky investments lie along that part of the efficiency boundary represented by MN. It follows that the smaller the gap between the borrowing (r_B) and lending (r_F) interest rates, then the smaller will be the segment of the original efficiency boundary of interest to investors. Therefore, let us now assume that the investor can lend *and* borrow money at the *same* risk-free interest rate (i.e. $r_B = r_F$). In such circumstances the efficiency boundary simply becomes the straight line drawn from r_F which is a *tangent* to the original risky portfolio efficiency boundary. The efficiency boundary that arises out of this assumption of identical risk-free lending and borrowing rates leads to some very important conclusions and is termed the '***capital market line***' (CML). It is illustrated in Figure 11.10.

The separation theorem

Figure 11.10 shows that there is now only *one* collection or portfolio of purely risky assets that investors would be interested in holding. This is called portfolio M in Figure 11.10. Thus investors who wished to locate on the CML somewhere between r_B and M would invest a proportion[8] of their funds in that portfolio of risky assets represented by M, and the remainder of their funds would be placed in the risk-free government bonds. Those investors who wished to locate on the CML *above* M would place *all* their own investment funds in the portfolio of risky assets M, borrow additional funds[9] at an interest rate of r_F, and invest those additional funds also in M.

This case, where it is assumed that investors can lend *and* borrow any amount of money at the risk-free interest rate of r_F, is important because of the fact that in such circumstances *all* risk-averse investors will be interested in only *one* portfolio of risky investments: portfolio M in Figure 11.10. They will either put all their investment funds into this portfolio; or only part of their funds and lend the rest at the risk-free interest rate (by investing in government bonds); or borrow additional funds and place all their own funds plus the borrowed funds into portfolio M. Therefore, whatever investment portfolio is constructed by an investor – in other words, *wherever* he or she chooses to locate on the CML – they will only be interested in one collection or portfolio of purely risky assets. This will be portfolio M. As a result we are now in a position of being able to identify the portfolio of risky assets that an investor would wish to hold (i.e. M), without any knowledge of his or her set of indifference curves (except to assume that they are generally risk-averse). This is the so-called '*separation theorem*'.[10] It has a significance similar to the separation theorem of the single-period investment–consumption model, in that decisions about investment in risky assets can be made on behalf of *all* investors without the need for any knowledge about the specific characteristics of their indifference curves.

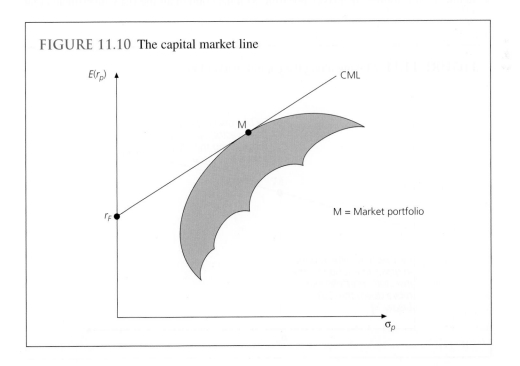

FIGURE 11.10 The capital market line

M = Market portfolio

In other words, we can distinguish between the individual investor's risk and expected return choice (i.e. where he or she decides to locate on the CML) and the choice of the optimal share portfolio. The optimal share portfolio is simply portfolio M and all investors can simply adjust the riskiness of their own portfolio, not by changing portfolio M, but by changing the level of lending or borrowing that they undertake (at the risk-free rate of interest). Therefore investors with different risk preferences will all hold the same risky portfolio of shares (i.e. portfolio M), but will have different proportions of borrowing or lending.

The introduction of the idea of the risky portfolio M helps to improve the practicality of portfolio theory for reasons other than just the separation theorem. We saw earlier that one of the main drawbacks of identifying the original risky asset efficiency boundary was the astronomical number of calculations that would be required. The presence of the CML neatly gets around this difficulty, as long as the location of the CML can be determined. Given that the CML represents a linear function, its location can be determined with knowledge of just two points: the risk-free return and the expected return and risk of the risky portfolio, M. Identification of the former is relatively straightforward whilst an acceptable proxy for the latter point – as we shall see in the following section – can be given by the expected return and risk of a general stock market index; for example, the FTSE all-share index in the UK or the FTSEurofirst 100 index in the euro zone etc.

The market portfolio

If all investors display the characteristics we ascribed earlier to a single investor (general risk aversion, rationality and consistency), then under the assumptions listed below, *all* investors[11] will wish to invest some or all of their funds in portfolio M of Figure 11.11. Further, as this will be the *only* combination or portfolio of risky investments that will be of interest to investors, and given that *someone* must hold each risky investment that is available, then it follows that risky portfolio M must contain all the risky investments that

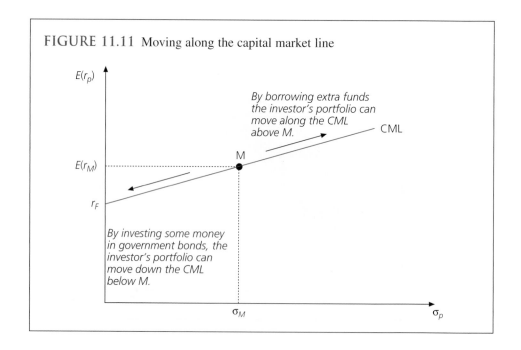

FIGURE 11.11 Moving along the capital market line

are available. That is to say, portfolio M must consist of shares in *all* the companies listed on the stock market. Hence portfolio M is termed the **market portfolio**.

An investor who wishes to hold the market portfolio as part of their overall investment portfolio would (at least in theory) hold shares in all the companies quoted on the stock market, in amounts *proportionate* to their total market values. As an example, suppose that there were only three listed companies: A, B and C and their total market values were €20 million, €10 million and €30 million, respectively. An investor who wished to invest €1800 in the market portfolio would buy €600 of shares in A, €300 of shares in B and €900 of shares in C.

The concept of the market portfolio produces a definition of equilibrium stock market prices. If the market portfolio contains the shares of all the quoted companies, then the market prices of those shares (and hence the return they are expected to produce) must be such that they are acceptable investments for inclusion in the market portfolio. In other words, share prices are at equilibrium when they produce an expected return that is just sufficient compensation for the risk that they involve.

It should also be noted that, given the risk reduction effect of diversification, then the market portfolio represents the *ultimate* diversified portfolio: it represents that portfolio of risky assets in which all the risk that is *possible* to eliminate, has been eliminated. However, the reader may understandably wish to question the practicality of the market portfolio concept. In practice, how can any investor seriously attempt to hold a risky portfolio that consists of shares in *all* quoted companies? (Remember, stock markets often have hundreds, if not thousands, of listed companies.) Furthermore, what exactly do we mean by 'the market'? Do we mean just the shares quoted on the stock market of the country where the investor is located – such as the DAX for a German investor, or the JSE for a South African investor –, or do we mean the shares in companies listed on *all* the world's stock exchanges? Do we limit our definition to shares, or do we extend it to cover all assets – such as property, precious metals and commodities? If we do extend it to include all assets, what about the ones that are not tradable or divisible?

Fortunately, several studies have shown that constructing a randomly selected portfolio of investments consisting of shares in only 15 to 20 different companies (instead of the approximately 3000+ different shares that are listed on some of the larger stock exchanges around the world), results in the elimination of around *90%* of the maximum amount of risk that it would be possible to eliminate through diversification. Figure 11.12 illustrates this relationship.

As a result, it is relatively easy to hold a portfolio of company shares that closely resembles the market portfolio in terms of both risk and expected return. Furthermore, in recent years, a number of investments have become available – such as mutual funds and exchange traded funds – that are designed to specifically track a particular country's stock market (or other), index.

Figure 11.12 illustrates not only the risk reduction effect of diversification but also the equally important fact that *not all* risk can be diversified away. There is an underlying rump of *non-diversifiable* risk. Various studies have shown that about 65% of *total* risk can, on average, be diversified away. The remaining 35% of total risk is non-diversifiable.

The assumptions

Many of the assumptions necessary for the conclusions reached in the foregoing analysis will be familiar, because they were used earlier in our development of the theory of financial decision-making. There are six main assumptions:

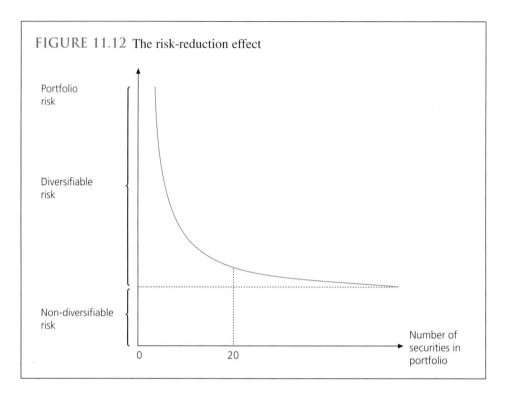

FIGURE 11.12 The risk-reduction effect

1. The investor's objective is to maximize the utility of wealth.
2. Investors make choices on the basis of risk and return. Return is measured by the arithmetic mean return from a portfolio of assets, and risk is measured by the standard deviation or variance of those returns.
3. All investors can lend and borrow unlimited amounts of cash at the risk-free interest rate.
4. No taxation, transaction costs or other market imperfections.
5. All investors have the same knowledge and expectations about the future and have access to the complete range of investment opportunities. Investors are all price-takers and have free access to all relevant information.
6. All investors have the same decision-making time horizon, i.e. the expected return on investments arises from expectations over the same time period.

These assumptions are important, and some of them are clearly unrealistic. However, the lack of realism of the model's assumptions is an issue of secondary importance. The main issue surrounds the *predictive ability* of the model: does the model correctly predict the expected return on portfolios of a particular level of risk? If it has substantial predictive power, then the lack of realism of its assumptions is of little concern. We shall touch upon the model's predictive ability in the next chapter, but (generally speaking) it *does* seem to possess fairly good (but not perfect) predictive power. Furthermore, when many of the above assumptions are relaxed we do find that the model appears to be remarkably robust and that its general conclusions continue to hold.

The market price of risk

The **slope** of the CML is of some interest. It can be calculated as:

$$[E(r_M) - r_F]/\sigma_M$$

where $E(r_M)$ and σ_M are the expected return and risk of the *market portfolio* and r_F is the risk-free return.

The slope of the CML indicates the 'risk-expected return' relationship of the whole capital market: in other words, it indicates the reward that investors will get (in terms of an expected return in excess of the risk-free return) for taking on risk. For this reason it is often referred to as the '***market price of risk***'.

As an example, suppose that the following values held:

$$E(r_M) = 16\%$$

$$\sigma_M = 3\%$$

$$r_F = 10\%$$

then the market price of risk would equal:

$$\frac{E(r_M) - r_F}{\sigma_M} = \frac{16\% - 10\%}{3\%} = 2$$

Thus the CML would have a slope of $+2$. This can be interpreted as indicating that for every 1% point of risk (standard deviation) taken on, the investor can expect to receive a return of 2% *above* the risk-free return. So if our investor Tom Scott is willing to take on 4% of risk in his investment portfolio (i.e. $\sigma_{Port} = 4\%$), he could expect to receive (on the basis of the figures above) a return of 8% *above* the risk-free return of 10%:

$$10\% + (2 \times 4\%) = 18\%$$

That is to say, if Tom Scott was willing to accept an investment risk of 4% then he could construct a portfolio yielding an expected return of 18%.

In general terms, the expected return from efficient portfolio '*j*' (where the term 'efficient' refers to a portfolio lying along the CML) is given by the expression for the CML function:

$$E(r_j) = r_F + \left[\frac{E(r_M) - r_F}{\sigma_M} \right] \times \sigma_j$$

or, more simply:

$$E(r_j) = r_F + \lambda.\sigma_j$$

where $\lambda = [E(r_M) - r_F] \div \sigma_M$ = the market price of risk.

Thus, the expected return on an efficient investment portfolio is equal to the risk-free return (r_F), plus the risk premium ($\lambda.\sigma_j$). The premium reflects the portfolio's own risk (σ_j), together with the market's risk attitude or risk-expected return trade-off (λ).

Market portfolio risk

Finally, there are two interconnected points about this analysis that are very important and which should be understood clearly. The first of these is to notice that the *market price of risk* indicates the amount of *additional* return that can be expected for each 1% of 'market portfolio risk' taken on (σ_M).

We know that the market portfolio represents the ultimate diversified portfolio and hence, by definition, the risk it contains is the risk that cannot be eliminated through diversification. Therefore the market price of risk indicates the additional expected return (in excess of the risk-free return) provided by the market to investors for each 1% of *non-diversifiable* risk taken on. The implied assumption here is that the market would *not* be willing to give investors any reward (in terms of expected return) for taking on risk that it is possible to eliminate through the diversification process. This is a conclusion of great importance and it will be expanded upon in the next chapter.

The second point is connected to the first. It is that the CML expression:

$$E(r_j) = r_F + \lambda \sigma_j$$

gives the return that should be expected from an *efficient* investment portfolio. Thus it only applies to investment portfolios lying along the CML (a rational risk-averse investor would not be interested in any other portfolios). The point of importance here is that this analysis, and in particular the expression for the CML, does not apply to *individual* investments (for example, it does not apply to the return we should expect from the shares of an individual company) – which could be termed an inefficient investment – but only to efficient investments, i.e. efficient portfolios. Once again, this point will be picked up in the following chapter.

SUMMARY

This very brief analysis of portfolio theory can be summarized as follows:

- The expected return on a share can be measured by its arithmetic mean return and its risk can be measured by the standard deviation of returns.

- When investments are combined in a two-asset portfolio, the expected return on the portfolio is equal to a weighted average of the returns expected on the two component investments.

- However, the risk of the portfolio is less than a weighted average of the risk of the two component investments. This is the risk reduction or elimination effect of diversification.

- Portfolio risk can easily be reduced by investing in less risky investments; but, as a result, the portfolio's expected return will also be reduced. However, portfolio diversification can reduce portfolio risk *without* a consequent reduction in expected return: this is the true meaning of the risk-reduction effect of diversification.

- From the two-asset portfolio analysis it follows that the greatest possible risk-reduction effect must be achievable with the greatest possible amount of diversification. This occurs when the portfolio includes investments in the shares of *all* quoted companies, and is termed the market portfolio.

- Not all risk is capable of being diversified away and so the market portfolio does contain a significant element of risk. However, risk which is capable of being diversified away will be eliminated from the market portfolio, leaving only non-diversifiable risk.

- The market portfolio, in terms of its risk-reduction characteristics, can be fairly easily approximated by a portfolio of 15 to 20 investments in different segments of the stock market. This is because the risk-reduction benefits of diversification arise fairly rapidly and most of the risk-reduction effect is achieved with only a relatively limited amount of diversification.

- Given that investors are rational and risk-averse, this means that they like expected return, but dislike risk. Thus investors will only be interested in holding one portfolio of shares (risky assets): the market portfolio (or its more practical 20-investment equivalent). This is because it provides the minimum possible amount of risk for its given level of expected return.

- Investors can then adjust the risk of their own personal portfolios (σ_p) so that they hold more or less risk than the market portfolio (σ_M) by either borrowing or lending at the risk-free rate of return, and so sliding their own personal investment portfolio up or down the CML from point M (see Figure 11.11).

- Therefore the equation of the CML indicates the return that can be expected by an investor from an efficient portfolio, which can be defined as one that is located on the CML.

- This return:

$$E(r_p) = r_F + \lambda\sigma_p$$

consists of two elements. The first is the return available on an investment with no risk at all (r_F). The second is the risk premium ($\lambda\sigma_p$), the additional return available as a reward to investors for taking on risk.

- The risk premium itself consists of two elements: λ and σ_p. The first element, λ, is the market price of risk and represents the going rate of reward on the stock market (in terms of expected return) for taking on risk. The second element, σ_p, is the number of percentage points of risk taken on by the particular efficient portfolio chosen (j).

- Finally, it is important to realize that the *only* source of an efficient portfolio's risk (σ_p) is the market portfolio risk. The risk of the market portfolio is, by definition, all non-diversifiable and so the risk premium only relates to non-diversifiable risk.

NOTES

1. This is the case in all but the most exceptional circumstances, as will be seen later.
2. It is assumed that the reader is familiar with the statistical term, *correlation coefficient*. This is the term often used in conjunction with two-variable linear regression analysis. It expresses the strength of the linear relationship between two variables. A fuller explanation than that given in the text will be found in any introductory book on general statistics.
3. These values have been calculated from the portfolio risk and expected return expressions, but they could have been estimated from Figure 11.1.
4. This expression is a simplified version of the original expression for portfolio risk, which can be applied when the correlation coefficient is perfectly negative, i.e. $= \sigma_p - 1$.

5. Indeed, *any* portfolio lying to the north-west of Z would be preferred, but the only portfolios that would not (in turn) be dominated themselves, are those lying along the north–west boundary line.

6. These investments are said to be risk-free as there is thought to be virtually no chance of default either on the interest payments or on the repayment amounts. (However, the recent world financial crisis and particularly how it has affected some countries in the eurozone, starts to cast some doubt about whether any investment is *truly* risk free.)

7. The efficient portfolios lying along AB could be called *efficient risky portfolios* in that they are all portfolios that consist of risky investments – the shares of companies.

8. Just what proportion would depend upon where the investor wished to locate between r_F and M.

9. Just how much would be borrowed would depend upon how far up the CML, above M, the investor wished to locate.

10. In fact it is often referred to as the 'Tobin' separation theorem after the author who developed the idea in order to distinguish it from the Hirshleifer separation theorem that we dealt with in an earlier chapter.

11. With the exception of the investor who wishes to hold a totally risk-free portfolio. That investor would place *all* of his investment funds in government bonds, in order to earn a certain return of r_F.

FURTHER READING

1. Many articles on portfolio theory are very mathematical and make difficult reading. A good overview is provided in J. Dickinson, 'Portfolio Theory', in *Issues in Finance* by M. Firth and S.M. Keane (eds), Philip Allen 1986.

2. Also of great interest from the father of portfolio theory is H.M. Markowitz, 'Foundations of Portfolio Theory', *Journal of Finance*, June 1991.

3. Three useful articles are W.H. Wagner and S. Lau, 'The Effects of Diversification on Risk', *Financial Analysts Journal*, November–December 1971; W.F. Sharpe, 'Risk Aversion in the Stock Market: Some Empirical Evidence', *Journal of Finance*, September 1965; and B.H. Solnik, 'Why not Diversify Internationally Rather than Domestically?', *Financial Analysts Journal*, July–August 1974.

4. E.J. Elton, M.J. Gruber, S.J. Brown and W.N. Goetzmann, *Modern Portfolio Theory and Investment Analysis: International Student Version*, 8th ed., Wiley 2010 provides a comprehensive coverage of portfolio theory.

QUIZ QUESTIONS

1   In a two-asset portfolio, what determines the degree of risk-reduction effect?

2   What is the expression for the risk of a two-asset portfolio?

3   Given the following:

State of world	Probability	Possible return: A	Possible return: B
I	0.30	28%	35%
II	0.40	18%	15%
III	0.30	6%	20%

What is the correlation coefficient of returns between investments A and B?

4   Given the information in question 3, how would you construct a portfolio to produce an expected return of 20%?

5   What is the expression for the risk and expected returns of an *N*-asset portfolio?

6   What is an 'efficient' portfolio?

7   What is the expression for the capital market line?

8 If the risk-free return (i.e. government bonds) was 10% and the expected return on the general stock market index was 16% and risk measured by standard deviation was 3%, how would you construct an efficient portfolio to produce a 15% expected return, and what would be its risk?

9 Given the information in question 8, and the fact that you have personal funds of €1000 to invest, how would you construct a portfolio giving an expected return of 20%, and what would be its risk?

10 Define the market portfolio.

(See the 'Answers to Quiz Questions' section at the back of the book.)

PROBLEMS

The answers to two of the following problems (those indicated by an asterisk) are available to students online. The answer to the remaining problem is available only to lecturers (see the 'Digital Resources' page for details).

1* In Utopia, a very restrictive investment market exists. Investors are able to invest in four types of security (in any combination): A, B, C and X. Securities A, B and C are all risky investments; their current market-derived expected (period) returns $E(r)$ and the standard deviation of these returns (σ) are given below:

Security	E(r)	σ
A	0.10	0.02
B	0.15	0.04
C	0.20	0.07

All are perfectly positively correlated with each other. Security X is a risk-free investment which yields a period return of 8%. Investors can also borrow unlimited amounts of cash at an interest rate of 8% per period. There is no taxation in Utopia.

Required:

(a) Draw to scale the area of possible risky portfolios. Draw the CML and identify the market portfolio.

(b) Calculate the market price of risk and explain what it represents.

(c) State briefly what conclusions you draw from your answer to (a) about the current state of the market for risky assets in Utopia.

(d) An investor in Utopia wishes to hold an efficient portfolio, yielding a 10% expected period return. How would this portfolio be composed and what would its risk be?

(e) Show how an investor in Utopia might construct an efficient portfolio yielding a 20% expected period return.

(f) State the main assumptions underlying portfolio theory and indicate briefly why its conclusions may be of importance for investment decision-making within individual companies.

2 Alpha plc, a UK manufacturing company, wishes to diversify its operations internationally by establishing equal-sized subsidiaries in two other countries. Because of the company's existing trading relationships, one should be in Europe and the other in the Middle East.

▶

▶

Five countries have been considered and the forecasts of possible present values of net cash flows (excluding outlay) have been calculated using a 20% discount rate. In addition, the calculation of the expected NPV and the risk (measured by standard deviation of NPV) has also been completed. These data are given below:

Saudi Arabia (SR m)		Switzerland (SFr m)		Denmark (kr m)	
Probability	Present value	Probability	Present value	Probability	Present value
0.30	+31.5	0.35	+9.2	0.30	+61.4
0.40	+33.0	0.40	+9.5	0.50	+64.4
0.30	+32.2	0.25	+9.8	0.20	+65.5

Kuwait (KD m)		Croatia (kn m)	
Probability	Present value	Probability	Present value
0.30	+2.4	0.35	+40.40
0.40	+2.5	0.40	+53.00
0.30	+3.4	0.25	+36.32

The expected initial outlay (in British pounds), in all cases is approximately £5.2 million and all of the projects have an expected life of 5 years. An investment analyst employed by Alpha plc has already started work on the decision and has calculated the ENPV and the risk of the Croatian project:

Kn m			£m	Outlay		£NPV		Probability		
40.40`	÷	8.80	=	4.6	−5.2	=	0.61	×	0.35	=	−0.21
53.00	÷	8.80	=	6.00	−5.2	=	+0.8	×	0.40	=	+0.32
36.32	÷	8.80	=	4.13	−5.2	=	−1.07	×	0.25	=	−0.27
								ENPV	=	£−0.16m

(£NPV)²		Probability		
0.37	×	0.35	=	0.13
0.64	×	0.40	=	0.26
1.14	×	0.25	=	0.29
		ENPV²	=	0.68

$$\text{Risk} = \sigma = \sqrt{0.68 - (-0.16)^2} = £0.80m$$

The corporate finance department of Alpha plc has estimated the following average exchange rates (number of units of overseas currency per £1) for the next 5 years:

Saudi riyal/£	6.00
Swiss franc/£	1.5
Danish krone/£	8.5
Kuwaiti dinar/£	0.45
Croatian kuna/£	8.8

▶

They have also estimated the correlation coefficients of ENPV between the countries.

Saudi Arabia/Switzerland	−0.15
Saudi Arabia/Croatia	+0.40
Saudi Arabia/Denmark	+0.60
Switzerland/Kuwait	+0.30
Denmark/Kuwait	+0.60
Croatia/Kuwait	+0.85

Required:

(a) The analyst looking at this investment decision has now left the firm. You are asked to complete the task by using the above information to advise the management of Alpha plc in which two countries to locate its proposed subsidiaries. Alpha plc is concerned with both the profitability and the riskiness of its investments.

(b) Critically discuss the shortcomings of your analysis.

3* Cape Town Consortium (Pty) Ltd has been specially formed to invest a total of 20 million rand to undertake two investment opportunities. The risk and return characteristics of the two projects – code-named Africom and Rovvos – are shown below:

	Africom	*Rovvos*
Expected return	12%	20%
Risk	3%	7%

Cape Town Consortium plans to invest 80% of the available investment funds in the Africom project and the remaining 20% in the Rovvos project. The partners in Cape Town Consortium believe that the correlation coefficient between the returns of the two investment projects is +0.1.

Required:

(a) Calculate the returns from the proposed portfolio of the two investment projects.

(b) Calculate the risk of the portfolio.

(c) Comment on your calculations in part (b) in the context of the risk-reducing effects of diversification.

(d) Suppose the correlation coefficient between Africom and Rovvos was −1.0. How should Cape Town Consortium invest its funds in order to obtain a zero-risk portfolio?

12 THE CAPITAL ASSET PRICING MODEL

LEARNING OBJECTIVES

The purpose of this chapter is to:

- Develop the concept of the 'security market line'.
- Derive the 'capital asset pricing model'.
- Examine the concepts of systematic and unsystematic risk.
- Discuss the validity and limitations of the 'capital asset pricing model'.
- Introduce 'arbitrage pricing' theory.
- Explain the significance of systematic and unsystematic risk.
- Discuss how the 'capital asset pricing model' may be utilized to generate risk-adjusted discount rates for investment appraisal.

THE SECURITY MARKET LINE

In the previous two chapters we have introduced approaches to the financial decision-making process in the face of uncertainty. We saw that on the basis of several assumptions about investors and their environment, investment decisions can be made on the criteria of expected return and the variability of return.

We then developed the idea of the capital market line (CML) which (if it can be held to apply in the real world) leads us to conclude that the capital markets display a *linear* risk-expected return relationship of the type:

$$E(r_j) = r_F + \lambda \sigma_j$$

Further, our analysis indicates that this relationship is not based simply on the *total* risk of individual investments – in other words, the variability of their possible returns – but on just one part of that risk: the *non-diversifiable* risk. The market would not provide a reward (in terms of an increased expected return) for that part of an investment's risk that could be eliminated by holding it as part of a well-diversified portfolio.

At this point it is worth recalling the purpose of our enquiry into the handling of uncertainty. We are concerned with building up a normative theory of managerial financial decision-making: a theory about how company managements should make physical capital investment decisions on behalf of their shareholders. Therefore, although the analysis in the previous chapter was concerned with investors (rather than managers) making financial decisions, its relevance to our purpose is obvious. We are interested in how shareholders, as investors, take decisions in the light of uncertainty because of the guidelines it can give us about how managers should take similar decisions on their shareholders' behalf.

Our brief consideration of capital investment appraisal under conditions of uncertainty that was made at the beginning of Chapter 10, led us to try to answer two questions: how to measure the *risk* of a capital investment project and how to identify the return that should be *expected* from it, given its level of risk. Although our development of portfolio theory will have given us some clues as to how both these questions can be answered, it has done no more than that, because it focused on the risk and expected return relationship of *portfolios* of assets. Our concern is with the relationship as it applies to *individual* assets. It is this point that is tackled in the current chapter.

In particular, we are going to develop a *share price valuation model*. In other words, for the time being at least, we are going to continue to look at stock exchange investment decision-making, but now in relation to investment in shares of individual companies, rather than portfolios. This share price valuation model is usually referred to as the '**capital asset pricing model**' (often known as the CAPM) and it arises directly out of the ideas and conclusions of portfolio theory.

However, it also involves the many unrealistic assumptions of our previous analysis. Nevertheless, the model is useful, in that it provides several significant insights into the major factors of share price determination, and so is of direct interest to decision-makers within companies. Indeed, it is worthwhile remembering that the realism or otherwise of a model's assumptions is an irrelevant issue in considering its validity. What is important is the *predictive power* of the model. In other words, despite its (unrealistic) assumptions and simplifications of the real world, does it appear to capture the main elements of the relationship it seeks to portray? We shall conclude that although the CAPM is *not* a perfect and complete representation of the real world, it appears to be a fairly good representation of the real world and is, in many ways, the best tool available to us.

Derivation of the security marmet line

The CML function provides an expression for the return that can be expected from an efficient portfolio investment, i.e. an investment in the market portfolio, plus either lending or borrowing at the risk-free rate of return. However, we can also use it to derive an expression for the expected return on an 'inefficient' investment, such as a risky portfolio, other than the market portfolio or, more importantly, an investment in the shares of a *single* company.

We already know from our analysis of the risk and expected return of a two-asset portfolio (where the two assets are shares in companies A and B) that the risk is given by the expression:

$$\sigma_p = \sqrt{[x^2\sigma_A^2 + (1-x)^2\sigma_B^2 + 2x(1-x)\sigma_A\sigma_B\rho_{A,B}]}$$

and that the magnitude of the risk-reduction effect of diversification is determined by the correlation coefficient. The further away the correlation coefficient is from $+1$, the greater is the risk-reduction effect.

From this expression, we can see that portfolio risk is made up of *three* elements. The first element – given by the term $[x^2\sigma_A^2]$ – is the contribution that investment A makes, *independently*, to the portfolio. Similarly, the second element, $[(1 - x)^2\sigma_B^2]$, is investment B's independent contribution to portfolio risk.

Then there is the third element: $[2x(1 - x)\sigma_A\sigma_B\rho_{A,B}]$, which is really composed of *two* identical parts:

$$x(1 - x)\sigma_A\sigma_B\rho_{A,B}$$

This represents the contribution made to the risk of the portfolio by the two investments *jointly*, and which is determined by their tendency to *co-vary* – or vary together (i.e. $\rho_{A,B}$).

Because investment A co-varies with investment B in an identical fashion to how investment B co-varies with investment A, there are two identical parts to the third element. Within each part, the term $\sigma_A\sigma_B\rho_{A,B}$ (known as the **covariance of returns** between investments A and B) effectively represents the *non-diversifiable* risk that each investment contributes to the portfolio.

We saw that when the correlation coefficient was $+1$, there was no risk-reduction effect. This is because the total risk of each investment would be *all* non-diversifiable. Hence, when $\rho_{A,B} = +1$, the portfolio risk expression:

$$\sigma_p = \sqrt{[x^2\sigma_A^2 + (1 - x)^2\sigma_B^2 + 2x(1 - x)\sigma_A\sigma_B]}$$

simplifies to:[1]

$$\sigma_{port} = x\sigma_A + (1 - x)\sigma_B$$

That is, the portfolio risk is just a weighted average of the risk of the portfolio components. However, when $\rho_{A,B} < +1$, then *not all* the total risk of each investment is non-diversifiable. Some of it can be diversified away and so:

$$\sigma_{port} < x\sigma_A + (1 - x)\sigma_B$$

which is the risk-reduction effect of diversification.

Furthermore, from our discussion of the Capital Market Line, we derived the expression for the expected return from an efficient portfolio as:

$$E(r_p) = r_F + \lambda\sigma_p$$

where all the portfolio's risk $-\sigma_p-$ consisted of non-diversifiable risk derived from the portfolio's holding of the market portfolio.

From this expression can be derived an expression for the return on an *inefficient* investment, such as the shares in Elbro Ingenieria SA, a company listed on the Madrid stock exchange:

$$E(r_{Ebro}) = r_F + \lambda\sigma_{Ebro}\rho_{Ebro, M}$$

Indeed, this is the general expression for the expected return from *any* non-efficient portfolio' investment and is termed the **security market line** (SML).

The CML and the SML

An examination of the equation for the SML shows how closely related it is to the CML equation:

$$\text{CML: } E(r_{port}) = r_F + \lambda \sigma_{port}$$

$$\text{SML: } E(r_{Ebro}) = r_F + \lambda \sigma_{Ebro} \rho_{Ebro, M}$$

In fact, in interpretation, they have exactly the same meaning.

The CML indicates that the return on an efficient portfolio consists of two elements. The first element is the return available for holding an investment with no risk at all – r_F – and the second is the additional return that can be expected as a reward for holding the investment's risk – the risk premium $-\lambda \sigma_{port}$.

The risk premium is the product of the market price risk (λ) and the risk taken on by the particular efficient portfolio[2] chosen (σ_{port}). The important point to remember here is that the amount of risk taken on arises purely from the portfolio's holding in the market portfolio. As the riskiness of the market portfolio is all non-diversifiable (by definition – it is the ultimate diversified portfolio), thus the risk premium given by the market is only for non-diversifiable risk.

Turning to the SML expression we can see that, similar to the CML, the expected return on the shares in an individual company consists of two elements: the risk-free return and a risk premium. However, the risk premium is now not simply the product of the market price of risk (λ) and the investment's risk (σ_{Ebro}), but is:

$$\sigma_{Ebro} \rho_{Ebro, M}$$

where $\sigma_{Ebro} \rho_{Ebro, M}$ is that part of Ebro's *total* risk that contributes to the non-diversifiable risk of the market portfolio. In other words, $\sigma_{Ebro} \rho_{Ebro, M}$ represents the non-diversifiable risk of the Ebro shares. Thus the risk premium is based not on the total risk of Ebro Ingenieria, but only on that part of total risk that cannot be diversified away, because, remember, the market only provides a risk premium for non-diversifiable risk. Example 1 puts some figures on this discussion to help clarify the point made.

EXAMPLE 1

Suppose we are given the following information about Ebro Ingenieria SA, a company listed on the Madrid stock exchange. The shares have a (total) risk of 8% and have a correlation coefficient with the market portfolio of +0.70:

$$\sigma_{Ebro} = 8\%$$

$$\rho_{Ebro,M} = +0.70$$

▶

▶

Also, if the risk-free return (r_F), is 3% and the market price of risk, (λ), is 2 then:

$$E(r_{Ebro}) = 3\% + [2 \times (8\% \times 0.70)]$$

$$E(r_{Ebro}) = 3\% + [2 \times 5.6\%]$$

$$E(r_{Ebro}) = 3\% + 11.2\% = 14.2\%$$

Therefore, the risk premium of 11.2 % is not based on Ebro's *total* risk of 8%, but only on part of that risk, 5.6%. This is because:

$$8\% \times 0.70 = 5.6\% = \text{non-diversifiable risk of Ebro}$$

The market will only give a premium for non-diversifiable risk because Ebro's *diversifiable* risk can be eliminated by holding the shares of Ebro as part of a well-diversified (i.e. efficient) share portfolio. Whether or not an investor in Ebro Ingenieria shares *does* actually hold them as part of a well-diversified portfolio is irrelevant as far as the stock market is concerned. The stock market will not provide a risk premium for holding a risk which can be easily eliminated through diversifying.

Thus if an investor *just* held Ebro shares, they would be holding a risk of 8%, but the return they could expect would only be based on a risk of 5.6%. So it can be seen how important it is to hold a well-diversified portfolio for an investor to get the expected return *deserved*, given the risk taken on.

THE CAPM EXPRESSION

In the foregoing discussion we have seen that the expected return on any individual/non-efficient investment is determined only by its non-diversifiable risk. More technically, this risk is referred to as '**systematic**' or '*market*' risk. Similarly, the diversifiable risk is known as '**unsystematic**' or '*unique*' risk.

The SML expression gives the return that an investor should expect from any non-efficient investment, given its level of *systematic* risk. The relationship thus described is usually known as the *capital asset pricing model* or the CAPM. Thus, it would state that the return that should be expected on Ebro shares is:

$$E(r_{Ebro}) = r_F + \lambda \sigma_{Ebro} \rho_{Ebro, M}$$

That is to say, the return that should be expected from an investment in ICI shares is equal to the risk-free return, plus a risk premium. The risk premium is determined by the market price of risk and the systematic risk level of Ebro shares.

Interpreting systematic and unsystematic risk

The CAPM provides the relationship between an investment's systematic risk and its expected return. Therefore, given the general risk-aversion of the market, investments with high levels of systematic risk can be expected to provide a high return and vice versa.

On the other hand, it would be possible to have an investment with a relatively high amount of total risk, but only a low expected return: conversely, an investment with a low level of total risk might have a relatively high expected return. In each case, the actual level of expected return depends upon the degree of correlation concerned. The former case would hold where the correlation coefficient was low, whereas the latter case might hold where the correlation coefficient was strongly positive. Example 2 illustrates such a situation.

EXAMPLE 2

We have the following information about two companies quoted on the Paris stock exchange:

Cralyon SA has a standard deviation of returns of 20% and a correlation coefficient with the market portfolio of +0.20.

Davmont Moteurs has a standard deviation of returns of only 8%, but has a correlation coefficient with the market portfolio of +0.90

The risk-free interest rate in France is 3% and the market risk premium is 2.

In terms of our notation:

$$r_F = 3\% \qquad \lambda = 2$$

$$\text{Cralyon SA:} \qquad \sigma_{Cralyon} = 20\%$$

$$\rho_{Cralyon, M} = +0.20$$

$$\text{Davmont Moteurs:} \qquad \sigma_{Davmont} = 8\%$$

$$\rho_{Davmont, M} = +0.90$$

Therfore, in terms of total risk, the shares in Cralyon are significantly *more risky* than Davmont shares. However:

Systematic risk of Cralyon:	20% × 0.2 = 4%
Systematic risk of Davmont:	8% × 0.9 = 7.2%
Expected return on Cralyon:	3% + (2 × 4%) = 11%
Expected return on Davmont:	3% + (2 × 7.2%) = 17.4%

Most of Cralyon's risk is capable of being diversified away and so its expected return is *relatively low*, although its total risk is high. Conversely, most of Davmont's risk is systematic and so *cannot* be diversified away. As a result, although its total risk is relatively low, its expected return is *relatively high*.

Because we will be interested in applying the CAPM to project investment appraisal, it is useful to consider the source or cause of systematic and unsystematic risk. Remembering that risk has to do with the variability of a share's return, and the return is, in turn, dependent upon movements in the market price (i.e. the capital gain or loss) and the level of dividends, then the determinants of risk are really the same as the determinants of share price movements and dividend levels.

This is an important area of the theory of financial decision-making and we will return to analyze it in depth in a later chapter. However, for the moment we will simply (and very tentatively) conclude that both share price movements and dividends are determined by the level or a firm's cash flow.[3] (Indeed, we should not consider such a conclusion as being contentious, given our discussion in Chapter 1.) Therefore it follows that the *total* risk of a company is determined by the variability of its cash flow: the greater the variability, the greater the risk, and vice versa.

Many factors affect the level, or variability, of a firm's cash flow over time. For example, the quality of its management, the state of its labour relations, the level of its advertising and the effectiveness of its research and development efforts will all affect the level of cash flow. However, in addition, there are other more general factors that will also affect a firm's cash flow. Examples would include such things as the rate of economic growth in the economy, the level of consumer demand, movements in exchange rates, rates of company tax and the level of interest rates.

All these factors can be roughly divided up into two groups. One group is those factors that are *specific* or special to the *individual* company (such as the quality of its management and the effectiveness of its research and development). The other group is the more *general* factors that affect *all* companies in the economy (to a greater or lesser extent) and not just the individual firm (e.g. the level of consumer demand and the level of taxes). It is this former group of factors that are the determinants of a company's specific or unsystematic risk, whereas the latter group of factors are the ones that determine the level of a company's market or systematic risk.

The logic of this division of 'risk causes' is fairly easy to follow. Factors that are special or *specific* to an *individual* company will be 'washed out' or diversified away, when the shares are held as part of a well-diversified portfolio. However, there is no such escape from the *market-wide* macroeconomic type factors that affect *all* firms and hence cannot be eliminated by diversification.

One of these company-specific factors might be the quality of a company's production engineers. If you held shares in two different companies, one with good production engineering and one with rather poor production engineering, then the good and the bad effects would tend to cancel each other out and so the impact of the production engineering function on your investment portfolio's performance would be diversified away.

On the other hand, if we take a market-wide factor such as the level of economic growth in the economy, then if there is a sharp fall in the level of economic growth, the shares in *both* companies are likely to be adversely affected (although not necessarily to the same extent), and so the effect of the fall in economic growth on your portfolio's performance cannot be diversified away.[4]

We shall return to the problem of identifying the sources of systematic risk at a later stage. However, it is worthwhile pointing out that, in practice, the identification of systematic and unsystematic risk factors is not as clear-cut as the foregoing discussion might seem to imply. There is a considerable 'grey area' of boundary between the two sets of factors.

The determinants of the systematic risk level

Finally, this is an appropriate place to discuss what determines the degree to which a particular firm's shares are exposed to systematic risk. In other words, why do some companies have a high level of systematic risk exposure and other companies have low systematic risk exposure?

If systematic risk can be defined as the extent to which a company's cash flow is affected by *economy-wide* or *non-company-specific* factors, then there are likely to be three main determinants of that systematic risk exposure:

1. The sensitivity of the company's revenues to the general level of economic activity in the economy and other macroeconomic factors.

2. The proportion of fixed to variable costs (i.e. the degree of cost sensitivity to changes in revenue levels).

3. The level of financial gearing or leverage (i.e. the amount of interest bearing debt/loans the company has, when compared to the amount of the shareholders' equity).

In other words, what makes a company risky in systematic risk terms is the degree to which the company's revenues are determined by macroeconomic factors largely outside the control of its management. This risk can then be either increased or reduced by the proportions of fixed and variable costs involved and further increased by exposure to debt financing costs (which are also fixed).

A company manufacturing machine tools might be seen as an example of having high revenue sensitivity. If the economy is growing strongly, demand for all kinds of products will increase. Manufacturers will take this opportunity to buy new machinery either to replace old ones or to increase capacity. However, if the economic situation is depressed then demand for many products will decline and it may not be necessary for manufacturers to buy any machinery at all, preferring to make do with existing machines until the economy begins to pick up. Thus the cash flows for a machine tool manufacturer can be expected to be particularly volatile, being especially sensitive to general economic conditions, and these general economic conditions cannot be diversified away in a portfolio.

On the other hand, a food retailer, such as a supermarket group, might be taken as an example of a business with a lower degree of revenue sensitivity. Generally speaking, in both good times and bad, the supermarket's revenue is likely to be little changed. In bad times people have still got to eat to live, while in good times spare cash will probably be spent on other things (such as leisure activities, new clothes and cars), rather than increasing the consumption of food.

Where a company has a high level of fixed costs relative to total costs, its net cash flows will be more volatile than would otherwise be the case. This is because it will still have to pay the fixed costs, no matter how high or low its revenue income might be. The level of debt financing is similar in that the company will still have to pay interest on the loans whatever is happening to its revenue cash flow.

These factors are particularly important for companies that have relatively volatile income flows. However, for a firm with low revenue sensitivity, the proportion of fixed to variable costs will make little difference to its riskiness. As its revenues are relatively stable, it should at all times be able to cover its operating and financing costs, whether they are fixed or variable.

Given the foregoing, and assuming that managers – like investors – are risk-averse, it should not surprise us to find that firms with high revenue sensitivity try to minimize the proportion of both fixed *financing* and fixed *operating* costs. On the other hand, the management of firms with low revenue sensitivity can afford to be more relaxed about such issues.

THE BETA VALUE

We now move on to the practical application of the CAPM and continue using the shares in Ebro Engenieria as an example. The CAPM model will provide the return that should be expected from an individual risky investment. But how are we to identify the several variables that are required?

If the 'market price of risk' (λ) term is expanded, the CAPM expression becomes:

$$E(r_{Ebro}) = r_F + \frac{[E(r_M) - r_F]}{\sigma_M} \times \sigma_{Ebro} \times \rho_{Ebro, M}$$

We will assume that the values of r_F and $E(r_M)$ are relatively easy to identify (using the return on government bonds and the expected return on the general stock market index, respectively). Accepting this, there remains the problem of identifying σ_M, σ_{Ebro} and $\rho_{Ebro, M}$. These could be estimated individually by examining the historical variability of the returns on the market portfolio, the returns on the shares in Ebro Ingenieria and their correlation with the market portfolio. However, fortunately, a much more straightforward estimation procedure exists (which we will examine shortly).

These three 'troublesome' elements (σ_M, σ_{Ebro} and $\rho_{Ebro, M}$) are usually *combined together* and termed the **beta value** of Ebro Ingenieria shares, so that the CAPM is then re-expressed in the much neater form:

$$E(r_{Ebro}) = r_F + [E(r_M) - r_F] \cdot \beta_{Ebro}$$

where:

$$\beta_{Ebro} = \frac{\sigma_{Ebro} \times \rho_{Ebro, M}}{\sigma_M}$$

Interpreting beta

The numerator of the beta value ($\sigma_{Ebro} \times \rho_{Ebro, M}$) represents the *systematic* risk of *Ebro shares*, and the denominator(σ_M) represents the *total* risk of the market portfolio which (as we know), is *all systematic* risk. Hence the beta value of Ebro shares is an index of the amount of Ebro's systematic risk, *relative* to that of the market portfolio. Example 3 illustrates this point.

EXAMPLE 3

Suppose we have the following data about Frère Carat, a Belgium company that is listed on the Euronext stock market, together with information about the market portfolio:

Standard deviation of Carat shares: 10%

Standard deviation of the market portfolio: 5%

Correlation coefficient between Carat and the market: +0.70

As a result we can now calculate the beta for Frère Carat shares:[5]

$$\beta_{Craft} = \frac{10\% \times 9(+ 0.70)}{5\%} = 1.40$$

▶

In other words, the shares in Frère Carat have a total risk of 10% (their standard deviation), but systematic risk of: $10\% \times (+0.70) = 7\%$. The other 3% of the company's total risk is unsystematic and would be eliminated when the shares are held as part of a widely diversified investment portfolio. As the market portfolio has only 5% of systematic risk, Frère Carat's shares have 40% more systematic risk than the market portfolio:

$$\left(\frac{7\% - 5\%}{5\%}\right) = 0.40 \text{ or } 40\%$$

Hence, Frère Carat's beta value of 1.40 expresses the company's systematic risk level *relative* to the average systematic risk level on the stock market (i.e. the risk of the market portfolio).

As further examples, a share with a beta of 2 would have *twice* as much systematic risk as the average, while a share with a beta of 0.67 would only have *two-thirds* the average level of systematic risk on the stock market.

The beta value of a company's shares also indicates the degree of responsiveness of the expected return on the shares, relative to movements in the expected return on the market. Beta does not indicate the degree of total volatility that can be expected in an investment's return, but only indicates the extent to which expected return is likely to react to overall market movements. For example, if the expected return on the market portfolio rises or falls by (say) 5%, then the expected return on the share will react as follows:

$E(r)$ will tend to rise or fall by $> 5\%$ if $\beta > 1$

$E(r)$ will tend to rise or fall by $< 5\%$ if $\beta < 1$

$E(r)$ will tend to rise or fall by $\approx 5\%$ if $\beta = 1$[6]

Beta can also be interpreted in terms of a share's risk premium. The beta value of a share indicates the relative magnitude of the change in the share's risk premium that will result from a change in the risk premium of the market portfolio. Example 4 provides some figures to illustrate this.

EXAMPLE 4

Landtonic is a small company listed on the London AIM 'junior' stock market. Its shares have a beta value of 1.22. The expected market return is 9% and the risk-free return is 4%. In terms of our notation:

$$r_F \quad\quad = 4\%$$
$$E(r_M) \quad = 9\%$$
$$\beta_{Landtonic} \quad = 1.22$$

Therefore the expected return on Landtonic's shares would be:

$$E(r_{Landtonic}) = 4\% + (9\% - 4\%) \times 1.22 = 10.1\%$$

► Thus an investment in Landtonic's shares provides investors with an expected risk premium of 6.1% (i.e.: 10.1% − 4%).

Suppose that the expected market return now increases by 2% to 11%. (Assume that r_F remains unchanged.) The risk premium on the market portfolio will then have risen by 2%, from 5% to 7%. However, Landtonic's expected risk premium will rise by more than this: 2.44%, because of its beta value being greater than 1: 2% × 1.22 = 2.44%. And so its overall expected return will rise from 10.1% to become: $E(r_{Landtonic})$ = 4% + (11% − 4%) × 1.22 = 12.54%.

In contrast, Avva Minerals, another small AIM-listed firm has a beta value of only 0.70. Therefore the expected return on AVVA's shares would be:

$$E(r_{Avva}) = 4\% + (9\% - 4\%) \times 0.70 = 7.5\%$$

Avva has a lower beta value than Landtonic, and so lower systematic risk, and so we would expect the shares to produce this lower return.

Once again, the expected market return now increases by 2% to 11% (and r_F remains unchanged). The risk premium on the market portfolio will then have risen by 2%, from 5% to 7%. However, because of its beta value being less than 1, Avva's expected return will *not* rise by 2%, but by only 1.4% (2% × 0.70 = 1.4%), to:

$$E(r_{Avva}) = 4\% + (11\% - 4\%) \times 0.70 = 8.9\%$$

Generally, the return on shares with a beta value **greater than 1** will *rise more* (and fall *more*), than the rise (or fall), in the return on the market portfolio. Conversely, the return on shares with a beta value of **less than 1** will *rise less* (and *fall less*) than the rise (or fall), in the market portfolio.

As a result, we can conclude that high beta shares (i.e. where $\beta > 1$) will tend to out-perform the return on the market portfolio (the return on the general stock market index), and low beta shares (i.e. where ($\beta < 1$) will tend to underperform the average return on the stock market. But, of course, this under- or over-performance comparison with the return on the market portfolio applies to *both* rises and falls in the return on the market portfolio. Therefore high beta shares can either be a good or a bad thing, depending on what is happening to the return on the general stock market index.

Finally, it is worthwhile making one point completely clear. The beta value can indicate the expected *change* in a share's return, relative to a *change* in the return on the market portfolio. What it *cannot do* is indicate the expected return on a share, relative to the expected return on the market portfolio. For this latter information, we also need to know the risk-free return. For example, if a share has a beta value of 1.4, then a rise of 3% in the expected return on the market portfolio would be expected to lead to a rise of 3% × 1.4 = 4.2% in the expected return on the share. However, if the expected return on the market portfolio is 9%, then we *cannot* say that the expected return from the share is 9% × 1.4 = 12.6%. This can only be found from using the CAPM itself: $E(r_{Shares}) = r_F + (9\% - r_F) \times 1.4$.

Portfolio betas

Thinking back to the discussion in the previous chapter about the risk and expected returns of a two-asset portfolio, we saw that although the expected return was a weighted average of the expected returns of the two portfolio components, the risk of the portfolio was *less than* the weighted average of the risk of the components. This risk reduction effect was caused by the diversification.

However, systematic risk, by definition, cannot be diversified away, and hence the systematic risk of a two-asset portfolio [7] *is* a weighted average of the systematic risk of the component investments. As beta gives an index of relative systematic risk, we can conclude that the beta value of a portfolio (as well as the expected return) **is** a weighted average of the betas of its component investments.

Thus if we were to construct a three-asset portfolio as follows:

Asset	E(r)	Beta	Proportion of money invested
A	14.4%	1.6	60%
B	12.8%	1.2	10%
C	10.8%	0.7	30%

then:

$$E(r_{port}) = (14.4\% \times 0.6) + (12.8\% \times 0.1) + (10.8\% \times 0.3) = 13.16\%$$

$$\text{and } \beta_{port} = (1.6 \times 0.6) + (1.2 \times 0.1) + (0.7 \times 0.3) = 1.29$$

This is an important characteristic of beta and we shall return to it later.

Measurement of beta

Example 3, concerning the shares in Frère Carat's shares, illustrated how a share's beta value could be estimated from its constituent components:

$$\beta_{shares} = \frac{\sigma_{shares} \times \rho_{shares, M}}{\sigma_M}$$

However, for real-world applications, there are obvious difficulties in being able to obtain the required data easily. Fortunately, a much more convenient method of estimating beta exists.

The beta value measures the degree to which a share's risk premium varies as the average risk premium on the stock market varies. It is not surprising, therefore, that this relationship can be observed directly from the stock market, by looking at how the return on a share varies as the return on the general stock market index (used as a surrogate for the market portfolio) varies.

If the historical average market risk premium is plotted on a graph against the historical risk premium on the shares of a particular company, then the resulting scatter diagram will reflect the general nature of the relationship that exists between the return on the company's shares and the return on the market portfolio.

The points plotted on the graph can be expected to scatter upwards to the right, indicating a positive relationship between the two variables:[8] in other words, movements in the return on the shares (whether up or down) will tend to follow movements in the return on the market portfolio. Figure 12.1 illustrates the situation. In practice, the return on the general stock market index is used to approximate the market portfolio.

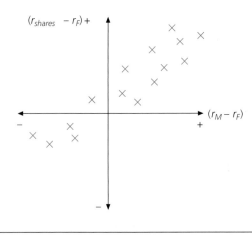

FIGURE 12.1 Scatter diagram of the share's risk premium plotted against the market portfolio's risk premium

Linear regression analysis can then be used to plot a straight 'line of best fit' through the scatter data.[9] This reflects the average relationship between the share's risk premium and the risk premium of the market portfolio.

This observed relationship is usually referred to as the '*market model*' and the linear regression line is termed the share's '*characteristic line*'. Example 5, together with Figure 12.2, illustrates this general procedure.

EXAMPLE 5

To find a share's characteristic line, we look backwards to the recent past – say over the last 3 years – and compare the share's risk premium with the market portfolio's risk premium (or the stock market index risk premium). Therefore, suppose it is now June 2015. Going back 3 years takes us back to June 2012. What we would do is to calculate what has been the annual risk premium on a share $(r_{share} - r_F)$, and the risk premium on the market portfolio $(r_M - r_F)$ over the last 3 years, moving up 1 month at a time. Let's use the shares in Verenigde NV as an example:

For example:

	$[r_{Verenigde} - r_F]$	$[r_M - r_F]$
June 2012 – June 2013	4%	3%
July 2012 – July 2013	6%	4.5%
August 2012 – August 2013	5%	4%
.	.	.
.	.	.
.	.	.
June 2014 – June 2015	7%	6%

▶

Each of these data pairs is then plotted onto a scatter diagram, such as in Figure 12.2, and a regression analysis undertaken to identify the α (alpha) and β (beta) coefficients of the regression equation, the *characteristic line*:

$$(r_{Verenigde} - r_F) = \alpha + \beta\,(r_M - r_F)$$

Suppose the regression equation is found to be:

$$(r_{Verenigde} - r_F) = 2\% + 1.30 \times (r_M - r_F)$$

The alpha coefficient (α) gives the *vertical* intercept point of the regression line and the beta coefficient (β) gives the *slope* of the regression line.

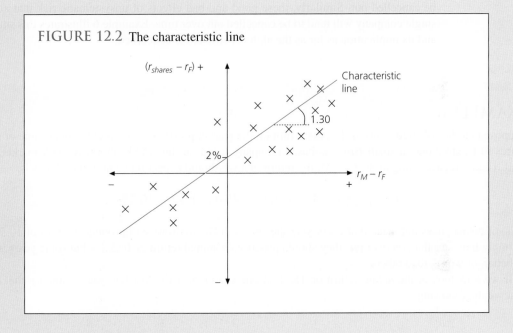

FIGURE 12.2 The characteristic line

In the example of the regression equation in Example 5, the 'alpha' coefficient had a value of 2% and the 'beta' coefficient a value of 1.30. Both of these have important meanings and we shall begin by looking at the meaning of the 'alpha' coefficient's value.

The alpha coefficient

In a perfect world the alpha coefficient of the regression equation should be zero. In other words, the regression line should go through the graph's origin (where the horizontal and vertical axes cross).

The regression/*characteristic* line shows the relationship between the average market risk premium (on the horizontal axis) and the share's risk premium (on the vertical axis). Logically, therefore, it follows that in a situation where the market portfolio risk premium is zero, the share should not have any risk premium either.

We can look at this in a different way. We have seen that a share's total risk is composed of both systematic and unsystematic elements. Systematic risk describes the exposure of the company's cash flow (and hence its financial performance, value and rate of return) to changes in the macroeconomic environment within which it operates. On the other hand, unsystematic risk is caused by factors specific to the individual company, such as the quality of its top management team and the state of its labour relations.

Portfolio theory shows us that investors can only expect to receive a return for holding systematic risk. The market will not provide a return for unsystematic risk because there is no need for any investor to hold it – it can easily be eliminated through holding a well-diversified investment portfolio.

However, it is very important to understand that this *does not* mean that unsystematic risk factors will not affect a company's financial performance and rate of return on its shares: of course they will. It is just that (as was explained earlier in this chapter) in a well-diversified investment portfolio, the good and bad effects of unsystematic risk will tend to be cancelled out. Similarly, these good and bad effects of unsystematic risk that affect a single company will tend to be cancelled out over time. Example 6 illustrates this situation and its implication as far as the alpha coefficient is concerned.

EXAMPLE 6

Suppose that the risk-free return is 4%, the return on the market portfolio is 9% and the beta value of the shares in Dentredrone, a small Brussels-based company listed on the NYSE alternext stock market, is 1.30. Therefore, according to the CAPM, the return that we should expect on Dentredone shares is:

$$E(r_{Dentredrone}) = 4\% + (9\% - 4\%) \times 1.30 = 10.5\%$$

This, of course, does not mean that every year the shares in Dentredrone will produce a return of 10.5%. It simply indicates that, *on average*, they should produce an annual return of 10.5% – but some years will be better, or worse, than others.

If we now look at the *actual* return on Dentredrone shares over the last few years, suppose that we observe the following:

Year	1	2	3	4
Actual return	12.3%	9.6%	6.1%	14.0%
Abnormal return	+1.8%	−0.9%	−4.4%	+3.5%

The '*abnormal return*' indicates by how much the *actual* return has been above or below the *expected* return. Now notice in this example that the average *actual* return is 10.5% (the expected return predicted by the CAPM), and the average *abnormal* return is zero:

$$12.3\% + 9.6\% + 6.1\% + 14.0\% = 42.0\% \div 4 = \mathbf{10.5\%}$$

$$+1.8\% - 0.9\% - 4.4\% + 3.5\% = 0\% \div 4 = \mathbf{0\%}$$

This is what *should* happen in a *perfect* world. The abnormal return each year is caused by the unsystematic risk factors (which are sometimes 'good', as in Year 1, and sometimes 'bad', as in Year 3), that affect the company's financial performance. However, over time, these effects should cancel out, leaving a zero

▶

▶ abnormal return and, therefore, leaving an average return equal to that expected by the CAPM. It is in this sense that we say that a share's characteristic line *should* pass through the graph's origin because the α or alpha coefficient of the regression equation measures the share's average abnormal return. However, life does not always work out quite as precisely as this example does. Suppose the actual returns on the Dentredrone shares were:

Year	1	2	3	4
Actual return	13.6%	9.2%	16.8%	10.4%
Abnormal return	+3.1%	−1.3%	+6.3%	−0.1%

In these circumstances the average return on the shares is 12.5% and the average abnormal return is +2%. In other words, although CAPM says that, given the share's relative systematic risk, they should give an average return of 10.5%, they have in fact actually given an average return which is 2% greater, at 12.5%.

This is the type of situation illustrated in Figure 12.2, where the share's characteristic line has an alpha value of +2%.

Some investors believe that alpha values can be used to provide investment decision advice. On the basis that on average, over time, the alpha value (or average abnormal return) should be zero, some investors believe that shares with negative alpha values should be sold and those with positive alpha values should be bought.

To see the logic at work here, we will use the Dentredrone shares from Example 6. In that example, according to the CAPM the shares should be expected to produce an annual return of 10.5% but over the last few years they have actually produced an average return of 12.5%: a positive abnormal return of +2%. Given that the average abnormal return *should* be zero, the reasoning is that over the next few years the *actual* average return on the shares should be only 8.5% – therefore having a *negative* alpha value of 2% – so as to bring the longer run average return back to its expected level of 10.5% and a zero alpha value.[10]

However, there is a well-known statistical fallacy in this logic. Suppose you toss a coin. We know that there is a 50% chance of 'heads' and a 50% chance of 'tails', and on average we should get as many heads as tails. Suppose we toss a coin five times and each time it comes up heads; what's the chance of tails when we toss the coin a sixth time? We may be tempted to think (as do the followers of alpha values) that, given there should be as many heads as tails, with five heads in a row there must be a *great* chance that next time it will be tails. However, statistics has no 'memory': the chance of a tail on the sixth throw remains at 50% as usual.

The beta value

Let us now return to Example 5. We have been looking at the meaning of the 'alpha' coefficient in the regression equation of the characteristic line. We can now look at the meaning of the regression equation's 'beta' coefficient.

The 'beta' coefficient describes the slope of the characteristic line and so indicates the degree to which the share's risk premium reacts to changes in the market portfolio's risk premium.

A slope (or 'beta' coefficient) of *greater* than 1 indicates that movements in the *share's* risk premium will be greater than movements in the market portfolio's risk premium. In our example, therefore, where the 'beta' coefficient had a value of 1.30, this means that a 1% increase or decrease in the market portfolio's risk premium will lead to a 1.3% increase or decrease in the share's risk premium.

Similarly, a 'beta' coefficient of *less* than 1 indicates that the share's risk premium under-responds to movements in the market portfolio risk premium. A 'beta' coefficient of 0.75 would imply that a 1% change in the market portfolio risk premium would lead to only a 0.75% change in the share's risk premium.

Finally, if the characteristic line has a slope of exactly 1, then movements in the share's risk premium will tend to be *the same* as movements in the market portfolio's risk premium.

This description of the behaviour of the share's risk premium relative to the market portfolio's risk premium is, of course, directly comparable to our earlier discussion of the meaning of a share's beta value. And it is from the 'beta' coefficient of the regression equation that the beta values of shares are, in practice, estimated. Thus, in Example 5, the shares in Verenigde NV would have had a beta value of 1.30.

Beta stability

The main problem with this approach to estimating a share's beta value is that, for decision-making, we really require an estimate of what *will be* the company's beta value in the future, so that we can estimate what *will be* the expected return. However, the approach used for estimating beta looks at the past, or historical, relationship between the share and the stock market, not the future relationship.

Therefore, whether this method is a satisfactory approach to estimating *future* beta values depends upon a single issue: how stable are beta values over time? If a company's beta value is found to change very little over time, then estimating the future beta on the basis of the past relationship may well be acceptable.

The beta value expresses the degree to which the company is exposed to systematic risk (relative to the market portfolio). Therefore it measures the degree to which the company's performance is affected by macroeconomic forces in the economy (e.g. the rate of economic growth, inflation levels, exchange rate movements, interest rates, etc.). Commonsense would lead us to suppose that companies are unlikely to change their sensitivity to these factors rapidly, unless some major event (such as a large-scale move into a new area of business) takes place within the company.

This is indeed what the evidence tends to show. Although there is some tendency, over time, for shares with high and low betas to move towards a beta of 1 (i.e. a general tendency for betas to regress towards the mean), generally speaking beta values are fairly stable and do not change substantially over relatively short (say, 5 years) periods of time.

A further estimation approach

Finally, as well as estimating beta from first principles using the equation for beta:

$$\beta_A = \frac{\sigma_A \rho_{A,M}}{\sigma_M} \text{ or } \beta_A = \frac{\text{Cov}(r_A, r_M)}{\sigma^2_M}$$

and in addition to estimating beta through regression analysis, Example 7 shows how a 'rough and ready' approximation of beta might be generated quite simply. (Notice that these two expressions in the above equations are identical; if the covariance term is expanded; the expression reduces, through cancellation, to equal the first expression.)

EXAMPLE 7

Süd-Meister AG is a small technology company listed on the Deutsche Borse. The DAX is the general German stock market index. Given the following data, the beta value of Süd-Meister shares could be estimated.

| | Süd-Meister | | DAX | | |
Year	Average share price (€)	Dividend per share (c)	Average DAX index	DAX dividend yield	Return on government bonds
3 years ago	1.39	7	6810	3%	7%
2 years ago	1.47	8.5	7155	5%	6%
1 year ago	1.63	9	7860	5.5%	5%
Current year	1.85	10	8640	5.5%	4%

Return on Süd-Meister shares:

1. Average percentage annual capital gain

   Let g = average annual capital gain in the share price:

   $$€1.39 \times (1 + g)^3 = €1.85$$

   therefore:

   $$g = (1.85 \div 1.39)^{1/3} - 1 = 0.10 \text{ or } \textbf{10\%}$$

2. Average annual dividend yield (dividend ÷ share price = dividend yield):

Year	Dividend yield
3 years ago	7 ÷ 1.39 = 0.050
2 years ago	8.5 ÷ 1.47 = 0.058
1 year ago	9 ÷ 1.63 = 0.055
Current year	10 ÷ 1.85 = 0.054
	0.217 ÷ 4 = 0.054 or **5.4%**

3. Therefore the return on Süd-Meister shares can be given as: average annual capital gain + average dividend yield = 10% +5.4% = **15.4%**

Return on the market portfolio (DAX stock market index):

1. Average annual percentage capital gain on the stock market index: Let g = average annual capital gain:

   $$6810 \times (1 + g)^3 = 8640$$

   therefore:

   $$g = [8640 \div 6810]^{1/3} - 1 = 0.0825 \text{ or } 8.25\%$$

▶

▶

2. Average annual DAX dividend yield:

$$3\% + 5\% + 5.5\% + 5.5\% = 19\% \div 4 = 4.75\%$$

3. Therefore the return on the DAX stock exchange index (acting as a surrogate for the market portfolio) is:

$$E(r_M) = 8.25\% + 4.75\% = 13\%$$

Average annual risk-free return:

$$7\% + 6\% + 5\% + 4\% = 22\% \div 4 = 5.5\%$$

Given the information gathered above:

$$E(r_{Süd\text{-}Meister}) = 15{:}4\%$$
$$E(r_M) = 13\%$$
$$r_F = 5.5\%$$

the CAPM can be used to estimate the beta value of company A shares:

$$E(r_{Süd\text{-}Meister}) = r_F + [E(r_M) - r_F] \times \beta_{Süd\text{-}Meister}$$

$$15.4\% = 5.5\% + [12.75\% - 5.5\%] \times \beta_{Süd\text{-}Meister}$$

$$\frac{15.4\% - 5.5\%}{12.75 - 5.5\%} = \beta_{süd\text{-}Meister} = 1.37$$

THE VALIDITY OF THE CAPM

The assumptions behind the CAPM

Does the CAPM accurately predict the return that, on average, is produced on the shares of a particular company? This is the key question. Does it work?

The CAPM is built upon a number of assumptions, some of which are realistic, others of which are not. Effectively we can divide the CAPM assumptions up into two groups. The model makes assumptions about *investors* and it makes assumptions about the *financial market environment* within which investments are bought and sold. As far as investors are concerned, the model assumes:

1. They are rational, risk-averse, utility maximizers.
2. They perceive utility in terms of return.
3. They measure risk by the standard deviation of returns.
4. They have a single-period investment time horizon.
5. They all have the same expectations about what the uncertain future holds.

Furthermore, the model assumes that financial markets are perfect and, specifically, that:

1. There are no taxes.
2. There are no transaction costs.
3. Investors can both lend and borrow at the risk-free rate of return.

To see whether these assumptions about the real world are reasonable, we first have to be clear as to what they mean. Saying that investors are 'rational' means that they always like *more*, than *less* – in other words, they always prefer a higher return to a lower return.

Risk-aversion means, as we know, that investors dislike investments where the outcome is uncertain. This does not mean that they are unwilling to take on risky investments, but that they require a *reward* for doing so: the greater the risk, the greater the required reward.

Utility maximization, again as we know, means that we assume investors want to make themselves as *well-off* as possible. In economic terms, they wish to achieve their highest possible utility/indifference curve.

All these assumed characteristics of investors appear fairly reasonable and do not pose any real problems. We can probably also agree that investors do measure being 'better-off' in terms of the return that the investment produces. However, whether they measure risk as the standard deviation of returns must be somewhat doubtful. A cynic might say that most investors don't even know what a standard deviation is, never mind what it measures! However, technically, the problem with standard deviation (and we touched upon this problem in our earlier discussion on utility) is that it is really only a satisfactory measure of risk if we can assume that the distribution of returns is symmetrical (i.e. normal). This is because when we say that investors are risk-averse, what we *really* mean is that investors dislike *downside* risk – nobody minds the upside potential of an investment. If the probability distribution of an investment's returns is normally distributed then standard deviation adequately measures *both* sides of risk. However, a problem arises if the distribution is not symmetrical, but is skewed either towards the upside or towards the downside. In such a situation, standard deviation is not going to provide an adequate measure of downside risk. Logically, the distribution of returns on a share must be skewed, because the upside potential is unlimited, whereas the maximum downside risk is limited to a loss of 100%.

The assumption that all investors have an investment time horizon of a single time period is highly suspect. People invest for different reasons. Some are investing on a speculative basis, looking for short-term profits. Others are investing with a much longer time horizon in view, saving for when they retire.

Finally, the assumption that all investors have the same expectations of the future – in other words, that they make a similar assessment of the probability distribution of returns on investments – must also be suspect. The future is unknown, and so we can only guess at what might happen. Human nature being what it is, some investors may well take a more optimistic view of the future than others.

We cannot accept that all the assumptions made about the financial environment are realistic. There are taxes and, more importantly, in many countries there are differences between the tax treatment of dividends and of capital gains. It is not simply a case of saying that the return on an investment is a combination of a dividend yield and a capital gain (or loss) on the share price. Because, if the two are taxed differently, how that total return is to be split between these two elements will be important. Not only that, investors in the same investments but with different tax situations will therefore receive different effective (i.e. after-tax) returns for the same risk.

Transaction costs also exist. Investors have to pay commission and other costs on share transactions, and there is a further cost to consider in the fact that, in practice, there is a (small) difference between the buying price and the selling price of a share.

Lastly, although investors can lend at the risk-free rate of interest (by investing in government bonds), they certainly *cannot* borrow at that rate.

Thus we must conclude that many of the assumptions that underlie the CAPM are clearly unrealistic. However, whether or not the assumptions that underlie the model are realistic is not a matter of importance. The real question is the one we started with: Does it work? Does the model have '*predictive power*'?

The empirical evidence

A model may have highly *realistic* assumptions, but if it has no *predictive power* it is largely worthless. On the other hand, a model may be constructed on very *unrealistic* assumptions and yet, *if it works*, then the unrealistic assumptions don't really matter.

So does the CAPM work? Do we, in an efficient, equilibrium stock market, observe the linear risk-return relationship shown in Figure 12.3? Unfortunately, the answer is not quite as simple as 'Let's take a look'. The reason, as was pointed out by Richard Roll in a now famous article (known as Roll's critique), published in 1977, is that in order to test the CAPM, we need to be able to identify the return on the market portfolio.[11] In practice, it is virtually impossible to do so.

Most researchers who have tried to test the CAPM to see if it works have used a stock market index as a surrogate of the market portfolio. But no stock market index includes all the companies quoted on the stock market but only (what they hope is) a representative selection. For example, in the UK there are well over 2000 stock exchange listed companies, but the FTSE all-share index only contains 630 of these investments.

Not only that but, as Roll pointed out, even if you did include all the companies quoted on the stock exchange, you are still excluding a wide range of other types of investments. These might include shares in unquoted companies, antiques, precious metals and stamp collections. Therefore it is virtually impossible to be able to identify the return on the *true* market portfolio of *all* capital assets.

Nevertheless, despite the problems put forward by Roll, hundreds of researchers have attempted to test the CAPM to see if it works, looking at the relationship between observed beta values and average returns.

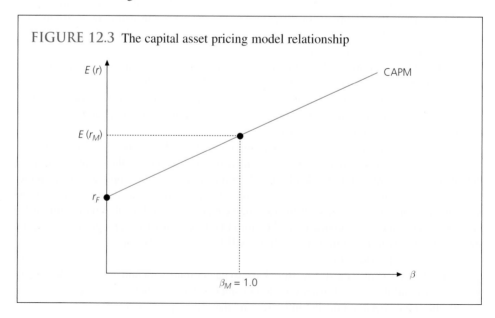

FIGURE 12.3 The capital asset pricing model relationship

The model is normally tested on the basis of 'risk premiums'. In other words, if we take the basic CAPM in terms of shares in company Z:

$$E(r_z) = r_F + [E(r_M) - r_F] \times \beta_z$$

and subtract the risk-free return from both sides of the equation:

$$E(r_z) - r_F = [E(r_M) - r_F] \times \beta_z$$

This then gives the risk premium on investment Z $[E(r_z) - r_F]$, equals the average risk premium on the stock market $[E(r_M) - r_F]$ times the beta value. We also add into the equation a 'vertical intercept term' – a – which should be zero. Thus:

$$E(r_z) - r_F = a + [E(r_M) - r_F] \times \beta_z$$

This intercept term plays an important role in the testing of the CAPM. As we know, the CAPM is a very simple model which states that the risk premium on an investment is *purely* a function of the average risk premium on the stock market *times* beta – a factor which is designed to measure the systematic risk of the investment relative to the average systematic risk of the stock market. If the 'a' vertical intercept term does not turn out to be zero, it indicates that some other factor(s), besides relative systematic risk, are involved in determining the investment's return.

The results of these tests show up three important things. The first is that there *does* appear to be a positive linear relationship between beta and the investment's return. So, fundamentally, we could conclude the CAPM does appear to be correct: high beta shares give higher returns, and low beta shares give lower returns.

However this conclusion, that the tests show the CAPM to be fundamentally correct, is controversial. Others would argue the reverse, because of the other two points the results show up. The first of these is that the 'a' intercept is *not* zero, but is positive. This indicates that there are other factors besides relative systematic risk that determine return.

A number of researchers have followed up this point and have tried to identify what these other factors may be. Two promising factors appear to be the company size and dividend policy. Smaller companies tend to give slightly higher returns than larger companies with the same beta value. Similarly, companies with high dividend yields give slightly greater returns than companies with similar beta values, but with lower dividend yields. However, it may well be that once the tax differences between dividend income and capital gains are taken into account this effect ceases to be significant.

Other researchers have found an apparent relationship between a company's price–earnings ratio (PER) (the ratio of share price/earnings per share), and its return. Companies with low PERs give higher returns than similar beta companies with higher PERs. However, it needs to be recognized that the earnings figure is based on historic accounting data whilst the price is based on market expectations. This does, however, imply that earnings figures might be a better predictor of future returns than we might often give them credit for.

Finally, other research has found evidence that returns on shares may have some element of *seasonality* in them. In other words, what determines the return is not only the beta, but also the position of the company within its seasonal cycle.

There is also other evidence which shows up problems with the CAPM. This is specifically in terms of Roll's criticisms that our usual measures of the market portfolio are inadequate. Evidence has been found that for some industries – such as companies in the oil industry and in natural resources – the CAPM is a particularly *poor* predictor because, it is argued, the market portfolio surrogate that is used is under-representative of those areas.

We said earlier that the empirical research has unearthed three real points of interest. The third of these is that the actual slope of the CAPM appears to be slightly less than the predicted slope. This is illustrated in Figure 12.4. In other words, low beta shares (those with $\beta < 1$) tend to give *slightly higher r* returns than CAPM would predict, while high beta shares ($\beta > 1$) tend to give *slightly lower* returns than CAPM would predict. No really convincing explanation for this phenomenon has been forthcoming.

Despite all the foregoing, these arguments should be kept in perspective. Although the CAPM is not *perfect*, it probably is a *fairly good* predictor of returns and it is certainly better than anything else that is available. The other point which should not be lost sight of is that, although there may be a number of other factors (e.g. company size and dividend policy), which go towards determining returns, it still appears that relative systematic risk (beta) is by far the most important of these factors.

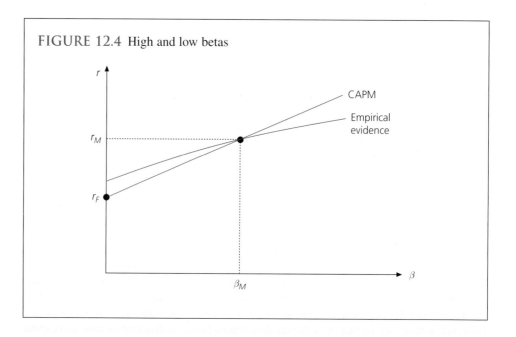

FIGURE 12.4 High and low betas

REAL WORLD VIEW: Divided opinion – is the CAPM still relevant today?

As we have seen in this chapter, the CAPM – although widely used and recognized – is not without controversy. Developed independently throughout the 1960s by various economists, it was celebrated as a neat framework to base investment decisions on. That some of its developers won a Nobel Prize for contributions to economics in 1990 is in itself testament to its widespread appeal and longevity. But does its 'neatness' and simplicity as a theoretical model actually serve to distort its true value in the real world?

The heart of this issue is whether such a theoretical and mathematical model can be applied both tangibly and reliably to the real situation it simulates. Broadly speaking, there are two camps. Many uphold the model's utility (and indeed the very notion that a mathematical formula is applicable when it comes to asset pricing), whereas detractors suggest that there is simply no convincing empirical evidence to back it up. *Financial Times* writer, John Kay, seemingly sides with the latter, intent on 'consign[ing] the CAPM to the dustbin of scientific history,' despite recognizing the fact that 'the model remains central to modern financial economics.'

The lampooning of scientifically derived theories that take a purely mathematical-logic approach to behavioural phenomena is nothing new – Kay cites an infamous 1974 journal article on 'The Economics of Brushing Teeth' as an example. The chief arguments against CAPM are that it fails to take into consideration market instability, unpredictability of behaviour and other key human aspects that can't be rationalized or reduced into a succinct model. Opponents also criticize the idea that all economic decisions are driven by the desire to 'maximize'. Nobel laureate Markowitz (whose work sowed the seeds for the creation of the CAPM) has since picked holes in the model, speaking around 2007 on the assumptions central to CAPM: 'None of these assumptions are realistic.'

Another issue is that 'simple rules of thumb and common sense' may in reality be just as effective, yet can be dismissed as unscientific, unquantifiable and hence unlikely to court favour of critics and investors seeking (or requiring) a methodical rule to justify decision-making.

As with all scientific theories, a model is often simply the 'best fit' of describing a situation, until a *better* fit comes along to take its place. Eugene Fama, himself a 2013 Nobel Prize winner who has also criticized the model in recent years, is one of several economists to develop an alternative. As the name suggests, his 'Fama–French three-factor model' incorporates multiple variables, rather than just the one of the CAPM. It is also arguably more robust through taking into account local factors. Other methods include Merton's portfolio problem and arbitrage pricing (discussed shortly in this chapter).

Financial columnist James Mackintosh, commenting on choice behind the 2013 Nobel Prize winners, suggests that the theories should be tempered by a degree of common sense: 'start with a rigorous, but false, model, then tweak it to take account of one's view of whether prices are cheap or expensive'.

So is the CAPM still relevant? The key is in knowing its limitations. Whilst not without its detractors, and despite the introduction of other, supposedly more reliable models, the CAPM – perhaps due to its utility – remains a prevalent model today.

ARBITRAGE PRICING THEORY

Detractors of the CAPM believe that a superior asset pricing model exists: the arbitrage pricing model or APM. In many ways, the CAPM can be viewed as being a *special* case of this more general model and, in that sense, the APM is probably superior to the CAPM. The 'only' problem is that, so far, researchers have had great difficulty in identifying the information that is needed to make it work in practice.

The APM looks very similar to the CAPM, but its origins are significantly different. Whereas the CAPM is a *single-factor* model, the APM is a *multi-factor* model. Instead of just a single beta value there is a whole set of beta values – one for each factor.

Arbitrage pricing theory (APT), out of which the APM arises, states that the expected return on an investment is dependent upon how that investment reacts to a set of individual macroeconomic factors (the degree of reaction being measured by the betas) and the risk premium associated with each of those macroeconomic factors.

This is, of course, exactly what the CAPM does – except that it only looks at *one* factor, the return on the market portfolio. CAPM looks at how the return on an investment reacts to changes in the return on the market portfolio (the investment's beta value) and the risk premium on the market portfolio ($E(r_M) - r_F$).

In contrast, APM states that the expected return on investment A, is given by:

$$E(r_A) = r_F + (r_{F1} - r_F)\beta_{F1} + (r_{F2} - r_F)\beta_{F2} + \dots$$

where *F1* and *F2* etc. refer to these individual macroeconomic factors.

The first problem with using the APM is that we are uncertain about the identity of all these macroeconomic factors (i.e. *F1, F2, F3*, etc.). Second, we are uncertain about how to measure the investment's sensitivity to changes in each of these factors (i.e. β_{F1}, β_{F2}, etc.). Finally, it is difficult to identify the risk premium of each of these macroeconomic factors (i.e. $(r_{F1} - r_F)$, $(r_{F2} - r_F)$, etc.).

In many ways the APM is a good idea but certainly, at present, it is still a long way from being (and may never be) of practical use. Nevertheless, some advances have been made, especially in terms of trying to identify the macroeconomic factors that determine an investment's return.

Several factors appear to have been identified as being important (some of which, such as inflation and money supply, industrial production and personal consumption, do have aspects of being interrelated). In particular, researchers have identified:

1. Changes in the level of industrial production in the economy.
2. Changes in the shape of the yield curve.
3. Changes in the default-risk premium (i.e. changes in the return required on bonds with different perceived risks of default).
4. Changes in the inflation rate.
5. Changes in the real interest rate.
6. The level of personal consumption.
7. The level of money supply in the economy.

All of these accord with common sense. Given that the value of the firm can be seen as the discounted present value of the future cash flow it is expected to generate, then it is changes to this value that will bring about changes to the return on the firm's shares. The index of industrial production (which is obviously similar in reality to the CAPM's market portfolio) is an obvious indicator of the firm's ability to generate future cash flows. Similarly, the other factors are all – to some extent – going to impact either on the level of the cash flows that the company is able to generate or on the discount rate used by the market to convert those expected cash flows to present value.

The idea is that all firms in the economy will react – to some extent – to change in these seven factors. Furthermore, all firms will react in a similar way. For example, an increase in the level of industrial production will be good news for them all, and so these factors will not be capable of being diversified away. However, not all firms will react to the same extent – some will be more affected than others. This degree of sensitivity would be measured by a set of beta values for each firm – one beta value for each factor. Finally, as none of these factors can be diversified away, they will each have a risk premium. In other words, there will be a reward for accepting the risk, of say, the impact of an unanticipated change in the level of inflation on a company's cash flow.

If we describe these seven factors as *F1–F7*, then we could try to measure the beta value of each factor on the same basis as we measure beta values for the CAPM. Thus for company A:

$$\beta_{A_{F_1}} = \frac{\sigma_A \times \rho_{A,F_1}}{\sigma_{F_1}} \qquad \beta_{A_{F_2}} = \frac{\sigma_A \times \rho_{A,F_2}}{\sigma_{F_2}}$$

where σ_A = standard deviation of returns on A shares, σ_{FI} = standard deviation of the level of industrial production, ρ_{AFI} = correlation coefficient between the returns on A shares and the level of industrial production, etc.

Some research has been undertaken applying the APM and, in particular, comparing its results with those of the CAPM. The outcome has been mixed. Some research has shown that the APM does give superior predictions to the CAPM in certain situations (usually when the industry group is effectively under-represented in the market portfolio). Other research, however, has indicated that the APM tells us very little that we don't already know from the far simpler CAPM.

Therefore the conclusion that we reach is the same conclusion that we reach in many other areas of corporate finance theory: we are a long way from the end of the road of truly knowing what the answers are to all the questions.

BETAS AND PROJECT INVESTMENT APPRAISAL

The project discount rate

The link between the CAPM and our quest for an NPV discount rate for project investment appraisal seems obvious. The CAPM can be used to generate the appropriate discount rate ($E(r_{project})$) having taken into account the systematic risk of the project:

$$E(r_{project}) = r_F + [E(r_M) - r_F]\beta_{project}$$

However, there are two major difficulties: one conceptual and one practical.

The conceptual difficulty concerns the fact that the CAPM is a single-period return model, whereas the discount rate required for an NPV calculation is obviously a multi-time period rate of return. As a result, strictly speaking, the CAPM-generated rate of return cannot be applied to an NPV calculation. One solution would be to derive a multi-time period capital asset pricing model – such models do exist. However, there are considerable difficulties involved with them which restricts their practical usefulness.

If it can be assumed that the risk-free return and the excess market return, i.e. $E(r_M - r_F)$, will remain *approximately* constant over the life of the project, then the single-period CAPM model can be used safely in a multi-time period analysis such as an NPV analysis. If such assumptions cannot be made with reasonable confidence – and one problem here is that the excess market return does show some degree of volatility over time – then at least we can try to allow for some of the multi-time period effects. For example, the annual yield to redemption on government bonds that has the same number of years to maturity as the life of the project can be taken as the estimate of the risk-free return. However, the basic problem of CAPM being a single-period model does remain.

Nevertheless, using the CAPM to provide an NPV discount rate is certainly a considerable improvement on estimating a discount rate on the basis of management's own subjective value judgement (as we saw in Chapter 9), or not taking risk into account at all. The pragmatic solution is to conclude that, in the light of these circumstances, if a CAPM-generated expected rate of return is to be used as an NPV discount rate, it should only be used with caution. But, having stated that, the CAPM does at least provide a framework for analyzing what should be a project's discount rate, and it is likely to provide an estimate that is of the correct order of magnitude, given the project's systematic risk. In short, the CAPM may not be the perfect way to estimate a project's discount rate, but it is the best way that we have available.

The project beta

The second difficulty concerns the identification of the project's beta value. Obviously this cannot be estimated in the way that a share's beta is estimated; nor would it be fruitful to consider trying to estimate a project's beta through estimating the individual components of the beta value expression.

One possible approach to solving the problem is to use the beta value of the *industry group* within which the project could be classified, as a surrogate for the beta value of the project. The industry beta value would simply be an average of the beta values of the firms within that industry.[12] Thus, if the project under appraisal was a cement production facility, then the average beta value of the quoted companies in the cement industry could be taken as an estimate of the project's beta. (However, some adjustments might have to be made to the beta value obtained in this way, if it were thought that the project's systematic risk characteristics differed significantly from those of the cement industry generally.)

Adjusting beta

How should such adjustments be made? What happens if a project does not fall neatly within an industrial classification (or the classification is thought to be too wide to be appropriate)? The answer to both these questions is that we require a clearer idea of the identification of systematic risk.

We know that systematic risk refers to the degree of sensitivity to macroeconomic changes. Thus to form a view about the systematic risk of a particular project, we need to examine the degree to which its cash flows – its revenue and cost flows – react to changes in the economy, such as changes in the business cycle or in rates of unemployment. In other words, how closely related are the project's cash inflows and outflows to macroeconomic forces?

The greater the degree to which the cash inflows are related (that is, the greater is their sensitivity to macroeconomic changes), then the greater is their systematic risk and the greater should be the project's beta value. The reverse will apply to the project cash outflows; thus, if the cash outflows are also sensitive to macroeconomic changes – i.e. the costs are variable rather than fixed – then this will tend to reduce the degree of the project's systematic risk. Conversely, if most of a project's costs are fixed and do not vary with macro economic changes, then this adds to the systematic risk.

A project with cash inflows that are highly sensitive to changes in macroeconomic factors, but with cash outflows that are mostly fixed and therefore are not sensitive to macroeconomic changes, would be classified as a highly (systematic) risky project. The opposite would be a project with mainly variable costs and a revenue flow that was relatively insensitive to macroeconomic changes.

Thus, if it is possible to identify a fairly narrow industrial classification within which a particular investment falls, then the beta value of that industry could be taken as an initial estimate of the project's beta. This can then be adjusted (on a necessarily subjective basis) to allow for the project's particular revenue and cost cash flow sensitivities, when they are thought to differ from the industry norm. In situations where a suitable industry classification does not exist, the relevant characteristics of the project's revenue and cost cash flows would have to be examined and an attempt made to match them to an industry (and its beta value) with cash flows that exhibit similar characteristics.

Finally, there is the situation where a stock exchange listed company is involved in the appraisal of a project that falls within the normal area of its business. Here the company's own beta value can provide the starting point, with adjustments being made to allow for the atypical aspects of the project's sensitivity to macroeconomic factors. However, even in these circumstances, the industry beta (if possible) is likely to be a more satisfactory starting point than the individual company beta. This is because the individual company beta – estimated from the slope of the regression line through the historical market relationship – will contain some estimation error.[13] Using an industry beta, which is an average of individual company betas, helps to reduce substantially the amount of this error (in much the same way that unsystematic risk is reduced through diversification).

This whole problem of identifying a suitable beta value to generate a discount rate for a project's investment appraisal is complex and we will return to this discussion at a later stage.

One final point

The CAPM is a model for pricing capital assets, e.g. shares. We know from the previous chapter that in the single-period world of the CAPM, the return on a share is given by:

$$r_j = \frac{(P_j 1 - P_j 0) + \text{Divs}}{P_j 0}$$

where $P_j 0$ is the current price per share in company j and $Pj1$ is the end of period price per share. Suppose we take the simplest possible case and assume that no dividend is paid during the time that the share is held. In such circumstances:

$$r_j = \frac{(P_j 1 - P_j 0)}{P_j 0}$$

From this, we can use the CAPM to determine what should be the current market price of the share:

$$\frac{E(P_j 1) - P_j 0}{P_j 0} = r_F + [E(r_M) - r_F]\beta_j$$

simplifying:

$$P_j0 = \frac{E(P_j1)}{1 + r_F + [E(r_M) - r_F]\beta_j}$$

and rearranging:

$$\frac{E(P_j1 - P_j0)}{P_j0} = r_F + [E(r_M) - r_F]\beta_j$$

In this expression, the denominator can be thought of as a risk-adjusted discount rate, where $[E(r_M) - r_F]\,\beta j$ represents the share's risk premium. Therefore, the current equilibrium share price is equal to the expected future share price, discounted to present value using a risk-adjusted discount rate: in other words the discount rate reflects the (systematic) risk of the shares.

This way of looking at CAPM is useful in the context of the foregoing discussion about using CAPM within an NPV analysis, because it shows CAPM as providing a risk-adjusted discount rate – albeit for just one time period. It is precisely this that we are seeking to use as an NPV discount rate in an investment appraisal, in the face of uncertainty.

This is not the end of our consideration either of the investment appraisal discount rate or the CAPM. We shall find that in the following chapters we will make repeated references to both topics. However, for the time being we will turn to look at some other aspects of risk and ways in which a company's management can respond.

SUMMARY

This chapter discussed how the CAPM is developed out of portfolio theory, and examined its meaning and use. The main points made were as follows:

- The CML expression deals with the expected return on an efficient portfolio investment. From this can be derived the expected return on an *inefficient* investment: the expected return on the shares of an individual company. Such an expression is termed the capital asset pricing model.

- In the CAPM, the risk premium is determined by the product of the market price of risk and the share's systematic risk level. This latter value is given by the product of the share's total risk (σ) and the degree to which the returns on the share are correlated to the returns on the market portfolio.

- Normally, in practice, a share's systematic risk is not measured in absolute terms, but in terms relative to the (systematic) risk of the market portfolio. This is indicated by the beta value.

- Shares with betas greater than one will have more systematic risk than the average level of systematic risk on the stock market (indicated by the risk of the market portfolio), and their share price behaviour will tend to be more volatile than the general stock market index.

- Shares with betas of less than one will have less systematic risk than the average, and their share price behaviour will tend to underperform in movements in the general market index.

- As high beta shares are more risky than average, they will be expected to produce a return higher than average. Low beta shares will similarly be expected to produce a return lower than average.

- Unsystematic, or diversifiable, risk is principally caused by company-specific factors (such as labour relations and management quality) which affect the performance of a company's cash flow. Such effects will be *washed away* in a well-diversified portfolio.

- Systematic, or non-diversifiable, risk is principally caused by macroeconomic factors that affect all firms in the stock market, to a greater or lesser extent. Such factors would include the rate of national economic growth and the level and volatility of exchange rates. The impact of these effects cannot be eradicated through diversification.

- A company's exposure to systematic risk is determined by the degree of its revenue sensitivity to these macroeconomic-type effects and also by its cost sensitivity – that is, its ratio of fixed to variable costs. Most importantly, the greater the revenue sensitivity, the greater the degree of systematic risk.

- Beta can, in theory, be measured from first principles using the beta expression of covariance over market variance: $Cov(r_A, r_M)/ \sigma^2_M$. However, it is usually estimated by the slope of the regression line of the relationship between the returns on the share and the returns on the market portfolio.

- Although the CAPM is developed under a set of rather unrealistic assumptions, the empirical evidence does tend to suggest that a positive, linear risk–return relationship, of the type described by the CAPM, does really exist. Despite the theoretical problems that exist in the testing of the model, and despite the evidence which suggests that systematic risk is not the sole determinant of return, we can conclude that the CAPM does appear to capture the essence of the relationship between risk and return on the stock market.

- The CAPM can be viewed as being a special, single-factor model, of a more general model: the arbitrage pricing theory model. However, although research has indicated that there may be a whole range of factors that determine an investment's return, the capture of the determinants within a multi-factor APT model is not yet developed as a practical tool.

- Finally, the use of CAPM to generate NPV discount rates for project appraisal was examined. A number of problems arise in this use of the CAPM, not least of which are the facts that the CAPM is a single-period model and NPV is a multi-period analysis and that project betas have to be estimated on the basis of industry betas. However, this application of the CAPM will be further developed at a later stage.

NOTES

1. The portfolio risk expression, when $\rho_{ab} = +1$, can be given as:

$$\sigma_p = \sqrt{[x^2\sigma^2_A + (1-x)^2\sigma^2_B + 2x(1-x)\sigma_A\sigma_B]}$$

Remembering that:

$$(a + b)^2 = a^2 + b^2 + 2ab$$

then:

$$\sigma_p = \sqrt{[x\sigma_A + (1 - x)\sigma_B]^2}$$

and:

$$\sigma_p = x\sigma_A + (1 - x)\sigma_B$$

2. That is, the risk taken on by the particular point the investor has chosen to locate his portfolio on the CML.

3. Perhaps a safer description at this stage would be to say that share price movements and dividends are determined by the expected future success of the company.

4. Although it is not considered here, there may well be a possibility of eliminating some country-specific macroeconomic factors by holding an internationally diversified portfolio.

5. In practice we do not have to calculate a share's beta value as beta values for shares listed on all significant stock markets are widely available and easily accessible.

6. The sign ' ≈ ' means 'approximately equal to'.

7. Or a portfolio of any number of assets.

8. The relationship would be positive in a 'correlation coefficient' sense. In other words, the return on the shares in the individual company will tend to move in the *same direction* as the return on the general stock market index.

9. Most introductory textbooks on statistics will show how such a line of best fit might be calculated from scatter diagram data.

10. The rationale of this advice is dealt with more fully in Chapter 16. Basically, there is an *inverse* relationship between a share's price and its return. Therefore, where the alpha value has been negative, the return has been *too* low in the past and so can be expected to rise in the future – by the share price falling. Hence the advice to sell negative alpha shares before the share price does actually fall.

11. Roll, 'A Critique of the Asset Pricing Theory's Tests', *Journal of Financial Economics,* March 1977.

12. In making such a calculation, the differing capital structures of the companies (i.e. the ratio of equity to fixed interest capital) must be taken into account. This topic will be returned to in a later chapter, after the issue of capital structure has been discussed.

13. Indicated by the scatter of the plots on the graph around the regression line. The greater the degree of scatter, the greater the degree of possible error.

FURTHER READING

1. Much of the CAPM literature is mathematically demanding. However, an excellent article which is very readable is the two parts of: F. Modigliani and G.A. Pogue, 'An Introduction to Risk and Return: Concepts and Evidence', *Financial Analysts Journal,* March–April and May–June 1974.

2. Another excellent review article is K. Peansell, 'The Capital Asset Pricing Model', in *Issues in Finance,* M. Firth and S.M. Keane (eds), Philip Allen 1986.

3. Two further excellent articles can be found in the book of readings edited by J.M. Stern and D.H. Chew, *The Revolution in Corporate Finance,* Blackwell 1992. They are: J. MacQueen, 'Beta is Dead! Long Live Beta!' and B. Rosenberg and A. Rudd, 'The Corporate Uses of Beta'.

4. On the empirical evidence and testing of the CAPM, see E.F. Fama and K.R. French, 'The Capital Asset Pricing Model: Theory and Evidence', *Journal of Economic Perspectives*, 18, 2004; H. Levy, 'The CAPM is Alive and Well: A Review and Synthesis', *European Financial Management,*

December 2009; E. Dimson, P. Marsh and M. Staunton, 'Global Evidence on the Equity Risk Premium', *Journal of Applied Corporate Finance*, Fall 2003 discuss the returns on equity in 16 countries in the 103 years from 1900 to 2002.

5. Roll's criticism of the CAPM tests makes difficult, but worthwhile, reading: R. Roll, 'A Critique of the Asset Pricing Theory's Tests', *Journal of Financial Economics,* March 1977. The article by Ross is also fairly demanding, but it is particularly interesting to see how the APT model is developed in an entirely different way to the CAPM: S.A. Ross, 'The Arbitrage Theory of Capital Asset Pricing', *Journal of Economic Theory,* December 1976.

6. Of direct relevance to the application of the CAPM to investment appraisal, there are a number of good articles, including: S.C. Myers and S. Turnbull, 'Capital Budgeting and the Capital Asset Pricing Model: Good News and Bad News', *Journal of Finance,* May 1977; H. Levy, 'Another Look at the CAPM', *Quarterly Review of Business and Economics,* Summer 1984; D.W. Mullins, 'Does the CAPM Work?', *Harvard Business Review,* January/February 1982; J.C. Van Horne, 'An Application of the CAPM to Divisional Required Returns', *Financial Management,* Spring 1980; and T.E. Conine and M. Tamarkin, 'Divisional Cost of Capital Estimation: Adjusting for Leverage', *Financial Management,* Spring 1985.

7. Finally, on APT, a clear overview is given by R. Bower and D. Logue, 'A Primer on Arbitrage Pricing Theory', in J.M. Stern and D.H. Chew (eds), *The Revolution in Corporate Finance,* Blackwell, 1992. Some empirical testing can be seen in N.F. Chen, R.W. Roll and S.A. Ross, 'Economic Forces and the Stock Market: Testing the APT and Alternative Asset Pricing Theories', *Journal of Business,* Autumn 1986. For a discussion on the possible APT model inputs, see C.B. McGowan and J.C. Francis, 'APT Factors and their Relationship to Macroeconomic Variables', in C.F. Lee *et al.* (eds), *Advances in Quantitative Analysis of Finance and Accounting,* JAI Press 1991; A. Ang and J. Chen, 'CAPM over the Long-run: 1926–2001', *Journal of Empirical Finance,* 14, 2007; J. Campbell and T. Vuolteenako, 'Bad Beta, Good Beta', *American Economic Review*, December 2004; E. Fama and K. French, 'The CAPM – Theory and Evidence', *Journal of Economic Perspectives,* Summer 2004; H. Levy, 'The CAPM is Alive and Well: A Review and Synthesis', *European Financial Management,* 16, 2010.

QUIZ QUESTIONS

1. Write down the standard CAPM expression for the expected return on company A shares.
2. What does beta measure?
3. What is unsystematic risk and what are its sources?
4. What determines a share's exposure to systematic risk?
5. Given the following information, what is company B's systematic risk, unsystematic risk and beta value?:

$$\sigma_B = 20\%$$

$$\sigma_M = 10\%$$

$$\rho_{B,M} = +0.6$$

6. What is company C's beta value, given the following information?:

$$Cov(r_C, r_M) = +73.5$$

$$\sigma_M = 7\%$$

7. Company D has a beta value of 1.2. It is thinking of undertaking a project with a beta value of 1.7. If, when accepted, the project will comprise 10% of the firm's total worth, what will be the subsequent beta value of the company?

8. Does an *overvalued* share lie above or below the CAPM line?

9. What is the principal difference between the CAPM and the APM?

10. Given the following information, what would be your advice concerning project X:

		Cash flow
0		−100
1		+ 60
2		+ 50
r_F	=	8%
$E(r_M)$	=	12%
$\beta_{industry}$	=	1.75

(See the 'Answers to Quiz Questions' section at the back of the book.)

PROBLEMS

The answers to three of the following problems (those indicated by an asterisk) are available to students online. The answer to the remaining problem is available only to lecturers (see the 'Digital Resources' page for details).

1* Hartmuth AG is a medium-sized software development company listed on the Frankfurt stock exchange. The company's directors would like to broaden the company's activities by acquiring a company that is involved in the development and marketing of computer gaming products.

   Hartmuth has identified three small gaming companies, of approximately equal worth of around €4 million each, as possible acquisition targets.

   Details of the market performance of these three companies are as follows:

Company	Beta factor	Total risk*	Risk specific to the company	Current dividend yield	Price–earnings ratio
Amter	0.67	30%	28%	11.1%	4.2
Börgö	1.14	36%	31%	9.5%	5.4
Claas	0.88	50%	48%	12.2%	4.7

*Risk is defined in terms of standard deviation and the unit of measurement is percentage returns.

The directors are unsure which of the three companies to acquire. At present, Hartmuth has a beta factor of 0.67, total risk (σ) of 30%, company-specific risk of 28% and a market worth of €62 million. The German DAX stock market index currently has a standard deviation of 16%.

▶

Required:

(a) Calculate the new market value and the new systematic (or market) risk of Hartmuth AG that would occur in each of three independent circumstances:

    (i)   if Hartmuth acquires company Amter

    (ii) if Hartmuth acquires company Börgö, and

    (iii) if Hartmuth acquires company Claas.

(b) Explain how diversification can reduce the total risk associated with Hartmuth's shares.

(c) Discuss why the directors of Hartmuth AG might wish to diversify, and suggest which of the three companies best meets the directors' requirements.

Discuss whether the shareholders of Hartmuth should welcome the proposed diversification.

2* Herve Vitold holds a well-diversified portfolio containing a large number of different companies' shares. He is considering investing in the quoted shares of *one* of two companies, Sanofi and Dolloré. The amount of money invested would be small, relative to the total value of his portfolio. He wishes to select whichever company's shares that will lead to the largest reduction in his portfolio risk, as measured by the variance of portfolio returns. The correlation coefficient of the returns on Sanofi's shares with the return on the market portfolio and with the returns on Herve Vitold's existing portfolio are expected to be 0.30 and 0.16 respectively over the coming years. The corresponding correlation coefficients for the returns on shares in Dolloré are 0.25 and 0.21, respectively. The standard deviations of returns for Sanofi and Dolloré are expected to be 35% and 30% respectively for the coming year and their expected returns for that period are 9% and 7% respectively.

Required:

(a) Advise M. Vitold on which of the two shares he should select for his portfolio in order to meet his objectives.

(b) Demonstrate why the expected return on an ordinary share in Sanofi is greater than that for Dolloré.

(c) Discuss how your advice might change if M. Vitold's portfolio contained shares in only a very small number of listed companies.

(d) Discuss why the relevant measure of risk may vary between a company's shareholders, debt holders and managers.

3* The government of Mauritius is considering how to protect its domestic cement industry. There is only one cement manufacturer in the country – CiMaurice – which is being adversely affected by competition from imported cement. Currently the government is considering banning imports of cement and – because that would leave CiMaurice with a monopoly – imposing government controls on the price of cement.

In this respect the government want to be able to compare the systematic riskiness of CiMaurice with that of its overseas competitors. With this knowledge, they hope to be able to determine a fair return for the company's shareholders and hence, the price that should be set for cement.

As a result, you have been called in by the government to try to estimate the company's beta value. Mauritius has a small stock exchange and CiMaurice is one of the listed companies. The government has provided you with the following information:

▶

	CiMaurice		Mauritius stock exchange		Return
	Average share price Rs	Dividend yield	Average SEM index	Average dividend yield	Government bonds
Current year	16.42	10%	1983	16%	15%
1 year ago	15.50	12%	1665	16%	16%
2 years ago	12.10	8%	1789	10%	14%
3 years ago	9.50	10%	1490	18%	15%

Required:

(a) Estimate the beta value of CiMaurice

(b) Comment on what effects you think that the government's action might have on the riskiness of CiMaurice.

4 John Smith has savings of £12 000. Of this amount he has invested £6000 in government bonds which currently yield a return of 6%. The remainder has been invested in a portfolio of four different companies' shares that are listed on the London stock exchange. Details of this portfolio are as follows:

Company	Expected return	Beta shares	Worth of shareholding
W	7.6%	0.20	£1 200
X	12.4%	0.80	£1 200
Y	15.6%	1.20	£1 200
Z	18.8%	1.60	£2 400

Required:

(a) Calculate the expected return and beta value of Mr Smith's savings portfolio.

(b) Mr Smith has decided that he wants an expected return of 12% on his savings portfolio. Show how he would achieve this by selling some of his government bonds and investing the proceeds in the market portfolio.

(c) If Mr Smith was *only* to invest in government bonds and the market portfolio, what savings portfolio would be required to give him an expected return of 10.32%?

(d) If Mr Smith wants to choose between his existing savings portfolio (as in (a)) and the one constructed in (c), which would you advise, and why?

(e) Explain the significance, if any, of both alpha and beta values to investors in quoted shares.

OPTION VALUATION

INTRODUCTION

The three previous chapters have looked at the nature of risk. In particular, we have seen that the total risk of an investment can be split into that part that can be eliminated through diversification, and that part of total risk which cannot be diversified away. Furthermore, we have seen that all investors dislike risk – they dislike the fact that an investment's outcome is uncertain – and therefore they demand a reward for undertaking a risky investment. The reward for risk-taking is in the form of the return that the investment is expected to yield; the more risky the investment, the greater must be the anticipated return.

An alternative approach to understanding the implication of risk-aversion is to say that more risky investments will be less valuable (and therefore be priced lower) than less risky investments. Suppose an investment is expected to produce a cash inflow of €110 with great certainty (i.e. very little risk). As such, you judge that you would require the reward of a 10% return to persuade you to undertake the investment. This implies that you would be willing to pay €100 to undertake the investment because, for an outlay of €100, the investment gives the required rate of return of 10%: (€110 − €100) ÷ €100 = 0.10 or 10%.

Now suppose another investment is also expected to produce a cash inflow of €110 but there is much greater uncertainty about whether this expected cash flow will actually occur (i.e. this investment is much *more* risky). As a result, let us say that, on this much more risky investment, you decide that you require a 37.5% return to persuade you to undertake the investment. This means that you are only willing to pay €80 to undertake that investment: (€110 − €80) ÷ €80 = 0.375 or 37.5%.

Thus, both investments are expected to produce a cash flow of €110, but the *more* risky investment is *less* valuable and is worth only €80; whilst the *less* risky investment is *more* valuable and is worth €100.

THE BASIC CHARACTERISTICS OF OPTIONS

However, as we know, risk is a 'two-way street'. An investment where the outcome is uncertain, can perform both better than expected (the upside potential), as well as worse than expected (the downside risk).

Although we assume that investors are generally risk-averse – in other words they dislike risky investments and so place a lower value on them, than investments with less risk – it is really only the *downside risk* of an investment that is disliked: upside potential is welcomed.

Option contracts are a type of financial security that can be used to provide protection against an investment's downside risk whilst, at the same time, allowing advantage to be taken of its upside potential. This characteristic of option contracts makes them highly desirable, and hence valuable. This value of an option is known as the option 'premium'.

When talking about stock markets, we can refer to the 'primary' stock market and the 'secondary' stock market. On the primary market, new shares are created (issued), by companies, who sell them to investors. Once investors have bought these shares on the **primary** market they can then, if they so wish, sell them on to other investors. This buying and selling of shares *between* investors, takes place on the **secondary** stock market. Options (or more correctly, option contracts) are financial securities, just like shares are financial securities. And, just like shares, we can talk about primary and secondary option markets.

On the primary option market, new options are created (the technical word used is that new options are '**written**') by *option writers,* who sell them on to investors. These investors can, if they so wish, sell on the options that they bought off the option writer, to other investors. This activity takes place on the secondary option market.

The distinction between buying options on the primary market and buying them on the secondary market is not important as far as we are concerned. However, the distinction between selling options on the primary market (i.e. writing options) and selling options – that the seller has already bought – on the secondary market, is very important. In this chapter, generally speaking, references to *selling* options will relate to activity on the *primary* market. Therefore, any reference to 'selling an option' will refer to the process of creating, or writing, an option by an option writer. When the selling process relates to an activity on the secondary market, the text will specifically mention that this is the case. Why this distinction is important will become clear at a later stage.

Types of options

There are many different types of options in the real world. In this book we will be concerned with three types of 'financial' options, as well as what are called 'real' options. The three financial options we will look at are:

- share options
- foreign currency options, and
- interest rate options.

The 'real' options are concerned with capital investment decisions and we will consider these types of options at the end of this chapter. In addition, we will look at interest rate options in the next chapter, when examining interest rate risk management; and foreign currency options, when we cover foreign exchange risk management in a later chapter. For the time being we will concentrate on share options.

OPTION TERMINOLOGY

Before we start to look more closely at the valuation of share options, we first have to introduce some option terminology.

Call options and put options

The owner of an equity **call** option has the right to **buy** a specific quantity of shares in a particular company, at a fixed price, which is called the exercise price (or strike price) of the option. Similarly, the owner of a **put** option has the right to **sell** a specific quantity of a particular share at a fixed exercise price.

Thus *call* options give the right to *buy*. *Put* options give the right to *sell*. However, it is important to note that the owner of a call (or a put) option only has the *right* to buy (or sell), but they do not have any *obligation* to do so.

Exchange-traded options and over-the-counter options

Options can be bought either in special 'option markets', where *standard* option contracts are traded, or from banks, where *tailor-made* options can be bought. The standardized options are known as '*traded options*' and the tailor-made options are known as '*OTC options*' (over-the-counter options). Standardized traded options tend to be slightly cheaper than similar, tailor-made OTC options.

'American' and 'European' options

As has been said, options give the owner the right to buy (a call) or sell (a put) a particular share at a fixed price. When this right expires it is known as the option's expiry date, or maturity date. If the option's owner decides to take up their right to buy (or sell), this is known as *exercising* the option.

American options can be exercised at any time, up to the option's expiry date. On the other hand, *European* options can only be exercised on the expiry date, and not before.

Exchange-traded options are always American options. OTC options – because they are tailor-made – can be either American or European. However, in practice, OTC options tend to be European options.

THE VALUATION OF OPTIONS

A key aspect of options is to understand what determines their value or price – in other words, what determines the **option premium**. This *market value of an option* – the option premium – consists of *two* elements: (a) the **intrinsic value,** and (b) the **time value**.

The intrinsic value of a call

The intrinsic value of an option is defined as the gain you would make if you exercised the option *immediately*. Therefore we can calculate the intrinsic value of a call option as the difference between the current share price and the option's exercise price:

> Intrinsic value of a call option = Current share price − Exercise price

For example, suppose you bought a call option some time ago, in respect of a share in the Webadz AG – a small software developer, based in 'Silicon Allee' in Berlin. The call option has an exercise price of 100 cents and it expires in 2.5-years' time. Let us assume that the option cost 5 cents to buy (its premium). Today, the current market price of Webadz shares is 115 cents, and so the intrinsic value of the option would be 115c − 100c = 15c. In other words, you could exercise your right today to buy a share in Webadz for 100 cents, then sell that share at its market price of 115 cents, and so make a *gain* of 15 cents giving you an overall *net profit* of 15c − 5c = 10c. This relationship between the exercise price, the market price, the premium paid and the resulting net profit is illustrated in Figure 13.1.

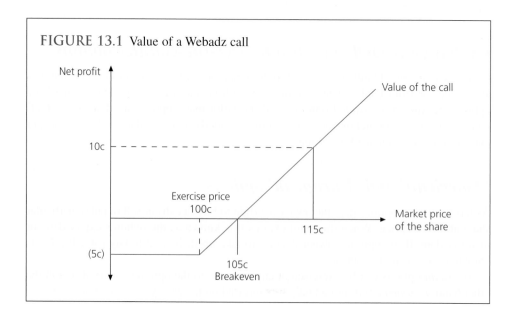

FIGURE 13.1 Value of a Webadz call

From this diagram we can see that the option will only become worth exercising (i.e. you make a gain on exercise) once the market price of the shares exceeds the exercise price of 100 cents. Furthermore, the *higher* the market price goes above 100c, the *greater* will be the gain on exercise and the greater will be the resulting net profit.

Also, notice that the breakeven market price – where the gain on exercise (or intrinsic value) equals the premium paid – can be calculated as:

Exercise price (100c) + Premium paid (5c) = Break even market price (105c)

The intrinsic value of a put

For a put option, the intrinsic value is the opposite of what it was for a call:

Intrinsic value of a put = Exercise price − Current share price

Suppose that you had bought a put option on the shares of Nanocerte – a French company involved with financial technology services – at an exercise price of 80 cents, for a premium of 10 cents. If the current market price of Nanocerte shares is 50 cents, then the option's intrinsic value is: 80c − 50c = 30c. In other words, you can currently buy a share in Nanocerte for 50 cents and then exercise your option to sell it for 80 cents, making a gain of 30 cents and a net profit of: 30c − 10c = 20c.

Again these relationships can be illustrated using a diagram (see Figure 13.2). In this case, the *lower* the market price of Nanocerte shares, the *greater* the gain on exercise (intrinsic value) and the greater is the net profit. However, the options would not be worth exercising if the market price of the shares was above 80 cents.

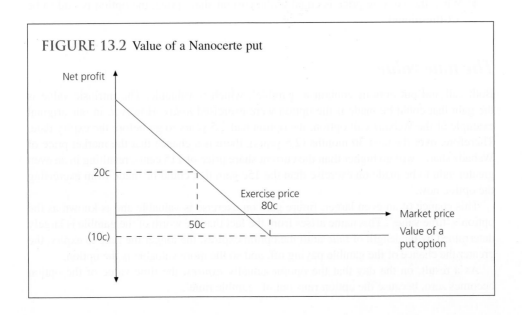

FIGURE 13.2 Value of a Nanocerte put

Minimum intrinsic value

It is important to realize that the intrinsic value of both call and put options **cannot** be negative. The minimum intrinsic value is *zero*. As a result, the maximum loss that can be incurred when buying either call or put options is simply the amount of the premium paid. The reason for this is that you are never forced to exercise an option. Remember that options give you a right, but not an obligation. If, upon exercise, you were to make a loss, you simply would *not* exercise the option. The option would be worthless and would be discarded, with the net result of the loss of the premium paid.

For example, if call options in Dynceed plc have an exercise price of £4.50 and the shares have a current market value of £3.80, then *exercising* the option would produce a loss:

Exercise the option to buy a share at:	£4.50
Sell the share at the current market price:	£3.80
Loss on exercise:	(65p)

Consequently, you would *not* exercise the option, and it would simply have a zero intrinsic value and a net loss of the premium that had been paid.

In-, out- and at-the-money options

Some more terminology:

- When an option's intrinsic value is positive, it is said to be '*in-the-money*'. Exercising an in-the-money option would produce a gain. An example of an in-the-money option would be Webadz.
- If the intrinsic value is zero (or potentially negative – as in the Dynceed example above), then it is said to be an **'out-of-the-money'** option.
- When the exercise price is equal to the current share price, the option is said to be **'at-the-money'**.

The time value

Both call and put options contain a 'gamble', which is valuable. The intrinsic value is the gain that could be made if the option were exercised *today*. However, in our original example of the Webadz call option, the option had 2.5 years to go before the expiry date. Therefore, over the next 30 months (2.5 years), there is a chance that the market price of Webadz shares will go higher than the current share price of 115 cents, resulting in an even greater gain to be made on exercise than the 15c gain that could be made from exercising the option now.

This chance of an even larger, future gain on exercise is valuable and is known as the option's 'time value'. This name arises from the fact that the worth of the gamble is largely determined by the length of *time* until the option expires: the longer the time to expiry, the greater the chance of the gamble paying off, and so the more valuable is the option.

As a result, on the day that the option actually *expires*, the time value of the option becomes zero, because the option runs out of 'gamble time'.

The market value

As a result, the 'market value' of an option – the premium payable – consists of these two elements:

$$\text{Market value} = \text{Intrinsic value} + \text{Time value}$$

and so, at all times:

- the market value of an option will be greater than its intrinsic value, **except** on the day of expiry, when the time value will be zero, and so the market value will *equal* the intrinsic value.

This then leads to an important observation: options would *never* (normally) be exercised *before* their expiry date. This is because the option would be more valuable if sold unexercised (for which you would receive its market value), than what it would be worth if exercised (for which you would receive only its intrinsic value).

Returning to our original example of Webadz call options; today the call option's *market value* would be greater than the 15 cents intrinsic value, and so the premium will be greater than 15c. Just what would be the *actual* premium we will come to shortly.

Finally, let us return for a moment to the distinction between American and European options. Although an American option can be exercised at any time up to its expiry date, we would never (normally) exercise *before* the expiry date: the option would be more valuable unexercised (its market value), than it would be exercised (its intrinsic value).

Determinants of intrinsic value

The intrinsic value of an option has already been defined as the gain that you can make from *immediate* exercise. Thus the intrinsic value is a function of two key determinants: (i) the option's exercise price, and (ii) the market price of the 'underlying' shares. In our example, the Webadz call options had an intrinsic value of 15 cents because of the 100c exercise price and the 115c Webadz share price. Obviously, a different exercise price, or a different market price, will change the intrinsic value:

- *Changing the exercise price.* For example, if the exercise price is *lower*, say only 90c, then the intrinsic value would have been *greater*: 115c − 90c = 25c intrinsic value. Similarly, a *higher* exercise price, say 112c, would have *reduced* the intrinsic value to: 115c − 112c = 3c. The intrinsic value becomes zero once the exercise price is greater than or equal to the market price of the share.

- *Changing the market price.* Returning to a 100c exercise price, if the Webadz share price now *increases* to 160c, then the intrinsic value of the options will also *increase*: 160c − 100c = 60c. Similarly, if the market price *falls* to 110c, then this will *reduce* the intrinsic value to: 110c − 100c = 10c. If the market price is less than or equal to the exercise price, the intrinsic value becomes zero.

Determinants of the time value

Three factors combine to determine an option's time value: (i) the length of time to expiry; (ii) the volatility (or variability) of the share's market price; and (iii) the time value of money.

- *(i) Time to expiry.* This point was referred to earlier. Quite simply, the longer the time to expiry, the greater is the chance that the gamble that the option contains, will pay off. Thus the longer is the time to expiry, the greater the value of the option and vice versa.

- *(ii) Volatility of the share price.* As we know, risk is a 'two-way street'. There is both a chance that the share price will move favourably, as well as adversely. Generally speaking, we say that investors do not like risk (i.e. they are risk-averse), because they don't like the prospect of an *adverse* movement. However, options protect investors from adverse movements, while allowing them to take advantage of any favourable movement. So with options, investors suddenly *like* the idea of risk in that, the more volatile/variable the share price is, the greater the chance of a favourable movement in the share price occurring (and also, of course, the greater the chance of an adverse movement but, of course, the option provides protection from that aspect). As a result, the *more volatile* the market price of the shares, the *greate*r the value of the option, and vice versa. This volatility of the share price is measured by the standard deviation of historic share price movements.

- *(iii) Time value of money.* Finally, the value of the option is affected by the time value of money, in the form of the risk-free interest rate. This is because, when valuing options, we have to take into account that the premium is payable *now*, but the exercise price is payable at some time *in the future*. Thus we need to find the present value of this future exercise price. The risk-free interest rate is used because the future exercise price is known with certainty. The higher is the risk-free interest rate, the lower is the present value of the future exercise price and so the greater will be the value of the option.

Determinants of the market value

Given the foregoing discussion, we can say that the market value of an option (i.e. its premium) is determined by a combination of five factors:

1. the exercise price
2. the current market share price
3. the time to expiry (in years)
4. the volatility of the share price
5. the (annual) time value of money.

These five determinants were combined by two American researchers, Black and Scholes, into a mathematically complex option valuation formula. It is not particularly helpful for us to go through the rather formidable mathematical derivation of the model (which involves stochastic calculus) within the context of this discussion. What is more important is to see how the model operates, as well as the reasoning that underlies it.

Before we start to look at the Black and Scholes option valuation model in detail, we should point out that there are two other factors that also have an impact on the value of options. One is whether they are European options (and so can only be exercised on the expiry date) or American options (and so can be exercised at any time up to their expiry date). The added flexibility of American options tends to make them slightly more valuable than the equivalent European option.

The other factor is the possibility of a dividend being paid on the shares before the expiry date of the options. The existence of a dividend provides a possible circumstance where American options might be exercised *before* the expiry date, in order to acquire the shares and so gain access to the dividend payment. The Black and Scholes model ignores the possibility of dividends and assumes that the options are European.

Finally, it should be pointed out that a number of different option valuation models have been developed over time. The Black and Scholes model has the distinction of being the first really practical model to be developed and, despite some difficulties in its application, the empirical research undertaken does tend to show that it remains an extremely good predictor of option values.

THE BLACK AND SCHOLES MODEL

Our look at the Black and Scholes model must necessarily begin with the introduction of some notation, as follows:

C = The market value of a call option (i.e. the option premium).

S = Current market price of the shares.

X = Option's exercise price.

Rf = Risk-free rate of interest.

T = Time, in years, until the option expires.

σ = Volatility (as measured by the standard deviation) of the share price.

$\log_e$ = Natural log.[1]

e = The mathematical constant: 2.718....

N = Cumulative area under the normal curve.

The model takes as its starting point the intrinsic value of a call option, but uses a slightly more sophisticated definition than the one that we have used earlier:

Intrinsic value of a call = Share price − *Present value* of the future exercise price

$$C = S - [X \times e^{-Rf \times T}]$$

but it then makes things a little more complicated by using *continuous* discounting, rather than the more normal type of discrete discounting that we use in NPV/IRR calculations. This is what the value: $e^{-Rf \times T}$ represents. (This discount factor could have been written as $(1 + Rf)^{-T}$, without too much loss or accuracy.)[2]

Finally, the share price, S, and the exercise price, X, both have to be adjusted to take into account the option's time (i.e. gamble) value. The share price is adjusted by a factor called $N(d_1)$, and the exercise price is also adjusted by another factor called $N(d_2)$. As a result we have the Black and Scholes option valuation model:

$$C = [S \times N(d_1)] - [X \times e^{-Rf \times T} \times N(d_2)]$$

where the two adjustment factors are:

$$(d_1) = \frac{\log_e\left(\dfrac{S}{X}\right) + (Rf \times T)}{\sigma \times \sqrt{T}} + \left(0.5 \times \sigma \times \sqrt{T}\right)$$

and:

$$(d_2) = (d_1) - \sigma \times \sqrt{T}$$

Notice that these two adjustment factors involve T – the time to expiry and also σ – the standard deviation/variability of the share price. In this way, they both adjust the values of the current share price and the present value of the future exercise price – and hence the value of the option – for the probability of possible future movements in the market price of the shares, up to the expiry date of the option.

Using the model

We can now use the Black and Scholes option valuation model to calculate the premium on the Webadz call options that we used in our original example. These options had a 100 cents exercise price and an expiry date of 2.5-years' time. The current Webadz share price was €1.15 (or 115 cents). Therefore, in terms of our notation:

$$S = 115c$$
$$X = 100c$$
$$T = 2.5$$

In addition, let us assume that the risk-free interest rate is 10% per year and the Webadz share price has a standard deviation/volatility of 20%. Therefore:

$$Rf = 0.10 \text{ (i.e. 10\%)}$$
$$\sigma = 0.20 \text{ (i.e. 20\%).}$$

Looking at the model and the two adjustment factors, it can be seen that in order to apply the model four initial calculations are required, as follows:

- $Rf \times T$ $=$ $0.10 \times 2.5 = \mathbf{0.25}$
- $e^{-Rf \times T}$ $=$ $e^{-0.10 \times 2.5} = e^{-0.25} = \mathbf{0.7788}$
- $\log_e [S \div X]$ $=$ $\log_e[115c \div 100c] = \log_e 1.15 = \mathbf{0.1398}$
- $\sigma \times \sqrt{T}$ $=$ $0.20 \times \sqrt{2.5} = 0.20 \times 1.5811 = \mathbf{0.3162}$

Having made these basic calculations, we can then proceed as follows:

The first thing we need to calculate is the adjustment factor value (d_1) which we can find as follows:

$$(d_1) = \frac{\log_e\left(\frac{S}{X}\right) + (Rf \times T)}{\sigma \times \sqrt{T}} + \left(0.5 \times \sigma \times \sqrt{T}\right)$$

$$(d_1) = \frac{0.1398 + 0.25}{0.3162} + (0.5 \times 0.3162) = +1.39$$

Having calculated (d_1) as $+1.39$, we can now calculate the second adjustment factor value (d_2):

$$(d_2) = (d_1) - \sqrt{T} \times \sigma$$

$$(d_2) = 1.39 - 0.3162 = +1.07$$

The third step is to now find the values for the $N(d_1)$ and $N(d_2)$ adjustment factors using the tables for the 'Area under the Normal Curve'. (These tables can be found at the end of the book.)

Using the Normal Curve tables, the (d_1) calculation of $+1.39$ has a value of 0.4177 and so: $N(d_1) = N(+1.39) = 0.50 + 0.4177 = \mathbf{0.9177}$ (See Figure 13.3 for an explanation as to why an extra 0.50 – or 50% – has to be added).

For $N(d_2)$, the (d_2) calculation of $+1.07$ has a value of 0.3577 in the Normal Curve tables and so: $N(d_2) = N(+1.07) = 0.50 + 0.3577 = \mathbf{0.8577}$ (See Figure 13.4).

[Note: If the values for (d_1) and/or (d_2) had been negative – as they will be for an out-of-the-money option – the negative sign is ignored when looking up the $(d_1$ or $d_2)$ value in the Normal Curve tables. The value for $N(d_1)$ and $N(d_2)$ will then be equal to 0.50 *minus* these

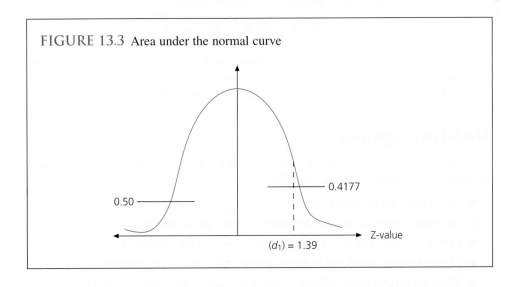

FIGURE 13.3 Area under the normal curve

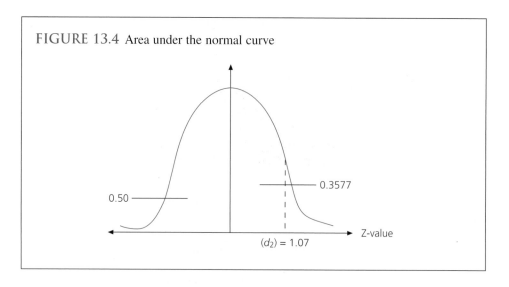

FIGURE 13.4 Area under the normal curve

Normal Curve table values. For example, if the (d_1) value was -1.68, then using the tables, and ignoring the negative sign, this has a value of 0.4535. In such circumstances, the value for $N(d_1)$ would be: $0.50 - 0.4535 = 0.0465$.]

We can now use the Black and Scholes model to find the value of the Webadz call options:

$$C = S \times N(d_1) - [X \times e^{-Rf \times T}] \times N(d_2)$$

$$C = [115c \times 0.9177] - [100c \times e^{-0.25}] \times 0.8577$$

$$C = 105.5c - [100c \times 0.7788] \times 0.8577$$

$$C = 105.5c - (77.88c \times 0.8577)$$

$$C = 105.5c - 66.8c = 38.7 \text{ cents}$$

Thus, on the basis of the data given, the Webadz call options would each have a market value/premium of 38.7 cents (and of course this could now be split up between the 15 cents intrinsic value and remainder of 23.7 cents which must be the time value).

Model assumptions

The basic Black and Scholes option valuation model is based on a number of (often rather unrealistic) assumptions. They are as follows:

- The options are European calls.
- No taxes or transaction costs are involved with option trading.
- Option investors can lend and borrow at an interest rate equal to Rf.
- The underlying shares can be freely bought and sold – even in fractional amounts.
- There are no dividends payable on the shares before the option's expiry date.
- Both Rf and the share's standard deviation remain constant over the life of the option.

Although many of these assumptions are unrealistic, in practice the basic model can be adjusted to take account of a more realistic situation.

Adjusting the model for dividends

As stated above, the Black and Scholes model specifically assumes that there will be no dividends due to be paid on the underlying shares before the option's expiry date. However, we can allow for the impact of dividends on the value of an option by simply reducing the current share price (S) by the *present value* of the future expected dividend payment. For example, suppose that Ukyima's current share price is 100 pence and it is expected to pay a 10 pence dividend per share in 3-months' time (the Ukyima options are due to expire in 6 months). The risk-free interest rate is 8%. Therefore, before we can use the Black and Scholes model to value Ukyima's calls, we first have to reduce the current share price of 100p by the present value of the 10p dividend expected in 3-months' time, where $T = 0.25$ (i.e. 25% of one year) and $Rf = 0.08$:

$$10p \times e^{-Rf \times T} = 10p \times e^{-0.08 \times 0.25} = 10p \times 0.980 = 9.8p$$

and so $S = 100p - 9.8p = 90.2p$ would be used in the Black and Scholes model.

Valuing put options

Although the Black and Scholes model only values call options, this does not mean that a separate model has to be developed to value put options, because there is a connection between the value of a call and the value of a put. This connection is given by the ***put–call parity*** equation which is developed below.

THE BUILDING BLOCKS OF INVESTMENT

There are four basic financial securities out of which all other investments can be constructed. They are:

1. investing in shares
2. investing in risk-free bonds
3. investing in call options in the shares
4. investing in put options in the shares.

With each one of these investments they can be either bought or sold. Thus you might buy shares in the hope that the price will go up, or you can sell shares in the expectation that the price will go down. Similarly you can buy risk-free bonds (that is, lend money), or you can sell risk-free bonds (that is, borrow money). Finally, with options, as we have seen, you can also either buy or sell them – both puts and calls.

For each of these four fundamental financial securities, in the diagrams that follow, we illustrate graphically their impact on an investor's wealth arising out of a change in the price of the underlying securities. This change in wealth (in cents) is given on each of the vertical axes and the change in the share price (again, in cents) is given on the horizontal axes.

We use the notation S to represent investments in shares: +S for buying shares and –S for selling shares. Similarly, we use the notation B, C and P for investments in bonds, call options and put options respectively.

Finally, the 'starting point' of each analysis is the graph's origin, where the axes intersect. The solid line shows the change in investment or wealth caused by a changing share price, when the security is bought. Similarly, the dashed line shows the change in investor's wealth caused by a changing share price, when the security is sold.

Investing in shares

Obviously, if you buy the shares, every 1 cent increase in the share price leads to a 1 cent increase in the investor's wealth, and vice versa. Conversely, if you sell shares, then every subsequent 1 cent increase in the value of the shares is effectively a 1 cent loss in the investor's wealth (Figure 13.5).

Investing in risk-free bonds

Technically, risk-free bonds are free of any risk of default and do not pay interest (Figure 13.6). You earn a risk-free rate of return through a *capital gain* in the value of the bond. Thus if B is the nominal or par value of the bond which is to be repaid, its current value will be its discounted present value: $B (1 + r_F)^{-T}$.

An example might help to make this clearer. If you have a bond that is due to be repaid at 100 cents in 1 year and the risk-free interest rate is 10%, then the bond's current value will be: $100c \times (1 + 0.10)^{-1} = 90.9c$. Buying the bond at 90.9c and being repaid at 100c gives a gain of: 9.1c (100c − 90.9c) which represents a return of 9.1c ÷ 90.9c ≈ 10%.

The rate of return that you receive (r_F) if you buy bonds, or the rate of return that you pay (r_F) if you sell bonds is entirely unaffected by any market changes as its return is risk-free and so is certain.

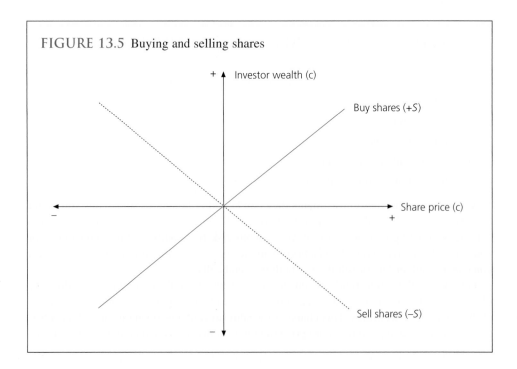

FIGURE 13.5 Buying and selling shares

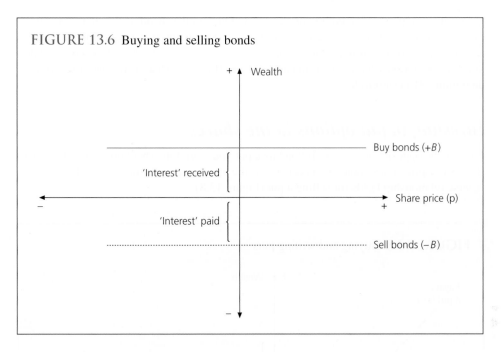

FIGURE 13.6 Buying and selling bonds

Finally, notice than in Figure 13.6 – for simplicity – the return on the risk free bonds is termed 'interest'.

Investing in call options in the shares

If you buy a call option, its cost – the premium you pay – is indicated on the vertical axis (Figure 13.7). The value of the option increases if the share price rises: a 1 cent increase in the value of the shares leads to a 1 cent increase in the value of the call option. Hence

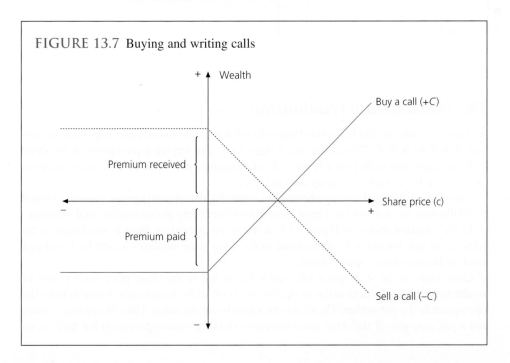

FIGURE 13.7 Buying and writing calls

the positive-sloping 45° solid line on the graph. On the other hand, if the share price falls, options cannot have negative values – all you can lose is the premium paid. The reverse relationship holds if you *sell* a call option. You receive a premium (the option's price) when you sell the option which is your maximum gain. But if the share price then rises you (as an option seller) start to lose.

Investing in put options in the shares

Puts are the opposite of calls. So if you buy a put you *gain* if the share price *falls*. However, if the share price rises, then all you can lose is the option premium that you paid. Again, the reverse relationship holds for selling a put (Figure 13.8).

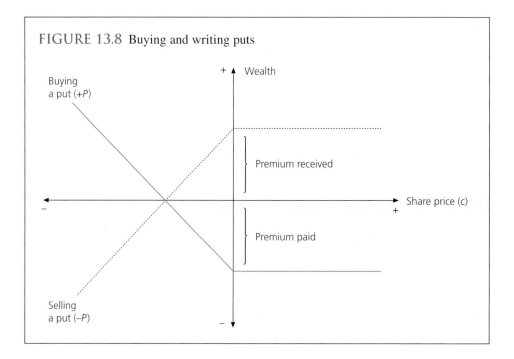

FIGURE 13.8 Buying and writing puts

The fundamental relationship

We can now state the fundamental relationship that exists between these four basic securities: $S + P = B + C$. That is, buying a share ($+S$) and buying a put option in the share ($+P$), is equivalent to buying a bond ($+B$) and buying a call option ($+C$) in the share (at the same exercise price and expiry date as the put).

This relationship can be seen to be true by combining the relevant figures. Figures 13.9 and 13.10 illustrate the left-hand and right-hand sides respectively of this fundamental equation.

In the situation shown in Figure 13.9, if the share price rises there is no change in the value of the put, but every 1 cent increase in the share price increases wealth by 1 cent as a result of the investment in the shares.

Conversely, if the share price falls, each 1 cent fall in the share price *loses* 1 cent of wealth from the investment in the share, but this is offset by 1 cent *gain* in wealth from the investment in the put option. Therefore one cancels out the other. Thus, if you buy a share and a put, you *gain* if the share price *increases* (less the option premium) but there is *no*

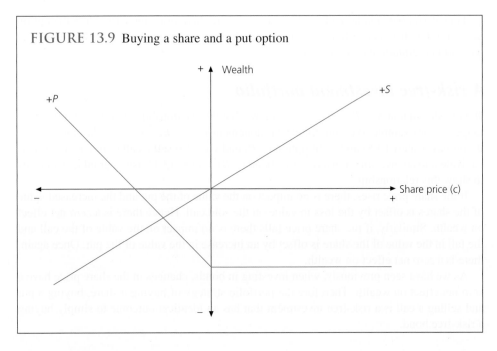

FIGURE 13.9 Buying a share and a put option

effect on your wealth from a *fall* in the share price (again, except for the loss of the option premium that you paid).

From Figure 13.10 we can see that the net outcome is *identical* to that arising from buying a share and a put option: if the share price rises there is no impact on the bond but each 1 cent increase in the share price leads to a 1 cent increase in the value of the call option and therefore in the investor's wealth. If the share price falls, there is no impact on the investor's wealth from either security.

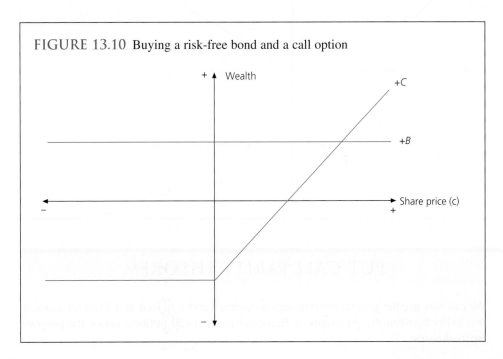

FIGURE 13.10 Buying a risk-free bond and a call option

Thus if you buy a bond and a call, you gain if the share price increases (less the option premium) but there is no effect on your wealth if the share price falls (except for the loss of the option premium that you have paid).

A risk-free investment portfolio

Having shown that $S + P = B + C$, it follows that the relationship should hold if we rearrange it. For example, one important rearrangement is $S + P - C = B$.[3] In other words, if you buy a share $(+S)$ and a put option $(+P)$ and you also sell a call option $(-C)$, this is equivalent to an investment in a risk-free bond $(+B)$. Figure 13.11 uses a graphical analysis to show this relationship.

If the share price rises, there is no impact on the value of the put and the increased value of the shares is offset by the loss in value on the sold call. Hence there is a *zero* net effect on wealth. Similarly, if the share price falls there is no impact on the value of the call and the fall in the value of the share is offset by an increase in the value of the put. Once again, there is a *zero* net effect on wealth.

As we have seen previously, when investing in bonds, changes in the share price have a zero net effect on wealth. Therefore the portfolio strategy of buying a share, buying a put and selling a call is a risk-free investment that has an identical outcome to simply buying a risk-free bond.

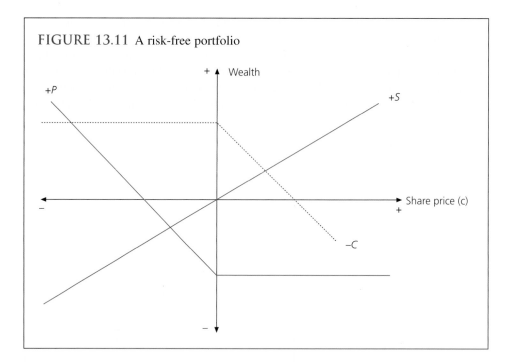

FIGURE 13.11 A risk-free portfolio

PUT–CALL PARITY THEOREM

We can now use the general relationships considered above to look at a fixed relationship that exists between the premiums of European put and call options, called the ***put–call parity theorem***.

In order to develop this theorem, we first need to show that not only does $S + P - C = B$, but also that the net outcome from a *portfolio* investment of $S + P - C$ is equal to the exercise price of the options, which we will call X.

As an example, we will use Maxyqube Ltd, a small mobile communications provider, that is quoted on the Johannesburg stock exchange. The company's shares have a current market value of R2.25 and both the call and put options in the shares have an exercise price of R2.25 (so the options are 'at-the-money') and have 2 years to maturity. Furthermore, suppose the annual risk-free rate of return is 6%. (We will see shortly why we need to know this.)

We will arrange the portfolio of investments in the following way:

1. buy a share $(+S)$ in Maxyqube,
2. buy a put option $(+P)$ in Maxyqube shares, and
3. sell a call option $(-C)$ in Maxyqube shares.

Let us now look at what the outcome would be under two alternative scenarios:

Scenario 1: The Maxyqube share price rises.

Scenario 2: The Maxyqube share price falls.

However, before doing so, it is important to remember that if, at expiry, the share price is *below* the exercise price, *call* options are worthless. Similarly, if at expiry, the share price is *above* the exercise price, *put* options are worthless.

SCENARIO 1

Scenario 1: In 2-years' time Maxyqube's share price has risen to R2.90

Value of the shares bought	R2.90
Value of put option bought	0
Value of call option sold	(40c)*
Net value of the investment portfolio =	R2.50 = Exercise price of the options

* Notice that you will lose 40 cents on the call options that you sold because on expiry they will be worth exercising, so the investor who bought the call from you will want to buy a Maxyqube share from you which is now worth R2.90 for only R2.50 – the exercise price – thus you lose 40 cents on the option being exercised.

We can see algebraically that the net outcome of the investment portfolio must *always* be equal to an amount X, which is equal to the exercise price of the option, *whatever* the stock market price of the shares on expiry:

Net value of portfolio = $S + P - C$, where:

S = value of share
P = value of put option
C = loss on call option sold = $(S - X)$

Again, remember that the value of the put option will be zero *(P = 0)*, as a rising share price makes them worthless. Therefore:

$$S + P - C = S = 0 - (S - X)$$

and so:

$$S + P - C = S + 0 - S + X = + X$$

or:

$$S + P - C = X$$

We obtain exactly the same result from the second scenario, where the share price, on the expiry of the options, has fallen.

SCENARIO 2

Scenario 2: In 2-years' time Maxyqube's share price has fallen to, say, R1.85.

Value of shares bought	R1.85
Value of put option	65c*
Value of call option	0
Net value of the investment portfolio =	R2.50 = Exercise price of the option

* You have bought a put option which allows you to sell a share, which is now worth only R1.85, for R2.50. Thus the value of the option is the resulting profit of 65 cents (R2.50 − R1.85).

Once again, the predictability of this outcome can be seen algebraically:

$$\text{Net value of portfolio: } S + P - C = S + (X - S) - 0 = + X$$

As the value of the portfolio at the expiry date, in all circumstances, will be equal to X (the exercise price of the option) then the present value of the portfolio's worth will be given by:

$$X \times e^{-Rf \times T}$$

Notice that the risk-free interest rate is used for discounting because, as we know, the $S + P - C$ portfolio has an outcome equivalent to a risk-free bond investment:

$$S + P - C = B$$

The present value of the portfolio in our example, given r_F is 6%, is:

$$100c \times e^{-0.06 \times 2}$$
$$100c \times 0.887 = 88.7c$$

As a result, we are now able to take this general relationship:

$$S + P - C = X \times e^{-Rf \times T}$$

rearrange it:

$$S - X \times e^{-Rf \times T} = C - P$$

and insert the known current data: $S = 100c$

$$X \times e^{-Rf \times T} = 88.7c$$

to give:

$$100c - 88.7c = C - P = 11.3c$$

This indicates that the value of the put option should be 11.3 cents *less* than the value of the call.

Put–call parity equation

We have, in this example, an illustration of how the put–call parity equation can be used to identify the price differential between call and put options:

$$S - X \times e^{-Rf \times T} = C - P$$

If the Black and Scholes model was then used to value the Maxyqube *call* options, then it would be possible to simultaneously derive the value of the Maxyqube put options as being worth 11.3 cents less than the value of the call.

Therefore we can state in general terms that the value of a put option, with the *same exercise price* and *expiry date* as a corresponding call option, is given by:

$$P = C + [X \times e^{-Rf \times T}] - S$$

This says that the value of a put is equal to the value of the call option (with the same exercise price and time to expiry), *plus* the present value (by using continuous discounting) of the future exercise price, *less* the current share price.

Let us now return to the Webadz AG shares from our original Black and Scholes example, but now suppose we want to find the value of a put option on Webadz shares with an exercise price of 100 cents and 2.5 years to expiry.

Assume that the current Webadz share price is €1.15, *Rf* is 10% and the standard deviation of the company's share price is 20%.

Therefore, to find the value of these puts, the first thing that we do is to find the value of the call options with the same exercise price and expiry date – which we have already done: 38.7 cents. Therefore:

$$P = 38.7c + [100c \times e^{-0.10 \times 2.5}] - 115c$$

$$P = 38.7c + [100p \times e^{-0.25}] - 115c$$

$$P = 38.7c + [100c \times 0.7788] - 115c$$

$$P = 38.7c + 77.9c - 115c = 1.6 \text{ cents}$$

Therefore, the put options on Webadz shares with a 100c exercise price and 2.5 years to expiry have a premium/market value of 1.6 cents. Because the options are currently out-of-the-money their intrinsic value is zero and the time value is 1.6 cents.

USING SHARE OPTIONS

Having seen how to value both calls and puts, we will now turn to what use can be made of options. However, in order to keep things simple, we will ignore the time value aspect and just assume that the option's premium is equal to its intrinsic value.

Speculating with calls

First, remember, that a 1 cent change in the value of the share price will lead to a 1 cent change in the (intrinsic) value of the call option.

Haji Riyad is a Saudi Arabian company quoted on the Saudi stock market – the Tadawul. The company's shares are currently priced at 125 Saudi riyals (SR). Call options are available with an exercise price of 100SR. Therefore their intrinsic value will be: 125SR − 100SR = 25SR.

Haji Riyad are due to announce their profits for the year in the next few days. You predict these will be higher than expected and so expect that the company's share price will rise as a result. You want to back your judgement by investing 50 000SR in Haji Riyad. There are two courses of action that you could take:

- Buy Haji Riyad shares: 50 000SR ÷ 125SR = 400 shares.
- Buy Haji Riyal call options: 50 000SR ÷ 25SR = 2000 call options.

Suppose that your prediction is correct and Haji Riyal's share price rises by 10SR to 135SR. As a result:

- Gain on the shares: 400 × 10SR = 4000SR.
- Profit on the shares: 4000SR / 50 000SR = 8%.
- Gain on the options: 2000 × 10SR = 20 000SR.
- Profit on the options: 20 000SR / 50 000S = 40%.

This is the so-called 'gearing effect' of speculating with options – they magnify your gain.

Limiting downside risk

The current share price of Bin Hayat shares is 50SR. Call options are available with an exercise price of 45SR. Therefore the intrinsic value of the calls is: 50SR − 45SR = 5SR.

We predict that Bin Hayat's share price will soon increase as a result of the company winning a large contract and so we want to invest in 10 000 shares. There are two possible courses of action:

- Buy 10 000 shares at a cost of: 10 000 × 50SR = 500 000SR.
- Buy 10 000 call options at a cost of: 10 000 × 5SR = 50 000SR.

If our prediction proves to be correct and the share price rises by 1 riyal, then we will make: 10 000 × 1SR = 10 000SR gain on *each* investment.

However, suppose that Bin Hayat fails to win the contract and as a result the share price actually falls. In such circumstances, the *maximum* we can lose on the investment in the company's shares is 500 000SR (i.e. the company goes into liquidation). But with the options, our maximum loss is limited to only 50 000SR. Investing in options *limits exposure* to the risk of a loss from speculation.

Speculating with puts

Remember that the characteristic of puts is that a fall in the share price will lead to a rise in the value of the put, and vice versa.

Waqaya is a pharmaceutical company. Its share price is 10SR. Put options are available with a 10.25SR exercise price. Their intrinsic value is: 10.25SR – 10SR = 0.25SR.

You own 10 000 shares in Waqaya. The company is currently testing a new drug and will shortly announce the test results. If the tests prove successful, Waqaya's share price will rise; if unsuccessful, the share price will fall. What do you do?

- take a chance that the results will be successful and hold onto the shares – and run the risk of making a loss if the tests are unsuccessful, or
- sell the shares now – and run the risk of missing out on making a profit if the tests turn out to be a success.

Better than *either* of these two courses of action is to use *put* options which will:

- protect you from a loss if the tests are unsuccessful, but
- allow you to profit if the tests are successful.

To use puts in this way you would retain your 10 000 Waqaya shares but, in addition, buy 10 000 Waqaya put options at a cost of: 10 000 × 0.25SR = 2500SR.

Suppose the tests are unsuccessful and the Waqaya share price falls by 2SR; then the intrinsic value of the puts will rise by 2SR. As a result:

Loss on the shares	10 000 × 2SR =	20 000SR
Gain on the puts	10 000 × 2SR =	20 000SR
Net effect		nil

The loss on the shares is offset by the gain on the puts, and the only cost incurred has been the 2500SR cost of the puts (which is like the cost of an insurance policy).

On the other hand, if the test results are successful and the Waqaya share price rises by 5SR to 15SR, then the intrinsic value of the put options becomes: 10.25SR − 15SR = 0. (Remember, intrinsic values cannot be negative.) As a result:

Gain on the shares	10 000 × 5SR	=	50 000SR
Loss on the puts	10 000 × 0.25SR	=	2 500SR
Net gain			47 500SR

These effects can be seen diagrammatically (Figure 13.12) and they can then be combined (Figure 13.13).

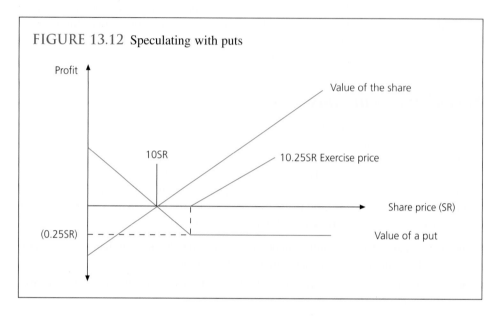

FIGURE 13.12 Speculating with puts

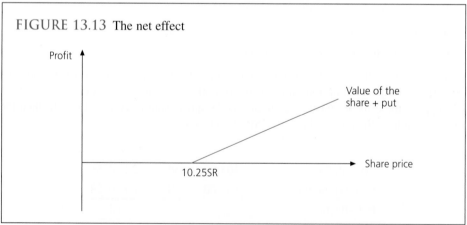

FIGURE 13.13 The net effect

Combining calls and puts

Suppose that we have the same scenario as in the previous example, except that currently you do not hold any shares in Waqaya. How might you be able to profit from the uncertainty surrounding Waqaya's future share price?

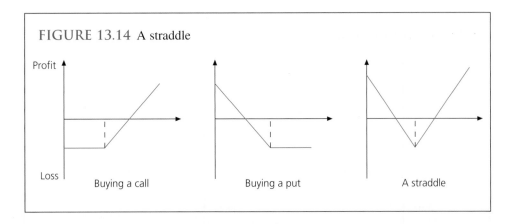

FIGURE 13.14 A straddle

You could re-create the previous situation – buy Waqaya shares and Waqaya puts – but then you would only gain on good news and simply would not lose on bad news. But if you *combine* both calls *and* puts in Waqaya shares, you can gain on both good *and* bad news. This process by which you buy both calls and puts with the same exercise price and the same expiry date is known as a 'straddle'.

So, if the test results are good, the profit on the calls, less the put premiums, equals the overall net profit. If the test results are bad, the profit on the puts, less the call premiums, equals the overall net profit. Again, we can see how this works diagrammatically (Figure 13.14).

This result may seem almost too good to be true: you profit *whichever way* the share price moves. However there is one problem. Namely, that you require a *significant* share price movement (in either direction) in order to generate a sufficient gain on one of the options to offset the premiums paid, and so result in an overall net profit.

Writing (selling) options

So far we have only considered buying calls and puts; but we can also *sell* calls and puts. Such an activity is usually referred to as *writing* options.

Selling options can be dangerous and care must be exercised. This is because when options are *bought* the potential gain is unlimited but the potential loss is restricted to the premiums paid. When options are *sold* the effect is reversed: the potential loss is unlimited, and the potential gain is simply the premiums received from the sale of the options. We can see the truth of this from Figure 13.15.

Writing options then introduces the interesting possibility of converting a risky shareholding into a risk-free investment. For example, an investor owns 10 000 shares in Afropak Ltd, a South African packaging company. If they also *buy* 10 000 Afropak at-the-money *puts* and *sell* 10 000 Afropak at-the-money *calls*, this effectively locks them in to the *current* worth of Afropak shares.

If Afropak's share price rises, the gain in the value of the shares would be offset by the loss on the calls sold – see Figure 13.15(B). On the other hand, if Afropak's share price falls, then the loss on the shares would be offset by a profit on the puts bought – see Figure 13.15(C).

Thus by combining a shareholding with buying puts and selling calls, we can effectively create a 'synthetic' risk-free investment – a risk-free hedge (albeit at a cost of the premiums payable).

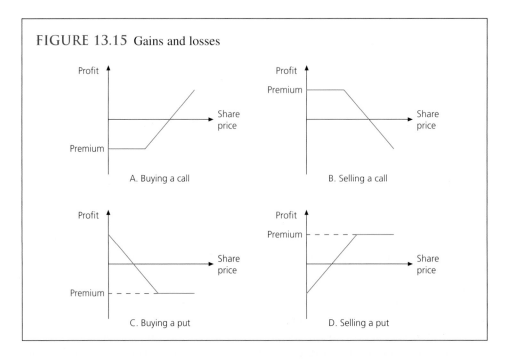

FIGURE 13.15 Gains and losses

THE OPTION 'GREEKS'

When an option reaches maturity (i.e. its expiry date), its value is simply determined by the difference between its exercise price and the share's market price (its intrinsic value). However, we know that before maturity its value is dependent upon a number of factors:

- exercise price
- share price
- time to expiry
- volatility of the share price
- risk-free interest rate.

Over time, with the exception of the exercise price, all of these factors can be expected to change. Each time they do change, this will lead to a change in the market value of the option. These interactions are represented by the so-called option 'Greeks':

- delta
- gamma
- theta
- vega
- rho (or phi).

Delta or the hedge ratio

The relationship between the change in the market value of the option and the change in the share price is given by the delta value (Figure 13.16). This can be defined as:

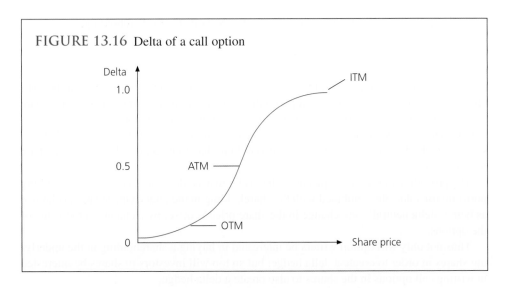

FIGURE 13.16 Delta of a call option

$$\frac{\text{Change in the market value of the option}}{\text{Change in the value of the shares}}$$

Delta can take on any value between 0 and +1 for call options and any value between 0 and –1 for puts:

- 'In-the-money' (ITM) options → Delta $> +0.50$ (or > -0.50 for puts)
- 'Out-of-the-money' (OTM) options → Delta $< +0.50$ (or < -0.50 for puts)
- 'At-the-money' (ATM) options → Delta $= 0.50$ (or –0.50 for puts).

For example, if call options in Noix de Coco SA shares have a delta of 0.60, this implies that the calls are 'in-the-money' and that a 10 cent change in the share price will lead to a:

$$10c \times 0.60 = 6 \text{ cents}$$

change in the value of the options. (Puts have negative deltas because the value of a put moves in the *opposite* direction to the movement in the share price.)

An option's delta is actually given by the value of $N(d_1)$ and, for us, its key interpretation is that it provides the 'hedge ratio'. Remember, for a call option writer (i.e. seller), the higher the share market price moves, the greater is the potential loss on the option when the holder exercises. What the *hedge ratio* does is it tells the option writer how to hedge (avoid) the risk of this loss by indicating the number of shares that would have to be held in order to offset any potential loss on the calls.

Thus in the Noix de Coco example, if the delta value is 0.60 and we have written call options in respect of 1000 shares, we would have to buy and hold: $1000 \times 0.60 = 600$ shares in Noix de Coco in order to offset any potential loss on the options. If Noix de Coco's share price then rose by 5 cents, the value of the calls would increase by: $5c \times 0.60 = 3c$ and so the option writer's loss on the calls would be:

$$1000 \text{ calls} \times 3c = €30$$

which would be *exactly* offset by the profit on the Noix de Coco shareholding:

$$600 \text{ shares} \times 5c = €30$$

However, the problem is that the option's delta value will not remain constant, but will change as the share price changes. Suppose the 5 cent movement in the Noix de Coco share price causes the delta to move to 0.68. The option writer must now hold: 1000 calls × 0.68 = 680 shares in order to hedge the position – they will need to buy an extra 80 Noix de Coco shares – and, of course, every time the shareholding has to be adjusted in this way, share transaction costs are involved.

The procedure that we have just described is known as 'delta hedging', and the resulting portfolio (of sold calls combined with the shareholding in the underlying shares), is known as being 'delta neutral': any change in the share price is offset by a change in the value of the options.

Thus not only will option writers be interested in buying a shareholding in the underlying shares in order to create a delta hedge: but so too will investors in shares be interested in writing call options in the shares to also create a delta hedge.

Gamma

Gamma can take on values between 0 and 1 (see Figure 13.17). It measures the degree to which the *delta* value moves as the share price moves. Thus the higher the gamma value, the *more sensitive* is the delta value to changes in the underlying share price and the more frequently will the shareholding have to be adjusted in order to maintain a delta neutral position.

Thus options with a high gamma value are both time-consuming (in terms of the frequency of share transactions required) and expensive (in terms of transaction costs) to keep at a delta neutral position.

What determines the gamma value is the uncertainty surrounding whether or not the options will be exercised. The greater the uncertainty, the higher will be the gamma value and vice versa. At-the-money options with only a short time to expiry may or may not be exercised – it would only take a small movement in the share price, in either direction, to

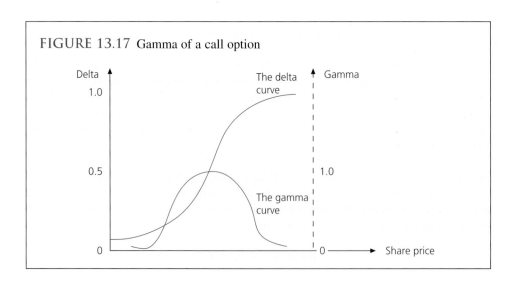

FIGURE 13.17 Gamma of a call option

change the decision – and so they will tend to have very high gamma values. On the other hand, options that are deeply in-the-money are almost certainly going to be exercised, and will have very low gamma values.

Theta

Theta measures the change in the option premium as the time to expiry (in days) changes. In other words theta describes how much of an option's time value is lost from day to day (see Figure 13.18).

Take, for example, a 3-month (i.e. 90-day) option. At the end of day 1 it will lose $\frac{1}{90}$ of its time value. At the end of day 2 it will lose $\frac{1}{89}$ of its time value, and so on. At the end of day 86 (now only 5 days to go before expiry), it will lose $\frac{1}{5}$ of its time value; then $\frac{1}{4}$ of its time value … until at the end of day 90 it has no time value left, and all that remains is its intrinsic value.

Time decay is almost constant for the first two-thirds of an option's life. At about 70% of the way through its life, it still retains around a half of its time value. The decay increases rapidly in the last one-third of its life, and during the last week it loses progressively one-seventh, one-sixth, etc. of its time value.

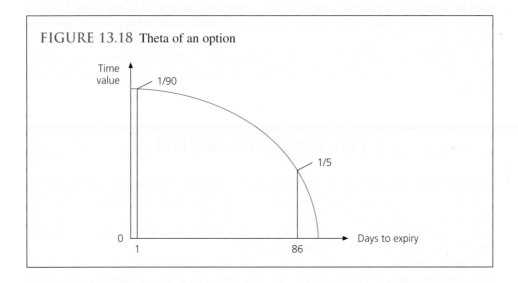

FIGURE 13.18 Theta of an option

Vega

An option's vega value measures the change in the value of the option as the volatility (standard deviation) of the share price changes. This is a simple linear relationship (see Figure 13.19), where the greater the share price volatility, the more valuable the option – because of the option's characteristic of protecting from downside risk, while allowing exposure to upside potential – and so the higher the option premium.

Rho (or Phi)

This is the last, and least used, of the Greeks. It simply measures the change in the option's premium in relation to changes in the value of the time value of money (Rf).

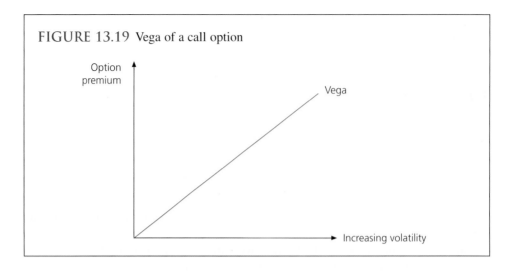

FIGURE 13.19 Vega of a call option

With share options, this Greek is usually referred to as rho. It has two possible names because, when used in conjunction with foreign currency options – say US$/€ options – we need to distinguish between the impact on the option premium of a change in the US risk-free rate of interest (phi) and the impact on the option premium of a change in the Eurozone risk-free interest rate (rho).

As the risk-free interest rate rises, so the value of a call option increases as a result of a fall in the present value of the future exercise price. For put options, the relationship is the reverse.

THE BINOMIAL MODEL

Before we leave the valuation of share options, it is helpful to look at their valuation from a simpler – but much more limited – perspective than the Black and Scholes model. This alternative approach to option valuation is known as the *binomial model* because it deals with a situation where there are only *two* possible future outcomes for a share's market price. This is illustrated in the following example.

Claudine Bartone is an investor who is considering a 12-month investment in the shares of a company called London Logistics plc. The shares each have a current market value of £2.50. However, Claudine believes that in 12-months' time, either the company's share price will have risen to £3.50, or it will have fallen to £1.50. (These are the only two possible future outcomes.)

London Logistics call options are available at an exercise price of £2.50 and with an expiry date of 12-months' time. The risk-free rate of interest is 6% per annum.

As we know (from Figure 13.11), shares and options can be combined so as to create a risk-free investment, called a hedge portfolio. Such an investment portfolio should, by definition, give *the same return as that available from investing in risk-free bonds*: 6% and it is this observation which provides the key to being able to value the London Logistics call options.

In order to do so, we first need to be able to determine the number of shares Claudine will need to hold and the number of call options she will need to buy or sell in order to provide a certain return of 6%, whichever one of the two future share price outcomes actually occurs.

If she purchases a share in London Logistics today for £2.50, in 12-months' time the anticipated outcome will be that the share is sold for either £3.50 or £1.50. As a result a purchaser of the London Logistics call options will find that, at the expiry date in 12-months' time will find that either, the share price has risen to £3.50 and the option is exercised, resulting in a gain of 100p, or the share price has fallen to £1.50 and the option is allowed to lapse as worthless.

Now, how can Claudine create a risk-free portfolio? We know that if the share price goes up, she will gain on her shareholding. Conversely, if the share price falls she will lose on her shareholding. Therefore, in order to set up a risk-free position, we will require the call option to provide for the *opposite* result to that arising from holding the shares.

We know that call options increase in value if the share price rises, and vice versa. Therefore, to achieve the desired effect, our investor will need to *sell* call options in London Logistics shares. So, if Claudine buys London Logistics shares and *sells* London Logistics call options, the investment outcomes from the two possible future states of the world will be:

If the share price rises

1. She receives £3.50 from the sale of the shares.
2. She loses £1 (i.e. £3.50 − £2.50) on the exercise of the option by its purchaser.

If the share price falls

1. She receives £1.50 from the sale of the shares.
2. The option buyer allows the option to lapse as it is worthless.

Let 'c' be the number of London Logistics call options Claudine *sells* for every one London Logistics share that she holds. Her net wealth at the end of the year will be:

If the share price rises

$$+£3.50 - (a \times £1)$$

If the share price falls

$$+£1.50 - 0$$

If the investment is to be risk-free, Claudine must achieve the same net wealth outcome in both share price scenarios. Thus:

$$£3.50 - [c \times £1] = £1.50 - 0$$

Solving for c gives:

$$\frac{£3.50 - £1.50}{£1} = c = 2$$

Therefore Claudine Bartone will need to *sell* two London Logistics call options for every one London Logistics share bought, in order to construct a risk-free hedge. The inverse of the 'c' value (½ or 0.50), is known as the '***hedge ratio***'. It represents the ratio of bought shares to sold calls required to construct a risk-free hedge portfolio.

More formally the hedge ratio can be defined as:

$$\frac{\text{Number of shares bought}}{\text{Number of calls sold}}$$

The 2:1 ratio of sold calls to bought shares will guarantee Claudine the same net wealth position in 12-months' time, whatever the share price scenario, as can be shown.

If the share price *rises* to £3.50, both the options that she sold will be exercised for £2.50. Therefore, she will have to sell two shares, worth £7 (2 × £3.50) for only £5 (2 × £2.50), making a loss of £2 as a result. As her one share in London Logistics is now worth £3.50, her net wealth will be **£1.50** (£3.50 – £2).

If the share price *falls* to £1.50, as this is below the £2.50 exercise price, both call options will expire as worthless. Therefore Claudine is simply left with her one London Logistics share worth **£1.50**, which would represent her net wealth.

We can now use Claudine Bartone's hedge portfolio to place a value on the current market price of the London Logistics call options. This is done by comparing the hedge portfolio with a risk-free bond yielding a return of 6%.

Our risk-free hedge portfolio gives a certain outcome in 12-months' time of £1.50. As this should represent an annual rate of return of 6% on the initial investment (I) the value of this initial investment can be found by solving:

$$I \times (1 + 0.06) = £1.50$$

$$I = \frac{£1.50}{(1 + 0.06)} = £1.42$$

Therefore, the net cost of buying one London Logistics share, *less* the proceeds from the sale of two London Logistics call options should be £1.42. Given that the current price of London Logistics shares is £3.50, this implies that the investor needs to sell the two call options for £2.08 (£3.50 − £1.42), or £1.04 each. This represents the current market price/ the option premium of the London Logistics company's call options: £1.04.

We could now, if we wanted, use the put–call parity theorem to value the company's put options. Given:

$$P = C + [X \times e^{-Rf \times T}] - S$$

then:

$$P = £1.04 + [£2.50 \times e^{-0.06 \times 1}] - £2.50$$

$$P = £1.04 + [£2.50 \times 0.942] - £2.50 = £0.895 \text{ or } 89.5\text{p}$$

Therefore, the London Logistics put options with an exercise price of £2.50 and a 12-month expiry date would each have a market value of 89.5p.

Obviously, this binomial valuation approach is very limited, as it only allows two possible future share price outcomes (although, it can be extended to look at more than just one time period forward). However, it is useful in that it introduces the idea of the hedge ratio: the ratio of sold calls to bought shares needed to construct a risk-free portfolio.

REAL OPTIONS

Finally, we turn to have a brief look at how option valuation theory might be of direct use in the evaluation of capital investments. The term 'real' options is used to refer to the *flexibility* that can be found in some *capital* investment decisions made by companies, and this flexibility has value – which can be measured using the Black and Scholes analysis. Examples of this investment flexibility would include such things as the possibility of delaying the start of an investment; the possibility of abandoning and investment at an earlier stage than planned; or the possibility of extending an investment's normal life.

Patent rights will often provide companies with the right of exclusivity to develop a new product for a specific period of time. As a result the company has the ability to delay the investment if it wishes to do so, in order to gather additional information or resolve some uncertainties – without fear of losing out to a competitor. Such 'breathing space' – the option to delay – can be very valuable. Similarly, a 'break-clause' in a long property lease gives valuable flexibility. A company may enter into a 10-year lease on a new building, but if there is a break clause after 5 years, the company has the valuable option to abandon its use of the building before the end of the full term. If the acquisition of a machine is under evaluation which has a normal productive life of 5 years, but there is the possibility of undertaking a refurbishment at the end of 5 years which would extend its life for a further 3 years, then this option to extend the normal life of the investment can be valuable.

In many circumstances the valuation of real options can be very problematic, because of the difficulty of identifying the precise nature of the option, or options, available. However, for our purposes in the context of the present chapter, we will use a fairly simple example to demonstrate the approach to valuing real options and the use to which it might be put.

Madrileña SA is a fruit juice bottling company, based in València. The company is currently evaluating the proposed purchase of a new bottling production line. The investment would require the immediate expenditure of €10 000 000 and is expected to generate a cash flow of €2 500 000 per year for the 5 years of its normal operating life. The company believes that 10% would be a suitable NPV discount rate to evaluate the investment. On this basis, the investment would not be worthwhile as it would incur a *negative* NPV:

- €10 000 000 + [€2 500 000 × A$_{5\ 10\%}$]
- €10 000 000 + [€2 500 000 × 3.791] = – €522 500 NPV

Madrileña is now informed by the equipment supplier that it would be possible to spend €3 000 000 refurbishing the production line at the end of 5 years. This would allow the line to be operated for a further 3 years, generating an expected cash flow of €2 000 000 per year. This additional cash flow is uncertain and has a standard deviation of 35%. The risk-free interest rate is 4%.

This option, in 5-years' time, to extend the machines' life for a further 3 years, can be valued on the basis of the Black and Scholes model where:

S = The present value of the expected additional cash flow

X = The cost of the refurbishment

T = The time when the refurbishment is undertaken

Rf = Risk-free interest rate, and

σ = The standard deviation of the post-refurbishment cash flow.

As a result: $S = [€2\ 000\ 000 \times A_{3\ 10}\% \times 1.10^{-5}]$

$S = [€2\ 000\ 000 \times 2.4869 \times 0.6209] = €3\ 088\ 232$

$X = €3\ 000\ 000$

$T = 5$ years

$Rf = 0.04$

$\sigma = 0.35$

and so: $Rf \times T = 0.20$

$e^{-Rf \times T} = 0.8187$

$\ln [S \div X] = +0.0290$

$\sigma \times \sqrt{T} = 0.7826$

and: $d_1 = +0.6839$

$d_2 = -0.0987$

$N(d_1) = 0.7517$

$N(d_2) = 0.4602$

therefore the option has a value of:

$$[0.7517 \times €3\ 088\ 232] - [0.4602 \times €3\ 000\ 000 \times 0.8187] = €1\ 191\ 127$$

and the overall NPV of the proposed bottling line, including the value of the 'real' option attached to it, now becomes: $- €522\ 500 + €1\ 191\ 127 = + €668\ 627$. Thus the proposed new bottling line's *overall* NPV is *positive*, making it a worthwhile investment.

SUMMARY

- Options confer a right, but not an obligation, on their holder to buy (or sell) a security, at a fixed price, on or before a future specific date.

- An option's intrinsic value is the gain that would be made if it had to be exercised immediately. This value can never be negative. An option's market value will always be greater than its intrinsic value, except at the final expiry date, when the two values will be the same.

- From an investor's viewpoint options confer two fundamental benefits: they magnify the investor's exposure to a security's upside potential and they also limit the investor's exposure to the security's downside risk.

- Options can either be bought or written (sold). When buying an option, the investor's profit potential is unlimited; however the loss is limited to the option premium paid. An option writer, on the other hand, has the potential for unlimited loss, with the possible gain limited to the option premium received.

- The market value of an option is a combination of its intrinsic value and its time value. The intrinsic value is a function of the exercise price, the current share price, the risk-free rate of interest and the time to expiry. The time (or gamble) value is a function both of the option's time to expiry and the volatility (or variability) in the price of the shares to which the option relates. This market value can be found via the Black and Scholes option valuation model.

- There are four fundamental financial securities that form the building blocks of all investments: shares (S); risk-free bonds (B); call options (C); and put options (P). They can be combined into a fundamental equality relationship: $S + P = B + C$.

- Given this fundamental relationship, it follows that a risk-free investment can be artificially created by the combination: $S + P - C = B$.

- Furthermore, the fundamental relationship can also be used to develop a fixed relationship between the premiums on calls and puts: the put–call parity (which uses continuous discounting): $P = C + [X \times e^{-Rf \times T}] - S$.

- The Black and Scholes model specifically excludes the possibility of dividends being paid on the underlying shares. However, the model can be easily adapted to provide a reasonable approximation for the impact of dividends by adjusting the share price for the present value of the expected dividend, before inserting its value in the Black and Scholes model.

- The option Greeks look at the sensitivity of the market value of the option to changes in the valuation variables. In particular, the delta value tells an option writer how much of the underlying security (to which the option relates) needs to be held in order to hedge their risk exposure.

- The valuation of options can be looked at from a far simpler, but more limited perspective, using a binomial option valuation model. It is based on the fact that a risk-free investment – known as a hedge portfolio – can be constructed out of shares and options. This hedge portfolio can then be compared with the return on a risk-free bond to identify the implied value of the option.

- Finally, real options that might be attached to capital investments can also be valued by applying the principles of the Black and Scholes option valuation model.

NOTES

1. On a scientific calculator the natural log button is normally designated as: 'ln'.
2. Normally in corporate finance, we use *discrete* discounting, which assumes that annual cash flows arise at a single point in time in the year. The discrete discounting factor is expressed as:

$$(1 + i)^{-n}$$

where 'i' is the annual rate of discount and 'n' is the number of years in the future that the cash flow arises.

The Black and Scholes model uses a more mathematically sophisticated version of discounting: *continuous* discounting. This assumes that the annual cash flow arises evenly and *continually* throughout the year. The continuous discounting factor employs the mathematical constant 'e' and is expressed as:

$$^{n}e^{-i \times n}$$

In reality, there is relatively little difference between the two discounting factors. For example if i, the discount rate, is 10% and n is 3 years, then:

$$(1 + i)^{-n} = (1 + 0.10)^{-3} = 0.7531$$

$$e^{-i \times n} = e^{-0.10 \times 3} = e^{-0.30} = 0.7408$$

3.   Think back to our earlier discussion, where we saw that simultaneously buying a call and selling a put is equivalent to buying the shares. Therefore, selling a call and buying a put is equivalent to selling the shares. Hence $+P - C = +S$. Thus on the left-hand side of the equation, $S + P - C = B$, shares are effectively being bought and sold.

FURTHER READING

1.   Much of the literature on options is very mathematical. For a general descriptive review see D.A. Ross and N.M. Cavalla, 'Options', in J. Rutherford and R.R. Montgomerie (eds), *Handbook of UK Corporate Finance,* Butterworths 1992; and F. Black, 'Fact and Fantasy in the Use of Options', *Financial Analysts Journal,* July–August 1975; F. Black, 'How we came up with the Option Formula', *Journal of Portfolio Management*, 15, 1989.

2.   For a more difficult review of option pricing, see J.C. Cox, S.A. Ross and M. Rubinstein, 'Option Pricing: A Simplified Approach', *Journal of Financial Economics,* March 1979.

3.   A good, clear introduction to options is given by D.B. Hemmings, 'An Introduction to Options', *Managerial Finance,* Summer 1982.

4.   F. Taylor *Mastering Derivatives Markets*, 3rd ed, FT/Prentice Hall 2006 and T.J. Andersen, *Global Derivatives a Strategic Management Perspective*, FT/Prentice Hall 2005 provide useful guides to derivatives in general, including options.

5.   Three interesting articles on the subject of real options are: R.L. McDonald, 'The Role of Real Options in Capital Budgeting: Theory and Practice', *Journal of Applied Corporate Finance*, Spring 2006; M. Amran, F. Li and C.A. Perkins, 'How Kimberly-Clark Uses Real Options', *Journal of Applied Corporate Finance*, Spring 2006 and A Dixit and R. Pindyck, 'The Options Approach to Capital Investment', *Harvard Business Review*, May–June 1995.

6.   S. Bartram, G. Brown and F. Fehle, 'International Evidence of Financial Derivative Usage', *Financial Management*, 38, 2009, looks at how widespread is the use of options and other financial derivatives.

QUIZ QUESTIONS

1   What is a European put option?
2   What is an American call option?
3   When will an option's intrinsic value be the same as its market value?
4   It is known that a company is bidding for a very large and profitable contract. If they win the contract, the share price is likely to rise, if they lose the contract, then it will fall. How might you try to profit from such a situation using options?
5   If you simultaneously buy a call and sell an identical put, what is the effect?
6   The market value of an option can be said to consist of two elements. What are they?
7   The Black and Scholes option pricing model is a function of five variables. What are they?
8   What are the four basic financial securities? What is the fundamental equality relationship that exists between them?
9   What is the put–call parity equation?
10   What is a delta risk?
     (See the 'Answers to Quiz Questions' section at the back of the book.)

PROBLEMS

The answers to these problems are available to students online (see the 'Digital Resources' page for details).

1 The shares of Cuccioli SpA are currently priced at €4.15. The call options have an exercise price of €4 and are due to expire in 3-months' time. The risk-free interest rate is 5% and Cuccioli's share price volatility – as measured by the standard deviation – is 22%.

Required:

(i) Calculate the premium on the Cuccioli call options.

(ii) Calculate the value of Cuccioli put options with an exercise price of €4 and a 3-month expiry.

(iii) How would an investor with 50 000 Cuccioli shares construct a delta neutral hedge using Cuccioli calls?

2 Using the Black and Scholes option valuation model and the put–call parity theorem, calculate the market value of both the call and put options of the following three companies:

	Sterx	Fegro	Oost
S	100c	100c	100c
X	95c	100c	110c
T	3 months	6 months	9 months
σ	30%	25%	20%
Rf	5%	10%	5%

INTEREST RATE RISK

LEARNING OBJECTIVES

The purpose of this chapter is to:

- Introduce the 'money market' and the concept of interest rate risk.
- Explore the basic short-term interest rate risk 'hedging' techniques of forward rate agreements (FRAs) and interest rate guarantees.
- Describe the concept of interest rate 'futures' and discuss their use.
- Introduce the longer-term interest rate risk hedging techniques of 'caps', 'collars' and 'floors'.
- Discuss and illustrate the use of interest rate 'swaps'.

INTRODUCTION

Our analysis of portfolio theory illustrated how risk exposure could be reduced through diversification. However, as we saw in Chapter 11, the management of companies should not be concerned with internal diversification for its own sake. In other words, companies should not be concerned with the management of unsystematic risk – which their shareholders can eliminate quite easily for themselves. However, systematic risk is different and if there is any way that companies can reduce exposure to systematic risk without also reducing cash flows, this is likely to be of benefit to investors.

In the previous chapter we saw how a combination of risky securities (shares) and call and put options could be combined so as to bring about a risk-free position. In this chapter we consider the use of options – and a variety of other hedging techniques – to manage one particular type of systematic risk that faces company management: interest rate risk.

A definition

Risk, as we know, describes a situation where the outcome is uncertain. In the economy, interest rates vary as a result of the interplay of a whole variety of macroeconomic factors and, as a result, the future direction and level of interest rates is uncertain.

Interest rate risk refers to the risk of an adverse movement in interest rates. This adverse movement may be an increase in interest rates if the company wishes to borrow money. But, on the other hand, if the company has surplus cash that it intends to place on deposit, an adverse movement would be represented by a fall in interest rates.

THE MONEY MARKETS

Before we look at some interest rate risk management techniques, we first need to set out some background information concerning the money markets. The 'money markets' can be used as a general term to describe the market-place where organizations can lend and borrow (relatively large) amounts of money for short periods of time. Typically, money can be lent and borrowed on the money markets for periods ranging from 'overnight' (which is from 3.00 pm on one day to 3.00 pm on the next day) to up to about 12 months.[1]

Money market interest rates are continuously changing in the light of supply and demand market forces (remember that interest rates are simply the 'price' of money and they respond to changes in demand in exactly the same way as does the price of anything else), and to the changing macroeconomic situation.

At any one point in time, money market interest rates are quoted for a variety of time periods (or maturities). Typically, these are: overnight, one week, one month, 3 months, 6 months and one year – although rates are also available for other maturities as well (e.g. 5 months).

These money market interest rates, although they refer to loans or deposits for periods of generally less than 1 year, are always quoted as an *annual* rate of interest. For example, money market interest rates may be quoted as follows:[2]

- overnight = 7%

- 1 week = 6½%

- 1 month = 6%

- 3 months = 5¾%

- 6 months = 5½%

- 1 year = 5%.

These rates are quoted in annual terms[3] to facilitate easy comparison. To calculate the actual interest rate over the specific time period, the annual rate has to be divided by the number of those time periods in the year. Translation of the annual rates into the rate per time period is as follows:

	Annual interest rate				Actual interest rate
Overnight	7%	÷	365	=	0.0192%/day
1 week	6½%	÷	52	=	0.125%/week
1 month	6%	÷	12	=	0.5%/month
3 months	5¾%	÷	4	=	1.4375%/quarter
6 months	5½%	÷	2	=	2.75%/half year
1 year	5%	÷	1	=	5%/year

Although money market interest rates are continually changing, once money is borrowed or deposited at a particular rate, then that rate is fixed for the time period concerned – irrespective of what subsequently happens to interest rates. Therefore, using the data in the table, if a company places €10 million on deposit for 6 months in the money market at an (annual) interest rate of 5½% then, whatever happens to interest rates over the next 6 months, they are locked into receiving €10 million $\times$ 0.055 $\times$ 6/12 = €275 000 interest for the deposit.

Finally, in these examples just a single interest rate for each maturity has been quoted. Given that money markets are where companies can lend *and* borrow short term, for each maturity there will be two rates – one (the borrowing rate) higher than the other (the lending rate). Thus if the 6-month money market interest rates were quoted at: 5½–6%, this means that money could be placed on deposit for 6 months at an annual interest rate of 5½% and money could be borrowed for 6 months at 6% per year interest.

FORWARD FORWARD LOANS

Suppose that CLS Elektronic's cash flow forecast indicates that, in 2-months' time, it will need to borrow €50 million for a 6-month period. The current 6-month money market interest rates are 5½ – 6%, but the company's finance director is concerned about the risk that, over the next 2 months, interest rates will rise. As a result, when CLS comes to borrow the €50 million in 2-months' time it will have to pay a significantly higher rate of interest that the current rate of 6%.

In these circumstances the company is exposed to *interest rate risk*: the risk that there may be an adverse movement (i.e. a rise) in interest rates by the time the loan is required. One way to avoid this uncertainty about what rate of interest the company will actually pay on the loan would be for it to hedge the risk using a '*forward forward*' loan.

This is achieved very simply. Instead of waiting for 2 months, the company would borrow €50 million now for *8 months*, and immediately place the borrowed money on deposit for the next 2 months until it is required. The net outcome is shown in Example 1.

EXAMPLE 1

Suppose the current money market interest rates are:

2 months:	5¼% – 5¾%
6 months:	5½% – 6%
8 months:	5⅝% – 6⅛%.

▶

CLS Elektronik *borrows* €50 million now for *8 months* at an annual rate of interest of $6\frac{1}{8}$%. It then places €50 million on *deposit* for *2 months* at an annual interest rate of 5¼%. Therefore CLS's *net* interest charge for having a €50 million loan available, for its own use, over the required 6-month time period is:

$$€50m \times 0.06125 \times 8/12 \quad = \quad €2\,041\,667 \text{ interest payable}$$
$$€50m \times 0.0525 \times 2/12 \quad = \quad \underline{€437\,500 \text{ interest received}}$$
$$\text{Net interest payable} \quad = \quad €1\,604\,167$$

The amount of net interest payable represents an interest rate on the required loan of:

$$\frac{€1\,604\,175}{€50\,000\,000} \times 100 = 3.21\% \text{ per 6 months}$$

$$3.21\% \times 2 = 6.42\% \text{ per year}$$

By undertaking a forward forward loan arrangement, the company avoids any uncertainty about the actual rate of interest it will have to pay on its €50 million 6-month loan which is required in 2-months' time: it will pay a *certain* 6.42% per year.

Notice that the current 6-month loan rate is 6% per year. Therefore the extra 0.42% annual rate of interest that the company pays through the use of a forward forward loan is, effectively, the cost of eliminating the risk. In a sense, the extra interest it pays on the loan, relative to the current interest rate, is like an insurance premium.

$$€50m \times 0.0042 \times \frac{6}{12} = €105\,000$$

CLS is paying a premium of €105 000 to be able to lock into *today's* interest rate for its *future* loan, thereby avoiding all uncertainty as to the loan's cost.

FORWARD RATE AGREEMENTS

Forward forward loans are relatively unusual nowadays, because more efficient ways have been developed that can often be used to achieve the same effect. However, as we shall see, the concept of the forward forward loan interest rate is still important.

Taking the same example as before, an alternative strategy for CLS Elektronik to follow would be for it to approach its bank with a request to fix the interest rate that the company will have to pay in 2-months' time on a €50 million 6-month loan. Essentially, what would be requested is termed a *Forward Rate Agreement* or FRA. This is a mechanism, by which a company can lock itself into a rate of interest today, on a future loan.

The bank is likely to respond positively to this proposal and agree to an FRA on a €50 million 6-month loan in 2-months' time at an annual rate of interest of 6.42%. Why 6.42%? Because the bank will have calculated what rate of interest the company could have locked into through a forward forward loan. It is this rate which mainly determines the rate at which an FRA is agreed.

Now although the effect of an FRA is as we have described it – the bank and the company are agreeing to the company being able to borrow €50 million for 6 months in

2-months' time at 6.42% interest – the actual *mechanics* of the arrangement are some-what different.

Having secured its FRA, CLS will then wait for 2 months before it borrows the €50 mil-lion it requires. Suppose it turns out that the finance director's original fears are justified, and during the intervening 2 months, 6-month loan interest rates have moved up sharply from 6% to 8%. As a result, when the company borrows the €50 million it has to pay 8% interest – the going market interest rate. But, it will also *receive* 'compensation' under its FRA, equal to the extra interest it has to pay: 8% − 6.42% = 1.58%. The net outcome is shown in Example 2.

EXAMPLE 2

CLS Elektronik will take out an FRA on a €50 million 6-month loan at 6.42% interest.

At the time when the loan is actually required interest rates have risen to 8%. As a result the company will *receive* 8% − 6.42% = 1.58% interest in compensation under its FRA agreement to bring its *net* interest cost back down to the agreed rate of 6.42%:

€50m × 0.08	× 6/12	=	€2 000 000	interest payable
€50m × 0.0158	× 6/12	=	€395 000	compensation received
Net interest payable		=	€1 605 000	

This is equivalent to an annual rate of interest on the loan of 6.42%, as agreed:

$$\frac{€1\,605\,000}{€50\,000\,000} \times 100 = 3.21\% \text{ per 6 months} \times 2 = 6.42\% \text{ per year}$$

Alternatively, having taken out its FRA at 6.42%, suppose that CLS then finds that when it takes out its loan in 2-months' time, interest rates have actually *fallen* to 5%. Under these circumstances, the company has to *pay* compensation under its FRA, equivalent to 1.42% in order to bring its effective interest charge on the loan up to the agreed rate. Example 3 illustrates this alternative situation.

EXAMPLE 3

CLS Elektronik takes out an FRA on a €50 million 6-month loan at 6.42% interest.

At the time when the loan is actually taken out, interest rates have *fallen* to 5%. As a result the company will *pay* compensation under its FRA equivalent to 6.42% − 5% = 1.42% interest.

€50m × 0.05	× 6/12	=	€1 250 000	interest payable
€50m × 0.0142	× 6/12	=	€355 000	compensation payable
Total effective loan cost		=	€1 605 000	

▶

▶

This is equivalent to an annual rate of interest on the loan of 6.42%, as agreed:

$$\frac{€1\,605\,000}{€50\,000\,000} \times 100 = 3.21\% \text{ per 6 months} \times 2 = 6.42\% \text{ per year.}$$

One important thing to understand is that the FRA is a totally *separate* contractual agreement from the loan itself. Therefore the financial institution (typically a bank) from which the company obtains its FRA may or may not be the same institution that eventually supplies the company with the subsequent loan.

This separation of the FRA contract from the loan contract is an important point, because it means that a company has the ability, if it so wishes, to enter into a forward rate agreement without any intention of borrowing money.

Other uses of FRAs

FRAs are normally supplied by banks. They are very widely used in practice and can extend up to about 2 years into the future. In our examples we have shown FRAs being used to hedge interest rate risk on a future loan. But this is by no means the only use of FRAs.

For example, Création Suisse is a furniture design company. The company believes that their revenues, and hence their operating profits, are *inversely* correlated with interest rate movements. In other words, when interest rates go up, their revenues, and hence their operating profits, go down – and vice versa. (The type of companies whose revenues are likely to be sensitive to interest rate movements in this way are those whose products form part of consumers' discretionary, rather than necessary, expenditure.)

A furniture design company like Création Suisse may well be in this situation. People don't have to buy new furniture in the way that they do have to buy food, and so will not buy new furniture when times are tough and financial resources are constrained. Création Suisse may argue therefore as follows: most of our customers own their own homes, and they have borrowed money in order to buy them. When interest rates go up, they are required to pay more interest on the loans they have taken out to pay for their homes. As a result, they have less money available to spend on furniture and so our sales will decline. Conversely, when interest rates fall, they have more spare money and may well use some of that to buy new furniture; hence our sales go up. In other words our sales are negatively correlated with interest rates.

Such a company is therefore also exposed to interest rate risk – the risk to its operating profitability of an adverse impact on its customers' buying activity from an increase in interest rates. A company in this situation could reduce its risk exposure by using FRAs. This would enable a company such as Création Suisse to receive compensation when interest rates go up and thus help to maintain its profitability.[4] Conversely, when interest rates go down, the company has to pay compensation under the FRA, but this is offset by rising sales and profitability. Thus a series of FRAs can be used to smooth out the impact on the company's operating profit of interest rate movements. Figure 14.1 illustrates this effect.

Another use of FRAs would be for a company with a high level of floating rate debt finance to use them in order to protect its level of profitability: if interest rates rose, the higher interest payments would be offset by compensation received under the FRAs, and vice versa.

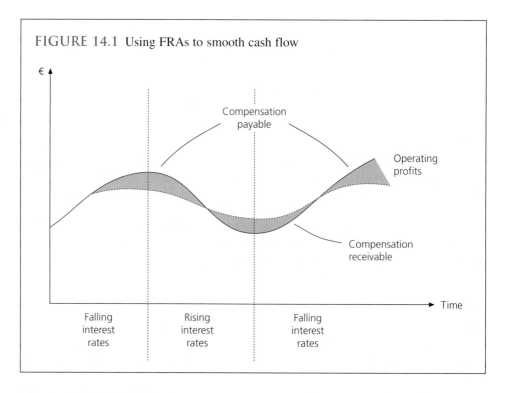

FIGURE 14.1 Using FRAs to smooth cash flow

The market in FRAs

The FRA market is very active and well developed on an inter-bank basis (i.e. with banks dealing between themselves). However, the market's development is relatively limited for non-bank users.

This slow development of FRAs by non-bank users is probably due to a combination of two factors. One is that the same hedging effect can be achieved by other means (e.g. see the later discussion on interest rate futures – although the use of FRAs avoids the 'margin' requirement of futures). The other reason is that banks will actually quote forward loan and deposit rates to their customers if requested. Therefore, returning to our original FRA example involving CLS Elektronik – which wanted to borrow €50 million for 6 months in 2-months' time, the company may well be able to get the bank to agree in advance an interest rate of 6.2% for the loan that is required in 2-months' time. (Notice that by fixing this future loan rate now, the bank is exposing *itself* to interest rate risk which it may well hedge by agreeing an FRA with another financial institution.)

A final point

There is a final point to notice about FRAs as a method of hedging a company's exposure to interest rate risk. In the previous chapter we noted how options had the characteristic of hedging against an adverse movement (downside risk), while allowing advantage to be taken of a favourable movement (upside potential). FRAs do *not* have this characteristic. They hedge the company, as we saw in Examples 2 and 3, against both an adverse movement in interest rates *and* a favourable movement. Instead, what they do is to *lock* a company into a *specific* rate of interest.

INTEREST RATE GUARANTEES

Interest rate guarantees (IRGs) or interest rate options (IROs), possess the characteristic that all options have: the ability to provide a hedge against adverse movements in interest rates, while also allowing advantage to be taken of any favourable movements.

If we return to the CLS Elektronik example used previously we can see that an IRG could be utilized to hedge interest rate risk exposure, as an alternative to an FRA. CLS Elektronik had wanted to borrow €50 million in 2-months' time for a 6-month period. To hedge their exposure to interest rate risk they could take out an option on the required loan – normally with a bank – at, say, an interest rate of 6.5% per annum.

If, in 2-months' time, interest rates have indeed risen as feared to 8%, then CLS can exercise its option to borrow €50 million for 6 months at 6.5% interest. On the other hand, if interest rates fall over the next 2 months to 5%, then the company can allow its option to lapse and, instead, it can borrow the €50 million on the money market at the current interest rate of 5%.

In this way it can be seen that interest rate guarantees – or options – can be used to hedge against adverse movements in interest rates; but they also allow the company to take advantage of any favourable movement in interest rates that may occur. The interest rate guarantee at 6.5% would guarantee that CLS Elektronik would not have to pay more than 6.5% interest on its €50m 6-month loan.

Pricing IRGs

Because of this additional advantage of IRGs – not only do they provide a hedge against a *rise* in interest rates, but they also allow advantage to be taken of a *fall* in rates – they are more expensive to buy as a hedging instrument than FRAs. The reason for this is that with an FRA, *both* parties to the agreement (the company on one side and the bank on the other side) obtain a hedge – the company gains a hedge against rising interest rates and the bank gains a hedge against falling interest rates (because, in such circumstances, the company will *pay* compensation to the bank with which it has the FRA). With an IRG, the bank is simply being paid to provide insurance to the company.

Having said that an interest rate option contract would be more expensive than a forward rate agreement, how would its price be set? The answer is by application of the Black and Scholes option valuation model which we examined in Chapter 13.

In that chapter we examined the general principles that underlie option valuation within the context of share options. Those same principles apply to all options, including IRGs. Thus the cost or value of an interest rate call option (an option to buy a loan at a fixed price/rate of interest) would be a function of five variables:

1. the current market rate of interest
2. the exercise price interest rate of the option
3. the length of time to expiry
4. the volatility of interest rates
5. the risk-free interest rate.

A simple illustration of applying the Black and Scholes model to an IRG is shown in Example 4.

EXAMPLE 4

Huta Kowski is a Polish steel foundry. The company is planning to borrow €1 million for 1 year, in 12-months' time. The current rate of interest on such loans is 5% and the risk-free rate of interest is 3% per year. Interest rate volatility in the recent past has been represented by a standard deviation of 10%. The expected cost of an IRG on the loan at 4% interest could be calculated as follows:

At the current rate of interest, the interest charge on the loan would be: €1 million × 0.05 = €50 000. The company wishes to buy an option with an interest rate exercise price of 4%, giving an interest charge on the loan of: €1 million × 0.04 = €40 000. Therefore in terms of our usual Black and Scholes notation:

$$S = 50000$$
$$X = 40000$$
$$T = 1$$
$$\sigma = 0.10$$
$$Rf = 0.03.$$

$$d_1 = \frac{\log(S \div X) + Rf \times T}{\sigma \times \sqrt{T}} + \frac{1}{2} \times \sigma \times \sqrt{T}$$

$$d_1 = \frac{\log(50\,000 \div 40\,000) + (0.03) \times 1}{0.1 \times \sqrt{1}} + \frac{1}{2} \times 0.10 \times \sqrt{1}$$

$$d_1 = 2.58$$

$$d_2 = d_1 - \sigma\sqrt{T}$$

$$d_2 = 2.58 - (0.10 \times \sqrt{1}) = 2.48$$

Using the tables of the area under the normal curve, this gives cumulative probabilities for the d_1 and d_2 values of:

$$N(d_1) = 0.4951 + 0.50 = 0.9951$$
$$N(d_2) = 0.4934 + 0.50 = 0.9934$$

and so C, the value of the option, can be found from the Black and Scholes model:

$$C = [N(d_1) \times S] - [X \times e^{-Rf \times T} \times N(d_2)]$$

$$C = [0.9951 \times €50\,000] - [€40\,000 \times e^{-0.03 \times 1} \times 0.9934]$$

$$C = €49\,755 - [€40\,000 \times 0.9704 \times 0.9934]$$

$$C = €49\,755 - €38\,560 = €11{,}195$$

Therefore the IRG would cost Huta Kowski €11,195 to purchase.

FRAs versus IRGs

Under what circumstances might a company choose to use an FRA, and when might it prefer an IRG? In order to answer this question, first notice that both arrangements can hedge the company against an *adverse* movement in interest rates.

Therefore, if a company wishes to borrow money at some time in the future and believes that between now and that future time interest rates will *rise*, it will hedge the risk using the *cheapest* means possible: it will hedge using an FRA.

However, suppose the company's management simply feel that market interest rates are volatile, and could go either up *or* down between now and when the loan will be required. Under these circumstances, the management may be willing to use the more expensive hedging instrument: an IRG – the obvious point at issue here being that if the company uses an FRA and interest rates then fall, the company will be unable to get the benefit of those lower rates. An IRG does not lock the company into paying a specific interest rate in the way that an FRA does.

OPTION CONTRACT MARKETS

In the previous chapter we discussed the general ideas underlying option contracts. One area that was briefly mentioned was that fundamentally there are two types of option 'markets' where options (of different sorts) are bought and sold. These are the 'OTC' market and the 'option exchange' market. Options that are bought on the OTC market are usually 'tailor-made' to the precise requirements of the purchaser. Because of their unique nature they are not readily tradable. In other words, having bought an OTC option, there is very little scope for being able to sell it on to a third party; all that can be done is hold it until a subsequent decision is taken to exercise it or allow it to lapse. The interest rate option in Example 4 would have been an OTC option, tailor-made to the precise requirement of Huta Kowski and the seller or writer of the OTC option would have been a bank.

In contrast, option contracts bought and sold on option exchanges are not tailor-made, but are *standardized* contracts. Therefore exchange-traded share options are for a standard number of shares in the company per contract (usually 1000) at a set (*not* negotiated) exercise price and for a set (*not* negotiated) future expiry date (usually, 9 months into the future). It is this standardization that makes them marketable. Therefore, having bought an exchange-traded option, apart from being able to hold the option and subsequently decide whether to exercise it or allow it to expire, you have also got the opportunity to sell it, unexpired and unexercised, to another investor. Share options, in particular, are usually in exchange-traded form, but options exchanges – of which there are several throughout the world – will usually trade options on a range of underlying financial assets, including shares, commodity prices, interest rates and foreign exchange rates. In addition, the traded option market often trades in another type of financial instrument, called a '*futures contract*'.

INTEREST RATE FUTURES

Of particular concern to us here is one specific type of futures contract: *interest rate futures*. Let us first have an informal look at them.

Futures contracts differ from options contracts in one fundamental way. As we know, options hedge against adverse events but allow you to take advantage of favourable events. By contrast, futures contracts have a 'locking-in' effect and so hedge you against both adverse *and* favourable movements in events.

We have just been discussing two types of option contracts: tailor-made OTC options and standardized exchange-traded options. In many ways we can make a similar distinction between FRAs and interest rate futures contracts. FRAs are tailor-made contracts that hedge the company against both adverse and favourable movements in interest rates. In a similar way, as we shall see, interest rate futures are standardized contracts that hedge against both adverse and favourable interest rate movements.

Formally, a futures contract is a standardized, legally binding agreement to buy or sell a specific asset at a fixed time in the future at a specific price. With futures – unlike options – investors cannot simply walk away from the contract and allow it to lapse. Either the investor takes a profit or accepts making a loss, depending on how prices move between when the contract was taken out and its future expiry (or 'delivery') date. Interest rate futures can appear a little confusing at first, but we will come to realize that they are, in fact, very easy to handle. Initially, we need to describe their basic characteristics.

Interest rate futures contracts are available in a number of different currencies, principally the US dollar, Japanese yen, European euro and British pound sterling. For the purposes of explanation we will use euro futures contracts, but in practice contracts would be used in whichever currency the company was facing interest rate risk. Therefore, if an Emirates company wanted to borrow some US dollars in the future and feared the risk of an increase in US dollar loan interest rates, then it would hedge with dollar futures contracts.

In addition, there are both short-term and long-term interest rate futures contracts. Naturally enough, short-term contracts are used to hedge against adverse movements in short-term interest rates, and long-term contracts are for movements in long-term interest rates. Given that, within the context of the present discussion, we are looking at relatively short-term interest rate risk – on money market loans and deposits – we will use short-term euro interest rate futures, as dealt in on the NYSE Euronext market in Amsterdam, for the purposes of explanation.

A single euro short-term interest rate futures contract relates to the interest that could be earned on a 3-month deposit of €1 000 000. Thus the 'unit of trading' is €1 000 000. One feature of futures markets is that you can only trade in *whole* contracts. Therefore you can trade in short-term euro interest rate contracts in €1 million 'steps' (i.e. €1m, €2m, etc.).

If a company were to buy or sell a euro futures contract, they would in fact be buying or selling the *interest* on a €1 million 3-month deposit. The rate of interest[5] is given by the 'price' of the futures contract (called the quotation) which is expressed on an 'index basis'. What is meant by this is that the price of each contract is equal to 100, less the annual rate of interest. Thus if the annual interest rate on the €1 million deposit was 6¾%, the price of the contracts would be quoted as: $100 - 6.75 = 93.25$.

Contracts are issued on a 3-monthly cycle – typically, March, June, September and December. Each one matures or expires towards the end of the month in question, typically on the third Wednesday of the month. Therefore the June contracts expire on the third Wednesday in June and the September contracts expire on the third Wednesday in September. At any one time, dealers in the futures market are faced with a choice of three different expiry dates. For example, suppose we are currently in February. You would be faced with a choice of March, June or September contracts. By the time we reach the third Wednesday in March, the March contracts will expire and new December contracts are created. Thus, at the end of March, the choice would be between June, September and December contracts.

Profits and losses on futures contracts are measured in 'ticks'. With interest rate futures, one tick represents price movements of 0.005% (i.e. 0.00005), in the annual interest rate. Therefore, for example, a 1% movement in interest rates represents 200 ticks.

The value of a tick of profit or loss is calculated on the basis of the amount of interest it represents:

$$\text{Contract size} \times \text{Contract duration} \times \text{Tick size}$$

Therefore, on euro 3-month interest rate futures contracts, the value of a tick can be calculated as:

$$\text{€1 000 000} \times {}^{3}\!/_{12} \times 0.00005 = \text{€12.50}$$

Finally, interest rate risk can be hedged by either buying or selling futures contracts. Whether they are bought or sold depends upon what represents an adverse movement in interest rates. For example, if a company wanted to hedge against the risk of an *increase* in interest rates (because it intends to take out a future loan) then it would hedge by selling futures – called a 'short hedge'. However, if it wanted to hedge against a *fall* in interest rates (because it was planning to place surplus cash on deposit in the future) then it will hedge by buying futures – a 'long hedge'.

We now know enough about interest rate futures to be able to look at an explanatory illustration of their use. This is shown in Example 5.

EXAMPLE 5

It is now 1 June. In 2-months' time, on 1 August, Van De Katoen – a European-wide business outsourcing company, is planning to borrow €3.9 million for a period of 3 months. Van De Katoen can currently borrow money at an annual interest rate of 8%, but the company's CFO fears that interest rates will have risen by August and so wishes to hedge using interest rate futures contracts. Currently the September 3-month interest rate futures contracts are priced at 93.

We will look at what action Van De Katoen needs to undertake in order to hedge this risk. First, though, we need to explain why the September interest rate futures contracts are going to be used to construct the hedge. Remember that it is now 1 June and so Van De Katoen would have a choice of three contracts: June, September and December contracts. The June contracts are of no use to the company, as they will have expired by the time they need to borrow the money on 1 August. This leaves a choice of either September or December contracts. Although *either* could be used, it is normal to use the contract with the *next* expiry date *after* the date when the loan is required.[6] We require the loan on 1 August and so the futures contracts with the next expiry date after that would be the September contracts.

The following actions would be necessary for the company to set up its hedged position:

1. The first action is for the CFO to set up a 'target' loan cost based on the existing interest rate. If there was no change in interest rates between now (1 June) and 1 August, then the loan would involve an interest cost target of:

$$\text{€3 900 000} \times 0.08 \times \frac{3}{12} = \text{€78 000 interest cost 'target'}$$

▶

As we shall see, the company's futures hedge will result in the company having an *actual* net interest cost which will be very close to this targeted cost of €78 000. (It may end up paying a little more or a little less than €78 000, for reasons we shall see presently.) This outcome will occur *whatever* happens to interest rates between 1 June and 1 August, when the loan is taken out.

2. The second action is to identify the number of futures contracts that are required to hedge the interest charge on the €3.9 million loan. Each contract is in respect of the interest on a deposit of €1 million and so the company will require €3.9 million ÷ €1 million = 3.9 contracts. Given that futures can only be dealt with in whole contracts, this means that Van De Katoen will round this figure up to four contracts. (Notice what this implies – the company is hedging the interest charges on a €3.9 million loan with futures contracts in respect of a total deposit of: $4 \times €1$ million = €4 million.)

3. The third and final action in setting up the hedge position is for Van De Katoen to decide whether they need to buy or sell the futures contracts. Remember the rule: to hedge a loan against rising interest rates, sell futures: to hedge a deposit against falling interest rates buy futures.[7] Here Van De Katoen wants to hedge a *loan* and so they will *sell* four September euro interest rate futures contracts at a price of 93 (their current market price on 1 June).

The reason for the buying and selling rule on futures contracts for deposits and loans respectively will become obvious as we proceed with the example. As we shall see, if Van De Katoen initially *sells* futures and then interest rates *go up*, it will end up making a *profit* on the futures which acts like compensation under an FRA, offsetting the higher interest charges on the loan. (Similarly, if the company initially *buys* futures and then interest rates *fall*, again it will make a *profit* on the futures which would compensate for the reduced interest earned on our deposited money as a result of the fall in interest rates.)

Therefore futures hedges work on a very simple basis, similar to the compensation that is paid or received under an FRA. With Van De Katoen's loan, if interest rates go up (an adverse interest rate movement) it will make an offsetting *profit* on the futures, and if interest rates go down (a favourable interest rate movement) it will make an offsetting *loss* on the futures. Thus, as was pointed out earlier, futures contracts hedge the company against *both* sides of risk: the risk of adverse *and* favourable movements in interest rates.

Having set up this hedged position on 1 June we can then move forwards 2 months to 1 August. This is the day Van De Katoen will need to borrow €3.9 million for 3 months.

Suppose that on 1 August short-term interest rates have risen to 10.5% and euro September interest rate futures contracts are now priced at 90.75:

1. The company has to borrow €3.9 million for 3 months at 10.5% interest. Thus the actual interest charge incurred by the company on the loan will be:

$$€3\,900\,000 \times 0.105 \times \frac{3}{12} = €102\,375$$

This can be compared against the target interest cost of €78 000 to show a 'loss' on target of: €102 375 − €78 000 = €24 375. In other words, because interest rates have risen by 2.5% over the 2-month period from 1 June to 1 August, Van De Katoen is having to pay €24 375 more interest on the loan than it had planned. However, what we shall see is that the company will make a profit on its futures contracts which will *approximately* offset this extra interest cost.

2. On 1 August, as well as borrowing €3.9 million, the company needs to 'close out' its futures position. It does this by transacting a deal in the futures market which is the *reverse* of the original transaction undertaken on 1 June. In that original transaction the company *sold* four September euro contracts;

and so – in order to close out its futures position – it now *buys* four September euro contracts, at their current (1 August) price of 90.75.

What have these two sets of futures transactions achieved? Originally, the company sold four September euro contracts at 93. Remember that the 'price' of the contracts represents an interest rate quoted on an index basis. Thus 93 represents: $100 - 93 = 7\%$ interest. Therefore what the company sold was the interest, at 7%, on four 3-month deposits of €1m each. This represents a total amount of interest of:

$$4 \times €1\,000\,000 = €4\,000\,000 \times 0.07 \times \frac{3}{12} = €70\,000$$

This interest was due to be delivered on the third Wednesday of September. However, futures contracts are very seldom left to 'mature' in this way. Instead, futures positions are usually 'closed out' before the delivery date by undertaking an offsetting transaction. This is just what Van De Katoen did in buying four September contracts at 90.75. What it was doing in this transaction was buying the interest of four €1 million 3-month deposits. Therefore how much interest had it bought? Remembering that 90.75 represents an interest rate of: $100 - 90.75 = 9.25\%$:

$$4 \times €1\,000\,000 = €4\,000\,000 \times 0.0925 \times \frac{3}{12} = €92\,500$$

In other words, through its futures transaction the company had *bought* €92 500 of interest and had *sold* €70 000 of interest. One set of futures contracts offsets (or cancels out) the other set of futures contracts and the company either receives the balance (if it has bought more interest than it has sold), or it has to pay off the balance (if it has sold more interest than it bought). In this way, it makes either a profit or a loss on its futures transactions.

In this example Van De Katoen receives more interest than it sold and so it makes a profit on its futures transaction of: €92 500 − €70 000 = €22 500. However, recall that we said earlier that profits and losses on futures contracts are usually measured in ticks. Therefore, how this profit would normally be calculated is as follows:

Contracts bought at: 90.75

Contracts sold at: 93.0

Profit per contract: $93 - 90.75 = 2.25\% \div 0.005\% = 450$ ticks

Total profit: 4 contracts × 450 ticks per contract = 1800 ticks

Value of profit: 1800 ticks × 12.50 per tick = €22 500.

Therefore, once the company closes out its futures position on 1 August, it will receive a profit from the futures market of €22 500 which will approximately (but not precisely) offset the extra interest charge on its €3.9 million loan.

Interest charge	€102 375
less Profit on futures	€22 500
Net interest cost	€79 875
Target interest cost	€78 000

Hedge efficiency

Notice in Example 5, how close the company's actual interest cost, net of the futures profit, is to the target cost set 2 months earlier of €78 000. How good a hedge this action has been is usually measured by the 'hedge efficiency ratio' of profit (on the futures) over loss[8] (on target):

$$\frac{\text{Profit}}{\text{Loss}} = \frac{€22\,500}{€24\,375} = 0.923 \text{ or } 92.3\% \text{ hedge efficiency}$$

The hedge efficiency ratio is calculated in such a way that if the net interest charge (€79 875) was *greater* than the target interest charge (€78 000) the hedge efficiency would be *less than* 100%. If the net interest charge was *less than* the target charge, the hedge efficiency would be *greater than* 100%, and if the net interest charge was exactly equal to the target charge, then the hedge efficiency ratio would be 100%: a 'perfect' hedge.

Futures will only provide a 100% efficient hedge through luck. There are two reasons for this. One is the fact that we can only deal in whole contracts. In Example 5, Van De Katoen would have liked to have hedged with 3.9 contracts, but had to round up to four whole contracts. Therefore, one reason why a perfect hedge is unlikely is this *standardized* nature (rather than being tailor-made to the company's precise requirements) of futures contracts. Euros can only be hedged in units of €1 million.

The other reason for the imprecise nature of a futures hedge is that the price of futures contracts will only move *approximately* in line with changes in the interest rate faced by the company. This disconnection between movements in market interest rates and movements in futures prices is referred to as 'basis risk'. In Example 5, the company's loan interest rate rose by 2.5% from 8% to 10.5%. However, the futures price only moved by 2.25% from 93 (i.e. 7%) to 90.75 (i.e. 9.25%).

For both these reasons, futures hedges are unlikely to be 100% efficient. However, in practice, the actual efficiency is likely to be fairly close to 100%. The other thing to remember is that these futures contracts hedge the company against both adverse and favourable movements in interest rates. In Example 5 there was an *adverse* movement in interest rates and so the futures contracts provide an offsetting *profit*. In Example 6, the opposite situation is illustrated by changing the scenario on 1 August.

EXAMPLE 6

In Example 5, on 1 June Van De Katoen sold four September euro interest rate futures contracts at 93 in order to hedge its risk on a €3.9 million 3-month loan required from 1 August.

Take this same situation, but now suppose that on 1 August loan interest rates had *fallen* from 8% (on 1 June) to 6.5% and euro futures are now quoted at 94.25. The following now occurs:

(a) The company borrows €3.9 million for 3 months at 6.5% incurring an interest charge of:

$$€3\,900\,000 \times 0.065 \times \frac{3}{12} = €63\,375$$

Target interest charge	= €78 000
'Profit' on target	= €14 625

▶

▶

Because interest rates have fallen – they have moved in the company's favour – the actual interest charge is significantly below the target level.

(b) The company needs to 'close out' its futures position by reversing the earlier deal. Therefore it now buys four September euro contracts which are priced at 94.25.

(c) The outcome from the futures transactions is:

Contracts bought at	94.25		
Contracts sold at	93		
Loss per contract	1.25%	=	250 ticks
Total loss on futures: 4 × 250 × €12.50		=	€12 500

(d)

Actual interest charge on €3.9 million loan	€63 375
plus loss on futures contracts	€12 500
Total costs	€75 875
Target cost of loan	£78 000

$$\text{Hedge efficiency:} \quad \frac{\text{Profit}}{\text{Loss}} = \frac{\text{€14625}}{\text{€12500}} = 1.17 \text{ or } 117\% \text{ hedge efficiency}$$

In this case the hedge efficiency is over 100% because the net cost of the loan to the company is *slightly less* than the target amount. Here the standardization of the contracts and the basis risk have combined to act slightly in the company's favour.

Maturity mismatch

Examples 5 and 6 both involved 3-month interest rate futures being used to hedge a 3-month loan. What would have happened if the company had required a loan for more or less than 3 months? This situation is known as a '*maturity mismatch*' and can be easily handled by adjusting the number of contracts dealt in with the hedge.

Taking Example 5, suppose Van De Kateon wanted to borrow €3.9 million for 6 months (rather than 3 months). It can still hedge its exposure to interest rate risk using 3-month interest rate futures, by *doubling* the number of contracts used from four to eight. The idea here is that, as the duration of the loan is twice that of the futures contract, it will require twice the number of contracts to hedge the risk. If the loan was for 9 months, then it would require *three times* the number of contracts: 4 × 3 = 12 contracts. Similarly, if the €3.9 million loan was required for only 2 months (i.e. the duration of the loan was only two-thirds of the duration of the futures contract) then the number of contracts required to hedge would be:

$$\frac{\text{€3.9m}}{\text{€1m}} = 3.9 \times \frac{2}{3} = 2.6 \text{ rounded up to 3 whole contracts}$$

Example 7 provides an illustration of a maturity mismatch on a short-term deposit.

EXAMPLE 7

Nova Royale is based in the UK and imports from and exports to several countries in the Eurozone. It is now early January. In April, Nova Royale is due to receive €3.95 million from a Belgian customer. Nove Royale's CFO has decided that, on receipt, the money will be placed on deposit for 5 months and then used to pay off a euro-denominated invoice that will then be due for payment in September. The current interest rate available on short-term euro deposit is 6% per annum, but the company's CFO fears that this will fall significantly in the next few weeks. As a result, the company decides to hedge its exposure to interest rate risk by using 3-month euro interest rate futures. The contract size is €1 million and June contracts are currently quoted at 94.

The CFO's target interest income on the euro deposit, on the basis of current interest rates, would be:

$$€3.95m \times 0.06 \times \frac{5}{12} = €98\,750$$

To set up the hedge the company will need to *buy* euro futures (as it is hedging a deposit and so fear *falling* euro interest rates). If there was *no* maturity mismatch, the number of contracts required would be: €3.95m ÷ €1m = 3.95.

However, because there is a maturity mismatch (3-month futures and a 5-month deposit), the required number of contracts has to be increased proportionally:

$$3.95 \times \frac{5}{3} = 6.58 = 7\,contracts$$

Therefore Nova Royale will buy seven euro June futures contracts at a price of 94 in order to hedge its exposure to interest rate risk.

In April, when the company receives the €3.9 million, it finds (as feared) that euro short-term interest rates have fallen to 4.75% per annum and June euro futures are quoted at 95.25.

As a result, Nova Royale then places the €3.95 million on 5-month deposit to yield:

$$€3.95m \times 0.0475 \times \frac{5}{12} = €78\,177$$

Target interest income	= €98 750
Loss on target	= €20 573

At the same time, the company will close out its position in the futures market by reversing the earlier deal and so it *sells* seven euro June contracts at 95.25.

The outcome of its futures trades is calculated as follows:

Contracts bought at	94
Contracts sold at	95.25
Profit per contract	1.25% = 250 ticks

Total profit = 7 × 250 × €12.50 = €21 875.
This results in a hedge efficiency of:

$$\frac{Profit}{Loss} = \frac{€21\,875}{€20\,573} = 1.063 \text{ or } 106.3\% \text{ hedge efficiency}$$

▶

In other words:

Target interest income	=	€98 750
Actual interest income	=	€78 177
plus Profit on futures	=	€21 875
Total income	=	€100 052

A strip hedge

As a final example of using interest rate futures, we now turn to have a look at the concept of the 'strip hedge'. Latech is a French software developer. The company has €10 million of surplus finance available to invest for the next 2 years, until it will be required to fund a major upgrade to its systems. Market conditions are such that interest rates in the eurozone on longer-term deposits are higher than on shorter-term deposits. (Technically, the 'yield curve' is rising.[9]) Therefore the company's CFO knows that she can get a better rate of interest investing the money longer term (say, in 2-year bonds), but the company's liquidity preference dictates that she would prefer to invest it in a series of short-term (3-month) deposits, in order to have easy access to the funds, in case an earlier than planned upgrade is required. However, the CFO would then run the risk of short-term interest rates falling over the next 2 years, and of being criticized by other board members for not taking the opportunity to lock into the higher longer-term rate.

There are a number of solutions available to solve the CFO's problem. One would be to hedge the interest rate risk using a 'strip' of futures contracts.

On the NYSE Euronext market, euro 3-month interest rate futures contracts extend out 24 months. Suppose it is early January 2016. The company is faced with the following futures prices (and their implied rates of interest):

	Quote	Implied interest rate (%)	
March 16	94.28	5.72	
June	94.44	5.56	
Sept.	94.36	5.64	
Dec.	94.16	5.84	Average
March 17	93.84	6.16	= 6.17%
June	93.50	6.50	
Sept.	93.15	6.85	
Dec.	92.91	7.09	

The company can then place the €10 million on a series of 3-month deposits over the next 2 years and buy ten €1m contracts, in each of the eight contract expiry dates which are available. By doing this, the company is maintaining easy access to the €10 million held on deposit while, at the same time locking itself into a 6.17% interest rate over the next 2 years and so avoiding the possibility of falling short-term interest rates over this period. Latech would close out each set of futures contracts at their expiry. If interest rates have gone up they will receive a higher rate of interest on the deposited money to offset the loss on the futures. If interest rates go down, the profit on the futures will offset the lower level of interest earned on the deposited cash.

Margin

Finally, we need to examine the concept of 'margin'. All futures deals (and traded option deals) are conducted through a futures market which effectively stands as a guarantor of the obligations of each party (the buyer and the seller of the contracts).

Futures contracts are 'zero sum games', in the sense that every deal has a buyer and a seller, and the profit made by one party equals the loss made by the other. The great fear of dealing in futures is that having made a profit on your futures, the other party (who has therefore made a loss) then defaults. This risk (referred to as counterparty credit risk) is overcome by the futures market requirement that whenever a futures position is 'opened' – this would occur in our examples when we set up the hedge by selling futures (to hedge a loan) or buying futures (to hedge a deposit) – a certain sum of money known as 'initial margin' must be placed on deposit with the futures market, to act as security against possible default. (The rules on margin amounts are quite complex and need not concern us here.)

Thereafter, at the end of every day until the company's futures position is closed out, the futures market calculates the profit or loss that has been made on the open futures position. This profit or loss is then added to or subtracted from the balance on the margin account. (This process of daily updating of profits and losses is known as being 'settled to market'.) If the company is making substantial losses on its open futures position, such that the balance on the margin account falls below some specified minimum (remember the margin is there to act as security against default), then the company is required by the futures market to place *further* money on deposit to 'top up' the margin account to its minimum required level. This additional margin is referred to as 'variation margin'. This requirement to place money on margin account is seen as one of the disadvantages of futures hedging as it exposes the company to the possibility of an uncertain future cash flow liability.

CAPS, COLLARS AND FLOORS

Forward forward loans, FRAs, IRGs or IROs and interest rate futures are all short-term hedging devices. They can only be used to hedge against adverse movements in interest rates in the relatively short-term future, up to a maximum of about 24 months ahead.

However, both IRGs and FRAs have equivalent, *longer-term*, hedging techniques. Interest rate caps, interest rate floors and interest rate collar agreements can all be considered longer-term versions of IRGs. They are hedging devices that are generally bought 'over-the-counter' from a bank and they can be used to limit a company's exposure to adverse movements in interest rates on longer-term loans and deposits, while at the same time allowing advantage to be taken of favourable movements.

Interest rate caps

For example, suppose a South African company, South Continental Shipping, wishes to raise a R15 million 7-year loan. The company's bank will only offer such a loan at a floating or variable rate of interest of SARB [10] plus 2%.

South Continental's CFO is unwilling to agree to these terms because he believes that interest rates are likely to rise in the future. If this was to happen, then the interest rate on the company's loan would rise also, and it is thought that too sharp a rise in future interest rates could seriously damage the company's profitability and liquidity.

One obvious solution would be for the company to raise the loan at a *fixed* rate of interest. However, the bank is unwilling to agree to such an arrangement because it too believes interest rates will rise and so does not want to get locked into a lending agreement at the low current levels of interest.

The solution would be for the CFO to accept the floating rate loan but, in addition, buy an interest rate cap agreement at, say, 6.5% on SARB. A cap agreement does what the name suggests – it places a 'cap' or 'limit' on how high an interest rate the company can be asked to pay on its floating rate loan. A cap on SARB of 6.5% means that if, during the term of the loan, if SARB goes above 6.5% (at which rate the company pays: 6.5% + 2% = 8.5%), the interest rate on the loan sticks at 8.5%. If SARB subsequently falls below 6.5%, the company's loan rate will also fall.

It is in this way that a cap operates as an *option* – limiting the company's exposure to an adverse movement in interest rates, while allowing it to take advantage of falling interest rates. How much this option would cost to buy depends very much on the circumstances. In particular, the cost is a function of the level at which the cap was set – a cap at 8% would cost less than a cap at 6.5% – and the perceived risk of rising interest rates in future. However, essentially, its cost would be determined in line with the factors contained in the Black and Scholes model.

Interest rate collars

One way of reducing the cost of the cap – and effectively converting the variable rate loan into a *semi-fixed* rate loan – is to simultaneously buy a cap – say at 6.5% – and *sell* an interest rate *floor agreement* at, say, 4%. This combined arrangement is known as a 'collar'. It places a limit on how high the interest rate can float up and on how low the interest rate can float down. In this example the CFO would be fixing the interest rate on the floating rate loan so that it doesn't exceed 8.5%, nor does it go below 6%.

A collar arrangement will obviously cost less than a cap because it provides protection to the bank as well as the company. (In this example the bank is protected from receiving a rate of interest on their loan of less than 6%.) Nevertheless, just how much an interest rate collar agreement would cost again depends upon the cap and floor rates set and the outlook for future interest rate movements.

Interest rate floors

Interest rate floor agreements on their own, or combined with a cap into a collar agreement, can also be used by companies to hedge interest rate risk on floating rate *deposits*. Thinking back to the example in our discussion of futures where we showed a Latech's CFO hedging interest risk on a short-term deposit through a *strip hedge* of futures contracts; an alternative would be a collar or floor agreement related to the deposited sum.

INTEREST RATE SWAPS

Just as caps, collars and floors are longer-term versions of IRGs/IROs, so interest rate swaps are a longer-term version of FRAs.

The market in swap agreements is both large and important, and has developed rapidly over a relatively short period of time. There are a great many variations now available, but we will confine ourselves at this stage to looking at the basic type of interest rate swap agreement. (At a later stage, when we come to consider foreign exchange risk, we will return to the idea of interest rate swaps.)

The basic interest rate swap agreement is where one company swaps a stream of *floating* rate interest payments (on a notional loan), with another company, for a stream of *fixed* interest payments. The companies involved in such an arrangement may deal directly with each other or, more typically, the deal would be arranged through an intermediary, such as a bank.

Suppose De Wit Construction has a €50 million 5-year loan at Euro-LIBOR plus 1% and Jahr Technologies has a €50 million 5-year loan at a fixed rate of interest of 7%. If they arrange a swap, each of the companies (called the counterparties) agrees to pay the other party's loan interest commitments. Thus, the effect is that De Wit has converted its floating rate loan into a fixed rate loan and Jahr has done the reverse.

If the two companies are of different credit risk (e.g. suppose De Wit had a better credit rating than Jahr and could borrow at a fixed rate of, say, 6%), then an up-front payment is made by one party to the other to offset the difference.

Interest rate swaps can be used in many situations. One situation is of immediate concern here – using a swap agreement to hedge against an adverse movement in interest rates. Suppose Werft-Rück has a €100 million long-term loan at a floating rate of interest. The CFO now believes, on an analysis of the macroeconomic situation, that over the next 3 years, say, interest rates are likely to rise. What they can do is enter into a 3-year swap agreement with a counterparty to swap into a fixed rate of interest for the next 3 years. At the end of this time, the company will revert back to paying a floating rate of interest, when hopefully interest rates will have started to fall back. Therefore, by this action, the CFO is hedging the company against the possibility of an adverse movement in interest rates over the next 3 years.

Swaptions

Alternatively, a company with a fixed interest loan which believed that interest rates were likely to fall over the next few years could swap into a floating rate of interest with the intention of taking advantage of the anticipated fall in interest rates. However, such a move could backfire on the company if, having arranged a swap into a floating rate of interest, interest rates subsequently rise.

One way around this would be for the company to arrange a cap agreement with the swap intermediary. If the floating rate of interest went above the cap, the company would only have to make interest payments at the capped level and the intermediary would finance the difference out of its own resources to the swap counterparty. Such an arrangement is known as a swap option or 'swaption'.

Quality spread or coupon swaps

Although not strictly to do with interest rate risk, we will take this opportunity to look at another common reason for the existence of swap agreements. This is in order to take advantage of slight inconsistencies between different capital markets. This is illustrated in Example 8.

EXAMPLE 8

Kingsland Advertising and Barwick Engineering are both UK companies and each want to raise a £100 million 10-year loan. Kingsland wishes to borrow at a fixed rate of interest, wanting to have certainty about its future interest liabilities. Barwick wishes to borrow at a floating rate because its finance director believes that interest rates are likely to fall in the future.

Kingsland has been offered a fixed interest loan at 8% or a floating rate loan at LIBOR[11] + 4.5%. Barwick has a better credit rating than Kingsland. As a result, it has been offered a fixed interest loan at 6% and a floating rate loan at LIBOR + 3%. These facts are tabulated below:

	Fixed interest	Floating rate	
Kingland	8%	LIBOR + 4.5 %	
Barwick	6 %	LIBOR + 3%	
Quality spread differential:	2%	− 1.5%	= 0.5%

Because of Barwick's superior credit rating, it is able to borrow money more cheaply than Kingsland – the so-called 'quality spread'. However, notice that the rate at which Barwick can borrow below that of Kingsland is not consistent between the two types of loan. Barwick can borrow 2% cheaper than Kingsland on fixed interest loans, but only 1.5% cheaper than Kingsland on floating rate loans. If the capital market were being consistent, we would expect Barwick's superior credit standing to have the *same* impact on both types of loan.

In circumstances such as these, when there is a difference in the quality spreads between the two types of loan, it is possible for both parties to benefit from a swap arrangement. In this example, the quality spread differential is 0.5% and therefore a swap agreement will result in a total interest saving between the two parties equal to this amount (before any fee charged by an intermediary for putting the two counterparties together). How this interest saving is split between the two parties is negotiable, but it is usually divided equally. If this were to be the case, then a swap agreement can be used which will result in each company getting the type of loan it wants at 0.25% less than the rate of interest it would normally have to pay. (You might think that 0.25% isn't much, but it represents a saving of £250 000 per year for 10 years on each company's £100 million loan.)

Therefore Kingsland will achieve the fixed interest loan that it wants at 8% − 0.25% = 7.75%; and Barwick will acquire a floating rate loan at LIBOR +3% − 0.25% = LIBOR + 2.75%.

The swap is put together on the following basis:

(a) The largest quality spread is first identified. The type of loan to which it applies is then borrowed by whichever company can borrow at the cheapest rate. This company is referred to as the 'lead' company. In this example the quality spread on fixed interest loans is the largest: 2% (the quality spread on floating rate loans being only 1.5%), and on this type of loan, Barwick can get the best rate: 6%. Therefore Barwick – as the "lead" company – borrows £100 million at a fixed rate of interest of 6%.

(b) The counterparty company – Kingsland – then borrows the other type of loan. Therefore Kingsland borrows £100 million at LIBOR + 4.5%.

▶

(c) The counterparty to the lead company (that is, Kingsland) then pays the lead company the normal rate of interest that it would pay on the type of loan it really wants, less the agreed swap saving. In this example we will assume that the total interest saving of 0.5% (the quality spread differential) will be split *equally* between the two parties: 0.25% each. Kingsland wants a fixed interest loan and would normally pay 8%. Therefore Kingsland pays Barwick 8% − 0.25% = 7.75% interest.

(d) Finally, the lead company – Barwick in our example – pays the interest on the loan that has been raised by the counterparty. Therefore Barwick pays Kingsland interest equal to LIBOR + 4.5%.

The outcome of this arrangement is as follows:

Kingsland:	Pays LIBOR + 4.5% on the loan raised
	Pays 7.75% interest to Barwick
	Receives LIBOR + 4.5% from Barwick
Net payment:	Kingsland pays 7.75% interest fixed.
Barwick:	Pays 6% interest on loan raised
	Pays LIBOR + 4.5% to Kingsland
	Receives 7.75% interest from Kingsland
Net payments:	Barwick pays 6% + LIBOR + 4.5% − 7.75% % = LIBOR + 2.75%

Therefore each company achieves the type of loan it requires, with an interest rate saving of 0.25% on the normal rate of interest that they would pay.

Advantages and disadvantages

Swap arrangements have a number of advantages. Principal amongst these is their flexibility and their low transaction costs. In terms of flexibility, they can usually be arranged in respect of any amount of money (typically €5 million to €50 million) and over virtually any time period. Furthermore they can be reversed, if desired, before the planned maturity date by re-swapping with other counterparties. Swap deals do not depend on being able to identify a suitable counterparty, as banks are often willing to act in this role themselves. (Indeed many large banks raise fixed interest debt with the express intention of using it to swap into floating rate debt with commercial organizations that do not have a sufficiently good credit standing to raise fixed interest loans directly.)

Transaction costs on swaps are relatively modest. Standardized legal documentation is usually used which reduces legal costs and competitive market forces restrain the level of fees demanded by intermediaries.

The main problem with swaps, and one which is often ignored by the parties concerned, is 'counterparty' risk – that is, the risk that your swap partner may default on their obligations. Thus, in Example 8, Barwick relies on Kingsland, the less creditworthy company, to meet its obligations to pay 7.75% interest each year. If Kingsland does default, Barwick can in turn stop paying LIBOR + 4.5% to Kingsland, but Barwick is still left with a type of loan (fixed interest) that it does not want. Using an intermediary is one way of reducing this risk, with the intermediary (for a fee) agreeing to take over the swap in the event of one of the counterparties defaulting.

SUMMARY

Interest rate risk can be defined as the risk of an adverse movement in interest rates.

- The basic hedging technique for interest rate risk is the forward forward loan, where the company borrows money before it is required, so as to lock itself into a particular rate of interest. This money is then placed on deposit to earn interest until the loan is actually required.

- FRAs represent a simpler and more convenient way of achieving the same hedging effect as that achieved with a forward forward loan. Under an FRA, the company either receives or pays compensation to offset an adverse or favourable movement in interest rates.

- Whereas FRAs hedge the company against both adverse *and* favourable movements in interest rates, IRGs are true options, in that they hedge the company against adverse interest rate movements, but allow it to take advantage of favourable movements.

- Another hedging instrument is the interest rate futures contract. Unlike FRAs, which are tailor-made to the firm's precise requirements, these are standardized hedging instruments which are traded on future markets. Like FRAs, they effectively lock the company into a specific rate of interest and so provide a hedge against both adverse and favourable interest rate movements.

- Interest rate caps, floors and collars are all longer-term versions of FRAs. Interest rate cap agreements place a limit on a company's exposure to the risk of rising interest rates on a floating rate loan. Floor agreements similarly place a limit to the risk of falling interest rates on a monetary deposit. Interest rate collar agreements can be used to effectively turn a floating rate loan into a semi-fixed rate loan by limiting interest rate movements in both directions.

- Interest rate swap agreements come in many forms. However, they are basically agreements to swap a stream of floating interest rate payments for a stream of future fixed interest rate payments and so provide a longer-term hedge against adverse movements in interest rates.

NOTES

1. Notice that, in reality, there is not a single money market, but rather a series of different, highly specialist money markets. However, for our purpose, we can treat the money markets as a single entity without any loss of understanding.

2. Notice that whether money market interest rates increase or decrease over time depends upon circumstances and the shape of the 'yield curve', that is discussed in Chapter 15.

3. Money market rates are quoted in terms of simple or 'nominal' annual interest rates. Thus the one month rate is, in the example in the text, $\frac{1}{2}\%$ per month. This gives a nominal annual rate of: $\frac{1}{2} \times 12 = 6\%$ per year. However, the effective annual interest rate – known as the APR, the annual percentage rate – is the compounded value of the monthly rate: $(1 + 0.005)^{12} - 1 = 0.06168$ or 6.168% per year. They are given in annual terms so as to facilitate ease of comparison between, say, the overnight rate and the 1-week rate. They are quoted in simple/nominal annual terms so that the actual interest rate per time period can be easily calculated. For example, the 6% 1-month rate is actually: $6\% \div 12 = \frac{1}{2}\%$ per 1 month.

4. It can be seen from this reasoning why banks are happy to enter into FRAs with commercial companies. Generally speaking, banks are more profitable when interest rates are high. Under an FRA, the bank receives compensation when interest rates fall, thus helping the bank to reduce its own risk exposure.

5. The interest rate on EURONEXT short-term euro futures reflects the European Bankers Federation Euribor offered rate – EBF Euribor – which is, effectively, the short-term rate that banks lend at between themselves.

6. In order to minimize 'basis risk' – of which more later.

7. The 'rule' is what it is because it produces the desired result. For example, if a loan is to be hedged, then we would want to make a 'profit' on a futures trade if interest rates rise – to offset the higher interest cost. If a futures hedge is set (termed 'opening up a futures position'), by selling futures contracts, then a profit *will be* generated if, subsequently, interest rates rise.

8. This 'loss' value of €24 375 is the difference between the actual loan interest paid (€102 375) and the target amount of interest (€78 000).

9. See Chapter 15 for a discussion of the yield curve.

10. SARB is the South African Reserve Bank repo interest rate, a floating rate of interest which is widely used as a benchmark interest rate for floating rate commercial loans in South Africa. In this case, the company is offered a loan at an interest rate that is 2% higher than SARB.

11. The London Inter-Bank Offered Rate. The floating rate of interest at which banks lend between each other.

FURTHER READING

1. Two good articles on the general area of financial futures, including interest rate futures: K.R. French, 'Pricing Financial Futures Contracts: An Introduction', *Journal of Applied Corporate Finance,* Winter 1989; B.W. Nocco and R.M. Stulz, 'Enterprise Risk Management: Theory and Practice', *Journal of Applied Corporate Finance*, Fall 2006.

2. For a specific examination of interest rate futures and option, see S.B. Block and T.J. Gallagher, 'The Use of Interest Rate Futures and Options by Corporate Financial Management', *Financial Management*, Autumn 1986.

3. Two interesting articles on swaps are: S.M. Turnbull, 'Swaps: A Zero Sum Game?', *Financial Management,* Spring 1987; and L.D. Wall and J.J. Pringle, 'Alternative Explanations of Interest Rate Swaps: A Theoretical and Empirical Analysis', *Financial Management,* Summer 1989.

4. A good general review article is: C.W. Smithson, 'A LEGO Approach to Financial Engineering: An Introduction to Forwards, Futures, Swaps and Options', *Midland Corporate Finance Journal,* Winter 1987.

5. F. Taylor, *Mastering Derivatives Markets*, 3rd ed., FT Prentice Hall 2006 and T.J. Andersen, *Global Derivatives a Strategic Management Perspective*, FT/Prentice Hall 2005, provide guidance regarding the management of interest rate risk through the use of derivatives; S. Bartram, G. Brown and F. Fehle, 'International Evidence of Financial Derivative Usage', *Financial Management*, 38, 2009 looks at the widespread use of derivatives in practice.

QUIZ QUESTIONS

1   If the 3-month money market interest rate is 8%, how much interest would you pay on a €1 million 3-month loan?

2   You wish to borrow €5 million for 3 months in 2-months' time. How would you set up a forward forward loan hedge?

3   If you had an FRA on a €10 million 6-month loan at 6.5% and, at the time the loan was taken out the market interest rate was 7%, would you pay or receive compensation, and how much?

4   What is the fundamental difference between an FRA and an IRG or IRO?

5 If you wish to hedge against a rising rate of interest on a floating rate loan, would you set up a hedge position by buying or selling interest rate futures?

6 If interest rate futures are priced at 93.75, what rate of interest does this imply?

7 What is 'basis risk'?

8 Why is it unlikely that a futures hedge will be 100% efficient?

9 Company A can borrow at a fixed rate of interest of 8% and also at LIBOR + 1%. Company B can borrow at a fixed rate of interest of 9.75% and at LIBOR + 2.75%. Is there an advantage to an interest rate swap?

(See the 'Answers to Quiz Questions' section at the back of the book.)

PROBLEMS

The answers to these problems are available online (see the 'Digital Resources' page for details).

1 Sabadelle SA has €14 million of fixed rate loans at an interest rate of 12% per year which are due to mature in 1 year. The company's CFO believes that interest rates are going to fall, but does not wish to redeem the loans because large penalties exist for early redemption. Sabadelle's bank has offered to arrange an interest rate swap for 1 year with a company that has obtained floating rate finance at euro LIBOR + $\frac{1}{8}$%. The bank will charge each of the companies an arrangement fee of €20 000 and the proposed terms of the swap are that Sabadelle will pay euro LIBOR plus $1\frac{1}{2}$% to the other company and receive from the company $11\frac{5}{8}$%.

Corporate tax is at 20% per year and the arrangement fee is a tax allowable expense. Sabadelle could issue floating rate debt at euro LIBOR + 2% and the other company could issue fixed rate debt at $11\frac{3}{4}$%.

Required:

(a) Evaluate whether Sabadelle SA would benefit from the interest rate swap:

    (i) if euro LIBOR remains at 10% for the whole year

    (ii) if euro LIBOR falls to 9% after 6 months.

(b) If euro LIBOR remains at 10%, evaluate whether both companies could benefit from the interest rate swap if the terms of the swap were altered. Any benefit would be equally shared.

2 (a) It is now 31 December and the CFO of Logistica Grupo is concerned about the volatility of interest rates. In 3-months' time, the company needs to borrow €5 million for a 6-month period. Current interest rates are 8% per year for the type of loan that Logistica would use, and the treasurer does not wish to pay more than this. He is considering using either:

    (i) a forward rate agreement (FRA), or

    (ii) interest rate futures, or

    (iii) an interest rate guarantee.

Required:

Explain briefly how each of these three alternatives might be useful to Logistica Grupo.

(b) The CFO of Logistica expects interest rates to increase by 2% during the next 3 months and has decided to hedge the interest rate risk using interest rate futures.

March euro 3-month time deposit futures are currently priced at 92.25. The standard contract size is €1 000 000 and the minimum price movement is one tick (the value of one tick is 0.005% per year of the contract size).

▶

Required:

Show the effect of using the futures market to hedge against interest rate movements:

  (i)   If interest rates increase by 2% and the futures market price also moves by 2%.
  (ii) If interest rates increase by 2% and the futures market moves by 1.5%.
  (iii) If interest rates fall by 1% and the futures market moves by 0.75%.

In each case, estimate the hedge efficiency.

  (c) If, as an alternative to interest rate futures, the CFO had been able to purchase IRGs at 8.5% for a premium of 0.2% of the size of the loan to be guaranteed, calculate whether the total cost of the loan after hedging in each of situations (i) to (iii) in (b) above would have been less with the futures hedge or with the guarantee. The guarantee would be effective for the entire 6-month period of the loan.

FINANCING DECISIONS

15 FINANCIAL MARKETS

LEARNING OBJECTIVES

The purpose of this chapter is to:

- Discuss the concept of financial market efficiency.
- Consider the nature of investor 'rationality' and implications of market inefficiency.
- Examine the 'term structure of interest rates' and the concept of the 'yield curve'.
- Discuss the theories concerning the shape of the yield curve.

INTRODUCTION

We now turn to look at some aspects of the company's financing decisions. More specifically, we shall be looking at how we can measure the economic (as opposed to the accounting) costs of the different types of finance which are available, in order to then begin consideration of the complex question concerning the company's capital structure decision.

However, before we turn to examine these topics, we first need to consider elements of the economic background against which financing decisions are made. In particular, in this chapter, we consider two important aspects of financial markets.

The first of these is a consideration of the extent to which the financial markets – and, in particular, the stock market – can be said to be 'efficient' in the pricing of company securities. In other words, we need to look at the degree to which we can rely on the stock market being able to correctly value a company's shares.

The second aspect of financial markets that we look at in this chapter is referred to as the 'term structure' of interest rates. This is concerned with the relationship between long- and short-term interest rates and the messages, or otherwise, that the term structure might give to the corporate treasurer when taking decisions about how the company's assets should be financed.

REAL WORLD VIEW: Increasing Capital in Saudi Banks

The Saudi Arabian Monetary Agency (SAMA) was established in 1952 in order to give the country necessary monetary control and regulation (its first task being the development of the Saudi Riyal). Since the 1980s, the SAMA has switched its main focus from controlling a booming economy to introducing financial market reforms.

Most recently, it has helped to guide banks through the financial crisis, and now modern Saudi banking systems are working on lowering their ratios of loans-to-deposits. Many banks in Saudi Arabia are doing this by increasing their capital up to 100% in order to increase their ability to lend without breaking credit concentration requirements.

Given the importance of the private sector in driving the 2014 economy, this policy seems like a way to stimulate loans and keep the Saudi banking system growing strong. However, according to a report by the National Commercial Bank, it is possible that this monetary policy may change once the USA withdraws its QE programme.

Will an increase of capital in banks help to stimulate the Saudi economy even further?

MARKET EFFICIENCY

A definition

The efficient markets hypothesis (EMH) holds that a stock market is efficient if the market price of a company's shares (or other financial securities, such as bonds) rapidly and correctly reflects all relevant information as it becomes available. In a truly efficient stock market, if all information turned out to be entirely reliable and complete, share prices could be relied upon to correctly reflect the true economic worth of the shares. In such a market, overvalued or undervalued shares would not exist. However, when we talk about market efficiency in the real world we have to recognize that we have no way of knowing what the future will bring and so we have to qualify our interpretation of the value of shares. We cannot claim that an efficient market means that share prices reflect *true* economic worth because that is determined by the future, but we can say that share prices fully and accurately reflect all available information that is relevant to their value. We will discuss what this actually means below.

Importance of market efficiency

The concept of an efficient stock market, and the degree to which the market actually is efficient, is of prime importance to the financial manager for a number of reasons.

Perhaps the most fundamental of these reasons relates back to our discussions in Chapter 1 about financial objectives. There we said that the fundamental objective behind financial management decision-making was the maximization of shareholder wealth. This was then 'translated' – in order to make it into an operational objective – into the maximization of the value of the company's shares.

With this in mind therefore, it is important that the financial manager can rely on the stock market to correctly value the company's shares. If the financial manager makes a decision that will increase shareholder wealth, then it is important that both the manager and the shareholders should have the implications of that decision correctly *signalled* to them, through a rise in the company's share price. A similar argument would also hold in a situation where a manager makes a decision that damages shareholder wealth. It is important that the stock market price of the company's shares gives accurate feedback to both the principals and their agents – to both managers and shareholders.

However, apart from this fundamental reason for making stock market efficiency highly desirable, there are a number of other reasons of almost equal importance. In the forefront of these is the market's risk–return relationship, which we examined in previous chapters, and the fact that a fundamental assumption that underlies the concept of portfolio theory is a belief that the stock market is reasonably efficient. This is because, in an efficient market, share prices are valued so as to give the return that they *should* be expected to produce (on average), given their relative systematic risk exposure.

If the stock market were *inefficient* at pricing shares, then we could not rely on the risk–return messages given by the CAPM. Indeed, in such circumstances, the concept of the market portfolio as the optimal share portfolio loses credibility. If the stock market were really inefficient, then the optimal share portfolio would be one which consisted of holdings in undervalued 'bargain' shares. Diversification, in its own right, would not necessarily be a desirable objective to achieve in such circumstances; investing in bargain shares which gave higher returns than they should, given their level of risk, would be the best investment objective.

A further implication of an inefficient stock market is that the CAPM would no longer be able to provide the financial manager with an NPV discount rate for project appraisal purposes. In fact, in an inefficient stock market, it would be virtually impossible for managers to take rational capital investment decisions on behalf of the company's shareholders. In our earlier discussion on NPV we saw that the discount rate was an opportunity cost, reflecting the return available elsewhere on similar risk investments. In an inefficient market it would be effectively impossible to identify such a rate of return, as different investments with the same degree of risk as the project might give different returns and it would be impossible for managers to ensure that they had identified the best available forgone rate of return to use as the NPV discount rate.

Finally, another important implication of market efficiency for financial managers concerns the importance of information disclosure. The stock market can only be expected to value a company's shares correctly on the basis of the information that has been disclosed. Therefore, if financial managers (and shareholders) want the stock market to correctly value the company's shares, they must ensure that they communicate sufficient information to the market to allow it to do so. In an efficient stock market, information disclosure is a key requirement.

Levels of market efficiency

Having discussed why the concept of market efficiency is important for financial managers, we now reach a crucial question. Is the stock market efficient in the pricing of shares? Do share prices quickly and correctly reflect the impact of new, relevant information?

It has become the norm to consider the efficiency of markets in terms of whether or not they are efficient at three different levels:

1. weak form efficiency
2. semi-strong form efficiency
3. strong form efficiency.

Although we should not get too concerned about the definitions of these levels, they do have important implications for the ways in which it might be possible to 'beat the market' as we will see in the next section.

Weak form efficiency is the lowest level of efficiency. It implies no more than that share prices fully reflect any information that may be obtained from studying and analyzing past movements in the share price. Thus if the market is weak form efficient, it will not be possible to identify mispriced shares – either undervalued or overvalued shares - by analyzing the past share price trends and patterns.

Semi-strong form efficiency is the next level. If the market is semi-strong efficient, it will also be efficient in the weak sense. Semi-strong efficiency implies that share prices fully reflect all the relevant, publicly disclosed information that is known about the company and its circumstances. Thus if the market is semi-strong efficient, it will not be possible to identify mispriced shares by analyzing publicly available information.

Finally, there is strong form efficiency. This is the most extreme form of market efficiency. If the stock market is strongly efficient, this implies that share prices reflect *all* relevant information about their value, even though some of that information may not have been publicly disclosed. Thus if the market is strong form efficient, it will not be possible to identify mispriced securities under any circumstances – including the use of information which has not yet been publicly disclosed, called 'inside information'.

MARKET EFFICIENCY AND SHARE DEALING

Most active stock market investors try to beat the market. What they try to do is to identify undervalued shares and buy them before their prices rise; similarly, they also look for overvalued shares in order to sell them before their prices fall. In other words, such investors are backing their own judgement about what the shares are worth, against the collective judgement of the stock market, as seen in the current price of the shares. Therefore they act as though the market were inefficient.

There are basically three forms of stock market analysis that investors use to help them try and identify overvalued or undervalued shares and these are linked to the levels of efficiency we have just discussed. They are technical analysis, fundamental analysis and the use of 'inside' information.

Technical analysts study charts of past share price movements (and hence are often referred to as 'chartists'), with the intention of discovering particular patterns of share price movements that appear to re-occur. Once these patterns have been identified then, in following the share price movements of a particular company, if they see one of these patterns *starting* to develop, this then gives them 'predictive power' and they are then able to predict the future share price movements and so can make buy and sell investment decisions.

Technical analysts believe that they have discovered hundreds of these re-occurring patterns; an example of one – termed a 'head and shoulders' pattern – is given in Figure 15.1. So, an analyst who is following the share price movement of Körbermetall shares, as in Figure 15.2, may conclude that the share price is currently reaching the top of a head and shoulders pattern, and therefore advises that the shares be sold now, before the share price falls.

Technical analysts do not know why, nor do they particularly want to know why, a particular share's price is predicted to rise or fall. All they know is that that is the movement implied by the developing pattern. However, it has to be said that if Chartism is to work, it implies that there are patterns in the behaviour of investors since it is very difficult to

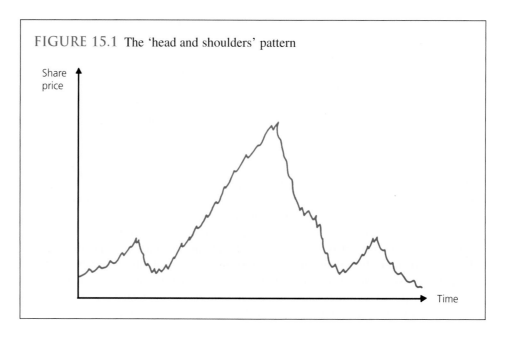

FIGURE 15.1 The 'head and shoulders' pattern

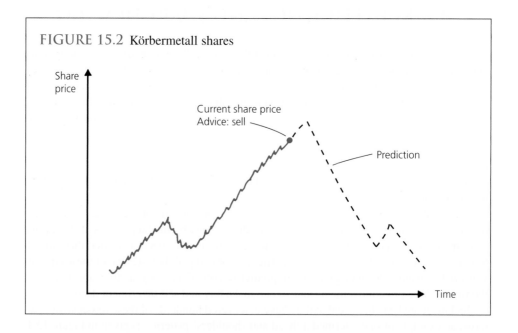

FIGURE 15.2 Körbermetall shares

see how there might be patterns in the real-world events driving the value of an individual company. We will return to investor behaviour later in the chapter.

Fundamental analysis takes a completely different approach. Fundamental analysts tend to specialize in particular sectors of the stock market, about which they become extremely knowledgeable. They cast very wide information-capture nets and then, on the basis of this information, and with the use of a share valuation model, determine what they think the shares *should be* worth. This value is then compared with the current *market price* of the shares and, if the analyst thinks the shares are worth more than the current market price, 'buy' advice is given. Conversely, if the analyst believes the shares to be overvalued on the market, 'sell' advice is given.

These analysts are called fundamental analysts because they look at the *fundamental factors* that lie behind a share's value: the revenues the company can be expected to generate, the costs that the company is expected to incur in the generation of those revenues, the uncertainty surrounding both the future costs and revenues and, finally, the price (or return) of comparable investments. Common sense suggests that it may well be possible to make profits from this type of analysis, if it is done thoughtfully and thoroughly, and it could be argued that these profits are in fact justified as the result of the effort put into information gathering and analysis. Furthermore, it is reasonable to suggest that fundamental analysts provide the mechanism by which the market attains the level of efficiency that it does.

The third approach to stock exchange investment is, in some forms and in some stock markets, illegal. But in many forms, and in a few stock markets, it is not. All investors are, in a sense, looking for 'inside information'. In other words they are looking for information, insights or connections which they believe are not yet fully reflected in a share's market price. It is in this sense – rather than in the illegal sense – that we refer to the use of inside information as the third approach to formulating stock exchange investment advice. (What is generally judged to be illegal in most stock markets is the use of 'price sensitive' information, *before* it has been publicly disclosed to the stock market, to make buy and sell decisions.)

The EMH has implications for all three approaches. Quite simply, if the market is weakly efficient, technical analysis is worthless. If there is any information to be gained from looking at past share price movements, that information – according to the weak efficiency definition – is *already* reflected in the current share price. Technical analysts would be unable to predict future share price movements on the basis of past share price movements.

If the market is semi-strong efficient, not only is technical analysis worthless, but so too is fundamental analysis. The implication of semi-strong efficiency is that, however wide the fundamental analyst's trawl for information, and however good their analysis of that information within their share valuation model, that information's implications are *already* impounded in the share's market price. Thus if the fundamental analyst believes the shares are overpriced or underpriced, it is unlikely that it is the analyst's valuation, rather than the market's valuation, which is incorrect.[1]

Finally, in a world of strong stock market efficiency, investors would not even be able to expect to profit from inside information. This is because, with strong efficiency, the share price reflects *all* relevant information about the company, whether or not that information is in the public domain.

THE EMPIRICAL EVIDENCE OF EMH

So, how efficient are the stock markets in practice? Can markets be relied upon to correctly value a company's shares, or is it possible to find shares which are being either overvalued or undervalued by the stock market?

The concept of market efficiency has been subject to more empirical testing than practically any other area in the theory of corporate finance (and indeed the social sciences more generally). This is not surprising since identification of inefficiencies might be expected to provide opportunities for substantial financial gains. For this reason some care needs to be taken about interpreting the results of empirical research in this area.

The tests of weak efficiency overwhelmingly suggest that all stock markets – both big and small, around the world – are efficient in the weak sense. The evidence on semi-strong efficiency is much more mixed – often as a result of difficulties in the testing procedures themselves. Nevertheless, we can conclude that the majority of the evidence suggests that most stock markets are semi-strong efficient, most of the time. Finally, no one would really expect the stock market to be strongly efficient; in order for this to be so, share prices would need to reflect information that had not been publicly disclosed. But despite this, there is some evidence that stock markets may be efficient – to a limited extent – even in the strong sense.

Weak efficiency

So far as weak efficiency is concerned, empirical studies show that share prices tend to follow a 'random walk'. This term can be misleading, in that it gives the impression that share prices move at random, without any reason.

In fact random walk means almost the opposite of this common sense interpretation. If share prices follow a random walk, the implication is that share prices *only* move when they have 'good reason' to do so – that is, they only move in response to the disclosure of new information that is relevant to their value. This might be something like the disclosure of the annual profits at an unexpected level, news of a major natural resource discovery or the announcement of a significant new customer. Given that new information like this occurs at *random* points in time, share price movements should also occur at random.

Therefore random walk implies that share prices only move when they have got good reason to move. If researchers can find evidence of non-random movements in share prices, this implies that the market is being inefficient because share prices are moving when they have *not* got a good reason to do so.

If share prices do follow a random walk, it then follows that technical analysis is worthless, in that it cannot have any predictive power: by definition, anything which moves at random cannot be predicted.

All sorts of different tests on random walk have been conducted by researchers, and the reading references at the end of this chapter indicate a selection of this work. However, virtually *none* of these tests have been able to discover any evidence of significant non-randomness in share price movements, indicating that probably all stock markets pass the weak efficiency test.

Semi-strong efficiency

A large number of ingenious tests have been devised to examine semi-strong efficiency and, although the results have been mixed, the majority of the tests have tended to support the hypothesis that most stock markets, most of the time, are semi-strong efficient.

A good example of a semi-strong test would be one of the very first that was carried out. It was undertaken in the USA by Fama, Fisher, Jensen and Roll and the results were published in 1969 (see the 'Further reading' section at the end of the chapter). They examined the price behaviour of shares where 'stock splits' were made. (Stock splits are sometimes called bonus or scrip issues – new shares are given to existing shareholders – free of charge – in some fixed proportion to their existing shareholding.)

For example, in a one-for-one stock split, one new share is issued free of charge for every existing share. Thus the number of shares in issue is doubled. In such an exercise nothing has happened to alter the *total worth* of the company but, as the number of shares has doubled, the market price per share can be expected to be *halved*.

Fama *et al.* looked at the 'abnormal returns' on the shares of such companies over the 30 months prior to the stock split and over the 30 months after the stock split. By 'abnormal return', what is meant is when the return on the shares is greater (a positive abnormal return) or less (a negative abnormal return) than the return *expected*, given the share's beta value.

What they found was that in the 30 months prior to the stock split announcement the shares gave a strong positive abnormal return (i.e. the price of the shares rose). Subsequent to the announcement, there was virtually no movement, on average, in the shares' return. Figure 15.3 illustrates the situation.

The implications of this finding are as follows. A stock split should not really have any effect on the wealth of shareholders. The company remains exactly the same as before and all that happens is that the number of shares in issue is increased, but nothing has happened to change the value of those shares in aggregate. (Using the earlier example, if you have 100 shares in Nimex priced at €2.50 each, your shareholding is worth €250. If the company undertakes a one-for-one stock split, this results in you now holding 200 shares in Nimex valued at only €1.25 each and the worth of your shareholding remains unchanged at €250.) Therefore why should a share's price tend to rise prior to a stock split? The answer to this question is that with stock splits there is often an effective *increase* in dividends. For example, in our one-for-one stock split the dividend *per share* might have been maintained, thereby effectively *doubling* the level of dividends paid out. And, of course, an increase in dividends would seem to cause an increase in shareholder wealth. Thus it would be reasonable to imply that a share's price tends to rise prior to the announcement of a scrip issue *in anticipation* that this event would be accompanied by an effective increase in dividends.

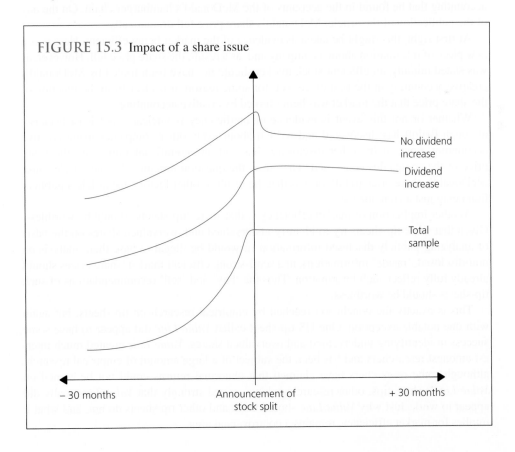

FIGURE 15.3 Impact of a share issue

No dividend increase

Dividend increase

Total sample

− 30 months

Announcement of stock split

+ 30 months

However, not all scrip issues are accompanied by an increase in dividends. Fama *et al.* divided their sample of stock-splitting companies into those which did and those which did not increase dividends at the time of the stock split. They then found that for those companies that did increase dividends there was, on average, no significant change in their returns after the stock split. In other words, the shares had risen in anticipation of the dividend increase and, once the increase had been announced, they maintained their new level.

This supports the idea of the efficiency of the stock market. The share price rose in anticipation of the information and, once the information was publicly disclosed, the share price already reflected the impact of that information.

On the other hand, those companies making a stock split and not increasing dividends, suffered on average, negative abnormal returns after the bonus issue: again, evidence that the shares had originally risen in anticipation of new information (about a dividend increase) but, when that expectation subsequently was unfulfilled, the price fell back. Again, this situation is illustrated in Figure 15.3.

The evidence on semi-strong efficiency, although very substantially in support of the concept, is less overwhelming than that for weak efficiency. Two examples of research that cast doubt on semi-strong efficiency are discussed here.

One of the implications of market efficiency is that the stock market should not be fooled by 'creative accounting'. In other words, the market should not be misled by companies artificially manipulating their reported profits by changing their accounting policies. Researchers have all tended to find this to be the situation, with one very notable exception. A researcher in the USA, Professor Briloff, wrote an article in a US business magazine (see the 'Further reading' section at the end of the chapter) about the large amount of creative accounting that he found in the accounts of the McDonald's hamburger chain. On the day of the publication of the article, McDonald's share price fell dramatically.

At first sight, this might be taken as evidence of the market being efficient. Here was a new piece of information about a company and, as a result, the share price fell. However, as was stated initially, an efficient stock market should not have been fooled by McDonald's creative accounting in the first place; yet, for some reason, it is clear from the reaction of the share price that the market was being fooled by creative accounting.

Whether or not this event is evidence of inefficiency is unclear – not least because, although Briloff has discovered and written about many other companies using creative accounting, none of his other disclosures has had any significant impact on the share price of the companies concerned. Therefore, the question remains: did the article cause McDonald's share price to fall, or was that the result of other factors, the article's publication being just a coincidence?

Another implication of market efficiency is that share 'tip-sheets' should be worthless. Given that share tip-sheets try to identify undervalued and overvalued shares on the basis of analyzing publicly disclosed information (it would be illegal to base their analysis on non-disclosed, 'inside' information), in a semi-strong efficient market, share prices should already fully reflect such information. Thus the 'buy' and 'sell' recommendations of such tip-sheets should be worthless.

This is exactly the conclusion reached by empirical research on tip-sheets, but again with one notable exception. One US tip-sheet called *Value Line* did appear to have some success in identifying undervalued and overvalued shares. *Value Line* created much interest amongst researchers and has been the subject of a large amount of empirical research; although some researchers have claimed that abnormal returns could not be earned on *Value Line*'s share tips, other researchers have argued strongly that *Value Line* really did appear to work. Just why *Value Line* should work and other tip-sheets do not, and what it implies for market efficiency, remains a controversial area.

Strong efficiency

Finally, there is strong market efficiency. As was stated earlier, no one really expects stock markets to be strongly efficient in the strict sense of the definition: if they were, share prices would have to reflect information of which the stock market was unaware – a rather unrealistic scenario. Furthermore, in such an efficient market, investors could not even profit from inside information, but we have the evidence of cases where investors have made large profits from the use of inside information – and have subsequently ended up in court and in jail.

Formal research into strong efficiency has been hampered by the fact that researchers require knowledge of inside information in order to test whether or not it has affected share prices. Not surprisingly, they have met with difficulty in obtaining such information to use in testing. Nevertheless, some inventive approaches have been used, particularly concerning the performance of institutional investors such as mutual funds and pension funds.

At one time institutional investment managers would have semi-private conversations with the top executives of the major companies in which they invested. In these meetings they were likely to gain insights and information about the company which was not available to investors generally. (Changes in the definition of insider dealing mean that this type of briefing is now much less likely.)

If the market is not efficient in the strong sense, then institutional investment managers should have been able to profit from this additional information. The empirical evidence suggests that they could not do so. For example, in another early study (1968) by Jensen which looked at the performance of 115 mutual funds (see the 'Further reading' section at the end of the chapter), no evidence was found of superior performance or, where there was a positive abnormal return, it was so small as to be eliminated in the mutual funds' management charges.

Conclusion

The evidence on market efficiency should not really be seen as surprising. It appears to indicate that new information divides itself up into that which is capable of being anticipated by the market (such as the level of profits for the year) and that which is not capable of being anticipated (such as a major factory fire).

The market appears to be very good at anticipating new information and the share price progressively reacts as these market 'guesses' become more confidently held. It is not surprising that this is the case, given the number of highly paid, intelligent people who are consistently striving to anticipate movements in share prices. It is equally unsurprising that no single analyst has been able to show that they can consistently act ahead of the rest.

In respect of that much smaller class of information, the information that is not capable of anticipation, the situation is different. Inside knowledge of this type of information (which is not the type likely to be obtained by unit trust managers) is likely to lead to an ability to 'beat' the stock market; though, of course, it is likely to be illegal to use the information in that way. In other words, it would appear logical that the market is not strongly efficient in the strictest sense of the definition.

On the other hand, the evidence also points to the fact that when unanticipated information does become publicly disclosed, share prices tend to react very rapidly as a result; again, too rapidly for most investors to react quickly enough to beat the share price movement. In this respect, the study by Patell and Wolfson (1984) is of particular interest.

So far as financial managers are concerned, the evidence is very substantially (but not entirely) in favour of semi-strong efficiency. Therefore, managers should be aware of the fact that the results of their decisions will be reflected in the company's share price, once those decisions have been communicated to the stock market.

THE TERM STRUCTURE OF INTEREST RATES

Let us now move on to examine another important aspect of financial markets. This is the relationship between short-term and long-term interest rates or rates of return, referred to as the 'term structure' of interest rates.

The yield to maturity

With an investment in corporate bonds,[2] the return that is received is a combination of two elements: the rate of interest that the bond pays (termed the coupon rate) and the capital gain or loss that may be made on the bond when it is sold on to a third party,[3] or when the loan is repaid by the issuer of the bond.

With some bonds, the interest element is intended to be the main or only source of return; others have a balance between interest and capital gain, while still others pay no interest at all (zero coupon bonds) and are designed to provide their return purely in the form of a capital gain.

With all of these different types of bonds, the '*yield to maturity*' is the annual rate of return that would be expected, if the bond was held until it was redeemed or repaid. The yield to maturity is calculated on the basis of the IRR on the cash flow that the bond generates for an investor, if held up to the date when the loan is repaid (that is, until it 'matures').

For example, Tromsø has issued some bonds. Each bond is currently priced in the market at €90.[4] The bonds have a 4% coupon (and so pay €4 of interest per year), and are due to be redeemed for €100 in 3-years' time.[5] Its 'redemption yield' or 'yield to maturity' is represented by '*i*' in the following expression – the IRR of the bond's future cash flow up to maturity:

$$-€90 + [€4 \times A_{3\,i}] + [€100 \times (1 + i)^{-3}] = 0 \text{ NPV}$$

At a 6% discount rate, NPV = + €4.65
At a 10% discount rate, NPV = − €4.92

$$\text{IRR} = 6\% + \left[\frac{+€4.65}{+€4.65 - (-€4.92)} \times (10\% - 6\%) \right] = 7.9\% \text{ Redemption yield}$$

What we observe in the financial markets is that bonds with the same risk, but with different maturities, have different redemption yields. The relationship between the redemption yield and the length of time to maturity is called the '*term structure of interest rates*' and is described by the yield curve.

The yield curve

Generally speaking, we find that shorter-term maturity bonds have a lower redemption yield, and longer-term maturity bonds have a higher yield, as shown in Figure 15.4.

However, the yield curve is not always rising in this way. It may be flat, or it may fall, as illustrated in Figure 15.5.

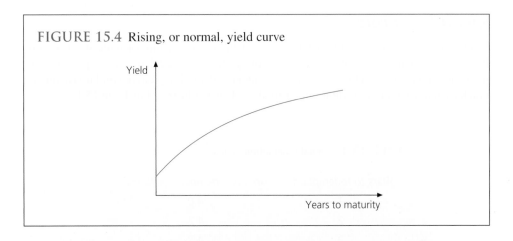

FIGURE 15.4 Rising, or normal, yield curve

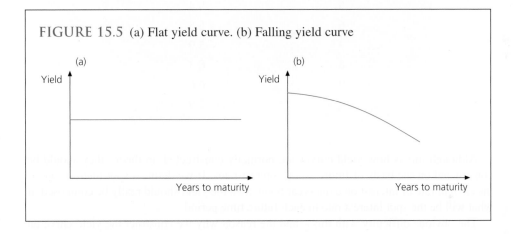

FIGURE 15.5 (a) Flat yield curve. (b) Falling yield curve

We need to examine the factors that underlie the term structure of interest rates, as it is obviously important both to investors and to companies.

Suppose the CFO of Ocaso Generali has €10 million that the company wants to invest for a period of 10 years. The CFO has a number of choices as to how this might be achieved. For example, the €10 million could be invested in bonds which mature in 10 years (i.e. 10-year bonds); or alternatively, the €10 million could be invested in a *succession* of ten one-year bonds (and there are many other alternatives, for example the €10 million could be invested in two consecutive 5-year bonds, etc.).

What course of action the company takes may well be determined by the term structure of interest rates. If the yield curve is *upward* sloping, the company may conclude that it would get a better return investing in the longer-term (10-year) bonds. But if the curve were *downward* sloping, it may conclude that it would do better with a sequence of one-year bond investments as one-year redemption yields are higher than the longer-term yields. A similar judgement would have to be made by a company CFO who wished to *borrow* money for, say, a 10-year period. They would have to decide between raising the finance with 10-year bonds or through a series of shorter-term bond issues.

Spot interest rates

Before we start to examine the determinants of the term structure of interest rates more closely, we first have to look again at how the yield curve is calculated. In practice, the yield curve is constructed by calculating the annual redemption yield of similar-risk bonds, which each have a different future maturity date. This is illustrated in Table 15.1.

TABLE 15.1 Annual redemption yields

Years to redemption	Annual redemption yield (%)
1	4.0
2	4.2
3	4.7
4	4.9
5	5.4
6	5.5
7	5.9
8	6.3
9	6.6
10	6.9

Although this is how yield curves are normally constructed, in theory they should be constructed on the basis of future 'spot' interest rates. If we define a spot interest rate as the *current* rate of interest on a one-year bond, then the yield should really be composed of what will be the spot interest rate in each future time period.

The obvious difficulty with this – and the reason why we construct the yield curve on the basis of redemption yields – is that we do not know what these future spot rates will be. However, the important question is: does it matter? The answer is that, yes, it may make a significant difference.

In our initial example, the redemption yield of the Tromsø bond was estimated to be 7.9% In other words the bond's discounted future cash flow had a present value of €90:

$$€4 \times (1 + 0.079)^{-1} + €4 \times (1 + 0.079)^{-2} + €104 \times (1 + 0.079)^{-3} = €90$$

On the other hand, given that the spot interest rate for each time period, *t,* is given the notation S*t*, then the true relationship should be:

$$€4 \times (1 + S_1)^{-1} + €4 (1 + S_1)^{-1} \times (1 + S_2)^{-1} + \\ €104 \times (1 + S_1)^{-1} \times (1 + S_2)^{-1} \times (1 + S_3)^{-1} = €90$$

In particular, whereas with the redemption yield, the interest rate is assumed to be the same in each future time period, this is *not* necessarily the case with spot rates.

For example, suppose that we knew what the future spot interest rates were:

$S_1 = 4\%$
$S_2 = 6\%$
$S_3 = 14\%$

then:

Present value:

Year 1:	$€4 \times (1 + 0.4)^{-1}$	$= €3.84$
Year 2:	$€4 \times (1 + 0.4)^{-1} \times (1 + 0.06)^{-1}$	$= €3.51$
Year 3:	$€104 \times (1 + 0.04)^{-1} \times (1 + 0.06)^{-1} \times (1 + 0.14)^{-1}$	$= €82.65$
		$€90$

This set of spot rates: 4%, 6% and 14% would represent the true term structure of interest rates over Years 1, 2 and 3. Therefore our estimated Year 3 rate of 7.9% (found from the redemption yield on a 3-year bond) differs significantly from the true Year 3 rate of 14%.

The point at issue is whether there is any difference between these two discounted cash flows:

$$€4 \times (1.079)^{-1} + €4 \times (1.079)^{-2} + €104 \times (1.079)^{-3} = €90$$

and:

$$€4 \times (1.04)^{-1} + €4 \times (1.04)^{-1} \times (1.06)^{-1} +$$
$$€104 \times (1.04)^{-1} \times (1.06)^{-1} \times (1.14)^{-1} = €90$$

As such, there is not. But suppose we wish to value a new 3-year bond with a coupon of, say, 5%. If we valued it on the basis of the redemption yield of 7.9%, or on the basis of the future spot rates of 4%, 6% and 14%, we would *not* get precisely the same value, as Example 1 illustrates.

EXAMPLE 1

Present value of a 3-year €100 bond with a 5% coupon rate at a 7.9% annual discount rate.[6]

$$[€5 \times A_{3,\,7.9\%}] + [€100 \times (1 + 0.079)^{-3}]$$
$$[€5 \times 2.582] + [€100 \times 0.796] = €92.51$$

The present value of this same bond using the spot interest rates:

Year 1:	4%
Year 2:	6%
Year 3:	14%

$$€5 \times (1 + 0.04)^{-1} + €5 \times (1 + 0.04)^{-1} \times (1 + 0.06)^{-1} +$$
$$€105 \times (1 + 0.04)^{-1} \times (1 + 0.06)^{-1} \times (1 + 0.14)^{-1} = €92.89$$

Is this difference important? It has the potential to be, especially with steeply rising or falling yield curves and significant differences in coupon rates. However, under most circumstances we can be reasonably satisfied that spot rates are fairly well approximated by the yield to maturity on bonds of differing maturity periods.

PURE EXPECTATIONS HYPOTHESIS

Let us now turn to examine the factors that underlie the term structure of interest rates. What determines whether the yield curve is flat, rising or falling? There are three main theories concerning the factors which determine the shape of the yield curve. The first – and the most fundamental – is called the Pure Expectations Hypothesis.

This holds that the yield curve is determined by the market's *expectations* about *future* interest rates. A rising yield curve reflects investors' expectations that interest rates will go up in the future. A falling yield curve reflects expectations of falling future interest rates. Finally, a flat yield curve reflects expectations of unchanged future interest rates. Furthermore, if this hypothesis holds true, the term structure of interest rates can be used to forecast future interest rates.

Suppose that the annual redemption yield on a one-year bond is 6% and on a two-year bond it is 7%. Therefore the yield curve is *rising*. This yield curve data can now be used to estimate the expected yield on a one-year bond, *12 months from now*. In other words, this yield curve data can be used to estimate what will be the *future* rate of interest, given the *current* one-year interest rate is 6%.

This can be estimated on the basis that the expectations hypothesis assumes that investors should be *indifferent* between investing in a single two-year bond (from Year 0 to Year 2) and investing in two consecutive one-year bonds (one from Year 0 to Year 1 and the other from Year 1 to Year 2).

Given that the current annual rate of return when investing for two years is 7% (investing in a two-year bond), and an annual return of 6% can be earned investing over the next 12 months (in a one-year bond), this implies that investors expect to be able to earn an annual rate of return of 7.63% on a one-year bond in 12-months' time. How the rate of 7.63% is calculated is illustrated in Example 2.

EXAMPLE 2

The annual return on one-year bonds is 6%.
The annual return on two-year bonds is 7%.
A company has €1000 to invest for 2 years. Investing in a two-year bonds will give:

$$€1000 \times (1 + 0.07)^2 = €1144.90$$

If the company invests €1000 in a one-year bonds, at the end of 12 months they will have:

$$€1000 \times (1 + 0.06)^1 = €1060$$

▶

Therefore what rate of return will the company then have to earn from investing that €1060 for a further year, to give *exactly the same* outcome from investing the €1000 in a 2-year bonds? This can be found as follows, where S_2 is the spot interest rate in the second year:

$$€1060 \times (1 + S_2) = €1144.90$$

$$S_2 = \frac{€1144.90}{€1060} - 1 = 0.0763 \text{ or } 7.63\%$$

Thus the current term structure of:

Years to maturity	*Annual* redemption yield
1	6%
2	7%

implies that (spot) interest rates are expected to rise next year from their current level of 6% to 7.63%. This is why two-year bonds currently give an annual redemption yield of 7%.

This analytical approach can be extended as far into the future as data will allow. Suppose that the term structure was: Year 1: 6%, Year 2: 7% and Year 3: 7.5%. We have already found the expected spot rate for next year: 7.63%. Therefore the expected spot rate for the *following year* can also be found. Example 3 provides the calculation.

EXAMPLE 3

$$(1 + 0.06)^1 \times (1 + 0.0763)^1 \times (1 + S_3)^1 = (1 + 0.075)^3$$

In other words, the capital plus interest received from an investment in a three-year bonds should be the same as the capital plus interest received from investing in three consecutive one-year bonds.[7]
  Solving for S_3 gives:

$$S_3 \times \frac{1.075^3}{1.06^1 \times 1.0763^1} - 1 = 0.089 \text{ or } 8.9\%$$

Therefore our forecast spot 1-year interest rates for the next 3 years are now:

Year 0:	6%
Year 1:	7.63%
Year 2:	8.9%

Forward interest rates

These *future* spot interest rates that we estimated in Examples 2 and 3, on the basis of the pure expectations hypothesis, are known as 'forward' interest rates. In other words we have estimated the current, 1-year forward and 2-year forward spot interest rates as estimates of the future spot rates.

The pure expectation theory states that forward rates are good predictors of future spot rates on the basis that, if they weren't, a profit could be made – what is termed an 'arbitrage gain' – from the situation. For instance, in our example, the one-year forward rate is 7.63%, but let us suppose that the expected spot rate in 12-months' time was a little higher than this – say 8%. This implies that money could be *borrowed* for two-years at 7% (remember, this is the current annual redemption yield on two-year bonds) and then *invested* in two consecutive one-year bonds and so make a profit, as Example 4 illustrates.

EXAMPLE 4

To illustrate how a profit can be made in such a situation we will take an investor who is going to borrow €100 000 for two years and invest that money in two consecutive one-year bonds:

1. Borrow €100 000 for two years at an annual rate of interest of 7%.

2. At the end of two years you will owe (capital, plus interest) €100 000 $\times (1 + 0.07)^2$ = €114 490.

3. The €100 000 that you have borrowed is invested in a one-year bond with a 6% redemption yield, producing: €100 000 $\times (1 + 0.06)^1$ = €106 000 in one year's time.

4. In one year's time this €106 000 is then reinvested for a further year at 8.5% (remember that this, we are assuming, is what the interest rate is expected to be in 12-months' time). This provides a total sum (capital plus interest) in two years' time of: €106,000 $\times (1 + 0.085)^1$ = €115 010.

5. This money can then be used to repay your €100 000 2-year loan, plus interest, providing you with an 'arbitrage' profit of: €115 010 − €114 490 = €520.

According to the expectations hypothesis, if such a profitable opportunity were to exist, many investors would like to take advantage of it. As a result there would be an increase in the demand to borrow two-year money (at 7%) and an increase in investors wishing to place money on deposit in one-year bonds. The supply and demand market forces arising out of this increased demand for two-year loans would force up 2-year redemption yields, and the increased availability (i.e. supply) of people wishing to lend would push down 1-year rates. These supply and demand market forces will stabilize interest rates at the point where no such profits are possible. That point of equilibrium is reached where spot interest rates and forward interest rates are in accord with the expectations hypothesis.

The transactions we have described here are referred to as 'arbitrage' (or 'interest' arbitrage) and the resulting profits are known as 'arbitrage gains'. Such situations – it is said – represent a disequilibrium in the market place (making money is never normally so easy), and are usually eliminated rapidly by supply and demand market forces that rapidly restore equilibrium.[8]

The Fisher Effect

Having examined the ideas that lie behind the pure expectations hypothesis, we can now turn to a related question: what determines these forward interest rates/the future spot interest rates? Why do people sometimes believe interest rates in the future will rise or fall (or stay the same)?

In order to answer this question, we need to return to the Fisher Effect, which we first met in Chapter 7. This states that:

$$(1 + \text{money interest rate}) = (1 + \text{real interest rate}) \times (1 + \text{inflation})$$

Adapting this slightly to our present needs:

$$(1 + \text{expected future spot interest rate}) = (1 + \text{expected future real interest rate})$$
$$\times (1 + \text{expected rate of inflation})$$

If we assume that the real interest rate remains *constant* (a reasonable assumption, at least in the shorter term), the Fisher relationship implies that it is the expected rate of *inflation* that determines expected future interest rates. In our earlier example, the spot rate was expected to go up from its current level of 6% to 7.63% next year and to 8.9% the following year. The Fisher Effect implies that this rise in future interest rates, arises from the fact that inflation is expected to increase from its current level.

Therefore, on the basis of the pure expectations hypothesis and the Fisher Effect, a *rising* yield curve would imply *rising* future inflation rates; a *falling* yield curve would imply *falling* inflation; and a *flat* yield curve would imply *no change* in future inflation rates.

Taxes and transaction costs

There are a number of problems with the pure expectations theory, when it states that a long-term bond and a series of short-term bonds should be seen by investors as *perfect substitutes* for each other. Two obvious problems are taxes and transaction costs.

Suppose we have *zero coupon* bonds that deliver their annual rate of return just in the form of a capital gain. Under these circumstances – and keeping in mind that capital gains are normally only taxed when they are realized – we would *not* be indifferent between a three-year bond and a series of three consecutive one-year bonds, referred to in Example 3.[9]

Returning to Example 3, we said that a 7.5% per annum yield to maturity on a three-year bond would be seen as being equivalent to a consecutive series of three one-year bonds yielding 6%, 7.63% and 8.9% respectively. However, they would not be equivalent if tax were taken into account.

There are two reasons for this. First, with the three-year bond, no tax would be payable until Year 3, when the total capital gain was realized, whereas with the series of one-year bonds a capital gain would be realized each year and so there would be a liability to pay tax on that capital gain each year. But not only would the timing of the tax payments be different, but so too would be the amounts of tax paid, both in absolute cash terms and in present value terms. Example 5 illustrates this conclusion with some calculations.

EXAMPLE 5

You can choose between investing €1000 in a three-year *zero coupon* bond yielding an annual return of 7%, or investing in a series of three one-year zero coupon bonds. The first bond gives a return of 6%, the second 7.63% and the third 8.9%.

Assume for purposes of this illustration that tax is paid on capital gains as soon as they arise, at a rate of 25%.

Invest in a single three-year bond:

Capital gain on the three-year bond:[10]

$$€1000 \times (1 + 0.07)^3 = €1225.04 - €1,000 = €225.04$$

Tax on the capital gain:

$$€225.04 \times 0.25 = €56.26$$

After tax amount available at Year 3:

$$€1225.04 - €56.26 = \textbf{€1168.78}$$

Repeating this analysis for the series of three consecutive investments in one-year bonds:

1st one-year bond

$$€1000 \times (1 + 0.06)^1 = €1060 - €1000 = €60 \times 0.25 = €15 \text{ tax}$$

$$€1060 - €15 = €1045 \text{ available for re-investment.}$$

2nd one-year bond

$$€1045 \times (1 + 0.0763)^1 = €1124.73 - €1045 = €79.73 \times 0.25 = €19.93 \text{ tax}$$

$$€1124.73 - €19.93 = €1104.80 \text{ available for re-investment.}$$

3rd one-year bond

$$€1104.80 \times (1 + 0.089)^1 = €1203.13 - €1104.80 = €98.33 \times 0.25 = €24.58 \text{ tax}$$

$$€1203.13 - €24.58 = \textbf{€1178.55} \text{ available.}$$

Therefore you are not indifferent to the two alternative investments, after taking tax into account. The three-year bond produces €1168.78, after tax, at Year 3. In contrast, the three consecutive one-year bonds produce €1178.55, after tax, at Year 3.

A second difficulty for the pure expectations hypothesis is provided by transaction costs. The problem with transaction costs is that their presence in the process of buying bonds (in terms of commission payable to an intermediary) means that, once again, investors are not going to view a single longer-term bond and a consecutive series of shorter-term bonds as perfect substitutes: the former is only going to incur *one* set of transaction costs; the latter is likely to incur *several* sets of transaction costs.

Liquidity preference

Perhaps a more serious problem with the pure expectations hypothesis is that it is developed in a world of certainty. Once the fact that the future is not certain is taken into account, problems arise for the perfect substitutability criterion. According to the pure expectations hypothesis, both borrowers and investors should be indifferent between long-term bonds and a series of short-term bonds.

However, the returns available on future short-term bonds are uncertain, and they may turn out to be above or below what the expectations hypothesis predicts. For instance, as we saw in the earlier example, suppose the annual yield to maturity on one and two-year bonds is 6% and 7% respectively. This implies that the current spot interest rate is 6% and the one-year forward spot interest rate will be 7.63%, because this would make a series of two consecutive one-year bonds give the same yield as a two-year bond. The problem that an investor in one-year bonds faces (and, for that matter, a borrower via the issue of one-year bonds) is that there is *no certainty* that the yield on one-year bonds in 12-months' time will be 7.63%. The yield may turn out to be more or less (or equal to) 7.63%, whereas the investor knows with certainty that by investing in a two-year bond, they can lock into 7% per annum *for certain*.

However, the liquidity preference hypothesis believes that, generally, investors prefer liquidity to certainty: if interest rates do go up, they want to be able to take advantage of that rise, rather than being locked into a lower rate. Thus they will prefer bonds with shorter maturities and, indeed will be willing to take a lower return than they could get on longer-term bonds in order to retain this flexibility.

It could be argued that other investors may prefer longer-term bonds to avoid the risks of falling yields on shorter-term bonds. However, the argument in favour of short-term bonds is based on the relationship between bond yields and bond prices. If you had invested in the two-year bond used in the earlier example and it then transpired that the yield on one-year bonds in 12-months' time was not 7.63% but had risen to 8%, the impact on the bond would be that its price or value would *fall*. It is this potential loss in the capital value on longer-term bonds that investors are felt to particularly dislike.

In addition, the liquidity preference hypothesis believes that borrowers have the opposite preference to investors. In other words, they like to borrow via long-term bonds so that they know their borrowing liabilities and, furthermore, they avoid the risk of having to re-borrow short-term bonds under adverse conditions (i.e. rising interest rates). This therefore leads borrowers to be willing to pay more for long-term loans.

The conclusion of this analysis is that both borrowers and lenders have 'liquidity preferences'. Investors are willing to take a lower yield on shorter-term bonds, and borrowers have to be offered a lower yield to persuade them to issue such debt. Conversely, borrowers are willing to pay a higher yield to obtain longer-term borrowing and investors have to be offered higher yields to persuade them to invest in longer-term bonds.

As a result, liquidity preference theory concludes that whatever is the term structure of interest rates arising out of the pure expectations hypothesis and the Fisher Effect, liquidity preferences of investors and borrowers will tend to bias longer-term bond yields upwards. This is why the 'normal' yield curve is upwards sloping, as shown earlier in Figure 15.4.

Segmented markets

Finally, there is a third argument at work, which is referred to as 'segmented markets'. This holds that the reason why the redemption yields of bonds differs for different maturities has little to do with future interest rate or inflation rate expectations, nor is it to do with liquidity premiums.

Instead, it is argued that markets for both lenders and borrowers are *segmented*. Some investors only want to invest short term, other investors only want to invest long term. Therefore, investing in a series of short-term bonds is held *not* to be an acceptable substitute for investing in a single long-term bond – an assumption that underpins the expectations hypothesis.

Similarly, some borrowers only want to borrow short term; other borrowers only want to borrow long term. In such circumstances borrowers and lenders prefer a specific maturity, irrespective of differences between long- and short-term interest rates, and therefore whether long-term interest rates are above or below or the same as short-term rates (in other words, whether the yield curve is rising, falling or is flat) is simply a function of *supply and demand market forces* in each segment of the market place.

Conclusion

Which theory is correct: pure expectations, liquidity preference or market segmentation? The truth probably lies somewhere between all three, but, generally speaking, the pure expectations hypothesis is seen as the bedrock factor in determining the term structure of interest rates.

The term structure probably does contain liquidity premiums to compensate for risk but, at the same time, more and more techniques and mechanisms are becoming available to limit exposure to interest rate risk – as we saw in the previous chapter – and its importance may, if anything, be diminishing.

Similarly, there are lenders and borrowers who are only interested in specific maturities, and who will select those maturities irrespective of the term structure. But not all borrowers and lenders will ignore the substitutability of a sequence of short-term bonds and a long-term bond. Therefore, if segmented supply and demand market forces have a significant impact on bonds of one particular maturity – for example, a shortage of supply may force up the long-term yield significantly above expected future spot rates – then at least some investors will seek to make arbitrage profits. Such arbitraging activities are then likely to bring the yield curve back down towards the configuration hypothesized by pure expectations.

SUMMARY

This chapter has examined the efficient markets hypothesis and its implications and the term structure of interest rates. The main points covered were:

- The efficient markets hypothesis examines the degree to which stock markets are efficient in reflecting relevant information in share prices.

- Weak efficiency occurs when market prices follow a random walk, thereby limiting the usefulness of technical analysis.

- Semi-strong efficiency occurs when share prices quickly and correctly reflect any relevant information as it arises in the public domain. Its occurrence limits the usefulness of fundamental analysis of share prices.

- Strong efficiency occurs when share prices reflect *all* relevant information, whether or not it is in the public domain. In such circumstances investors could not even expect to profit from the possession of inside information.

- The empirical evidence overwhelmingly supports weak efficiency, and substantially supports semi-strong efficiency. On strong efficiency, the empirical evidence is less clear but, realistically, markets are unlikely to be strongly efficient.

- The implications for financial managers of semi-strong efficiency, in particular, are important. It implies that project NPVs will be reflected in share prices; the timing of capital-raising exercises is unimportant from the viewpoint of whether a company's shares are currently 'cheap' or 'expensive' and this casts doubt on the takeover of a publicly quoted company ever being expected to produce a positive NPV.

- The relationship between a bond's redemption yield and the length of time until its maturity is described by the term structure of interest rates, and is illustrated by the yield curve.

- The yield curve usually rises over time, but it may be flat or fall over time.

- There are a number of theories that attempt to explain the shape of the yield curve. The pure expectations hypothesis holds that the yield curve reflects expectations about future interest rates, which, in turn, reflect expectations about future inflation rates.

- Another explanation for the shape of the yield curve is given by the liquidity preference theory, which holds that, because the future is uncertain, lenders prefer to lend short term and borrowers like to borrow longer term. Hence lenders are willing to accept lower short-term interest rates because of their preference and borrowers are willing to offer higher long-term rates because of their preference. Hence the 'normal' shape of the yield curve.

- A third explanation is given by the market segmentation argument, which holds that the markets for long- and short-term bonds are unconnected. People do not see a series of short-term bonds as a substitute for a single longer-term bond. Thus long- and short-term bond maturity yields are simply a function of supply and demand market forces.

NOTES

1. There is an interesting paradox here. Fundamental analysis is worthless in the sense that analysts are unable to identify undervalued or overvalued shares, except through luck. However, fundamental analysts have a *usefulness* to the stock market as a whole, in that they help to keep the market 'on its toes' and efficient. In other words, their efforts to seek out bargains go towards ensuring that share prices react swiftly to the disclosure of new, relevant information. The paradox here is that an efficient market needs investors who think it is inefficient, in order to keep it efficient.

2. In other words, the investor is effectively lending a company money, in return for which they receive a certificate – the 'bond' – which acknowledges the loan.

3. These bonds are marketable securities and so can be bought and sold on financial markets, where their price will reflect current interest rates, as well as supply and demand market pressures.

4. We will look more closely at the pricing of bonds in Chapter 16.

5. Bonds are normally issued in €100 units. Therefore €100 is known as the 'par' or redemption value of the bonds, and it represents the amount that will be repaid when the loan reaches maturity.

6. The annuity factor is calculated as:

$$A_{3,7.9\%} = \frac{1 - [1 + 0.079]^{-3}}{0.079} = 2.582$$
$$\text{and } [1 + 0.079]^{-3} = 0.796$$

7. Or from an investment in a two-year bond followed by re-investment of the proceeds in a one-year bond:

$$(1 + 0.07)^2 \times (1 + S_3)^1 = (1 + 0.075)^3$$

8. Notice that you could also make an arbitrage gain if the expected spot rate were less than the forwards rate, by borrowing short term and lending longer term.

9. This example is used for the purposes of exposition, and is not intended to be realistic. The tax rates on zero coupon bonds can often be quite complex. This example is purely designed to show that tax does potentially provide a problem for the pure expectations theory.

10. The bond will cost €1000 to buy now. It does not provide any interest payments but, at the end of 3 years a total of €1225.04 is repaid, giving a total capital gain of €225.04, equivalent to an annual rate of return – before tax – of 7%.

FURTHER READING

1. There is a vast amount of research in this area and the reading on market efficiency is almost limitless. However, a really good, classic introduction is B.G. Malkiel, *A Random Walk Down Wall Street,* Norton 1985.

2. A good review of the original research into EMH is given by E.F. Fama, 'Efficient Capital Markets: A Review of Theory and Empirical Work', *Journal of Finance,* May 1970.

3. The October 1987 stock market crash made many people stop and rethink their ideas of EMH. However, see: K. Brown and S. Tinic, 'How Rational Investors Deal with Uncertainty (or, Reports of the Death of Efficient Markets Theory are Greatly Exaggerated)', in J.M. Stern and D.H. Chew (eds), *The Revolution in Corporate Finance,* Blackwell 1992.

4. A really classic article on EMH research is that by R. Ball and P. Brown, 'An Empirical Evaluation of Accounting Income Numbers', *Journal of Accounting Research,* Autumn 1968. But this can be contrasted with E.F. Fama and K.R. French, 'Business Conditions and Expected Returns on Stocks and Bonds', *Journal of Financial Economics,* November 1989.

5. For evidence on possible exceptions to market efficiency, see: G. Hawawini and D.B. Kein, 'On the Predictability of Common Stock Returns: World-Wide Evidence' in R.A. Jarrow, V. Maksimovic and W.T. Ziema (eds), *Finance,* North Holland 1994. On the other hand, E.R. Dawson and J.M. Steeley, 'On the Existence of Visual Technical Patterns in the UK Stock Market', *Journal of Business Finance and Accounting* 30 (1 & 2) 2003 find little evidence of exploitable patterns in share price movements; and, finally, for a thoughtful discussion on EMH anomalies see E.F. Fama, 'Dissecting Anomalies', *Journal of Finance*, August 2008.

6. For an example of a test on semi-strong efficiency see: E.F. Fama, L. Fisher, M. Jensen and R. Roll, 'The Adjustment of Stock Prices to New Information', *International Economic Review,* February 1969.

7. On the arguments surrounding Briloff's evidence, see: G. Foster, 'Briloff and the Capital Markets', *Journal of Accounting Research,* June 1979.

8. On the evidence of the performance of unit trusts, see: M. Jensen, 'The Performance of Mutual Funds in the Period 1945–64', *Journal of Finance,* May 1968; and B.G. Malkiel, 'Returns from Investing in Equity Mutual Funds: 1971 to 1991', *Journal of Finance,* June 1995.

9. The speed of stock market reaction to the public disclosure of new information can be seen in J.M. Patell and M.A. Wolfson, 'The Intraday Speed of Adjustment of Stock Prices to Earnings and Dividend Announcements', *Journal of Financial Economics,* June 1984.

10. R. Ball, 'The Global Financial Crisis and the Efficient Markets Hypothesis: What Have We Learned?', *Journal of Applied Corporate Finance,* (4) 2009 looks at the situation after the world-wide financial crisis in 2007–8.

11. There is a growing literature concerning the behavioural aspects of investors. W. Forbes, *Behavioural Finance,* Wiley 2009 provides a thorough introduction to the area. A. Shleifer, *Inefficient Markets,* Oxford University Press 2000 discusses a range of implications related to the possibility of inefficient markets. There is also a considerable amount of interesting material in P A Adler and P Adler, *The Social Dynamics of Financial Markets,* JAI Press 1984. Students wishing to go further in this area are referred to H. Shefrin, *A Behavioural Approach to Asset Pricing,* Elsevier 2005 and D. Hirschleifer, 'Investor Psychology and Asset Pricing', *The Journal of Finance,* August 2001.

12. For a deeper analysis of the term structure of interest rates, see R. Roll, *The Behaviour of Interest Rates: An Application of the Efficient Market Model to US Treasury Bills,* Basic Books 1970.

QUIZ QUESTIONS

1 What are the three levels of market efficiency?
2 What are the implications of semi-strong market efficiency for financial managers?
3 What are the implications of EMH for stock exchange investment analysis?
4 Why do share prices follow a random walk?
5 What does a technical analyst attempt to do?
6 What is the shape of a 'normal' yield curve?
7 What is the pure expectations hypothesis?
8 What is the liquidity preference theory?
9 What does a falling yield curve imply about future inflation rates, according to the pure expectations hypothesis?
10 The yield on a one-year bond is 5% and on a two-year bond it is 6.5%. What is the implied one-year interest rate that is expected next year?

(See the 'Answers to Quiz Questions' section at the back of the book.)

PROBLEMS

The answers to these problems are available online (see the 'Digital Resources' page for details).

1 The following statement contains several errors. Explain what these errors are.
'According to the efficient market hypothesis all share prices are correct at all times. This is achieved by prices moving randomly when new information is publicly announced. New information from published accounts is the only determinant of the random movements in share price. 'Fundamental and technical analysts of the stock market serve no function in making the market efficient and cannot predict future share prices. Corporate financial managers are also unable to predict future share prices.'

2 You are given the following annual redemption yields on corporate bonds of equal risk:

Years to redemption	Redemption yield (%)
1	6
2	5.75
3	5.50
4	5
5	4.5

Required:

(a) Estimate spot interest rates for the next 5 years.

(b) Plot the yield curve.

(c) If the real interest rate is expected to be 2% per annum, forecast inflation rates over the next 5 years.

(d) If you expect the spot interest rate to be 7% next year (S_2) show why you would prefer to invest in two consecutive one-year bonds, rather than in one two-year bond.

THE COST OF CAPITAL

LEARNING OBJECTIVES

The purpose of this chapter is to:

- Develop the concept of the cost of equity capital.
- Introduce the dividend valuation model.
- Discuss the use of the CAPM to identify the cost of equity capital.
- Compare the use of the dividend valuation model and the CAPM to identify the cost of equity capital.
- Explore the different types of debt capital and to examine how the cost of debt might be calculated.

THE FINANCING DECISION

So far, our analysis has largely been confined to an evaluation of capital project invest-ment appraisal and the problem of risk. We have not considered how any particular invest-ment project should be financed – or indeed – whether the method of finance makes any difference.

This exclusion of any consideration about the financing method has been assisted by the assumption of a perfect capital market, which implies that if a company can identify a project that has a non-negative NPV, when discounted at a rate that reflects its level of sys-tematic risk, then the required finance will be made available by the capital market.[1] Thus the question of financing has appeared to be irrelevant to the investment decision.

In this chapter, and in the three that follow, we start to examine whether the question of project financing is really irrelevant and, if it is not, then what factors should be considered when evaluating different methods or sources of finance.

It is perhaps wise at this point to make very much the same sort of observation that was made at the outset of our analysis of the handling of risk in decision-making. Just as our knowledge of how we should take account of risk is still incomplete, this is also the case in terms of the financing decision, especially in terms of the decision concerning the 'optimal' capital structure of companies.

In this chapter, we examine much the same area as we did in Chapter 12 on the CAPM – the rate of return on financial securities (e.g. the shares of companies) but, in one sense, from a different perspective. This is the area of the cost of company capital. We do this first, in order to begin to examine the decision itself. We shall see in the following chapter that the cost of capital concept can also provide us (under certain restrictive circumstances) with a capital investment appraisal discount rate.

Chapters 18 and 19 look directly at the implications for the firm and its owners of the financing decision. Chapter 20 then examines how capital investment decisions and financing decisions interact and how such interactions may be analyzed.

Types of long-term finance

Generally speaking, capital investment projects are financed from three alternative (but not necessarily mutually exclusive) sources: finance directly supplied by the capital markets in the form of ordinary share capital; finance directly supplied by the capital markets in the form of interest-bearing medium- and long-term loans; and finance internally generated by the firm in the form of retained profits. There are other sources of long-term finance – one important one may be government grants[2] – but in the main these three sources of finance predominate.

These various types of finance differ from each other in several ways, including how they are issued, the obligations that they impose on a firm's management and how they are affected by the tax system. They also differ significantly in terms of risk. Our analysis of the CAPM showed that the return required on any investment should reflect the systematic risk involved. Therefore, if these different types of capital have different levels of systematic risk, then we can expect their returns to reflect these differences.

Finally, although we shall be examining the expected returns required by the suppliers of corporate finance, because we are interested in what these returns are from the viewpoint of management, they will be referred to as the '*costs*' of the various types of capital.

THE COST OF EQUITY CAPITAL

Physical and financial investments

In our analysis in Chapter 4, using the single-period investment-consumption model we distinguished between *physical* investment decisions and *financial* investment decisions. In fact the distinction between financial and physical investments is almost entirely artificial, so far as decision-making is concerned.

A physical (or real) investment could be defined as involving cash (i.e. consumption power) being spent in order to combine and operate productive resources (the factors of production) so as to generate a saleable output (of either goods or services), which can be exchanged for cash. A financial investment still involves an outlay of cash – it is lent on the financial markets – but now a third party undertakes the physical investment.

Individuals or companies borrow money through the medium of the financial markets in order to undertake physical investments, with the hope that the investment will produce a sufficient cash return in the future, to allow a surplus to remain once the borrowed funds (capital plus interest) have been repaid. Obviously, this is a highly simplified view of the distinction between physical and financial investments, but it is essentially correct.

The required return on equity capital

There are many ways in which money can be invested on the capital market. One is to buy the shares issued by a company (either directly from the company or from a third party in the form of an existing shareholder) so that the company, rather than the investor personally, undertakes the physical investments.

An essential characteristic of an investment in shares or equity capital, which differentiates it from most other forms of capital market investment, is that the investment never comes to maturity, i.e. it is permanent and is never repaid.[3] (However, shares are *negotiable*: the permanent investment in a company can be sold on to another investor. These transactions form the bulk of stock exchange dealings.) Because of this characteristic of equity capital, those making such investments to a company are held to be the legal owners of the company.

To find what is the expected return required by shareholders on their capital, we shall return to our earlier discussion on the objective of financial management decision-making. The objective, we said, could be stated as the maximization of the (current) market value of the company's ordinary share capital. This was a surrogate for maximizing the dividend flow to shareholders *through time* (which in itself was a surrogate for wealth maximization) because it is this dividend flow (including a future terminal cash flow) that gives a share its market value.

We also know that cash flows are uncertain, and that cash flows which arise at different points in time cannot be directly compared, but must first be converted to values at one point in time (usually, the present time is chosen). Thus the market value of a share in a company represents the sum of its expected future dividend flow, discounted to present value.

This particular line of reasoning leads to the *share valuation model* known as the 'dividend valuation model': the market price of a company's shares equals the sum of its future expected dividend flow, to infinity, discounted to present value. In this model, what is of particular interest to us is the *discount rate* implied by a particular stock market share price. This discount rate represents the return an investor can expect to obtain on the shares. This is illustrated in Example 1.

EXAMPLE 1

Shares in Zenith SA are expected to produce a 45 cents dividend at the end of each year, in perpetuity. If the share has a market value of €5, this represents the sum of the expected future discounted dividend stream:

$$€5 = €0.45 \times (1 + i)^{-1} + €0.45 \times (1 + i)^{-2}.......+ €0.45 \times (1 + i)^{-\infty}$$

As this is a perpetuity, the sum reduces to:

$$€5 = \frac{€0.45}{i} \quad \text{and so} \quad i = \frac{€0.45}{€5} = 0.09 \text{ or } 9\%$$

▶

▶

Therefore i, the rate of discount implied, given the share's market value, is 9%. It is this *interest or discount rate* that reduces the sum of the future expected 45 cent dividend flow to a present value of €5.[4]

So, 9% must be the expected return that is required by ordinary shareholders in Zenith, taking into consideration the systematic riskiness of the future expected dividend flow. (This, in turn, depends upon the systematic riskiness of the expected returns from the physical investments which the company has undertaken.) In other words, if an investor bought a share in the company for €5 and received a 45 cent dividend each year, then that investor would be getting a 9% annual return on the money invested.

Defining the cost of equity capital

If equity capital were to be the only source of investment funds used by the company in Example 1, and the shareholders required an expected return of 9% on their investment, then 9% could be taken by management as representing the discount rate to be used in the company's project appraisal NPV calculations. The reasoning behind this is that investors have implicitly specified a 9% return through the price set on the shares in the stock market. The shares are priced at €5 because, on this basis, investors can expect to receive a 9% return. Why is an expected 9% return required? Because this must be the going rate of return, elsewhere on the stock market, for investments of the *same* level of systematic risk.

If shareholders can obtain a return of 9% elsewhere on the stock market for a similar level of risk, the inference is that the company's management must earn at least this rate of return on any physical investments they wish to undertake with shareholders' funds (providing, of course, that they are of a similar systematic risk class as the average for the company). If they cannot find projects yielding *at least* such expected returns (given the risk level) then they should not invest. They should give the money back to shareholders – perhaps in the form of a dividend – because shareholders *themselves* can invest that money elsewhere to yield a 9% expected return. Thus 9% becomes – from the perspective of management – *the cost* of using equity capital to invest in projects. (Notice that this cost is, in fact, an *opportunity* cost.)

The discount rate that reduces the sum of a share's expected future dividend flow to a present value equal to its market price is called the '*cost of equity capital*'. It is the minimum expected return required by shareholders from the investment of their funds, by the company's management. However, the cost of equity capital is an appropriate discount rate to use in NPV calculations *only* in circumstances where the project being appraised has the same level of systematic risk (i.e. the same beta value) as the systematic risk of the company's *existing* cash flows (i.e. those cash flows generated by capital investment projects that have already been undertaken).

This is a very important (and limiting) proviso, but it is obvious from our previous analysis. A rate of return is appropriate for a given risk level, and so a company's cost of equity capital is a required rate of return relative to its *existing* level of risk. Therefore, this will be appropriate to use as a discount rate for project evaluation only if the project's risk is *similar* to the company's risk.

If the project has a *different* level of risk, then the company's existing cost of capital is not the appropriate discount rate. In these circumstances, we would have to rely upon a CAPM/beta type of analysis as discussed in Chapter 12, in order to identify the correct rate of discount.

EXPECTED RETURN, DIVIDENDS AND MARKET PRICE

Workings of the stock market

Before proceeding to consider further how the required expected return on equity is to be estimated, let us examine the nature of the relationship between expected return, dividends and market price. In order to do so we shall be taking a simplified but generally correct view of the workings of stock markets.

With the company discussed in Example 1 above, shareholders in Zenith required an expected return (or yield) of 9%. On the basis of an expected annual dividend per share of 45 cents in perpetuity, this produced a market value of €5 per share. Now, in the following analysis, the riskiness of the expected future dividend flow will remain unchanged.

Suppose something happens which leads investors, in general, to believe that the company will now pay an annual dividend per share in future of 50 cents, instead of 45 cents. At the market price of €5 the share now yields a return of: €0.50/€5 = 10%. This 10% return is above the required return (of 9%) for this level of risk, and so investors will start to *buy* the company's shares because they represent a 'bargain' priced at only €5.

Stock exchanges work through a supply and demand market mechanism, and therefore this increased demand for the company's ordinary shares will force up the market price. Suppose, in response to this increased demand, the market price rises to €5.20 per share. At this new price, the shares are still yielding an excessively high return: €0.50/€5.20 = 9.6%, and so demand will continue. In fact the price of the share should rise until its price equates with the required yield of 9%. So the market price will settle at €0.50/0.09 = €5.56 (approx.) per share. (Any further increase in share price will cause the share to have too *low* an expected return, investors will wish to sell, and so the reverse process will start, with the share price falling until it produces the required yield of 9%.)

A changing required return

This example illustrates the *positive* relationship that exists between the dividend expectations of a share and its market price. Increases or decreases in the expected dividend flow will cause a respective rise or fall in market value, with the linchpin of the mechanism being the required expected return.

Similarly, suppose an event occurs which causes investors to change the level of a share's required rate of return. For example, because a company's expected future dividend flow is viewed, for some reason, as becoming more or less risky than before; or because alternative investments have become more or less attractive in terms of their risk-return. Then a consequent change in market price will occur until the revised required yield has established itself. There is an *inverse* relationship between required return and market price.

As an example, suppose that we return to the original situation of Zenith shares with a market price of €5 per share, a constant annual expected dividend of 45 cents and hence an expected return of 9%. Suppose that, for some reason, rates of return throughout the economy rise. (One possible reason might be that the government has increased the return it gives on government stock and so this has pushed up all rates of return in the economy.) As a result, investments with a similar level of systematic risk to that of Zenith rise to (say) 12%.

This means that the Zenith shares are no longer giving a sufficient return at 9%. In consequence, investors will start to *sell* the shares, and this selling pressure will cause the share price to *fall*. How far the share price will fall is determined by what is the new level of required expected return. In this case, the shares will fall in price until they reach €3.75, at which point they too now produce a return of 12% – as do comparable risk investments. Hence the share price has fallen, but the expected return has *risen*.

The share price–return relationship

At first sight these relationships between the market price of a share and its return can appear confusing. If the share price *rises,* then the return *falls,* and vice versa.

If we return to the figures in Example 1, suppose an investor – Franz Foubert – buys shares in Zenith when they are €5 each. Franz receives an annual dividend of 45 cents, and so he earns an annual rate of return on his investment of: €0.45/€5 = 9%. Nothing then happens to change the level of the expected annual dividend – it remains at 45 cents – however suppose, for some reason, the Zenith share price now rises to €6. As a result the return on the shares will now fall to: €0.45/€6 = 0.075 or 7.5%.

However notice what this means. It does not mean that Franz Foubert's return has fallen to 7.5%. By buying the shares at €5, Franz has effectively locked into receiving a 9% return on his investment for as long as he continues to hold the shares. This is because he only paid €5 a share and continues to receive an annual dividend of 45 cents, giving him a 9% rate of return on the investment.

The rise in the share price simply means that *new* investors in the shares receive the lower return of 7.5%, because they have to pay €6 a share in order to get the annual dividend of 45 cents. Thus not only does the rising share price not lower Franz Foubert's return, it also makes him *better off* relative to new investors. His 'better-offness' manifests itself in the fact that he has made a capital gain on his shares: their price has risen from €5 to €6.

What does this one euro capital gain represent? Suppose that Franz had originally spent €600 buying 120 shares in Zenith at €5 each. Therefore Franz receives a total annual dividend of €54 (120 × 45c). Once the share price has risen to €6, new investors investing €600 could only buy 100 shares in Zenith and would receive an annual dividend of €45 (100 × 45c). Therefore Franz receives €9 *more* dividend than they get. The sum of these extra dividends, to infinity, discounted back to present value at the *new* cost of equity capital is: €9 ÷ 0.075 = €120, which is the total capital gain that Franz Foubert has made on his shares:

Purchase cost:	120 × €5	=	€600
Current value:	120 × €6	=	€720
Capital gain		=	€120

Therefore, what does the one euro per share capital represent? It represents the present value of the additional dividends that Franz receives, relative to *new* investors.

The shareholder and the market

An individual investor has to decide whether to buy, hold or sell shares in any particular company. It is not the individual shareholder's actions, but those of the market as a whole (i.e. all investors collectively) that determines a share's expected yield. Therefore individual investors have to estimate a share's future expected dividend flow and from this, together with the share's market price, they will be able to derive its expected yield or return.

What action individual shareholders then take (buy, sell or hold) depends upon their own personal attitudes to risk and the return they require for bearing varying amounts of it. Other things being equal, if investors believe that the share's expected yield is *at least* sufficient compensation for the risk that owning the share involves, then they will buy; if *just* sufficient they will hold; if *less than* sufficient they will sell. The actions of individual shareholders will have very little (if any), direct effect on the market price. However, if many investors have a similar attitude to the required 'risk-expected return' trade-off, then they all[5] are likely to undertake similar action and the share's market price will adjust accordingly. Hence the position of market equilibrium is achieved, as was referred to in our discussion of the market portfolio and the capital market line (CML).

APPLYING THE DIVIDEND VALUATION MODEL

Introduction

At first sight, the dividend valuation model may appear to be a rather naive and incomplete model of share price behaviour. It implies that share prices are only determined by the expected future level of dividends and the systematic risk of the future dividend flow.[6]

If we think back to how we defined the return on a share for the purposes of portfolio theory, we said that the return was composed of two elements: the dividend and the capital gain (or loss) on the share price. At first sight, the dividend valuation model appears to be ignoring this second element of a share's return – the capital gain.

However, the dividend valuation model does *not* ignore the idea of capital gains and losses on the share price. Instead, what the model implies is that what *causes* a capital gain (or loss) is *changed expectations* as to the future level (or riskiness) of the expected dividends.

In addition, notice how the underlying logic of the dividend valuation model fits in with the general assertion made earlier in this book: that values are applied to objects (including shares) in order to allow decisions to be made about them, and an object's current value, on the assumption of a rational, economic model is based on the net stream of future benefits it will produce (or, rather more correctly, that it is expected to produce). Furthermore, we have already recognized the importance of cash and cash flow in economic wealth-maximizing decisions, and the dividend valuation model, being a cash flow valuation model, is therefore in close accord with this reasoning.

The model

If we make use of the following notation:

$P_E =$ market price per share

$V_E =$ total market value of equity $= P_E \times$ number of shares in issue

$d_t =$ dividend per share paid in time t

$D_t =$ total dividend paid to equity holders at time $t = d_t \times$ number of shares in issue

$K_E =$ cost of equity capital (expected return on equity).

Then the dividend valuation model can be expressed in general terms as:

$$\text{either } V_E = \sum_{t=1}^{\infty} \frac{D_t}{(1 + K_E)^t} \text{ or } P_E = \sum_{t=1}^{\infty} \frac{d_t}{(1 + K_E)^t}$$

The only difference between the two expressions is that the first displays the model in terms of the *total* market value of the equity, whereas the second displays the model in terms of the market value *per share*.

If we assume that the future expected dividend flow will remain at a constant level for all future time periods (i.e. a level in perpetuity), then the model can be simplified into the form we used in the earlier example that explained the relationship between expected return, dividend flow and market price:

$$V_E = \frac{D}{K_E} \text{ or } P_E = \frac{d}{K_E}$$

Bid and offer prices

There are several additional points to be made in connection with this model. The first concerns the value of P_E (and consequently V_E) that is to be used.

Shares are normally given two prices: a bid (selling) price and an offer (buying) price.[7] However, we are retaining the assumption of a perfect capital market, and one of the sub-assumptions of this is that there are no transaction costs involved in buying and selling shares. As the difference between the buying and selling prices is a type of transaction cost, this assumption allows us neatly to side-step the problem of having two share prices and instead assume that there is no difference between the bid and offer price. Therefore we will use what is referred to as the share's 'middle price'. This is usually the price seen quoted in the pages of the financial press.

Cum dividend and ex dividend

The second point to be made concerns the fact that market prices of ordinary shares can sometimes be quoted either 'cum div' (with dividend), or 'ex div' (without dividend). When a dividend payout is proposed there has to be a cut-off point in terms of who has rights to receive the dividend. If the cut-off point was the close of trading on 31 March, a share that is sold before close of trading on that day is sold *cum div*, which is to say that the investor buying the share also buys the right to the dividend. Any shares that are sold after close of trading on 31 March are sold without the transfer of rights to the dividend, in other words it is the seller that receives the dividend. As a general rule, the price of the shares will *fall* by the value of the dividend, at the point at which it goes ex div (at close of trading on 31 March in our example).

Suppose a company is expected to pay a 10 cent dividend per share in perpetuity and shareholders require an expected return of 8%. The dividend valuation model can be used to estimate the share's market value: $P_E = 10c / 0.08 = 125c$ or €1.25. This is the ex div market price of the shares (i.e. it is the market price of the share at that point in the company's year when the next 10 cent dividend is due to be paid in approximately 12-months' time), because the dividend valuation model is based on the arithmetic of

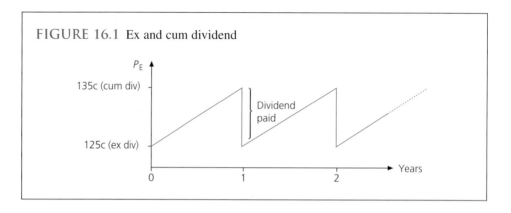

FIGURE 16.1 Ex and cum dividend

an 'immediate' annuity, and so it automatically assumes that the first/next dividend payment will occur in 12-months' time.[8]

Assuming that there are no changes in investors' expectations and that all expectations are fulfilled, a share's market price will follow a 'dogs-tooth' pattern over time. Using the example above, the share's market price will rise steadily over the next 12 months from the ex div market price of 125 cents until, just prior to the payment of the next dividend, it will have a price of *135 cents* (125 cents plus the forthcoming dividend of 10 cents). This latter figure is the share's *cum div* price. Once the share has gone ex div the market price falls back to the ex div price of 125 cents and so restarts the slow rise over the year towards the next dividend.

Figure 16.1 illustrates this highly simplified account of a share's market price movements over time in a perfect market, with unchanging and fulfilled expectations about the future.

As the dividend valuation model employs ex div market prices, so any cum div share prices have to be adjusted accordingly. For example, if a share was expected to yield a constant annual dividend of 22 cents and it had a current market price of €1.32 cum div, then its equivalent ex div price would be the cum div price, less the expected forthcoming dividend: 132c − 22c = 110c. The share's required return would thus be: 22c / 110c = 0.20 or 20%. From now on we shall use P_E (and, consequently, V_E) to represent the ex div market price of a share.[9]

The dividend growth model

Up to this point we have made use of a simplified version of the dividend valuation model which assumes a constant, level flow of expected dividends through time. This may well be quite realistic.[10] There are several examples of companies that have been observed to pay (approximately) constant dividends per share over relatively long periods of time. However, it is important to realize that such an assumption is not an assumption of the general dividend valuation model, but of just the simplified version of it, which we have been using as an example.

If it is believed that a company's flow of future dividends is likely to be a more complex pattern than the one we have assumed, then that more complex pattern can be taken account of within the more general model. We are using the simplified model purely for reasons of arithmetic convenience.

An alternative simplifying assumption about the future pattern of a share's dividends is not that they are constant, but that they *grow* at a *constant annual rate*, in perpetuity. The calculations in the panel show how this 'dividend growth' model can be derived as:[11]

$$P_E = \frac{d_1}{K_E - g} \quad \text{or as}: P_E = \frac{d_0(1 + g)}{K_E - g}$$

where

d_0 = current dividend per share (i.e. at t_0)

d_1 = expected dividend per share in 12-months' time (i.e. t_1)

K_E = cost of equity capital

P_E = ex div market price per share

g = constant annual growth rate of dividends.

Notice that both versions of the model are equivalent, because $d_1 = d_0(1 + g)$. In other words, next year's dividend equals this year's dividend, times one plus the growth rate.

The arithmetic of the model

$$P_E = \frac{d_1}{(1 + K_E)} + \frac{d_1(1 + g)}{(1 + K_E)^2} + \frac{d_1(1 + g)^2}{(1 + K_E)^3} \cdots + \frac{d_1(1 + g)^{N-1}}{(1 + K_E)^N} \tag{1}$$

multiplying each side by $(1 + g)/(1 + K_E)$ gives:

$$\frac{P_E(1 + g)}{(1 + K_E)} = \frac{d_1(1 + g)}{(1 + K_E)^2} + \frac{d_1(1 + g)^3}{(1 + K_E)^3} \cdots + \frac{d_1(1 + g)^N}{(1 + K_E)^{N+1}} \tag{2}$$

subtracting equation (2) from equation (1) gives:

$$P_E - \frac{P_E(1 + g)}{(1 + K_E)} = \frac{d_1}{(1 + K_E)} - \frac{d_1(1 + g)^N}{(1 + K_E)^{N+1}} \tag{3}$$

as long as $K_E > g$ then, as N approaches infinity so $d_1(1 + g)/(1 + K_E)N + 1$ approaches zero and therefore:

$$P_E - \frac{P_E(1 + g)}{(1 + K_E)} = \frac{d_1}{(1 + K_E)} \tag{4}$$

multiplying equation (4) by $(1 + K_E)$ gives:

$$P_E(1 + K_E) - P_E(1 + g) = d_1$$

$$P_E(K_E - g) = d_1 \tag{5}$$

therefore:

$$P_E = \frac{d_1}{K_E - g} \tag{6}$$

Just as the constant dividend model can be rearranged to give the cost of equity capital:

$$K_E = \frac{d}{P_E}$$

so too can the dividend growth model:

$$K_E = \frac{d_1}{P_E} + g \text{ or } K_E = \frac{d_0(1 + g)}{P_E} + g$$

Therefore if a company's equity has an ex div market price per share of 210 cents and a constant expected annual dividend growth rate of 5%, and a dividend of 20 cents has just been paid, the cost of equity capital or expected return on equity would be:

$$K_E = \frac{20c \times (1 + 0.05)}{210c} + 0.05 = 0.15 \text{ or } 15\%$$

The dividend growth rate

There are two main approaches to estimating 'g' (the constant expected dividend growth rate) in practice. One is to take the *average* past rate of growth of dividends and assume that this rate will continue unchanged in the future. If need be, this rate can be adjusted to take account of any additional information that leads to the belief that the past growth rate will not be approximately reflected in the future growth rate.

As an example, suppose the past pattern of dividends per share is given by:

Year	Dividends per share (cents)
t_{-4}	8.0
t_{-3}	9.0
t_{-2}	9.5
t_{-1}	10.5
t_0	12.0

The dividends per share have grown over a 4-year period (i.e. five items of data produce 4 years of growth), from 8 cents to 12 cents. This represents an average annual rate of growth (g) of:

$$8c \times (1 + g)^4 = 12c$$

$$1 + g = \left[\frac{12c}{8c} \right]^{1/4} = 1.067$$

$$g = 1.067 - 1 = 0.1067 \text{ or } 10.67\%$$

The other approach, originally put forward by the American economist Myron Gordon, examines the *basis* of dividend growth and attempts to *derive* a future growth rate rather than just to extrapolate a past growth rate.

Gordon started from the idea that a company cannot pay out a growing level of dividends each year without a growing level of profitability/earnings. Nor can a company be expected to generate a growing level of annual earnings without a growing investment in the company's fixed asset base.

Therefore, on the basis of a number of limiting assumptions which are listed below, Gordon argued that if the company retained a constant proportion of earnings (profits) each year (*b*) and reinvested them (the growing investment base) to earn an annual rate of return of *r* (the growing level of earnings), then the company would be able to sustain an annual dividend growth rate (*g*) equal to the product of *r* and *b*.

$$g = rb$$

Assuming a constant proportion (*b*) of each year's earnings (E_t) are reinvested to earn a constant annual rate of return (*r*), then the annual earnings pattern is:

$$
\begin{aligned}
E_1 & \\
E_2 &= E_1 + rbE_1 = E_1(1 + rb) \\
E_3 &= E_2 + rbE_2 = E_1(1 + rb) + rbE_1(1 + rb) \\
&\qquad\qquad\quad = E_1(1 + rb)(1 + rb) \\
&\qquad\qquad\quad = E_1(1 + rb)^2 \\
&\qquad\qquad\quad \vdots \\
E_N &\qquad\qquad\quad = E_1(1 + rb)^{N-1}
\end{aligned}
$$

The annual dividend pattern is therefore:

$$
\begin{aligned}
D_1 &= (1 - b)E_1 \\
D_2 &= (1 - b)E_2 = (1 - b)E_1(1 + rb) \\
D_3 &= (1 - b)E_3 = (1 - b)E_1(1 + rb)^2 \\
&\vdots \\
D_N &= (1 - b)E_N = (1 - b)E_1(1 + rb)^{N-1}
\end{aligned}
$$

Therefore each year the annual dividends grow by an amount equal to (1 + *rb*) times the previous year's dividends: an annual rate of dividend growth of *rb*. In practice, given the validity of the assumptions, *b* and *r* would be estimated as follows:

$$b = \frac{\text{Earnings} - \text{Dividends}}{\text{Earnings}}$$

$$r = \frac{\text{Earnings}}{\text{Book value of capital employed}}$$

and the dividend growth model (which is often known as the Gordon growth model in this form) becomes:

$$P_E = \frac{d_0(1 + rb)}{K_E - rb}$$

The assumptions that underlie the Gordon dividend growth model are as follows:

1. An all-equity company.
2. Retained profits (earnings) are the only source of additional investment capital.
3. A constant proportion of net profits is retained each year for re-investment.
4. Projects financed through retained profits produce a constant annual return.

Notice that this particular version of the dividend valuation model is only applicable to companies that have an *all-equity* capital structure, because if debt capital is involved (a case examined in the next section), then it causes problems in keeping r and b, and hence g, constant.[12]

A changing dividend growth rate

We can modify the dividend growth model to allow for changing growth rates (although it has to be said that it would be unusual to know that growth rates would change in three, five or however many years' time). Suppose we were given the following information about the Dresden Pharma. The company has just paid an annual dividend of 5 cents per share. Dividends per share are expected to grow at 10% per year for the next 3 years, and then will only grow by 5% per year thereafter. Shares in other companies with a similar level of systematic risk to Dresden yield a 15% return on equity.

The dividend growth model can be adapted from a situation where it assumes a *single*, constant rate of dividend growth, to handle this type of situation where there are *two* rates of dividend growth. Example 2 takes this information to estimate the current, ex div value of Dresden Pharma shares.

EXAMPLE 2

Dresden Pharma have just paid a 5 cents dividend per share. This dividend per share is expected to grow at 10% per year until Year 3. Thereafter it will grow at 5% per year. A discount rate of 15% is thought to reflect the systematic risk involved.

The current value of Dresden shares will equal the sum of the future expected dividends (to infinity), discounted back to present value:

Year			
0	5c	=	5c
1	5c $(1.10)^1$	=	5.5c
2	5c $(1.10)^2$	=	6.05c
3	5c $(1.10)^3$	=	6.655c

▶

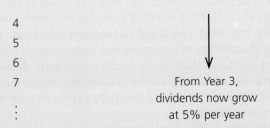

4
5
6
7
⋮

From Year 3,
dividends now grow
at 5% per year

Notice that the dividend valuation model's assumption of a constant dividend growth rate does hold true from Year 3 onwards. Therefore the standard model can be adapted to value Dresden shares at Year 3:

Standard model

$$P_{E0} = \frac{d_0 \times (1 + g)}{K_E - g}$$

Adapted model

$$P_{E3} = \frac{d_3 \times (1 + g)}{K_E - g}$$

In terms of the adapted model:

$$d_3 = 6.655c$$
$$g = 0.05$$
$$K_E = 0.15$$

$$P_{E3} = \frac{6.655c \times (1 + 0.05)}{0.15 - 0.05} = 69.9 \text{ cents}$$

Notice what this represents. It is the sum of the future expected dividends from Year 4 onwards (remember $d_3 \times (1 + g) = d_4$), discounted back to Year 3.

We can now find the *current* ex div value of Dresden Pharma shares based on the present value sum of the future dividend flow:[13]

Year	Dividend				PV
1	5.5c	×	$(1 + 0.15)^{-1}$	=	4.8c
2	6.05c	×	$(1 + 0.15)^{-2}$	=	4.6c
3	(6.655c + 69.9c p)	×	$(1 + 0.15)^{-3}$	=	50.3c
	↑		P_{E0}	=	59.7c

Sum of the dividends
from Year 4
onwards, discounted
back to Year 3

Therefore the current ex div value of the Dresden Pharma shares is approximately 59.7 cents per share.

The cost of retained earnings

One of the most important sources of corporate long-term investment capital is retained earnings – i.e. that part of net cash flow generated by a company's past investment projects which, at the time it arises, is retained within the firm rather than being distributed to shareholders as part of the dividend flow. Because retained earnings arise from sources internal to the company, rather than externally (such as a new equity issue), there is a temptation to believe that this source of capital is somehow 'costless'.

In fact, both from a legal and an economic standpoint, retained earnings belong to the ordinary shareholders of a company and so the 'cost' of retained earnings, or the minimum expected return that their use in investment projects should generate, is exactly the same as the expected return required by shareholders on new equity: the cost of equity capital. Retained earnings form part of the equity capital of a company and their cost is therefore a reflection of this fact.

This has already been implicitly taken into account in that the *market* value of equity was used in the specification of K_E, and the market value reflects *both* the nominal value of a company's equity capital *and* the value of the retained earnings. (In practice retained earnings are a slightly cheaper source of capital than a new issue of equity because of the issue costs incurred with the latter, but this rather minor point will be dealt with in Chapter 21.)

CAPM AND THE COST OF EQUITY CAPITAL

We have now looked at how we can estimate the cost of equity capital using the dividend valuation model (DVM). However, if we pick up on a point made right at the start of this chapter, we said that the cost of equity capital is really the return on equity capital. Whether it is called a 'cost' or a 'return' depends upon whose point of view we are taking.

From management's viewpoint, it is a *cost* of capital. In fact, it represents an *opportunity cost* of capital: the minimum return that they must seek to earn when investing shareholders' funds. However, from the investors' viewpoint, it represents the *rate of return* they can expect to receive if they were to invest in the company's shares. If we think of the cost of equity capital as the return on equity, we have already seen in Chapter 12 how this may be identified – by using the CAPM.

This means that a company's cost of equity capital can be estimated in *two* different ways. Either the dividend valuation model can be used to find K_E (as we have seen) or the CAPM can be used to estimate $E(r_{shares})$. Essentially K_E and $E(r_{shares})$ can be seen as two different sets of notation representing the same thing: the cost or return on equity capital.

Example 3 illustrates the use of both models in this way.

EXAMPLE 3

Mota-Energia is a long-established petroleum refiner, quoted on the Lisbon Euronext stock exchange. Its current balance sheet, in summarized form, is as follows:

		(Euros millions)
	Non-current assets	200
	Net current assets	60
	Total assets	260
Financed by:		
	Share capital	20
	Reserves	240
	Total liabilities	260

▶

The company's shares are currently priced at €2.14 *cum div* on the stock market. Over the last year the company produced earnings after tax of €40 million from which the stock market is expecting a total net dividend payout of €30 million or 12 cents per share.

The dividend per share record of the company, over the last 5 years, is as follows:

	Year	Dividend share (cents)
	t_{-5}	9.85
	t_{-4}	10.40
	t_{-3}	10.85
	t_{-2}	11.20
	t_{-1}	11.70
(expected)	t_0	12.0

The current return on Portuguese government bonds is 5%, the market return is 9% and Mota-Energia has an equity beta of 0.90.

The company wishes to estimate its cost of equity capital. Given the available information, this can be found both from using the capital asset pricing model and from using the dividend valuation model:

Using the CAPM:

$$E(r_{\text{Mota-Energia}}) = 5\% + (9\% - 5\%) \times 0.90 = 9.5\%$$

Using the dividend valuation model:

From the information on the historical dividend record, it would appear that the dividend growth version of the model is most appropriate. There are two possible approaches to estimating the *future* dividend growth rate:

(a)   On the basis of the past dividend growth rate.
(b)   On the basis of the Gordon model: *rb*.

(a)   Past dividend growth rate:

$$9.85c \times (1 + g)^5 = 12c$$

$$(1 + g)^5 = \frac{12c}{9.85c}$$

$$(1 + g) = \left[\frac{12c}{9.85c} \right]^{1/5}$$

$$g = 1.218^{0.20} - 1$$

$$g = 1.04 - 1 = 0.04 \text{ or } 4\%$$

(b) Gordon rb:

$$b = \frac{€40 - €30}{€40} = 0.25$$

$$r = \frac{€40}{€260} = 0.154$$

$$g = 0.154 \times 0.25 = 0.0385 \text{ or } 3.85\%$$

As both give an estimate of the dividend growth rate of approximately 4%, that figure will be used in the dividend valuation model:

$$d_0 = 12c$$

$$P_E = 214c - 12c = 202c$$

$$g = 0.04$$

$$K_E = \frac{12c \times (1 + 0.04)}{202c} + 0.04 = 0.102 \text{ or } 10.2\%$$

Therefore, given the estimates of the two share valuation models of 9.5% and 10.2%, Mota-Energia should use 10% as its estimated cost of equity capital.

CAPM VERSUS THE DVM

Given, as we have seen in Example 3, that there are two ways in which we can estimate the cost of equity capital, does it matter which approach we use? Putting this question more directly: will the DVM provide approximately the same estimate as the CAPM? The answer is that, in the real world, they probably will **not** do so (unlike in Example 3).

There are four main reasons for this conclusion. The first is that the two models are significantly different, in that the CAPM is a *normative* model and the DVM is a *positive* model. What is meant by a 'normative model' is that CAPM gives the return that *should be* expected from the shares given their relative systematic risk. In contrast, the DVM as a 'positive model' indicates what *is* the return on the share, given its current market price and dividend; and its expected dividend growth rate. Therefore the two models may give significantly different estimates of K_E because 'what should be' is not always 'what actually is'.

For example, suppose that CAPM estimates that the expected return on the shares should be 20%. Sometimes it will be more than 20%, sometimes less, but on average it should be 20%. Therefore when, at a particular moment in time, we use the DVM to calculate the cost of equity capital, the shares may not be priced at that time to give the average rate of return that CAPM suggests we should expect.

A second reason why the two models may not provide similar estimates of the cost of equity capital is that the CAPM is a *single* time period model; while the DVM is a *multi-time* period model.

The CAPM is a single time period model in that – as we saw – the rate of return is calculated over just a single time period. On the other hand, the DVM is very much a multi-time period model, with the share price being the sum of the future expected dividend, to infinity. The CAPM therefore provides just a single time period rate of return, while the DVM provides an average multi-time period rate of return. The one will not always be the same as the other.

A third reason for possible differences between the two models is that the CAPM (as was noted in the brief discussion of the arbitrage pricing model in Chapter 12) is a single-factor model. As such, CAPM may not be capturing all the determinants of return and so the model may be 'incomplete'. For example, there is some evidence to suggest that company size plays a part in determining return, with small companies apparently providing a slightly greater return than larger companies of the same beta value.[14]

The final reason for the two models not giving the same estimate of the cost of equity capital concerns inaccuracies in the input data (of the 'garbage in, garbage out' variety). The DVM requires three items of data, as was noted in the preceding paragraph, and there are potential problems with at least two of them.

We have discussed the fact that we input into the model the ex div share price. The problem here is that share prices are quoted ex div for approximately 5 to 6 weeks; if, during this time period, the share price has been volatile, then we are faced with the problem of deciding on the best *representative* value of the ex div share price.

The second data input problem is the more serious. This concerns the estimation of the future rate of growth of dividends (g). We have seen two possible ways of estimating g; one from the past rate of growth of dividends, and one on the basis of rb. Neither method is satisfactory. Trying to estimate the *future* on the basis of the *past* is never a good forecasting technique, unless there are positive reasons to believe that the past will be replicated in the future. No such justification exists here. On the other hand, we have already commented upon the fact that the estimation of g using rb relies on assumptions that are wholly unrealistic. (There is a third potential data input problem concerning the dividend valuation model. This concerns the impact of tax on the dividend value and the fact that different investors may – under some tax regimes – bear a different tax charge on the dividend and so produce different costs of equity capital for different investors.)

It is not only the DVM which suffers from problems of accurate data input; so too does the CAPM. Like the DVM, the CAPM requires three items of data: r_F, $[E(r_M) - r_F]$ and β.

The problem that arises with the risk-free rate of return, r_F, is that we use the return on government bonds as the measure of r_F, but this return is only risk-free/certain in terms of its *money* return. What is still uncertain is the *purchasing power* of that money return, because the future rate of inflation is unknown.

For example, suppose the annual rate of return on government bonds is 5%. All this means is that if you invest €100 now in government bonds, you are certain to receive back €105 in 12-months' time. What is uncertain is *the purchasing power* of that €105 in 12-months' time, because we don't know what the rate of price inflation over the next 12 months will be. What is needed is a *real* risk-free return – that is a risk-free return in terms of purchasing power; however, such a number cannot be satisfactorily identified.

The second data problem concerns the average market risk premium: $[E(r_M) - r_F]$. The problem here is that this average risk premium is extremely volatile. In recent years, it has been as great as 13% and as low as 4%. Indeed, it is so volatile that researchers are usually forced to use a long-run (50 years) average of this figure in order to get a reasonably stable estimate. Having done this, it is then somewhat uncomfortable to have to assume that over the next time period the market risk premium will be the same as this very long-run average figure.[15]

The final item of data that is required by the CAPM is beta. The problem here lies in how beta values are estimated in the real world. We saw that normally betas are estimated using regression analysis of *past* data. What we really require in order to use CAPM is a *forward-looking*, or future, beta but in practice we estimate beta by looking backwards at the past relationship between the return on the shares and the return on the market portfolio.

As such, there would be no problem with this backwards-looking approach as long as we could rely on beta values remaining fairly stable over time. This prompts the question: do beta values remain stable over time? The answer depends (to some extent) on how you wish to interpret the evidence. Beta values certainly do move over time, as companies change their exposure to systematic risk. But, on the other hand, they tend to move relatively slowly. However, the estimation of beta remains a far from ideal situation.

Therefore, on the basis of all these reasons, we would not necessarily expect the dividend valuation model and the capital asset pricing model to produce the *same* estimates of the cost of equity capital. However, of the two, we can probably conclude that the CAPM is *likely* to provide the more reliable figure. The reason for reaching this conclusion is the fact that the dividend valuation model – in its practical application – really does have an almost insurmountable problem with regard to identifying a reliable estimate of the future rate of growth of dividends.

THE COST OF DEBT CAPITAL

We came across the idea of the cost of debt capital in Chapter 15 when discussing the term structure of interest rates, although we referred to it then as the 'redemption yield'. In our foregoing discussion on the cost of equity capital, we said that the *cost* of equity and the *return* on equity were essentially the same thing. The former term was used when looking at things from management's viewpoint and the latter term was used when looking at things from the shareholder's viewpoint. In a similar way, the term 'redemption yield' looks at the calculation from the investor's or lender's viewpoint, while the 'cost of debt capital' takes the management's viewpoint.

However, as we shall see, the redemption yield on bonds and the cost of debt capital are *not* the same in one important respect. When looking at the cost of debt capital from the company's point of view, we need to take into account the fact that companies normally receive *tax relief* on debt interest. However we will come to this point later. Let's start by looking at the cost of debt capital from first principles.

Debt versus equity capital

So far we have examined the cost of equity capital. We now turn our attention to the other[16] major source of finance: loan finance. This comes in a great variety of forms, and so we will assign it the generic term of 'debt capital'.

Debt capital can be defined as a loan made to a company which is normally repaid at some future date. Debt capital differs from ordinary share capital in two fundamental ways.

First, investors in debt capital do not become part-owners of the company but are merely creditors, because they are only lending money to the company for a fixed period.[17] At the end of this period, the loan is repaid: the debt capital is said to be redeemed. In contrast, equity capital represents a *permanent* investment which is never repaid except in very special circumstances (such as company liquidation).

Second, the holders or suppliers of debt capital usually receive a contractually fixed annual percentage return on their loan, which is specified when the debt capital is issued and which is known as the coupon rate. Again, this contrasts with the situation of the suppliers of equity capital whose annual return – the dividend – is not at all contractually fixed and the exact level is set, year by year, at the discretion of the directors.

In addition to these two fundamental differences between debt and equity capital, debt capital is ranked ahead of equity for payment of the annual return. In other words, legally, interest on debt capital must be paid in full before any dividend may be paid to the suppliers of equity. Thus, if there is any shortfall in company earnings in any year, it is the ordinary shareholders who are more likely to suffer than the debt holders.

Debt capital therefore represents a loan with a contractually fixed rate of return, a contractually fixed time of repayment and preferential payment treatment over equity capital. In an uncertain world, all three factors combine to make the debt capital of any given company a substantially *less risky* investment for a supplier of capital, than that company's share capital.

As debt can be viewed as less risky than shares, it follows that the required expected return on a company's debt[18] will be less than that required on its equity capital. In a *certain* world, debt and equity capital would logically require the same return from any given company; but in an *uncertain* world the required returns differ.

The interest valuation model

We know that sometimes shares are quoted (i.e. they are traded on a stock market), and sometimes they are unquoted. The point was made in Chapter 1 that, for convenience, we shall normally be dealing with a stock exchange quoted company in our development of the theory of financial management.

Debt capital is similar to equity capital in that some debt capital is quoted whilst other debt capital (in fact, the majority) is unquoted. Again, for convenience we shall deal initially with quoted debt capital, although we will return later to the problem with unquoted debt. For clarity, we will refer to quoted debt capital as 'bonds'.

In order to examine the cost of debt capital we shall use the principles upon which the dividend valuation model was based in order to develop a *bond* valuation model. Therefore, we can say that the market value of a bond is determined by the sum of the future cash flows it will produce, discounted to present value. These future cash flows usually consist of the expected future interest flow and (if they are redeemable bonds), their future redemption or repayment amount.

'Plain vanilla' bonds

Typically, bonds are normally issued in units of €100. Thus each bond represents €100 of loan or debt capital and the €100 is termed the bond's 'nominal' or 'par' value.

Attached to each unit are details of the interest rate that will be paid by the borrower, expressed as a percentage of the nominal value. This interest rate is referred to as the 'nominal' interest rate or 'coupon' rate.[19] In addition, the bond will contain details of when it is to be repaid (its redemption date) and the amount or value at which it will be redeemed (which is normally its par value of €100).

A company might issue €25 million worth of (€100) bonds with a coupon rate of 8% and redemption due in 5-years' time at par value (i.e. €100 per bond is due to be repaid). This is the standard form of bond and is sometimes known as a 'plain vanilla' bond. There are many variations on this basic type, as we shall see.

Pricing bonds

Bonds, like shares, are traded in supply and demand markets. As a result, the market price of a bond depends upon supply and demand market forces. Essentially, what drives these market forces is the difference between the *current* market interest rate for investments of the same risk level as the bond, and the bond's own *coupon* rate. Thus, if a bond has a coupon rate *below* current market interest rates, its market value will be *below* its nominal value of €100, and vice versa. This relationship is demonstrated in Example 4.

EXAMPLE 4

To help understand this relationship between market and coupon interest rates, we will look at an example using – for simplicity – an irredeemable €100 bond (i.e. a bond that is never due to be repaid), with a coupon rate of 5%. It is therefore expected to produce an annual cash flow of €5 of interest, in perpetuity (i.e. €100 × 0.05 = €5).

The *current* market interest rate (for *similar risk* investments) is 8%. If the bond's perpetuity stream of interest payments is discounted back to present value at this current interest rate, its present value sum is: €5 ÷ 0.08 = €62.50. This represents the bond's current market value.

The bond has a *market* value of only €62.50, against a nominal value of €100, because that is how much would be needed to be invested today, at the current interest rate of 8%, to produce annual interest of €5: €62.50 × 0.08 = €5.

Using a similar form of analysis, if market interest rates then fell to 4%, the value of the bond would rise to: €5 ÷ 0.04 = €125. Finally, if market interest rates were the *same* as the bond's coupon rate, then the bond would have a market value equal to its nominal value: €5 ÷ 0.05 = €100.

The opportunity cost of debt capital

It is at this point that an important fact emerges. We are concerned with finding the 'cost' to a company of the various types of capital it might use to finance an investment project, in order to use this cost as a possible discount or cut-off rate in the appraisal process. For such a use we might easily believe that the bond's *coupon* rate, rather than the current market interest rate (assuming they differ), reflects the cost to the firm of using this source of capital. However, such a belief would be incorrect.

This possible misunderstanding really arises from an incorrect interpretation of the word 'cost'. Cost of capital does *not* refer to how much the capital costs the firm to buy – in other words, the interest rate that the company is paying – but refers to the best available return (at that risk level) available elsewhere, that the firm forgoes when it applies the capital to a particular investment project: it is the *opportunity cost* of debt capital that we need to identify.

Therefore, as far as the investment appraisal and the cost of debt capital is concerned, it is the *current market* interest rate that is important; not the (*historic*) *coupon* rate. Example 5 demonstrates the logic behind this statement.

EXAMPLE 5

Formosa SA issued some bonds a few years ago at a coupon rate of 6%. (At the time of issue, 6% would have been the current market interest rate for debt capital of that risk level. Bonds will normally always be issued at a coupon rate equal to the current market interest rate at the time of issue.) Today, the current market interest rate (for similar risk bonds) is 8%.

Formosa has now identified an investment project which requires an outlay of €1 million and which is expected to produce a net cash flow of €290 000 per year for 4 years. It proposes to finance the investment by using part of the proceeds of the bond issue. Therefore it calculates the project's NPV using the bond's coupon rate of 6% as the discount rate.

▶

▶

Project cash flows (€000s)

Year	0	1	2	3	4
	−1000	+290	+290	+290	+290

At a 5% discount rate:

$$NPV = -1000 + [290 \times A_{4\,6\%}] = €4879\ NPV$$

As a result, the project has a *positive* NPV of €4879 and so the company undertakes the investment.

However, if we recall our analysis of the logic of the NPV decision rule, we can see that such a discount rate is incorrect. In discounting a project's cash flow to produce a positive or negative NPV, an implicit comparison is automatically being made between the returns from investing in the project and the returns that could be achieved by investing the investment's €1 000 000 cost on the capital market. Hence we use the *market* interest rate as the discount rate.

Therefore, discounting the project by 6% means that an *incorrect comparison* is being carried out: in fact, as an alternative to the project, an interest rate of 8% can be earned for the same level of risk. Therefore discounting the investment's cash flow at 8% gives an NPV of:

$$NPV = -1000 + [290 \times A_{4\,8\%}] = -€39\,491\ NPV$$

As the project has a *negative* NPV at the current market rate of discount, it should *not* be undertaken. The €1 000 000 required outlay could be better employed deposited on the money market at 8% where it could, for example, produce the following flows (€000s):

Year	0	1	2	3	4
	−1000	+301.92	+301.92	+301.92	+301.92

Compare this flow with that expected from the project. (In other words, given an 8% interest rate, €1 000 000 now can produce an annuity of €301 920 a year for 4 years. The proposed investment only produces a cash flow of €290 000 per year.)

The cost of irredeemable debt capital

We will now turn to look systematically at how to go about estimating a company's (opportunity) cost of debt capital. To start, we will examine the simplest type of debt capital: irredeemable or undated bonds. These are bonds that are not expected to be repaid and whose interest payments form a perpetuity cash flow. We will make use of the following notation:[20]

P_B = market price per bond, ex interest

V_B = total market value of the bonds = P_B × number of bonds issued

i — annual interest paid per bond

I — total annual interest = i × number of bonds issued.

The general valuation model for irredeemable bonds is:

$$V_B = \frac{I}{K_D} \text{ or, on a per unit basis, } P_B = \frac{i}{K_D}$$

Where K_D is the current market rate of interest (for similar risk securities). In other words, K_D is the (opportunity) cost of debt capital. Therefore, the models can be switched around to provide this cost of debt directly:

$$K_D = \frac{I}{V_B} \text{ or, similarly, } K_D = \frac{i}{P_B}$$

For example, a company has issued irredeemable bonds at a coupon rate of 7.5% and each bond currently has a market value of €93.75, ex interest. The company's cost of debt capital can then be estimated as: $K_D \times$ €7.50 ÷ €93.75 = 0.08 or 8%. We can conclude from this that, for an investment of the bond's risk level, the current market interest rate is 8%.

Because we are dealing with an uncertain world, just as we talked in terms of K_E being the expected return on equity, so we should talk in terms of the expected return to bond holders. Although a company's debt is less risky than a company's shares, they are not risk-less investment.[21] (Sometimes bonds can be a very risky investment, for instance in cases where there is a substantial probability that the issuing company will be unable to meet the future interest and redemption payments, if the bond is redeemable.)

In calculating the cost of debt capital by means of the formula $K_D = I/V_B$ (or i/P_B) we are calculating what is called the bond's 'yield to maturity', or 'redemption yield'. This is the maximum rate of return (as opposed to the expected return) that the bond will produce at its current market price, assuming that all future contractual payments attached to the bond will be met by the issuing company.

However, taking this as a reasonable assumption, then the figure calculated for K_D is likely to be a fairly accurate estimate of the cost of debt capital for investment appraisal purposes. If the going concern concept is not thought applicable to a particular company, its marginal cost of debt capital should be based on the alternative cash flow which its debt is expected to yield.

REAL WORLD VIEW: Negative Yields, the Role of Rating Agencies and Lending to Countries

Throughout this chapter, we have addressed issues surrounding the cost of capital. A seemingly unusual example of raising capital, which has drawn headlines in recent years, is the curious phenomenon of lending with *negative* yields – or implementing what has been referred to as 'Negative Interest Rate Policy' (NIRP). In the summer of 2012, for example, the government of Germany sold bonds totalling €4.17 billion on a 2-year note, with a yield averaging minus 0.06%. In real terms, this meant that the government not only borrowed money from investors, but was in effect paid for the pleasure (as opposed to being charged interest on the loan). On the face of it, this doesn't appear to have been an attractive proposition for the investors. However, the negative interest rate is perhaps indicative of the degree of risk aversion in the European debt markets at that time; arguably Germany was deemed to be the safest borrower, when the alternative options may have incurred significant losses.

This trend has been witnessed across Europe, with Switzerland amongst others showing a negative yield on its bonds. In the secondary market, 2-year debts from Austria, Finland and the Netherlands dropped below 0%. Outside the eurozone, short-term debts showed negative return in Denmark as well.

It is interesting to note that since 2007, rating agencies (who give large-scale borrowing ratings dependent upon how likely their debt is to be paid back and hence play a significant role in the flow of international capital) have been criticized.

Michael Barnier, the Internal Market Commissioner, said that: 'Ratings have a direct impact on the markets and the wider economy… And rating agencies have made serious mistakes in the past.' In May 2014, and in the context of a fractious international climate, the Russian Deputy Finance Minister, Sergei Storchak, emphasized Russia's desire to move away from traditional international ratings agencies, noting that a break was simply 'a matter of time'.

As of 2014, Standard & Poor's rating agency rate the following countries as AAA (the top rating): Australia, Denmark, Finland, Germany, Hong Kong, Liechtenstein, Luxembourg, Norway, Singapore, Sweden, Switzerland and the UK.

What might be the longer-term issues of negative interest? How important do you believe agency ratings to be? Do you think that these ratings could have a negative impact on countries whose economies are already struggling?

The cost of redeemable debt

The cost of redeemable debt is found by estimating the IRR of the bond's cash flow. This can be found by using the linear interpolation method that was used in the earlier discussion about the IRR. Example 6 illustrates the approach.[22]

EXAMPLE 6

Gold Coast Construction, a South African company, issued R10 000 000 worth of 5% R1000 bonds 7 years ago. They are due to be redeemed at par in 3-years' time. The bonds have a current market price of R1010 (i.e. per R1000 unit) cum interest.

Gold Coast's cost of debt capital can be estimated as follows. First, the equivalent ex interest price of the bonds would be: R1010 −£50 (i.e. the annual amount of interest payable) = R960. Then, if the company were to issue an identical bond now, its cash flow would be:

Year	0	1	2	3
	+R960	−R50	−R50	−R1050

The company would be able to sell the bond for R960 but it would then have to pay out R50 of interest at the end of each of the next 3 years. In addition, in 3-years' time, the bond would have to be repaid at its R1000 par value.

Using linear interpolation to find the IRR of this cash flow:

At a 4% discount rate:

$$+960 - [50 \times A_{3\,4\%}] - [1000 \times 1.04^{-3}] = -58.76 \text{ NPV}$$

▶

▶

At a 16% discount rate:

$$+960 - [50 \times A_{3\ 16\%}] - [1000 \times 1.16^{-3}] = +207\ \text{NPV}$$

Therefore K_D, the IRR, can be estimated as:

$$K_D = 4\% + \left[\frac{-58.76}{-58.76 - (+207)} \times (16\% - 4\%) \right] = 0.066\ \text{or}\ 6.6\%^{23}$$

Furthermore, the total market value, ex interest, of the company's bonds can be calculated as:

$$V_B = \text{R}10\,000\,000 \times \frac{\text{R}\,960}{\text{R}\,1000} = \text{R}9\,600\,000$$

Finally, notice that a *very rough* approximation to the cost of redeemable debt can be obtained as follows:

$$K_D = \text{coupon rate} + \text{average annual capital gain}$$

The bonds issued by Gold Coast Construction have a 5% coupon. As the current ex interest price is R960 and they are redeemable at R1000, then the capital gain is approximately: R40 ÷ R960 = 4.17%. As this capital gain is made when the bonds are redeemed in 3-years' time, the average annual capital gain is: 4.17% ÷ 3 = 1.4%.

Thus Gold Coast's cost of debt capital could be roughly approximated as:

$$5\% + 1.4\% = 6.4\%$$

Semi-annual interest payments

In our examples so far we have assumed the bonds pay their interest annually. However, in practice, semi-annual payments of interest are more usual. For example, suppose a bond had a coupon rate of 10%, with interest paid semi-annually. Each year, €10 of interest in total would be paid, with €5 being paid mid-year and the other €5 being paid at year-end. In these more realistic circumstances, calculating the cost of debt capital is a little more complicated. Example 7 illustrates such a situation.

EXAMPLE 7

Garaventa AG has issued 12% bonds with interest due to be paid semi-annually. The bonds have a current market value of €114 ex interest and are due to be repaid at their €100 par value in 3-years' time. What is Garaventa's cost of debt capital?

▶

▶

Each year €12 of interest is paid in two instalments of €6. Therefore, on the basis of half-year time periods, the bond's cash flow is:

Time period	0	1 to 6	6
	€114	− €6 per time period	− €100

The IRR of this cash flow can be estimated using linear interpolation, as usual:

At a 4% discount rate:

$$+114 - [6 \times A_{6\,4\%}] - [100 \times 1.04^{-6}] = +3.52 \text{ NPV}$$

At a 6% discount rate:

$$+114 - [6 \times A_{6\,6\%}] - [100 \times 1.06^{-6}] = +14 \text{ NPV}$$

IRR of the cash flow:

$$4\% + \left[\frac{+3.52}{+3.52 - (+14)} \times (6\% - 4\%) \right] = 3.33\%$$

Notice that this IRR relates to a *half-yearly* cash flow. And so it has to be adjusted on to an *annual* basis in order to estimate the *annual* cost of debt capital for Garaventa:

$$(1 + 0.0333)^2 - 1 = 0.068 \text{ or } 6.8\% \text{ per year}$$

Discount or zero coupon bonds

All the examples used so far have been of 'plain vanilla' bonds. In other words, the bonds are issued and redeemed by the company at their nominal value and the company pays a specified rate of interest to the investor.

Although there are, as was mentioned earlier, a great number of variations on this standard type of debt capital, it is convenient at this stage to look at one important type of bond which is significantly different. This is the discount bond or zero coupon bond. These differ from plain vanillas in that they are *not* issued by the company at their nominal value, but at a *discount* on this value. For example, some bonds may be issued at €75 for every €100 of nominal value. Therefore when the company issues one of these bonds with a €100 nominal value, they only receive €75 from the lender.

The other way in which these bonds differ from plain vanillas is that they do not usually pay any interest. The investor obtains a return in the form of a capital gain only, because the bonds are redeemed at their nominal value. Example 8 illustrates the circumstances in which a company might issue discount or zero coupon bonds, and the procedure that we follow to calculate their cost of debt capital.

EXAMPLE 8

Silvertown Property plc wants to raise a 3-year loan in order to buy a vacant plot of land on which to construct an office block. The cost of the land, together with the construction costs, will amount to £150 million. Therefore Silvertown plans to borrow this amount and repay the loan in 3-years' time, when it hopes to sell the building for £250 million. Because this investment will not generate any cash inflow until the building is sold, the company decides *not* to issue plain vanilla bonds, which would require interest to be paid each year (for which the company would have no cash inflow available) but instead to issue discount/zero coupon bonds.

The company decides to issue zero coupon bonds with a total nominal value of £200 million. These will be issued at a 25% discount on their nominal value, they will carry a zero coupon rate and will be redeemed at their nominal value in 3-years' time. The resulting cost of debt capital for Silvertown Property would be calculated as follows:

First, notice that the issue will raise the £150 million required: £200 million $\times$ (1 − 0.25) = £150 million. This means that each bond with a nominal value of £100 (but paying no interest) will be issued in return for a loan of £75 from investors.

As usual, the cost of debt capital is the IRR of the bond's cash flow:

Year	0	3
Cash flow	+75	−£100

$$NPV \text{ at } 6\% = -£8.96$$

$$NPV \text{ at } 12\% = +£3.82$$

Using linear interpolation:

$$IRR = 6\% + \left(\frac{-8.96}{-8.96 - 3.82} \times (12\% - 6\%) \right) = 10.2\%$$

The cost of debt capital of Silvertown's discount bonds is 10.2%

Low coupon bonds

One obvious variation are bonds that lie midway between the two 'extremes' of plain vanilla bonds and discount/zero coupon bonds. Such bonds *do* pay a rate of interest, but at a lower level than a plain vanilla would pay. In order to compensate investors for this lower rate of interest, they are also issued at a discount to their nominal value – but at a smaller discount than zero coupon bonds would be issued at. Such bonds are usually termed low coupon bonds.

A plain vanilla bond is usually issued by a company at its €100 nominal value, with a coupon rate that reflects the current market interest rate at the time of issue. Subsequent changes in the market interest rate then cause the market value of the plain vanilla bond to rise above or fall below its nominal value of €100. An investor who buys a plain vanilla bond at its time of issue (and so pays €100 for it) and who then holds it until maturity when the €100 is repaid, receives an annual rate of return equal to the coupon rate. Thus the return received is purely in terms of the interest payments.

On the other hand, as we have just seen in Example 8, an investor in a discount bond receives no interest, but derives a return in the form of a capital gain.

Low coupon bonds fall somewhere between these two extremes where an investor who buys a bond at the point of issue will get part of their return in the form of interest payments and part of their return in the form of a capital gain on redemption. Example 9 illustrates this case.

EXAMPLE 9

Kapinski Holidays is based in Zurich. The company wants to raise a SFr100 million 5-year loan at a coupon rate of 3%. The current annual rate of return on similar risk securities is 8%. The company will therefore have to issue the bonds at a 20% discount on their nominal value in order to give investors (approximately) their required rate of return: At a 20% discount, each SFr100 nominal bond will be issued at SFr80. (And so the company will have to issue bonds with a total nominal value of SFr100 million $\times$ 100/80 = SFr125 million in order to raise the SFr100 million required.)

Therefore the yield to maturity can be found from the IRR of the bond's cash flow:

Year	0	1 to 5	5
	+ SFr80	− SFr3	− SFr100

$$\text{NPV at } 6\% = -\text{SFr7.37}$$

$$\text{NPV at } 10\% = +\text{SFr6.54}$$

Using linear interpolation:

$$\text{IRR} = 6\% \left(\frac{-7.37}{-7.37 - 6.54} \times (10\% - 6\%) \right) = 8.1\%$$

Thus when priced at SFr80 and with a 3% coupon rate, these bonds will give a rate of return or redemption yield of approximately 8.1%, which is similar to the yield on securities with the same level of risk.

The impact of corporation tax

The company requires knowledge of its cost of debt capital for investment appraisal purposes and so, from this viewpoint, the expected return which the supplier of debt capital receives – the redemption yield – is *not* the main focus of attention. The point of importance is the cash flow that *the company* must pay out in order to service the debt.

In this respect, taxation has an important effect when the country's tax regime (as most tax regimes usually do), allows companies to offset debt interest (but not capital redemption payments) against their corporation tax liability. Therefore, as far as company investment appraisal is concerned, it is the *after* corporation tax receipt cost of debt capital which is important.

So far, we have ignored taxation in the calculation of K_D, and so we have, in effect, been calculating a *before-tax* cost of debt capital: K_D. If T represents the current rate of corporation tax – and assuming it is expected to remain a constant over the life of the debt – then the after-tax cost of *irredeemable* bonds can be found as:

$$K_{D_{AT}} = \frac{i(1 - T)}{P_B} \text{ or } K_{D_{AT}} = K_{D_{BT}}(1 - T)$$

For *redeemable* bonds, their after-tax cost can be found by solving the IRR of the following cash flow:

$$P_B = i(1 - T) \times A_{N, Kd} - R(1 + K_D)^{-N} = 0 \text{ NPV}$$

where *n* equals the number of years to redemption and *R* represents the redemption value of the bonds. Example 10 illustrates the calculations required.

EXAMPLE 10

(a) Klodawa Tecnik operates in the German telecoms market. The company issued 25 million of 8% *irredeemable* bonds some years ago. Their current market price is $106.50 ex interest. Corporation tax in Germany is charged at 19%. Therefore the Klodawa's after-tax cost of debt capital is:

$$K_D = \frac{€8 \times (1 - 0.19)}{€106.50} = 0.061 \text{ or } 6.1\%$$

The total market value of the bonds is:

$$V_B = €25m \times \frac{€106.50}{€100} = €26\,625\,000$$

(b) Dansk Jet is a Danish aeronautical engineering company. It has issued 50 million Danish krone of 9% 1000kr bonds. They are due to be *redeemed* in 4-years' time at par. Their current market value is 1040kr ex interest. Corporation tax in Denmark is charged at 25%. The company's current cost of debt capital is found by solving the IRR of the following cash flow:

$$+1040 - [90 \times (1 - 0.25) \times A_{4, Kd}] - 1000 \times (1 + K_D)^{-4} = 0 \text{ NPV}$$

At 4%, the cash flow's NPV is: −64.48 NPV
At 10%, the cash flow's NPV is: +143.03 NPV.
Using linear interpolation, the after-tax cost of debt capital can be estimated as:

$$K_D = 4\% + \left[\frac{-64.48}{-64.48 - (+143.03)} \times (10\% - 4\%) \right] = 0.0586 \text{ or } 5.86\%$$

▶

▶

And the total market value of the company's bonds would be:

$$V_B = 50\text{m kr} \times \frac{1040 \text{ kr}}{1000 \text{ kr}} = 52\,000\,000 \text{ kr}$$

The reasons why this adjustment to take account of tax must be made can be easily demonstrated. If a company issues €100 bonds with a 10% coupon rate and pays corporation tax at 20%, then the company does not actually pay €10 interest per bond per year (although the bond holder actually receives €10 of interest per year). As interest is allowable against corporation tax, the company only pays €10 $(1 - 0.25) = $ €7.50. The balance of interest of €2.50 can be viewed as being paid by the tax authorities (through a reduced corporate tax liability). This obviously causes the effective cost of debt (to the company) to fall substantially below the before-tax rate that the lender receives.

Unquoted debt

So far, we have only considered debt capital that has been quoted on a stock exchange (referred to as a 'public' issue of debt) and so has a market price. However, most debt capital – such as bank loans – is unquoted (or termed a 'private' issue). It is possible to *estimate* the cost of unquoted debt, but only if the cost of similar-risk quoted debt is known. We cannot obtain the cost of unquoted debt directly because – as we have seen in the previous examples – in order to find a cost of debt we need a market value. However, if we have some similar-risk quoted debt, its cost can be used as an estimate of the unquoted debt's cost, on the basis that similar risk securities should yield the same return. Example 11 illustrates this situation.

EXAMPLE 11

Auto Technology is a US company. It has issued $12 million of 8% $100 bonds which are redeemable at par in 3-years' time. Each bond currently has a market price of $92 ex interest. In addition the company has a $6 million 3-year bank loan fixed at 10% interest.

As both the quoted and unquoted debt (i.e. the bank loan) of Auto Technology rank equally for payment purposes, they can be assumed to be of similar risk. The company's tax rate is 33%.

The after-tax cost of the quoted debt capital (i.e. the bonds) is given by the IRR of its cash flow:

Year	0	1 to 3	3
	+$92	$8(1 − 0.33)	−$100

NPV at 4% = − $11:77
NPV at 10% = + $3.54

▶

Interpolating:

$$IRR = 4\% + \left[\frac{-11.77}{-11.77 - (+3.54)} \times (10\% - 4\%) \right] = 0.086 \text{ or } 8.6\%$$

Therefore the after-tax cost of debt capital of the quoted bonds of Auto Technology is: $K_{DQ} = 8.6\%$ and their total market value is: $V_{BQ} = \$12$ million $\times 0.92 = \$11.04$ million. As the *unquoted* bank loan is thought to be of similar risk, then the after-tax cost of the company's unquoted debt (10% bank loan) is also:

$$K_{DUQ} = K_{DQ} = 8.6\%$$

Floating rate debt

Up to this point, all our examples have involved debt capital which paid a fixed rate of interest. However, a great deal of debt capital raised by companies pays a rate of interest that is not *fixed*, but which *varies* with movements in current market interest rates.

This type of debt capital is known as *floating* or *variable rate* debt. Typically, the debt will pay interest at a fixed 'margin' (or 'spread') over a floating benchmark or reference interest rate.

The terms 'benchmark' and 'reference' interest rate are used to describe a widely recognized rate of interest which varies over time in response to supply and demand market pressures and other macroeconomic forces. Two well-known benchmark interest rates are the 'interbank' rates and the central bank 'prime' or 'base' rates. Examples of interbank rates would be Euribor (the Euro Interbank Offered Rate), and LIBOR (the London InterBank Offered Rate). But such benchmark rates exist in most financial centres, such as SIBOR (the Saudi Interbank Offered Rate), and JIBAR (the Johannesburg Interbank Agreed Rate). These interbank rates represent the rate of interest at which banks lend between themselves. Bank prime and base rates – such as the South African SARB, the eurozone ECB re-financing rate and the British BoE rate – represent the minimum rate of interest at which a country's central bank will lend money to their country's commercial banks.

If a company raises a loan at 'SIBOR +3%', the company will be paying a rate of interest on its loan equal to whatever rate SIBOR is, plus an extra 3%. (This 3% is the fixed margin or spread.) And so, if SIBOR is 6%, the company pays 9% interest on its loan; if SIBOR falls to 5%, the company's loan interest rate will fall to 8%.

How often a company's loan interest rate is altered in this way is known as the 'rollover' period. Interbank rates are continually changing (usually only by very small amounts), and it would cause obvious administrative problems if a company's loan interest rate moved continually as well. Therefore, to avoid this problem, loans with floating rates of interest have their interest rate re-set periodically. In practice, one of the most common rollover periods is 3 months. If we take our example of a loan at SIBOR +3% with a 3-month rollover, this means that every 3 months the interest rate that the company will pay on its loan over the following 3 months is re-set.

Suppose the company has interest rollover dates of 1 January, 1 April, 1 July and 1 October each year. If on 1 January SIBOR is 6%, the company pays 9% (6% + 3%) interest on its loan over the next 3 months. If by 1 April SIBOR has now risen to 7.5%, the company will then pay 10.5% interest on its loan over the next 3-month time period, and so on.

However, notice that these interest rates in this example would be annual rates of interest. Thus the actual rate of interest paid over the 3 months 1 January–1 April would have been: 9% × 3/12 = 2.25%. Similarly, in the next 3-month period, they would pay 10.5% × 3/12 = 2.625%.

As far as calculating the after-tax cost of debt capital is concerned, floating rate debt causes very little problem. In such circumstances K_D is simply the current interest rate that is payable on the debt and the total market value of the debt will always be equal to its total nominal value. This is because, as we have already noted, what causes the market price of fixed interest debt to move is changes in the difference between the fixed coupon rate on the debt and the current market interest rate. With floating rate debt this situation does not occur because the interest rate paid moves in line with market interest rates. Hence the market value and the nominal value of floating rate debt will always be the same. Example 12 illustrates the situation with the most common type of floating rate debt, a bank loan.

EXAMPLE 12

České Podia a.s. is based in the Czech Republic. It has a Kč50 million (50 million koruna) bank loan, repayable in 7-years' time. The interest rate payable is 2% over bank base rate. The Czech corporation tax rate is 19%. The Czech bank base rate is currently 8%. The company wishes to calculate its after-tax cost of the bank loan. This can be done as follows:

The company currently pays an interest rate of:

$$8\% + 2\% = 10\%$$

therefore:

$$K_D = 10\% \times (1 - 0.19) = 8.1\%$$

The 'market value' of the bank loan is equal to its nominal value of Kč50 million.

CONVERTIBLE DEBT

Convertible debt is a really interesting type of long-term capital because it is a 'hybrid' – it is part debt capital and part equity capital. Another way of viewing it would be as deferred equity capital.

Typically, convertible debt capital is similar to fixed interest redeemable debt capital, with one important exception. This is that, at the redemption date, the holders have an *option*: they can either have the loan repaid (usually at its nominal/par value), or they can convert the debt's redemption value into the company's shares, at a fixed price per share.

Therefore convertible debt is debt capital with a call option attached in respect of the company's shares. It is the presence of this option that makes valuing convertible debt, and calculating its cost, a difficult area.

Some definitions

Let us begin with some definitions. Suppose that Cyber Sovereign – a UK company – has issued £50 million worth of £100 convertible bonds paying a fixed rate of interest (coupon) of 5% and which are redeemable at par in 4-years' time, or convertible into 25 shares. Cyber Sovereign's shares are currently priced at £2.50 each.

The 'conversion' ratio is the number of shares into which each £100 unit of debt can be converted. Therefore, in this example, the conversion ratio is 25, i.e. each £100 bond can be converted into 25 shares. The conversion price is effectively the exercise price of the option. In this case as each £100 bond can be converted into 25 shares, this gives a conversion price or exercise price of: £100 ÷ 25 = £4 per share.

The 'conversion premium' is the percentage by which the conversion price exceeds the current share price. Therefore, in our example, the conversion premium is:

$$\frac{400p - 250p}{250p} = 0.60 \text{ or } 60\%$$

Advantages of convertibles

Convertibles can be attractive securities, both from the viewpoint of the company and for the investor. As we saw with low coupon bonds, investors are willing to accept a lower rate of interest as long as it is compensated with the possibility of a capital gain. With low coupon bonds, the capital gain element was provided by the company selling the bonds at a discount to their nominal value.

The investor also has the potential to make a capital gain with convertible debt out of the option element. If, at the time of conversion, the market price of the company's shares is *above* the conversion price, the investor will be able to make a capital gain upon exercising the option to convert. Therefore, just as with low coupon bonds, the investor is willing to accept a lower than normal interest rate on convertible debt because they offer this prospect of a compensating capital gain in the future. Thus the potential saving in interest costs makes them attractive securities from the company's viewpoint – and, as we have discussed in Chapter 13, options can be highly desirable from an investor's viewpoint.

There is of course a further advantage to convertible debt from a company's point of view. A normal (or 'straight') issue of debt usually has to be repaid at some future point in time, with the consequent negative impact on the company's cash resources. In contrast, with luck, convertible debt will not have to be repaid, because investors will convert into shares instead.

The downside to this advantage, of course, is that if investors do convert into shares in the future, then that may lead to a reduction, (i.e. dilution), in the company's earnings per share at that time.

Cost of convertible debt

Let us now turn to the question of the valuation of convertible debt and its cost of capital. As was stated previously, convertible debt can be viewed as a combination of a plain vanilla bond plus a call option in the company's shares. As such, it would appear relatively simple to value each of these components individually and then combine them to find the value of the convertible.

Finding the value of the bond element is straightforward: it is simply the sum of the future expected cash flows discounted to present value at a rate that reflects its risk. The real problem lies in the valuation of the option element.

The Black and Scholes valuation model can only be of partial help, for two reasons. One is that the Black and Scholes model assumes that the company's shares do not pay out any dividends, when in reality they will do. The other is that convertible debt normally is 'callable' by the company.

What this means can be seen if we return to our earlier example of Cyber Sovereign's convertible debt with an option to convert or redeem in 4-years' time. Usually, the company will give itself the right to force investors to convert earlier than 4-years' time if it wishes. This is what is meant by the term 'callable'.

An investor who buys convertible debt is buying a straight bond plus a call option on the company's share and simultaneously *selling* a call option to the company. The arithmetic of even a simplified example is really too complex for us to investigate within the context of this book. However, what we can do is look at what would be the *minimum* value of a convertible bond. This minimum value must be the greater of its value as straight debt and its current conversion value. Example 13 illustrates this situation. It is important to realize that the bond's actual value will always be greater than this minimum value, in much the same way that we saw that the actual value of an option is always greater than its intrinsic value (except on expiry).

EXAMPLE 13

Claas Media GmbH has issued some convertible bonds with a coupon rate of 6%. Each bond has a €100 nominal value and is redeemable at par in 3-years' time or convertible into 40 shares. The company's current share price is €2.10 and similar-risk debt securities are expected to produce a 14% redemption yield. We want to place a *minimum* value on these convertible bonds.

The value of the bond as straight debt can be found from the sum of the future interest and redemption cash flows, discounted to present value at 14%:

$$\text{Value of the bond: } [\text{€6} \times A_{3\ 14\%}] + [\text{€100} \times 1.14^{-3}] = \text{€81.43}$$

The current *conversion value* of the bond, given its conversion ratio of 40, is:

$$\text{Conversion value: } 40 \times \text{€2.10} = \text{€84}$$

Therefore the convertible bond's *minimum* value will be the *higher* of these two values – its value as a straight bond and its value converted into the company's shares: €84.

Finally, we will conclude with a simple example of how we might attempt to identify the after-tax cost of convertible debt. This is shown in Example 14. You will quickly notice that the validity of the calculation rests entirely on the assumption that the firm is able to estimate the worth of the shares at the future redemption/conversion date.

EXAMPLE 14

Crédit Générale SA has issued €50 million of 6% bonds which are either repayable at par in 3-years' time, or convertible into shares at €2.50 each. The bonds are currently priced at €102.97 ex interest.

▶

The company's shares have a market price of €2.20 *ex div*, this year's dividend of 10 cents having just been paid. Dividends are expected to grow in the future at 10% per year. Corporation tax in France is at 33%.

In order to find the after-tax cost of capital of these convertible bonds, the first thing to do is to determine whether bond holders are likely to redeem or convert their bonds in 3-years' time. In order to do this we have to estimate what will be the worth of the company's shares in 3-years' time.

Crédit Générale's cost of equity capital can be found by using the dividend growth model:

$$K_E = \frac{10c \times (1 + 0.10)}{220c} + 0.10 = 0.15 \text{ or } 15\%$$

If dividends are to grow at 10% per year, then the dividend in 3-years' time will be:

$$10c \times (1 + 0.10) = 13.31c$$

And so the estimated market price of the shares in 3-years' time can be found from a further application of the dividend valuation model:

$$P_{E,t3} = \frac{13.31c \times (1 + 0.10)}{0.15 - 0.10} = 293 \text{ cents (approx) or } €2.93$$

As the conversion price of the shares is €2.50 and the estimated value of the shares at the time of conversion is €2.93, it will be worthwhile for bond holders to convert: the share price (€2.93) is expected to be *above* the call option exercise price (€2.50).

At a conversion price of €2.50, the conversion ratio is:

$$€100 \div €2.50 = 40$$

and so the shares are expected to be worth:

$$40 \times €2.93 = €117.20$$

which, of course, is greater than the bond's redemption value of €100.

Finally, the after-tax cost of the convertible bonds can be estimated from the IRR of the bond's cash flow:

Year	0	1 to 3	3
	+€102.97	−€6(1 − 0.33)	− €117.20

NPV at 4% discount rate: −€12.31

NPV at 16% discount rate: +€18.90

Interpolating:

$$\text{IRR} = 4\% + \left(\frac{-12.31}{-12.31 - (+18.90)} \times (16\% - 4\%) \right) = 8.73\%$$

Therefore the after-tax cost of Crédit Générale's convertible bonds is estimated to be 8.73%.

Implicit and explicit costs of debt capital

As a final point, it is important to remember that financial decisions are principally made on behalf of and for the benefit of the shareholders, the legal owners of a company. As far as debt holders are concerned, management's only wish is to fulfil their contractual obligations to them in terms of interest and redemption payments.

In this respect, in this chapter we have only considered the *explicit* cost of debt capital, but there is also an *implicit* cost that company managements must take into account. This implicit cost of debt arises from risk considerations that directly affect the ordinary shareholders. We shall examine this aspect in detail later, in Chapter 18 on capital structure, but it is as well to be aware at this stage that debt capital does have a cost that is additional to its explicit cost, which is what we have been calculating.

SUMMARY

This chapter has examined the costs of equity and debt capital. The main points covered were:

- The dividend valuation model states that the share price is equal to the present value sum of the future expected dividends, discounted to present value.

- The discount rate in such an analysis reflects the current rate of return on similar systematic risk investments. This rate of return is known as the cost of equity capital and represents the opportunity cost, to management, of using shareholders' funds to undertake capital investment projects.

- Normally two, alternative, simplifying assumptions are used about the future flow of dividends represented in the model: either dividends per share are assumed to remain at a constant level in the future, or they are expected to grow at a constant annual rate.

- Assuming dividend growth, the growth rate can either be estimated on the basis of the past rate of growth of dividends; or by using the Gordon approach. This states that the dividend growth rate – under certain assumptions – is the product of the earnings retention rate and the company's return on capital.

- A company's cost of equity capital can also be estimated using the capital asset pricing model. However, there are a number of significant differences between the two models, which cannot be expected to produce similar estimates.

- In a similar way to shares, debt capital is also valued on the present value sum of the future expected interest and redemption cash flow.

- The discount rate in such an analysis reflects the current rate of return on similar risk investments. As such, it again represents the opportunity cost, to management, of using debt capital to finance projects.

- In other words, if managers wish to maximize shareholder wealth they should not invest debt capital to earn a lower rate of return than could be earned elsewhere in the capital market from a similar risk investment.

- Debt capital is issued by companies in many different forms. It may be issued privately or through a public issue. It may be at a fixed or floating rate of interest. With fixed interest debt, there are again many possible variations from 'plain vanilla' bonds to 'zero coupon' bonds.

- Finally there is convertible debt, which can be seen as a hybrid: part equity and part debt. From a cost of capital point of view, this type of capital poses particular problems because of the option element that it contains.

NOTES

1. The exception to this was our discussion as to how our DCF appraisal techniques coped with the problem of capital rationing.
2. Another source is lease finance. This will be explicitly considered at a later stage.
3. Except under very exceptional circumstances, such as liquidation.
4. This is assuming that the rate of discount remains a constant at 9% in perpetuity. Alternatively, we could view the 9% as the *average* rate of discount over this time period.
5. Or, if not all, at least a sufficient number to move the market price.
6. It should be pointed out that the dividend valuation model does not, itself, make any distinction between systematic and unsystematic risk. However, from our knowledge of portfolio theory and the CAPM we can infer that the dividend valuation model implies a consideration of systematic rather than total risk.
7. The 'middleman' who makes the market for shares in a stock exchange is called a market-maker. The difference between the bid and offer price represents the market maker's profit: buying shares at the lower price and selling shares at the higher price.
8. For a detailed explanation of immediate annuities, see the Appendix to Chapter 5 on compounding and discounting. Remember that the key characteristic of such annuities is that the first cash flow (i.e. the first dividend) arises in 12-months' time.
9. We have only examined the situation where a single annual dividend is paid. Where, say, dividends are paid twice a year (an interim and a final dividend) there are, in effect, two ex/cum div situations. For example, suppose a 5 cents per share dividend is paid half-yearly on a share with an ex div market value of 100 cents. We cannot say that $K_E = 10/100 = 0.10$ as this only represents the share's nominal annual return. The effective annual return would be given by:

$$5c \div 100c = 5\% \text{ per half-year}$$
$$K_E = (1 + 0.05)^2 - 1 = 0.1025 \text{ or } 10.25\% \text{ per year.}$$

10. This assumption could be relaxed so that dividends through time, on average, are assumed to be a constant, but to do so can lead to problems, where the discount rate changes over time.
11. Obviously the model can also be presented in terms of total market values: $V_E = D_1/(K_E - g)$.
12. Obviously Gordon's variant of the dividend growth model is very simplistic, but it may well be a self-fulfilling predictor of share market values if investors generally believe that g can be estimated as rb and so partly base their market actions on such calculations.
13. We have left the Year 0 dividend out of the calculation at this stage because we want the current *ex div* share price. The current *cum div* share price would be: 59.7c + 5c = 64.7 cents.
14. Incidentally, the problem of whether or not the model is 'complete' is only one that affects normative models. This is never a problem of positive models. The DVM is not saying what actually determines K_E. All it is saying is that given P_E, d_0 and g, then it follows that the return on the share is K_E.
15. Dimson *et al.* 2003 provide a useful survey of the levels of market risk premium that demonstrates how this has varied over a number of years.
16. The reader should remember that in analyzing the cost of equity capital we have covered the 'cost' both of directly raised equity capital and the 'cost' of retained earnings.
17. Irredeemable or *undated* debt capital does exist, where the loan is never repaid (except in liquidation), but is uncommon.
18. Just like shares, loans are not homogeneous in terms of risk. The riskiness of any particular loan depends upon a number of factors including the riskiness of the company raising the loan, the security (if any) attached to the loan and how it ranks for payment with other debt capital issued by the company.
19. The term 'coupon' rate is used because on some older bonds there used to be a strip of perforated coupons. Each year the bond holder detached one of the coupons and sent it into the company in order to claim the interest payment.
20. Debt market values follow a dog's-tooth pattern similar to those of equity market values. Just as we only dealt with ex div equity market values – adjusting a cum div value if necessary to an equivalent ex div basis – so similarly the debt valuation model only deals with ex interest bond values.

21. However, the amount of risk involved may be very small.
22. It is worthwhile noting that if redeemable bonds have an ex interest market price of €100 and they are redeemable at par value, then their cost of debt capital does equal their coupon rate.
23. Notice that when calculating the IRR we obtained a negative NPV at the low discount rate and a positive NPV at the higher discount rate. This is the opposite of our previous experience with project IRRs. This is because the cash flow – an inflow followed by a series of outflows – is the opposite of a normal project's cash flow.

FURTHER READING

1. The two most interesting original articles on the cost of capital are: D. Durand, 'Growth Stocks and the St. Petersburg Paradox', *Journal of Finance,* September 1957 and M.J. Gordon, 'Dividends, Earnings and Stock Prices', *Review of Economics and Statistics,* May 1959.

2. Some other contributions of interest are: M.J. Gordon and L.I. Gould, 'The Cost of Equity Capital: A Reconsideration', *Journal of Finance,* June 1978; A. Chen, 'Recent Developments in the Cost of Debt Capital', *Journal of Finance,* June 1978; R.S. Pindyck, 'Risk Inflation and the Stock Market', *American Economic Review,* June 1984.

3. For some practical attempts to measure cost of capital, see: L.J. Gitman and V.A. Mercurio, 'Cost of Capital Techniques Used by Major US Firms', *Financial Management,* Winter 1982; J.J. Siegal, 'The Application of the DCF Methodology for Determining the Cost of Equity Capital', *Financial Management,* Spring 1985; R. Harris, 'Using Analysts' Forecasts to Estimate Shareholders' Required Returns', *Financial Management,* Spring 1986; and D.F. Scott and J.W. Petty, 'Determining the Cost of Common Equity Capital: The Direct Method', *Journal of Business Research,* March 1980; E. Dimson, P. Marsh and M. Staunton, 'Global Evidence on the Equity Risk Premium', *Journal of Applied Corporate Finance,* (4) 2003 provide an excellent survey of the market risk premium over a significant period of time; E. Fama and K. French, 'The Equity Premium', *Journal of Finance,* April 2002 look at potential returns. R. Mehra and E. Prescott, 'The Equity Premium: What We Have Learned in 20 Years' in R. Mehra (ed), *Handbook of Investments: Equity Risk Premium,* Elsevier 2006 provides an overview of the risk premium issue; M.R. King, 'The Cost of Equity for Global Banks: A CAPM Perspective From 1990 to 2009', *BIS Quarterly Review,* September 2009.

QUIZ QUESTIONS

1 Given the following information, estimate the company's cost of equity capital:

$$P_E = \text{€1.47 cum div dividend share record} \qquad t_{-3} \quad 11.25c$$
$$d_0 = \text{13 cents} \qquad\qquad\qquad\qquad\qquad\qquad t_{-2} \quad 12c$$
$$\qquad\qquad\qquad\qquad\qquad\qquad\qquad\qquad\qquad\qquad t_{-1} \quad 12.5c$$
$$\qquad\qquad\qquad\qquad\qquad\qquad\qquad\qquad\qquad\qquad t_{-0} \quad 13c$$

2 What are the assumptions behind the $g = rb$ model?

3 Estimate the company's after-tax cost of debt capital and the total market value of the debt capital ex interest:

€12 million 15% €100 bonds. Redeemable in 4 years at €110 per cent. Current market price is €128 cum interest. Corporation tax is at 33%.

4 If a company had issued £10 million of 12% unquoted debt, redeemable in 3 years at par and similar in risk to those in question 3, what is the total market worth of the debt issue?

5   What is the after-tax cost of debt capital of an issue of 18% bonds which is redeemable at par in 7-years' time and whose current market price is €118 cum interest? Corporation tax is charged at 20%.

6   A company has issued R50 million of zero coupon bonds, due for repayment in 3-years' time at par. Their current market price is R87. What is the company's cost of debt capital?

7   Define the following:
   (a)   plain vanilla bonds
   (b)   discount bonds
   (c)   conversion ratio
   (d)   conversion price
   (e)   conversion premium.

8   What are the advantages of convertible debt?

9   A company has issued €25 million of 5% convertible bonds, redeemable in 4-years' time or convertible into 50 shares. The current price of the bonds is €88 ex interest and the current market price of the company's shares is €1.65 ex div. If the share price is expected to rise by 8% per year in future, calculate the after-tax cost of the convertibles. The corporation tax rate is 20%.

10   What is the minimum value of a convertible?
   (See the 'Answers to the Quiz Questions' section at the back of the book.)

PROBLEMS

The answers to two of the following problems (those indicated by an asterisk) are available to students online. The answer to the remaining problem is available only to lecturers (see the 'Digital Resources' page for details).

1*   Hääl Grupp is a successful food retailing company, based in Estonia, and quoted on the Tallinn stock exchange. Over the last 5 years it has increased its share of the Estonian retail food market by 30%. Hääl has a current share price of €9.94 per share. The company's recent dividend record is shown below:

	t_{-4}	t_{-3}	t_{-2}	t_{-1}	Current year
Dividend per share (cents)	4.86	5.86	7.5	9.0	11.0

Required:

(a)   Estimate the cost of equity capital for the Hääl Grupp using:

   (i)   dividend growth model

   (ii)   capital asset pricing model (you should assume a risk-free rate of interest of 14%, a beta of 0.8 and a market return of 8%).

(b)   Discuss whether the assumptions underlying the models used in part (a) are realistic and explain how the effects of using these assumptions are reflected in the results obtained.

(c)   Explain why managers need to know the cost of the equity capital of their companies.

▶

2*   You work for a French aeronautical company – Sanofi-Rhŏne SA. A work colleague has recently been moved to another company. Your CEO has asked you to take over from your colleague and to provide urgently needed estimates of the discount rate to be used in appraising a large new capital investment. You have been given your colleague's working notes, which you believe to be numerically accurate.

Working notes estimates for the next 5 years (annual averages)

Stock market total return on equity	16%
Sanofi-Rhŏne dividend yield	7%
Sanofi-Rhŏne share price rise	14%
Standard deviation of total stock market return on equity	10%
Standard deviation of Sanofi-Rhŏne's total return on equity	20%
Correlation coefficient between Sanofi-Rhŏne return on equity and total stock market return on equity	+0.7
Correlation coefficient between total return on the new capital investment and total market return on equity	+0.5
Growth rate of Sanofi-Rhŏne earnings	12%
Growth rate of Sanofi-Rhŏne dividends	11%
Growth rate of Sanofi-Rhŏne sales	13%
Government bond yield	12%

The after-tax earnings available to the company's shareholders in the most recent year were €5 400 000, of which €2 140 000 was distributed as dividends. The company has 10 million shares in issue, which are currently trading on the stock exchange at €3.21. The company pays corporation tax in France is at 33%.

Required:

(a) Estimate Sanofi-Rhŏne's cost of equity capital using:

   (i)   the dividend valuation model

   (ii) the capital asset pricing model.

(b) Why might you not expect these two models to produce similar values for the cost of equity capital?

3   Bolar plc is quoted on the London stock exchange. It currently has three types of marketable debt in its capital structure.

   (a) Unsecured 14% £100 bonds with a redemption date of 30 June in 3.5-years' time. Interest is payable annually on 31 December. Their current market price is £95 ex interest per bond.

   (b) Secured 10% debentures, redeemable by the company on 31 December in 3 to 5-years' time. Interest of £5 per debenture is payable every 6 months on 30 June and 31 December each year. Their current market price is £91.50 ex interest.

   (c) Unsecured 8% convertible debentures. These are convertible in 2-years' time into 40 shares, or in 4-years' time into 30 shares. If not converted, the debentures will be redeemable in 10-years' time. Interest is payable annually on 1 January and the current market price is £93 cum interest.

All the debt has a unit par value of £100. All of Bolar's marketable debt is redeemable at its par value. Assume that it is now 31 December. Ignore tax.

▶

Required:

(a) Calculate the annual redemption yields for each of the three types of debt. For the convertible debenture estimate the annual yield if the company's share price, currently 190 pence, increases by:

   (i)   5% per year

   (ii) 10% per year.

   Assume that, if conversion occurs, the shares would immediately be sold, and that the ex-interest value of convertible debentures is expected to be £88.50 in 2-years' time and £92 in 4-years' time.

(b) Explain briefly why the redemption yields in your answer to (a) above differ.

WEIGHTED AVERAGE COST OF CAPITAL

The purpose of this chapter is to:

- Introduce an initial discussion about a company's capital structure.
- Develop the 'pool of funds' concept.
- Outline the calculation of the weighted average cost of capital for a company.
- Explore the assumptions behind the use of the weighted average cost of capital as a discount rate in investment appraisal.

THE PROJECT DISCOUNT RATE

At the outset of Chapter 16 it was stated that – apart from other uses principally concerned with the capital structure decision – the cost of capital analysis could possibly provide another way (as an alternative to the CAPM) of identifying a discount rate/cut-off rate for DCF investment appraisal techniques. It is this that we now examine in detail.

The capital structures of commercial companies can be separated into two types. Companies can have either a capital structure which consists *entirely* of equity capital, or they can have a *mixed* capital structure, where debt capital and equity capital are held in varying proportions. Of these, the mixed capital structure is the more common in practice (especially amongst stock exchange quoted companies) but the equity financed company provides us with a much less complex situation, and so initially we shall examine the question of the investment appraisal discount rate in terms of an all-equity financed company.

All-equity financed companies

Suppose that a company has an all-equity capital structure and intends to remain as such (at least up to the horizon of its current planning). Under a number of limiting assumptions, we can state that its current cost of equity capital could properly be used as the discount rate for investment appraisal.

This rate, the expected return required by the ordinary shareholders, could be used because it represents the minimum acceptable return for a project undertaken by the company, in opportunity cost terms. The cost of equity capital represents the opportunity cost of the shareholders' capital, in that it reflects the return that they could earn elsewhere (for a similar level of risk). Therefore their capital should be applied to a particular capital investment project undertaken by the company's management, only if it is expected to yield this return, as a minimum.

This condition applies whether the project is being financed by a new equity issue (ignoring any issue costs), or by funds from an equity issue made in the past, or by using retained net earnings. In all cases, the investment capital being used represents shareholders' funds, and the company should only use such funds if each project to which they are applied is expected to earn at least this minimum return. Use of the NPV decision rule, with the cost of equity capital as the discount rate, will ensure that this is the case.

Two limiting assumptions

There are two important limiting assumptions to this advice. The first is that the company is assumed to be evaluating projects which, if they were accepted, would not cause any significant change in the company's overall level of risk. That is, the acceptance of the project would not cause investors generally to view the company's expected future cash flows as having changed in their level of uncertainty. The reason for this assumption is obvious. The market-derived cost of equity capital is the required return relevant only to the company's *existing* level of risk and so would be an inappropriate rate to apply to a project that had a *different* level of risk.

The second limiting assumption is that the project being appraised is small, relative to the overall size of the company – i.e. the project represents a 'marginal' investment. The reason for this assumption is as follows. The company's cost of equity capital is a *marginal* cost; it refers to the minimum expected return required from a relatively small (i.e. marginal) investment in the shares of the company. This is so because the current share price that is used in the cost of equity calculation is the price at which a relatively small quantity of the company's shares can be currently bought or sold – if a large quantity of shares were involved, then a separate price would have to be negotiated. Therefore, the cost of equity capital is only appropriate for the evaluation of a project which represents a marginal change in the company's total investment.

If either of these assumptions is violated, then the company's cost of equity capital will not necessarily provide an appropriate rate of discount for project investment appraisal. Of the two, it is the first which is the most important and which is likely to cause the most problems in practice: projects will often have a level of risk which is *not* the same as the company's current average risk level.

Mixed capital structure companies

Where a company's capital structure is composed of both debt and equity capital, with their differing opportunity costs, what discount rate should be used for investment appraisal purposes? The short answer to this question, which we shall expand upon and attempt to justify, is that a *weighted average* of the costs of all the individual components of the capital structure should be used: the company's weighted average cost of capital.

On the surface this can appear to be strange advice. Assume a company possesses a capital structure of which (measured in current stock market values) half is equity with a cost of (say) 20% and half is debt with a cost of (say) 10%. Using the proportion of each type of capital in the overall structure as the weights, we find that the company's weighted average cost of capital (which we shall call K_0) is given by:

$$(0.50 \times 20\%) + (0.50 \times 10\%) = 15\%$$

Now, suppose an investment project is identified by the company – called Project Alpha – which requires a cash outlay of €1 million and the company proposes to raise the capital through a *bond* issue at the current market rate of interest of 10%. The cost – in the everyday sense of the word – of the capital put into the project would be 10%, and so it would appear logical to use this as the NPV discount rate: if the project yields a return greater than 10% (i.e. it has a positive NPV at a 10% discount rate), the company must find the project beneficial.

In contrast to this, we have stated that the company's weighted average cost or capital should be the discount rate used for project evaluation: 15%.[1] But why should the company require a minimum return of 15%, when it appears that the project would be worthwhile as long as it yields a return in excess of 10%?

For instance, if the project were found to have a yield (i.e. an IRR) of 14%, evaluating it using K_0 (of 15%) as the discount rate would lead to its rejection, on the grounds of having a negative NPV, even though it appears to produce a return 4% above its cost. To use K_0 as the discount rate appears to be nonsensical.

For another view of things suppose the same company later has another investment opportunity – called Project Beta – which it is proposed to finance through an issue of *equity* capital (whose cost is 20%). If the project yields a return of 17% (say), it would have a positive NPV when discounted by a 15% K_0 and so would be accepted. Once again, the use of K_0 appears to lead to a nonsensical decision: acceptance of a project which does not generate sufficient return to cover the cost (20%) of the capital outlay required.

A constant capital structure

What lies behind the advice that the company's weighted average cost of capital (WACC) should be used as the NPV discount rate (or as the minimum required IRR), rather than the cost of the *specific type* of capital that is being used to finance the project? The fundamental reason is that it is assumed that the company intends to maintain its existing capital structure of debt and equity capital. (Just why a company should wish to do so will be dealt with in the following chapter on the capital structure decision. However, for the moment, let us accept that management have judged that the company's existing capital structure is somehow ideal and so wish to retain it.)

This implies that how any individual project is financed is purely a function of chance circumstances. Sometimes it may be more convenient for a company to raise debt, sometimes equity. However, using our example above, if the company intends to maintain its existing 50:50 debt–equity mix in the medium to longer term (although it may fluctuate a little in the short term as first debt is raised and then equity is raised), then the *average cost* of its capital is 15%. It therefore follows that all projects should be evaluated against this average, overall required rate of return.

In the example above, the really nonsensical decision would be for the company to use the cost of the *specific* source of finance as the NPV discount rate. It could then find itself accepting the Project Alpha which gave a 14% return, and then rejecting Project Beta which would have given a 17% return.

Using the company's WACC as the NPV discount rate avoids the possibility of such an erroneous sequence of decisions: use of the WACC would *reject* the 14% Project Alpha and would *accept* the 17% Project Beta. Given the company's average cost of capital is 15%, this now seems a sensible sequence of decisions.

'Pool of funds' concept

The above line of argument is often referred to as the *'pool of funds'* concept. The argument runs as follows. It is neither practical nor especially sensible to try to identify a particular source of investment cash, physically, with a particular project. Once cash enters a company, it enters the general 'pool' of capital within that company, and it is out of this pool that investment funds are drawn in order to be applied to particular investment projects.

Not unnaturally, the cost involved in using funds out of this pool of capital is the weighted average of all the individual capital inputs. Therefore, on the assumption that a company's capital structure (and hence the make-up of its capital pool) remains stable in the medium to longer term, it is the weighted average of these capital costs that must be the minimum acceptable return for any investment project. Neither the cost of what appears to be the individual source of capital used, nor the K_0 of the short-term capital structure fluctuation, are appropriate for designating a minimum acceptable return in opportunity cost terms.

The arguments for the use of the weighted average cost of capital as the investment appraisal discount rate are not perfect, and they are made under a number of assumptions that may or may not be borne out in practice. We have already noted these when examining the all-equity company case: unchanging capital structure, unchanging company risk, marginal projects. But if we return to the example we used previously, we can see that using K_0 produces the most sensible long-term investment decision advice. As we are assuming that the projects are similarly risky, the first – Project Alpha – (yielding a 14% return) should be rejected as it does not generate the expected return required by the company in the medium to longer term, whereas it is correct to accept the second project – Project Beta – (yielding 17%) because it does meet this requirement.

THE CALCULATION OF K_0

Let us now turn to examine how the WACC is calculated and how a company's capital structure is measured. The two questions are to some extent interlinked, but we shall start with the calculation of K_0.

The formal derivation

A company's WACC is derived in a way that is analogous to other costs of company capital. It is the linchpin of the relationship between the expected *total* future net cash flow of the company (i.e. dividends plus interest cash flows) and the current *total* market value of the company (i.e. debt capital plus equity).

In other words, using as a basis the logic which underpins the dividend valuation model, a company's *total* market value must be based on the sum of the expected future *total* net cash flow, discounted to present value. This cash flow can be split into two separate streams: interest payments (and loan capital repayments) and dividend payments. Assuming that a company has not issued redeemable debt capital, then the WACC could be found by solving the following equation for K_0 (i.e. K_0 is given by the IRR of the cash flow):

$$V_E + V_B - \sum_{t=1}^{\infty} \frac{D_t}{(1 + K_0)^t} - \sum_{t=1}^{\infty} \frac{I_t}{(1 + K_0)^t} = 0$$

where V_E and V_B are the current total market values of equity and bonds (i.e. debt), and D_t and I_t are the total dividend and interest payments made at time t.

If the assumption of only irredeemable debt is joined by an assumption of a constant annual dividend in perpetuity,[2] then the expression for K_0 simplifies as follows:

$$V_E + V_B - \frac{D}{K_0} - \frac{I}{K_0} = 0$$

Multiplying both sides by K_0 and rearranging, gives:

$$V_E K_0 + V_B K_0 - D - I = 0$$
$$K_0(V_E + V_B) = D + I$$
$$K_0 = \frac{D + I}{V_E + V_B}$$

On the basis that, under the cash flow assumptions made, $V_E = D/K_E$ and so $D = V_E \times K_E$ and similarly $I = V_B \times K_B$, and so:

$$K_0 = \frac{(V_E \times K_E) + (V_B \times K_B)}{(V_E + V_B)} \quad \text{or}$$

$$K_0 = K_E \times \left(\frac{V_E}{V_E + V_B} \right) + K_B \times \left(\frac{V_B}{V_E + V_B} \right)$$

From this simplification we can see why the discount rate to be used in project appraisal is the WACC and that the weights to be applied to the individual costs of capital are the market values of each capital source, as a proportion of the company's total market value.

In this derivation of K_0, we have ignored the presence of corporation tax and the fact that the company receives tax relief on its interest payments. If tax is to be included – as indeed it should be given that in an NPV analysis we require the *after-tax* discount rate to be applied to the *after-tax* project cash flows – then the after-tax relief cost of debt capital should be used in the calculation of K_0:

$$K_0 = K_E \times \left(\frac{V_E}{V_E + V_B} \right) + K_{B_{AT}} \times \left(\frac{V_B}{V_E + V_B} \right)$$

The assumptions behind the use of the WACC

Given this formal derivation of the weighted average cost of capital, we can now see that there are in fact four assumptions that have to be complied with if it is to be used as an NPV discount rate.

1. The project should be marginal. That is, the project should be small relative to the size of the firm.
2. The project should be financed in such a way as not to change the company's existing capital structure.
3. The project should have the same degree of systematic risk as the existing average systematic risk level of the company.
4. All cash flows (i.e. dividends, interest and project cash flows) should be level perpetuities.

The first assumption is required because both K_E and K_B represent marginal costs of capital. That is, they represent the return available on relatively small investments in the equity and debt securities of the company. Therefore K_0, in turn, also represents a marginal cost of capital: the overall return on a relatively small investment in the company. It therefore follows that, strictly speaking, the WACC should only be used as an NPV discount rate on projects which are also relatively small.

The second assumption is required because, if the project is financed in such a way that the capital structure of the company is *changed*, then obviously the weights in the WACC calculation will change. This, we would expect, would then lead to a change in the value of K_0.

However, there is also another reason why K_0 might be expected to change if the company's capital structure is changed. It was pointed out in Chapter 16 that a company's debt capital is a less risky investment than a company's equity capital. This is because, legally, a company must pay its debt interest in full before equity dividends can be paid. In bad years, there is a chance that equity holders will miss out on their dividends whilst debt holders will have a legal right to their interest. Should a company be unable to pay interest to its debt holders it will have to come to some sort of arrangement with them or the likelihood is that it will find itself going into liquidation.

Because equity is more risky than debt (for the provider of the funds rather than the company), the expected return on a company's equity capital is greater than is the expected return on its debt. This extra return that equity holders receive is compensation for the risk that arises from being at the back of the payout queue (both in terms of income and in terms of getting back their money should the company be liquidated) and is called the 'financial risk premium'.

Obviously, other things being equal, the more debt interest the company has to pay, the greater is the risk for equity holders that the firm will have insufficient cash flow to pay them their dividend, all the cash flow having gone to paying interest charges. Therefore, the more debt interest the company has to pay out, the greater will be the financial risk premium demanded by equity holders – that is, the greater will be K_E. Therefore, unless projects are financed so as *not to* change the capital structure, K_0 would also be expected to change because of the resulting change in K_E.

In these circumstances the question would then appear to be: which K_0 should be used: the company's *existing* K_0 or the *new* K_0 that applies once the capital structure is changed? The answer, in fact, is that neither would be correct.

Why this is so will be explained more fully in Chapter 21. For now, all we will say is that if the company is thinking of undertaking a project and wants to finance it in such a way that the capital structure will change, then two decisions are involved. The company is making a capital investment decision *and* is also making a capital structure decision. The NPV technique is a capital investment appraisal technique *only*. It cannot cope with a simultaneous capital structure decision as well. Therefore, if we are to use a company's WACC as an NPV discount rate, we need to assume that the capital structure will remain unchanged.

The third assumption is required because – as we know – the NPV discount rate should reflect the systematic risk of the project. The company's WACC is its overall rate of return. Like any other market-derived rate of return it reflects the systematic risk involved – the systematic risk of the overall company. Therefore K_0 would only be a suitable NPV discount rate if the project had a similar level of systematic risk.

Finally, there is the fourth assumption. From the formal derivation of the WACC calculation it can be seen that, strictly speaking, the WACC model is a level perpetuity cash flow model. Therefore the company's K_0, calculated on the basis of that model, should really only be applied to projects which themselves have perpetuity cash flows.

How much of a problem will these assumptions cause in practice? The first and last assumptions will cause little difficulty. Most projects evaluated are relatively small when compared to the size of the company. Even if they were not, the violation of the first assumption is unlikely to lead to a serious distortion of the investment appraisal.

A similar conclusion can be reached over the last of these four assumptions. The fact that the company may have redeemable debt (and so a non-perpetuity dividend flow) is likely to make little difference in practice. The WACC can still be calculated as an average of the costs of equity and debt, weighted by their market value proportions. Similarly, the fact that the project is almost certainly not going to have perpetuity cash flows is unlikely to bias the investment appraisal unduly, when using K_0 as the discount rate.

The second assumption does cause problems. These are normally avoided by accepting that the capital structure may change in the short run, but is likely to be maintained in the medium to long term, and so K_0 should be calculated on the company's longer-run (or target) capital structure. However, if financing the project causes a significant change in capital structure, then an NPV–WACC approach to the investment appraisal is not appropriate. What is an appropriate approach will be discussed in Chapter 21.

That leaves the third assumption about risk. It is here that we run into real difficulties.

THE WACC AND PROJECT RISK

If the company is a single-product company (such as a cement manufacturer), and the project under consideration is a general expansion of its existing business, then it may well be safe to assume that the project does have the same degree of systematic risk as the existing risk of the company. However, if the project represents a move into a new area of business, then the existing WACC would not be an appropriate discount rate to use.

However, very few companies are single-product companies. Most companies are, to some extent, diversified. In such circumstances the company's WACC does not reflect the systematic risk of any *one* particular area of its business. It reflects its average level of systematic risk throughout *all* its areas of business.

Therefore, for a diversified company, its WACC is going to be an unsuitable discount rate for project appraisal purposes. Its WACC is unlikely to reflect the systematic risk of any particular project, except by chance. Example 1 is an illustration of this problem. As can be seen, the company's WACC is estimated to be 17.5% but notice the different ways in which the WACC can be calculated.

EXAMPLE 1

Intesta Lombardo SpA is an Italian company based in Genoa. The company has two main divisions. One operates a chain of supermarkets while the other manufactures office furniture. The company is financed by both debt and equity capital.

The total market value of the company's equity is €30.3 million ex div. The company has recently paid this year's dividend which totalled €4 million. This was in line with the company's policy of increasing dividends by 6% per year. In addition, Intesta Lombardo has issued €12.625 million of 8% €100 irredeemable bonds. They are currently quoted at €80 per cent, ex interest.

The company's equity has a beta value of 1.71 and its debt beta[3] is estimated at 0.29. The supermarket industry has an average beta of 0.80 while office furniture manufacturers have an average beta of 1.92. Intesta's business is divided (approximately) equally between its two divisions.

The risk-free interest rate is 8% and the return on the Milan stock market index is 15%. Ignore tax. Intesta currently uses its WACC to evaluate *all* projects, but is now thinking of using a different discount rate for each one of its divisions.

WACC calculation

This can be arrived at through *three* different routes:

Approach 1

(i)   Cost of equity capital:

$$K_E = \frac{€4m \times (1 + 0.06)}{€30.3m} + 0.06 = 0.20 \text{ or } 20\%$$

Total market value of equity = V_E = £30.3m

(ii) Cost of debt capital:

$$K_D = \frac{€8}{€80} = 0.10 \text{ or } 10\%$$

Total market value of bonds: V_B = €12.625m × 0.80 = €10.1m
Total market value of the company: $V_0 = V_E + V_B$ = €40.4m

(iii) Weighted average cost of capital:

$$K_0 = \left(20\% \times \frac{30.3}{40.4}\right) + \left(10\% \times \frac{10.1}{40.4}\right) = 17.5\%$$

Approach 2

(i)   Cost of equity capital:

$$K_E = 8\% + [15\% - 8\%] \times 1.71 = 20\% \text{ (approx.)}$$

(ii) Cost of debt capital:

$$K_D = 8\% + [15\% - 8\%] \times 0.29 = 10\% \text{ (approx.)}$$

(iii) Weighted average cost of capital:

$$K_0 = \left(20\% \times \frac{30.3}{40.4}\right) + \left(10\% \times \frac{10.1}{40.4}\right) = 17.5\%$$

▶

▶

Approach 3

(i) Weighted average cost of capital:

$$\beta_{INESTA} = \left[\beta_{EQUITY} \times \frac{V_E}{V_O} \right] + \left[\beta_{DEBT} \times \frac{V_B}{V_O} \right]$$

$$\beta_{ROCHA} = \left(1.72 \times \frac{30.3}{40.4} \right) + \left(0.29 \times \frac{10.1}{40.4} \right) = 1.355$$

$$K_{0\ INESTA} = 8\% + (15\% - 8\%) \times 1.355 = 17.5\%$$

(ii) Divisional discount rates:
Supermarket division

$$\text{Required return} = 8\% + (15\% - 8\%) \times 0.80 = 13.6\%$$

Office furniture division

$$\text{Required return} = 8\% + (15\% - 8\%) \times 1.92 = 21.4\%$$

Finally, notice that:

$$(21.4\% \times 0.50) + (13.6\% \times 0.50) = 17.5\%[4]$$

The third of the three WACC calculations in Example 1 shows that WACC reflects the company's average systematic risk level, which is represented by its weighted average beta value of 1.355.

The CAPM can be used to calculate specific discount rates for each division, based on the beta value of their industry groups. Therefore, the minimum required rate of return from the supermarket division should only be 13.6%, given its relatively low systematic risk. On the other hand, the minimum required rate of return from the office furniture division is 21.4%, reflecting its relatively high degree of systematic risk.

On this basis, we can see that if Intesta Lombardo were to evaluate all its capital investments using its WACC as the NPV discount rate, it would be using *too high* a discount rate for projects in the *low-risk* supermarket division (17.5% > 13.6%), and it would be using *too low* a discount rate for projects in the *higher-risk* office furniture division (17.5% < 21.4%).

Example 1 highlights the danger of companies using a single required rate of return (i.e. their WACC) across the whole of their business, without taking into account the specific level of systematic risk of individual divisions. This potential danger is diagrammatically illustrated in Figure 17.1.

If the company simply applies its WACC to all projects, then it will incorrectly accept the high-risk projects whose risk and expected return characteristics locate in shaded area A. Conversely, it will incorrectly reject low-risk projects whose risk and return characteristics locate in shaded area B.

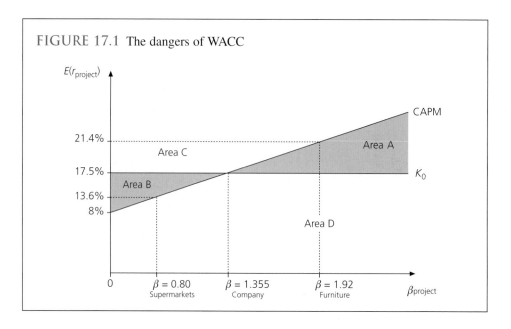

FIGURE 17.1 The dangers of WACC

With projects whose risk and return characteristics locate in either areas C or D, there is no problem. Area C projects will be correctly accepted by the WACC. Area D projects will be correctly rejected. However, the danger lies with area A and B projects.

Returning to Example 1, the company's supermarket division could be quite needlessly rejecting what are perfectly acceptable (area B) projects because too high a minimum return is being specified. But, even worse, the furniture manufacturing division may be accepting projects, thinking they will produce a positive NPV, when in reality, they can be expected to generate *negative* NPVs. The mistake arises because too low a discount rate is being used for the risk involved.

For project appraisal purposes, what is always required is an NPV discount rate that is tailor-made to reflect the *individual* systematic risk level of the investment project that is under evaluation. The company's WACC does not provide this (except, as was mentioned before, if the company is in a single area of business and the project represents a simple expansion of that existing business), but the CAPM can provide it.

The absence of tax

We will pick up on this analysis in Chapter 21. However, it is important to note that Example 1 did not include tax. Tax makes a significant difference to the analysis, as we shall see.

Conclusion

The conclusion of our analysis, to this point, is as follows. The company's WACC represents its *overall* rate of return (and hence the notation of K_0 for the WACC), and reflects its *overall* level of systematic risk.

Traditionally, the WACC has been used as an NPV discount rate for project appraisal purposes.[5] However, we have seen that four assumptions need to hold good if an NPV/WACC analysis is to be correct. Although three out of those four assumptions may be thought to cause little real difficulty, *one* of the assumptions does have the potential to cause *real* problems: that of risk differences.

We have seen in Example 1 how this problem may be overcome by using a discount rate calculated specifically to reflect an individual project's systematic risk, rather than using the company's WACC. However, we have not yet finished with this analysis and will return to it in Chapter 21, where we will also address two other related problems: what happens if the project is *non*-marginal and what happens if the project is to be financed in such a way that the company *does* significantly change its capital structure?

In the three following chapters we will put the issue of the NPV discount rate to one side. Instead, we shall turn to look directly at the financing decision and try to answer two questions: does it matter whether individual projects are financed with debt or equity capital (or some mixture of the two), and does it matter what overall debt-equity mix (the company's capital *gearing* or *leverage* ratio) is used to finance its assets?

SUMMARY

The main points made were as follows:

- A company's overall cost of capital can be calculated on the basis of an average of the costs of the individual sources of capital, weighted by the market-valued proportions of those individual sources of capital: the WACC.

- The cost of a specific source of capital should *never* be used as an NPV discount rate. Instead, the company's overall WACC should be used.

- The WACC provides a suitable discount rate, given the validity of four assumptions: the project is marginal; no change in capital structure; no change in systematic risk level; and all level perpetuity cash flows.

- Of these four assumptions, the second and third are crucial. If a project is financed so as to cause a change in capital structure then an NPV/WACC analysis appears inappropriate. NPV is an investment appraisal technique and it cannot adequately handle a simultaneous capital structure decision.

- The third assumption is crucial because of the logic of NPV: the discount rate reflects the return available elsewhere on an investment with similar systematic risk to the project under appraisal.

- A company's WACC reflects its existing systematic risk level. Therefore to provide a suitable discount rate the project must have that level of risk also. In the real world such an assumption is likely to be very suspect.

- It is concluded that, in most circumstances it is likely to be safer to generate a discount rate from CAPM, which is tailor-made to the project's systematic risk level, rather than to use WACC.

NOTES

1. We are deliberately ignoring the fact here that the issue of bonds might affect the company's capital structure and so affect the weights and hence the value of K_0. The effect of this change, and whether or not the company's *existing* K_0 or *new* K_0 should be used as the discount rate, will be dealt with later.

2. Therefore both the interest cash flow and the dividend cash flow are level perpetuity cash flows.
3. Although so far we have only talked about the beta value of shares, debt capital also possesses systematic risk and so will have a beta value.
4. Weights of 50% (i.e. 0.50) are used in this calculation as we are told that Intesta's business is divided equally between its two divisions.
5. The WACC can also be used as the minimum required IRR.

FURTHER READING

1. There are a number of interesting articles which are, in the main, critical of the use of the WACC as an NPV discount rate. For example, see: F.D. Arditti, 'The Weighted Average Cost of Capital: Some Questions on its Definition, Interpretation and Use', *Journal of Finance*, September 1973; and M.J. Brennan, 'A New Look at the Weighted Average Cost of Capital', *Journal of Business Finance*, Summer 1973.

2. Particularly good, in this context, are: S.M. Keane, 'The Cost of Capital as a Financial Decision Tool', *Journal of Business Finance and Accounting*, Autumn 1978; H.P. Lanser, 'Valuation, Gains from Leverage and the Weighted Average Cost of Capital as a Cut-off Rate', *Engineering Economist*, Fall 1983; and E.F. Brigham and T.C. Tapley, 'Financial Leverage and the Use of the NPV Criterion: A Re-examination', *Financial Management*, Summer 1985. Finally there are some interesting research outcomes to be seen in E. Lee, M. Walker and H. Christensen, 'The Cost of Capital in Europe', *Certified Accountants Educational Trust*, 2006.

QUIZ QUESTIONS

1 El Técnicas is an energy supply company, quoted on the Bolsa de Madrid stock exchange. You are given the following information about the company:
Current dividend per share: 5 cents.
Current share price: 88 cents cum div.
Dividend growth rate: 7%.
Number of shares: 25 million.
€25 million 15% €100 irredeemable bonds.
Current market price: €110 per bond, ex int.
€10 million unquoted 12% irredeemable debt.
€3 million 7-year bank loan at Euribor +4%.
Euribor: 10%.
Tax: 35%.
Required: Calculate the WACC of El Técnicas.

2 What is the argument for why the cost of a *specific* source of capital should not be used as the NPV discount rate?

3 What are the assumptions behind the use of WACC as an NPV discount rate?

4 What is the problem faced by a diversified company wishing to use its WACC as an NPV discount rate?

5 Why is the CAPM likely to produce a superior NPV discount rate than WACC?

6 Why is the company's effective cost of debt capital likely to be *less than* the rate available to investors, given similar risk?

7 If the company can borrow more cheaply than can investors, what implications does this have for the company's capital structure?

8 How is a company's capital structure measured?

(See the 'Answers to the Quiz Questions' section at the back of the book.)

PROBLEMS

The answers to two of the following problems (those indicated by an asterisk) are available to students online. The answer to the remaining problem is available only to lecturers (see the 'Digital Resources' page for details).

1* Osmine Pipework manufactures fluid control systems. The company is considering investment in a new factory to cope with increased demand for its products. Detailed forecasts of the expected cash flows that would result have been made, and it is estimated that an initial capital investment of £2.5 million is required. The company's current (t_0) share capital consists of 3 million shares, and the market price per share is £1.35 ex div. The dividends for the last 5 years have been as follows:

Year	t_{-4}	t_{-3}	t_{-2}	t_{-1}	t_0
Dividend per share (pence)	10.0	10.8	11.6	13.6	13.6

Osmine currently has in issue £800 000 of 8% £100 debentures redeemable in 4-years' time. The current market price of these debentures is £82.50 ex interest. The company also has outstanding a £900 000 bank loan repayable in 8-years' time. The rate of interest on this loan is variable, being fixed at 1.5% above the BoE base rate which is currently 10%.

Required:

(a) Calculate the WACC for Osmine Pipework.

(b) Explain briefly to the directors of Osmin Pipework what assumptions they are making if the WACC calculated in (a) above is used to discount the expected cash flows of the factory investment.

(c) Describe the practical problems that might be encountered when attempting to compute the WACC for a large stock exchange quoted company.

2* Bontoni Groupo is a holding company owning shares in various subsidiary companies. The board of directors is currently considering several investment opportunities that will further increase the range of the group's business activities. The board would like to use discounted cash flow techniques in their evaluation of these projects but as yet no WACC has been calculated, to be used as a discount rate.

  Bontoni Groupo has 8 million shares in issue. The current ex div market price per share is €1.10, a dividend of 10 cents per share having been paid recently. The company's financial analysts have calculated that 18% is the most appropriate after-tax cost of equity capital. Extracts from the latest balance sheet for the group are given below:

	Bontoni Groupo
	(€000s)
Share capital	2 000
Reserves	5 705
Shareholders' funds	7 705
3% irredeemable €100 bonds	1 400
9% redeemable €100 bonds	1 500
6% Unquoted bonds	2 000
Bank loan	1 540

All debt interest is payable annually and all the current year's payments will be made shortly. The current *cum interest* market prices for €100 bonds are €31.60 and €103.26 for the 3% and 9% bonds respectively. Both the 9% debentures and the 6% bonds are redeemable at par in 10-years' time. The 6% unquoted bonds are not traded on the open market, but the analyst estimates that its effective pre-tax cost is 10% per annum. The bank loan bears interest at 2% above Euribor (which is currently 11%) and is repayable in 6 years. The effective corporation tax rate of Bontonio Groupo is 30%.

Required:

(i)   Calculate the effective after-tax WACC as required by the board of directors.

(ii) Outline the fundamental assumptions that are made whenever the WACC of a company is used as the discount rate in NPV calculations.

3. Schwarz Tek GmbH is a divisionalized company, quoted on the Deutsche Börse stock exchange. Two of its divisions are currently evaluating investment proposals and have submitted them to the corporate board for approval. The project cash flows are as follows:

Cyber Systems division	(€000s)	Silicon Chip division	(€000s)
Year: 0	−200	Year: 0	−150
1	+100	1	+ 75
2	+100	2	+ 48.36
3	+ 79.3	3	+ 75

The following information about the company is available: Current balance sheet (summarized):

		(€000s)
Assets:	Non-current assets	7 500
	Net current assets	2 460
		9 960
Finance:	30 million shares	3 000
	Reserves	6 960
		9 960

Dividend/share and earnings/share record

Year	Dividend (cents)	Earnings (cents)
t_{-4}	5.12	6.19
t_{-3}	5.32	6.44
t_{-2}	5.53	6.69
t_{-1}	5.76	6.90
t_0 (current year)	5.99	7.31

The current total market value of the company's shares is €13.35 million, *ex div*. Schwarz Tek has a beta of 1.16. The systems industry has a beta of 1.50 and the silicon chip industry has a beta of 0.50. The annual return on 3-year government bonds is currently 11% and the expected return on the DAX stock market index is 17%. Ignore tax.

Required:

(a) Schwarz Tek usually evaluates all investment proposals with NPV, using the cost of company capital as the discount rate. Estimate this discount rate and evaluate both projects.

(b) Advise the company as to why it should evaluate projects using *risk-adjusted* discount rates. Estimate an appropriate rate for each project and re-evaluate them both.

(c) Comment and explain, with the help of a diagram, the implications of your answers to parts (a) and (b). Assume all-equity financing throughout.

18 CAPITAL STRUCTURE IN A SIMPLE WORLD

LEARNING OBJECTIVES

The purpose of this chapter is to:

- Introduce the Modigliani and Miller (M and M) capital structure analysis.

- Discuss the concepts of 'business' and 'financial' risk.

- Explore the relationship between a company's cost of equity and its capital structure.

- Develop the 'arbitrage' proof that capital structure should have no impact on a company's WACC.

- Examine the assumptions and the implications of the M and M analysis.

AN OPTIMAL CAPITAL STRUCTURE

Can any particular ratio of debt to equity finance in a company's capital structure be said to be *optimal*, in terms of helping to increase the wealth of ordinary shareholders? This is an important question for several reasons.

First, and most importantly, up to this stage we have assumed that management could increase the wealth of ordinary shareholders *only* by the decisions they made about physical investment projects. However, if an optimal gearing ratio exists, then it would mean that a company's management could increase shareholder wealth, not only by making good investment decisions, but also by making good financing/capital structure decisions.

A second reason for the importance of the question about the existence of an optimal capital structure is the implications that it has for the approach which we have developed to investment decision-making. Hitherto, we have assumed that the question of *how* a particular investment project is to be financed (the financing decision) can be taken *separately* from the investment decision itself (as a direct result of the separation theorem). The investment decision has therefore been examined in isolation from any consideration as to how it might be financed. If the financing decision can be shown to be important for the company – in terms of the desired capital structure – then we may have to revise our approach to investment appraisal and capital investment decision-making.

A third reason could also be proposed. In suggesting the possible use of the WACC for discounting and appraisal purposes, we assumed that a company's capital structure would remain constant. This assumption would obviously gain support if it could be shown that an optimal capital structure does exist for a company. Because, then, management would wish to attain, and remain at, that particular gearing ratio.

The capital structure decision was first rigorously analyzed by two American economists, Modigliani and Miller (universally known in the abbreviated form of M and M), in a justly famous article that appeared in 1958 (see the 'Further reading' section at the end of the chapter). Much of our analysis in this section will be based upon the approach that they took.

Initially we will assume that there is no tax. This is known formally as the 'Modigliani and Miller, *no tax*, capital structure hypothesis'.

The total market value model

We introduced the term 'gearing' or 'leverage' when examining the costs of the various sources of capital that are available to a company. We can define the term as the ratio of the total market value of a company's debt capital to the total market value of its equity capital.[1] The distinction between debt and equity was important because each type of capital bore a different level of risk: debt capital was a less risky investment in a company than an equity capital investment in that same company.

This risk differential resulted from the fact that debt capital interest had first claim on a company's annual net profits, ahead of equity dividends. In addition, debt capital had repayment preference over equity capital in circumstances of company liquidation. As a result of this risk differential, the suppliers of debt capital to a company would require a lower return than the suppliers of equity, because they bore less risk.

In order to calculate the costs of the different capital sources, two valuation models were constructed, both based on the premise that an object's value is determined by the flow of future net benefits which it produces. Therefore, a company's equity capital derived its value from the sum of the (discounted) flow of future dividends which it was expected to produce. Similarly, debt capital was valued on the basis of the sum of the future expected (discounted) interest flow and the future capital redemption payment.

From these two valuation models, it follows that the *total* market value of a company (debt plus equity), V_0, must be derived from its expected future (discounted) net cash flow – which consists of its future dividend flow and its future interest and capital redemption cash flow. It will be helpful, for later analysis, to restate this in terms of the notation used earlier when analyzing a company's cost of capital.

Table 18.1 gives this restatement (ignoring taxation for the present), under the assumption of constant annual dividends in perpetuity and irredeemable debentures. If we let $[V_E \times K_E] + [V_B \times K_D] = Y$, and if we assume that none of a company's net cash flow is retained but is paid out in full each year as dividends and interest, then Y is a constant and so a company's total market value is given by:

$$V_0 = \frac{Y}{K_0}$$

TABLE 18.1

If Y is the company's total annual cash flow which is assumed to be a level perpetuity that is paid out each year as dividends and interest:

$$V_E = \frac{Y - V_B \times K_D}{K_E} \tag{1}$$

$$V_E \times K_E = Y - V_B \times K_D \tag{2}$$

Taking expression (2) and factoring out V_0:

$$\frac{V_0 \times V_E \times K_E}{V_0} = Y - \frac{V_B \times K_D \times V_0}{V_0} \tag{3}$$

$$\frac{V_0 \times V_E \times K_E}{V_0} + \frac{V_B \times K_D \times V_0}{V_0} = Y \tag{4}$$

$$V_0 \left[\frac{V_E \times K_E}{V_0} + \frac{V_B \times K_D}{V_0} \right] = Y \tag{5}$$

$$V_0 = \frac{Y}{\dfrac{V_E \times K_E}{V_G} + \dfrac{V_B \times K_D}{V_0}} = \frac{Y}{K_0} \tag{6}$$

where $V_E \times K_E = D$ and $V_B \times K_D = I$

Gearing and V_0 in a no-tax world

The question that we wish to examine is whether or not a company's gearing ratio (i.e. its capital structure) can affect its total market value.[2] From the above it should be clear that changing a company's gearing ratio will affect its total market value (V_0) *only* if it causes a change in either the company's annual net cash flow (Y), or its WACC (K_0). However, we can argue that changing the gearing ratio of a company will *not* affect either of these factors, as follows.

Changing the gearing ratio cannot have any effect on the company's annual cash flow (Y), as that is determined by the assets in which the company has invested, and not by how those assets are financed. The only effect that changing the gearing has on the firm's annual cash flow is that it changes the proportions of the cash flow that are paid out as dividends and interest. The more highly geared the firm, the greater is the proportion of its annual cash flow paid out as interest and the smaller the proportion paid out as dividends, and vice versa.

Changing the gearing ratio will also not affect the value of K_0. The company's WACC reflects the average return required by the suppliers of the capital. Its level is determined (as in any rate of return) by the degree of systematic risk in the *company's* overall cash flow. There is no reason why changing the gearing ratio should affect the systematic risk of the cash flow being generated by the company's assets, and hence changing the gearing ratio will not affect K_0.[3]

From this analysis we can draw two important conclusions. The first is that simply changing a company's capital structure cannot (by itself) change the company's total market value. Thus, companies can only enhance their shareholders' wealth by making good investment decisions. The financing decision (through which a company's capital structure or gearing ratio can be changed) cannot affect shareholder wealth.

The second conclusion is that companies whose assets display the same degree of systematic risk can be expected to have the same WACC, even though they may have entirely different gearing ratios. This is because it is the systematic risk of the company's collection of assets which determines its overall return of K_0.

The assumptions

These ideas are illustrated in Example 1 below, but before proceeding further with this analysis, we should first make explicit the very important assumptions upon which it is based. These are:

1. At any given level of risk, individuals and companies can all borrow at the same rate of interest, which remains constant regardless of the gearing.
2. There are no costs attached to market transactions, the supply of information or the process of bankruptcy.[4]
3. There is no difference between corporate borrowing and personal borrowing in terms of risk (e.g. there is no limited liability advantage for companies).
4. There is no taxation.

EXAMPLE 1

An investor is starting a company – Iberia Cervejas – to produce a zero-alcohol beer. The required equipment would cost €100 000. The investment involves a level of systematic risk which requires an expected annual return of 15%. Therefore the investment would be expected to produce an annual net cash flow of €15 000 in perpetuity. This cash flow will be fully paid out each year, to the suppliers of the €100 000 of finance.

Three different financing options are being considered to set up the company:

1. The investment is financed entirely by €100 000 of equity capital.
2. €50 000 of 10% debt (the current market cost of debt capital) is borrowed, with the remaining €50 000 supplied as equity capital.
3. €80 000 of 10% debt is borrowed, with the balance provided by equity capital.

Table 18.2 illustrates the returns to equity and debt, the WACC and the total value of Iberia Cervejas that would result from each of these three financing options.

TABLE 18.2

	Option 1	Option 2	Option 3
Investment annual cash flow	€15 000	€15 000	€15 000
Less interest payment	—	€5 000	€8 000
Dividend payments	€15 000	€10 000	€7 000
K_E: Return on equity (D/V_E)	15%	20%	35%
K_D: Return on debt (I/V_B)	—	10%	10%
K_0: WACC (Y/V_0)	15%	15%	15%
Total value of the company (Y/K_0)	€100 000	€100 000	€100 000

It should be noted that Example 1 does nothing to prove or disprove the relationship between a company's gearing ratio and its WACC that was argued in the previous section. Rather, it is based upon that relationship, in that it assumes that K_0 remains unchanged, despite the different gearing ratios. As a result of that assumption (and the four assumptions listed above) the rest follows.

This example serves a very useful purpose in that it highlights the fact that although K_0 remains unchanged as gearing changes, the cost of equity capital does change. It is the relationship between gearing and K_E that is now examined.

BUSINESS AND FINANCIAL RISK

In the earlier discussion of portfolio theory and the CAPM we saw that an investment's total risk could be split up into two components: systematic (or non-diversifiable) risk and unsystematic (or diversifiable) risk. Further, we saw that it was *only* an investment's systematic risk that determined its expected return. We can now split a company's systematic risk into two further components: systematic business risk and systematic financial risk.

The business risk of a company relates to the riskiness of its operating cash flows. In other words, business risk relates to the systematic risk of the net cash flows that result from the operation of the company's assets. Both the equity and the debt holders in a company bear this risk. However, financial risk refers to some *additional* systematic risk which is borne *only* by the equity holders of a geared company.[5]

In Chapter 16, when we discussed the cost of debt capital, it was pointed out that K_D was only the *explicit* cost of debt capital and that there was another cost, an implicit (or hidden) cost. This implicit cost is caused by the presence of financial risk.

Financial risk arises directly out of the gearing process and is borne by the equity shareholders in a geared company. It is caused through debt capital having priority over equity capital in both the distribution of the company's annual net cash flow (as interest and dividends) and in any final liquidation distribution. As interest payments to debt holders must legally be paid in full by the company before any dividend payments can be made, the greater the proportion of debt capital within a company's capital structure, the greater the probability that the company will have no cash remaining with which to pay a dividend. This risk of a reduced or zero dividend, which is borne by ordinary shareholders, is termed financial risk, and its severity is likely to increase as a company increases its level of gearing.

Diagrammatically, a company's expected annual net operating cash flow can be portrayed as a probability distribution. In an all-equity company (on the assumption of no retention by the company of this net cash flow) the probability distribution of the net operating cash flow also represents the probability distribution of the dividend flow. Gearing up has the effect of imposing a fixed annual charge on this distribution (the interest payments), so shifting the dividend payment probability distribution to the left (see Figure 18.1). The greater the proportion of debt in the capital structure, the further will be the leftward movement and the greater will be the proportion of the dividend probability distribution falling within the negative portion of the horizontal axis. Thus the greater is the risk of a reduced or zero dividend, as gearing is increased.

Thus financial risk arises from the fact that equity holders are always at the back of the annual 'payout queue'. The more highly geared the company, the greater the amount of interest that has to be paid before dividends can be paid (i.e. the longer the queue in front of the equity holders), and hence the greater amount of financial risk borne by ordinary shareholders.

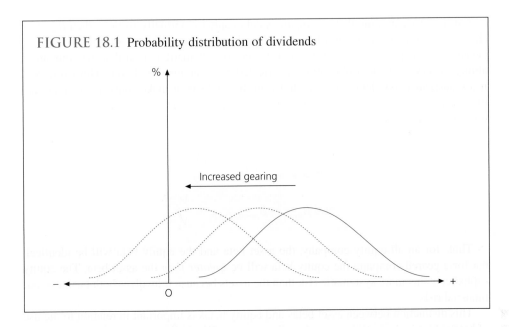

FIGURE 18.1 Probability distribution of dividends

This financial risk is systematic risk, in that it cannot be diversified away. As a result, shareholders will require a higher expected return on their capital for bearing increased amounts of financial risk. Therefore as a company increases its level of gearing, the amount of financial risk borne by ordinary shareholders increases and, in consequence, the cost of equity capital rises.

This effect was seen in Example 1 and in Table 18.2. As the gearing ratio increases, the return on equity rises from 15% to 35%. In Option 1 (the all-equity situation), the 15% return on equity simply reflects the business risk of the assets. However, the 20% return in Option 2 reflects a 15% return for holding the business risk of the assets, *plus* a 5% return for holding the financial risk represented by the level of gearing involved. Further, it is important to note that the shareholders have not gained in moving (say) from Option 1 to Option 2. The higher return on equity in Option 2 simply reflects the higher risks involved in holding equity capital in that situation.

Asset betas and gearing

Given that beta values are used as an index of systematic risk, it follows from the above that we can distinguish between the beta value of a geared company's equity and the beta value of its assets. The reason for this is that the assets will only contain business systematic risk, whereas the equity will contain both business and financial systematic risk.

We know from our discussion of the CAPM in Chapter 12 that the beta value of a *collection* of securities is a *weighted average* of the beta values of the individual securities. This observation allows us to conclude therefore that the beta value of an asset is a weighted average of the beta values of the collection of securities that finance that asset. (In reality this relationship is determined the other way around. The betas of the financing securities will be determined by the systematic risk of the asset they are financing.) Hence:

$$\beta_{company\ assets} = \beta_{equity} \times \frac{V_E}{V_0} + \beta_{debt} \times \frac{V_B}{V_0}$$

Further, if we assume that a company's debt capital is virtually riskless, then $\beta_{debt} \approx 0$. (In reality the debt beta for most companies is likely to be very low, but not zero. This is because debt capital – like equity – is exposed to systematic risk in that the company's ability to service its debt obligations is affected by economic conditions. However, even if a realistically low debt beta is included in the analysis, it makes only a very marginal impact on the outcome.) Therefore, maintaining the assumption of a zero debt beta, the relationship simplifies to:

$$\beta_{company\ assets} = \beta_{equity} \times \frac{V_E}{V_0}$$

$$\text{and } \beta_{equity} = \beta_{company\ assets} \times \frac{V_0}{V_E}$$

Thus, for an all-equity company, the asset beta and the equity beta will be identical, but for a geared company the equity beta will be *greater than* the asset beta. The equity capital contains more systematic risk than the assets because it involves both business *and* financial risk.

This distinction between asset betas and equity betas is important in relation to the use of beta values in determining a *project* discount rate. We shall return to examine this in the following chapter. Table 18.3 develops the relationship further.[6] The key points to keep in mind are that the equity beta measures the systematic business risk *and* the systematic financial risk of the shares, while the asset beta measures the company's systematic business risk only.

TABLE 18.3

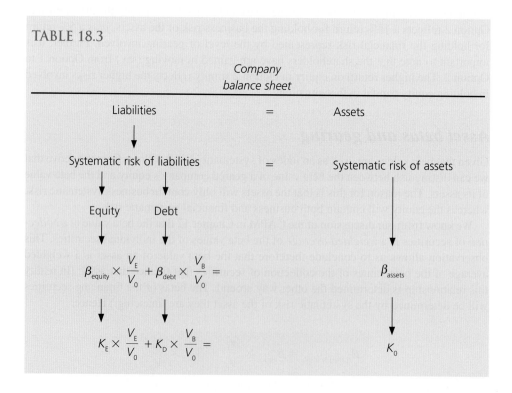

Gearing and K_E

We shall turn now to examine the relationship between gearing and the cost of equity capital, but all the while retaining our set of specified assumptions. The relationship can be derived from the dividend valuation model, as is shown in Table 18.4.

TABLE 18.4

Given the relationship:

$$V_0 = \frac{Y}{K_0} \qquad (1)$$

then:

$$Y = V_0 K_0 = V_E K_0 + V_B K_0 \qquad (2)$$

The dividend valuation model can be expressed as:

$$K_E = \frac{D}{V_E} \equiv \frac{Y - V_B K_D}{V_E} \qquad (3)$$

Substituting the definition of Y given in (2):

$$K_E = \frac{V_E K_0}{V_E} + \frac{V_B K_0}{V_E} - \frac{V_B K_D}{V_E} \qquad (4)$$

Cancelling and simplifying:

$$K_E = K_0 + (K_0 - K_D)\frac{V_B}{V_E} \qquad (5)$$

From the final line of Table 18.4 it can be seen that the cost of equity capital of a company consists of two elements, K_0 (which reflects the expected return required for the business risk of the company's assets), plus $(K_0 - K_D) \times V_B/V_E$. This latter element represents the financial risk premium and is a positive linear function of the gearing ratio.

Therefore, returning to Example 1 used earlier, and using the *third* financing option which involves €80 000 of debt and €20 000 of equity:

$$
\begin{aligned}
K_0 &= 15\% \\
K_D &= 10\% \\
V_B &= \text{€80 000} \\
V_E &= \text{€20 000}
\end{aligned}
$$

hence:

$$K_E = 15\% + (15\% - 10\%) \times \frac{80\,000}{20\,000} = 35\%$$

Earlier, we concluded that companies with assets that had the same degree of business risk (the same asset betas) would have the same weighted average costs of capital, whatever their gearing ratios. Therefore a slightly different (but equivalent) way of expressing the relationship between gearing and the cost of equity capital can be given:

$$K_{E_g} = K_{E_{ug}} + (K_{E_{ug}} - K_D)\frac{V_B}{V_E}$$

where K_{E_g} = cost of equity capital of a geared company and $K_{E_{ug}}$ = cost of equity capital of a similar business risk, but all-equity financed company.

The graphical relationship

The relationship between a company's gearing ratio and the costs of its various types of capital is shown in Figure 18.2. The lower diagram illustrates the fact that the total worth of a company's assets (and hence the total worth of the company) remains constant, however the assets are financed. Although, once again, it should be pointed out that this set of relationships – often referred to as the 'M and M No Tax Case' – was developed under the four sets of assumptions specified earlier.

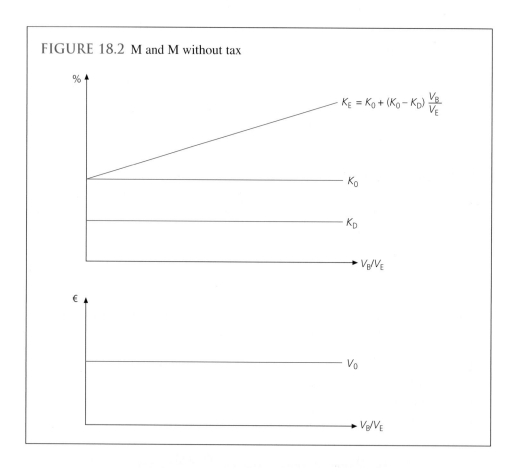

FIGURE 18.2 M and M without tax

THE ARBITRAGE PROOF

All the conclusions that we have drawn from the foregoing analysis are based on the initial premise that a company's gearing ratio does not itself determine or affect either its WACC or its total market value; but what reason do we have for believing this initial premise to be correct? Modigliani and Miller showed that if this was found *not* to hold true in practice (for example, if two companies with the same degree of business risk were found to have different WACCs) then that would represent a short-lived *disequilibrium* situation.

In such circumstances, 'arbitrager' traders would move into the market, selling shares in the company with the lower-valued K_0 and buying shares in the company with the higher valued K_0. They would do so because they could profit from such transactions.

These arbitrage traders would continue to trade until supply and demand market forces caused the WACCs of the two companies to become equal. This equating of the WACCs would be brought about through normal market supply and demand forces (selling shares causing the price to fall and vice versa). Once this position was reached, no further gains could be made, and equilibrium would have been restored.

The word 'arbitrage' is a technical term referring to a situation where two identical goods are selling for different prices and where it is possible to trade in both. If such a situation arises, then it will not persist for long as traders will start to *buy* at the lower price and *sell* at the higher price, thereby making a profit. Buying pressure (increased demand) will force up the price of the lower priced goods and selling pressure (increased supply) will force down the price of the higher priced goods.

Although stock market investors do not often refer to this process in the share market by the term *arbitrage*, many of their transactions are arbitrage deals. The same is true of many commodity transactions on the commodity exchanges – but there traders do refer to them by the technical name of arbitrage, as do foreign exchange dealers. In fact arbitrage is a very common form of transaction in many different markets.

An arbitrage example

Suppose that there are two companies, Arno and Bruno, with identical levels of business risk, although their annual net cash flows are of different magnitudes. Data on the two companies are given in Table 18.5.

TABLE 18.5

	Company	
	Arno	Bruno
Year	$1 \rightarrow \infty$	$1 \rightarrow \infty$
	(€000s)	(€000s)
Annual dividends (D)	1 000	2 000
Annual interest (I)		400
Annual cash flow (Y)	1 000	2 400
Equity market value (V_E)	6 250	12 000
Debt market value (V_B)		4 000
Total market value (V_0)	6 250	16 000
Equity cost of capital ($K_E = D/V_E$)	0.16	0.166
Debt cost of capital ($K_D = I/V_B$)	—	0.10
Weighted average cost of capital ($K_0 = Y/V_0$)	0.16	0.15
Number of shares in issue	6.5m	10m
Market price per share (P_E)	50 cents	120 cents

Because these two companies have identical levels of business risk, their WACCs *should be* the same. As they are not, an arbitrage opportunity exists: specifically for shareholders in Bruno company (the company with the lower K_0) to sell out of Bruno shares and buy into Arno company shares.

As an example, suppose an investor – Carlos – owns shares in Bruno which have a current market value of €30 000. The shares can be expected to produce an annual dividend of €30 000 × 0.166 = €5000. For this expected annual dividend flow Carlos is bearing two types of risk: he holds the business risk of the company, and he also holds financial risk, as Bruno is geared.

If Carlos were to sell his €30 000 shareholding and simply invest the proceeds in Arno shares, the two investments (shares in Arno, compared with shares in Bruno) would *not be* comparable, as Arno has an all-equity capital structure; thus although the business risk of the two investments would be the same, the shareholding in Arno would result in no additional financial risk being held.

To be able to compare 'like with like' would require Carlos to maintain the *same* level of financial risk when holding shares in Arno as that held as a shareholder in Bruno. To do so, Carlos would need to substitute 'home-made' gearing (or home-made financial risk) for the 'corporate' gearing that he held as a shareholder in Bruno.

Bruno company has borrowed (at the market rate of interest, K_D) €1 for every €3 of its shareholders' equity capital (i.e. Bruno company's debt–equity ratio is 1:3), and so Carlos would need to borrow €1 (at the market interest rate of 10%) for every €3 of his own cash. As a result, Carlos would borrow €10 000 and, by so doing, maintains his existing level of financial risk.

Carlos has now a total of €40 000 (€10 000 borrowed and €30 000 of his own money from the sale of the Bruno shares) and all of this is now invested in the shares of Arno. He thereby maintains both the business *and* the financial risk levels he held as a shareholder in Bruno.

This shareholding in Arno can be expected to produce an annual dividend of €40 000 × 0.16 = €6400. Out of this Carlos has to pay an annual interest charge on his loan of €10 000 × 0.10 = €1000, leaving him a net annual expected cash flow of €5400. Thus Carlos – through this arbitrage transaction – has increased his annual income by €400 – from €5000 to €5400 – with *no change* in *either* his business *or* financial risk levels.

Other shareholders in Bruno will also see this opportunity to make an arbitrage gain and will undertake similar transactions. The net result will be that selling pressure on Bruno's shares will force the market price down to a point at which the WACCs of the two companies equate. Once this point is reached, there will be no further gains to be made from arbitrage dealings and so the price will stabilize: equilibrium will have been attained.

If the (not too unreasonable) assumption is made that the market correctly prices Arno's equity and Bruno's debt, then the foregoing analysis suggests that the market value of Bruno's equity will fall sufficiently far to raise the company's WACC to 16% (i.e. equal to that of Arno). The equilibrium value of Bruno's equity can then be calculated, as is shown in Table 18.6.

Thus, the market value of Bruno company's equity capital will fall from €12 million to €11 million. In other words, the shares will fall in price from 120 cents each to 110 cents each.

TABLE 18.6

In equilibrium the WACC of Bruno company will be 16% (that is, equal to the WACC of Arno). Therefore the equilibrium total market value of Bruno is (€000s).

$$V_0 = \frac{€2400}{0.16} = €15\,000$$

Given that Bruno's debt is correctly valued at €4000, then the equilibrium value of Bruno's equity will be:

$$V_E = €15\,000 - €4000 = €11\,000$$

At which point:

$$K_E = \frac{€2000}{€11\,000} = 0.182 \text{ approx.}$$

which is exactly what is predicted by the M and M expression for the cost of equity capital:

$$K_E = 0.16 + [0.16 - 0.10] \times \frac{€4000}{€11\,000} = 0.182 \text{ approx.}$$

[However notice that this expression will only provide K_E when equilibrium values of K_0 (or K_{EU}); K_D; V_E and V_B are used.]

Reverse arbitrage

Now suppose that the stock market gets things slightly wrong and overreacts to the arbitrage transactions taking place, with the result that Bruno's shares fall in price to 104 cents per share. The situation would be as follows (figures in €000s).

Bruno company: $K_E = €2000/€10\,400 = 0.1923$
$$K_D = €400/€4000 = 0.10$$
$$K_0 = €2400/€14\,400 = 0.166$$

As Bruno's WACC is now *above* that of Arno, there would be an arbitrage opportunity in a move *from* the shares in Arno *into* Bruno company shares. However, notice that such a move, unlike the previous example, would involve going from an all-equity company to a geared company. This situation is sometimes referred to as *reverse* arbitrage, but it is rather misleading to do so as it is simply another arbitrage transaction, but now the mechanics of the move differ.

For example, suppose that there is an investor – Daniella – who holds €5000 worth of shares in Arno. She currently expects to receive an annual dividend of €5000 × 0.16 = €800. This is in exchange for holding *just* the business risk of Arno. As Arno is all-equity financed the shareholder, Daniella, bears no financial risk. Thus the problem is now how does she sell her shares in Arno and move into Bruno company shares – to take advantage of the temporary disequilibrium price of Bruno's equity – while maintaining her current level of zero financial risk?

One approach would be for Daniella to buy both the debt and equity of Bruno in the same proportion as Bruno's debt–equity ratio. Therefore Daniella would sell her shares in Arno for €5000 and buy €4 of Bruno's debt for every €10.40 of Bruno's equity that was bought (Bruno's debt-equity ratio is now €4 million: €10.4 million). Thus she would buy €3611.11 of Bruno's equity and €1388.89 of Bruno's debt.

This process by which the investor maintains her zero financial risk level can be explained in several ways. Perhaps the most intuitively appealing is to argue that although she takes on a positive amount of financial risk through her equity holding in Bruno, she *also* takes on a *negative* amount of financial risk through her debt holding. The net effect of holding both securities, in a combination equal to the company's gearing ratio, is that the financial risk is cancelled out.[7]

The effect of this reverse arbitrage transaction would be to give the investor an annual expected dividend of €3611.11 × 0.1923 = €694.42 and annual interest of €1388.89 × 0.10 = €138.89. Thus a total annual income of €833.31 would be expected, which represents a gain of €33.31 over her original investment in Arno's shares, with no change in the risk borne.

Once again, other investors are likely to identify the opportunity to make this arbitrage gain and will act in a similar fashion. Their combined effect will be to bring about an equilibrium position and the equating of the WACCs of the two companies.

Two further points

In both the example of 'normal arbitrage' and of 'reverse arbitrage' there has been a concern to maintain a particular level of financial risk in order to allow investment returns to be comparable. However, in both cases, this was done on the basis of Bruno's gearing ratio when in disequilibrium. Bruno's equilibrium debt–equity ratio is 4:11. Therefore a more precise approach to holding financial risk at a given level would be to utilize this equilibrium ratio.

Thus in the normal arbitrage example, Carlos would have substituted home-made for corporate gearing by borrowing 10 909.09 and the resulting arbitrage gain would have been slightly higher at €454.54. Similarly, in the reverse arbitrage example, Daniella would have brought €1333.33 of Bruno's debt and €3666.67 of its equity. This again would result in a slightly increased arbitrage gain of €838.43.

Finally, what if an investor identifies the possibility for gain by arbitraging between two geared companies? In these circumstances, both mechanisms have to be employed. For example suppose company X had a debt-equity ratio of 1:3 whereas company Z had a debt-equity ratio of 2:1. A shareholder in X wishes to move to Z in order to take an arbitrage gain but also wishes to maintain his existing level of financial risk. This can be achieved by selling his shareholding in X, borrowing €1 for every €3 of sale proceeds and then applying the whole amount (borrowings plus own cash) to buying both the debt and equity of Z in the proportion of €2 of debt for every €1 of equity.

REAL WORLD VIEW: Cost of Capital by Industry

In an annual study in 2013, KPMG looked at Cost of Capital in the German and Swiss markets, analyzing how different industries and sectors determine the WACC. This is the minimum return a company must earn on its assets, to avoid losing investment.

The average WACC on companies surveyed was 7.9%, almost the same as the previous year (8.1%). It is interesting to note that the lowest WACC was 5.8% for the energy and natural resources sector, and 8.8% for the automotive sector.

The difference in average WACC depends partly on growth: 'different approaches were adopted in the different industries for growth rate calculation. Surveyed companies of the automotive industry predominantly applied a growth rate based on past industry sales (40 percent, previous year: 20 percent).'

Clearly, it is important not to generalize between industries; some industries rely much more heavily on capital assets than others. For example, an NYU list from January 2014 shows that a large amount of US companies with the lowest cost of capital are finance-based (e.g. bank at 5.03%, regional bank at 5.19%, brokerage and investment banking at 5.55%, non-bank and insurance financial services at 5.41% and re-insurance at 5.20%). Meanwhile the companies with the higher cost of capital are those which arguably require larger amounts of capital assets (e.g. auto parts at 9.38%, beverage at 9.54%, broadcasting at 9.20% and oilfield services/equipment at 9.01%).

CONCLUSIONS

The analysis up to this point allows three important conclusions to be made. The first is that companies with this *same* level of business risk should, in equilibrium, have the *same* weighted expected cost of capital.

Second, *changes* in a company's gearing ratio should leave its WACC *unchanged*. The increased return required by ordinary shareholders that arises out of an increase in gearing represents the compensation required for bearing additional financial risk. It is determined by the expression: $K_E = K_0 + (K_0 - K_D) \times V_B/V_E$.

Finally, and perhaps most importantly, the analysis leads us to conclude that the financing decision is relatively *unimportant*. It can have no impact on the value of the company and so does not affect the wealth of shareholders.

In respect of the second of these three conclusions, the M and M analysis can be expressed in very simple terms: as a company increases its gearing, two effects occur. The first is that the company gains an *advantage* in that debt capital is cheaper than equity capital. The reason for this is that debt is a lower risk security than equity as debt holders get preferential 'payout' treatment, hence debt requires a lower expected return.

The second effect is that the company incurs a *disadvantage* in that the expected return required by equity capital increases. This is because increasing the gearing increases the financial risk held by equity and so forces up the required expected return, by way of compensation.

These two effects – the advantage and the disadvantage – are two different sides of the same coin. They both arise through the same phenomenon: debt holders are paid before equity holders. (In fact we can go further than this and say that the money required to pay the additional return to shareholders arises from the savings made from using lower-cost debt.) Therefore it is not surprising that the two effects exactly cancel each other out, so that the net effect is zero: changing the gearing leaves the company's total market value and its WACC unaltered.

The assumptions

Having outlined the basic M and M capital structure hypothesis, and before proceeding to examine alternative theories about the relationship between a company's gearing ratio and the cost of its equity capital, let us now take a closer look at the many assumptions upon which the M and M hypothesis is based. In particular, we shall look at the assumptions underlying the arbitrage process which helps to restore the M and M equilibrium position in the presence of short-run disequilibrium stock market prices and which is held up as proof of their capital structure theory.

Arbitrage, as we know, is a technical term to describe a supply and demand market process which prevents perfect substitutes from selling at different prices in the same market. The key phrase here is 'perfect substitutes' and so, for the arbitrage process to act as a proof of the M and M hypothesis, shares in an all-equity company must be seen as (or must be able to be made) a perfect substitute for shares in a geared company.

We know from the valuation principles, which were defined originally, that value results from the future flow of net benefits and the certainty (or otherwise) attached to that future flow. Therefore, if we take two companies with the same expected annual cash flow and the same level of business risk, it follows that they should have identical total market values. However, we also know that if one company is all-equity and one company is geared, their shares are *not* perfect substitutes for each other, because the shares in the geared company include an additional risk element: financial risk.

In order to make the shares in the two companies perfect substitutes, in terms of the risk borne in holding them, the investors in the geared company must be able to substitute home-made gearing (i.e. personally gear-up themselves) for corporate gearing. (We saw this process being undertaken by Carlos in the first example used above.) To be able to do so, there must be no difference between the cost and risk of *corporate* borrowing (and hence gearing) and the cost and risk of *individual* borrowing (gearing). This requires two assumptions of highly questionable real-world validity: individuals and companies must be able to borrow at the same rate of interest and the facility of limited liability for companies either must not exist, or must also extend to individuals.

In practice, individuals almost invariably have to pay a *higher* rate of interest on borrowed money than do companies, and in that borrowing their liability is unlimited, whereas companies have the protection of limited liability. Therefore, quite plainly, corporate and individual borrowing differs both in terms of cost *and* of risk, and so this requirement of the arbitrage process, as far as share dealings are concerned, appears to be unfulfilled.

However, the discrepancy between theory and practice can be resolved to some extent by the fact that for share prices to regain an equilibrium position, not *all* investors have to arbitrage in order to cause the necessary price changes through the supply and demand market mechanism. Just sufficient share transactions are required to 'move the market'. There are many limited liability companies with substantial holdings of shares in other companies, who could themselves undertake arbitrage transactions (and thereby avoid the problems outlined above), and so bring about market equilibrium.

This counter-argument, against the real-world invalidity of the two assumptions required for effective stock market arbitraging, appears reasonably sound – at least in theory – although it should be pointed out that there is some evidence to suggest that many institutional investors do not readily indulge in arbitrage transactions. However, there is another assumption involved in the arbitrage process which in practice does not hold, and so causes frictional problems: the assumption that all market transactions are undertaken at no cost (i.e. no stockbrokers' fees or commissions).

In practice, market transaction costs are usually relatively low. Such costs are therefore unlikely to interfere with the smooth and efficient operation of arbitraging (e.g. where the gain that might accrue to an investor from arbitraging may be completely offset by the transaction costs involved), except where the arbitrage gains are very small, because the amount of disequilibrium remaining (and hence the level of arbitrage gains) is itself small.

Thus, although transaction costs will (as always) interfere with the economic mechanism, the degree of interference may well be relatively unimportant. We shall return to this assumption in Chapter 19, for it contains another, implicit assumption, that bankruptcy costs are zero. But before doing so, we shall examine the effects of two other much more problematic assumptions within the hypothesis: that the cost of debt capital remains constant whatever the level of gearing, and that there is no taxation.

A rising cost of debt

The M and M analysis assumes that the cost of debt remains constant and does not change as the level of gearing changes. This assumption is hard to justify in practice. Logically, as a company gears up, the cost of debt should *increase*, so that K_D approaches what would have been the cost of *equity* capital, if the company had remained ungeared. This is because, at the extreme of 100% gearing point (if such a thing was possible), the risks borne by the suppliers of debt capital would be exactly the same as the risks borne by equity capital, if the company were all-equity financed.

The problem with a rising cost of debt capital is that, for the company's WACC to remain *constant*, the company's cost of *equity* capital must start to *decline*, to offset the rise in the cost of debt. Figure 18.3 illustrates this rather unlikely situation.

To deal with the reality of a rising cost of debt, M and M initially offered a rather ingenious solution. This reasoned that as a company gears up to *very* high levels, the shares become *exceptionally* risky – so risky that they begin to attract a different type of investor: risk-seeking, '*gambler*' investors. To these investors, the shares now become increasingly attractive as gearing reaches very high levels. As a result of the share buying activity of these gambler investors, the company's share price starts to *rise* and, as a consequence, its cost of equity starts to *fall*.

The practicality of this explanation for the behaviour of the cost of equity at very high levels of gearing has got to be viewed with considerable scepticism. However, there is an inescapable logic here. We have seen that the return required by an investor is directly related to the amount of risk to which investors are exposed. Ignoring the fact that different types of risk might emerge as a company becomes very highly geared, we can see that the required return on the business as a whole – its WACC – *must remain constant*, and so there must be a more realistic way of accommodating the reality of a rising cost of debt within an analysis of the capital structure decision. This we will examine in the following chapter.

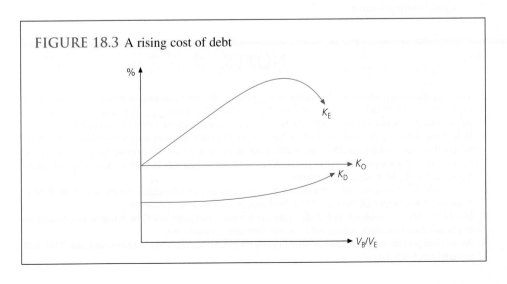

FIGURE 18.3 A rising cost of debt

SUMMARY

- This chapter has developed the M and M no-tax capital structure hypothesis. The basic conclusion is that the capital structure decision cannot affect shareholder wealth and so is irrelevant to the company's financial objective of shareholder wealth maximization.

- The analysis is presented in two stages. The first concerns the firm valuation model: $V_0 = Y \div K_0$ and the fact that K_0 is determined by the risk of Y. Gearing determines how Y is divided up between dividends and interest, but has no effect on the risk of Y and so has no effect on K_0. It is from this analysis that the basic conclusion follows.

- Further, assuming K_D remains a constant, then it is shown that K_E is a positive, linear function of the gearing ratio, given by the expansion:

$$K_E - K_0 + [K_0 - K_D] \times \frac{V_B}{V_E}$$

- Thus the first stage of the analysis gives a constant K_0 at all levels of gearing and the second stage gives a constant K_D and a linearly increasing K_E. Finally, given the overall firm valuation model, as neither Y nor K_0 changes with gearing, nor will V_0. Graphically this was seen in Figure 18.2.

- A secondary conclusion of the M and M analysis is that what determines a company's overall return (K_0) is its *business* risk – that is, the general uncertainty surrounding its net operating cash flow. As this is unaffected by gearing, it therefore follows that companies with the same degree of business risk (that is, the same asset betas), will all have the same K_0, even though they might have different capital structures.

- Finally, M and M show that this conclusion *must* hold in an equilibrium capital market. If not, and companies in the same business risk class had different WACCs, then this would represent an arbitrage opportunity.

- If such arbitrage opportunities arise then investors will move in quickly to take advantage – and so make a profit – and the effect will be to re-establish the market equilibrium position.

NOTES

1. There are numerous definitions of gearing in use, perhaps the most common of which is the ratio of the total market value of debt capital to total market value of the company (i.e. debt plus equity). In those circumstances, the proportion of debt can be quoted as a percentage of a firm's total capital.

2. In fact, remembering the objective that we have assigned to management decision–making – the maximization of *shareholder* wealth – we really want to know whether the gearing ratio can affect the market value of a company's *equity* capital. We shall reconcile changes in total market value and equity market value at a later stage in the analysis.

3. As a result, the assumption of an unchanging capital structure as a condition for the use of the WACC as an investment appraisal discount rate would appear to be no longer necessary.

4. In other words, it is assumed that if the company becomes bankrupt it will be possible to liquidate its assets and distribute them amongst the various claimants without cost.

5. As we shall see, the equity holders of an *all-equity* financed company *only* hold business risk. They will not hold any financial risk.

6. The reader may like to refer back to Example 1 in the previous chapter to see this relationship in action.
7. It should be noticed that this cancelling-out process does not mean that the financial risk has been eliminated in a diversification sense. Financial risk is systematic and therefore non-diversifiable.

FURTHER READING

1. At the end of this chapter we have only really reached the half-way point in our analysis of the capital structure decision. However, obviously M and M's original article, together with some contemporary observations, are well worthwhile: F. Modigliani and M. Miller, 'The Cost of Capital Corporation Finance and the Theory of Investment', *American Economic Review,* June 1958; J.F. Weston, 'A Test of Cost of Capital Propositions', *Southern Economic Journal,* October 1963; and R.F. Wippern, 'Financial Structure and the Value of the Firm', *Journal of Finance,* December 1966.

2. Another interesting article that can be usefully read at this stage, which compares how capital structures differ in different countries, is: R.G. Rajan and L. Zingales, 'What Do We Know About Capital Structure? Some Evidence From International Data', *Journal of Finance*, December 1995.

QUIZ QUESTIONS

1 If a company had a cost of equity capital of 20% and a cost of debt of 10% and a 1:4 debt–equity ratio, what would be the company's cost of capital, if it was all-equity financed?

2 Given the information in question 1, if the company were to change its gearing ratio from 1:4 to 3:5 what would be the change in its K_E and K_0?

3 Two companies, Allo and Bella, are in the same business risk class. Allo is all-equity and Bella has a gearing ratio of 1:3. You have €100 worth of shares in Allo. Show how you would arbitrage into Bella.

4 In an arbitrage transaction, what is the purpose of home-made gearing?

5 What is financial risk and who bears it?

6 A company has a gearing ratio of 1:2. Its cost of equity capital is 20% and its cost of debt is 10%. If $E(r_M) = 15\%$ and $r_F = 10\%$, what is the company's asset beta?

7 Given the information in question 6, if the company were to change its gearing from 1:2 to 2:5, what would be the company's revised equity beta? (Assume K_D remains unchanged at 10%.)

8 Given the information in question 6, another company also has a cost of equity of 20% and a cost of debt of 10%. However it has a debt–equity ratio of 2:5. Are they in the same business risk class?

(See the 'Answers to Quiz Questions' section at the back of the book.)

PROBLEMS

The answers to two of the following problems (those indicated by an asterisk) are available to students online. The answer to the remaining problem is available only to lecturers via the website (see the 'Digital Resources' page for details).

1* Quis plc and Zanda plc are two companies whose shares are quoted on the London stock exchange. Their assets have the same level of systematic risk. Each company has a constant annual earnings flow (before dividends and interest) of £5 million. This level of earnings is expected to be maintained by both companies in the future.

▶

Quis plc has issued £8 million of 9% irredeemable bonds; each £100 bond is currently quoted at £50, ex interest. Zanda plc has no debt. Each of Quis's 17.2 million shares is currently quoted at £1, ex div, while Zanda has issued 46.4 million shares each of which has a market price of 50p, ex div. Both companies pay out the entire earnings flow each year as dividends and interest.

Jill Gamma holds 464 000 shares in Zanda. as part of her well-diversified investment portfolio. Her market analysis leads her to believe that Quis shares are currently underpriced, because of a temporary disequilibrium in the market. As a result, she is considering selling her Zanda shares and investing in Quis shares instead.

Required:

(a) Suggest how Ms Gamma could undertake the arbitrage deal so as to maintain her current level of financial risk. Explain briefly why you think your suggested approach will maintain her financial risk level. What would be her resulting gains?

(b) What would be the equilibrium share price of Quis's equity if other investors also undertook arbitrage deals?

Assume that the market prices of Quis's bonds and Zanda's shares are in equilibrium. Assume no taxation.

2* Cabernet and Chardonnay are two bio-tech companies in the same business risk class. Cabernet is quoted on the Paris Bourse and has a debt–equity ratio of 1:3. The company's equity has a beta of 1.6 and the debt capital can be assumed to be riskless. Chardonnay is an unquoted, private company which is all-equity financed.

The expected return on the CAC stock market index is 16%. The return on government bonds (and also the return on Cabernet's debt) is 10%.

Assume that both Cabernet and Chardonnay pay out constant annual dividends. Cabernet's debt is irredeemable. Ignore taxation.

Required:

(a) Explain precisely what is meant by the term 'same business risk class'. Estimate the beta value of Chardonnay's equity.

(b) Estimate the WACC of each company and comment briefly on the significance of your figures in respect of the M and M (no-tax) capital structure hypothesis.

(c) Jean Davide is a small shareholder in Chardonnay. He has just received his regular dividend of €1500. Jean has now been offered €10 000 for his shareholding. However, he does not know whether or not to sell his shares as he relies heavily on his annual dividend from the company.

(d) Explain how Jean Davide can make himself better off, with no change in risk, by selling his shares in Chardonnay and investing in Cabernet. What would be his resulting gain?

(e) Assuming Cabernet's debt and equity capital are at their equilibrium value, estimate the equilibrium value of Jean's shareholding in Chardonnay.

3 Burda has an all-equity capital structure. Krone is very highly geared. Both companies come within the same business risk class. You are given the following information:

	Krone	Burda
	Years 1→∞	Years 1→∞
Annual dividends	€100 000	€180 000
Annual interest	€80 000	—
Total annual cash earnings	€180 000	€180 000
Total market value of equity	€400 000	€1 800 000
Total market value of debt	€1 000 000	—

There is a perfect capital market, no taxation, no transaction costs and no difference between corporate and private gearing.

Required:

(a) What would you conclude from the above information?

(b) Draw a diagram or diagrams (not to scale) to illustrate the current situation and to show what would happen if arbitragers entered the market.

(c) Illustrate the gain to be made from arbitrage by an individual currently holding €1000 worth of shares in one of the above companies (i.e. there are only arbitrage gains to be made from trading one way; therefore, you have to specify initially the direction of arbitrage).

Assume that the ordinary shares of Burda and the bonds of Krone are in equilibrium.

CAPITAL STRUCTURE IN A COMPLEX WORLD

LEARNING OBJECTIVES

The purpose of this chapter is to:

- Examine the impact of taxation on the M and M analysis of capital structure.
- Apply the M and M equations to examine the impact of capital structure on a company's costs of capital.
- Discuss the problems caused for the M and M analysis through real-world complications.
- Describe the 'traditional' theory of capital structure.
- Discuss the impact on the capital structure decision caused by the introduction of personal taxes, as well as corporate taxes.

TAXATION AND CAPITAL STRUCTURE

In Chapter 18 we examined the M and M no-tax capital structure hypothesis. In this chapter we will look at the M and M *with-tax* analysis and we shall see that, as a result, the conclusion that we reached in Chapter 18 – that the capital structure decision is unimportant, as it has no impact on the overall value of the company and so no impact on shareholder wealth – will be radically changed.

In the analysis of the capital structure problem in Chapter 18 (under the set of simplifying assumptions used) we stated that the total market value of a company could be defined as: $V_0 = Y/K_0$. Therefore, a company's gearing ratio could only affect its total market value (V_0) if it affected either the company's expected annual net cash flow (Y) or its weighted average cost of capital (K_0). With the introduction of a taxation regime which allows debt capital interest to be set off against tax liability, a company *will* be able to increase its expected annual net after-tax cash flow (Y) by gearing up.

Table 19.1 shows that a geared company's total after-tax cash flow can now be split into two elements: the after-tax cash flow that would arise if it were all equity financed, plus the tax relief it receives on the debt interest payments.[1] Therefore the total after-tax cash flow of the company will *increase* as it increases its gearing. This is because the more highly geared the company becomes, the more debt interest it pays, the greater the amount of tax relief it obtains and hence the smaller is the amount of tax paid. In such circumstances, the company would theoretically maximize its total market value by gearing up so that its capital structure consists of virtually all debt and just a token amount of equity to determine ownership.

TABLE 19.1

The dividend and interest valuation models indicate that the total value of a company is equal to the present value sum of the future expected dividend and interest cash flow streams. Still assuming all-level perpetuity cash flow streams, where X represents the annual operating net cash flow *before* interest and taxes:

$$V_E = \frac{(X - V_B K_D)(1 - T)}{K_{E_{ug}}} \tag{1}$$

$$V_B = \frac{V_B \times K_D}{K_D} \tag{2}$$

$$V_0 = \frac{(X - V_B K_D)(1 - T)}{K_E} + \frac{V_B K_D}{K_D} \tag{3}$$

Looking at the total cash flow

$$(X - V_B K_D)(1 - T) + V_B K_D$$

and expanding the terms:

$$X - XT - V_B K_D + V_B K_D T + V_B K_D$$

Cancelling and simplifying:

$$X(1 - T) + V_B K_D T$$

Thus the company's after-tax cash flow is what it would be if it were all-equity financed – $X(1 - T)$ – *plus* the value of the interest tax relief – $V_B K_D T$. The total value of the company is found by discounting these annual cash flows to present value. The discount rate to be applied to $X(1 - T)$ is the cost of equity capital that would apply to the company if it were all-equity financed ($K_{E_{ug}}$). The discount rate to be applied to $V_B K_D T$ (i.e. the interest rate that reflects the risk involved) is K_D. Thus:

$$V_0 = \frac{X(1 - T)}{K_{E_{ug}}} + \frac{V_B K_D T}{K_D} \tag{4}$$

$$V_0 = \frac{X(1 - T)}{K_{E_{ug}}} + V_B T \tag{5}$$

Hence, the more highly geared the company becomes, the larger becomes the second term – $V_B.T$ – (the first term remains unchanged), and so the greater becomes the value of the company.

In other words, taking the final expression for V_0 in Table 19.1:

$$V_0 = \frac{X(1-T)}{K_{E_{ug}}} + V_B T \qquad (5)$$

this can be interpreted as follows: The total market value of a geared company (V_0) is equal to what it would be worth if it was all-equity financed:

$$\left(\frac{X(1-T)}{K_{E_{ug}}} \right)$$

plus the present value of tax relief on debt interest, $V_B T$. Expression (5) can be rewritten as:

$$V_{0_g} = V_{E_{ug}} + V_B T$$

where V_0 is the total market value of a geared company, $V_{E_{ug}}$ represents what the company would be worth if it were all-equity financed and $V_B T$ represents the present value worth of the tax relief on debt interest – which is often referred to as the 'tax shield'.

Therefore, under the assumption of tax relief being available on debt interest, the total market value of the company is an increasing function of the level of gearing. What effect does gearing now have on both a company's cost of equity capital and its weighted average cost of capital? To answer that question we must once again examine the relationships involved.

Taxation and the WACC

The revised relationship between the gearing ratio and WACC can be derived both intuitively and analytically. Let us start with the intuitive explanation.

We saw in a world without tax that there was both an advantage ($K_D < K_E$) and a disadvantage (financial risk $\rightarrow$ increased K_E) to gearing up. However, these two effects exactly offset each other and so the net effect was zero: K_0 remained unaffected by gearing changes.

With the introduction of tax, there is now an *additional* advantage to gearing up: the tax relief obtained on the debt interest. Further, this advantage is *cumulative* – the more highly geared a company becomes, the more tax relief it obtains and the smaller its tax liability becomes. Thus we could intuitively argue that in a world where there was tax relief on debt interest, we would expect a company's *after-tax* WACC to be progressively *lowered* as it *increased* its level of gearing.

Indeed, this conclusion can also be inferred from the WACC expression. In this expression, the cost of debt capital is 'after tax' and as a company gears up, a progressively greater weight is given to this 'cheap' capital:

$$K_0 = K_E \times \frac{V_E}{V_0} + K_D(1-T) \times \frac{V_B}{V_0}$$

A more analytical derivation of the relationship between the WACC and gearing is given in Table 19.2 (where $K_{E_{ug}}$ represents the cost of equity capital of a *similar business risk*, but *all-equity* financed company).

The derivation of the WACC in Table 19.2 shows that (as we intuitively reasoned), as a company increases the proportion of debt in its capital structure, so the WACC declines. In fact, the WACC is a *negative* linear function of the ratio V_B/V_0.

TABLE 19.2

Starting with the company valuation expression derived in Table 19.1:

$$V_0 = \frac{X(1-T)}{K_{E_{ug}}} + V_B T \tag{1}$$

Multiplying through by $K_{E_{ug}}$:

$$V_0 K_{E_{ug}} = X(1-T) + V_B T K_{E_{ug}} \tag{2}$$

Rearranging and factoring out V_0:

$$V_0 K_{E_{ug}} - V_B T K_{E_{ug}} = X(1-T) \tag{3}$$

$$V_0 K_{E_{ug}} - \frac{V_0 V_B T K_{E_{ug}}}{V_0} = X(1-T) \tag{4}$$

$$V_0 \left(K_{E_{ug}} - \frac{V_B T K_{E_{ug}}}{V_0} \right) = X(1-T) \tag{5}$$

$$V_0 \frac{X(1-T)}{K_{E_{ug}}[1-(V_B T/V_0)]} \tag{6}$$

given that:

$$V_0 = X(1-T)/K_0$$

then:

$$K_0 = K_{E_{ug}}[1-(V_B T/V_0)]$$

The cost of equity capital

The cost of equity capital's relationship with the gearing ratio can also be intuitively derived. We know that the expected return required by equity rises (in a world of no taxes), as gearing is increased, because of the increasing burden of financial risk on shareholders. The financial risk arises because debt interest has to be paid in full to lenders, before any dividends can be paid to shareholders.

In a taxed world, debt interest payments are, effectively, subsidized by the tax authorities. Thus if the company had interest of €100 to pay and corporation tax was at 20%, then €20 out of the €100 of interest payable would be provided for through a reduced tax liability. Therefore, in a taxed world, although the cost of equity capital would still be expected to increase with increased gearing, because of the presence of financial risk, it would do so at a *slower rate* than in a tax-free world. The presence of subsidized interest payments effectively reduces gearing ratios from the viewpoint of shareholders and their financing risk.

Once again, this intuitive argument can be shown, analytically, to hold good. Table 19.3 illustrates the relationship. What we derive is an expression that is very similar to the cost

TABLE 19.3

The WACC can be calculated either as:

$$K_0 = \frac{V_E}{V_0} \times K_{E_g} + \frac{V_B}{V_0} \times K_D(1 - T)$$

or:

$$K_0 = K_{E_{ug}}\left(1 - \frac{V_B T}{V_0}\right)$$

therefore:

$$\frac{V_E}{V_0} \times K_{E_g} + \frac{V_B}{V_0} \times K_D(1 - T) = K_{E_{ug}}\left(1 - \frac{V_B T}{V_0}\right) \tag{1}$$

Multiplying through by V_0 and rearranging:

$$K_{E_g} = \frac{K_{E_{ug}}(V_0 - TV_B)}{V_E} - \frac{V_B K_D}{V_E} + \frac{V_B K_D T}{V_E}$$

$$= \frac{K_{E_{ug}} V_E}{V_E} + \frac{K_{E_{ug}} V_B}{V_E} - \frac{K_{E_{ug}} TV_B}{V_E} - \frac{V_B K_D}{V_E} + \frac{V_B K_D T}{V_E} \tag{2}$$

$$= K_{E_{ug}} + \frac{K_{E_{ug}} V_B}{V_E}(1 - T) - \frac{K_D V_B}{V_E}(1 - T)$$

$$K_{E_g} = K_{E_{ug}} + (K_{E_{ug}} - K_D)\frac{V_B(1 - T)}{V_E} \tag{3}$$

of equity capital function in an untaxed world, except that the effect of the gearing ratio is reduced by the presence of taxation. As a result, the amount of debt in the gearing ratio is measured as $V_B(1 - T)$, rather than just V_B.

The graphical relationship

The relationship between the various costs of capital and the gearing ratio is shown graphically in Figure 19.1. (Note that although the WACC is a *linear* function of V_B/V_0, it is an *asymptotic* function of V_B/V_E.)

Therefore, we can reiterate the conclusion of the M and M with-tax capital structure hypothesis: companies should try to use as much as possible. The more highly geared the company, the lower will be K_0, the higher will be V_0 and the greater will be shareholder wealth. This increase in shareholder wealth comes about through the tax shield, for it is the shareholders who gain the benefit of the company, receiving tax relief on debt interest and so paying less tax.

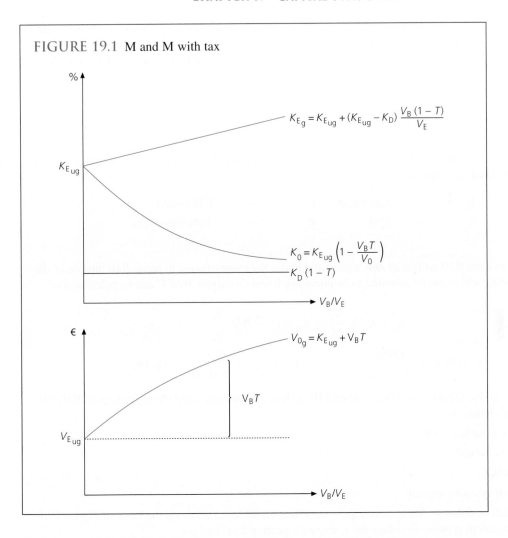

FIGURE 19.1 M and M with tax

USING THE M AND M EQUATIONS

The M and M with-tax analysis produces three fundamental equations, as we have seen:

$$K_{E_g} = K_{E_g} + (K_{E_g} - K_D) - \frac{V_B \times (1 - T)}{V_E} \qquad (1)$$

$$K_0 = K_{E_{ug}} \left(1 - \frac{V_B T}{V_0}\right) \qquad (2)$$

$$V_{0_g} = V_{E_{ug}} + V_B T \qquad (3)$$

These equations can be utilized to illustrate the impact of changes in the company's capital structure on the company's total market value, its various costs of capital and on shareholder wealth. We will use two examples. In Example 1, a company undertakes an 'artificial' change to its capital structure by issuing new equity capital and using the money to 'repay' debt. Thus the new finance is not increasing the assets of the company, but is being used to simply change the company's capital structure (to *reduce* its level of gearing).

EXAMPLE 1

Impala Telkom is a small South African-based telecoms company. The company has a geared capital structure, with details as follows:

$$V_E \quad = \quad \text{R80 million} \qquad V_B \qquad = \qquad \text{R35 million}$$

$$K_{E_g} \quad = \quad 20\% \qquad K_D \qquad = \qquad 10\% \text{ before tax}$$

$$T \qquad = \qquad 28\%$$

Impala wants to issue R10 million of new equity and to use the money raised to repay R10 million of the company's bonds (which can be assumed to be undated). Impala's current WACC can be calculated as:

$$K_0 = K_{E_g} \times \frac{V_E}{V_0} + K_D \times (1 - T) \times \frac{V_B}{V_0}$$

$$K_0 = 20\% \times \frac{\text{R80m}}{\text{R115m}} + 10\% \times (1 - 0.28) \times \frac{\text{R35m}}{\text{R115m}} = 16.1\%$$

We will now examine the impact of the issue of R10 million of new equity and the repayment of R10 million of Impala's bonds on:

1. Impala's total market value
2. Shareholders' wealth
3. Impala's WACC
4. Impala's cost of equity capital.

However, before doing so, we can *anticipate* the effect on all four factors on the basis of Figure 19.1. Impala's management propose to *reduce* the company's gearing level and so:

1. The company's total market value (V_0) will *fall*
2. Shareholder wealth will *fall* because of a reduction in the size of the tax shield
3. The company's WACC will *rise*
4. The company's K_E will *fall*.

Let us now look at the precise effects of Impala's proposed change in capital structure, taking each of those four impacts in order.

1. Using the *current* data, in the M and M equation:

$$V_0 = V_{E_{ug}} + V_B T$$

to solve for $V_{E_{ug}}$:

$$\text{R115m} = V_{E_{ug}} + \text{R35m} \times 0.28$$

$$\text{R115m} - \text{R9.8m} = V_{E_{ug}} = \text{R105.2 million}$$

▶

Therefore if Impala's assets were all-equity financed, the company's total market value would be R105.2 million. The company's current total market value is R115 million because of the tax shield – the tax relief that Impala receives because of its interest liabilities.

If Impala now raises R10 million of new equity and uses the finance to reduce its outstanding debt from R35 million to R25 million then, again using:

$$V_0 = V_{E_{ug}} + V_B T$$

we can find the *new* total market value of the company:

$$V_0 = R105.2m + R25m \times 0.28 = R112.2 \text{ million}$$

Impala's total market value has been reduced from R115 million to R112.2 million (a reduction of R2.8 million), because it has lost the tax shield on the R10 million of repaid debt equal to R10m × 0.28 = R2.8m (remember, the value of the tax shield is given by: $V_B T$).

2. The change in the company's capital structure will lead to a fall in shareholder wealth equal to the lost tax shield of R2.8 million. This can be demonstrated as follows:

Currently:	V_E	=	R80m
Given:	V_0	=	$V_E + V_B$
Therefore:	V_E	=	$V_0 - V_B$

and so *after* the change in capital structure:

$$V_E = R112.2m - R25m = R87.2 \text{ million}$$

Therefore the total market value of the equity has risen from R80 million to R87.2 million but, remember, shareholders have invested an extra R10 million in the company. As the value of their shares has only gone up by R7.2 million, there has been a loss in their wealth of: R10m − R7.2m = R2.8m.

3. Using the *current* data in the M and M equation:

$$K_0 = K_{E_{ug}} \times \left(1 - \frac{V_B T}{V_0}\right)$$

we can solve for $K_{E_{ug}}$:

$$16.1\% = K_{E_{ug}} \times \left[1 - \frac{R35m \times 0.28}{R115m}\right]$$

$$\frac{16.1\%}{0.915} = K_{E_{ug}} = 17.6\%$$

This would be Impala's cost of equity capital, if the company were all-equity financed. Therefore 17.6% represents the return required for just Impala's *business* risk. At present Impala's shareholders receive a return (K_E) of 20% because they also bear financial risk from Impala's current level of gearing. If Impala now issues an extra R10 million of equity and repays R10 million of debt, then again using:

$$K_0 = K_{E_{ug}} \times \left(1 - \frac{V_B T}{V_0}\right)$$

we can find the company's *new* WACC:

$$K_0 = 17.6\% \times \left(1 - \frac{R25m \times 0.28}{R112.2m}\right) = 16.5\%$$

Therefore the change in capital structure has increased WACC from its existing level of 16.1% to 16.5%.

4. Finally, the M and M equation for K_E, together with our calculation of $K_{E_{ug}} = 17.6\%$ can be used to identify the company's new cost of equity capital:

$$K_{E_g} = K_{E_{ug}} + (K_{E_{ug}} - K_{DBT}) \times \frac{V_B \times (1 - T)}{V_E}$$

$$K_{E_g} = 17.6\% + (17.6\% - 10\%) \times \frac{R25m \times (1 - 0.28)}{R87.2m} = 19.17\%$$

Thus, Impala's cost of equity capital will fall from 20% to 19.17% with the proposed reduction in the company's gearing ratio.

In Example 2, a company is issuing debt capital in order to finance a capital investment. In this case the finance is increasing the assets of the company, as well as changing its capital structure.

EXAMPLE 2

Berne Biotech AG is a Swiss-based, all-equity financed company with a total worth of SFr12 million (SFr = Swiss Francs) and a cost of equity capital of 18%. Berne intends to invest in a SFr3 million capital investment to expand the company's existing manufacturing capacity. The investment has a +SFr1 million NPV.

The company intends to finance the project with a SFr 3 million irredeemable bonds issued at the current market interest rate of 4%. The corporation tax rate is 18%. What is the impact of the project and its finance on Berne Biotech's:

1. total market value, V_0

2. shareholders' wealth

3. WACC, and

4. cost of equity capital?

Taking each of these in turn:

1. At present, because Berne Biotech is all-equity financed:

$$V_0 = V_E = V_{E_{ug}} = SFr12 \text{ million}$$

The new V_0 arising out of the change in capital structure can be found from the M and M equation:

$$V_0 = V_{E_{ug}} + V_B T$$

therefore:

$$V_0 = \text{SFr12m} + [\text{SFr3m} \times 0.18] = \text{SFr12.54 million}$$

However, we must not forget that, in this example, SFr3 million of *additional* assets are being added to the company, *plus* the project's positive NPV. Thus the new total market value of the company, after taking into account not only the change in capital structure, but also the SFr3 million of newly added assets (i.e. the capital investment) and the project's NPV is given by:

$$V_0 = \text{SFr12.54m} + \text{SFr3m} + \text{SFr1m} = \text{SFr16.54 million}$$

This is made up as follows:

Existing total market value of company:	SFr12m
+ Extra tax shield:	SFr0.54m
+ Extra capital investment:	SFr3m
+ Project's NPV:	SFr1m
= New total market value of the company:	SFr16.54m

2. Given that $V_0 = V_E + V_B$, then the post-investment total market value of the equity of Berne Biotech will be:

$$V_E = V_0 - V_B$$
$$V_E = \text{SFr16.54m} - \text{SFr3m} = \text{SFr13.54 million}$$

Therefore shareholder wealth, represented by the total market value of the equity, has increased by: SFr13.54m − SFr12m = SFr1.54m. This is composed of two separate elements: the NPV of the project (SFr1 million) and the tax shield on the debt interest (SFr0.54 million).

3. Given the fact that Berne is currently all-equity financed, then:

$$K_0 = K_E = K_{E_{ug}} = 18\%$$

Using the M and M equation, the new WACC can be calculated:

$$K_0 = K_{E_{ug}} \times \left(1 - \frac{V_B T}{V_0}\right)$$

$$K_0 = 18\% \times \left(1 - \frac{\text{SFr3m} \times 0.18}{\text{SFr16.54m}}\right) = 17.4\%$$

Thus the increase in Berne's gearing will cause its WACC to fall from 18% (its current K_E) to 17.4%.

4. Using the M and M equation:

$$K_{E_g} = K_{E_{ug}} + (K_{E_{ug}} - K_{D_{BT}}) \times \frac{V_B(1 - T)}{V_E}$$

the company's new cost of equity capital can be estimated:

$$K_{E_{ug}} = 18\% + (18\% - 4\%) \times \frac{\text{SFr3m} \times (1 - 0.18)}{\text{SFr13.54m}} = 20.54\%$$

▶

Therefore the change in Berne Biotech's capital structure causes its cost of equity capital to increase from 18% to 20.54%. This is because, before the capital structure change, Berne's shareholders only bore the company's *business* risk, as it was all-equity financed. However, after the issue of SFr3 million of debt, the company's shareholders are starting to bear *financial* risk as well, and so their return rises by 2.54% (the financial risk premium) to 20.54%.

Arbitrage in a taxed world

Before we leave the M and M analysis, it is worthwhile to point out that the arbitrage analysis that we looked at in Chapter 18 can be adapted to a taxed world. To show how we can do so, we will refer back to the two examples that were used in Chapter 18.

In the first arbitrage example, which was set out in Table 18.5, our investor, Carlos, was moving from a geared company (Bruno company) to an all-equity financed company (Arno company). In order to be able to compare like with like, our investor had to substitute home-made or personal gearing for corporate gearing. This was done by the arbitrager borrowing money, at an interest rate equal to K_D, such that:

$$\left(\begin{matrix} \text{Borrowed} & & \text{Share} \\ \text{funds} & : & \text{sale} \\ & & \text{proceeds} \end{matrix} \right) = V_B : V_E \text{ of Bruno company}$$

With tax in the analysis, the procedure remains exactly the same, except that the arbitrager borrows money in the ratio:

$$\left(\begin{matrix} \text{Borrowed} & & \text{Share} \\ \text{funds} & : & \text{sale} \\ & & \text{proceeds} \end{matrix} \right) = V_B \times (1 - T) : V_E \text{ of Bruno company}$$

Therefore, in that example, given that Bruno's gearing ratio – $V_B:V_E$ – was 1:3, and now assuming a corporation tax rate of 20%, our arbitrager would borrow money in the ratio: $1 \times (1 - 0.20) : 3$ or 0.80 : 3. In other words, the arbitrager Carlos would borrow 80 cents for every €3 of share sale proceeds in order to maintain his existing level of financial risk.

A similar adjustment is made in the 'reverse arbitrage' situation. In that example, in the previous chapter, our arbitrager bought both debt and equity in the geared company in the same ratio as the company's gearing ratio. This now changes so that both debt and equity is bought in the ratio $V_B \times (1 - T):V_E$.

In our reverse arbitrage example the $V_B:V_E$ ratio was 4:10.40. Again, assuming a corporate tax rate of 20%, the arbitrager (in this case it was Daniella), instead of buying €4 of debt for every €10.40 of equity, she would buy debt and equity in the ratio of $4 \times (1 - 0.20):10.40$, or €3.20 of debt for every €10.40 of equity.

M AND M IN THE REAL WORLD

The M and M *with tax* analysis suggests that companies should gear themselves up to the maximum possible extent. However, in the real world, the evidence is that companies generally do not borrow at anything like the levels that M and M's analysis suggests should happen. So far as European companies are concerned, the average level of gearing is such that debt capital represents about 30% to 35% of total capital. This fact suggests that our model is too simple – it must be excluding some important aspects about the financing decision and its effects.

Agency costs

One possible reason why we do not find companies gearing up to the high levels suggested by the M and M *with tax* analysis is that there are some 'hidden' costs of debt capital that we have so far ignored. One particular group of these is referred to as 'agency costs'.

Agency costs arise out of what is known as the principal–agent problem.[2] This problem is concerned with how the instructions or objectives, and the rewards, given to agents (i.e. management) can be formulated so that the agents, acting in their own interests, also act in the interest of the principals (i.e. the suppliers of company capital). In other words, the principal–agent problem is concerned with the external financial control of a company's management, by the suppliers of its finance.

In respect of debt finance, the suppliers of debt finance are concerned that they are not fooled or misled by a company's management. For example, a situation could occur where a management raise finance for a supposed investment in a low-risk project but, once the debt is issued, they use the money to invest in a high-risk project. In such circumstances the debt holders are likely to suffer because their expected rate of return would not properly reflect the risk of their investment.

In order to try to avoid this sort of situation we find that debt suppliers often impose very restrictive conditions (or covenants) on loan agreements that constrain management's freedom of action. For example, debt covenants may restrict the level of dividends that may be paid (to prevent shareholders stripping the firm of cash, to the detriment of debt holders); or they may restrict the level of additional debt finance that can be raised (in order to maintain a given degree of security); or they may restrict management from disposing of major fixed assets without the debt holders' agreement.

All of these examples represent constraints on management – they constrain their freedom of action – and are known as 'agency costs'. All agents realize that they are going to be controlled or constrained by their principals, but that does not mean that agents actually *like* these agency costs that they are forced to bear. They do not like them – and will often attempt to minimize them.

The more money the suppliers of debt capital lend to a company – that is the more highly geared the company becomes – then the more constraints they are likely to impose on the management in order to secure their investment. Hence it could be argued that management may well limit the level of a company's gearing in order to avoid the more onerous of these agency costs. As a result we do not find, in practice, companies gearing up to the high levels suggested by the M and M analysis.

Bankruptcy costs

Another cost that may be viewed as a part of the general agency costs is that of bankruptcy (the forced liquidation of a company because its liabilities exceed its assets). In the previous analysis it was always assumed, implicitly, that companies could go bankrupt costlessly, but what happens when the possibility and the associated costs of corporate bankruptcy are introduced?

The *probability* of a company becoming bankrupt is likely to be (amongst other things) an *increasing* function of a company's gearing ratio but, as far as the capital structure problem is concerned, the important factor is the substantial cost that may be involved in a company's liquidation or bankruptcy. If a company that was forced into bankruptcy could be liquidated costlessly (i.e. if its assets could be sold off at their 'correct' market values and if there were no legal or administrative costs), then the fact that the probability of bankruptcy is an increasing function of the gearing ratio would not have any adverse effect on the total market value of a company.

Unfortunately, in the real world, the costs of bankruptcy are considerable. As well as very substantial administrative and legal costs, the company's specialized assets may have to be disposed of at less than their operational values, because they have lost their going-concern/synergy value and because their sale has to take place hurriedly in an imperfect market. These costs (in whole or in part) will come out of the liquidated pool of funds which is destined to be returned to shareholders. Therefore, bankruptcy involves a company's shareholders in a cost they would otherwise not have incurred and so it is effectively responsible for causing a reduction in their level of wealth.

All shareholders, whether they are shareholders in geared or all-equity companies, face the (hopefully small) probability that their company may be forced into bankruptcy. This fact is just one component of the concept of business risk and, as such, is allowed for in the expected value of the future dividend flow and the required expected return on equity capital. However, the act of gearing up by a company has the effect of positively adding to the probability of its bankruptcy, due to the fact that if a company is unable to meet its fixed debt interest payments, then the debt holders have the legal right to liquidate the company in order to repossess their capital and unpaid interest.

Therefore, as a company increases its level of gearing, an increasing proportion of its expected annual cash flow is likely to be paid out as interest. But, as the future is uncertain, the company's future annual cash flows are *variable* and uncertain, while debt interest represents a *fixed*, contractual obligation, and so there is also an increasing chance that the company's cash flows will not be sufficient to meet these debt interest payments. A succession of such years for a geared company will almost certainly lead to bankruptcy and the incursion of its associated costs.

Thus, as gearing increases, so too does the probability of bankruptcy and hence the 'expected' cost of bankruptcy (where the expected cost of bankruptcy = cost of bankruptcy × probability of bankruptcy). Given this analysis, the M and M expression for the total market value of a geared company might be altered to:

$$V_{0_g} = V_{E_{ug}} + V_B T - E_{[BANKRUPTCY]}$$

where $E_{[BANKRUPTCY]}$ represents the expected cost of bankruptcy defined as the probability × the cost of bankruptcy. As a result, it could be argued that management restrict the company's level of gearing because V_0 (and so shareholder wealth) *reduces* at very high levels of gearing. Figure 19.2 illustrates the possible situation.

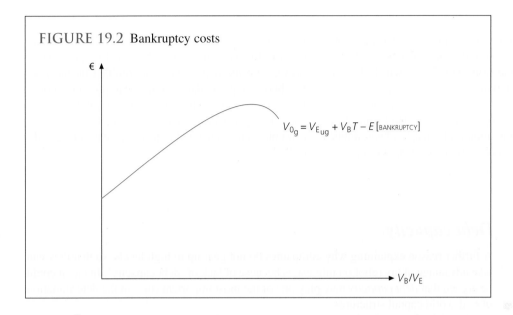

FIGURE 19.2 Bankruptcy costs

$$V_{0_g} = V_{E_{ug}} + V_B T - E\,[\text{BANKRUPTCY}]$$

Therefore bankruptcy costs would appear to provide yet another reason why we do not find companies with very high gearing ratios: there is this additional implicit cost which is borne by shareholders. However, these expected costs may not be the most important element in the role that the possibility of bankruptcy plays in limiting gearing ratios.

Shareholders can generally be expected to hold well diversified portfolios. Therefore, if one particular company within an investment portfolio goes into liquidation, the associated costs will be incurred by the investor, but they are likely to be relatively small. In contrast, the management of a company hold 'undiversified portfolios' as far as their labour is concerned (i.e. they only work for the one company) and so, to them, the cost of bankruptcy is *very* substantial – they lose their employment. Therefore we might conclude that management – for their own, personal, reasons – are also likely to want to restrict the level of gearing, in order to restrict the probability of bankruptcy and hence avoid the very substantial personal costs involved.

REAL WORLD VIEW: The True Cost of Bankruptcy

Bankruptcy laws vary around the world. In the USA, companies often use the trade-off theory of capital structure as a decision whether or not to go into bankruptcy. This is because the costs of bankruptcy can actually be extremely high, thus reducing the value of company assets.

For example, the Enron bankruptcy in 2001 (see also the *Real World View* in Chapter 2) was the world's sixth largest corporate bankruptcy,

estimated to have cost around $23 billion in liabilities. The legal fees alone of this bankruptcy came to $756.6 million.

Another example is the city of Detroit, Michigan, which filed for Chapter 9 bankruptcy in July 2013. By October, Detroit owed almost $23 million in fees to various consultants, advisors and lawyers: all as part of the discussions about entering into the bankruptcy process. Of course, the bankruptcy of a city leads to more complications: which parts of it are assets that can be sold? The problem with Detroit lies in its art collection, only 5% of which does not have donor restrictions.

Meanwhile in the EU, as reported in 2011, a low bankruptcy discharge time in England and Wales saw an increasing amount of what has been dubbed 'bankruptcy tourism', particularly from German and Irish small businesses and entrepreneurs. Europeans can file for bankruptcy anywhere in Europe, hence opening up the opportunity for troubled businesses to choose a particular country that presents more favourable options. This means that a debt discharge wait of 12 years in Ireland or seven in Germany, for example, can be changed to just one year in England or Wales.

Debt capacity

A further reason explaining why companies do not gear up to high levels, so that they can take advantage of tax relief on interest, is because of lack of 'debt capacity'. In fact it could be argued that *debt capacity* may play one of the most important roles in the determination of real-world capital structures.

Most debt finance that is lent to companies by banks and other debt suppliers is *secured* against the assets of the company. Relatively little debt capital is unsecured. The idea behind securing a loan against the company's assets is obvious. If the company defaults on the loan agreement, the lender has the legal right to seize the assets against which the loan was secured, sell those assets, and so recover their loan capital (and any unpaid interest) out of the sale proceeds (any money that remains after this process would be returned to shareholders).

From the foregoing, it will be obvious that not all assets make good security for loans and that some assets provide better security for a loan than other assets. Perhaps the two most important characteristics of an asset in determining its suitability to act as security against a loan are:

1. the 'quality' of the second-hand market in the asset
2. the asset's rate of depreciation.

The quality of the second-hand market refers to the ease (or otherwise) with which a seized asset could be sold. Thus the better the quality of the second-hand market, the more suitable is the asset as loan security. Similarly, an asset which depreciates rapidly (in reality rather than accounting terms) is going to offer poor security. The value of the asset may then be worth significantly less than the outstanding value of the loan – particularly in the latter years of a loan's terms.

If a company wishes to acquire a building costing, say, €1 million and the lender is willing to loan €900 000 against the security of the asset, then the building would be said to have a *90% debt capacity*. However, if a company wished to purchase €1 million worth of specialized industrial equipment, the lender may only be willing to lend, say, €300 000 against the security of that particular asset. That asset only has a debt capacity of 30%.

A building could be expected to have a *high* debt capacity because of its active second-hand market and its slow rate of depreciation (it could even appreciate). Specialized industrial machinery, on the other hand, is likely to have a relatively *low* debt capacity because it probably has a poor second-hand market and a relatively high rate of depreciation.

Therefore, from this discussion on debt capacity, we may conclude that high levels of corporate gearing are unusual, not because of a positive management decision to limit the amount of gearing, but simply because the company has run out of debt capacity. In other words the capital structure decision may be determined more by the *suppliers* of debt capital, rather than by the *managers* of the company.

Tax exhaustion

A final possible reason for observed gearing levels is 'tax exhaustion'. Debt financing is attractive to companies (and, to some extent, to shareholders), because of the tax relief allowable on the interest payments. As a company increases the gearing level, so it increases its annual interest payments and it also increases the amount of tax relief that it gains. The term 'tax exhaustion' refers to the situation where a company does not have a sufficient tax liability to be able to take advantage of all the tax relief that it has available.

At the point of tax exhaustion therefore, the effective cost of debt capital rises significantly from $K_D(1 - T)$ to simply K_D. Once this position is reached, debt capital loses much of its attraction for the company, and so we have a fourth possible reason for the fact that observed levels of corporate gearing are less than would be expected from the M and M *with tax* analysis.

FURTHER VIEWS ON CAPITAL STRUCTURE

The M and M analysis of the capital structure problem, whether in a taxed or a tax-free world, is based upon a number of assumptions about the environment, including the tax regime and the working of the capital markets. On the basis of these assumptions, their analysis produces rigorous conclusions about the nature of the trade-off between financial risk and gearing and about the behaviour of a company's cost of equity capital, its WACC and also its total market value, as the gearing ratio changes.

In addition, an important conclusion arising from the discussion, as far as company managements and shareholders are concerned, is that gearing up (i.e. increasing the proportion of debt in a company's capital structure) enhances the total market value of the company – and hence increases shareholders' wealth – through the tax relief that is allowable on corporate debt interest.

However, when we examine the real world we find that companies do not follow this conclusion to its logical extreme and gear up so that 99%+ of capital is debt. We then concluded that there must be some relevant factors that were missing from the analysis, of which we considered four possibilities: agency costs, bankruptcy costs, debt capacity and tax exhaustion. What can we conclude from this discussion? Perhaps the safest conclusion that we can make is that the capital structure decision (and hence the financing decision) is both complex and difficult. In particular the costs of increased gearing cause identification problems that prevent any general decision advice being formulated.

In this next section we will examine two further views of the capital structure decision faced by companies. The first is referred to as the 'traditional' view, as it is a view that is often casually subscribed to, without much rigorous analysis being applied. The second is a further development by Miller (of M and M) who had some additional thoughts on the matter.

The traditional view of capital structure

It is often held that the generally accepted wisdom of investors, analysts and company managements alike (hence the term 'traditional' view) is that there are both advantages and disadvantages, as far as the maximization of shareholders' wealth is concerned, to corporate gearing. It is believed that at relatively *low levels* of gearing the advantages *outweigh* the disadvantages and so the market value of the company gradually rises but that, after a while, the relationship *reverses* and the disadvantages start to outweigh the advantages, so that further increases in gearing cause the company's market value to decline. Figure 19.3 sketches the various relationships involved in this traditional view of capital structure.

The main advantage of gearing is seen to be that, because corporate debt interest is allowable against taxation, a company is able to raise capital at an effective cost which is substantially below the market rate (i.e. debt capital is held to be 'cheap' capital because of interest tax relief). The main disadvantage arises from the fact that increased gearing results in an increased level of financial risk being borne by the company's shareholders. This, in turn, leads the shareholders to require a higher expected return on their capital (i.e. an increased K_E), by way of compensation.

A further disadvantage can also be suggested. This is that, at relatively high gearing levels, because of the quantity of debt finance that has been raised, *primary* and *subordinated* issues of debt start being made, where some debt holders receive interest payments before other debt holders and, as a result, some debt holders – the subordinate debt holders – start to bear their own version of financial risk. The subordinated debt holders therefore require an increased rate of interest in compensation. As a result, a company's *average* cost of debt (K_D), as well as the cost of equity, starts to rise as gearing levels reach higher levels.

In contrast to this traditional view of capital structure, the M and M hypothesis was that, in a tax-free environment, the advantages and disadvantages of gearing exactly offset each other at all gearing ratios; whereas in a taxed world, the advantages consistently outweigh

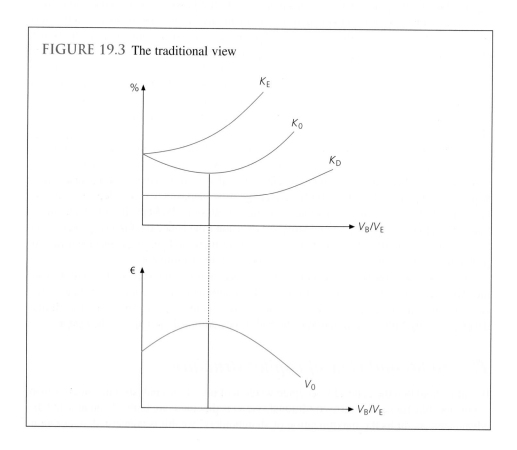

FIGURE 19.3 The traditional view

the disadvantages at all levels of gearing. However, the real point of difference between the M and M and traditional views is the exact nature of the relationship between the cost of equity capital and the gearing ratio.

Whereas in the M and M hypothesis the increased return required by equity capital as compensation for bearing financial risk rises at a constant rate as the gearing level increases, the traditional view is that this required expected return rises at an increasing rate, i.e. at a rate which is, at relatively low levels of gearing, below that hypothesized by M and M, but which increases above the return required by equity in the M and M model, at higher gearing ratios.

In this respect it is interesting to note that as financial risk is systematic, the CAPM analysis would probably lead us to expect a positive linear relationship between the cost of equity and the gearing ratio (if it is only financial risk that is causing the cost of equity to rise). Thus CAPM would support the M and M hypothesis.

As far as the rising cost of debt argument is concerned, the M and M analysis simply assumes that K_D remains a constant at all gearing levels. Whether K_D would actually rise at a high gearing level is debatable. Our discussion on debt capacity would suggest that as long as the company can provide suitable security for its debt, then debt holders are not likely to bear their own version of financial risk as gearing increases. Thus the assumption of a constant K_D may well be realistic – up to the level of gearing at which the firm's overall debt capacity is reached.

The traditional view of capital structure is just that: a view or reflection of what is traditionally believed to be the relationship between a company's various costs of capital and the gearing ratio, and it has never rested on a rigorous theoretical model as does the M and M hypothesis. Several writers have expressed the traditional view of capital structure in algebraic form, but none has been able to show satisfactorily, in the way in which M and M used the existence of arbitrage transactions, why the cost of equity capital should have a non-linear relationship with the gearing ratio, as argued by the traditionalist view.

The most notable feature about the traditionalist view of capital structure (which follows on from the assumed nature of the K_E function) is the U-shaped WACC curve and the corresponding inverted-U total market value curve. At low gearing levels, the advantages outweigh the disadvantages, and so K_0 is pulled down; and as a result V_0 rises. But, as the company continues to gear up, the advantages now start to become outweighed by the disadvantages, K_0 rises and consequently V_0 falls.

This leads firmly to the conclusion that each company has an optimal capital structure that minimizes its WACC and so maximizes its total market value. Company managements must search for this particular gearing ratio (which is likely to vary from company to company and may well vary over time for any one particular company), and so the financing decision is elevated to a position of importance almost on a par with the investment decision itself.

Corporate and personal taxes

The M and M analysis of the capital structure decision in a taxed world implies that tax relief on debt interest would encourage companies to gear up to as high a level as possible. The greater the level of gearing, the greater would be the tax subsidy on debt financing accruing to the company. However M and M only considered *corporate* taxes. It was left to a subsequent analysis by Miller (1977)[3] to include the effects of *personal* as well as corporate taxes. Miller's arguments, although they can be developed intuitively, are complex and they are briefly outlined below.

Miller showed that when personal as well as corporate taxes are taken into account, then the expression for the value of the tax shield (the present value of the tax relief on corporate debt) changes. Thus the M and M expression:

$$V_{0_g} = V_{E_{ug}} + V_B T$$

changes to:

$$V_{0_g} = V_{E_{ug}} + V_B \left[1 - \frac{(1 - T_C)(1 - T_E)}{1 - T_D} \right]$$

where:

$$
\begin{aligned}
T_C &= \text{corporate tax rate} \\
T_E &= \text{personal tax rate on } \textit{equity} \text{ income} \\
T_D &= \text{personal tax rate on } \textit{debt} \text{ income.}
\end{aligned}
$$

In a homogeneous personal tax regime where all personal income is taxed at the *same* rate, then $T_E = T_D$ and so Miller's expression for V_{0_g} reduces back to:

$$V_0 = V_{E_{ug}} + V_B T_C$$

In other words, homogeneous personal taxes were an implicit assumption of the M and M with-tax analysis.

However in the real world, the personal tax regime is heterogeneous where $T_E \neq T_D$. In such circumstances Miller argued that, effectively, $T_E = 0$ as shareholders can avoid taxes on dividends by taking dividends as capital gains (i.e. selling cum div and re-purchasing at ex div), which effectively escape personal tax in many tax regimes.[4] In addition he put forward a macroeconomic argument that, in an equilibrium market for corporate debt $T_D = T_C$.

It is this latter argument that lies at the heart of Miller's analysis and it is the most controversial part of his thesis. He argued that the existence of tax relief on debt interest – but not on equity dividends – would make debt capital more attractive than equity capital to companies. However, given that the market for corporate debt capital operates under the laws of supply and demand, companies would have to offer a higher return on debt (K_D) in order to generate a greater supply of debt.

Assuming a certain world in which investors hold either debt or equity, to persuade an equity supplier to switch over to become a debt supplier (because the company would prefer debt), the company must offer an after-personal tax return on debt at least equal to the after-personal tax return on equity. Then, remembering that $T_E = 0$, the after-personal tax return on debt must, at a minimum, be:

$$K_D (1 - T_D) = K_E$$

Therefore, the minimum interest rate the company must pay on debt capital is:

$$K_D = \frac{K_E}{1 - T_D}$$

If the previous expression gives the minimum debt interest rate the company must offer to persuade equity investors to switch to debt, what then is the maximum interest rate the company would be willing to pay? This would be where the after-corporate tax cost of debt was equal to the cost of equity:

$$K_D(1 - T_C) = K_E$$

At that point, the company would be indifferent between equity and debt finance as the effective cost of each would be the same. In other words, the highest interest rate they would be willing to pay would be:

$$K_D = \frac{K_E}{1 - T_D}$$

Given a supply and demand market for corporate debt, as long as the interest rate: $K_D < K_E/(1 - T_C)$ companies would want to *issue* debt (i.e. borrow). And, as long as $K_D \geq K_E/(1 - T_D)$, investors would be willing to *supply* debt (i.e. lend). Thus an equilibrium position in the corporate debt market – where supply and demand equated – would occur where:

$$\frac{K_E}{1 - T_C} = K_D = \frac{K_E}{1 - T_D}$$

In other words, equilibrium would occur where $T_C = T_D$; where the corporate tax rate equals the personal tax rate of marginal (or incremental) investors in corporate bonds. This is shown graphically in Figure 19.4.

From this analysis, the conclusion can be drawn that, from the viewpoint of an individual company, it will be indifferent between raising debt or equity finance as the effective cost of each will be the same. (Obviously a non-tax paying company would strongly prefer *equity* finance because $K_D > K_E$.) All the advantages of the tax relief on debt interest will go to the suppliers of debt capital whose own personal T_D is less than T_C. This is represented by the shaded area on Figure 19.4.

This conclusion can be seen from the fact that Miller's expression for V_{0_g}:

$$V_{0_g} = V_{E_{ug}} + V_B\left[1 - \frac{(1 - T_C)(1 - T_E)}{1 - T_D}\right]$$

reduces, when $T_E = 0$ and $T_D = T_C$, to:

$$V_0 = V_{E_{ug}}$$

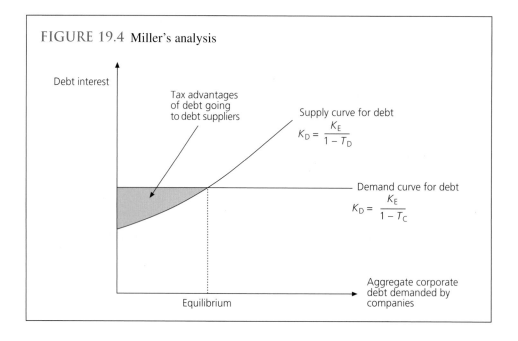

FIGURE 19.4 Miller's analysis

The value of the tax shield now becomes zero. There is *no advantage* to gearing and so one capital structure is therefore as good as another. (Notice that this conclusion is, rather ironically, identical to that of the original M and M no-tax capital structure hypothesis.) Hence the financing/capital structure decision is relegated to being a matter of little importance for corporate financial management.

Whether Miller's argument holds true in practice is unclear. As supportive evidence, he draws attention to the fact that if debt does possess a net advantage due to tax relief on interest, then companies would be expected to move to higher gearing ratios at times of high rates of corporation tax and vice versa. (In other words, the higher the rate of corporation tax, the greater the tax advantage of debt.) However, he claims that there is little evidence to suggest that this does occur, which therefore supports his argument. Miller's evidence has been subject to criticism and hence there are some doubts about the empirical validity of his hypothesis. Nevertheless, his argument does caution against *over-exaggerating* the tax advantages of debt capital, and it provides another way of explaining observed gearing ratios: companies do not gear up to high levels, not only because there are hidden costs involved in doing so, but also because the gains are themselves rather small.

CONCLUSION

In concluding our examination of the capital structure problem, all we can say is that it would appear that the financing decision may be of some importance, in so far as a company's capital structure can have both beneficial and detrimental effects on its total market value and, consequently, on the market value of the ordinary shares. However, the exact nature of the relationship in real life between a company's gearing level, its total market value and the costs of its various types of capital remains unclear. What we have seen is that gearing can be a double-edged sword and hence should always be treated with caution. We must also recognize that because the market valuation of equity is constantly changing, so will be the gearing of the company. This probably means that there can be no optimal long-term target gearing ratio for companies and aiming to remain within a range is more likely to provide a workable approach to the problem.

CAPITAL STRUCTURE IN PRACTICE

The pecking order theory

At the start of this book we stated that we would examine how companies *should* make financial decisions. Thus we were looking at the 'normative' theory of financial decision-making. We then went on to say that a normative theory cannot be developed in isolation from what actually happens in practice and that therefore we would also have to examine the *practice* of financial management decision-making. Nowhere is this more important than in the area of capital structure.

As the previous two chapters have shown, the theory of the capital structure decision does not give company managements any clear advice. The Modigliani and Miller with-tax analysis concludes that companies should gear up as much as possible. The traditional view concludes that some gearing will be advantageous, but not too much – and just what is the optimal gearing ratio for any particular company is a matter of trial and error. Finally, Miller's analysis concludes – under specific assumptions about the personal tax regime, which may or may not be valid – that the capital structure decision has no impact on the value of a company and so is an irrelevance from the viewpoint of shareholder wealth.

These 'standard' theories of capital structure, both as developed by M and M and by the proponents of the traditional view, see the capital structure decision as a trade-off between the advantages and disadvantages of debt financing.

However, in the real world we find companies have all sorts of capital structures. Some are all-equity financed, some have a modest amount of debt financing, whilst still others are highly geared.

An alternative view of the gearing decision was developed by Myers to try to explain, at least in part, this observed variety of different capital structures. It is known as the '*pecking order theory*' and it has begun to attract increasing interest as a theory that provides a *behavioural* insight into the practice of the capital structure decision.

The issue of timing

When a company's managers are faced with a decision about whether to raise equity or debt finance, besides all the usual factors that have to be taken into account – such as tax relief on interest, risk of default, etc. – there is also the issue of whether it is the right *time* to issue new equity or debt finance. On some occasions managers will judge that it is the right time to raise equity and on other occasions, it is the right time to raise debt.

Managers will judge that it's a good time to raise new *equity* finance when they believe that the company's share price is relatively *high* (to the point of being overvalued by the market). Conversely they will *not* want to issue new equity when they consider that the share price is *low* (the company's shares are seen as being cheap or undervalued). As a result, managers prefer to issue debt (i.e. gear-up) when the share price is low – and so it is not a good time to raise equity – and to issue equity (i.e. reduce gearing) when the share price is high.

The suggestion is that this so-called *timing* consideration may be a more important factor in the actual capital structure decision than any of the more traditional considerations, such as tax shield.

The decision by companies to take the timing factor into account may be very sensible because of the presence of '*asymmetrical* information'. What this term refers to is the fact that managers within the company are likely to have a much better idea of the *true* worth of the company's shares than do outside investors, because they will have much more recent and more detailed information about the company's present and future prospects. Thus management may well be able to identify situations (or at least, believe they can), where the stock market is mispricing (either overvaluing, or undervaluing) the company's shares.

Market signals

However, given the existence of reasonably efficient financial markets, investors will be aware of these management thought processes and so may see an issue of new equity by a company as a signal that the management believe the shares to be *overvalued*. As a result, investors may start to sell the company's shares, causing the price to fall.

Likewise, a new issue of debt may be seen as a signal that the management believe that the shares are *undervalued*. In response, investors will start to buy the undervalued shares, and so push up the share price.

If a company's managers feel that the shares are undervalued, they will want to issue debt (rather than equity) and, at the same time, they will not mind giving out the signal that they believe the shares to be undervalued.

However, and this is a key point, if the manager's think that the shares are *over*valued then, on the basis of our previous reasoning, they will want to issue equity. The problem is that such a move will signal their belief the shares are overvalued and so may prompt investors to sell and so cause the share price to fall. Therefore, in order to avoid such an undesirable result, managers may choose to issue debt – rather than equity – even when they believe the company's shares to be overvalued.

The conclusion therefore of this line of reasoning – up to this point – is that managers will want to issue debt in both undervalued *and* overvalued share price scenarios. They will never want to issue equity. (However, this is only an interim conclusion – we have yet to finish the argument.)

Consideration of debt

The next stage of the argument is to consider the cost of debt in the analysis. A company's cost of debt can be seen as consisting of two elements: the risk-free rate of interest and a risk premium. The risk premium payable by a company will be a function of its risk of default, as perceived by the financial markets. The greater the perceived risk of the company defaulting on its debt obligations, the higher the risk premium demanded by lenders, and vice versa.

Now suppose that the company's managers consider that debt finance is cheap (i.e. the interest cost is lower than it should be because lenders are *underestimating* the risk of default). In such circumstances the managers will want to issue more debt to take advantage of its cheapness (or underpricing).[5]

Alternatively, suppose that the management believe that the cost of debt is too high because lenders are *overestimating* the risks of default. In these circumstances, they will *not* want to issue any new debt, but will prefer to issue equity.

Once again, in a reasonably efficient debt market, lenders will read signals into new issues of debt. In particular, they may view an issue of new debt as signalling that the management view debt as cheap because the risk of default is being underestimated by the market. In such circumstances the financial market will revise its view of the perceived risk of default and so raise the company's cost of debt as a result.

The financing dilemma

Therefore management face a dilemma. If they issue equity there is a risk the market will interpret this as a signal that the shares are overvalued and so will start to sell the company's shares, causing the share price to fall.

On the other hand, if they issue debt, the market will interpret this as a signal that the management believe that the market is underestimating the company's risk of default, and so will respond by raising the company's cost of debt (by raising the required risk premium).

The solution to this financing dilemma is simple. Rely as much as possible on internally generated finance (retained earnings) and so avoid the possible adverse signals given out by either external equity or debt financing.

'Pecking order' rules

This reasoning then leads to a 'pecking order' of rules for the financing decision:

- *Rule 1*: Finance the company as much as possible through the use of retained earnings.

- *Rule 2*: If external finance has to be used (because the management have identified more profitable, [i.e. +NPV], investments than can be financed with retained earnings alone), then they should issue debt until the company's debt capacity is reached and only then, if +NPV projects still remain to be financed, issue equity.

This second rule needs some further explanation. The argument is that the more risky the source of finance, the greater the difficulty the financial markets have in assessing the degree of risk, and so the greater the chance of the market mispricing that particular source of finance. Debt, as we know, is less risky that equity and so the market finds debt much easier to price and value than equity. Therefore, out of choice, issue debt rather than equity.

Furthermore, when issuing debt, issue less risky debt first, and then issue progressively more risky debt. For example, initially the company should try to issue low risk *secured* debt. When there are no more assets available to act as security, then issue *unsecured* debt. Finally, it will only be when the company's debt capacity is reached (i.e. the company is unable to raise any more debt) that the management should consider issuing new equity finance. Hence, the idea of a financing *pecking order*: first use retained earnings; then secured debt; then unsecured debt; and then finally equity.

Conclusions

The key conclusion of the pecking order theory is that the company's capital structure decision is *not* determined by a trade-off consideration of the costs and benefits of using debt. Instead it is a function of:

- The amount of finance required to undertake all the profitable (+NPV) projects that have been identified by the company.

- The amount of retained earning available.

- The debt capacity of the company.

If a company's retained earnings are sufficient to finance all +NPV projects, then it will remain all-equity financed. If, once all retained earnings have been utilized, it still has unfunded +NPV projects, then it will start to issue debt and so gear-up. Once it reaches its debt capacity and there still remain unfunded +NPV projects, it will only then start to issue equity and so lower its gearing.

Finally, there are two other implications of the pecking order theory. One is that we would expect to find that more profitable companies would use less debt – because of the greater availability of retained earnings (and the empirical evidence suggests that this may well be the case). The other implication is more concerned with managerial behaviour. Companies could be expected to build up cash reserves (held in the form of marketable securities) so that if at any future point in time the retained earnings available are insufficient to finance all the +NPV projects, then they will not be *forced* to raise external finance, but can instead utilize the stored-up cash resources.

REAL-WORLD CONSIDERATIONS

Finally, before we leave the capital structure decision, let us turn to look at some more practical considerations. Suppose a financial manager is faced with the problem of needing to raise additional long-term capital. The immediate decision is, should just equity capital be raised, and so lower the company's gearing; or should just debt capital be raised, and so increase the company's gearing; or should a mixture of both debt and equity be raised so as to approximately maintain the company's existing gearing ratio?

As we know, the theory of capital structure gives very little guidance to the manager and in such circumstances, managers tend to take comfort from the idea that there is 'safety in numbers'. In other words, when the theory gives no clear indication as to what course of action should be taken, the safest thing is to do what everybody else does. Thus one of the most important considerations in the capital structure decision in the real world may be the average level of gearing for the *industry group*. Therefore, generally speaking, we may expect companies to be rather cautious about moving their gearing ratios away from their industry average level of gearing.

Additionally, whilst in the theory of capital structure, gearing has always been measured in terms of *market* values (i.e. V_B/V_E), in the real world gearing tends to be measured in terms of the accounting *balance sheet* values. Thus instead of V_E being used, the balance sheet value of 'shareholders' funds' (issued share capital plus all reserves) is used. Similarly, instead of the total market value of debt, V_B, being used, the balance sheet value (i.e. nominal value) of debt is used. Example 3 shows such an approach in more detail and illustrates how a company's gearing might be measured in practice by stock market investment analysts.

EXAMPLE 3

The following is the summarized balance sheet of Costa SA:

		(€)
Non-current assets		400 000
Inventories	150 000	
Receivables	100 000	
Cash	50 000	300 000

▶

Payables	80 000	
Short-term bank loan	100 000	180 000
Net current assets		120 000
Total assets		520 000
Financed by:		
Share capital		50 000
Reserves		300 000
Shareholders' funds		350 000
12% bonds		170 000
		520 000

Its gearing ratio can be measured as:

$$\frac{\text{Long-term debt} + \text{Short-term debt} - \text{Cash balances}}{\text{Shareholders' funds}}$$

this gives:

$$\frac{170\,000 + 100\,000 - 50\,000}{350\,000} = 0.629 \text{ or } 62.9\%$$

When we move away from the theory and look at the real world, accounting balance sheet values are used rather than market values for reasons of practicality. Whereas, for a quoted company, it is easy to calculate the total market value of the equity (V_E), this is not the case with the total market value of the debt (V_B).

The vast majority of corporate debt capital is issued privately and so is unquoted. Therefore it does not have a market value that can be observed. Rather than go to the trouble and difficulty of trying to estimate what its market value might be, nominal balance sheet values of debt are used.

Consequently, if the balance sheet value of debt is to be used, the view is that it would be inconsistent if market values of equity were used. As a result, gearing ratios tend to be calculated on the basis shown in Example 3, using book/balance sheet values of both debt and equity. However, as we have seen in the previous chapter, many assets are not represented in the balance sheet at all and those that are represented are shown at historic cost and not value. Accountants seem to accept historic cost (generally unadjusted for changing prices) because they claim it to be more objective than other values. In truth this is not so and all that can really be said in favour of historic cost is that it is more easily verifiable than the alternatives. (There are many accounting textbooks that deal with this issue and a list of appropriate references is included at the end of this chapter.)

EARNINGS PER SHARE AND GEARING

Risk and return

In taking the capital structure decision in practice, financial managers will be aware of the relationship between risk and return. Therefore they will know that if the company's level of gearing is increased, that will in turn, lead to an increase in the amount of risk – financial risk – borne by the shareholders. As a result, shareholders will require some additional reward in compensation.

In finance theory (and in practice) the reward for risk-taking is the return on the investment which, in terms of equity capital, is a combination of dividend yield plus percentage capital gain. However, financial managers requires a more direct and immediate measure of the reward for risk-taking when trying to assess whether they should, for example, increase the gearing of the company. In other words, they need to be able to assess whether the company will be able to generate sufficient extra return to compensate the shareholders for an increased level of financial risk.

This more direct and immediate measure of reward for risk-taking is provided by the accounting profit (or earnings) concept in terms of EPS – earnings per share. In practice, the financial manager will tend to make capital structure decisions on the basis of the gearing ratio measured in terms of accounting balance sheet values and the subsequent impact on earnings per share, the final decision being, of course, a matter of judgement. Example 4 illustrates such an approach.

EXAMPLE 4

Compañia Cerveja is based in Madrid. It wants to undertake a project to expand its current manufacturing capacity that will cost €5 million. The project has already been evaluated and is thought to have a positive NPV.

The decision now facing management is how to finance the project. Two alternative financing 'packages' are under consideration:

1. Issue 2.5 million new shares at 2 euros each, or

2. Issue €5 million long-term bonds at a fixed rate of interest of 9%.

The project is expected to generate an extra €1 million of earnings (before tax and interest) each year. The company pays tax at 30% and follows a policy of paying a constant dividend per share.

The current Income Statement and balance sheet are as follows:

Income statement	(€m)
Profit before interest and tax	4.4
Interest	1.2
Taxable profit	3.2
Tax	0.96
Profit after tax and interest	2.24
Dividends	0.4
Retained earnings	1.84

▶

Balance sheet	(€m)
Non-current assets	14.0
Net current assets	12.0
Total assets	26.00
Financed by:	
4 million shares	1.0
Reserves	15.5
Shareholder funds	16.5
12% long-term loan	9.5
	26.0

The current gearing and the current EPS can be calculated as follows:

$$\text{Gearing}: \frac{€9.5m}{€16.5m} = 0.576 \text{ or } 57.6\%$$

$$\text{EPS}: \frac{\text{Earning after tax and interest}}{\text{Number of shares in issue}} = \frac{€2.24m}{4m} = €0.56 \text{ or } 56 \text{ cents}$$

Each financing package can be evaluated, in turn, by looking at what will be its impact on the gearing ratio and EPS:

Finance Package 1	(€m)
Profit before interest and tax	4.4
Additional profits from project	1.0
	5.4
Interest on existing loans	1.2
Taxable profit	4.2
Tax	1.26
Profits available for shareholders	2.94
Dividends*	0.65
Retained earnings	2.29

* Currently €0.4 million of dividends are paid on 4 million shares. This represents a dividend per share of 10 cents. This financing package requires the issue of 2.5 million extra shares making a total of 6.5 million shares in total. If the company's policy of a constant dividend per share is to be maintained then the total amount of dividends paid will rise to €0.65 million.

$$\text{Gearing}: \frac{€9.5m}{€16.5m + €5m^* + €0.45m^{**}} = 0.433 \text{ or } 43.3\%$$

$$\text{EPS}: \frac{€2.94m}{6.5m} = €0.45 \text{ or } 45 \text{ cents}$$

* This is the extra €5 million of shareholders' funds arising from the issue of €5 million of extra equity capital.

▶

** In the existing balance sheet, the €1.84 million of retained earnings from the existing profit and loss account will already be included in the reserves figure of €15.5 million. The project, financed by Package 1, would raise the retained earnings figure by €0.45 million from €1.84 million to €2.29 million. These *extra* retained earnings – of €0.45m – have to be added to the value of shareholders' funds.

Finance Package 2	(€m)
Profit before interest and tax	4.4
Additional profit from project	1.0
	5.4
Interest on existing loans	1.2
Interest on new loan	0.45
Taxable profit	3.75
Tax	1.13
Profit available for shareholders	2.62
Dividends	0.4
Retained earnings	2.22

$$\text{Gearing}: \frac{€9.5m + €5m}{€16.5m + €0.38m} = 0.859 \text{ or } 85.9\%$$

$$\text{EPS}: \frac{€2.62m}{4m} = €0.655 \text{ or } 65.5 \text{ cents}$$

Summary	Gearing	EPS
Existing situation	57.6%	56c
Finance Package 1	43.3%	45c
Finance Package 2	85.9%	65.5c

The use of judgement

It is far from clear, as the summary in Example 4 shows, just what would be the correct judgement to make in practice between the two financing packages. The first package produces a reduction in gearing – and so a reduction in financial risk – but at the cost of a significant fall in EPS. On the other hand, the second financing package leads to a sharp increase in gearing with only a relatively small rise in EPS.

It is up to the financial manager to judge whether shareholders would be willing to bear the 'cost' (in terms of a lower EPS) of the reduced exposure to financial risk provided by finance package 1; or whether they would be willing to bear the cost of increased financial risk (as measured by the rise in the gearing ratio) in order to gain the reward of an increase in EPS provided by finance package 2.

Although the impact of the change in capital structure on 'reward' can be quite directly related to changes in EPS, the impact on financial risk is more difficult to judge through the measure of gearing alone. However, the quality of this latter measure could be improved by knowing what the average level of gearing is for Cerveja's industry group.

Thus, if the average gearing level of Cerveja's industry group was 90%, then the financial manager might well feel that the second package should be preferred to the first. The second package improves EPS while still leaving shareholders with a less than the industry average exposure to financial risk. In contrast, the first package reduces still further the shareholders' already (relatively) low exposure to financial risk, at a significant cost in terms of EPS.

However, if the industry average gearing was only 25%, then the conclusion reached in the judgement of the financial manager might well be different.

Interest cover ratio

An additional way of judging the impact of gearing on financial risk exposure is through the interest cover ratio. This can be defined as:

$$\frac{\text{Earnings before interest and tax}}{\text{Interest liabilities}}$$

The idea here is that the lower the ratio, the greater the probability that the company may default on interest payments and be forced into bankruptcy.

Using the data from Example 4, the interest cover ratios can be calculated as follows:

Existing situation:	€4.4m/ €1.2m	=	3.67
Financing Package 1:	€5.4m/ €1.2m	=	4.5
Financing Package 2:	€5.4m/ €1.65m	=	3.3

This ratio can therefore be used to highlight the significance of the changes in gearing and to give some insight of the significance of a move from a gearing ratio of 57.6% to 85.9%. But of course, as was commented upon previously, knowledge of Cerveja's industry group average interest cover would assist in bringing a greater depth of understanding to the interpretation of these data.

DEGREE OF OPERATING GEARING

In the discussion in the previous section on EPS and gearing, what was being examined was the risk and return relationship of just one type of systematic risk: systematic *financial* risk. That discussion therefore raises an additional question: how, in practice, are financial managers going to make a judgement concerning changes in systematic *business* risk?

Business and financial risk

In Chapter 12 we looked at the determinants of systematic and unsystematic risk, while in Chapter 18 we introduced the concept of business and financial risk. This present discussion provides a good opportunity to make clear the relationship between these different types of risk.

Portfolio theory teaches that a share's total risk is divided up into systematic and unsystematic risk. Modigliani and Miller's capital structure theory teaches that a share's total risk is divided into business and financial risk.

Unsystematic risk, as we know, arises from company-specific factors that have an impact on the level and variability of a firm's cash flow. Such factors as the ability of a company's senior management team, the state of its labour relations and the quality of its research and development work would all be examples.

On the other hand, systematic risk arises from the impact upon the firm of other factors which are not specific to the individual company, but which affect all companies (to a greater or lesser extent) throughout the stock market. These market-wide, macroeconomic-type factors include things like the rate of national economic growth, interest rate levels and exchange rate volatility. Such factors do not just affect the *individual* company, but affect *all* companies throughout the stock market.

In Chapter 12, when discussing the determinants of an individual company's exposure to these systematic risk factors (and hence its beta value), we state that, apart from gearing there are two main determinants:

1. The sensitivity of a company's revenues to the general level of economic activity in the economy and other macroeconomic factors.
2. The proportion of fixed to variable costs, both in terms of operating costs (e.g. wages, materials, energy costs) and financing costs (e.g. interest and dividend payments).

The *greater* the revenue sensitivity, and the *greater* the proportion of fixed costs, then the *greater* the company's exposure to systematic risk (and the higher its beta value as a result).

Given all these different strands, the relationship between business and financial risk, and between systematic and unsystematic risk can now be explored.

Financial risk is really concerned with the proportion of fixed financing costs (interest payments that must be made), to variable financing costs (dividend payments which need not necessarily be made). Thus financial risk is part of a share's systematic risk.

Just as financial risk arises out of how a firm is financed, so business risk arises out of the risky nature and characteristics of a firm's business. Thus business risk encompasses not only systematic risk – in terms of the revenue sensitivity of the business and the proportion of fixed to variable operating costs that the nature of the business involves – but also unsystematic risk in terms of the ability of the senior management team, the labour relations and other company-specific factors which affect the business. Figure 19.5 attempts to show these interrelationships more clearly.

We can now return to the problem of deriving a *practical* measure of systematic business risk. What is required is a way of measuring systematic business risk, in the same way that the gearing ratio (and, to some extent, the interest cover ratio) can be seen as a practical attempt to measure changes in systematic financial risk.

Systematic business risk can be approached through the concept of the degree of operating gearing (DOG). This can be defined as:

$$\frac{\text{Revenues} - \text{Variable operating costs}}{\text{Earnings before interest and tax}}$$

The DOG measure indicates the percentage change in earnings before interest and tax (EBIT) for every 1% change in revenues. Example 5 illustrates the calculation.

FIGURE 19.5 M and M and the CAPM

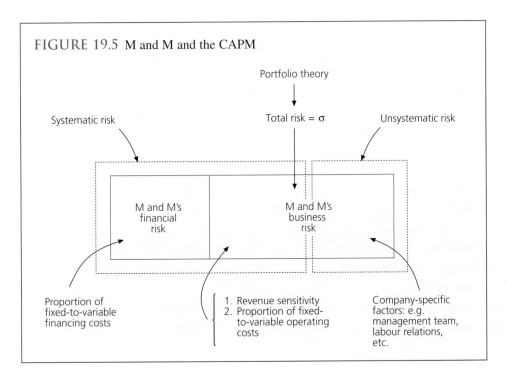

EXAMPLE 5

Zumbaba Ltd is a producer of building bricks in Southern Africa. Its income statement is as follows:

		(Rm)
Revenues		500
Wages	150	
Materials	120	
Variable overheads	55	(325)
Fixed overheads		(75)
Earnings before interest and tax		100

$$DOG = \frac{R500m - R325m}{R100m} = R1.75 \text{ million}$$

The degree of operating gearing is 1.75 which indicates that for every 1% change in Zumbaba's revenues, there will be a 1.75% change in the company's earnings before interest and tax. For example, if revenue increased by 10%, then EBIT should increase by 17.5% – from R100m to R117.5m. Conversely, if revenues, for example, fell by 5%, then EBIT should fall by 5% × 1.75 = 8.75%, from R100m to R91.25m.

▶

This can be seen to be the case as follows (notice the assumption that the percentage change in revenues will be reflected in the variable – but not the fixed – operating costs):

10% Increase in revenues		(Rm)
Revenues		550
Wages	165	
Materials	132	
Variable overheads	60.5	(357.5)
Fixed overheads		(75)
EBIT		117.5
5% fall in revenues		
Revenues		475
Wages	142.5	
Materials	114	
Variable overheads	52.25	(308.75)
Fixed overheads		(75)
		91.25

The meaning of DOG

The degree of operating gearing can be taken as a practical measure of systematic business risk, in the sense that it focuses on the proportion of fixed to variable operating costs and the impact that that proportion has on earnings, given changes to the company's revenues.

The greater the proportion of fixed to variable operating costs, the larger will be the DOG value. The larger the DOG value, the greater the impact on EBIT of changes in revenues. Thus the DOG value links revenue sensitivity to the subsequent variability of earnings.

Just as with the gearing ratio, so the DOG value is far from being a perfect measure of systematic business risk. It is limited in a number of important ways.

Certainly, if the value of the DOG increases for a particular company, then it is relatively safe to conclude that its business risk has also increased (and vice versa). However the DOG must be used with care when trying to compare the business risk of one company with that of another. If the two companies are in the same area of business, and therefore have comparable degrees of revenue sensitivity, then it would be safe to conclude that the company with the larger DOG value has the greater exposure to systematic risk.

However, the DOG is of very little use for comparing the relative business risk of two companies with significantly *different* revenue sensitivities. A high DOG value may not mean that a company has a high degree of business risk, if that company has a very low degree of revenue sensitivity. Similarly, a company may well have a high level of systematic business risk – even though it has a low DOG value – because it has such a high degree of revenue sensitivity.

Thus the DOG value, like the gearing ratio, must be used with care in order to make a judgement about risk. However, it can be helpful to financial managers who are faced with the practicalities of decisions involving trade-offs between systematic business risk and return. Example 6 illustrates such a case.

EXAMPLE 6

The Al Dallah Group is a Saudi-based oil exploration company. It is considering the acquisition of an oil-drilling rig which uses a new technology. The investment has already been evaluated and has been shown to have a positive NPV. However, it is expected to affect the company's proportion of fixed to variable operating costs.

The relevant part of the company's existing income statement is as follows:

		(SRm)
Revenues		800
Wage costs	180	
Material costs	200	
Energy costs	150	
Variable overheads	100	(630)
Fixed overheads		(70)
Earnings before interest and tax		100

The new drilling rig will not affect revenues but it will lower the wages cost of the company by 10%, the material costs by 5% and the energy costs by 20%. However, fixed overheads will increase by 50%.

The company's existing DOG value is:

$$DOG = \frac{SR800m - SR630m}{SR100m} = SR1.70 \text{ million}$$

With the new machine, the company's income statement would be revised as follows:

		(SRm)
Revenues		800
Wage costs	162	
Material costs	190	
Energy costs	120	
Variable overheads	100	(572)
Fixed overheads		(105)
Earnings before interest and tax		123

$$DOG = \frac{SR800m - SR572m}{SR123m} = SR1.85 \text{ million}$$

The new drilling rig would increase the company's exposure to systematic business risk – the DOG value has increased from 1.70 to 1.85. However, this is compensated for by the fact that EBIT rises by SR23m from SR100m to SR123m. Whether the additional earnings justify the additional risk is a matter of judgement on the part of management.

In practice, the final decision could not be taken on these data alone. Information on the Al Dallah Group's revenue sensitivity and the DOG values of its competitors would also be required.

SUMMARY

This chapter has discussed the M and M with-tax capital structure hypothesis, the traditional view of capital structure, Miller's 1977 analysis of debt and taxes and the 'real-world' determinants of capital structure.

- The M and M with-tax analysis shows that as a company increases its gearing there are three effects: the *advantage* that debt costs less than equity ($K_D < K_E$); the *disadvantage* that gearing increases financial risk and so the cost of equity rises; and the *advantage* that gearing brings further tax relief and so reduces the tax liability of the firm.

- The M and M no-tax analysis shows how the first two effects exactly offset each other (not surprisingly, because they both arise from the same source: the ordering of the 'payout queue' of debt and equity holders). This leaves a net advantage. As gearing increases, the after-tax WACC declines and V_0 rises.

- Assuming a constant cost of debt, then it follows that K_{E_g} is a positive linear function of the gearing ratio.

- Therefore the conclusion of the analysis is that companies should attempt to gear up as much as possible: the higher the gearing, the lower is K_0, the higher is V_0 and the greater is the increase in shareholder wealth.

- However, against this view is the traditional view which, like the M and M analysis, sees that there are both advantages and disadvantages to gearing. However, the traditional view holds that at low gearing levels the advantages outweigh the disadvantages and so the WACC is lowered. However at high gearing the reverse relationship holds and so the WACC rises.

- As a result, the company's WACC is U-shaped and the optimal gearing ratio is located where K_0 is minimized and V_0 is maximized. At that point shareholder wealth is also maximized.

- The empirical evidence does very little to solve the conflict between the two approaches because of a lack of company data for high gearing levels, which is where the two theories significantly diverge.

- However, empirically we find that companies tend *not to* gear up to the high levels the M and M analysis would lead us to expect, suggesting either that the WACC curve *is* U-shaped or that the M and M analysis excludes some important variables.

- There is no reason – either of an analytical or of an empirical nature – to suggest that the WACC function is really U-shaped. Therefore this leads us to conclude that the M and M analysis excludes some important factors in the real-world capital structure decision.

- These important real-world determinants are thought to include: bankruptcy costs, agency costs, debt capacity and tax exhaustion.

- Finally, the Miller analysis suggests that when personal taxes are included in the analysis and given two somewhat contentious arguments about personal tax rates, then it can be shown that the value of the tax shield on corporate debt interest reduces to zero. This is not to say that companies do not get tax relief on debt interest. Rather it implies that even allowing for tax relief on debt interest, the use of debt capital confers no benefits on shareholders' wealth.

- The chapter has also looked at some of the more practical considerations concerning how financial managers approach the capital structure decision. The main points covered were as follows:

- The pecking order theory is based on the idea of asymmetric information between a company's managers and external investors. This may lead to investors reading signals into management's financing decisions that indicate that either the share price is overvalued on the stock market, or the cost of debt is too low.

- As a result, managers will want to avoid the possibility of giving these undesirable signals and so they will wish to reply, as much as possible, on internally generated sources of finance: retained earnings.

- Only when all internally generated sources of finance have been exhausted will they wish to consider raising external finance. When external finance is required, given that the more risky the finance the greater the possibility of mispricing by financial markets, they will issue new finance in order of riskiness. Thus secured debt will be issued first, followed by unsecured debt and then, only after the company's debt capacity is reached, might new equity finance be issued.

- In practice gearing is usually measured in terms of accounting balance sheet values rather than market values.

- The risk and return trade-off in the capital structure decision is viewed in terms of the impact on the gearing ratio and on earnings per share.

- In practice the capital structure decision is a matter of judgement rather than arithmetic calculation.

- Financial risk is totally systematic and is the risk that is measured through the gearing ratio in the capital structure decision.

- Business risk is partially systematic and partially unsystematic. In practice, an attempt can be made to measure systematic business risk through the DOG ratio.

NOTES

1. From this point on, K_D will refer to the *before-tax* cost of debt capital. References to the after-tax cost of debt will be designated K_{DAT}, as before, or $K_D(1 - T)$, where T is the rate of corporation tax.
2. This we encountered in Chapter 1.
3. See item 1 in the 'Further reading' section below.
4. There are other ways as well by which investors can avoid personal taxes on equity investment, such as investing through pension fund schemes.
5. In fact the circumstances when management think that debt finance is cheap, are likely also to be the same circumstances where they believe their equity to be overvalued: both shareholders and lenders are being too optimistic about the company's future prospects. Thus one reaction of management will be to say 'issue equity because it's overvalued', while another reaction would be to say, 'issue debt because it's cheap'.

FURTHER READING

1. There are many articles on this area that are of interest. The basic ones of course are the two by M and M (F. Modigliani and M. Miller), 'The Cost of Capital, Corporation Finance and the Theory of Investment', *American Economic Review*, June 1958; and 'Corporation Income Taxes and the Cost

of Capital', *American Economic Review*, June 1963; and, in addition, the later analysis by Miller: M.H. Miller, 'Debt and Taxes', *Journal of Finance*, May 1977. There is also Miller's Nobel Prize lecture: M.H. Miller, 'Leverage', *Journal of Finance*, June 1991.

2. A good overview is provided in: S.C. Myers, 'The Capital Structure Puzzle', *Journal of Finance*, July 1984 and this is extended in J. Rutterford, 'An International Perspective on the Capital Structure Puzzle', *Midland Corporate Finance Journal*, Autumn 1985 and M. Barclay and C. Smith, 'The Capital Structure Puzzle: Another Look at the Evidence', in J. Rutterford, M. Upton and D. Kodwani (eds) Financial Strategy, 2nd ed. Wiley 2006. Another good overview is to be found in J. Board, 'Modigliani and Miller', in M. Firth and S.M. Keane (eds), *Issues in Finance*, Philip Allen 1986.

3. In terms of Miller's analysis there have been some thoughtful articles: H. de Angelo and R.W. Mausulis, 'Leverage and Dividend Irrelevancy under Corporate and Personal Taxation', *Journal of Finance*, May 1980; V.A. Aivazain and J.L. Callen, 'Miller's Irrelevance Mechanism', *Journal of Finance*, March 1987; J. Cordes and S. Sheffrin, 'Estimating the Tax Advantage of Corporate Debt', *Journal of Finance*, March 1983; and A. Kane, A.J. Marcus and R.L. McDonald, 'How Big is the Tax Advantage of Debt?', *Journal of Finance*, July 1984.

4. On the real-world factors behind the capital structure decision, articles of interest include: A. Barnea, R.A. Haugen and L.W. Senbet, 'Market Imperfections, Agency Problems and Capital Structure: A Review', *Financial Management*, Summer 1981; J.S. Ang and J.H. Chua, 'Corporate Bankruptcy and Job Losses Among Top Level Managers' *Financial Management*, Winter 1981; S.G. Rhee and F.L. McCarthy, 'Corporate Debt Capacity and Capital Budgeting Analysis', *Financial Management*, Summer 1982; and A. Agrawal and G.N. Mandelher, 'Managerial Incentives and Corporate Investment and Financing Decisions', *Journal of Finance*, September 1987.

5. Finally, there has been some interesting empirical work published: Recent work is consistent with some earlier findings. P. Marsh, 'The Choice Between Equity and Debt: An Empirical Study', *Journal of Finance*, March 1982 shows the relevance of company size, bankruptcy risk and asset structure as determinants of debt levels. A. Bevan and J. Danbolt, 'Testing for Inconsistencies in the Estimation of UK Capital Structure Determinants', *Applied Financial Economics*, 14, 2004 and also P. Brealey and P. Bunn, 'The Determination of UK Corporate Capital Gearing', *Bank of England Quarterly Bulletin*, Autumn 2005, found evidence that gearing is related to company size, asset structure and profitability. M. Frank and V. Goyal, 'Capital Structure Decisions: Which Factors are Reliably Important', *Financial Management*, Spring 2009 provide similar findings. Finally, some interesting survey evidence is provided in: J. Graham and C. Harvey, 'How CFOs Make Capital Budgeting and Capital Structure Decisions', *Journal of Finance*, Spring 2002.

QUIZ QUESTIONS

1 Given the following facts about a company:

$$K_E \quad = \quad 25\%$$
$$K_D \quad = \quad 10\% \text{ pre-tax}$$
$$V_B{:}V_E \quad = \quad 1{:}3$$
$$T_C \quad = \quad 35\%$$

What is the cost of equity capital of a similar business risk, all-equity financed, company?

2 Given the information in question 1, what would be its K_0 if it moved its gearing ratio from 1:3 to 1:2?

3 An all-equity financed company is currently worth €40 million. It is thinking of issuing €10 million of 8% irredeemable bonds to repurchase €10 million of equity. Given a corporate tax rate of 25%, what would be the effect on shareholder wealth?

4 What is the M and M expression for K_0 in a taxed world?

5 What does the 'tax shield' represent?

6 What is meant by debt capacity?

7 Given a company which has issued $10 million of debt (i.e. its current market value), has a gearing ratio of 1:3, a probability of going bankrupt of 5% and estimated bankruptcy costs of $1 million; what would the company be worth if it was all-equity financed assuming a corporate tax rate of 40%?

8 What is Miller's expression for the total market value of a geared company?

9 How would the gearing ratio of a company be calculated in practice?

10 How is 'earnings per share' calculated?

11 If a company had a gearing ratio of 50% would that be considered a high or low level of gearing?

12 Is financial risk unsystematic?

13 What determines the systematic part of business risk?

14 How is DOG calculated?

15 What information does DOG provide?

16 If one company had a DOG of 1.50 and another company in the same industry had a DOG of 2.50, what conclusion could you draw?

(See the 'Answers to Quiz Questions' section at the back of the book.)

PROBLEMS

The answers to four of the following problems (those indicated by an asterisk) are available to students online. The answer to the remaining problem is available only to lecturers (see the 'Digital Resources' page for details).

1* Kraftechnik AG and Innoptik AG are two German companies operating in *different* industries. Kraftechnik operates in an industry for which the average asset beta (i.e. the ungeared beta after removing the impact of financial risk) is 0.5; the corresponding beta is 1.5 for the industry of Innoptik. The current earnings before interest and tax for Kraftechnik are €500 000 and for Innoptik €1 200 000. These levels of earnings are expected to be maintained for the indefinite future, and neither company retains any earnings. The rate of return on riskless lending and borrowing opportunities is 3% per annum, and the return on the market portfolio is 8%. Both rates are expected to remain constant indefinitely.

Kraftechnik and Innoptik each have 5% irredeemable bonds with a market value of €1 000 000 in their capital structures. At these levels of gearing there is an 8% chance of Kraftechnik becoming bankrupt, and a 10% chance of Innoptik becoming bankrupt. In both cases, the present value of the associated after-tax costs of bankruptcy is expected to be €500 000.

The rate of corporation tax will be 30% for the foreseeable future and all debt interest is expected to be tax deductible.

Required:

(a) Calculate the total market values and debt/equity ratios of Kraftechnik and Innoptik.

(b) Discuss why the directors of some companies may choose high gearing ratios, whereas others may choose to have very low levels of debt in their capital structures.

2 Given below are extracts from the annual financial statements of four companies, together with information concerning their stock market performance. Companies A and B are producers of fruit juices and other drinks from the beverages sector. The principal activities of companies C and D are the distribution and service of electronic components, microprocessor systems and related equipment. Company D is also involved in the manufacture of steel building products.

▶

		Company		
	A	B	C	D
Latest financial statement extracts:				
Shareholders' funds (€m)	90.4	65.4	5.9	33.3
Long-term bonds (€m)	2.8	5.8	—	1.1
Dividend per share (cents)	4.3	8.2	2.4	9.9
Annual dividend growth since 2012	12%	10%	19%	22%
Current stock market details:				
Equity market value (€m)	68.0	63.2	68.8	123.4
Market value of long-term loans (€m)	0.6	0.1	—	0.3
Equity beta value	0.75	0.88	1.24	1.26
Share price (€)	1.64	2.80	3.03	4.70

You should assume that the return on government bonds is 4% and that the return on all long-term corporate loans is 7%. The market premium for risk (i.e. the difference between the return on the stock market index and the return on government bonds) should be assumed to be 5%.

Required:

(a)   Calculate the WACC for each of the four companies, assuming a corporation tax rate of 30%.

(b)   Using both the information given in the question, and the results of your calculations in part (a), explain why the WACCs differ between the four companies.

3*   The government of Woland has used a number of different corporation tax systems in recent years. Three years ago (t_{-1}) corporate profits were not taxable; however, in t_{-2} a corporate income tax at 50% of taxable profits was introduced. Under this tax regime debt interest was *not* allowed as a charge against taxable profits. In t_{-1} the government modified the tax system, allowing interest on corporate borrowings as a charge against taxable profits. Finally, in the current year (t_0), capital allowances and debt interest were allowed as charges against taxable profits. The size of these allowances were such that no companies in Woland paid any tax.

The total market value of the equity of two companies, Wolskie and Fabryke and the market value of the bonds in Fabryke at the end of each of the 4 years are:

		t_{-3}	t_{-2}	t_{-1}	t_0
		($000s)	($000s)	($000s)	($000s)
Wolskie	Equity	1 000	510	520	980
Fabryke	Equity	800	370	440	790
	Bonds	200	140	160	190

Both companies have had identical earnings streams over the 4-year period; and identical business risk characteristics; and to have paid out all their earnings as dividends at the end of each year. Neither company was expected to exhibit any growth during the 4-year period, although the levels of earnings expectations and the rates of return on corporate shares varied between years.

Explain the relative values of Wolskie and Fabryke under the differing tax systems in Woland over the past 4 years.

4* Latost plc wishes to raise £10 million in external finance by issuing either ordinary shares, or 8% bonds.

Summarized income statement

	(£000s)
Turnover	45 320
Operating profit	11 170
Interest	2 280
Profit before tax	8 890
Tax	3 112
Earnings available to shareholders	5 778
Dividend	3 467
Retained earnings	2 311

Summarized balance sheet

	(£000s)	(£000s)
Non-current assets		24 260
Current assets	28 130	
Less: Current liabilities*	18 370	9 760
13% bonds		34 020
		12 000
Net assets		22 020
Shareholders' funds		
10 million shares		5 000
Reserves		17 020
		22 020

* Including a short-term loan of £6 million. The share price is 350p.

Required:

Prepare a brief report, with supporting evidence, recommending which of these two alternative financing sources the company should use. State clearly any assumptions that you make.

5* (a)   What is meant by business risk?
Outline the major factors that determine a company's business risk and comment upon how controllable these factors are by a company.

(b)   Discuss to what extent business risk is of relevance to an investor owning a well-diversified portfolio.

(c)   Frontier Corporation is a US manufacturing company. It plans to purchase a new machine in the near future which will reduce the company's direct labour costs, but will increase fixed costs by $85 000 per year. Direct labour costs are expected to fall by 20% per unit of production. The new machine will cost $820 000 and will be financed by a 5-year fixed rate loan at an interest cost of 10% per year, with the principal repayable at the maturity of the loan. The company normally pays half of after-tax earnings as dividends, subject to the constraint that if after-tax earnings *fall* the dividend per share is kept *constant*.
Frontier Corporation expects its volume of sales to increase by 15% during the current financial year. Summarized extracts from the company's most recent financial accounts are detailed below.

▶

Income statement

	($000s)	($000s)
Turnover		3 381
Operating expenses		
Wages and salaries	1 220	
Raw materials	873	
Direct selling expenses	100	
General administration (all fixed)	346	
Other costs (all fixed)	380	2 919
Profit before interest and tax		462
Interest		84
Profit before tax		378
Corporation tax		151
Profit available to ordinary shareholders		227

Balance sheet

	($000s)	($000s)
Non-current assets		1 480
Current assets	1 720	
Less current liabilities	1 120	600
Net assets		1 510
3.2 million shares		800
Reserves		710
		1 510

The US tax rate is 40%.

Required:

State clearly any assumptions that you make.

(a) Evaluate the effect of the purchase of the machine on both the degree of operating gearing and the financial gearing of Frontier Corporation, comparing the position at the start of the current financial year with the expected position at the end of the current financial year.

(b) What are the implications for the shareholders of Frontier Corporation as a result of the purchase of the machine:

   (i)   if turnover increases by the expected 15%

   (ii) if turnover falls by 10%?

INVESTMENT AND FINANCING INTERACTIONS

LEARNING OBJECTIVES

The purpose of this chapter is to:

- Investigate the connection between the different company valuation models and their implied approach to investment decision-making.
- Demonstrate that 'adjusted present value' (APV) is the only investment appraisal technique that can correctly evaluate a situation where the company's gearing is changing as a result of financing the investment.
- Provide a worked example of the APV technique.
- Demonstrate the ability of the APV technique to handle other real-world complications in addition to a changing capital structure.
- Demonstrate that combining NPV with a risk-adjusted WACC may provide a simpler approach to capturing investment and financing interactions.
- Evaluate the 'lease or buy' decision, both on the basis of the traditional approach and on the basis of an APV analysis.

COMPANY VALUATION AND INVESTMENT APPRAISAL

The Hirshleifer separation theorem that was developed in Chapter 4, led to the conclusion that decision-makers could appraise capital investment opportunities without reference to how they are to be financed. However, that model was developed under a very restrictive set of assumptions, including that of a perfect capital market.

In Chapter 19 we saw that when we allow for some real-world capital market imperfections (in particular, taxation, agency and bankruptcy costs) the separation theorem starts to break down. As a result, in practice, there are likely to be some significant interactions between capital investment and financing decisions.

The question of concern in this chapter is how are we to take account of such interactions? As a starting point, we are going to examine the relationship between different company valuation models and alternative approaches to investment appraisal. Before doing so, however, we must set out the assumptions upon which the analysis is based. There are five in total:

1. All cash flows represent level perpetuities.
2. Investors are rational, risk-averse and base decisions on expected return and variance of returns.
3. Capital markets are perfect and in equilibrium.
4. Bankruptcy is costless.
5. Companies are each located at a 'target' gearing ratio at which they wish to remain.

It is obvious that some of these assumptions are unlikely to hold true in the real world. However, the assumptions are useful, as they help to simplify our initial analysis. Afterwards, we can consider what would be the likely impact of changing these assumptions on to a more realistic basis.

We start our analysis by briefly considering the different approaches to the valuation of companies that have been developed. There are four models that are of interest but, as we will demonstrate, they are basically all consistent with each other. The four models are:

1. the dividend and interest valuation model
2. the adjusted present value model
3. the Modigliani and Miller valuation models
4. the traditional valuation model.

1. THE DIVIDEND AND INTEREST VALUATION MODEL

The dividend valuation model states that the total market value of a company's equity reflects the sum of the future expected dividend flow, discounted to present value. A similar statement can be made about the total market value of debt capital. Thus – using our usual notation – the total market value of the firm is given by the sum of the equity and the debt market values:

$$V_0 = \frac{(X - V_B K_D)(1 - T)}{K_{E_g}} + \frac{V_B K_D}{K_D}$$

If the company's annual cash flow is taken as its dividend *plus* interest cash flow:

$$(X - V_B K_D) \times (1 - T) = \text{Annual dividend flow}$$

$$V_B \times K_D = \text{Annual interest flow}$$

then the company's total annual cash flow can be expressed as follows:

$$(X - V_B K_D)(1 - T) + V_B K_D = X - XT - V_B K_D T + V_B K_D T + V_B K_D$$

$$= X(1 - T) + V_B K_D T$$

where $X(1 - T)$ represents the annual after-tax cash flow that would occur if the company had been all-equity financed, and where $V_B K_D T$ represents the annual amount of tax relief the company gains from having to pay debt interest.

2. ADJUSTED PRESENT VALUE MODEL

Taking the two annual cash flow streams (dividends plus interest), as given above, and discounting each to present value, we arrive at an alternative expression for the total market value of the company:

$$V_0 = \frac{X(1 - T)}{K_{E_{ug}}} + \frac{V_B K_D T}{K_D} = \frac{X(1 - T)}{K_{E_{ug}}} + V_B T$$

Notice that each cash flow is discounted at a rate that best reflects its risk. Thus $X(1 - T)$ is discounted by what would have been the company's cost of equity capital if it were all equity financed and $V_B K_D T$ is discounted at the cost of debt capital.

This company valuation model is termed the adjusted present value (APV) model, as the company is first valued as if it were all-equity financed ($\frac{X(1 - T)}{K_{E_{ug}}}$), and then this value is *adjusted* to allow for the tax relief on debt capital ($V_B T$).

3. THE M AND M VALUATION MODEL

If the APV model is multiplied through by $K_{E_{ug}}$ and V_0 is factored out, then a third valuation model is arrived at:

$$K_{E_{ug}} V_0 - V_B T K_{E_{ug}} = X(1 - T)$$

$$K_{E_{ug}} V_0 - \frac{V_0 V_B T K_{E_{ug}}}{V_0} = X(1 - T)$$

$$V_0 = \frac{X(1 - T)}{K_{E_{ug}} [1 - (T V_B / V_0)]}$$

This values the firm as the present value of the future expected after-tax cash flow. Here the discount rate is the *M and M* weighted average cost of capital, and this implicitly takes the tax relief on debt interest into account. Hence it is applied simply to the after-tax cash flows that would arise if the firm were all-equity financed.

4. THE TRADITIONAL VALUATION MODEL

Finally, returning to the dividend valuation model, but now factoring out V_0, a fourth company valuation model is derived:

$$V_E = \frac{(X - V_B K_D)(1 - T)}{K_{E_g}}$$

$$V_E K_{E_g} = X(1 - T) - K_D V_B(1 - T)$$

$$\frac{V_0 V_E K_{E_g}}{V_0} + \frac{K_D V_B V_0(1 - T)}{V_0} = X(1 - T)$$

$$V_0 = \frac{X(1 - T)}{\dfrac{V_E}{V_0} K_{E_g} + \dfrac{V_B}{V_0} K_D(1 - T)}$$

Here the numerator is the same as with the previous model, but now the denominator is the traditional expression for the WACC. Once again, the effect of the tax relief on debt interest is implicitly allowed for in the discount rate.

APPROACHES TO INVESTMENT APPRAISAL

All four models of company valuation are equivalent, as long as the set of five assumptions, specified initially, all hold good. However, it should be noted that each model implicitly reflects a different approach to investment appraisal. The dividend and interest valuation model reflects a dividend flow approach; the APV valuation model reflects a risk-adjusted present value approach, and the M and M and traditional valuation models each reflect the standard NPV approach.

Maintaining the gearing ratio

An example may help to illustrate these different approaches. Suppose we have the following data about a small company called Claasburg (remember that we have the assumption of all-level perpetuity cash flows):

V_E	=	€400 000				
V_B	=	€100 000		K_E	=	18.375%
D	=	€ 73 500	therefore	K_D	=	10%
I	=	€ 10 000		K_0	=	16%
T	=	35%				

The company is considering an investment project that costs €100 000, and which is expected to produce an annual *after-tax* net cash flow of €28 000 in perpetuity.[1] It would not involve the company in any change in risk.

Given that Claasburg wishes to remain at its current (target) gearing ratio of 1:4 (debt–equity), how is the investment to be financed? It would not be correct to simply finance the project with €20 000 of debt and €80 000 of equity, as this ignores the project's NPV which would accrue to the equity holders. Instead a somewhat more lengthy analysis is required.

If the company is going to maintain its current gearing ratio (and there is no change in risk caused by the project's acceptance), then K_0 will remain at 16%. Hence the project's annual *net cash inflows* will have a present value of:

$$\frac{€28\ 000}{0.16} + €175\ 000$$

If there is to be no change in the gearing ratio, this increase in company value must be split between debt and equity in the ratio 1:4. Therefore, as a result of the project, the market value of the debt should increase by €35 000 and the market value of the equity should rise by €140 000 (35 000: 140 000 equals 1:4).

The increase in the market value of the debt issued by the company implies that €35 000 of new debt is raised in order to undertake the project. The remaining €65 000 of the €100 000 required outlay would therefore come from the equity holders.

The total value of the company's equity would rise by €140 000 because the equity holders have invested an extra €65 000 and, in addition, they will receive the €75 000 worth of the project's positive NPV:

$$- €100\ 000 + \frac{€28\,000}{0.16} = + €75\ 000\ \text{NPV}$$

Therefore the total market value of Claasburg's equity capital will rise by: €65 000 + €75 000 = €140 000.

Having decided that the investment project will be financed by €35 000 of debt capital (at a K_D of 10%), and €65 000 of equity capital, in order to maintain the existing gearing ratio, let us now examine the application of each of the four possible approaches to investment appraisal.

Dividend flow approach

This approach evaluates the project on the basis of examining the total market value of the equity *before* (V_E) and *after* (V_E^*) the investment is undertaken. The decision rule is to accept the project as long as it does not cause a *reduction* in shareholder wealth:

$$V_E^* - (V_E + \text{newly issued equity}) \geq 0$$

where $V_E^* = D^*/K_E^*$ (the asterisk refers to the situation *post*-investment).

As there is to be no change in the gearing ratio (and hence no change in financial risk): $K_E^* = K_E = 18.375\%$. But what about the post-investment annual dividend flow? This can be found as follows:

		(€)
Pre-tax project cash flow	=	€43 077
less interest payable on new debt	=	€3 500
Taxable cash flow	=	€39 577
less tax at 35%	=	€13 852
Additional dividends	=	25 725
Existing dividends	=	73 500
Post-investment dividends = D*	=	99 225

$$\text{hence } V_E^* = \frac{€99\,225}{0.18375} = €540\,000$$

and the difference between this post-investment total market value of the equity and the pre-investment value of the equity, plus the value of the new equity investment, will give the resulting increase in shareholder wealth:

€540 000 − (€400 000 + €65 000) = €75 000 increase in shareholder wealth.

APV approach

The second approach uses the APV. Here, the project's net cash flow is evaluated as if it were *all-equity financed*, and then the benefits of the tax relief from the new debt capital are added on. The decision rule is to accept the project as long as the APV's total worth is greater than the outlay required:

$$(V_{project-outlay}) \geq 0$$

$$\text{where } V_{project} = \frac{X(1-T)}{K_{E_{ug}}} + V_B T$$

The first task here is to identify what would be the discount rate if all-equity financing were involved. For this, use can be made of the M and M expression:

$$K_{E_g} = K_{E_g} + (K_{E_g} - K_D)\frac{V_B(1-T)}{V_E}$$

This can be switched around to solve for $K_{E_{ug}}$:

$$K_{E_{ug}} = \frac{V_E K_{E_g} + V_B K_D(1-T)}{V_E + V_B(1-T)}$$

which in the case of the present example gives a value for $K_{E_{ug}}$ of:

$$\frac{(€400\,000 \times 0.18375) + (€100\,000 \times 0.10) \times (1 - 0.35)}{€400\,000 + €100\,000 \times (1 - 0.35)} = 0.172$$

Therefore the value of the investment opportunity can now be found:

$$V_{project} = \frac{€28\,000}{0.172} + (€35\,000 \times 0.35)$$
$$= €162\,500 + €12\,250 = €175\,000$$

As the value of Claasburg's investment project is €75 000 *more than* its €100 000 cost, it should be accepted.

NPV approach

With this approach either the M and M or traditional expressions can be used for calculating the company's WACC of 16%. The decision rule is to accept the project as long as it has a non-negative NPV:

$$- €100\,000 + \frac{€28\,000}{0.16} = + €75\,000\,\text{NPV}$$

Therefore the project should be accepted. It will increase the wealth of Claasburg's shareholders by €75 000.

A changing capital structure

The equivalence of all three approaches (and all four company valuation models), should be obvious from the above example. However, it should also be noted that in order to determine how the project should be financed, in order to maintain the existing gearing ratio, the project's worth had first to be found. In other words, the analysis contains a 'circularity' which can be problematic.

To highlight this problem, and the difficulties it causes, we will examine a situation where Claasburg finances the investment in such a way that it does *not* maintain its existing gearing ratio. For example, suppose Claasburg proposed to finance the project with an €80 000 issue of 10% irredeemable bonds and €20 000 of equity.

In order to utilize the dividend flow approach, we need to find V_E^*. This is given by $V_E^* = D^*/K_E^*$.

The post-investment dividend flow is easy enough to find (€96 300), but we cannot identify what will be the *post-investment* cost of equity capital. This can only be found by first knowing what will be the *post-investment* gearing ratio which, in turn, we cannot identify until we know the worth of the project.

If we are prevented from using the dividend flow approach, what about using the NPV/WACC approach? Again we face a difficulty. We cannot use the *existing* WACC for obvious reasons: it reflects the *existing* capital structure, which will change if the project is accepted. Further – even if we wished to use it – we could not identify the *post-investment* WACC, for the same reasons as we could not use the dividend flow approach.

One possible way around the difficulty is as follows. The M and M capital structure analysis shows that there are *three* effects arising directly from an increase in corporate gearing. Two of these, the *advantage* of the cost of debt being 'cheaper' than equity and the *disadvantage* of the cost of equity rising because of increased financial risk, exactly offset each other. This leaves one net advantage: the tax relief on debt interest.

We know that what lies behind the use of the WACC as an NPV discount rate, is the assumption of an unchanging capital structure. In using the WACC, the net advantage of debt capital is taken into account by using the after-tax cost of debt capital. Thus, if the project were appraised using the company's *existing* WACC, the implicit assumption would be that it was being financed with €35 000 of debt (because it is this amount of debt that will maintain the existing gearing).

In this current example, Claasburg is proposing to finance the project using €80 000 of debt. The advantage to the company that accrues from using the €45 000 extra debt (i.e. €80 000 − €35 000) is given by the present value of the tax relief:

$$V_B T = €45\,000 \times 0.35 = €15\,750$$

If the project were to be financed with the existing gearing ratio, then K_0 would remain unchanged at 16% and the NPV of the project would be:

$$- €100\,000 + \frac{€28\,000}{0.16} = + €75\,000\,\text{NPV}$$

Hence the total benefits of the project are given by its worth if there were no change in capital structure (€75 000), *plus* the worth of the change in capital structure (€15 750). This represents a total of €90 750. However, once more notice the circular nature of the analysis. It can only be accurate if we know how the project should be financed in order to maintain the *existing* gearing ratio (i.e. a €35 000 : €65 000 debt:equity ratio).

That brings us to the APV approach. Given the company's existing gearing ratio and its existing cost of equity capital, we have previously calculated that – if the company were all-equity financed – its cost of equity capital would be (approximately) 17.2%. Hence the 'pure' value of the investment opportunity under consideration – which can be referred to as the '*base-case present value*' – is (as before):

$$- €100\,000 + \frac{€28\,000}{0.172} = + €62\,750\,\text{NPV}$$

The present value of the tax relief on the €80 000 of debt used to finance the investment is:

$$€80\,000 \times 0.35 = €28\,000$$

Therefore the *adjusted* (base-case) present value of the investment proposal can be calculated as:

$$€62\,750 + €28\,000 = €90\,750$$

Adjusted present value

Of all three approaches to the appraisal of the project used in the example above only the APV approach was capable of handling the situation where the company's existing gearing ratio was not being maintained. Furthermore, in the example used, we also saw that it is not as straightforward as it might initially appear for a company to finance a project in such a way as *not to* change the existing capital structure. (Where we had a gearing ratio of 1:4 the €100 000 project in question had to be financed by a 35:65 debt:equity mix and not simply 1:4.)

From the Claasburg example we must conclude that, unless a project is going to be financed in such a way as to leave the capital structure unchanged (or if we have an M and M no-tax world, where capital structure is irrelevant), APV is the *only* safe way of ensuring that all the effects of a project – together with its financing method – are going to be captured in the appraisal.

However, before we examine the use of the APV technique in greater detail, let us first clarify the basic approach that it uses. Adjusted present value essentially uses a 'divide and conquer' approach to capital investment appraisal. As we saw in the previous example, it first evaluates the project assuming that it is all-equity financed. This is referred to as the project's *base-case present value*. Then this figure is *adjusted* to take into account any 'side-effects' that might arise through the financing method used. Although these side-effects can be numerous, the principal one, again as we saw in the Claasburg example, is likely to be the tax relief on the interest paid on the debt capital used.

The base-case discount rate

In the example used to illustrate the basic mechanics of the APV technique the base-case discount rate was calculated by taking the geared company's K_E and then using a rearranged version of the M and M expression for the cost of equity capital in a taxed world:

$$K_{E_g} = K_{E_{ug}} + (K_{E_{ug}} - K_D)\frac{V_B(1-T)}{V_E}$$

was rearranged to find $K_{E_{ug}}$, the all-equity cost of equity capital:

$$K_{E_{ug}} = \frac{V_E K_{E_g} + V_B K_D(1-T)}{V_E + V_B(1-T)}$$

This approach is a perfectly acceptable means of identifying the base-case discount rate ($K_{E_{ug}}$), but *only* in *one* set of circumstances.

In the Claasburg example used in the previous section, we assumed that the project had the same degree of systematic risk as the company's existing average systematic risk level. Given this assumption, the approach used for calculating the base-case discount rate is satisfactory. However, as we have already discussed at an earlier stage when criticizing the use of the WACC as an NPV discount rate, such an assumption is often likely to be unrealistic in practice.

Therefore, if we wish to use the APV technique but feel that we cannot legitimately assume that the project's systematic risk reflects the company's average systematic risk, how can a suitable base-case discount rate be calculated? The answer is – as it was before in our discussion about the use of the WACC – to use the capital asset pricing model.

ASSET BETAS AND GEARING

In Chapter 12 we discussed the possible use of the CAPM to generate an NPV discount rate that was *tailor-made* to reflect the systematic risk level of the project under evaluation. This could be achieved by using, as a surrogate for the project's beta, the beta value of the project's industry group (or it might be based on the beta of an individual company specializing in a business very similar to the project being considered). The *industry beta* would simply be the average equity beta value of all the quoted companies within that particular industry.

Later, in Chapter 18, we saw how capital structure caused *financial risk* and that financial risk formed part of the *total* systematic risk borne by the equity capital in a company. This therefore implies that if we are to use an *industry* beta to act as a surrogate for a *project's* beta, then account must be taken of any difference between the industry's gearing ratio and the gearing ratio used to finance the project.

This could be done through the expression we developed in Chapter 18:

$$\beta_{assets} = \beta_{equity} \times \frac{V_E}{V_0} + \beta_{debt} \times \frac{V_B}{V_0}$$

where the industry's asset beta could be *re-geared* to reflect how the project is financed. Example 1 is a simple illustration of this situation. We will develop a more complex example of the calculation of a risk-adjusted WACC at a later point in this chapter.

EXAMPLE 1

For simplicity, we will assume that the debt beta is zero. As a result:

$$\beta_{assets} = \beta_{equity} \times \frac{V_E}{V_0} + \beta_{debt} \times \frac{V_B}{V_0}$$

Reduces to:

$$\beta_{assets} = \beta_{equity} \times \frac{V_E}{V_0}$$

We can now make use of this expression[2] to generate a suitable NPV discount rate.

Suppose an investment project involves *cement manufacturing*. The project is to be financed using a 1:3 gearing ratio (i.e. debt:equity) and the cement industry group has an average equity beta of 1:2 and the average cement industry gearing ratio of 1:4.

The industry's equity beta could be *ungeared* and then *re-geared* to reflect how the project is financed as follows:

$$\beta_{industry\ assets} = 1.2 \times \frac{4}{4 + 1} = 0.96$$

▶

▶

$$\beta_{\text{industry assets + project gearing}} = 0.96 \times \frac{3 + 1}{3} = 1.28$$

The beta value of 1.28 could then be put into the CAPM to provide a value for the *project's* cost of equity capital. This, together with the cost of debt used to finance the project and the project's gearing ratio, could then be used to calculate a WACC for the project and be used as an NPV discount rate.

However, we must be careful with Example 1, because it is only applicable in a *no-tax* situation.[3] This is because the expression used for identifying the asset beta does not take into account the fact that tax relief on debt capital effectively reduces the financial risk borne by equity at any particular gearing level.

Asset betas and tax

Let us now look at how asset betas can be found in a *taxed* world. Taking the M and M expression for the total market value of a geared company in a taxed world:

$$V_{0_g} = V_{E_{ug}} + V_B T$$

where: V_{0_g} = total market value of a geared company

$V_{E_{ug}}$ = what the company would be worth if it was all equity financed

$V_B T$ = present value of the tax relief on debt interest:

This expression can be restated as follows:

$$V_{E_g} + V_B = V_{E_{ug}} + V_B T$$
$$V_{E_{ug}} = V_{E_g} + V_B - V_B T$$
$$V_{E_{ug}} = V_{E_g} + V_B (1 - T)$$

Furthermore, on the basis that the beta value of a company's assets is reflected in a weighted average of the beta values of the individual securities that finance those assets, then we can formulate this expression in terms of beta values:

$$\beta_{\text{assets}} = \beta_{\text{equity}} \times \frac{V_E}{V_E + V_B(1 - T)} + \beta_{\text{debt}} \times \frac{V_B(1 - T)}{V_E + V_B(1 - T)}$$

This is therefore our *revised* expression for calculating asset betas in a *taxed* world.

However, before we start to apply this expression, one word of caution has to be sounded. One assumption that has been maintained throughout this analysis is that of perpetuity cash flows. This is not a *necessary assumption* of the APV technique, but it is an assumption of the expression we have developed for estimating an asset beta in a *taxed* world.

Therefore if this expression is used in a situation where the cash flows are not perpetuities, then it should be recognized that there will be some degree of error. However, when estimating an industry's asset beta, this assumption's lack of validity may not be substantial and so the error is likely to be relatively minor.

Applying the APV technique

Example 2 illustrates the use of the APV technique in a relatively simple situation. However, it should be noted that, even here, a traditional NPV/WACC approach would have great difficulty in arriving at a satisfactory evaluation of the project.

EXAMPLE 2

The problem

Kinevik AB is a small marine engineering company, based in Stockholm. It is currently considering diversifying into the automotive engineering industry. The particular project under evaluation would require capital expenditure of kr 1 000 000 and would have a zero value at the end of its 4-year life. It is estimated that the project would generate an annual net cash flow (revenues less operating cash costs) of kr 326 000.

The proposal is to finance the project with a kr800 000 4-year term loan from Kinevik's bank. The project would have sufficient *debt capacity*[4] to support such a loan and the annual interest rate would be 8%. The bank would also charge an administration fee on the loan of kr 15 000. In addition, the company would use kr 200 000 of retained earnings.

The automotive engineering industry has an average equity beta of 1.90 and its debt capital can be considered to be virtually risk-free and so can be assumed to have a zero beta value. The average gearing (debt:equity) ratio in the industry is 3:4.

Kinevik pays corporation tax at 22% at the end of each year. Tax relief is available on both capital expenditure and debt interest.

The annual return on government bonds is 4%. The average annual stock market return is 9%.

The company wishes to evaluate the proposed investment using an APV analysis.

The solution

The starting point is to identify the NPV of the project *as if it were all-equity financed* – that is the base-case present value:

1. *Base-case discount rate*
   Using:

$$\beta_{assets} = \beta_{equity} \times \frac{V_E}{V_0} + \beta_{debt} \times \frac{V_B}{V_0}$$

and given the assumption that debt capital can be considered to be virtually risk-free and so $\beta_{debt} = 0$, this reduces to:

therefore[1]:

$$\beta_{assets} = \beta_{equity} \times \frac{V_E}{V_0}$$

Therefore the asset beta of the automotive engineering industry can be calculated as:

$$\beta_{\text{automotive industry assets}} = 1.90 \times \frac{4}{4 + 3(1 - 0.22)} = 1.20$$

and now using CAPM:

Base-case discount rate $= R_F + [R_M - R_F] \cdot \beta_{\text{asset}}$

Base-case discount rate $= 4\% + [9\% - 4\%] \times 1.2 = 10\%$

This is the return required from Kinevik's automotive industry project, due to its systematic business risk (principally, its revenue sensitivity and its proportion of fixed to variable operating costs).

2. *Tax relief on capital expenditure.*

kr 1 000 000 ÷ 4 years = kr 250 000 × 0.22 = kr 55 000 per year tax relief.

3. *Base-case present value*

Year	0	1	2	3	4
	(1 000 000)				
Capex tax relief		55 000	55 000	55 000	55 000
Net cash flow		326 000	326 000	326 000	326 000
Tax on cash flow		(71 720)	(71 720)	(71 720)	(71 720)
After-tax cash flow	(1 000 000)	309 280	309 280	309 280	309 280

As the project's net cash flow is an annuity, we can use annuity discount factors to calculate its base-case present value, using the base-case discount rate of 10%:

$$- \text{kr 1 000 000} + (\text{kr 309 280} \times A_{4\ 10\%})$$

$- \text{kr 1 000 000} + (\text{kr 309 2800} \times 3.1699) = - \text{kr 19 613}$ base-case present value

Notice that, at this stage of the analysis, the project has a negative present value, so it is not a worthwhile investment. However:

4. *Present value of the financing side-effects*

(i) *Present value of the tax relief on interest / 'tax shield'*

Annual interest: kr 800 000 × 0.08 = kr 64 000
Annual tax relief: kr 64 000 × 0.22 = kr 14 080 £11 200 × 0.35 = £3920
Present value of tax relief: kr 14 080 × $A_{4\ 8\%}$ = kr 14 080 × 3.3121 = + kr 46 634

Notice that the pre-tax cost of debt capital is used as the discount rate. This rate is used as the best rate to reflect the low-risk nature of the tax relief cash flow. (The after-tax cost of debt is not used as this would represent 'double counting' of the debt interest tax relief.)

(ii) *Present value of capital issue costs*

Administration fee: kr 15 000
Tax relief on the fee: kr 15 000 × 0.22 = kr 3300

▶

As we would assume that both the administration fee and its tax relief would occur immediately (i.e. at Year 0), then these are both present value figures.

5. *Adjusted present value*

		(kr)
Base-case present value	:	(19 613)
Present value of tax shield	:	46 634
Administration fee	:	(15 000)
Fee tax relief	:	3 300
Adjusted present value	:	+ kr 15 321

Although the project would have been rejected if it had been all-equity financed (NPV: – kr 19 613), it is worthwhile accepting the project because of its proposed financing method: its overall APV is positive. Therefore, if the project is accepted it will increase shareholder wealth by kr 15 321.

APV and debt capacity

There is a further point to be made about Example 2. This concerns the reference to *debt capacity*. It can be seen from the analysis used in the example that debt capacity is valuable. A project's debt capacity indicates its ability to act as security for a loan. It is the tax relief available from such a loan which gives debt capacity its value.

This then raises a potential problem. Some projects may be undertaken where the amount of debt finance that is used effectively *under-gears* the project, leaving spare – or unused – debt capacity. Alternatively, a project might be financed by more debt capital than the project itself can support. In other words, the project might be *over-geared*, because of the availability of unused debt capacity elsewhere in the company.

The problem here concerns how the project should be evaluated via APV. Should the present value of the tax shield be based on the *actual amount* of debt financing used, or on the *theoretical amount* of debt financing the project's own debt capacity would allow it to raise?

The answer is that the tax shield should be based on the *theoretical* level of financing – i.e. on the full debt capacity of the project – as to do otherwise would lead to the danger of 'cross-subsidization'. Example 3 shows two possible situations.

EXAMPLE 3

Böhler Tec is a software developer based in Vienna. The company is considering buying a new generation of storage area network (SAN). The SAN is expected to cost €100 000 and – for the purposes of this example– has an infinitely long life. The investment has a debt capacity of 80% of its cost (and therefore could 'support' a loan of: 0.80 × €100 000 = €80 000). Böhler Tec decide to finance the project with €50 000 of equity and €50 000 of irredeemable bonds at 10% interest. The corporation tax rate in Austria is 25% and is payable at the end of each year. There are no other costs involved.

▶

The SAN project's base-case present value is negative: $-$ €16 500. If the present value of the tax shield is based on the *actual level* of debt financing its value is:

$$\frac{€50\,000 \times 0.10 \times 0.25}{0.10} = €12\,500$$

However, based on the theoretical amount of debt the project could support (€80 000), the tax shield then valued at:

$$\frac{€80\,000 \times 0.10 \times 0.25}{0.10} = €20\,000$$

Therefore, in the former case the APV would be *negative* and the project (incorrectly) rejected. In the latter case the project should, quite properly, be accepted, because of its positive APV (i.e. $-$€16 000 + €20 000 = $+$ €4000 APV). This latter analysis is correct because, although the project is not actually utilizing the whole of its debt capacity, the company has got the ability to raise an additional €30 000 of debt finance *in the future* (€80 000 $-$ €50 000), secured against this project's unused debt capacity. Hence, its value should be credited to the project.

Suppose Böhler Tec decided to undertake the SAN project, with the proposed level of financing. Some time later the company is evaluating an investment in a bit-mapped graphic catalyst (BMGC). The BMGC project requires €80 000 of capital expenditure and it has a 50% debt capacity. However, instead of just using €40 000 of 10% debt, the company proposes to use €70 000 of 10% debt, €40 000 of which is secured against the BMGC project's own assets, in line with its debt capacity, and €30 000 secured against the unused debt capacity arising from the earlier acceptance of the SAN project.

If the BMGC project has a negative base-case present value of €12 000, then its APV might be either positive or negative, depending on the tax shield chosen.

On the basis of debt financing of €70 000, the present value of the tax shield is:

$$\frac{€70\,000 \times 0.10 \times 0.25}{0.10} = €17\,500$$

Thus the project would be accepted with an APV of: $-$£12 000 + €17 500 = $+$ €5500. However, on the basis of the debt financing which the project can support in its own right (€40 000) the present value of the tax shield is:

$$\frac{€40\,000 \times 0.10 \times 0.25}{0.10} = €10\,000$$

In this case the project's APV is negative: $-$€12 000 + €10 000 = $-$€2000 and so should be rejected. The latter analysis is, of course, correct. In the former analysis, the present value of the tax shield contains a 'subsidy' from the SAN project equal to the value of the SAN project's unused debt capacity:

$$\frac{€30\,000 \times 0.10 \times 0.25}{0.10} = €7500$$

Quite simply, to be acceptable, a project should be capable of generating a positive APV *in its own right*. Logically, we should not *cross-subsidize* between projects in the evaluation process.

A more complex example

A more complex problem is illustrated in Example 4. Here the APV analysis takes account not only of the tax relief on debt interest, but also of a 'low cost' loan and capital issue costs. (In practice, any number of side-effects can be included in the analysis by just adding them on to the base-case present value.)

EXAMPLE 4

The problem

London Technology Solutions (LTS) is considering investing in two new pieces of equipment in order to extend its range of services. One is a high-powered 3-D laser scanner and the other is a 3-D printer. The scanner will cost £60 000 and the 3-D printer will cost £40 000. The investment in the two pieces of equipment is expected to produce a net annual cash flow, before tax, of £37 000 and have a life of 4 years. At the end of its life the two machines will be worthless.

For this type of investment the company would normally expect to finance 75% of the capital expenditure with debt capital with a maturity equal to that of the project's life. Thus they would expect to raise £45 000 of debt to purchase the scanner and £30 000 of debt to purchase the printer. In each case, the remainder of the finance required would be met from an issue of equity capital. Debt issue costs (bank administration fees), are expected to be 2.5% of the amount of debt raised.

Because the UK government wishes to promote the purchase and operation of 3-D printing technology, they will make a loan available to LTS (repayable at the end of 3 years) for 100% of the printer's cost, at a *subsidized* rate of interest of only 6%. This is in contrast to LTS's current market cost of debt of 10%. However, as a result of this facility, the company will only raise £35 000 of debt to finance the scanner, so that the overall debt ratio of the project remains at around 75%.

The entire investment project (i.e. the scanner plus printer), falls within an industry category having an equity beta value of 1.52 and an average debt:equity ratio of 1:3. The risk-free return and market return are 6% and 14.33%, respectively. LTS pays corporation tax in the UK at 20%. For simplicity, assume that tax is paid at each year-end and that there is tax relief available on both capital expenditure (spread evenly over the investment's life), and debt interest, but not on debt issue costs. Also assume that debt betas are zero.

The solution

Base-case present value of the project
The base-rate discount rate can be calculated as follows:

$$\beta_{project} = 1.52 \times \frac{3}{3 + 1 \times (1 - 0.20)} = 1.2$$

$$\text{Base-case discount rate} = 6\% + [14.33\% - 6\%] \times 1.2 = 16\%$$

and so the base-case present value:

(i)   Annual project cash flow: £37 000

(ii)   Tax charge on this cash flow: £37 000 × 0.20 = £7400

(iii)   Annual tax relief on capital expenditure: £100 000 × 0.20 = £20 000 ÷ 4 = £5000

(iv)   Annual after-tax cash flow: £37 000 − £7400 + £5000 = £34 600

(v)   Base-case present value: −£100 000 + [£34 600 × A$_{4\,16\%}$]

▶

▶

$$-£100\ 000 + [£34\ 600 \times 2.7982] = -£3182$$

Financing side-effects

(i) Present value of tax relief on debt interest:
Scanner

$$[£35\ 000 \times 0.10 \times 0.20] \times A_{4\,0.10} = £2219$$

Printer

$$[£40\ 000 \times 0.06 \times 0.20] \times A_{4\,10\%} = £1521$$

Therefore, total tax relief: £2219 + £1521 = £3740

(ii) Present value of cheap loan
Interest saving after tax:

$$£40\ 000 \times (0.10 - 0.06)\,(1 - 0.20) \times A_{4\,10\%} = £4057\ PV$$

(iii) Debt issue costs:
$$£75\ 000 \times 0.025 \quad -£1875$$

Adjusted present value

Base present value of project	£(3 182)
+ present value of tax relief on interest	£ 3 740
+ present value of cheap loan	£ 4 057
− issue costs	£(1 875)
APV	+£2 740

Therefore the project should be accepted; it has a positive APV of + £2740.

A final point

The logic behind the APV technique is simple: different risk cash flows should be evaluated separately using discount rates that specifically reflect the systematic risk level involved. For this reason, the technique is sometimes referred to as the '*valuation of components rule*' (VCR).

In a more sophisticated analysis of a large project, more than one discount rate may be used to calculate the base-case present value. For example, it may be thought that a project's revenues are significantly more (systematic) risky than its cost cash flows. Therefore, the present value of the revenues may be calculated separately from the present value of its costs, using a different discount rate in each case. Alternatively, it could be legitimately argued that the capital expenditure tax relief cash flows are particularly low-risk and so should have a separate discount rate applied to them which specifically reflects their low-risk nature.

Conclusions

In conclusion, what can be said about investment and financing interactions? It should be noted that, in most cases (except for such situations as found in Example 4), the major financing side-effect arises from the tax shield. However, in this respect, we should be cautious and not forget the conclusion of Miller's 1977 analysis that suggested that the *true* worth of the tax shield *may be* zero.

Whether or not Miller's analysis holds good in the real world is still subject to empirical testing. However, it may well be realistic to suggest that the value of the tax shield, even if it is not zero, is substantially less than the value placed upon it by the M and M with-tax analysis.

In such a case, an APV analysis – although technically more correct in most circumstances than a 'traditional' WACC/NPV analysis – may add very little to the project evaluation. In other words, given all the general uncertainties surrounding any investment appraisal, an NPV/WACC analysis may be thought to be sufficiently accurate.

However, in contrast to the above comment, it should also be pointed out that in very major projects (sometimes referred to as 'giant' projects) the financing package attached to the project often plays a crucial role. In such circumstances an APV analysis would be strongly desirable.

RISK-ADJUSTED WACC

An APV analysis is particularly applicable to the evaluation of major capital investments, which often involve quite complex financing arrangements. However, in many other circumstances, we might be able to conclude that an NPV/WACC analysis will provide a sufficiently accurate investment appraisal and provide good decision advice.

As we have already noted, the most problematic assumption lying behind an NPV/ WACC analysis is that the project has the *same* systematic risk as the company. Where this is not the case, but where the project is relatively small and the company is intending to maintain its existing capital structure, it is still reasonable to use an NPV/WACC analysis if the WACC is *adjusted* to take into account the different systematic risk that the project involves.

Example 1 gave a very simple illustration of this approach. In Example 5 we now give a full-scale illustration of the calculation of a risk-adjusted WACC that can then be used as an NPV discount rate in the type of situation described in the previous paragraph.

EXAMPLE 5

The problem

Kumba Cement is based in Durban, South Africa. The company has a debt:equity ratio of 1:4 and a pre-tax cost of debt capital of 12%. It is considering whether to diversify its operations by undertaking a sugar production project. The company realizes that it cannot use its WACC as an NPV discount rate in order to evaluate the project, as the systematic risk of cement manufacturing is unlikely to be the same as that of sugar production. In order to solve this problem, Kumba Cement has obtained information about Afrisugar Ltd, a large sugar producer:

Afrisugar Ltd

$$\beta_{equity} = 1.40 \qquad \beta_{debt} = 0.15$$
$$V_B : V_E = 2:3$$

In addition, the current return on South African government bonds is 10% and the return on the Johannesburg stock market portfolio is estimated to be 17%. Corporation tax in South Africa is at 33%.

Kumba Cement intends to use this information about Afrisugar to generate a risk-adjusted WACC: an NPV discount rate which will reflect both the systematic business risk of the sugar production project and the systematic financial risk of the company undertaking the project – Kumba Cement.

The solution

There are two possible approaches to the generation of a suitable discount rate. Both are shown here for the purposes of illustration:

Approach 1

This is completed in four stages.

1. The data concerning Afrisugar can be used to estimate *an asset* beta for sugar production.

$$\text{using: } \beta_{asset} = \beta_{equity} \times \frac{V_E}{V_E + V_B(1-T)} + \beta_{debt} \times \frac{V_B(1-T)}{V_E + V_B(1-T)}$$

$$\beta_{asset \atop Afrisugar} = 1.40 \times \frac{3}{3 + 2(1-0.33)} + 0.15 \times \frac{2(1-0.33)}{3 + 2(1-0.33)}$$

$$\beta_{asset \atop Afrisugar} = 0.968 + 0.046 = 1.014$$

This asset beta reflects Afrisugar's *systematic business risk* of the sugar producing business, and therefore can be used as an estimate for the asset beta of Kumba Cement's sugar manufacturing project:

$$\beta_{asset \atop project} = \beta_{asset \atop Afrisugar} = 1.014$$

2. The second stage of the analysis is to 're-gear' this asset beta with Kumba Cement's capital structure to estimate an *equity beta* for Kumba's sugar project. Before doing so, however, we need to estimate a debt beta for the project.

    Given that Kumba has a pre-tax cost of debt of 12%, the debt beta can be estimated from the CAPM:

$$K_D = r_F + [E(r_M) - r_F] \times \beta_{debt}$$

therefore:

$$12\% = 10\% + (17\% - 10\%) \times \beta_{debt}$$

$$\frac{12\% - 10\%}{(17\% - 10\%)} = \beta_{debt} = 0.286$$

An equity beta for the project can now be estimated, again using:

$$\beta_{\substack{asset \\ project}} = \beta_{\substack{equity \\ project}} \times \frac{V_E}{V_E + V_B(1-T)} + \beta_{\substack{debt \\ project}} \times \frac{V_B(1-T)}{V_E + V_B(1-T)}$$

where:

$$1.014 = \beta_{\substack{equity \\ project}} \times \frac{4}{4 + 1(1-0.33)} + 0.286 \times \frac{1.(1-0.33)}{4 + 1(1-0.33)}$$

$$1.014 = \beta_{\substack{equity \\ project}} \times 0.854 + 0.041$$

$$\frac{1.014 - 0.041}{0.856} = \beta_{\substack{equity \\ project}} = 1.137$$

This equity beta reflects the systematic risk of the shareholders' funds invested by Kumba Cement in the sugar project: it reflects the systematic business risk of sugar production, and the systematic financial risk of Kumba Cement's capital structure.

3. The third stage is to take the project's equity beta and use CAPM to generate a cost of equity capital for the project. Therefore, using the CAPM:

$$K_{\substack{E \\ project}} = r_F + (E(r_M) - r_F) \times \beta_{\substack{equity \\ project}}$$

$$K_{\substack{0 \\ project}} = 10\% + (17\% - 10\%) \times 1.137 = 17.96\%$$

Thus, this estimates that Kumba Cement's shareholders will require a 17.96% return on their funds that are to be invested in the sugar production project, to reward them for the project's systematic business risk and the company's financial risk.

4. The final stage of the analysis is to use Kumba Cement's capital structure to calculate a risk-adjusted WACC for the sugar project, using:

$$K_{\substack{0 \\ project}} = K_{\substack{E \\ project}} \times \frac{V_E}{V_0} + K_D(1-T) \times \frac{V_B}{V_0}$$

$$K_{\substack{0 \\ project}} = 17.96\% \times \frac{4}{4+1} + 12\%(1-0.33) \times \frac{1}{4+1} = 15.97\%$$

Approach 2

This is more direct and makes use of the fact that the asset beta, when inputted into the CAPM, generates $K_{E_{ug}}$. This is on the basis that the asset beta measures systematic business risk *only* and so, when put into CAPM, it generates the return required for the systematic business risk. As we know from the capital structure analysis in Chapter 19, $K_{E_{ug}}$ is the cost of equity capital in an *all-equity* financed company: such a company *only* has systematic business risk.

1. The first stage is exactly the same as in the previous approach: the project's asset beta is estimated on the basis of Afrisugar's asset beta.
   Therefore:

$$\beta_{\substack{asset \\ project}} = 1.014$$

▶

2. This can be input into the CAPM to estimate $K_{E_{ug}}$ for the project;

$$K_{E_{ug}} = r_F + (E(r_M) - r_F) \times \beta_{asset_{project}}$$

$$K_{E_{ug}} = 10\% + (17\% - 10\%) \times 1.014 = 17.1\%$$

This represents the expected return required on the project, given its systematic business risk.

3. Finally, the M and M equation for the WACC can be used – using Kumba Cement's capital structure – to provide an estimate of a risk-adjusted WACC for the project:

$$K_{0_{project}} = K_{E_{ug}} \times \left(1 - \frac{V_B \times T}{V_0}\right)$$

$$K_{0_{project}} = 17.1\% \times \left(1 - \frac{1 \times 0.33}{4 + 1}\right) = 15.97\%$$

Notice that *both* approaches produce *exactly* the same result; a risk-adjusted, after-tax WACC of 15.97% (say 16%), which could then be used in an NPV analysis of Kumba Cement's sugar production project.

LEASE OR PURCHASE DECISION

Financial and operating leases

Many companies use *leasing* to obtain the services of an asset, as an alternative to outright purchase. Therefore it can be seen as a source of finance and hence the 'lease or purchase' decision can be classed as a financing decision.[5]

The evaluation of the lease or purchase decision has been problematic mainly because it cannot really be viewed as a *pure* financing decision, as it also involves interactions with the investment decision.[6] In this section, we will examine how the lease or purchase decision should be evaluated in the light of our development of the APV technique.

The process of leasing involves one party (the lessor) purchasing an asset and *renting* out the use of that asset to another party (the lessee). Thus the lessee is able to operate the asset without actually being the legal owner.

It is usual for lease contracts to be classified into either *financial* or *operating* leases. The main characteristics of a financial lease are as follows. The lessor will lease the machine to the lessee, with the intention of receiving the full purchase price of the leased asset, plus a rate of return on capital, through the lease payments. For this reason, a financial lease cannot usually be cancelled or terminated early by either party. Therefore with this type of lease, the lessee – although not the legal owner – holds all the 'risks of asset ownership' (e.g. the risk of technological obsolescence and the risk that the demand for the asset's services will be below expectations). The lessor holds no risk, other than the risk of the lessee's default on the lease payments. Hence a financial lease is virtually indistinguishable from more normal debt capital – both in theory and in practice.

Operating leases are very different. They are generally short term and usually represent the rental of an asset to carry out a particular job. Characteristically, the asset will be used by many different lessees over its life. The lessor does not necessarily expect to recover the full cost of the asset, plus a return on capital, out of the lease payments, but will also take account of the expected second-hand value of the asset at the termination of the leasing agreement. Therefore, with an operating lease, the lessee does not bear any of the risks of ownership (these are borne instead by the lessor) because of the option to cancel the agreement at short notice. Where such a lease is entered into on a longer-term basis, it can be viewed not so much as a form of finance (although that is what it is), but more of a *marketing* device. In other words the manufacturer of an asset may offer the asset's services through an operating lease as a marketing device to encourage 'sales'.

The evaluation of an operating lease is relatively straightforward. Because the lease is terminable at short notice, the lease payments are treated as just another operating cost of the asset involved. Hence a straightforward NPV analysis can be used, where the (after-tax) lease payment cash flows are included along with all the other cash flows involved, and which are then discounted to present value by a discount rate that reflects the asset's systematic risk.

Evaluating a financial lease

We stated earlier that a financial lease is effectively the equivalent of debt capital in that, from a gearing viewpoint, the present value of a lease contract liability would be seen in the same terms as the liability on straightforward debt finance. However, the APV analysis of lease finance differs somewhat from that involving debt finance.

Example 6 illustrates the APV technique being applied to a lease versus loan-purchase decision. This can then be contrasted with the evaluation of the same project in Example 7, but which is undertaken along the lines of a *more traditional* lease versus purchase analysis. The anomalies in this second example should be fairly obvious – given what we know about risk and return relationships. (The fact that the two analyses produce the same conclusion is, of course, fortuitous.)

EXAMPLE 6

The problem

Premier Steel is a UK-based manufacturer of high tensile steel ingots. The company is considering undertaking a project that consists of the acquisition and operation of a steel press machine. The machine would cost £1 000 000 and would have a zero scrap value at the end of its 4-year life. It is expected to produce the following net cash flows (i.e. revenues less operating costs), pre-tax:

Year	Cash flow
1	+600 000
2	+500 000
3	+200 000
4	+60 000

The machine could either be bought outright or acquired via a financial lease. Purchase would be made through a £600 000 4-year term loan at 8% interest, secured against the machine (which has a 60% debt

▶

capacity), together with £400 000 of retained earnings. The lease agreement requires four payments of £270 000, paid annually in advance.

It is thought that the project is required to produce an after-tax return of at least 20% to be acceptable. This can be assumed to represent an adequate base-case discount rate.

Corporation tax in the UK is charged at 20%, payable at each year-end. Tax relief on capital expenditure is allowable evenly over the life of an investment. Tax relief is also allowable on interest and lease payments.

The analysis

In this type of situation, an APV analysis has to be undertaken on the basis of a pair of *mutually exclusive* alternatives: the project purchased and the project leased. (For simplicity, calculations will be rounded to the nearest £1000.)

(a) *Project purchased (£000s)*

Base-case present value:

Year	0	1	2	3	4
Outlay	(1 000)				
Net cash flow		600	500	200	60
Tax charge		(120)	(100)	(40)	(12)
After-tax c/f	(1 000)	480	400	160	48
20% discount	× 1	×.8333	×.6944	×.5787	×.4823
	(1 000)	400	278	93	23

Base-case *present value*: −£206 000

Present value of financing side-effects

1. Present value of tax relief on capital expenditure:

(i)   £1 000 000 × 0.20 = £200 000 tax relief ÷ 4 = £50 000 per year.

(ii) Given the low-risk/certain nature of this cash flow, it will be discounted at present value using the company's (before tax) cost of debt – 8% – to reflect this fact:

$$£50\ 000 \times A_{4\ 8\%} = £50\ 000 \times 3.3121 = £166\ 000$$

2. Present value of tax shield on interest payments:

Annual interest	:	£600 000 × 0.08 = £48 000
Annual tax relief	:	£48 000 × 0.20 = £9600
Present value of tax relief	:	£9600 × $A_{4\ 8\%}$ = £9600 × 3.3121 = £32 000

Adjusted present value

Base-case present value	− £206 000
Present value of tax relief	+ £166 000
Present value of tax shield	+ £32 000
APV	− £8 000

▶

Therefore the project is not worthwhile if loan-purchased by Premier Steel, it has a *negative* APV.

(b) *Project leased*

Base-case present value: −£206 000

present value of financing side-effects

(i)   Present value of lease payments:

$$-£270\ 000 - [£270\ 000 \times A_{3\ 8\%}]$$
$$-£270\ 000 - [£270\ 000 \times 2.5771] = -£966\ 000\ PV$$

(ii)   Present value of tax relief on lease payments:

$$£270\ 000 \times 0.20 = £54\ 000 \text{ per year tax relief}$$
$$£54\ 000 \times A_{4\ 8\%} = £54\ 000 \times 3.3121 = £179\ 000\ PV$$

(iii) Present value of capital expenditure saved: +£1 000 000

Adjusted present value

Base-case present value	:	−£ 206 000
Present value of lease payments	:	−£ 966 000
Present value of tax relief	:	+£ 179 000
Present value of saved capital expenditure	:	+£ 1 000 000
APV	:	+£ 7 000

Therefore the project *is* a worthwhile investment if Premier Steel use a lease, as it has a *positive* APV.

EXAMPLE 7

A more traditional approach to lease versus purchase decisions (although there are many variations) is to treat the analysis as a two-stage decision. The first stage is to compare the present value *cost* of leasing against the *cost* of purchase. The second stage is to then evaluate the project using the *least-cost* method of acquisition as the 'outlay'. In the first stage of the decision the after-tax cost of debt is used to reflect the low-risk nature of the cash flows and to take into account the tax-deductibility of debt. In the second stage, a discount rate is used which reflects the project's own systematic risk level.

Stage one

After-tax cost of debt: 8% (1 − 0.20) = 6.4% = discount factor.

Present value cost of leasing

(i)   Annual lease payments: £270 000 Years 0 to 3.

(ii)   Annual tax relief on lease payments: £270 000 × 0.20 = £54 000 Years 1 to 4.

▶

(iii)   Present value of lease payments at 6.4% discount rate:

$$£270\ 000 + [£270\ 000 \times A_{3\ 6.4\%}]$$

where: $A_{3\ 6.4\%} = \dfrac{1 - [1 + 0.064]^{-3}}{0.064} = 2.6533$

$$£270\ 000 + [£270\ 000 \times 2.6533] = £986\ 391$$

(iv)   Present value of tax relief at 6.4% discount rate:

$$£54\ 000 \times A_{4\ 6.4\%}$$

where: $A_{4\ 6.4\%} = \dfrac{1 - [1 + 0.064]^{-4}}{0.064} = 3.4336$

$$£54\ 000 \times 3.4336 = £185\ 414$$

(v)   Present value of leasing: £986 391 − £185 414 = £800 977

Present Value cost of purchase

(i)   Cost of purchase: £1 000 000

(ii)   Annual tax relief on capital expenditure: £1 000 000 × 0.20 ÷ 4 = £50 000

(iii)   Present value of tax relief (discounted at 6.4%):

$$£50\ 000 \times A_{4\ 6.4\%} = £50\ 000 \times 3.4336 = £171\ 680$$

(iv)   After-tax present value cost of purchase:

$$£1\ 000\ 000 - £171\ 680 = £828\ 320$$

Therefore, it is cheaper to acquire the machine with a lease (costing £800 977 in present value terms), rather than purchase (which costs £828 320 after-tax in present value terms).

Stage two

Project's NPV analysis

(i)   Effective present value cost of the investment: £800 977

(ii)   After tax cash flows:

Year	0	1	2	3
Net revenues	£600 000	£500 000	£400 000	£60 000
less Tax	£120 000	£100 000	£80 000	£12 000
Net cash flow	£480 000	£400 000	£320 000	£48 000

(iii)   Present value of after tax cash flow (using 20% discount factor):

Year	Net cash flow	×	20% discount rate	=	Present value cash flow
1	£480 000	×	0.8333	=	£399 984
2	£400 000	×	0.6944	=	£277 760
3	£320 000	×	0.5787	=	£185 184
4	£48 000	×	0.4823	=	£ 23 150
Total present value of after tax net cash flow					£886 078

(iv)   Net present value:

$$-£800\ 977 + £886\ 078 = +\ £85\ 101\ \text{NPV}$$

Therefore Premier Steel's project is worth undertaking via a financial lease agreement.

SUMMARY

This chapter has investigated investment and financing decision interactions.

- Four different valuation models were analyzed. All four were found to be equivalent, given a set of restrictive assumptions which included a fixed or unchanging gearing ratio.
- Given these assumptions, all four valuation models were capable of correctly evaluating a capital investment proposal.
- However, when the assumption of an unchanging gearing ratio is relaxed, all become, effectively, unworkable – with the exception of the APV model.
- The APV model is a very general model and, because it takes a 'divide and conquer' approach – evaluating each different risk cash flow separately – it can handle highly complex capital investment appraisals, together with the associated financing implications.
- In circumstances where an NPV/WACC analysis would be satisfactory, if it were not for the fact that the project's systematic risk is not the same as that of the company, then a risk-adjusted WACC can be estimated to reflect the project's systematic business risk specifically, together with the financial risk of the company's capital structure.
- Finally, the lease versus purchase decision was analyzed using an APV/valuation by components rule approach. Here it was seen that the analysis had to be conducted on the basis of a mutually exclusive investment decision

NOTES

1.   In other words, €43 077 per year, pre-tax: €43 077 × (1 − 0.35) = €28 000.
2.   An alternative, equivalent expression, after Hamada (1972), which is widely used is:

$$\beta_{assets} = \beta_{equity} \Big/ \left(1 + \frac{V_D}{V_E}\right)$$

but notice this expression specifically assumes $\beta_{debt} = 0$.

3. Because of this, in Example 1 there is really no need to re-gear the industry's asset beta of 0.96. This could be used in CAPM to generate a suitable discount rate for the project, which would be equal to the project's WACC. This is because, in a no-tax world, capital structure – although it does affect K_E – does not affect the overall return required.

4. The concept of 'debt capacity' was first discussed in Chapter 19. In this example, it is assumed that the lender is willing to accept the project's assets as sufficient security for the kr 800 000 loan required.

5. Some approaches treat the decision as an investment decision.

6. For a survey of the different approaches, see Bower (1973).

FURTHER READING

1. Two excellent articles which look at the whole area of investment and financing decisions, their interactions and the use of CAPM are: M.E. Rubinstein, 'A Mean-Variance Synthesis of Corporate Financial Theory', *Journal of Finance*, March 1973; and R.S. Hamada, 'The Effect of the Firm's Capital Structure on the Systematic Risks of Common Stocks', *Journal of Finance*, May 1972. In addition, a worthwhile reference on debt betas is: M. Weinstein, 'The Systematic Risk of Corporate Bonds', *Journal of Financial and Quantitative Analysis*, September 1981.

2. In addition, the following articles are of interest in providing a general overview: A.K. Makhaya and H.E. Thompson, 'Comparison of Alternative Models for Estimating the Cost of Equity Capital for Electric Utilities', *Journal of Economics and Business*, February 1984; and I.E. Brick and D.G. Weaver, 'A Comparison of Capital Budgeting Techniques in Identifying Profitable Investments', *Financial Management*, Winter 1984.

3. As far as APV is concerned, the original article is: S.C. Myers, 'Interactions of Corporate Financing and Investment Decisions – Implications for Capital Budgeting', *Journal of Finance*, March 1974. However, a good introductory article is to be found in R. Taggart, 'Capital Budgeting and the Financing Decision: An Exposition', *Financial Management*, Summer 1977 or in T.A. Luehrman, 'Using APV: A Better Tool for Valuing Operations', *Harvard Business Review*, May–June 1997, which is an easy to read account of APV.

4. L. Booth, 'Capital Cash Flows, APV and Valuation', *European Financial Management*, January 2007 compares different methods of decision making including APV. Other articles of interest include: D.R. Chamber, R.S. Harris and J.J. Pringle, 'Treatment of Financing Mix in Analysing Investment Opportunities', *Financial Management*, Summer 1982; R.C. Greenfield, M.R. Randall and J.D. Woods, 'Financial Leverage and the Use of the NPV Investment Criterion', *Financial Management*, Autumn 1983; I. Cooper and J.R. Franks, 'The Interaction of Investment and Financing Decisions when a Firm has Unused Tax Credits', *Journal of Finance*, May 1983; and R.S. Ruback, 'Capital Cash Flows: A Simple Approach to Valuing Risky Cash Flows', *Financial Management*, Summer 2002, which contains a useful discussion about using the WACC.

5. A good introductory article on the lease decision is R.S. Bower, 'Issues in Lease Financing', *Financing Management*, Winter 1973. In addition, three other articles worth reading are: L.D. Schall, 'Evaluation of Lease Financing Contracts', *Midland Corporate Finance Journal*, Spring 1985; J. Ang and P.P. Peterson, 'The Leasing Puzzle', *Journal of Finance*, September 1984; and H.H. Weingartner, 'Leasing, Asset Lives and Uncertainty: Guide to Decision Making', *Financial Management*, Summer 1987. Finally an interesting perspective is given by J.C. Drury and S. Braund, 'The Leasing Decision: A Comparison of Theory and Practice', *Accounting and Business Research*, Summer 1990.

QUIZ QUESTIONS

1   If a company has a debt:equity gearing ratio of 1:3 why will financing a €1000 project with €250 of debt and €750 of equity not necessarily maintain the firm's existing capital structure?

2   What does the base-case discount rate represent?

3   What does the base-case present value of a project represent?

4   Distinguish between an operating lease and a financial lease.

5   If an industry's equity beta is 1.45 and its debt beta is 0.25 with an average gearing rate of 2:5, what is its assets beta, given a 35% corporate tax rate?

6   Given the information in question 5, estimate the beta value for the industry's average level of financial risk.

7   What is debt capacity?

8   A project costs R5000. It will be financed with a R3000 5-year loan at 10% interest. The corporation tax rate is 28%, and the project has a 50% debt capacity. What is the present value of its tax shield?

   (See the 'Answers to Quiz Questions' section at the back of the book.)

PROBLEMS

The answers to the following two problems are available to students online (see the 'Digital Resources' page for details).

1   Africa Industries (Pty) Ltd, an industrial conglomerate, is currently evaluating a project to produce a new electronic lock mechanism recently developed by the company. The project will require an immediate outlay of R100 000 on production machinery. This would have a zero scrap value at all times and would not be an allowable expense against tax. The project is expected to have a 3-year life and produce a net annual cash flow of R67 000 in each year. The amount would be subject to corporation tax.

   Although the project only has a debt capacity of 30% of cost, the company has unused debt capacity elsewhere and so proposes to finance the project with a R40 000 3-year loan, with an annual interest charge of 10%, together with a R30 000 issue of equity and R30 000 of retained earnings. The new equity issue will incur administration costs amounting to 2% of the money raised and the debt capital will incur a fee of 1%. Both sets of issue costs are allowable against tax.

   The electronics sector has an equity beta of 1.26 and an average gearing ratio of 1:3 (debt:equity). The industry's debt can be assumed to have a beta of 0.10. The after-tax return on South African government bonds is 7% and the after-tax return on the Johannesburg stock market index is 15.5%. Corporation tax is charged at a rate of 28% at each year-end.

   Required:

   (a)   Evaluate the project for the management of Africa Industries (Pty) Ltd.

   (b)   How would your evaluation change if the manufacturer of the production machinery offered you a 3-year R100 000 interest-free loan (with an issue cost of 1%)?

2   Doppelbacher AG is a widely diversified industrial company, based in Vienna. It has recently acquired the rights to manufacture a special type of mechanical folding widget patented by a Japanese company. The rights – which last for 5 years – were bought by Doppelbacher's CFO shortly before he left for another company.

▶

The Doppelbacher's chief engineer has now been given the task of assessing whether manufacture is likely to be a worthwhile investment for the company. His decision, already presented to the board, is to reject the project on the basis of an indicated negative NPV.

However, the chairman of Doppelbacher is uneasy about the chief engineer's analysis and has called you in as a financial consultant for advice. From the chief engineer's report, you establish the following facts:

Cash flows:

	Capital (€000s)	Sales (€000s)	Operating expenses (€000s)	Tax (€000s)	Net cash flow (€000s)
Immediately	(1300)				(1 300)
End-year 1–5		1 800	(1 450)	(140)	210
End-year 5	600				600

NPV calculation:

	Net cash flow (€000s)	Discount factor (10%)	Present value (€000s)
Immediately	(1 300)	1.0000	(1 300)
End-year 1–5	210	3.9708	834
End-year 5	600	0.6209	372
Total NPV			(94)

The chief engineer's analysis is based on the following:

(a)   The company's market research department have estimated sales of 100 000 units per annum at €11 per unit.

(b)   The estimate of annual operating expenses consists of the following:

	(€000s)
Direct materials @ €2.50 per unit	250
Direct labour @ €3.20 per unit	320
Production overhead @ €3.80 per unit	380
Interest @ 10%	120
Administration, selling and distribution expenses	380
Total	1 450

The labour rate is based on a time allocation of apprentice workers on a fixed rate. Each apprentice worker costs the company €15 000 per annum, and this contract would necessitate employing 11 new ones. The company would need to spend €270 000 training these new employees in the first year, but this is not included specifically above as such costs are incorporated in production overhead expenses.

Production overhead is calculated on an allocated rate per labour hour of which 20% relates to variable overhead. Specific items of fixed overhead incurred as a result of this contract are:

Depreciation	€80 000 per annum
Supervisory labour	€56 000 per annum
Rent of additional property	€12 000 per annum

▶

Interest is based on the latest interest rate information, and it is the company's intention to finance this project with a €1.2 million 5-year term loan at 10% interest, plus €100 000 of retained earnings.

Administration, selling and distribution expenses are charged on the basis of a fixed rate on sales, 25% of these expenses are variable.

(c) The tax charge is based on a rate of 25%, which is the company's current marginal rate of corporation tax.

(d) The project is discounted at the anticipated interest rate.

(e) The capital cost of €1.3 million represents €1 million for plant and machinery, and €300 000 for working capital. It is anticipated that the plant and machinery will have a resale value of €600 000 at the end of 5 years.

In addition to the above, you ascertain the following:

(i)   The company's marginal tax rate will fall to 20% after Year 1.

(ii) The company will claim tax relief on net capital expenditure (cost less terminal value), spread evenly over its life.

(iii) Tax is payable at the end of each year.

(iv) The production machinery is estimated to have a 50% debt capacity. Working capital only has a 10% debt capacity. However, the company is, at present, all-equity financed and so has a considerable amount of unused debt capacity.

(v)   Manufacturing companies with similar characteristics to the proposed project have average equity and debt betas of 2.29 and 0.15 respectively. Their average gearing ratio is 2:3 and their average marginal rate of corporation tax is 20%.

(vi) The current after-tax risk-free return on European Central Bank bonds is estimated at 8%. The average return on the Vienna stock market index is 15.9%.

Required:

Draft a report to the chairman of Doppelbacher:

(a) presenting a revised assessment to assist them in their decision-making

(b) discussing any differences between your assessment and that of the ex-CFO, briefly discussing the basis of adjusted present value as a decision-making criterion.

THE DIVIDEND DECISION

The purpose of this chapter is to:

■ Explain the M and M dividend decision analysis.

■ Discuss the traditional view of the dividend decision.

■ Examine the dividend decision in the light of imperfect financial markets.

DIVIDEND POLICY IN PERFECT CAPITAL MARKETS

The dividend decision is the third major category of corporate long-term financial decisions that we shall investigate. In a similar vein to both the capital investment decision and the capital structure decision, we shall pursue the question: can management affect shareholder wealth through the dividend decision?

The dividend decision is, perhaps, the least analyzed and most elusive and controversial of the three areas of financial decision-making. Indeed, one of the most celebrated academic articles on the subject is entitled 'The Dividend Puzzle' (Black, 1976: see the 'Further reading' section at the end of this chapter).

Consequently, the theory in this area is the least complete. The complications and confusions surrounding the dividend decision arise principally because it is the linchpin to both the investment and financing decisions. It therefore becomes difficult to abstract the dividend decision from these influences so that it may be examined, initially at least, in isolation.

The problem of the dividend decision can be stated in the form of two questions: does the *pattern* of the dividend flow through time to shareholders affect the market value of the equity capital? If it does, can one particular pattern of dividends then be identified which would maximize the equity's market value? However, the meaning of these two questions can appear ambiguous, and so we shall start by clarifying the nature of our enquiry into the dividend decision.

The fundamental valuation model that we have used tells us that the market value of a company's equity capital is given by the summation of the expected future dividend stream, discounted to present value. In this sense, the *amount* of dividends paid out to shareholders, over time,[1] can clearly be said to affect the market value of a company's shares. However, the question that we shall explore is whether or not the *pattern* of the expected dividend flow is a determinant of equity market value, rather than the *magnitude* of the present value of the sum of the future expected dividend flow.

As far as a company's management is concerned, the dividend decision problem is one of *allocation*. How, at the end of each accounting period (for simplicity we shall assume this to be a 12-month period, although in practice the dividend decision is usually made either semi-annually (twice-yearly), or quarterly), should the company's net after-tax cash flow be allocated amongst the 'competing ends'?

There is a possible three-way split of 'competing ends' to be made: *interest payments* to the suppliers of debt capital, *dividend payments* to shareholders, and *retention* within the company for application to investment opportunities. As it is the capital structure decision that largely determines the level of interest payments, we are left with the question as to how the annual net of tax *and interest* cash flow (we could call it the distributable cash earnings) should be divided up between dividend payments and retention within the company for reinvestment.

REAL WORLD VIEW: Dividends at easyJet and the John Lewis Partnership

The John Lewis Partnership is one of the largest private companies in the UK, incorporating both John Lewis department stores and Waitrose supermarkets. It is also an employee-owned company, with staff known as 'Partners'.

As well as a strong pension scheme, insurance, and a 'long leave' after 25 years at the company, Partners receive an annual bonus as a share of the company's profit. 2013 saw the first bonus over £200 million: a 17% bonus for staff (around £4000 for the average full-time employee).

Outside shareholders in the John Lewis Partnership are not paid dividends, and the employees are allowed a certain amount of say in how profits are invested and allocated.

In contrast, easyJet announced in November 2013 that it was giving dividends of a similar figure to the John Lewis Partnership's (£175 million). This time, however, the dividends were being paid out to shareholders, at 44.1p per share.

Although this looks on the surface like an act of goodwill on easyJet's part, it is worth noting that this donation saved them significant sums of money on corporate taxes. These savings could be calculated at 10p per share.

Dividends as a residual

We can start the analysis of the dividend decision by recalling the basic single-period investment–consumption model which existed in a world of perfect capital markets and no taxation. We shall also assume that there are no sources of capital available to management which are external to the company. Figure 21.1 illustrates the model.

In terms of the dividend decision, the company management must decide at time t_0 what proportion of the company's wealth OA (this could be viewed as being equivalent to the distributable cash earnings referred to above) should be invested within the company and

FIGURE 21.1 The dividend decision

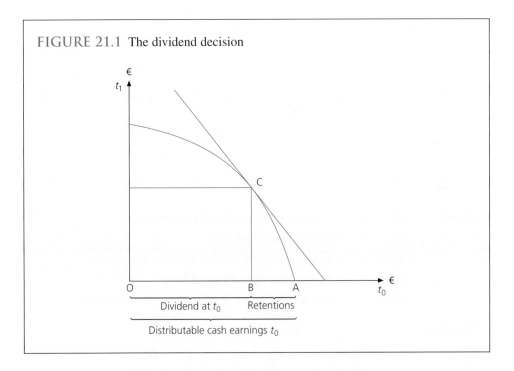

what proportion should be paid out as a dividend. We know that for *optimality* (i.e. for the maximization of shareholder wealth) the company should retain amount AB and distribute amount OB.

Therefore, notice that the decision on the division of amount OA was taken only with reference to the physical investment opportunities available and the perfect capital market rate of interest. The amount OB distributed as dividend to the company owners at time t_0 was purely the cash residual that was left *after* the investment decision had been made.

From this, we can derive a rather obvious dividend decision rule, which states that the distributable cash earnings should be retained within the company for reinvestment, as long as there are investment opportunities available which satisfy the NPV decision rule. Once this supply of investment opportunities has been exhausted (i.e. the company has moved to point C in Figure 21.1) any distributable cash earnings remaining uninvested should be paid out to shareholders as a dividend.

This is the so-called 'dividend irrelevancy hypothesis' which was first explicitly formulated by Modigliani and Miller, but the name of the hypothesis – at this stage – is somewhat misleading: dividends themselves are not irrelevant (as we know from the dividend valuation model), it is the *pattern* of dividends which is irrelevant. They should be treated purely as a residual which arises once the investment decision is made.

In reaching this conclusion, M and M approached the problem of the dividend decision from a different, but equivalent, viewpoint. We shall illustrate this by means of an example, the data for which are illustrated in Table 21.1.

Suppose an all-equity financed company normally pays out its entire net cash flow each year as dividend. The company has previously undertaken investments which will generate an annual perpetuity net cash flow of €1000. The current market value of the company would be given by the present value sum of this future expected dividend flow (V_E).

The management has now discovered a project that they wish to undertake at t_1. The project costs €1000 and, rather than raise an extra €1000 from shareholders (by selling

TABLE 21.1

	t_1	t_2	t_3	t_n
$V_E = \sum\limits_{t=1}^{n} \dfrac{D_t}{(1 + K_E)^t}$ =	+1 000	+1 000	+1 000 ...	+1 000
$NPV = \sum\limits_{t=1}^{2} \dfrac{A_t}{(1 + K_E)^t}$ =	−1 000	+1 500		
$V_E^* = \sum\limits_{t=1}^{n} \dfrac{D_t^*}{(1 + K_E)^t}$ =	0	+2 500	+1 000 ...	+1 000

where: V_E =   current market value of the equity
D_t =   existing dividend flow
V_E^* =   post-investment market value of the equity
D_t^* =   post-investment dividend flow
NPV   =   net present value of the proposed investment

therefore: $V_E^* = V_E + NPV$

or: $$\sum_{t=1}^{n} \frac{D_t^*}{(1 + K_E)^t} = \sum_{t=1}^{n} \frac{D_t}{(1 + K_E)^t} + \sum_{t=1}^{2} \frac{A_t}{(1 + K_E)^t}$$

To undertake the proposed investment: $V_E^* > V_E$ therefore: NPV > 0.

them some new shares), they decide to retain the dividend that was due to be paid at t_1. The project will produce a net cash inflow of €1300 at t_2 and the management propose to pay this out as *additional* dividend at that time.

Thus the *new* market value of the equity (V_E^*) would be given by the present value sum of the *revised* expected future dividend flow. The revised present value of the dividend flow can be seen as consisting of two components: the original present value dividend flow (V_E) plus the present value of the project's cash flow (NPV_p).

The company would only undertake the proposed investment if the revised market value of the equity was greater than (or at least equal to) the existing market value of the equity: $V_E^* > V_E$. To ensure this, the NPV of the project must be greater than or equal to zero. The conclusion that can be drawn from this is that what has enhanced shareholder wealth was the investment decision alone. The decision on dividend policy was irrelevant. The dividend decision was purely a residual of the investment decision.[2]

However it must be remembered that the M and M argument is set in the perfect no-tax world of their initial capital structure hypothesis. As a counter to this view, we now turn to examine the more *traditional* view of dividend policy which holds that the *pattern* of the dividend flow is relevant and *does* affect the market value of the shares.

Dividend patterns and the valuation model

Suppose that a company with an all-equity capital structure has made sufficient investments in the past to generate an annual net cash inflow of Y, in perpetuity. A constant proportion of this cash flow, b, is reinvested each year in projects which yield an average rate of return of r, whilst the remainder of each year's cash flow is paid out as dividends. As a result, Gordon's version of the basic dividend valuation growth model[3] can be applied to estimate the current market value of the company's equity capital:

$$V_E = \frac{Y(1-b)(1+rb)}{K_E - rb}$$

Assuming a given value for Y and for K_E, we can see that the value for V_E produced by the model is dependent on the values given to r and b. It is the effect of different values of b that is of interest, because it is this that reflects the dividend decision: different values of b produce different dividend flow patterns over time.

The effect of the retention proportion on the market value of the equity depends upon the value of r relative to K_E. Where $r > K_E$, then V_E increases as b increases: where $r < K_E$, the reverse relationship holds, and where $r = K_E$, then V_E is unaffected by changes in b.

But notice that what remains unaffected in such a situation is the *wealth* of shareholders. For example, if $Y = €100$ and $K_E = r = 0.20$ then, when $b = 0$, $V_E = €500$ and when $b = 0.1$, $V_E = €510$. Shareholder *wealth* can be seen to be unaffected by changes in b by the fact that when $b = 0$, they received a dividend of €100 and their shares had a market value of €500. Total wealth was therefore €600. When $b = 0.1$, they received a dividend of €90, €10 being reinvested, and their shares had a market value of €510. Total wealth is unchanged at €90 + €510 = €600.

At first sight, therefore, it may well appear that the dividend decision can affect the market value of the equity (because it determines b), but how the dividend decision affects V_E depends upon the relationship of r to K_E. But really, it is not the *dividend decision* that is causing the market value of the equity to change, but the *investment decisions* which follow, i.e. it is the investment of the retained earnings which causes fluctuations in the equity market value.

We are seeing here, once again, confirmation of the NPV investment appraisal rule: increasing b will lead to an enhancement of equity market value *only* if the retained cash flows are being invested in projects yielding positive NPVs when discounted by K_E (i.e. when the project's yield or IRR $> K_E$). Retention of distributable cash flow for investment in projects yielding negative NPVs (i.e. $r < K_E$) serves merely to reduce the current market value of the company's equity capital.

TRADITIONAL VIEW OF THE DIVIDEND DECISION

Notwithstanding the foregoing analysis, the traditional view[4] of the dividend decision is that at any particular point of time €1 of dividends (i.e. distributed cash flow) is somehow *more valuable* than €1 of retained cash flow – even though the cash flow may have been retained for investment in a project yielding a substantial positive NPV. This is sometimes referred to as the 'bird in the hand' argument (and at other times the 'bird in the hand *fallacy*').

Proponents of this traditional view use the dividend growth model to support their argument in the following way. So far in this analysis, in using the dividend growth model, we have held K_E constant as b was varied. The traditionalists argue that this cannot be done, because K_E is partly a function of the value of b, because of the presence of risk. The cost of equity capital, as we have calculated it, is really no more than an average of a whole family of discount rates, each of which is related to a cash flow in a specific period. Therefore a company, by retaining a part of its current period cash flow, is replacing a *certain* cash flow 'now' with an *uncertain* future cash flow (i.e. the future dividends generated by the investment financed by the cash retention). This increased uncertainty will effectively raise the discount rate used against these future flows and so will cause K_E (the average discount rate) also to rise.

Thus, increasing the value of b is likely to lead to an increase in the value of K_E and so equity market values can be said to be affected by dividend policy itself and not simply through the effects of the investment undertaken with the retention, because dividend policy can alter the riskiness of the expected future dividend flow. The optimal dividend-retention policy must be that which trades off the beneficial effects of retention and profitable reinvestment (i.e. an increased value for b on the assumption that $r > K_E$), against the detrimental effects of increased risk, so as to maximize the market value of the equity.

An arbitrage criticism

The arguments of the traditionalists do not really stand up to a close theoretical examination, if the existence of a perfect capital market is assumed. The main counter-argument that can be put forward is that if two companies are identical in every respect except that their dividend–retention ratios differ, and if the stock market values retained earnings differently from dividends, the market prices of the two companies will be in disequilibrium (i.e. two identical goods will be selling at different prices in the same market). This will allow investors to undertake profitable arbitrage transactions, substituting 'home-made' dividends for corporate dividends by selling part of their shareholding.

The following analysis illustrates this substitution in showing the irrelevance of dividend pattern and the opportunities which exist for arbitraging *if* a traditional view of dividend retention persists in the stock market.

We will assume that we have a perfect capital market in which there are no taxes or transaction costs and that the market interest rate of return is 10%. Gebrüder AG is an all-equity company that has made previous investments which are sufficient, in total, to generate an annual cash flow of €1000 in perpetuity. All this cash flow is paid out each year as dividends. Thus the company has a total market value of €1000/0.10 = €10 000. Each of the company's 1000 shares therefore has a market value of €10 and receives an annual dividend of €1.

Suppose Hans Böhmer owns 100 of the company's shares. Thus the market value of his shareholding is €1000, from which he receives an annual dividend of €100.

Gebrüder has just paid the current year's dividend and has informed shareholders that next year's dividend (at time t_1) will be withheld so as to invest in a project that will yield a net cash inflow of €2000 at time t_2. All of the project's cash inflow will be paid out, at that time, as an *additional* dividend.

The project's NPV will be: $-€1000 \times (1 + 0.10)^{-1} + €2000 \times (1 + 0.10)^{-2} = + €743.70$ and the company's revised dividend flow, and hence its revised market value, at t_0 is as follows:

	t_1	t_2	t_3...
Existing cash flow	+1 000	+1 000	+1 000...
Project cash flow	−1 000	+2 000	
Revised dividend flow		+3 000	+1 000...

$$V_E = \sum_{t=0}^{\infty} \frac{D_t}{(1 + 0.10)^t} = €10\,743.70$$

As a result of its intentions, the company's market value has risen by €743.70 which is the NPV of the project. Hans' shareholding will have risen in value by €74.37 to €1074.37.

However, suppose that Hans needs his €100 per year dividend from the company for consumption purposes and is therefore alarmed at the news that there will be no dividend payout next year (t_1). There are two main alternative courses of action which Hans may take to replace the withheld dividend, neither of which will reduce the current level of the investor's wealth of £1074.37. He can either sell part of his shareholding to generate sufficient cash to replace the dividend missed at t_1 (i.e. €100), or he can borrow the €100 at the perfect market rate of interest of 10%.[5] Let us examine the mechanics of this first alternative.

At time t_1, the company's total market value is the sum of the discounted future dividend flow:

	t_1	t_2	t_3	t_4 ...
Dividend flow	0	+3 000	+1 000	+1 000 ...

$$V_{E_n} = \sum_{t=1}^{\infty} \frac{D_t}{(1 + 0.10)^t} = €11\,818.20$$

Therefore each of the company's 1000 shares has an approximate market value of €11.82, and our investor's shareholding is worth approximately €1182 (100 × €11.82). If Hans now sells sufficient shares to produce €100 in cash as a substitute for the forgone dividend, he will sell €100 ÷ €11.82 = 8.46 shares,[6] leaving a shareholding of 91.54 shares in the company.

At time t_2 the company has €3000 to be distributed as dividends so each share receives a dividend of €3 and so Hans will receive a total dividend of: 91.54 × €3 = €274.62. Of this, €100 is required for consumption, leaving a balance of €174.62 available to re-purchase shares in the company and so recover the original shareholding position.

The ex div market value of the company at time t_2 will be €10 000 (the discounted sum of the future dividend flow) and so the individual share price is €10. Hans can now buy back the 8.46 shares previously sold at a cost of €84.60, leaving him with additional cash at time t_2 of €174.62 − €84.60 = €90.02. Thus Hans has effectively used 'home-made' dividends at time t_1 as a substitute for the company dividends which the management decided to retain. In doing so, his wealth position remains unchanged as the present value (i.e. at time t_0) of €90.02 at t_2 is £74.37 – the amount by which Hans Böhme's shareholding increased in value at time t_0 when the company's decision was announced.

A similar analysis could be undertaken where Hans, the investor, borrows €100 at t_1 (at the market interest rate), and repays capital and interest at t_2, using his increased dividend payment at that time. The net outcome will be exactly the same as before.

It should be clear from this example that if stock markets valued retained earnings *less favourably* than dividends, there would be opportunities for profitable arbitrage transactions to take place (with investors either buying shares in companies which are increasing their cash flow retention proportions – as they will be undervalued – or selling shares in companies which are reducing their retention proportions, as they are likely to be overvalued). These arbitrage transactions should rapidly produce 'correct' market valuations.

The possibility of external finance

Up to this point in our consideration of the dividend decision, we have only considered situations in which the only source of investment capital has been retained earnings. If we now widen the analysis to include the opportunity for companies to raise *external* finance for investment, what now becomes of the dividend decision?

When the possibility of external finance was excluded, the decision rule for company managements wishing to maximize shareholder wealth was to apply each year's cash earnings to investment in projects with positive NPVs. If all such projects had been undertaken before all the net cash earnings had been allocated, then the remaining earnings could be paid out as a dividend. Thus the dividend 'policy' was to treat dividends as a *residual* to the investment decision.

Dividends cannot be said to be 'irrelevant' in such circumstances. They are very relevant because, unless they are treated as a residual of the investment decision, they will be preventing 'profitable' investment from being undertaken and so will result in the shareholders' wealth failing to achieve the maximum.

Once the possibility of raising external finance is allowed, dividends no longer need to act as a residual but become *truly* irrelevant. This is because the payment of a dividend can no longer be held to prevent profitable, (i.e. +NPV), investments from being undertaken, because the required finance can always be raised externally.

However, the raising of external finance in such circumstances – be it either debt or equity – is also likely (but not certain) to change a company's gearing ratio, and so the dividend decision can be said to be *truly* irrelevant only if, at the same time, it is accepted that changes in a company's gearing ratio leave its market value unaffected. If not, then dividend policy may well indirectly affect equity market values. As we are assuming a tax-free world of perfect capital markets, we can also assume that the conclusions of the initial M and M capital structure hypothesis will hold and so the dividend policy becomes truly irrelevant.

It is worthwhile noticing that this interdependence of the two M and M hypotheses works in both directions: not only does dividend irrelevancy depend on the capital structure hypothesis, but in turn the capital structure hypothesis holds true only if a company's dividend–retention ratio leaves its market value unaffected. For example, suppose that the greater the proportion of cash earnings paid out as dividends, the higher would be the market value of a company's equity capital. In such circumstances capital structure could not be said to be independent of market values because, other things being equal, the smaller the proportion of retained earnings the higher would be the company's market value, and vice versa.

The introduction of the possibility of external finance also leaves the traditional view largely unaffected. Dividend policy still retains its importance on the basis that current dividends are more highly valued than future dividends generated by retained earnings. But in addition, just as the two M and M hypotheses are in tandem, so too are the traditional views of dividends and capital structure. Therefore a company's dividend policy also gains importance from the fact that it is a partial determinant of the level of retained earnings and so can affect the company's market value through changing the gearing ratio. The exact effects of a company's dividend policy through such influences are not certain, but are dependent on its location on the U-shaped WACC curve.

DIVIDEND POLICY IN AN IMPERFECT MARKET

'Clientele' effect

Once we move away from the assumption of a perfect capital market and a tax-free world, the dividend decision becomes much more problematical. In particular, there are a number of different capital market imperfections which are likely to interfere seriously with the hypothesis of dividend irrelevancy.

The dividend irrelevancy argument has been founded on the perfect capital market approach/separation theorem of our initial single-period investment–consumption analysis. The pattern of cash flows that the company provides the shareholder through the dividend policy is irrelevant, because each individual shareholder can adjust this dividend pattern to fit his or her desired consumption pattern by use of the capital market. It was this characteristic which allowed company managements to avoid the problem of having to identify the indifference curves of individual shareholders, when making investment decisions on their behalf.

However, capital market imperfections such as share sale and purchase transaction costs, differential lending and borrowing interest rates, and the presence of absolute capital rationing for the individual shareholder, all interfere with this process.

Quite simply, these capital market imperfections mean that an individual cannot *costlessly* adjust their dividend pattern to fit their preferred consumption pattern; indeed the cost of doing so may be relatively high.[7] In such circumstances, simple wealth maximization (i.e. in terms of the current market value of the equity) may not be a unique desire of shareholders, as the pattern of wealth receipt also becomes important.

In these circumstances, the company's dividend policy takes on a new dimension. Shareholders may positively prefer companies to supply them with a dividend pattern which matches fairly closely their desired consumption pattern, thereby relieving them of having to adjust this cash flow themselves.

In practice, companies often do this by following a consistent and easily identifiable dividend policy, but whether this is done explicitly for these reasons given above is open to argument. As an example, many companies strongly follow a policy in which dividend reduction is regarded as a sign of weakness and an increased dividend will be declared only if management are convinced that the new dividend level can be at least sustained, if not improved upon, in future years. In this way, shareholders whose own consumption pattern closely follows the dividend pattern of the company will be attracted by the knowledge that they are unlikely to need to resort to the imperfect capital market in order to make dividend/consumption pattern adjustments.

Unfortunately, the fact that an easily identifiable dividend pattern may mean that shareholders avoid the costs of adjustment, does not mean that such advantage is necessarily gained costlessly. Indeed, the cost which is directly saved by the shareholder may be more than offset by the consequential cost to the company (which will, in turn, rebound on to the shareholders).

This consequential cost may come about in that, by paying a dividend, the company is left with insufficient finance to undertake a profitable investment (i.e. one with a positive NPV) and so the investment opportunity is missed. Alternatively, because a dividend has been paid, the company has to raise finance for an investment from an external source which involves the incurrence of issue costs.

It may be thought that the dividend decision in this situation resolves into a straightforward cost minimization trade-off, but a problem arises with the identification and quantification of the costs incurred or avoided by the shareholders and the fact that they are unlikely to be the same for each individual shareholder. So we are reduced to concluding that in an imperfect capital market, probably the best approach that a company can hope to take is to follow a *consistent* dividend policy[8] and hope that the particular policy chosen does not incur too heavy cost penalties, relative to the transaction and opportunity cost savings made by shareholders. Such a policy is often referred to as arising from the 'clientele' effect. By following a consistent dividend policy, the company attracts to it a clientele of shareholders whose consumption pattern accords with the dividend pattern.

Dividends as signals

Another capital market imperfection that bears on the dividend decision concerns the need for information in an uncertain world. Capital markets are imperfect in the sense that information is neither costless nor universally available, and so decisions have often to be made by stock market investors on the basis of imperfect and incomplete information.

In such circumstances, a company's dividend declaration – a free and universally available piece of data – is often thought to signal information about its future performance. In fact, given that information about a company's future performance prospects is fairly sparse – especially to the individual investor – any information that becomes available is seized upon and embodied with a measure of importance which may often be in excess of its real value.

In these terms, the dividend decision once again gains in importance. If the stock market places such an (albeit maybe unjustified) *informational* content on the dividend declaration, then a company will not be acting so as to maximize its shareholders' wealth if it ignores this fact. It is most likely for this reason that many stock exchange quoted companies follow the dividend policy referred to earlier, where a dividend is reduced or passed completely only in the most dire financial circumstances.

This *signalling* effect of the dividend declaration is an important issue for companies. Several studies have shown that an increase or decrease over the *expected* level of dividends does precipitate a rise or fall (respectively) in the market share price. Hence the dividend declaration effect on the share price may be a major (if not *the* major) consideration in the decision. However, there is also evidence that where a company has a good reason for reducing the amount of dividends paid out (e.g. it has identified an exceptional investment opportunity), *and* can adequately transmit information about this to shareholders, it is unlikely to suffer as the result of reducing its dividend payout.

Tax considerations

Taxation and especially differential rates of personal income tax, a taxation distinction between income and capital gains, and the fact that a company might have both private and corporate shareholders, who are taxed under different tax regimes, form a serious capital market imperfection which interferes with the dividend irrelevancy approach. The major problem with the presence of taxation is that it can interfere with the *value equivalence* between dividends and retained earnings. As a result, some shareholders may prefer 'home-made' dividends (generated through selling part of their shareholding) because the rate of capital gains tax may be lower than their marginal income tax rate, which would be imposed upon company-distributed dividends. In contrast, other shareholders may prefer company-distributed dividends because their marginal tax rate results in *less* tax being paid than the combined effect of the capital gains tax and transaction costs incurred in the process of providing home-made dividends.

Once again, in the face of different taxation rates and different taxation regimes, we must conclude by saying that if a company follows a widely recognized, consistent dividend policy, then it can be expected to attract that group of shareholders on whom the particular dividend policy chosen has the most favourable (or least harmful) taxation effects.

In reaching this conclusion, there still remains the problem of what action the company should take in the face of significant changes in the taxation regime, as far as dividends are concerned. Should it try to adjust its dividend policy so as to bring about the most favourable outcome to its existing shareholders, or should it continue with its existing policy in the hope that new shareholders, to whom the company's dividend policy is now favourable in terms of taxation, will be attracted and so replace some of the existing shareholders?

The optimal decision in such circumstances requires an accurate evaluation of the cost trade-off concerned (on the basis that the objective of financial management is to benefit existing shareholders) between the cost to the company of changing its dividend policy[9] and the cost to its shareholders of not changing its policy. Both costs will be difficult to quantify in precise terms, but both may possibly be substantial and so should not be ignored.

THE EMPIRICAL EVIDENCE

Much of the empirical work on dividend policy has been carried out in the USA. Therefore some of these results must be interpreted with care as they will reflect the specifics of the US, 'classical' tax system which can differ from the systems found in other countries. However, the empirical evidence does appear to confirm the view that companies believe that the dividend decision is important and cannot be treated simply as a by-product of investment and financing decisions. For example Lintner (1956) in a survey of companies found that many did try to pay out an approximately constant proportion of earnings each year. At the same time there was a reluctance to match dividend growth with earnings growth and as a result dividend growth lagged behind earnings growth. These results were confirmed in a later study by Fama and Babiak (1968) which estimated that dividend growth lagged 2 to 3 years behind earnings growth.

This evidence does seem to support the signalling effect of dividends. Management appear to go to some lengths to ensure that dividends are only increased when they are confident that they will be able to maintain at least that new level of dividends in the future (Bray *et al.*, 2005). The fear is that, if they were forced to reduce dividends after an over-optimistic increase in the previous year, the market would read into the dividend decision unfavourable information.

If dividends are really seen by investors as a means of sending signals then we would expect share prices to react to unexpected changes in dividend policy. Pettit's 1972 study found exactly this reaction and these results were confirmed by later studies, such as Mougoué and Rao (2003) and Baker *et al.* (2002).

As far as clienteles are concerned, there is a great deal of evidence to support their existence. The original empirical evidence is that of Elton and Gruber (1970). They were particularly concerned about tax clienteles and the fact that some investors would strongly prefer to receive their returns in the form of capital gains rather than dividends, whilst other investors would prefer the reverse. Their evidence suggests that tax clienteles do exist: that shareholders in high dividend-paying companies have lower tax rates than shareholders in low dividend-paying companies.

Miller and Scholes (1978) cast doubt on Elton and Gruber's evidence. They essentially use an arbitrage argument based on earlier work by Brennan (1970). If tax clienteles do really exist, as evidenced by Elton and Gruber's results, this *should* present arbitrage opportunities: low-rate taxpayers should be able to profit from the higher-rate taxpayers' preference for capital gains and vice versa.

However, Elton and Gruber's original findings have been subsequently supported by many more recent studies including Becker *et al.* (2011) who found clear evidence that older investors preferred dividend paying shares and Dhanani (2005), who found from a survey of UK managers that signalling and dividend clienteles were important considerations in the dividend decision.

CONCLUSION

In truth, we really do not know whether dividend policy can affect shareholders' wealth. Whilst the bulk of the empirical evidence tends to suggest that either dividend policy *is* important, or is *thought to be* important much of the research needs to be treated with some caution.

However difficult it might be to carry out meaningful research in this area, it does seem that the dividend decision should be taken with care, given the imperfections of the real-world capital market. The benefit or otherwise of a particular dividend decision depends to a great extent upon how the individual shareholders are personally affected by the various market imperfections. It is likely, given a random selection of stock market investors, that the market imperfections with respect to dividends will affect individual shareholders in a number of conflicting ways, thus making a consensus dividend policy an unlikely possibility. The only escape from this dilemma for a company that intends to maximize the wealth of its shareholders is to follow a consistent dividend policy, which then allows the individual shareholder to judge its desirability in relation to his or her own personal circumstances.

SUMMARY

This chapter has looked at the dividend decision. However, it is difficult to reach any firm conclusions.

- In a perfect capital market world of no taxes, the dividend decision can be seen to be irrelevant. A shareholder receives his annual return in two elements: the dividend and the capital gain. The decision about what proportion of a firm's net distributable cash flow to retain and what proportion to pay out as dividends is therefore simply a decision as to how the overall return on the shares should be packaged. How large should be the capital gain package and how large should be the dividend package? However, the overall return itself is left unaffected by the decision.

- When capital market imperfections such as taxes, transaction costs and imperfect information are introduced, then it is possible for the dividend decision to begin to take on importance.

- Where dividends and capital gains are treated differently from the viewpoint of personal taxes and capital gains cannot be costlessly converted into income (nor dividends reinvested) without incurring transaction costs, it can be argued that companies should follow a stable and consistent dividend policy so as to attract to themselves a clientele of investors whose own personal tax position, and need (or otherwise) for income, suits that particular dividend policy.

- In addition to the clientele effect, the dividend decision may also be held to have an information content which it signals to the market. If this is so, then dividend policy is important in that management should ensure that their company's dividend decision does not give the wrong signal to the market.

- Although the empirical evidence is mixed and although some findings have been disputed, it does appear that the evidence points to the dividend decision being important both from a clientele and a signalling effect viewpoint.

NOTES

1. Including any cash on winding up or sale.
2. The reader may find it worthwhile to reflect how the M and M dividend irrelevancy hypothesis is also just a natural continuation of their capital structure hypothesis.
3. The model's numerator is slightly more fully defined than when it was first introduced in Chapter 16.
4. So-called because it is one which is widely held amongst both stock market investors and analysts.
5. A third possible alternative is a combination of the two courses of action.
6. For simplicity, we are assuming here that shares are divisible. The fact that this is not true in practice can be viewed as a slight market imperfection.
7. In the case of absolute capital rationing for the individual, the cost of some consumption patterns can be seen as infinitely high.
8. It is important to notice that it is not constant dividends that are being advocated, but a constant policy. This policy may be to treat dividends as a residual of the investment decision, and hence may result in a highly erratic dividend flow, but a constant policy.
9. A cost that will ultimately be felt by the shareholders.

FURTHER READING

1. The basic reading on dividend policy must be: M.H. Miller and F. Modigliani, 'Dividend Policy, Growth and the Valuation of Shares', *Journal of Business*, October 1961; and F. Black, 'The Dividend Puzzle', *Journal of Portfolio Management*, Winter 1976. For general empirical evidence on dividend policy, see J. Lintner, 'Distribution of Incomes of Corporations among Dividends, Retained Earnings and Taxes', *American Economic Review*, May 1956, and E.F. Fama and H. Babiak, 'Dividend Policy: An Empirical Analysis', *Journal of the American Statistical Association*, December 1968.

2. Good reviews of the literature can be found in F. Allen and R. Michaely, 'Payout Policy', in G. Constantinides, M. Harris and R. Stulz (eds), *Handbook of the Economics of Finance: Corporate Finance*, North-Holland 2003 and in H. DeAngelo, L. DeAngelo and D. Skinner, 'Corporate Payout Policy', *Foundations and Trends in Finance*, 3, 2008.

3. In addition, an interesting test of dividend irrelevancy is: G. Richardson, S.E. Sefcik and R. Thompson, 'A Test of Dividend Irrelevancy Using Volume Reactions to a Change in Dividend Policy', *Journal of Financial Economics*, December 1986.

4. For evidence on the information content of dividends, see: T.W. Foster and D. Vickrey, 'The Information Content of Stock Dividend Announcements', *Accounting Review*, April 1978; R.R. Pettit, 'Dividend Announcements, Security Performance and Capital Market Efficiency', *Journal of Finance*,

December 1972; J. Aharony and I. Swary, 'Quarterly Dividends and Earnings Announcements and Stockholders Returns', *Journal of Finance*, March 1980; P. Asquith and D.W. Mullins, 'The Impact of Initiating Dividend Payments on Shareholder Wealth', *Journal of Business*, January 1983; J.R. Woolridge and C. Ghosh, 'Dividend Cuts: Do They Always Signal Bad News?', *Midland Corporate Finance Journal*, Summer 1985; and A.R. Ofer and D.R. Siegal, 'Corporate Financial Policy, Information and Market Expectations: An Empirical Investigation of Dividends', *Journal of Finance*, September 1987. Finally, in relation to investor rationality, see C. Ghosh and J. Woolridge, 'Stock Market Reaction to Growth-Induced Dividend Cuts: Are Investors Myopic?', *Management and Decision Economics*, March 1989. H. Baker, G. Powell and E. Veit, 'Revisiting Managerial Perspectives on Dividend Policy', *Journal of Economics and Finance*, 2002: 26: 267–283.

5. On dividend policy, taxes and the clientele effect see: E.J. Elton and M.J. Gruber, 'Marginal Stockholders Tax Rates and the Clientele Effect', *Review of Economics and Statistics*, February 1970; M. Miller and M. Scholes, 'Dividends and Taxes: Some Empirical Evidence', *Journal of Financial Economics*, December 1978; R.H. Litzenberger and K. Ramaswamy, 'The Effect on Dividends on Common Stock Prices: Tax Effects or Information Effects?', *Journal of Finance*, May 1982; and J.R. Woolridge, 'Dividend Changes and Security Prices', *Journal of Finance*, December 1983; J. Graham and A. Kumar 'Do Dividend Clienteles Exist? Evidence on Dividend Preferences of Retail Investors', *Journal of Finance,* June 2006. W. Moser and A. Puckett, 'Dividend Tax Clienteles: Evidence from Tax Law Changes', *Journal of the American Taxation Association*, Spring 2009 provide evidence of an institutional investor clientele effect.

6. Two further, interesting articles are: H.K. Barker, G.E. Farrelly and R.B. Edelman, 'A Survey of Management Views on Dividend Policy', *Financial Management*, Autumn 1985; M.H. Miller, 'Behaviour Rationality in Finance: The Case of Dividends', *Journal of Business*, October 1986.

7. Finally, bringing the research into dividend policy up to date, see A. Kalay and M. Lemmon, 'Payout Policy', in B.E. Eckbo (ed.), *Handbook of Empirical Corporate Finance*, Elsevier 2007; B. Becker, Z. Ivkovic and S. Weisbeener, 'Local Dividend Clienteles', *Journal of Finance*, 66, 2011; L. Shao, C.C. Kwok and O. Guedhami, 'National Culture and Dividend Policy', *Journal of International Business Studies*, 41, 2010; and A. Wood, 'Death of the Dividend?', in J. Rutterford, M. Upton and D. Kodwani (eds), *Financial Strategy*, Wiley. 2006.

QUIZ QUESTIONS

1   Why might the dividend decision be said to be irrelevant?
2   What is the argument about dividends being a residual to investment decision?
3   What is the link between dividend irrelevancy and capital structure irrelevancy?
4   What is the bird-in-the-hand argument?
5   Which investors prefer capital gains to dividends?
6   If a clientele effect exists, what does it imply for dividend policy?
7   What empirical evidence is there to support the signalling effect of dividends?
8   In the real world, would it be wise for a company to retain a dividend which shareholders were expecting, in order to invest in a positive NPV project?
    (See the 'Answers to Quiz Questions' section at the back of the book.)

PROBLEMS

The answers to two of the following problems (those indicated by an asterisk) are available to students online. The answer to the remaining problem is available only to lecturers (see the 'Digital Resources' page for details).

1* Pulini SpA is an all-equity industrial services company quoted on the Milan stock exchange. It has issued one million shares. The dividends paid by Pulini have remained constant at €150 000 per annum and the market generally believes that dividends will continue at this level indefinitely, given the information presently available. The current dividend of Pulini is about to be declared and the current market price per share is €1.40.

The company has recently signed a contract to service factory equipment for an annual fee of €80 000, payable at the start of each year. The first annual fee has just been received. The contract, which is to commence immediately, will need the annual purchase of specialized materials costing €22 400 payable at the end of each year, and will incur no other incremental costs. The contract will continue indefinitely and will have the same risk as the existing operations of Pulini. No details of the contract have been communicated or leaked to the stock market.

Required:

(a) Estimate the cum div market value of Pulini SpA in each of the three following situations:

   (i)   The details of the contract are not communicated to the stock market, and the dividends paid out continue to be €150 000.

   (ii) The details of the contract are communicated and believed by the stock market, but the dividends paid out remain at €150 000.

   (iii) The details of the contract are *not* communicated to the stock market, but all the additional cash flow from the new contract is paid out as additional dividends.

(b) Discuss whether a company can affect its market price by altering its dividend policy.

(c) Outline the factors that might influence company management when deciding on the level of dividends to be declared.

   Ignore taxation in part (a), but not in parts (b) and (c).

2   During the world economic downturn in 2009–2012, Saint-Vinci Leasing SA ran into severe financial difficulties due to mistakes its management had made in the commercial aircraft leasing business in which it operated. Between 2009 and 2013 it made large operating losses and had to stop paying dividends. However, late in 2014 a new management team was installed in the company – at the instigation of the institutional shareholders and non-executive directors. This new management rapidly turned the company around by restructuring its business and focusing on the international leasing of private jets and the company is once again profitable.

As a result, at the board meeting held recently at the end of the company's financial year – which had seen a further increase in profits – the directors discussed whether or not the company should resume paying dividends. However opinions were divided. The chairman thought that a stable dividend policy should be introduced as quickly as possible. The CFO thought that dividend policy was unimportant as he remembered quite clearly from his MBA finance course that dividends are irrelevant. Finally, the treasurer was of the opinion that the company should only pay an annual dividend if there were not sufficient profitable projects available to absorb all the company's earnings. Thus the amount paid out in dividends should purely be this residual.

Required:
Discuss dividend policy with special reference to the comments made by the board members of Saint-Vinci Leasing SA.

3* Joseph and Auguste Pavin each own 50% of the issued ordinary share capital of Hevas International, a small property development company, but neither plays any part in its management. The company presently has €300 000 available in its bank account which it is proposing to invest in a construction project which is expected to produce cash inflows of €80 000 in Year 1, €100 000 in Year 2, and €170 000 after 3 years. No other cash flows are expected to be associated with the project. If the €300 000 is not used on this project it will be paid out as a dividend to Joseph and Auguste. If the project is accepted the cash inflows it produces will be paid out in full as dividends as they arise.

Auguste is in agreement with the company investing in the proposed project, but Joseph wants to be able to buy a new Ferrari supercar and claims that the company is not acting in his best interests if it fails to pay the money as dividend to enable him to do so. Hevas International is able both to lend and borrow money at 4% interest.

▶

Required:

(a)   Calculate the NPV of the proposed construction project.

(b)   Explain whether the company is acting in the best interests of *both* its shareholders by accepting the project if:

    (i)   Joseph and Auguste may both borrow money at 4% interest.

    (ii)   Joseph and Auguste can only borrow money at 10% interest.

(c)   Comment briefly on the implications of your answers to (a) and (b) above for corporate financial decision theory.

Ignore taxation.

INTERNATIONAL ISSUES

FOREIGN EXCHANGE

LEARNING OBJECTIVES

The purpose of this chapter is to:

- Examine the nature of foreign exchange rates.
- Discuss the 'spot' and 'forward' foreign exchange markets.
- Review the basic types of exchange rate systems.
- Examine the determinants of exchange rates.

INTRODUCTION

In the three final chapters of this book, we turn to look at some aspects of international financial management. In this chapter we examine the background to international financial management in terms of foreign exchange markets and the causes of movements in foreign exchange rates.

Then, in Chapter 23, we look at how importers and exporters may hedge their exposure to the risk of adverse movements in exchange rates. In that discussion, we will see a number of risk management techniques that parallel the techniques examined on interest rate risk management.

Finally, in Chapter 24, we look at an area of considerable importance and complexity: the overseas capital investment decision. This topic helps to bring together much of what has been discussed through the earlier part of the book.

In the current chapter we examine in detail the basics of foreign exchange. We will find that, although it does not contain anything that is difficult, there is a certain degree of complexity. A study of foreign exchange rewards a reader's attention to detail. It is these details that we address in this chapter.

EXCHANGE RATES

Currency exchange rates are important in corporate finance because of international trade. A German company may have exported goods to a UK company and received payment in British pounds. That German exporter will therefore need to exchange the pounds into their own currency – into euros – by *selling* the pounds and *buying* euros in exchange. Similarly, a South African company may have imported goods from a US company and find that they are required to make payment in US$. Therefore the South African importer will have to *buy* US$ – to pay off their invoice – in exchange for *selling* South African rand.

A crucial factor in both transactions is the *rate* of exchange. The German company will want to know how many euros they will receive from the receipt of the pounds from their export sale. The South African company will want to know what is the cost – in South African rand – of their imported goods.

Our look at foreign exchange will not only cover what determines exchange rates between different currencies, but also how companies deal with the fact that exchange rates (in most circumstances) are not *constant*, but tend to move in an unpredictable manner. This is the issue of foreign exchange risk – the risk of an adverse movement in exchange rates. Thus with foreign exchange we have yet another area of corporate risk management.

Direct and indirect quotes

The starting point for our analysis is to consider how exchange rates are actually given – how they are *quoted* – in the foreign exchange markets (i.e. the markets where currencies are bought and sold). Exchange rates are simply the price of one currency in terms of another currency. Therefore if we take, as an example, the exchange rate between the euro and the British pound, this could *either* be expressed as the price of one pound, in terms of euros – say £1 = €1.25 – *or* it can be expressed as the price of one euro, in terms of pounds – €1 = £0.80. In other words, pounds cost €1.25 and euros cost £0.80 or 80 pence.

When dealing with exchange rates, companies refer to their own currency as the 'domestic' or 'home' currency and other currencies as 'foreign' currencies. Given this terminology, exchange rates can be given/quoted as either a 'direct' quote or an 'indirect' quote.

Direct quote: This gives the *number of units* of the *home* currency that are exchanged for every *single unit* of the *foreign* currency.

Indirect quote: This gives the number of units of the *foreign* currency that are exchanged for every single unit of the *home* currency.

Different countries quote exchange rates in different ways, some use a direct quote format, and others use an indirect quote format. Countries within the eurozone tend to use the **direct quote** format and so that is the format we will use when discussing foreign exchange and the management of foreign exchange risk. However, this is obviously a potential source of confusion and misunderstanding and so, as a general warning, whenever unfamiliar exchange rates are involved, care must be taken to identify the particular quote format that is being used. There is a lot of difference when quoting the exchange rate between euros and pounds as 0.80 or as 1.25.

So to be clear, in this book we will always give exchange rates in the direct quote format, giving the number of units of the home currency that can be exchanged for a single unit of the foreign currency.

Furthermore, when quoting these exchange rates, we will use the (internationally recognized) currency *code* rather than the currency *symbol*. Therefore, in reference to the British pound, we will not use the currency *symbol* – £ – but the currency *code* – GBP. Similarly with the South African rand, we won't use the currency symbol – R – but the code – ZAR.

Finally, when looking at a pair of currencies, for example the exchange rate between the South African rand and the US dollar – ZAR/USD – the *first* currency will be the *home* currency (here it is the South African rand), and the *second* currency will be the *foreign* currency (here it is the US dollar); and it will be given as a *direct* quote. For example: **ZAR/USD 10.68** will mean that the exchange rate is R10.68 = $1, where the rand is the home currency and the US dollar is the foreign currency. Similarly ZAR/EUR 14.72 means R14.72 = €1.

The final point to note is that in the examples above, the exchange rate was given to two decimal places. In practice, the number of decimal places used is largely dependent upon the size of the number before the decimal point. The smaller the number before the decimal point, the greater the number of decimal places are required for accuracy. For example SAR/JPY 0.037 means 0.037 Saudi riyals = 1 Japanese yen. On the other hand JPY/SAR 27.13 means 27.13 yen = 1 riyal.

Buying and selling rates

If the exchange rate between the British pound and the euro is given as EUR/GBP 1.2550, this means that €1.2550 = £1. In other words, €1 and 25½ cents = £1; where the ½ cent is known in foreign exchange markets as 50 'basis points' (or 'pips'). Just as *cents* represent one-hundredth of a euro; so *basis points* represent one-hundredth of a cent. So while ½ cent would be referred to as 50 basis points; ¼ cent would be referred to as 25 basis points.

Finally, the EUR/GBR exchange rate would be referred to as: 'one-twenty-five-fifty'. That is one euro, twenty five cents and fifty basis points equals one pound.

When a single exchange rate is quoted, such as: EUR/USD 0.7325, this is known as a 'middle rate'. However, in practice, a *pair* of exchange rates is normally quoted, such as EUR/USD 0.7300 – 0.7350 where the first rate is the rate that you can *sell* the foreign currency and the second is the rate you can *buy* the foreign currency. Thus if you want to buy $1000 the cost would be: $1000 × 0.7350 = €735. On the other hand, if you wanted to sell $1000, the receipt would only be: $1000 × 0.7300 = €730. (If only a single, *middle* rate is provided, then it is usually assumed, for simplicity, that the foreign currency can be both bought *and* sold at that rate.)

FOREIGN EXCHANGE MARKETS

We can identify two FX markets, both of which are run by the international banks. These are the 'spot' FX market and the 'forward' FX market. The spot market is where companies can buy and sell currencies for immediate (i.e. on the spot) exchange or delivery. (In practice, exchange of currencies takes place 2 days later.) The forward market is where companies can arrange a *deal now* to buy or sell a *specific* amount of currency at a *specific* rate of exchange (the forward rate) for exchange/delivery on a *specific future date* (the forward date).

Foreign exchange markets are like any other market, in that they exist only if there is sufficient demand. Therefore although spot markets exist for most of the world's more important currencies, for many of the more minor (called 'exotic'), currencies there is no forward market, because there is insufficient demand.

Where a forward market exists, just how far forward in time can be dealt again depends upon the level of demand. The four most heavily traded currencies in the world are the US dollar, the euro, the British pound and the Japanese yen, and the forward market amongst these currencies can stretch up to 10 years forward. More usually, most forward market rates extend up to about 12 months into the future; but some only extend 3 months forward, or less.

The point about the 'depth' of the forward market is made because sometimes a company might be faced with an FX problem where the obvious solution is to use the forward market. However, the forward market in the required currency may not exist or, even if it did, it may not extend far enough forward in time for the company's purposes.

Nevertheless, given the depth of any particular forward market, a currency exchange deal can be arranged for *any* time period forward, up to its maximum depth. Therefore suppose it is 1 July and a French company wants to buy US$10 million for delivery on 23 September – that is in 84 days' time – then they can arrange a deal to buy €10 million, precisely 84 days forward.

This means that, unlike the spot market where there is a *single* pair of exchange rates (the buying and selling rates) at which you can deal for immediate delivery of currencies, on the forward market there are a whole *range* of pairs of exchange rates – one pair for each possible future date. Therefore, in the above example involving the purchase of US$10 million, the company would be quoted the 84 days EUR/USD forward rate.

'Standard' periods of time for forward exchange rates are 1 month, 3 months and 12 months and these rates – together with the spot rate – are normally instantly available. Other forward rates, such as an 84-day forward rate, have to be specifically quoted by the banks.

Discounts and premiums

In practice, spot and forward rates may be given as follows:

EUR/USD spot	0.7300 – 0.7350
1 month forward	0.7320 – 0.7375
3 months forward	0.7355 – 0.7445

However, it is more likely that instead of the forward rates being expressed like this, they are given as a rate of 'premium' on the spot rate:

EUR/USD spot	0.7300 – 0.7350
1 month forward	0.20c – 0.25c premium
3 months forward	0.55c – 0.95c premium

To obtain the actual forward rate, the premium is *added* to the spot rate. Notice that these rates of premium are always very small amounts of money. For example 0.20c is not 20 cents, but is just 20 basis points. Therefore:

EUR/USD spot	0.7300 – 0.7350
+ premium	0.0020 – 0.0025
1 month forward	0.7320 – 0.7375

EUR/USD spot	0.7300 – 0.7350
+ premium	0.0055 – 0.0095
3 months forward	0.7355 – 0.7445

Also, notice that when forward rates are *larger* numbers than spot rates (e.g. EUR/USD spot 0.7300 – 0.7350 < 3 months forward 0.7355 – 0.7445), the forward rates are at a *premium* to the spot rate. To see what this means, look at the situation in the example above. If a company wanted to buy US dollars at spot, every $1 would cost 73.50 cents, but if the company bought dollars 3 months forward, each $1 would be more expensive, costing 74.45 cents. Therefore, in the forward markets, the dollar is becoming more expensive to buy. Putting this more technically, the markets expect the dollar to strengthen or *appreciate* against the euro. (And the euro is therefore depreciating, or becoming less valuable against the dollar.) More generally, if forward rates are at a premium, the foreign currency is appreciating against the home currency.

The opposite of rates of premium are discounts. When forward rates are quoted at a discount, we subtract the discount from the spot rate to find the forward rate. Therefore, whenever forward rates are *smaller* numbers than spot rates, the forward rates are at a discount and this signifies that the foreign currency is *depreciating* against the home currency. As an example of this we will use the exchange rate between the South African rand (the home currency) and the Australian dollar (the foreign currency):

ZAR/AUD spot	9.56 – 9.60
1 month forward	0.10c – 0.12c discount
3 months forward	0.23c – 0.28c

and so:

ZAR/AUD spot	9.56 – 9.60
– discount	0.10 – 0.08
1 month forward	9.46 – 9.52

ZAR/AUD spot	9.56 – 9.60
– discount	0.23 – 0.18
3 months forward	9.33 – 9.42

Here the Australian dollar/the foreign currency is depreciating against the rand – it is becoming less valuable, or cheaper. Buying Australian dollars at spot costs R9.60 per A$. However, buying 3 months forward only costs R9.42 per A$.

Rates of depreciation and appreciation

Suppose we have a situation where the EUR/USD rate for buying US$ at spot is 0.7350 and the 12-month forward rate is 5.25c premium. We know that the actual forward rate can be found by adding the premium to the spot rate:

EUR/USD spot	0.7350
+ premium	0.0325
12 months forward	0.7675

As we know, because the forward rate is at a premium, this indicates that the foreign currency is *appreciating*, and this can be seen when the actual forward rate is calculated – the US dollar is *more expensive* to buy 12 months forward (€0.7675 = $1), than it costs at spot (€0.7350 = $1). This rate of appreciation in the dollar can be expressed in percentage terms, as follows:

$$\frac{0.0325}{0.7350} = 0.0442 \text{ or a 4.42\% rate of appreciation}$$

As a result, there is an alternative way in which the forward rate can be calculated:

$$\text{spot rate} \times (1 + \text{rate of appreciation}) = \text{the forward rate}$$

and so:

$$\text{EUR/USD spot } 0.7350 \times (1 + 0.0442) = 0.7675 \text{ 12 months forward}$$

Similarly, if the EUR/USD forward rate was at a discount, then expressing the discount as a percentage of the spot rate would represent the percentage rate of depreciation in the dollar. In these circumstances:

$$\text{spot rate} \times (1 - \text{rate of depreciation}) = \text{forward rate}$$

Example 1 illustrates some possible applications of these observations.

EXAMPLE 1

Suppose we have the following information:

EUR/USD spot: 0.7325
12 months forward: *2 cent* premium

Then: €0.02 ÷ €0.7325 = 0.027 or 2.7%. Therefore the forward rate represents a 2.7% appreciation in the US dollar, giving:

$$\text{Spot: } €0.7325 \times (1 + 0.027) = €0.7525 \text{ 12 months forward}$$

Using this approach, forward rates can then be calculated on the basis of expected annual rates of appreciation or depreciation. For example, suppose that the current EUR/GBP spot rate is €1.2550 and the pound is expected to depreciate by 3% per year over the next 2 years and then appreciate by 2% per year for the following 3 years. The EUR/GBP forward rates for the next 5 years can then be calculated as follows:

Current spot:	€1.2550 × (1 − 0.03) = 1.2134	1 year forward.
	€1.2134 × (1 − 0.03) = 1.1808	2 years forward
	€1.1808 × (1 + 0.02) = 1.2044	3 years forward
	€1.2044 × (1 + 0.02) = 1.2285	4 years forward
	€1.2285 × (1 + 0.02) = 1.2531	5 years forward

Exchange/delivery of currencies

With forward market deals, no money is exchanged at the time of the transaction, but only at the future agreed date of exchange. Therefore if a forward market deal is agreed now to buy USD1 million 3 months forward at EUR/USD 0.7420, then, in 3-months' time you must give the bank: $1 million $\times$ 0.7420 = €742,000, and, in exchange, they will give you $1 million.

We can distinguish between two types of FX forward contract: *fixed* forward contracts (normally simply referred to as forward contracts), and *time option* forward contracts (normally known as 'option' forward contracts). The former are by far the most common; the latter are used only infrequently.

With a EUR/USD fixed forward contract, exchange of currencies must take place on the agreed future date. Thus if you sell US$10 million 3 months forward, in 3-months' time (*to the very day*) you must hand over $10 million to the bank and they will give you the euro amount as specified at the agreed rate of exchange. In contrast, an option forward contract allows you – the financial manager (and not the bank) – to exchange dollars for euros *at any time* between two specified future dates. Therefore, if you sold US$10 million, 3 to 5 months forward, you could exchange dollars for euros at any time you wanted during that period. (You could not exchange *before* 3 months or *after* 5 months, but could exchange at any time between the two dates.)

When might a financial manager use such contracts? Suppose a Belgian company exporting to the USA and it invoices its US customer for US$500 000 on 3-months' credit. If the exporter could rely on the US customer paying precisely on time in 3 months, then they could arrange a deal now with the bank to sell US$500 000 3 months forward.

However, suppose the exporter could not rely on its customer paying the invoice on time, and past experience with the customer indicated that they could be up to 4 weeks late in payment. In such circumstances they could use a (time) option forward contract to arrange a deal with the bank to sell US$500 000 3 to 4 months forward. In this way, whenever the customer does actually pay up within 3 to 4-months' time, the exporter can activate its deal with the bank to sell the US$500 000 at the agreed rate of exchange.

The problem with option forward contracts is that the company gets a poor deal as far as the forward exchange rate is concerned. Taking the previous example, if the company was to tell the bank that it wanted to sell US$500 000 3 to 4 months forward, the bank would look at the 3-months' and the 4-months' forward rates and would only agree to the deal at whichever was the *worst* rate of exchange from the company's point of view.

> Suppose: EUR/USD spot: 0.7320 – 0.7330
> 3 months forward: 0.7360 – 0.7375
> 4 months forward: 0.7380 – 0.7400

Between the two forward selling US$ rates of 0.7360 and 0.7380 the company would prefer to deal at 0.7380, but the bank will only agree to the deal at 0.7360. (At 0.7380 the company would receive: $500 000 $\times$ 0.7380 = €369 000. At 0.7360, the company will only receive: $500 000 $\times$ 0.7360 = €368 000.) Therefore, whenever the US$500 000 is exchanged between 3- and 4-months' time, the deal would be done at 0.7380 and the company would only receive €368 000 in exchange for US$500 000.

It is for this reason that option forward contracts are unusual in practice – they are seen as being rather 'unprofessional' in the FX markets because they result in an unfavourable rate of exchange. Consequently, exporters go to great trouble to ensure that their export customers do pay up on time.

Using the same example, what would happen if the exporter arranged to sell the US$500 000 through a fixed forward contract, 3 months forward, and then shortly before payment is due, they hear that payment will be delayed for a further month? In such circumstances the company can arrange to have the US$500 000 sale contract 'rolled forward' for a further month. However, such a situation is undesirable because it could turn out to be expensive. Example 2 makes this clear.

EXAMPLE 2

Metallo NV is a Belgium company. It has exported goods to a US company and is due to receive US$500 000 on 1 March and arranges a forward contract sale at a EUR/USD exchange rate of €0.7360. (Therefore the company is expecting to receive US$500 000 × 0.7360 = €368 000.) Metallo learns on 1 March that payment will be delayed by 1 month until 1 April. The spot EUR/USD rate on 1 March is €0.7410 – 0.7420 and the 1-month forward EUR/US$ rate is €0.7390 – 0.7405.

The bank will roll Metallo's foreign exchange deal forward until 1 April, but will charge an amount effectively equal to the cost of *purchasing* US$500 000 to be able to meet the company's sale obligation on 1 March and undertaking a 1-month forward sale of US$500 000 to the new date of 1 April:

1. Purchase of spot US$ on 1 March	:	US$500 000 × 0.7420	=	(€371 000) cost
2. Original 3-month forward sale of US$	:	US$500 000 × 0.7360	=	€368 000 receipt
3. New 1-month forward sale of US$	:	US$500 000 × 0.7390	=	€369 500 receipt
New revised receipt	:			€366 500
Original planned forward sale receipt	:			€368 000
Fee charged by the bank to 'roll forward' 1 month	:			€1500 cost

Therefore the 1-month delay in the receipt of the US$500 000 will cost the exporter €1500, plus the time value of money (1 month's lost interest on the invoice's proceeds).

EXCHANGE RATE SYSTEMS

We now need to look a little more closely at foreign exchange markets. To do so, we will first look at some history.

In 1944 there was an historic meeting in the USA, at a place called Bretton Woods, where the world's leading trading countries agreed on a system of *fixed* exchange rates. Each country's currency was set at a fixed rate of exchange against the US dollar. The reason for this agreement was that it was generally recognized that the Second World War was coming to an end and that moves would have to be made to resume international trade and so expand the world's economy. In order to help this process governments wanted to make it just as easy for, say, a UK company to sell to a customer in New York as it was for it to sell to a customer in London. With fixed exchange rates (for example the USD/GBP rate was fixed at US$4 = £1), this process can help in that if a UK company sells some goods to a London customer for £250 000, those same goods can just as easily be sold to a New York customer for US$1 million. UK exporters invoicing their US customer for US$1 million would know precisely what they would receive, in terms of pounds, because the exchange rate was fixed.

However, although a system of fixed exchange rates is good for importers and exporters and for the promotion of international trade, such a system is inherently *unstable*, as it tries to deny the power and influence of supply and demand that the currency market forces. The result is that every so often these market forces became overpowering and the fixed exchange rate has to be reset at a new level. (Currencies are said to be *devalued* or *revalued* at such times.)

This system of fixed exchange rates lasted a surprisingly long time (up until 1971–72). It was able to do so because the centrepiece was the US dollar (which was backed/ guaranteed by gold), and during this time the US economy was so strong and so dominated the world economy that the supply and demand currency market forces were generally kept in check.

The Bretton Woods system fell apart in the early 1970s under two influences. One was the cost of the Vietnam War, which began to seriously damage the strength of the US economy in the late 1960s. The other, in the early 1970s, was the first of several oil price 'shocks', in which the oil-producing countries sharply increased the price of oil through the OPEC cartel. As a result, since around 1971–72, the great majority of world trade has carried on with a system of 'floating' exchange rates, where exchange rates have been allowed to move in response to supply and demand currency market forces.

Clean and dirty floats

In such a system we find two types of foreign exchange regime. One is called a 'clean' float and the other a 'dirty' or 'managed' float. Where a currency is allowed to float clean, the government of the country concerned is indicating that they are willing to allow the exchange rate to go in whatever direction market forces push it. Thus, in the early 1980s, the British government stated that sterling was in a clean float and so if there were a demand to buy sterling it would be allowed to appreciate; if there were selling pressure, then it would be allowed to depreciate.

Few governments are willing to leave their currencies completely at the mercy of market forces in this way; more commonly, governments try to operate a dirty or managed float. This means that most governments have a policy (which may or may not be made public), on the range of movement within which they are willing to allow their currency to float. If the currency appreciates significantly beyond this range, then the country's central bank starts selling the currency on the foreign exchange markets to counter the buying pressure and, hopefully, to force the exchange rate back to a politically more acceptable level. Similarly, if market forces depreciate the exchange rate below an acceptable level, the central bank begins buying the currency to push the exchange rate back up to a more acceptable level. Thus, the government attempts to 'manage' its currency's exchange rate.

The problem with a floating exchange rate is that it causes difficulties for international trade because it exposes companies to *foreign exchange risk* – that is the risk of an *adverse* movement in exchange rates and *uncertainty* as to what will be the cost or receipt, in their own currency, of an import or export deal. For example, say the exchange rate between the South African rand and the euro is currently ZAR/EUR: 14.57 (i.e. €1 = R14.57), and a South African company exports goods to France, invoicing their French customer for €1 million on 3-months' credit. The export company is *expecting* to receive the equivalent of R14.57 million, but is uncertain just what €1 million will be worth in terms of rand in 3-months' time, because they don't know what the exchange rate will be then. The possibility exists that the exchange rate could move to, say, ZAR/EUR; 14.30 in 3-months' time and so instead of receiving the expected R14.57 million from their export sale, they will only receive R14.30 million – a shortfall of R270 000.

DETERMINANTS OF FX RATES

We now turn to investigate the answers to three questions:

1. What causes foreign exchange rates to *move*?
2. What determines *forward* exchange rates?
3. What determines *future* spot rates?

Although we will deal with each of these questions individually, the answers to all three are interrelated (as we shall see), in that the answer to each question also affects the answer to the other two questions. The complexity means that, in practice, although we know the answers to all three questions, it is difficult (if not impossible) to predict future exchange rates because of these interactions.

Supply and demand

As noted earlier, exchange rates are simply the price of one currency in terms of another. Therefore if the EUR/GBP spot middle rate is 1.2150, this indicates that pounds cost €1.2150 each and €1 is worth 82.30 pence (i.e. $1 \div 1.2150 = 0.8230$). The prices of currencies are just like the prices of anything else, in that they respond to supply and demand market forces. Therefore if very large quantities of US$ are being bought on currency markets, the price of the US$ will rise – the US$ will *appreciate* in value. Conversely, if a lot of US$ are being sold on currency markets, this selling pressure will force down the price of the dollar – it will *depreciate*.

Therefore the simple answer to the question: 'what causes foreign exchange rates to move?' is supply and demand market forces in the currency markets. These market forces come from two principal sources. The first is speculators and speculation (so-called 'hot money') and the second is international trade and 'real' investment. Some estimates suggest that as much as 90% of these market forces arise out of currency speculation, and only 10% arise out of the buying and selling of foreign exchange for the purposes of international trade.

Individuals and financial institutions speculate on exchange rates – based on expectations about changes in macroeconomic and microeconomic factors – in much the same way as they might speculate on stock markets. If you think the shares of Avadé NV look cheap, you might buy them in anticipation of their price rising as soon as their true worth becomes more generally recognized. (You might also like to invest in Avadé because it pays out a high level of dividends.) Similarly, if the spot exchange rate between the Singapore dollar and the euro is EUR/SGD: 0.5710 and you think that the Singapore dollar is undervalued at only 57.1 cents each, you might want to buy S$ in anticipation of the currency appreciating. (Alternatively, if you think that Singapore interest rates might go up in the future you might want to buy S$ in order to place the currency on deposit and so benefit from the higher rate of interest.) In this way speculative market forces play a major role in the movement of exchange rates.

Currency market supply and demand forces also arise from the demands of international trade and investment. A Japanese company exports to Germany and receives euros in payment. That company will wish to sell those euro receipts in order to buy their own currency – the yen. Similarly, a UK company may import goods from Saudi Arabia and be invoiced in Saudi riyals. As a result, that UK company will need to sell pounds in order to buy riyals with which to pay the invoice.

These demands to buy and sell currencies arising out of import/export transactions also play their part in moving exchange rates in one way or another. So too will another form of international trade: international investment in assets. Suppose a Dutch company wishes to build a factory in Australia. It will need to sell euros in order to buy Australian dollars to be able to pay for the cost of building the factory in Australia.

Finally, there are also the supply and demand market forces arising out of international finance. A US company may wish to borrow money and decides to borrow Swiss francs to take advantage of lower interest rates in Switzerland than in the USA. Once that loan is raised, it will want to sell the francs in order to buy the US dollars that it requires. Over the life of the loan, it will periodically have to sell US dollars in order to buy Swiss francs to be able to pay the interest on the loan and eventually, repay the loan principal.

Thus the forces of supply and demand, both from speculators and from companies involved with international trade, financing and investment (as well as from governments engaged in the management of their floating exchange rates) are the factors lying behind movements in exchange rates.

Interest rates

Let us now turn to answer the second question. If the current EUR/USD spot rate (as determined by supply and demand market forces) is 0.7310 – 0.7320, what, for instance, determines why the 12-month forward rate is at a 1.25c – 1.40c premium?

The answer lies with the interest rate parity theorem (IRPT), which effectively works on the principle that international financial markets are *efficient*. There are no 'bargain' rates of interest to be had on loans/deposits in one currency rather than another. What you might seek to gain from a more *favourable* rate of interest in one currency rather than another, you are likely to lose in an *adverse* movement in exchange rates. Quite literally, exchange rates move to effectively bring about interest rate *parity* (or equality), amongst different currencies. This process is illustrated in Example 3.

EXAMPLE 3

Société Demlux is a small software company based in Luxembourg. The company has €500 000 of cash which will be required in 12-months' time to pay a corporation tax liability. In the meantime, the company's CFO wants to place the money safely on deposit in 12-month government bonds.

The interest on ECB (European Central Bank) bonds is 2% per year and the interest rate on British government bonds is 3% per year. The EUR/GBP exchange rates are as follows:

Spot EUR/GBP	1.2140 – 1.2150
12 months forward	1.2032 – 1.2050

Demlux's CFO is wondering whether she should place the spare funds on deposit in euros, at 2% interest, or in pounds, at 3% interest.

▶

If the €500 000 is invested in euros, at the end of 12 months the company will have: €500 000 × 1.02 = €510 000.

Alternatively, the CFO could sell the euros at spot and buy pounds, to give: €500 000 ÷ 1.2150 = £411 522.63.

These pounds could then be invested for 12 months at 3% interest to give: £411 522.63 × 1.03 = £423 868.31 in 12-months' time.

Finally, to avoid any uncertainty concerning future exchange rates, these pounds could be sold 12-months forward to give: £423 868.31 × 1.2032 = €510 000.[1]

This is *exactly* the amount of money that would have been received by Demlux if the money had simply been placed on deposit in euros at only 2% interest, because the interest rate parity theorem holds that forward rates are set to effectively bring about parity (or equality) between interest rates in different currencies.

Therefore we can conclude from the IRPT that forward rates are determined by the *differential* between interest rates in the different countries. The forward rates of the currency of the country with the lower rate of interest will appreciate against the currency of the country with the higher rate of interest by approximately the interest differential. In this example: 3% − 2% = 1%.

The precise rate of change is given by the following formula (given here in terms of EUR/GBP, but notice that the euro is the 'home' currency and pound is the 'foreign' currency):

$$\frac{\text{Eurozone interest rate} - \text{UK interest rate}}{1 + \text{UK interest rate}} = \% \text{ change in £}$$

or more generally:

$$\frac{\text{Home interest rate} - \text{Foreign interest rate}}{1 + \text{Foreign interest rate}} = \% \text{ change in the Foreign currency}$$

If this % change is 'positive' the Foreign currency is appreciating, but, if this % change is 'negative' the Foreign currency is depreciating.

Therefore, in our example:

$$\frac{0.02 - 0.03}{1 + 0.03} = -0.009709$$

or a 0.9709% depreciation in the pound $\begin{bmatrix} -\text{Foreign currency is depreciating} \\ +\text{Foreign currency is appreciating} \end{bmatrix}$

SpotEUR/GBP: $1.2150 \times (1 - 0.009709) = 1.2032$

1.2032: the 12-month EUR/GBP forward rate

The reason why IRPT determines forward rates is quite simple. If IRPT did not determine forward rates, it would be possible simply to make risk-free gains by borrowing money in one currency – at a lower interest rate – and placing it on deposit in another currency – at a higher interest rate. Such gains are referred to as 'arbitrage' profits and, if they were possible, then we would have a 'money machine' – and in the real world money machines just cannot exist.

This point can be illustrated by extending the example involving Société Demlux. Suppose Demlux's CFO was considering *borrowing* €500 000 at 2% interest and then placing the money on deposit, in

▶

pounds, at 3% interest. Now, instead of the 12-month forward rate for selling pounds being 1.2032 (which IRPT says it should be) it is in fact just 1.2100. As a result the following would occur:

- €500 000 borrowed for 12 months
- Interest payable at year-end: €500 000 × 0.02 = €10 000
- Convert the euros into pounds at spot: €500 000 ÷ 1.2150 = £411 522.63
- Place the pounds on deposit for 12 months to give: £411 522.63 × 1.03 = £423 868.31
- Sell the pounds 12-months forward to give: £423 868.31 × 1.2100 = €512 880.66
- Repay the euro loan plus interest: €510 000
- Resulting arbitrage profit: €2 880.66

If the EUR/GBP 12-month forward rate was – as IRPT says it should be – 1.2032, then there would have been *no* arbitrage gain to be made from such an exercise.

Finally, there is an important point that is often misunderstood. This is that this 12-month forward rate is technically called an 'unbiased estimator' of what *will be* the EUR/GBP spot rate in 12-months' time. Although this may well hold true in the longer run, generally speaking, forward rates are rather *poor estimates* of future spot rates. What may determine *actual* future spot rates is the subject of our third question.

Inflation

The main determinant of *future* spot exchange rates is given by another theorem, the purchasing power parity theorem (PPPT). This states that exchange rates should move to effectively bring about *purchasing power* parity between the currencies of different countries.

The PPPT as such is not as robust a theorem as IRPT, in that IRPT determines forward rates almost precisely. In contrast, PPPT will be a major influence behind future spot exchange rates, but is not the only influence (as we know from our discussion on supply and demand market forces).

The rationale behind the PPPT begins with the 'law of one price'. This law (given here in terms of EUR/USD) states that the euro price of a good, divided by the exchange rate, equals the dollar price of the same good. For example, suppose that a particular make of tablet computer costs €2000 in France and the spot EUR/USD rate is 0.7350. The 'law of one price' suggests that the US price of that same tablet computer will be: €2000 ÷ 0.7350 = US$2721 (more precisely: US$2721.09).

The reasoning behind the law is (once again), arbitrage. Suppose that the tablet computer could be bought in the USA for only US$2500. This would mean that the computers could be bought in the USA for the euro equivalent of US$2500 × 0.7350 = €1837.50 and then exported to France where they could be sold for €2000, making an (arbitrage) profit of €162.50 on each transaction. If this were to occur, the situation would not last long. The increased demand for tablet computers in the USA (by potential exporters) would force up their dollar price and the increased supply of those same tablet computers in France (from importers) would force down the euro price. These supply and demand market forces would continue until the law (and so equilibrium) re-established itself.

Like the PPPT itself, the law of one price is not a very robust or powerful law, because it does not apply to all goods, for two fairly obvious reasons. The first is that to operate efficiently, the transportation cost of the goods concerned must be small relative to the good's value. Thus the law will not work for low-cost, bulky items. However, it does work quite well for things such as gold and other precious metals, commodities (tea, coffee, tin, rubber, etc.), IT hardware and industrial equipment.

The second limitation on the working of the law is that it does not operate unless the goods are *physically* capable of being traded internationally. This requirement therefore excludes one very important group of assets from the law's influence: land and buildings. (You cannot buy a factory in the USA and physically transport it to mainland Europe.)

Assuming that the law of one price does tend to work for a significant amount of goods, let us continue with the example of the tablet computers and assume that the expected annual rates of inflation over the next 12 months in France and in the USA are 2% and 4% respectively.

As a result, we would expect the tablet computer to cost €2000 × (1 + 0.02) = €2040 in France in 12-months' time, and to cost US$2721 × (1 + 0.04) = US$2830 in the USA. Therefore, in order to maintain the law of one price, this implies that the EUR/USD spot rate in 12-months' time will be 0.7208 (i.e. €2040 ÷ $2830), so that €2040 ÷ 0.7208 = US$2830.

This is what is meant by the purchasing power parity theorem. Exchange rates move to maintain purchasing power parity between different currencies – that is, they move to maintain the law of one price. Therefore, the answer to the question as to what determines *future* spot rates is inflation differentials between different countries: the currency of the country with the higher rate of inflation will depreciate against the currency of the country with the lower rate of inflation by approximately the inflation differential. In our example, this differential is: 4% − 2% = 2% and so the dollar will depreciate by approximately 2% against the euro over the year.

The precise rate of change in the exchange, in terms of EUR/USD (again note which is the 'home' and which is the 'foreign' currency) is given by a formula which is very similar to that for IRPT:

$$\frac{\text{Eurozone inflation rate} - \text{US inflation rate}}{1 + \text{US inflation rate rate}} = \% \text{ change in US\$}$$

or more generally:

$$\frac{\text{Home inflation rate} - \text{Foreign inflation rate}}{1 + \text{Foreign inflation rate}} = \% \text{ change in the foreign currency}$$

If this % change is 'positive' the foreign currency is appreciating, but, if this % change is 'negative' the foreign currency is depreciating.

Using the data in our example, the percentage rate of change in the EUR/USD spot exchange rate in 12-months' time is:

$$\frac{0.02 - 0.04}{1 + 0.04} = -0.01923$$

or a 1.923% depreciation in the US dollar $\begin{bmatrix} - \text{Foreign currency is depreciating} \\ + \text{Foreign currency is appreciating} \end{bmatrix}$

SpotEUR / USD: 0.7350 × (1 − 0.01923) = 0.7209

and so, 0.7209: is the expected EUR/GBP spot rate in 12-months' time

Forecasting exchange rates

In this way, we can use estimates of future rates of inflation to estimate future spot exchange rates. Example 4 shows how this process works.

EXAMPLE 4

Kraftfabrik AG is a German manufacturing company which imports a key raw material from South Africa. The company wants to try to forecast the EUR/ZAR spot rates over the next 3 years. The current EUR/ZAR spot rate for buying the South African rand is 0.0695 and estimates of eurozone and South African inflation rates over the next 3 years are as follows:

	Inflation rates	
	Eurozone	South Africa
Year 1	2%	5%
Year 2	2%	4%
Year 3	4%	3%

Year 1 EUR/ZAR spot forecast.

$$\frac{0.02 - 0.05}{1 + 0.05} = -0.0286$$

Therefore the ZAR is forecast to depreciate by 2.86% to:

$$0.0695 \times (1 - 0.0286) = €0.0675 = R1$$

Year 2 EUR/ZAR spot forecast.

$$\frac{0.02 - 0.04}{1 + 0.04} = -0.0192$$

Therefore the ZAR is forecast to depreciate by 1.92% to:

$$0.0675 \times (1 - 0.0192) = €0.0662 = R1$$

Year 3 EUR/ZAR spot forecast.

$$\frac{0.04 - 0.03}{1 + 0.03} = +0.0097$$

Therefore the ZAR is forecast to *appreciate* by 0.97% to:

$$0.0662 \times (1 + 0.0097) = €0.0668 = R1$$

The calculations in Example 4 are very imprecise estimates of future EUR/ZAR spot rates for two reasons. The first is that the inflation differentials are themselves only estimates. The second reason is that at Years 1, 2 and 3 the *actual* spot rate will also be affected by supply and demand market forces *at that time*.

SUMMARY

- Exchange rates are really currency prices, of which there is a buying and a selling price (or rate).

- Exchange rates can either be quoted as 'spot' or 'forward' rates. Spot rates are for the immediate delivery (exchange) of currencies. Forward rates are for the delivery of currencies at specific future dates.

- Forward rates are normally quoted as a 'discount' or 'premium' to the spot rate. A discount is subtracted from the spot rate; a premium is added to the spot rate. A discount signals that the 'foreign' currency is depreciating (and the 'home' currency is appreciating); a premium signals that the foreign currency is appreciating.

- There are two types of forward FX contract: 'fixed' forward contracts and 'time option' forward contracts. Fixed forward contracts are for the exchange of currencies at a specific future date. Time option forward contracts are for the exchange of currencies at any time between two future dates.

- Exchange rate systems can either be fixed, floating or semi-fixed. Since 1972, most of the world's currencies have been in a system of floating exchange rates.

- Finally, within a system of floating exchange rates, there are three factors which cause exchange rates to move: the forces of supply and demand; interest differentials between countries, and inflation differentials between countries.

NOTE

1. Approximately, due to rounding error.

FURTHER READING

At this stage we are only half-way through our examination of foreign exchange risk management. However, there are a number of good books which give a deeper analysis of the foreign exchange markets and the causes of exchange rate movements.

1. From a UK perspective, see J.A. Donaldson, *Corporate Currency Risk,* Financial Times Business Information 1984 and Chapters 1–6 of A. Buckley, *Multinational Finance,* Prentice Hall 1992.

2. Although it is written from a US perspective, another excellent book is D.K. Eiteman, A.I. Stonehill and M.H. Moffett, *Multinational Business Finance,* Addison-Wesley 1992. See especially Chapters 2 and 4.

3. On the 'robustness' of PPPT, see: A.M. Taylor and M.P. Taylor, 'The Purchasing Power Parity Debate', *Journal of Economic perspectives*, Autumn 2004.

QUIZ QUESTIONS

Assuming:

Spot EUR/AUD	0.6725 – 0.6735
1 month forward:	0.0010 – 0.0015 premium

1 What are the EUR/AUD 1-month forward rates?
2 Is the Australian dollar (AUD) appreciating or depreciating against the euro?
3 What is the Australian dollar cost of selling €350 000 at spot?
4 What is the euro receipt from the 1-month forward sale of A$450 000?
5 Given a EUR/AUD spot rate of 0.6725 – 0.6735, and if you are told that the Australian dollar is expected to depreciate by 3% per year for the next 4 years and is then likely to appreciate by 10% per year thereafter, estimate the EUR/AUD spot rate in 6-years' time.
6 If EUR/GBP spot is 0.8160 and $/£ 12-month forward is 0.8082 and the yield on UK government is 5%, what is the yield on European Central Bank bonds?
7 US inflation is expected to be 5% next year and UK inflation 3%. If the current GBP/USD spot rate is 0.6120, forecast the spot rate in 12-months' time.
8 The current EUR/CHF spot rate is 0.8240. Inflation forecasts for the next 3 years are:

Eurozone	Switzerland	Year
2%	1%	1
3%	3%	2
4%	2%	3

Forecast the spot rates over the next 3 years.
(See the 'Answers to Quiz Questions' section at the back of the book.)

PROBLEMS

The answers to the following problems are available to students online (see the 'Digital Resources' page for details).

1 What causes exchange rates to move?
2 Describe the different types of exchange rate system.

FOREIGN EXCHANGE HEDGING

LEARNING OBJECTIVES

The purpose of this chapter is to:

■ Define the different types of foreign exchange risk.

■ Explain forward and money market hedging.

■ Demonstrate futures market hedging.

■ Demonstrate the use of option hedges.

FOREIGN EXCHANGE RISK DEFINITIONS

Risk, as we know, means uncertainty of outcome and so foreign exchange risk refers to the uncertainty of outcome that arises because exchange rates move unpredictably. Three types of foreign exchange risk can be identified:

1. transaction risk

2. translation risk

3. economic risk.

Transaction risk can be defined as being the risk that movements in exchange rates will adversely affect the value – in terms of the company's own domestic currency – of future foreign currency cash flows, arising out of import and export transactions. Therefore it arises when the company has either receivables or payables which are denominated in a foreign currency. Companies are also exposed to transaction risk if they undertake 'real' investment (e.g. building a factory) in a foreign country. That real investment will be expected to generate a future stream of positive net cash flows denominated in the foreign currency.

Finally, companies are also exposed to transaction risk if they borrow money denominated in a foreign currency. On such loans, they have future foreign currency interest and capital repayment liabilities on which they are exposed to the risk of movements in exchange rates.

The second type of foreign exchange risk, translation risk, arises when foreign currency assets and liabilities have to be *translated* into the company's own domestic currency, so as to be included in the company's balance sheet. Many people would argue that although *transaction* risk can have a real impact on the value of the firm and shareholder wealth, this is *not* the case with *translation* risk. Translation risk is seen here as an 'accounting problem', and not one which affects the real worth of companies, in that it has *no* cash flow impact. If we assume that markets are efficient then it follows that accounting problems such as this do not represent a real risk at all. The only real (as opposed to perceived) problem arising from translation of foreign currency items would thus be one resulting from market inefficiencies relating to the interpretation of financial data.

The exposure of companies to translation risk arises principally from having medium- to long-term assets (such as foreign investment projects) or liabilities (typically, loans) denominated in foreign currencies which have to be translated at each year-end into the company's own domestic currency to be included in the balance sheet.

Finally, economic exposure to foreign exchange risk arises from the possibility that the present value of the company's future expected foreign currency cash flows – in terms of their own domestic currency – may alter through changes in exchange rates. By this definition, economic foreign exchange risk can be viewed as a longer-term version of transaction risk. Thus future export sales that the company may hope to achieve, and future net foreign currency cash flows that it is hoped will arise from a foreign investment project, will all generate exposure to economic foreign exchange risk.

For present purposes, our attention is focused on the problem of foreign exchange *transaction risk*, and particularly the risk faced by importers and exports.

TRANSACTION RISK HEDGING

Eirtech Ltd is an Irish biotechnology company, based in Dublin. The company has exported goods worth €1 million to a customer in the USA and, because the current EUR/USD spot selling rate is 0.7042, they invoice their US customer for US$1.42 million on their normal terms of trade of 3-months' credit. That Irish exporter is faced with foreign exchange risk: it is uncertain what will be the euro revenues generated from the export deal. Although they know that it is going to receive USD1.42 million in 3-months' time, it doesn't know how many euros those dollars will buy when it comes to sell them in 3-months' time, because it doesn't know what the EUR/USD spot rate will be in 3-months' time. (Remember, exchange rates float in a relatively unpredictable way.)

What can be done about this foreign exchange risk? One answer is simple. Instead of invoicing the customer for US$1.42 million, Eirtech could invoice the customer for €1 million. The exporter will then have *no uncertainty* as to the euro revenues from the export sale: €1 million.

The only problem with this course of action is that the foreign exchange risk does not disappear. Instead, the exporter is simply pushing the risk onto the importing customer, who now faces uncertainty about the *dollar cost* of paying for those imported goods, because they too do not know what will be the EUR/USD spot rate in 3-months' time when the €1 million will have to be purchased, in order to pay the invoice. Pushing the foreign exchange risk onto the customer in this way is perfectly acceptable as a solution to the exporter's foreign exchange risk problem *if* the customer allows this. In other words, if the exporter has some sort of *monopoly power* and there is no other source of supply for the goods, then the customer may well simply have to accept the foreign exchange risk being pushed onto it in this way.

However, in most circumstances, export markets are highly competitive and so exporters are unable to operate in that way, for fear of losing the business to a rival who is willing to invoice the customer in the customer's own currency. Thus this solution to the exporter's foreign exchange risk problem is often unrealistic or unavailable.

Do nothing

An alternative would be for the exporter to invoice its customer for US$1.42 million, on 3-months credit, and then to do *nothing* about the foreign exchange risk, but just accept the chance that there may be an adverse movement in exchange rates over the credit period. This course of action may be perfectly acceptable, provided two conditions apply:

1. The amount of money involved is relatively small (in relation to the company's business).

2. The company does not expect exchange rates to move significantly in an adverse direction.

On this latter condition, there is of course the problem of how the company is going to be able to predict future exchange rates. One way is to look at the forward rates. If the EUR/USD 3-month forward rate is at a premium, this indicates an appreciation in the value of the US$ relative to the euro. Such a movement in exchange rates would be in the exporter's favour – it is owed money, US$1.42 million, in a currency that is appreciating – becoming more valuable – over time. In such circumstances, the exporter may be tempted not to do anything about its exposure to foreign exchange risk in the hope that, if anything, exchange rates may move in its favour.

However, the problem with this is that, as we know, forward rates are *not* very good predictors of future spot rates. Forward rates are determined by IRPT, while actual future spot rates are determined by PPPT, and supply and demand market forces at that future point in time. Therefore the fact that 3-month forward rates are at a premium is no guarantee that in 3-months' time the dollar will have appreciated from its current spot exchange rate. As a result, and given that a large amount of money – US$1.42 million – is involved, the exporter would be foolish to take a chance on foreign exchange risk, doing nothing to reduce or eliminate it. Therefore how can the exporter avoid – '*hedge*' – its potential exposure to foreign exchange risk?

Natural hedging or netting

There are a number of hedging techniques. The first that we can look at is the easiest and most obvious: foreign currency 'netting' or 'natural hedging'. The opportunity for this arises when a company is both an importer and an exporter and so has assets and liabilities denominated in the same foreign currency *and* with the same maturity date.

For example, suppose a German company exports to the USA and has invoiced a customer for US$1 million payable in 3-months' time. In addition, it has also imported some goods on 3-months' credit and has been invoiced for US$0.8 million. Effectively, the US$0.8 million liability can be paid by partially utilizing the US$1 million due to be received in 3-months' time. Therefore one amount can be *netted off* against the other, leaving the balancing US$0.2 million asset to be hedged by other means. As a result, the German exporter now only has an exposure to the risk of an adverse movement in exchange rates on US$200 000.

Forward market hedging

A second hedging device – and the most widely used in practice – is the *forward market* hedge. In the above example, the company could hedge the net US$0.2 million that is due to be received by the company in 3-months' time by using a forward contract: it could enter into a contract now, agreeing to sell US$0.2 million in 3-months' time, at a pre-determined fixed rate of exchange – the 3-month forward rate. As a result, there will be no uncertainty as to the euro value of the net US$0.2 million receivable in 3-months' time.

Example 1 will help make this clear, but now using the case of an importer.

EXAMPLE 1

Mechatronics AG is a German company. It has imported some electronic components from Brazil and has been invoiced for R$10 million (10 million Brazilian real), payable in 6-months' time. The current EUR/BRL exchange rates are as follows:

EUR/BRL spot	0.3205 – 0.3215
6 months forward	0.0070 – 0.0085 premium

The first thing to notice is that the forward rate here is at a *premium*, indicating that the foreign currency – the real – is expected to appreciate. This would represent an adverse movement from the Mechatronics point of view: they owe money in a currency (the Brazilian real), which is expected to appreciate against their own (euros). Therefore, it would be unwise not to hedge their exposure to foreign exchange risk.

To hedge in the forward market, the company would buy R$10 million. 6 months forward (remember, they need to buy Brazilian reals in order to be able to pay the invoice).

To calculate the actual 6-month forward rates, the premium has to be *added* to the spot rate:

EUR/BRL spot	0.3205 – 0.3215
plus premium	0.0070 – 0.0085
6 months forward	0.3275 – 0.3300

Given that the first of the pair of exchange rates is the rate for selling the foreign currency and the second is the rate for buying the foreign currency, then the euro cost of buying R$10 million 6 months forward is: R$10m × 0.3300 = €3.3 million. By using this forward market hedge, the German importer – Mechatronics – has no uncertainty about the cost in its own currency (€3.3m), of having to pay the R$10 million invoice in 6-months' time.

Money market hedging

A third hedging technique is called a 'money market' or 'financial' hedge. Although at first sight this will look more complicated than a forward market hedge, it has a very simple underlying logic.

Suppose a French company exports to Canada and invoices its customer for C$0.5 million on 3-months' credit. Current data are given in Table 23.1.

TABLE 23.1

Exchange rates:

EUR/CAD spot	0.6535 – 0.6545
3 month forward	0.6500 – 0.6512

3-month money market interest rates:

C$: 4.0% per annum

€: 2.0% per annum

The money market[1] is where companies (and individuals) can lend and borrow money for a short period of time. This time period can be as short as 'overnight' (which means from 3.00 p.m. one afternoon to 3.00 p.m. the next day) or as long as 12 months. Each time period in the money market has its own interest rate and in this example we are given the interest rate for lending and borrowing for a 3-month time period. It is important to remember that money market interest rates, for whatever time period, are *always* given in nominal *annual* terms. Thus the 3-month euro money market rate does not represent the actual amount of interest that is payable on a 3-months' loan or deposit. To get the actual rate of interest over 3 months, the *annual* interest rate has to be divided by 4 (i.e. 4×3 months = 12 months). Thus the 3-month euro interest rate is actually: $2\% \div 4 = 0.5\%$. Finally, and fairly obviously, note that the Canadian dollar rate is the rate applicable for Canadian dollar loans and deposits and the euro rate is for euro-denominated loans and deposits.

The 'money market hedge' uses what is termed the 'matching principle'. The French company has a C$0.5 million *asset* which is due to mature in 3-months' time. It hedges its risk exposure on these dollars by creating a *matching* C$0.5 million *liability*, which also matures in 3-months' time. This liability is created by taking out a 3-month Canadian dollar loan. The company will borrow C$x for 3 months, at an interest rate of $(4\% \div 4) = 1\%$ so that capital (C$x), plus accumulated interest will amount to precisely C$0.5 million at the end of 3 months. Therefore, the size of the loan can be calculated as follows:

$$C\$x \times (1 + 0.01) = C\$0.5 \text{ million}$$
$$C\$x = C\$0.5m \div 1.01 = C\$495\,049$$

How the money market hedge works is as follows: the French company invoices its Canadian customer for C$0.5 million on 3-months' credit. Simultaneously, it borrows C$495 049 from a bank for 3 months and immediately sells those Canadian dollars, at spot, to convert them into C$495 049 × 0.6545 = €324 010. This euro amount represents its receipt from the export deal. And, in 3-months' time when it receives C$0.5 million from the customer in settlement of the invoice, it then uses these Canadian dollars to repay its Canadian dollar loan which by now has accumulated (capital plus interest) to C$0.5 million.

Therefore, in this example, by using a money market hedge the French exporter receives €324 010 *now*. An alternative would have been for the French company to use a forward

market hedge and sell the C$0.5 million 3 months forward, to yield C$0.5 million ×
0.6512 = €325 600, which would be received in *3-months' time*.

Comparing hedges

If we contrast these two possible hedges, we can determine which one would be best: the
money market hedge, where the company receives €324 010 immediately, or the forward
market hedge where it receives €325 600 in 3-months' time.

These two amounts cannot be compared directly, because of the time value of money.
Either we have to compound the €324 010 forward for 3 months, or we have to discount
the €325 600 back 3 months. In this situation, it is easier to compound forward the euros
received from the money market hedge. The interest rate we would use would be the euro
3-month interest rate: 2% ÷ 4 = 0.5%. The result is shown in Table 23.2.

TABLE 23.2

	Now	3-months' time
Forward market hedge:		€325 600
Money market hedge:	€324 010 × (1 + 0.005)	= €325 630

We can now compare like with like and as €325 630 is very slightly more than
€325 600, the company's best hedge strategy in this example is to use the
money market hedge.

However, notice how very similar are the outcomes of the two hedges. This is
not a coincidence, but is because of the fact that the 3-month forward rate is
determined by the IRPT which uses the Canadian dollar and euro interest rates:

$$\frac{\text{EUR interest} - \text{CAD interest}}{1 + \text{CAD interest}} = \frac{0.02 - 0.04}{1 + 0.04} = -0.0192 \text{ a } 1.92\% \text{ depreciation in the CAD}$$

Therefore EUR/CAD spot × (1 − 0.0182) = 0.6419 3-month forward rate

---

Leading hedge

In this last example, the case of an exporter was used, but it will be helpful also to look at an
example using an importer. However, before doing so, we can continue to use the existing
example to look at another hedging strategy: 'leading the payment'.

In this context, 'leading' refers simply to asking the Canadian customer to forgo the
3-month credit period and to pay the invoice *immediately*. As a result, the French exporter
will receive the Canadian dollars immediately and can then sell them at spot for euros, and
so has no foreign exchange risk.

Obviously, the Canadian customer is unlikely to be willing to forgo the credit period
without being given some sort of discount on the full invoiced amount. The maximum discount that the exporter would be willing to give would be where the euro outcome resulting
from the customer leading the payment was the same as the euro outcome from the best
hedge: in this case, the money market hedge where C$324 010 is received immediately.
The identification of the discount is given in Table 23.3.

TABLE 23.3

If C$x represents the C$ received now from the Canadian customer leading the payment:

$$C\$x \div 0.6545 = €324\,010$$

$$C\$x = €324\,010 \div 0.6545 = C\$495\,050$$

If the Canadian customer were to pay C$495 050 immediately and forgo the credit period this would imply a discount of:

$$\frac{C\$500\,000 - C\$495050}{C\$500\,000} = 0.01\,or\,1\%\ discount$$

Therefore 1% would be the maximum discount the French exporter would be willing to offer to get the Canadian customer to lead the payment. Offering a greater discount than this would mean that the exporter would receive fewer euros than they would from using a money market hedge, with the Canadian customer paying the invoice in full after 3 months.

Another money market hedge

Let us now return to another example of using a money market hedge, but now with an importer facing foreign exchange risk. This is given in Example 2.

EXAMPLE 2

Al-Kharafi is a Kuwaiti global logistics company. It has recently bought a fleet of new trucks from a major Indian motor manufacturer and has been invoiced for 280 million rupees payable in 6-months' time. The exchange rates between the Kuwaiti dinar (KWD) and the Indian rupee (INR), together with money market interest rates are given below:

Exchange rates:

KWD/INR spot	0.00462 – 0.00472
6 months forward	0.00448 – 0.00461

6-month money market interest rates:

Kuwaiti dinars	3% per annum
Indian rupees	8% per annum

Once again, the matching principle is used but here the Kuwaiti importer has a rupee liability (which matures in 6-months' time), and so needs to create a matching rupee asset in order to hedge.

The rupee asset is created by the importer buying a quantity of Indian rupees at spot – IRx – and placing them on 6-month rupee deposit at an interest rate of: $8\% \div 2 = 4\%$ so that capital and interest accumulate to IR280 million at the end of 6 months. At that time, the contents of the rupee deposit account are then used to pay off the IR28 million invoice.

▶

The amount of rupees needed to be placed on deposit can be calculated as:

IRx × (1 + 0.04) = IR280 million
IRx = IR280m ÷ 1.04 = IR269 230 769

The cost of buying IR269 230 769 at spot will be:

IR269 230 769 × 0.00472 = K$1 270 769

This is the cost *now,* in dinars, of the Kuwaiti company's import deal. Thus the Kuwaiti importer has no foreign exchange risk: Al-Kharafi has no uncertainty as to the dinar cost of the new truck fleet.

Once again, we could compare the outcome of this money market hedge with a forward market hedge.

If Al-Kharafi was to buy IR280 million 6 months forward, the invoice would have a dinar cost of IR280m × 0.00461 = K$1 290 800 payable in 6-months' time. This can now be compared with the money market cost of K$1 270 769 payable immediately by compounding this latter amount forward 6 months at the 6-month dinar interest rate of: 3% ÷ 2 = 1.5%:

$$K\$1\ 270\ 769 \times (1 + 0.015) = K\$1\ 289\ 830$$

Once again we observe that there is virtually no difference in the two outcomes – because financial markets, including foreign exchange markets, are efficient.

FOREIGN EXCHANGE FUTURES CONTRACTS

We can now turn to yet another hedging device using foreign exchange futures contracts.[2] In effect, there is very little difference between a company hedging on the forward market and hedging on the futures market, except that on the forward market the foreign exchange deal is *tailor-made* to the company's precise requirements: forward deals can be conducted for any amount of money, for (virtually) any currency and for (virtually) any time period forward. In contrast, futures deals are in the form of *standardized* contracts of a fixed amount of money and are available in only a limited range of currencies and for a limited range of forward time periods.

Because of the standardized nature of futures contracts, as opposed to the tailor-made nature of forward contracts, the transaction costs (e.g. commission payments) on futures are likely to be lower than on forward contracts for small foreign exchange hedging transactions (say, less than €500 000). Therefore it is in these circumstances that futures hedges would appear to be a sensible alternative to other foreign exchange hedging techniques. However, as we shall see, a futures hedge is more complex and more difficult to understand, than the very simple forward market hedges and so their use as a foreign exchange hedge is very much secondary to their use for speculation on currency movements.

A single futures contract is in respect of a fixed, standard amount of one currency being exchanged for a given amount of another currency for delivery exchange on a specific, standard future date. Futures contracts are available in a limited range of major trading currencies, including: EUR/USD, GBP/USD and JPY/USD and also in some developing economy currencies. Futures contracts can be obtained from a variety of futures exchanges around the world, but all except the Chicago Mercantile Exchange – CME – have only a very limited range of currency pairs. Beside the CME, the main currency exchange that deal in currency futures is the Europe-wide Euronext market, and it is the Euronext USD/EUR futures contract that we will use as an example, during our discussion of futures hedging.

Each futures contract is in respect of a fixed amount of currency. Therefore, for example, the Euronext USD/EUR futures contracts have a contract size of US$20 000. Deals can be done in *whole* contracts only. (It is in this sense that futures contracts are *standardized*.) Therefore a US dollar/euro deal can only be hedged in US$20 000 steps: US$20 000 (1 contract), US$40 000 (2 contracts), etc. If you wished to hedge US$135 000, it could not be hedged precisely. It could either be under-hedged at 6 contracts (US$120 000) or overhedged at 7 contracts (US$140 00).

Futures contracts can be either bought or sold in the futures market, and the 'price' of the contract is effectively the exchange rate at which the deal is done. However, on the Euronext market, futures are priced on the basis of 'euros per US$100'. Therefore, if we buy one USD/EUR contract priced at €72, this is equivalent to a EUR/USD exchange rate of: €72 ÷ 100 = €0.72; and so we are buying US$20 000 in exchange for US$20 000 × 0.72 = €14 400. Similarly, if we sold 8 USD/EUR contracts at €72, we would be selling: 8 × US$20 000 = US$160 000 in exchange for: US$160 000 × 0.72 = €115 200.

On the Euronext market the futures prices move in units of one-tenth of a cent,[3] i.e. €0.0001, and this is known as the 'tick size'. Each €0.0001 movement in the futures price is worth €2 – known as the 'tick value'. (This tick value is derived as follows: US$20 000 contract size × 0.0001 = €2.)

Finally, contracts are issued on a 3-monthly cycle (typically: March, June, September and December) with three different contracts available at any one time. For example, suppose that it is early February; at that time we would have a choice available of March, June and September contracts. Each of these contracts would be due to expire towards the end of the month concerned (typically, the third Friday of the month). Therefore, if we bought two USD/EUR March futures contracts priced at €73, we would be buying 2 × US$20 000 = US$40 000 in exchange for US$40 000 × 0.73 = €28 800, with exchange of currencies being due on the third Friday in March.

As soon as the third Friday in March is reached, the March contracts expire (i.e. they are no longer available to be bought and sold) and a new contract is created: December contracts, to ensure that a choice of three different dated contracts are available (now: June, September and December).

A futures hedge

At first sight, futures contracts can be confusing, but their mechanics are really quite simple as can be seen in Example 3.

EXAMPLE 3

It is now January. Munichmetall GmbH, a German steel producer, invoices its US customer, Drake Inc., for US$325 000 payable in June. Current spot EUR/USD is 0.7320 – 0.7345 and the available USD/EUR Euronext contracts are:

▶

▶

March contracts	€73.15
June contracts	€73.30
September contracts	€73.55

The futures contract size is US$20 000.

Target outcome

Munichmetall is due to receive US$325 000 in June. If exchange rates do not move between now and 1 June, they will be able to sell the dollars and receive:

$$US\$325\ 000 \times 0.7320 = €237\ 900$$

This amount therefore represents what can be called the 'target outcome', in that the company will hope to be able to arrange hedge protection that will result in them actually receiving an amount in euros as close as possible to this figure of €237 900.

Which contracts?

The first decision concerns which contracts to use to hedge the company's foreign exchange risk exposure. In order to achieve the most efficient futures hedge, the company would use the contract whose expiry date is as close as possible to the expected date of the foreign currency receipt or payment. As Munichmetall is due to receive the US dollars at the end of June, the June futures contracts are the obvious choice.

Number of contracts

In order to set up the hedge, the next thing is to determine how many of the June USD/EUR contracts will be required. The amount of money needed to be hedged is US$325 000 and as the futures contracts are in units of US$20 000 this is equivalent to: US$325 000 ÷ US$20 000 = 16.25 contracts.

However, remember, only *whole* contracts can be dealt with on the futures market and we normally round to the nearest whole number of contracts – in this case, down to 16 contracts.

To buy or sell futures?

The next thing to decide is whether Munichmetall needs to buy or to sell 16 USD/EUR June futures contracts in order to hedge its foreign exchange risk exposure. The answer to this can be found as follows. Look at the currency in which the futures contract size is denominated. In this example, that currency is US dollars – the contract size is US$20 000. Now look to see what the company is doing with this currency in the 'cash market'. As Munichmetall is due to be receiving US dollars, it will want to *sell* these dollars (in exchange for euros) in the cash market, therefore to hedge it will need to *sell* USD/EUR futures. (If Munich metal was *importing* goods and had a US$ invoice to *pay*, it would need to *buy* dollars in the cash market – to pay the invoice – and so would hedge by *buying* futures.) Therefore, in order to undertake a futures hedge, Munichmetall will sell 16 USD/EUR June futures at €73.30.

'Profit' or 'loss' on target

No further action is then taken until June when Munichmetall receives US$325 000 from Drake Inc. Suppose, at that time, we find:

| EUR/USD spot | 0.7210 – 0.7228 |
| June USD/EUR futures | €72.24 |

▶

▶

Munichmetall will then sell the US$325 000 0 for euros on the spot market to yield:

$$US\$325\ 000 \times 0.7210 = €234\ 325$$

The target outcome was €237 900 and so there has been a shortfall of: €237 900 − €234 325 = €3575 caused by the depreciation in the dollar between January (when the exchange rate for selling dollars was 0.7320) and June (when the exchange rate has moved to 0.7210). However, as we shall see, this shortfall will be *offset* by a profit on the futures contracts that were bought in January.

Closing out the futures position

What Munichmetall now needs to do is 'close out' its futures position. It does this by *reversing* the earlier deal. In that earlier futures deal it *sold* 16 USD/EUR June futures contracts and so now, in order to close out its futures position, it *buys* 16 USD/EUR June contracts at their current price of €72.24.

Profits or loss on futures

To see the profit that Munichmetall has made on its futures dealings, we need to understand what its two futures transactions really imply.

It originally sold 16 USD/EUR June contracts at €73.30. Therefore it was selling 16 × US$20 000 = UD$320 000 for exchange/delivery in June in exchange for the receipt of: US$320 000 × [€73.30 ÷ 100] = €234 560.

The company then bought 16 USD/EUR June futures at €72.24. Therefore it was arranging to *buy* 16 × US$20 000 = US$320 000 for delivery in June. It is in this way that the company *closes out* its futures position: it has got contracts to both buy *and* sell US$320 000 for June delivery and so one set of contracts cancels out the other.

However, in the second futures deal, the US$320 000 was *bought* for June delivery at a cost of: US$320 000 × [€72.24 ÷ 100] = €231 168. As the euro receipt from the original dollar sale was greater than the euro cost of the dollar purchase, the company receives the difference as the *profit* on its futures deal: €234 560 − €231 168 = €3392. This is shown more clearly below:

First futures transaction: Sold US$320 000	Receipt	€234 560
Second futures transaction: Bought US$320 000	Cost	€231 168
	Profit	€3 392

Hedge efficiency

As a result, the net euro outcome for Munichmetall – in comparison to its 'target outcome' – is:

Receipt from spot sale of US$320 000	€234 325
Profit from futures transaction	€3 392
Total euro outcome	€237 717
Target £ outcome	€237 900

The success of the company's hedging can be measured by the 'hedge efficiency' ratio. This is given by profit ÷ loss where the 'profit' is that made on the futures transaction and the 'loss' is the shortfall in the cash market against the target outcome caused by the adverse movement in exchange rates. Therefore the hedge efficiency is:

$$\frac{€3392}{€3575} = 0.948 \text{ or } 94.9\% \text{ hedge efficiency}$$

In Example 3, the hedge efficiency was 94.9%.[4] Where the 'profit' exactly matches the 'loss', then we shall get 100% hedge efficiency. In practice 100% efficiency is unlikely to occur, except by chance – it is likely to be a little below (as it is in this example) or a little above 100%.

There are two reasons why a *perfect* 100% hedge efficiency is unlikely. One is that we can only deal in whole contracts. In Example 3, Munichmetall would have liked to have dealt in 16.25 futures contracts, but instead had to deal in just 16 contracts. The second reason why a perfect hedge is unlikely is because futures contract prices move approximately, but do not move precisely in line with exchange rates (this is referred to as 'basis risk'). For both these reasons, future hedges, unlike tailor-made forward market hedges, are unlikely to be perfectly efficient.

The 'lock in' effect

We saw that with a forward market hedge, the company effectively 'locks itself in' to a specific rate of exchange and so is effectively hedged not only against an *adverse* movement in exchange rates, but is also hedged against a *favourable* movement.

For example, suppose an Italian exporter invoices a South African customer for R10 million on 3-months' credit and hedges by selling R10 million forward for 3 months at 0.0686. This means that the exporter will receive R10 million × 0.0686 = €686 000 in 3-months' time, whatever happens to the EUR/ZAR exchange rate over the next 3 months. Therefore if in 3-months' time spot EUR/ZAR is 0.0672, it will be very glad that they hedged the R10 million at 0.0686. But, on the other hand, if spot EUR/ZAR in 3-months' time moved to 0.07250, it would be rather sorry about having hedged, because selling the R10 million spot would have yielded R10 million × 0.0725 = €725 000.

However, the key purpose of hedging is to avoid uncertainty of outcome – not to look back regretfully with the benefit of hindsight. (You might insure my house against fire; at the end of the year you don't regret having done so just because it hasn't burnt down.) The purpose of this example is to emphasize the point that a forward market hedge has the effect of hedging against both adverse *and* favourable movements in exchange rates. In other words, the company selling goods overseas makes its profit from selling those goods rather than speculating in currency movements.

This 'lock in' characteristic of a forward market hedge is also a characteristic of a futures market hedge. In Example 3, we saw that an *adverse* movement in exchange rates (the EUR/USD rate moved from 0.7320 in January to 0.7210 in June) caused a shortfall of €3575 to be made in the cash market in June when compared against the target outcome. However, this shortfall was then offset by a *profit* on the futures trades.

We would also find that the reverse situation holds: if there had been a *favourable* movement in exchange rates so that a surplus was made in June on the cash market when compared against the target outcome, then this surplus would, once again, have been offset – but this time by a *loss* on the futures trades.

Margin

Companies deal in futures via futures markets (or exchanges). The world's largest futures exchange is the CME and the main Europe-wide exchange is Euronex. However there are futures exchanges in most financial centres, all around the world (although by no means do all deal in *currency* futures), and many are linked together through the Intercontinental Exchange (ICE).

One important element of futures trading is the concept of 'margin'. Margin is essentially a deposit held by the futures exchange on behalf of futures traders as security against the trader defaulting upon their trading obligations. Therefore, in our futures example, when the Munichmetall sets up its hedge position in January (by selling 16 USD/EUR June contracts), it would have had to deposit some cash (or government securities) with Euronext for as long as its futures position remained 'open' (remember, the company in our example did not 'close out' its position until June). This initial deposit put up by the futures trader is called 'initial margin'. At the end of each working day that the futures position remains open, the futures exchange calculates whether a profit or loss has been made on the futures. This process is known as being 'marked to market'. If a profit has been made, it is then added to the balance of the trader's margin account. If a loss is made, that loss is subtracted from the balance on the margin account. If the balance on the margin account falls below some predetermined minimum, then the trader has to deposit *extra* money – called 'variation margin' – to bring the margin account balance up to the minimum permitted level.

Margin rules vary between different futures exchanges. However, for example, on the Euronext futures exchange the initial margin is €625 *per contract* and the minimum permitted balance on margin account is €500 *per contract*. Therefore Munichmetall would have had to put up initial margin of: 16 × €625 = €10 000 as security against their possible default on the obligations and if the balance of their margin account fell below: 16 × €500 = €8000 then additional variation margin would have had to be contributed.

REAL WORLD VIEW: Chinese Foreign Exchange Hedging

One issue that affects international trade and manufacturing overseas for the financial benefits is currency volatility. Traditionally, and particularly owing to favourable exchange rates (amongst other factors), the Pearl River Delta in China has been an attractive production proposition for many Western businesses, giving it the nickname 'the factory of the world'. Yet as of March 2014, with the Bank of China's rise of the trading band from 1 per cent (in April 2012) to 2 per cent, the Chinese yuan has become increasingly volatile, which could have significant operational consequences for international business and the export market. Following the announcement, value of the yuan depreciated rapidly to its lowest point in almost a year, with the expectation that it would then rise back to a notable strength.

As an article in the *South China Morning Post* suggests, currency volatility is placed highly as a growing concern alongside industrial reform, a shortage or labour, and rising wage costs. As the Chinese Manufacturers' Association of Hong Kong vice-president, Johnny Yeung Chi-hung, has noted, 'Yuan movement is getting increasingly hard to predict.' This fluctuation as the result of the band widening could be troublesome, having an impact on the hedging of risks to combat currency instability, such as the buying of forward contracts for those exporters who benefit from a weak Yuan.

This move from the Bank of China may simply be a snapshot of wider reforms to allow currency to float freely, although the complexity of balancing the interests of the various international stakeholders involved will necessitate careful future consideration for China to remain a competitive force in global industry.

FORWARD VERSUS FUTURES

It is interesting to compare the advantages of forward market hedging to futures market hedging. In this respect, futures have two advantages over forward hedges for smaller users of the foreign exchange markets:

1. The initial margin required is often considerably *less* than the deposit that may be required by banks from small companies wishing to use forward contracts.
2. The relatively small unit size of individual futures contracts (e.g. USD/EUR futures are for US$20 000 per contract) means that small importers and exporters can use the futures market and so avoid the relatively higher commissions charged by banks on small forward market deals.

For larger companies, in particular, the forward markets have many benefits:

1. Forward exchange rates are, to some extent, negotiable and so a large company can use its market power with a bank to negotiate a favourable forward market rate. In contrast, futures prices are simply market determined and are non-negotiable.
2. The banking system is open 24 hours a day, 7 days a week (on an international basis) and so companies can deal on the forward markets at any time. In contrast, futures markets are shut overnight, at weekends and on public holidays.
3. Many futures markets are relatively small and so a company wishing to hedge a very large amount of foreign exchange may find that the market is not liquid enough for their needs (i.e. their futures deals may be large enough to actually move the market prices against them).
4. Variation margin requirements are assessed on a daily basis and so a company which hedges using futures faces the possibility of an unpredictable and uncontrollable cash flow while their futures position remains open.
5. Finally, and as has been mentioned before, futures, unlike forward contracts, are only available in a limited range of major currencies and for only a restricted forward time period.

FOREIGN EXCHANGE OPTIONS CONTRACTS

We can now turn to look at a final foreign exchange hedging instrument: foreign exchange option contracts. In doing so, we will build on our knowledge of option valuation from Chapter 13.

As has already been pointed out, futures and forward contracts hedge the company against both adverse *and* favourable movements in exchange rates. It is in this respect that foreign currency options differ. A currency option can be used to hedge the company against an adverse movement in exchange rates whilst, at the same time, allowing the company to take advantage of a *favourable* movement in exchange rates.

Because of this advantage, hedging with options is *more expensive* than hedging with either futures or forward contracts. Consequently, companies will tend to hedge with futures/forward contracts if they are confident of an adverse movement in exchange rates, because this would be the cheapest way of hedging. However, if exchange rates are simply volatile and it is thought that the rate movement could just as easily be favourable as adverse, then companies *may* choose to use options to hedge – even though the cost is greater – so as to be able to take advantage of a possible favourable exchange rate movement, should one occur.

Options differ from forward and futures contracts in that, with a forward contract, the agreed exchange of currencies *must* take place; similarly, a company *must* close out its futures position. However, with an option contract, the company has a *choice* (or *option*): either it can exchange currencies as agreed (that is, it is said to '*exercise*' the option) or it can simply walk away from the whole arrangement if it is better off so doing (that is, it allows the option to '*lapse*'). Example 4 demonstrates the simple ideas behind the use of currency option contracts (which can be found on most currency futures exchanges, such as Euronext).

EXAMPLE 4

Synthélabo is a small French biotechnology company. It is due to pay US\$2.4 million in 3-months' time in patent licence permissions. In order to hedge its foreign exchange risk, it has bought a USD/EUR option contract to buy US\$2.4 million in 3-months' time at a EUR/USD exchange rate of: 0.7300.

If, in 3-months' time, spot EUR/USD is 0.7350, the company will choose to *exercise* the option and buy US\$2.4 million through the option contract at an exchange rate of only 0.7300. To do so costs: US\$2.4 million × 0.7300 = €1 752 000; whereas to buy US\$2.4 million spot would cost US\$2.4 million × 0.7350 = €1 764 000. A saving of €12 000. However, if in 3-months' time EUR/USD spot was 0.7220, the company would choose to allow the option to *lapse* and instead, buy US\$2.4 million on the spot market at a cost of only: US\$2.4 million × 0.7220 = €1 732 800. A saving of €19 200 over the cost of exercising the option.

Thus, in the first scenario, the company was *protected* against the *adverse* movement in exchange rates, while in the second scenario, the company was able to take *advantage* of the *favourable* movement in exchange rates. What the option was effectively doing was fixing the *maximum* euro cost of buying the required US\$2.4 million at €1 752 000. If the US\$2.4 million could have been bought at a *lower* cost on the spot market, then the company was allowed to walk away from the option contract.

Over-the-counter options

There are two basic types of foreign exchange option contract: *OTC* (over-the-counter), options and *traded* currency options. These are analogous to the *tailor-made* forward contracts and the *standardized* futures contracts, respectively.

Just as the banks operate the foreign exchange forward markets, they also deal in OTC currency options. These OTC options are available for any amount of money, in virtually any currency and for virtually any time period forward. Thus the OTC option contract is tailor-made to the firm's precise requirements. An illustration of a tailor-made OTC option is shown in Example 5.

EXAMPLE 5

Suppose a Spanish exporter invoices a UK customer for £1 350 000 on 3-months' credit. The 3 month EUR/GBP forward rate is 1.2150 – 1.2190. Thus the Spanish exporter could hedge by selling the £1 350 000 million 3 months forward and, as a result, the company would receive £1 350 000 × 1.2150 = €1 640 250 in 3-months' time, whatever happens to the EUR/GBP exchange rate in the meantime.

▶

▶

Alternatively, the Spanish exporter could hedge their exposure to foreign exchange risk by buying an OTC option to sell £1 350 000 3 months forward at, say, €1.2150. Then, in 3-months' time, if EUR/GBP spot is *below* €1.2150, say €1.2100, they will choose to exercise the option to sell the pounds for: £1 350 000 × 1.2150 = €1 640 250. However, if the EUR/GBP spot is *above* €1.2150, say €1.2200 then they will allow the option to *lapse* and sell the £1 350 000 on the spot market to yield, in this example, £1 350 000 × 1.2200 = €1 647 000.

Therefore the option protects the exporter from an *adverse* movement in the EUR/GBP exchange rate over the next 3 months, but allows it to take advantage of any *favourable* movement.

Traded currency options

Traded currency option contracts[5] are, in many ways, similar to futures contracts. They are available from Euronext (futures markets usually deal in option contracts as well as futures) in a limited range of currencies, with a standard amount of money per contract. For example, USD/EUR options have a contract size of €10 000. They are priced in US dollars per €100, the tick size is US$0.01 and so the tick value is US$1 per contract.

Just as with futures, traded currency options are normally issued on a 3-month cycle – typically March, June, September and December – with three contract dates available at any one time. Thus, in February, you could deal in March, June or September contracts. Once the March contracts expire (at the end of March), a new series of contracts, for December, will be created.

Calls and put

As we know, there are two basic types of options: 'call' options and 'put' options. A currency call option is an option to buy a particular currency and a currency put option is an option to sell a particular currency.

Option contracts, for hedging purposes, are *only* bought. But, a company can either buy call options (options to buy a particular currency), or it can buy put options (options to sell a particular currency). Therefore if a company bought a USD/EUR *put* option they would be buying a contract to *sell* €10 000 in exchange for US dollars. Similarly, if they bought a USD/EUR *call*, they would be buying a contract to *buy* €10 000 in exchange for US dollars.

Exercise price

Finally, the financial manager is usually faced with a choice of a range of different exchange rates (the 'exercise' or 'strike' price) with traded currency options. Typically, one is approximately equal to the spot rate, some a little below and others a little above.

Suppose a Portuguese exporter was due to receive US dollars in April. June EUR/USD option contracts (as with futures, we would usually hedge with the contracts with the *next* expiry date after we were due to receive payment) are available at the following USD/EUR exchange rates (Remember that the contracts are priced in US dollars per €100.): US$136, US$138 and US$140. How is the exporter to decide on the choice of option exchange rate?

Obviously an exchange rate of €100 = US$136 is more attractive to the exporter (who is due to receive US dollars), than an exchange rate at €100 = US$140, because at USD/EUR: 136 they are ensuring that they will receive a *greater minimum amount* of euros than they will receive at USD/EUR: 140. However, there is a cost trade-off problem here. As we shall see, the *more favourable* is the option exchange rate (the option exercise price), the *more expensive* is the option cost and vice versa.

Therefore the decision about what exchange rate the option should be taken at is a matter of managerial judgement. If the management believe that there is a strong possibility of a significant *adverse* movement in the spot rates, then they may judge that it is worth the higher cost to ensure a higher minimum euro outcome. On the other hand, if management feel that a *favourable* movement in exchange rates is the most likely outcome (but they still want to hedge the risk that their expectations may be wrong) then they may decide to select the less favourable – and hence cheaper – option exchange rate.

SETTING UP AN OPTION HEDGE

We will now make use of an illustration. This is given in Example 6.

EXAMPLE 6

Suppose it is June. Ruhrberger AG is a German manufacturer of concrete pumps. The company has invoiced Dubai Noor LLC, an overseas customer, for US$240 000, payable on 31 December. Data are as follows:

Current EUR/USD spot   0.7280 – 0.7320

December EUR/USD option contracts (contract size €10 000, pricing USD/€100):

| | December options | |
Exercise price	Calls	Puts
US$136	3.60	1.24
US$138	2.25	4.44
US$140	1.20	7.30

Premiums in US cents/€

Suppose Ruhrberger wishes to hedge its foreign exchange risk exposure using traded options with an exercise price of US$138 = €100 so as to ensure a minimum euro receipt from the export deal of: US$240 000 ÷ 1.38 = €173 913.

Number of contracts

The first task is to decide how many options need to be bought in order to hedge the US$240 000. The contract size is €10 000 and so we first need to convert the dollar invoiced amount into euros at the exchange rate given by the exercise price chosen:

$$US\$240\ 000 \div 1.38 = €173\ 913 \div €10\ 000 = 17.4 \text{ contracts}$$

As we can only deal in whole contracts, we would normally round this to the nearest whole number of contracts – 17 USD/EUR option contracts (and so, in this case, leave the US dollars very slightly under-hedged).

▶

▶

Calls or puts?

The next task is to decide whether Ruhrberger needs to buy USD/EUR call options or put options in order to hedge its foreign exchange risk exposure. The rule used is similar to that used with futures contracts: look to see what the company wishes to do to the 'currency of the contract size' in the cash market. In this example, the currency of the contract size is *euros* and in the cash market the firm will be receiving US$240 000 which it will wish to sell in order to buy euros. Therefore, in the cash market the firm will want to *buy* euros and so it hedges its foreign exchange risk by buying options to buy euros: call options. Therefore Ruhrberger will buy 17 USD/EUR December call option contracts at an exercise price of US$138.

Contract cost

Finally, what is the cost of these option contracts? The cost is given by the option 'premium' data given in the table above. December USD/EUR calls at an exercise price of US$138 cost 2.25 US cents per euro of option value. Therefore the total cost of the 17 option contracts can be calculated as:

$$17 \times €10\ 000 = €170\ 000 \times 2.25¢ = US\$3825$$

This cost will be payable immediately, at a euro spot cost of: US$3825 × 0.7320 = €2800.

The operation of the hedge

The next stage of the example is to see the effect of Ruhrberger's hedged position.

Suppose that on 31 December, when the company receives the US$240 000 from Dubai Noor, the following is the situation in the foreign exchange markets:

Scenario A: EUR/USD spot   0.7455 − 0.7495
Scenario B: EUR/USD spot   0.7010 − 0.7050

Scenario A:

Ruhrberger faces a choice. It can either sell its US$240 000 through the exercise of the options at an exchange rate of USD1.38 = €1 or it can allow the options to lapse and sell the $240 000 on the spot market at an exchange rate of €0.7455 = US$1. This can be seen as follows:

Exercise the options   US$240 000 ÷ 1.38 = €173 913
Spot sale   US$240 000 × 0.7455 = €178 920

Obviously, as the spot rate has moved favourably, the best course of action is for Ruhrberger to sell the US dollars spot, as this gives a more favourable rate of exchange, and so allow the options to lapse, yielding a euro outcome of €178 920 from the export trade.

Scenario B:

Again, Ruhrberger has a choice of either exercising the options at an exchange rate of US$1.38 = €1 or allowing the options to lapse and selling the US dollar spot at an exchange rate of €0.7010 = US$1.

In this scenario, *exercise of the options* provides the company with a more favourable exchange rate than that obtainable from a spot rate of exchange:

Exercise the options   US$240 000 ÷ 1.38 = €173 913
Spot sale   US$240 000 × 0.7010 = €168 240

The 17 USD/EUR call options with an exercise price of US$1.38 give Ruhrberger the right to buy (call): 17 × €10 000 = €170 000 in exchange for US dollars at an exchange rate of US$1.38 = €1.

▶

Therefore, in order to exercise the options, the company will have to pay over: €170 000 × 1.38 = US$234 600 out of the proceeds of the export trade. The balance of the US dollars: US$240 000 – US$234 600 = US$5,400 will be sold by Ruhrberger, at spot, for: US$5400 × 0.7010 = €3785.40.

Therefore the net outcome of exercising the options is as follows:

Euro receipt from the exercise of the options	€170 000
plus euro receipt from the spot sale of the surplus dollars	€3 785.40
Total euro receipt	€173 785.40

This total euro receipt figure could be compared with the euro receipt from the spot sale of $240 000:

$$US\$240\ 000 \times 0.7010 = €168\ 240$$

Therefore, in Scenario B we have an example where the options are exercised so as to protect the company from the adverse movement in the EUR/USD spot exchange rate, away from the option exercise price of US$138 (or US$1.38 = €1).

An importer case

The previous example used an exporting scenario. Let us now consider the case of an importer, which is illustrated in Example 7.

EXAMPLE 7

Roccade NV is a technology solutions company based in the Netherlands. The company has been supplied with CAD assistance from a specialist UK computer design company. Roccade has now been invoiced for £478 000 payable in 5-months' time, on 30 June.

Current EUR/GBP spot   1.2230 – 1.22500

June GBP/EUR option contracts: (contract size £10 000, pricing euros per £100)

	June options	
Exercise price	Calls	Puts
€120	2.15	1.12
€122	1.10	2.05
€124	0.25	3.20

Premiums in euro cents/£

The company is concerned that exchange rates might move adversely over the next few months and so decides to hedge using options with an exercise price of €1.20.

Number of contracts

£478 000 ÷ £10 000 = 47.8 rounded to 48 contracts.

▶

Calls or puts?

In the cash market, the company will need to buy pounds (and thus sell euros), in order to pay the invoice. Thus, in order to hedge they will want the option to buy pounds: calls.

Hedge

To hedge the company will buy 48 June GBP/EUR call options at an exercise price of €120 (equivalent to an exchange rate of €1.20 = £1).

Premium cost

$$48 \times £10\ 000 = £480\ 000 \text{ at } 2.15c \text{ per } £ = €10\ 320$$

On 30 June

Let us assume that on 30 June the EUR/GBP spot rate is now 1.2505 − 1.2525. The company faces a choice: should it buy the pounds on the spot market, or through the exercise of the options?

As the spot rate for buying pounds is €1.2525 = £1, and the option exercise price is €1.20 = £1 (i.e. €120 × £100), it will obviously be cheaper to pay the invoice through the exercise of the options. Therefore Roccade will exercise its 48 June call options, as follows: Exercise the options to buy 48 × £10 000 = £480 000 at a cost of £480 000 × 1.20 = €576 000. These pounds can then be used to pay off the £478 000 invoice and the £2 000 balance can be sold at spot to give: £2 000 ÷ 1.2505 = €1600. As a result the net cost of paying the £478 000 invoice is: €576 000 − €1600 = €574 400. This can then be compared to the cost of allowing the options to lapse and buying the entire £478 000 required at spot: £478 000 ×1.2525 = €598 695. This represents a saving to the company of: €598 695 − €574 400 = €24 295.

An important variation

In both of the examples above, Ruhrberger AG and Roccade NV, the foreign exchange was due to be received or paid on the day that the options were due to expire. However, this type of situation is a very special case and the analysis would be slightly different if, for example, Roccade had to pay the £478 000 on a date before 30 June (say 1 June).

Options are a little like an insurance policy. Thus June GBP/EUR calls with an exercise price of €120 ensure that the company will be able to buy a specific quantity of pounds at an exchange rate that will not be worse than €1.20 = £1. If the spot market provides a better exchange rate, the spot market can be used instead, if it provides a worse exchange rate, the options are exercised. So the choice faced by Roccade on 30 June was to buy £478 000 either on the spot market or by exercising the options at €120 (per £100). In the example, it turned out to be better to exercise the options. Had circumstances been different and the spot rate had been advantageous, the options would not have been exercised and they would have been discarded as worthless.

However, what would have happened if the £478 000 was due on 1 June and on that day Roccade could get a *better* exchange rate on the spot market than the options' exercise exchange rate of €1.20 = £1? Although the options would then not be exercised on 1 June, they would not be worthless and would *not* be simply discarded. The June options still have a month to run and, as a result, they will always have some value. Therefore they could be sold on to another investor (or even kept as a speculative investment in case it should turn out to be worthwhile exercising it at a later date).

Thus the choice facing Roccade on 1 June is not simply to exercise the options or let them lapse. It is rather:

1. buy the pounds through exercise of the options

2. buy the pounds at spot and sell on the options.

Suppose we return to Example 7 and the case of Roccade NV, but now on the assumption that the invoice is going to be paid on 1 June. The 48 June call options in the original example would still have been purchased. Then, on 1 June suppose we find:

EUR/GBP spot   1.1775 − 1.1815

June GBP/EUR option contracts: (contract size £10 000, pricing euros per £100)

	June options	
Exercise price	Calls	Puts
€120	0.95	0.62
€122	0.32	1.04
€124	0.18	1.88
Premiums in euro cents/£		

The company holds 48 options that relate to: $48 \times £10\ 000 = £480\ 000$. These are call options with an exercise price of €1.20. This gives the company the right to buy £480 000 at a cost of: $£480\ 000 \times 1.20 = €576\ 000$. Of the £480 000, £478 000 is required to pay off the invoice and the surplus of £2000 can be sold at spot to give: $£2000 \times 1.1875 = €2375$.

Thus the result of exercising the option is:

Cost of exercise	€576 000
less euro receipt from sale of surplus pounds	(€2 375)
Total net cost	€573 625

The alternative would be to buy the £478 000 at spot and sell on the unexercised options.

The cost of buying the £478 000 at spot would be $£478\ 000 \times 1.1915 = €569\ 537$. The receipt from the sale of the unexercised options would be: 48 options $\times £10\ 000 \times 0.95c = €4560$. As a result:

Cost of the spot purchase of pounds	€ 569 537
less receipt from the option sale	(€ 560)
Net cost	€ 564 977

Thus, in this case, it is better to buy the required £478 000 at spot and sell on the unexercised options, than it is to exercise the options.

EARLY EXERCISE

We noted above that, in circumstances where foreign exchange is due to be paid or received on a date *before* the option's expiry date, there were the following alternatives open to the company:

1. exercise the options
2. use the spot market and sell on the unexercised options.

In practice we will find that under normal circumstances, alternative 2 will *always* produce a better outcome than alternative 1. The reason for this arises out of a conclusion that we reached in Chapter 13 when looking at the valuation of options. The conclusion was that, under normal circumstances, options would never be exercised *before* their expiry date. The reason being that such options would be more valuable if sold on unexercised (whereby both the intrinsic value and the time value would be received) rather than exercised (where only their intrinsic value would be received).

CONTINGENT EXPOSURE TO FOREIGN EXCHANGE RISK

Importers and exporters use foreign exchange options as an alternative to hedging with either forward or future contracts, even though to do so incurs greater costs – the option premiums payable – in order to be able to take advantage of any favourable movement in exchange rates that might occur. However, there is one set of circumstances where using options is the *only* feasible hedging method and futures and forward market hedges are inappropriate. This occurs when a company has a *contingent* exposure to foreign exchange risk.

Suppose a German civil engineering contractor is bidding to undertake an overseas contract. The bid (and payment) must be made in US dollars and be submitted by, say, 1 March. The winning bid will be awarded the contract on, say, 1 June with payment being made on completion of the contract on 1 September.

If the German company decides it is willing to undertake the contract for payment of €5 million and given that the spot EUR/USD rate on 1 March is 0.7245, it enters a bid of: €5m ÷ 0.7245 = US$6.9 million.

The problem that the company faces is that as soon as it makes its bid to undertake the contract for a payment of US$6.9 million it is exposed to the risk of an adverse movement in exchange rates between 1 March and 1 September, when payment would be eventually received. However, the company cannot simply hedge its foreign exchange risk by selling US$6.9 million forward to 1 September (or by using the futures market), because with such contracts exchange of currencies *must* take place, (or the futures position closed out). The company may not end up winning the contract and so will not receive the US$6.9 million it would have contracted to sell forward on 1 September. This is because its exposure to foreign exchange risk on 1 March is *contingent* on another event occurring: it is contingent on winning the contract.

In such circumstances, an option hedge is ideal. On 1 March the company could buy an option to sell US$6.9 million forward to 1 September at an exercise price of €0.7245 = US$1. Then, if it won the contract it would be assured of receiving at least: US$6.9m × 0.7245 = €5 million. If it lost the contract and the EUR/USD rate is no better than 0.7245 on the option's expiry date, then it could simply allow its option to lapse.

Therefore it is in the face of *contingent* exposures to foreign exchange risk that we are more likely to see companies hedging through the options market.

TRADED OPTIONS VERSUS OTC OPTIONS

To complete our look at foreign exchange options, we will contrast the advantages and disadvantages of traded versus OTC options.

There are seven specific points to be made:

1. OTC options are available in a wide range of currencies, while traded currency options are only available in a narrow range of major trading currencies and a very few 'emerging market' currencies.

2. OTC options are available in 'cross currencies' (e.g. ZAR/JPY), while trade options are usually only available in currencies against the US$.

3. OTC options are available for any exercise date up to 1 year forward (or even longer). Traded options do not usually extend more than 9 months forward.

4. OTC option prices/'premiums' are determined by the bank which sells them, whereas traded option premiums are market determined (and so are non-negotiable). This means that a large company may be able to use its financial strength to negotiate a more favourable deal on OTC options. Conversely, small companies may find that they get a more favourable premium quoted on the traded market where their lack of financial muscle does not affect the cost of the deal.

5. OTC options may be more suitable for very large transactions which may be more difficult to arrange on a traded option exchange because of the danger of such a large single 'trade' moving the market price.

6. The banking system which deals in OTC options is a global, 24-hour, 365 days a year market which is never closed. Traded option markets have only very limited facilities for trading 'out of hours' (e.g. evenings, weekends and public holidays).

7. Traded options are freely marketable because of their uniform/standardized nature and so are liquid. In contrast, OTC options are not readily saleable and hence are essentially illiquid securities.

SUMMARY

- There are three 'types' of foreign exchange risk: transaction risk; translation risk; and economic risk. The focus of this chapter is on transaction risk – the risk to which importers and exporters are exposed.

- Many exporters try to avoid exposure to foreign exchange risk by invoicing in their own currency. However, this simply transfers the foreign exchange risk to the customer. In competitive export markets customers are unlikely to be willing to have the risk exposure imposed upon them in this way and will demand that they be invoiced in their own currency, not the currency of the exporter.

- Other exporters, although exposed to foreign exchange risk, undertake no hedging and so leave their exposure open. In many circumstances this action is unwise as exchange rates can move significantly over short time periods and so turn a potentially profitable export sale into a loss-making sale.

- The basic hedging technique is netting, where assets and liabilities in the same currency and with the same maturity can be offset against each other.

- Another hedging technique which is very widely used is to forward market hedge, where foreign currency is bought or sold forward in time, thus locking the company into a specific rate of exchange and so avoiding the uncertainty of a possible adverse movement in exchange rates.

- A money market hedge achieves the same effect as a forward market hedge, but involves the creation of a matching foreign currency asset or liability. The nature of this hedging technique is such that it is only likely to be used if a forward market hedge is not available (because there is no forward market or its depth forward is insufficient).

- Forward market and money market hedges are tailor-made to the precise requirements of the company suffering the foreign exchange exposure. In contrast, a futures market hedge provides standardized hedging contracts which, while providing roughly the same hedge effect as either a forward or money market hedge, will not provide the company with 100% hedge efficiency.

- Finally, foreign exchange risk can be hedged through the use of foreign currency options. The key difference that exists between options and all other hedging devices is that options protect the firm from an *adverse* movement in interest rates, while allowing advantage to be taken of *favourable* movements. All other hedging techniques lock the firm into a specific exchange rate and so hedge against both adverse and favourable foreign exchange movements.

NOTES

1. As we have seen in Chapter 14, when discussing interest rate risk management.
2. Once again, futures contracts were first encountered in our discussion on interest rate risk in Chapter 14.
3. In reality the tick size on the Euronext market is €0.01 because futures prices are quoted as 'euros per US$100'. Thus one USD/EUR contract at €72 is worth: US$20 000 × €72/100 = €14 400. If the price changes to €72.01, then the contract value changes by €2: US$20 000 × €72.01/100 = €14 402.
4. Notice how the hedge efficiency is calculated. If the profit is greater than the loss, the hedge efficiency is greater than 100%. If the profit is less than the loss, the hedge efficiency is less than 100%.
5. Of course options have been encountered before in Chapters 13 and 14.

FURTHER READING

1. Both books referred to as further reading for Chapter 25 – Buckley (1992) and Eiteman, Stonehill and Moffett (1992) – contain good coverage of foreign exchange risk.
2. Two good articles are D.P. Walker, 'What is Foreign Exchange Risk?', *Managerial Finance*, Summer 1982; and P.A. Beck and M. Glaum, 'The Management of Foreign Exchange Risk in UK Multinationals', *Accounting and Business Research*, Winter 1990.
3. Finally, for an interesting overview and discussion of corporate hedging see B.W. Nocco and R.M. Stulz, 'Enterprise Risk Management: Theory and Practice', *Journal of Applied Corporate Finance*, Fall 2006; K. Aretz and S.M. Bartram, 'Corporate Hedging and Shareholder Value', *Journal of Financial Research*, 33, 2010 and S. Bartram, G. Brown and F. Fehle, 'International Evidence of Financial Derivative Usage', *Social Science Research Network*, October 2006.

QUIZ QUESTIONS

1 What determines spot exchange rates?

2 How does the IRPT determine forward rates?

3 Why are forward rates not good predictors of future spot rates?

4

EUR/CAD spot	0.6535 − 0.6545
3 months forward	0.6500 − 0.6512
3-month money market interest rates	C$: 4.0% per year
	€: 2.0% per year

A Spanish company exports goods to the USA and invoices its customer for US$100 000 on 3-months' credit.

(a) Undertake a forward market hedge.

(b) Undertake a money market hedge.

(c) Which hedge is best?

5 A South African company has put in a bid for a contract in the USA. In order to hedge the foreign exchange risk exposure they have bought an OTC put option in respect of US$100 000, 6 months forward at an exercise price of ZAR/USD: R10.41. What action will they take in 6-months' time, if:

(a) They win the contract and:

   (i) ZAR/USD spot is R11.25?

   (ii) ZAR/USD spot is R 9.25?

(b) They lose the contract and:

   (i) ZAR/USD spot is R11.25?

   (ii) ZAR/USD spot is R9.25?

6 EUR/USD 5-month forward rate 0.7285, 6-month forward rate 0.7298. A German company wishes to hedge via a 5- to 6-months time option forward US dollar sale contract. What will be the contract's exchange rate?

7 What advantages do OTC options have over traded currency options?

8 An Italian company exports goods to the USA and invoices its customer for US$526 000 payable in August. It is now June.

Spot EUR/USD   0.7320 − 0.7345

September USD/EUR futures contracts are priced at €73.55 (per US$100). The contract size is US$20 000.

Required:

(a) Set up the futures hedge.

(b) Calculate the hedge efficiency if, in August:

Spot EUR/USD   0.7210 − 0.7228

9 A Greek company imports goods from the USA and is invoiced for US$297 500 payable in October.

EUR/USD spot rate   0.7280 – 0.7300

October forward   0.7320 – 0.7345

(a) Show how a forward market hedge would be carried out.

(b) Show how a futures market hedge would be carried out. (One USD/EUR futures contract represents US$20 000 and December sterling futures are priced at €73.15 per US$100.)

(c) What would be the result if the futures market hedge in EUR/USD spot turned out to be 0.7335 − 0.7360 in October, and December USD/EUR futures were priced at €73.55?

(See the 'Answers to Quiz Questions' section at the back of the book.)

PROBLEMS

The answers to the following problems are available to students online.

1   Fiddécreme is a medium-sized French electronics company with export and import trade with the USA. The following transactions are due within the next 6 months. Transactions are in the currency specified.

   (i)   Purchases of semiconductor components, cash payment due in 3 months: €116 000.

   (ii)   Sale of application-specific integrated circuits (ASIC), cash receipt due in 3 months: US$197 000.

   (iii) Purchase of digital signal processors for resale, cash payment due in 6 months: US $447 000.

   (iv)   Sale of ASICs, cash receipt due in 6 months: US$154 000.

Exchange rates (Euronext market)

	EUR/USD
Spot	0.7230 – 0.7248
3 months forward	0.0082 – 0.0088 discount
6 months forward	0.0115 – 0.0122 discount
Money market interest rates	
Euros: 3.5% per year.	
US dollars: 2.5% per year	

USD/EUR option (Euronext market) (Prices are US$ per €100, contract size €10 000)

Exercise price	March calls	March puts	June calls	June puts
US$138	2.25	4.44	3.16	4.90

Assume that it is now the end of December, with 3 months to expiry of the March contracts.

Required

   (i)   Calculate the net euro receipts/payments that Fiddécreme might expect for both its 3- and 6-month transactions if the company hedges foreign exchange risk on:
   1.   the forward foreign exchange market
   2.   the money market.

   (ii)   If the actual spot rate in 6-months' time was with hindsight exactly the present 6-months forward rate, calculate whether Fiddécreme would have been better to hedge through foreign currency options rather than the forward market or money market.

   (iii) Explain briefly what you consider to be the main advantage of foreign currency options.

2   Böhlor GmbH is a medium-sized coffee producer company, based in Vienna. It is now 1 December and the following transactions have been contractually agreed:

   (i)   Sale of ground coffee, cash receipt due 1 February of US$197 000.
   (ii)   Purchase of production equipment, invoice payable 1 May, for US$447 000.
   (iii) Sale of ground coffee, US$154 000 cash receipt due 1 May.

▶

EUR/USD exchange rates

Spot   0.7280 − 0.7320
Forward 1 February   0.7310 − 0.7355
Forward 1May   0.7340 − 0.7395

EUR/USD futures prices (contract size US$20 000, pricing euros per US$100)

March contracts   73.25
June contracts   73.85

Money market interest rates

Euros   4% per annum
US dollars   5% per annum

Required:

(a) Hedge Böhlor's foreign exchange risk exposure on the forward markets.

(b) Hedge Böhlor's foreign exchange risk exposure on the money markets.

(c) Compare the forward market hedge outcome to that of the money market hedge.

(d) Calculate the hedge efficiency that Böhlor could achieve on its foreign exchange risk exposure using a futures market hedge, if:

    (i)

    1 February spot EUR/USD   0.7350 − 0.7390

    March EUR/USD futures contracts   €74.00

    (ii)

    1 May spot EUR/USD   0.7295 − 0.7335

    June EUR/USD futures contracts   €73.00

FOREIGN DIRECT INVESTMENT

INTRODUCTION

Domestic versus foreign projects

The appraisal of capital investments in foreign countries involves several difficulties not present in domestic project appraisal. Principal among these difficulties are the following:

1. Exchange rates fluctuate over time, in an essentially unpredictable way. Therefore a foreign investment's cash flows are exposed to the risk of adverse foreign exchange movements.

2. There are a variety of ways in which a foreign government (the 'host' government) might take action which adversely discriminates against investments owned by a foreign company, *after* the investment has been undertaken. Such actions might range from the imposition of a penal rate of taxation, and/or restrictions on the remittance of project net cash flows back to the parent, to confiscation of the project's assets without compensation. These possibilities are referred to as 'country risk'.

3. There is the problem of correctly evaluating the systematic risk and expected rate of return on the project within an international, rather than domestic, context.

4. Finally, there is the problem of the correct project appraisal procedure. In particular, should the analysis be undertaken from the viewpoint of the project itself, or from the viewpoint of the parent company? This problem arises because of differences that can occur between a project's net cash flows, and a project's net cash flows that are available for repatriation back to the parent company.

This chapter examines these difficulties and the way in which they might be overcome. It builds on the previous two chapters which looked at the foreign exchange markets and the way that management can hedge foreign exchange risk.

The basic approach

A capital investment project in a foreign country generates a stream of net cash flows in the currency of its host country. How is the parent company to evaluate those cash flows in an NPV analysis? We can formulate two possible approaches to the problem which should provide exactly the same expected result.

Using as an example a UK company investing in the USA, the two alternative approaches are:

1. The project's US dollar cash flows are discounted at the dollar discount rate to generate a US$ NPV. This can then be converted at the GBP/USD spot rate to give an NPV denominated in pounds – the currency of the project's parent company.

2. The project's US dollar cash flows are converted to pound cash flows. These pound cash flows are then discounted at the pound discount rate to generate an NPV in pounds.

Notice how each approach starts off at exactly the same point (the project's US dollar cash flows), and ends up at exactly the same point (the NPV in UK pounds). Both approaches are illustrated in Example 1.

As both approaches provide exactly the same results, given our estimates and given that the IRPT holds, which approach should be used in practice is likely to depend on what information is available, and how difficult it might be to forecast the information that may *not* be available. Generally, it may be assumed that management might be more cautious about forecasting future exchange rates than they would be about forecasting the required US dollar rate of return (i.e. discount rate). Therefore Approach 1 may be the more likely one to be found in practice. There is, however, a lack of empirical evidence on the matter.

EXAMPLE 1

Cracker plc is a UK-based engineering company. It is considering undertaking an investment project in the USA, which has a cost of US$10 million and an expected life of 3 years. The investment would be financed out of the company's internal financial resources. The project cash flows are expected to be as follows:

Year	($m)
0	−10
1	+5
2	+6
3	+4

▶

▶

The GBP/USD spot rate is 0.6000 and the US dollar is expected to depreciate against the pound by 4% per year. A similar risk UK-based project would be expected to earn a minimum return of 20%.

Initial evaluation:

Adapting the IRPT, the project's dollar discount rate can be estimated:
GBP/USD IRPT:

$$\frac{\text{UK interest} - \text{US interest}}{1 + \text{US interest}} = \% \text{ change in US\$ dollar exchange rate}$$

Adapting the IRPT to find the US$ discount rate for the US project:

$$\frac{\text{UK discount rate} - \text{US\$ discount rate}}{1 + \text{US\$ discount rate}} = \% \text{ change in US\$ dollar exchange rate}$$

$$\frac{0.20 - \text{US\$ discount rate}}{1 + \text{US\$ discount rate}} = -0.04 \, (4\% \text{depreciation in US\$})$$

$$0.20 - \text{US\$ discount rate} = -0.04 \times (1 + \text{US\$ discount rate})$$

$$0.20 - \text{US\$ discount rate} = -0.04 - 0.04 \times \text{US\$ discount rate}$$

$$0.20 + 0.04 = 0.96 \times \text{US\$ discount rate}$$

$$\text{US\$ discount rate} = \frac{0.24}{0.96} = 0.25 \text{ or } 25\%$$

The future expected GBR/USD spot rates for Years 1 to 3 can also be estimated by adapting the IRPT: Given the IRPT:

$$\frac{1 + \text{ Home currency interest rate}}{1 + \text{ Foreign currency interest rate}} = \frac{\text{Forward exchange rate}}{\text{Spot exchange rate}}$$

This can be rearranged and adapted to give an estimate of the future spot rates:

$$\frac{1 + \text{ UK discount rate}}{1 + \text{ US discount rate}} \times \text{Spot GBP/USD} = \text{Estimated future GBP/USD spot rate}$$

and so:

$$\frac{1 + 0.20}{1 + 0.25} \times 0.6000 = 0.5760 \text{ Year 1 estimated spot rate}$$

$$\frac{1 + 0.20}{1 + 0.25} \times 0.5760 = 0.5530 \text{ Year 2 estimated spot rate}$$

$$\frac{1 + 0.20}{1 + 0.25} \times 0.5530 = 0.5308 \text{ Year 3 estimated spot rate}$$

▶

Approach 1 (US$ cash flows and US$ discount rate):

Year	US$m	×	25% discount factor		US$m present value cash flow
0	−10	×	1.0000	=	−6.0
1	+5	×	0.8000	=	+4
2	+6	×	0.6400	=	+3.84
3	+4	×	0.5120	=	+2.048

NPV: −US$0.112 × 0.6000 = **−£0.07m NPV**

Approach 2 (US$ converted to £ and discounted by UK discount rate):

Year	US$m	×	GBP/USD	=	£m	×	20% discount factor		£ present value cash flow
0	−10	×	0.6000	=	−6.0	×	1.0000	=	−6.0
1	+5	×	0.5760	=	+2.88	×	0.8333	=	+2.4
2	+6	×	0.5530	=	+3.318	×	0.6944	=	+2.3
3	+4	×	0.5120	=	+2.123	×	0.5787	=	+1.23

NPV: **−£0.07m**

REAL WORLD VIEW: Opening Up the Saudi Market

The Tadawul, Saudi Arabia's Stock Exchange, is not only the largest but also the most liquid market of the Arab World. Daily trading totals around £787 million, while its market capitalization of over £250 billion is greater than that of Thailand. In March 2014, strong performers included the Saudi Paper Manufacturing Co. and the National Agricultural Marketing Co. (Thimar), with shares rising notably.

It is easy to see how this lucrative market would be attractive to international traders, yet traditional barriers have made it difficult for Western investors, and particularly individuals, to enter. Firstly, Saudi trading practice has necessitated involvement of intermediary parties or participation in member trading firms to make deals, in addition to mutual funds, equity swaps and exchange-traded funds (ETF), leading to greater commission costs. Furthermore, differences in standards and regulations compared to Western markets have also stalled external participation in the past.

However, as commentators have noted, in recent years several notable developments have acted to open up the Tadawul to foreign traders. These began in February 2013, when the Capital Market Authority (the governing body) appointed a new head in Mohammed Bin Abdulmalik Al Sheikh, formerly of the World Bank. This was followed by plans to confirm a regulatory structure to allow foreign stock owners in and to issue credit ratings for domestic companies. Another major step was the introduction of a weekend from Friday to Saturday, in place of the 3-day closure previously in operation. All these changes, along with others, represent a concerted effort to correlate the stock exchange with the Gulf Cooperation Council markets and, indeed, broader international trading standards.

Commentators have speculated that these moves are an attempt to stay competitive against other markets in the region, notably the UAE, Qatar and Kuwait. The recent promotion of the UAE and Qatar to 'emerging markets' potentially brings considerable foreign investment which Saudi Arabia may seek to emulate.

PROJECT CASH FLOWS

Whichever approach to the appraisal of overseas projects is used, both take as their starting point the project's net cash flows denominated in the host country's currency. It is here that some controversy is found.

The point of dispute is whether the project's net cash flows should be viewed from the standpoint of the project itself, or from the standpoint of the parent. In other words should the year-by-year net operating cash flows of the project be evaluated, or should the project's net cash flows that are available to be remitted back to the parent, be evaluated?

With foreign country projects these two cash flows can often differ significantly, because of host country restrictions on the repatriation of project net cash flows. Example 2 shows how crucial the difference might be.

EXAMPLE 2

Belgatek SA is a medium-sized Belgian mobile telecoms company. The company is considering a capital investment project in a small southern African country, whose currency is the South African rand. The telecom investment's net cash flows – in rand – are:

Year	Rm
0	−10
1	+8
2	+4
3	+3.5

At the current EUR/ZAR spot rate of 0.0670, the project will require an outlay of €670 000 which the company will finance out of its own internal financial resources. Given the systematic risk involved, it is thought that 20% is a suitable required rate of return in rand terms.

The southern African country's laws permit foreign projects to remit back to their parents a maximum annual cash flow equal to 10% of the project's cost. Any surplus (or blocked) cash flows have to be placed on special government deposit at an interest rate of 5%. All blocked funds can be remitted back to the foreign parent company at the end of the project's life.

From the viewpoint of **the project**, it produces a *positive* NPV and so is acceptable:

Year	Rm	×	20% discount rate		Present value cash flow
0	−10	×	1	=	−10
1	+8	×	0.8333	=	+6.67
2	+4	×	0.6944	=	+2.78
3	+3.5	×	0.5787	=	+2.02
					R+1.47m NPV

$$+ \text{R1.47m} \times 0.0670 = \text{€98 490 NPV}$$

▶

However, from the viewpoint of Belgatek – **the parent company** – the project is undesirable, as it has a *negative* NPV:

Year	1	2	3
Project cash flow	8	4	3.5
Blocked funds	—	7	10.35
Interest on blocked funds	—	0.35	0.52
Total cash flow	+8	11.35	14.37
less Repatriated cash flow	1	1	14.37
Blocked funds	+7	+10.35	—

Year	Rm	×	20% discount rate		Present value cash flow
0	−10	×	1	=	−10
1	+1	×	0.8333	=	+0.83
2	+1	×	0.6944	=	+0.69
3	+14.37	×	0.5787	=	+8.32
					− R 0.16m NPV

$$-R\ 0.16m \times 0.0670 = -€10\ 720\ \text{NPV}$$

Although there has been some controversy over this matter, it is difficult to understand why. It should appear obvious that, as it is the *parent company* that is investing in the project, the project must be evaluated from the *parent's* viewpoint. That is to say, what is important is the NPV of the project's cash flows that are available to be remitted back to the parent. The fact that the project used in Example 2 has a positive NPV when viewed in its own right must be irrelevant. However good an investment might appear to be, there is little point in undertaking that investment if the investor cannot enjoy its benefits. Thus Belgatek, acting on its shareholders' behalf, are not going to be interested in undertaking the project if it does not represent a positive NPV investment from *their point of view*.

Overseas currency finance

The conclusion reached above then raises an interesting point as far as *financing* is concerned. One of the fundamental principles of capital investment appraisal is that the financing decision can be kept *separate* from the investment decision. This then leads us always to exclude *financing* cash flows in calculating a project's NPV. (Notice that this approach even held in an APV analysis. The base case present value did not include any financing cash flows.)

The reason for this is not that the financing cash flows are being ignored, but that their present value is always equal – by definition – to the amount of finance involved. Therefore, the outlay on a project at 'Year 0' reflects the present value of the financing cash flows involved with the outlay. Example 3 simply illustrates this point, which has been made in earlier chapters, but which is of particular importance as far as overseas project appraisal is concerned.

EXAMPLE 3

A company wishes to buy some new equipment for €1000. It has a net operating cash flow of €450 per year for each of the 3 years of its life and a zero scrap value. Given the systematic risk of the project, a 15% discount rate is thought suitable for evaluation purposes.

The machine is to be financed by a 3-year €1000 term loan at 10% interest. Ignoring tax (which would just be a complication, but which would not change the conclusions drawn), the approach used is to calculate the project's NPV, without *apparently* taking either the loan interest payments or loan repayment into account:

$$-€1000 + [€450 \times A_{3\ 15\%}] = +€27.44\ NPV$$

However, the loan cash flows are *not* being ignored. The loan incurs the following cash flows.

Year	€
0	
1	−100
2	−100
3	−1100

Applying the principle that the discount rate should always reflect the risk of the cash flow, the discount rate that would best reflect the risk of the loan cash flow would be the loan interest rate itself; and so:

Year	€		10% discount rate		Present value cash flow
0					
1	−100	×	0.9091	=	− 90.91
2	−100	×	0.8264	=	− 82.64
3	−1100	×	0.7513	=	− 826.43
Present value of financing cash				Flow	− €1000[1]

Therefore, in entering the project's outlay of £1000 in the NPV analysis we are implicitly entering the *present value* of the financing cash flows involved with the project.

However, problems can arise as far as this principle is concerned when part or all of a foreign project's finance is raised in the foreign country rather than – what has been implicitly assumed so far – via the export of the parent company's home currency. This is because the foreign financing can affect the amount of the project's cash flows available to be remitted back to the parent. To illustrate this, let us return to Belgatek and the project dealt with in Example 2, but now involve some foreign currency financing. Example 4 gives the details.

EXAMPLE 4

Belgatek now propose to finance the southern African telecom project (referred to in Example 2) as a joint venture (JV) with investors in the host country. These investors will put up 50% of the required R10 million and so will invest R5 million into the project. Belgatek will invest the remainder of the required cash; R5m × 0.0670 = €335 000 for the other 50% of the telecom investment. The company plans to pay out each year's entire net cash flow as dividends.

▶

With this financing proposal, from the *project's viewpoint*, its NPV remains at +R1.47million. However, from the *Belgian parent's* viewpoint, the revised financing plans *alter* their analysis:

Year	1	2	3
project cash flow	+8	+4	+3.5
less JV partner dividends	−4	−2	−1.75
plus blocked funds		+3	+4.15
plus interest		+0.15	+0.21
Total cash flow	+4	+5.15	+6.11
Repatriated c/f	−1	−1	−6.11
Blocked funds	+3	+4.15	—

Year	Rm	×	20% discount rate		Present value cash flows
0	−5²	×	1	=	−5
1	+1	×	0.8333	=	+0.83
2	+1	×	0.6944	=	+0.69
3	+6.11	×	0.5787	=	+3.54
			NPV		+R0.06m

$$+R60\ 000 \times 0.0670 = +€4020 \text{ NPV}$$

As a result the southern African telecoms project, which formerly produced a *negative* NPV, now produces a *positive* NPV.

In Example 4 it can be seen that because of the change in the source of the finance (South African rand rather than euros for 50% of the financing requirement), the resulting impact on the cash flows available to the parent now makes this particular project worthwhile.

Example 4 contains a very important conclusion as far as foreign project appraisal is concerned: the cash flows of any finance raised in the host country *must* be included in the NPV evaluation of the project if there are restrictions imposed on the repatriation of the project's cash flows back to the parent. If there are no restrictions on net cash flow remittance back to the parent, then the project should be appraised in the same way as any domestic project – *excluding* all the financing cash flows.

PROJECT DISCOUNT RATE

The conclusion reached in the above section then leads on to the problem of identifying the correct discount rate to use (whether Approach 1 is applied and a foreign currency discount rate is required, or Approach 2 is applied and a home currency discount rate is needed).

With both the Cracker company in Example 1 and the Belgatek company example used in Example 2, the problem was deliberately avoided by using all-equity financing (i.e. both investments were said to be financed out of their company's internal financial resources). In such a case the discount rate simply has to reflect the systematic *business risk* of the investment project.

The all-equity financing used in the first two examples also helped avoid having to make a distinction between taxed and no-tax cases. Therefore the analysis to date applies equally to both situations. However, we know from previous chapters that as soon as we start to look seriously at the choice and identification of the discount rate, we must distinguish between taxed and no-tax situations. For the moment, we will proceed on the assumption that there are no taxes.

What would happen in the original Belgatek example (Example 2) if the company had originally intended to finance the project with the €670 000 required by using €335 000 in the form of Belgatek's retained profits and the other €335 000 would be raised via a 3-year term loan? In these circumstances, the euro discount rate would have been the project's WACC.

However, what if Belgatek then decided to raise the 3-year term loan in the southern African country, in South African rand? In these circumstances, as far as the project appraisal from the parent's viewpoint is concerned, what would be evaluated would be the project's cash flows available for repatriation back to the parent. The point here is that these cash flows would be the ones that were available for equity only (the debt interest having been paid in rand). As a result, the discount rate to apply to these cash flows would be one which reflected the project's business risk, *plus* the financial risk that arises from the gearing – in other words the cost of *equity* capital for the investment. Example 5 illustrates the situation, making use of the Belgatek example data.

EXAMPLE 5

Belgatek SA had decided to use a 20% discount rate in rand terms because it had identified the project's asset beta to be 2.0. In South Africa, the current return on government bonds is 8% and the return on the Johannesburg Stock Exchange index is 14%. Therefore, using the CAPM:

$$8\% + [14\% - 8\%] \times 2.0 = 20\%$$

The company now proposes to finance the R10 million project by exporting sufficient euros to finance half the project (€335 000), and then raise a 3-year R5 million term loan in the southern African country for the remainder of the investment. The interest rate on the loan would be 8% as it would be viewed in the southern African country as being virtually risk-free.

Given the relationship:

$$\beta_{asset} = \beta_{equity} \times \frac{V_E}{V_o}$$

Rearranging:

$$\beta_{equity} = \beta_{asset} \times \frac{V_o}{V_E}$$

$$\beta_{asset} = 2.0 \times \frac{2}{1} = 4.0$$

and so the rand return required on the telecom project, from the viewpoint of the parent company's equity, can be estimated via the CAPM:

$$\text{Investment's required return} = 8\% + [14\% - 8\%] \times 4.0 = 32\%$$

The project's NPV analysis is now as follows:

South African rand cash flows

Year	1	2	3
Project cash flows	+8	+4	+3.5
less interest payments	−0.4	−0.4	−0.4
less loan repayment			−5.0
plus blocked funds		+6.6	+9.53
plus interest		+0.33	+0.48
Total cash flow	+7.6	+10.53	+8.11
Repatriated c/f	−1	−1	−8.11
Blocked funds	+6.6	+9.53	—

Year	Rm	×	32% discount rate		Present value cash flow
0	−5	×	1	=	−5.00
1	+1	×	0.7576	=	+0.758
2	+1	×	0.5739	=	+0.574
3	+8.11	×	0.4348	=	+3.526
			NPV		−R 0.142m

$$-\text{R142 000} \times 0.0670 = -€9514 \text{ NPV}$$

From the parent company's viewpoint, the telecom project is not a worthwhile investment, it has a negative NPV of €9514.

Foreign projects in a taxed world

Just as with domestic projects, so it is with overseas projects: the only really satisfactory approach to use in a taxed world is an APV analysis. But with such an analysis, because of the importance of having to look at the project's cash flows from the *parent company's* viewpoint, a greater decomposition of the various elements is required than we have so far used with APV. As a result, the analysis becomes very much more complex.

However, a more simple approach, which should still produce an analysis with an acceptable degree of accuracy, can be suggested. This would involve using the approach used in Example 5 to produce a modified base-case present value and then allowing for just the home-based financing side-effects.

In this approach, the base-case cash flows would be the project cash flows remittable to the parent and the base-case discount rate would, effectively, be the cost of equity capital which reflected the combined business and financial risk of this cash flow. Example 6 provides an example of this analysis.

EXAMPLE 6

Maximalwert AG is a German conglomerate with investments in a wide range of different industrial sectors and countries. It is thinking of undertaking a capital investment in an overseas country whose currency is the US dollar. The following information is available:

Project:	Cost: US$12m
	Life: 3 years
	Scrap value at Year 3: zero
	Operating cash flow US$8m year, pre-tax
Finance:	The US$12m finance required will be provided by:
	US$4m 3-year term loan at 8%
	€1.5m 3-year term loan at 7%
	€4.1m of retained profits
	These financing arrangements fully utilize the project's debt capacity and the €4.1m + €1.5m = €5.6m/0.70 = US$8m.
Risk:	The project is in an area that the company knows well as far as Eurozone investment is concerned and an asset beta of 1.34 is usually applied.
	In the eurozone, the risk-free rate of return is 6% and the return on the Frankfurt stock market index is 9.3%.
Market Data	
Tax and other data:	The German corporate tax rate is 30%, payable at the end of each year. The corporate tax rate of the host country is 40%, also payable at each year-end. In the investment's host country, straight-line depreciation on cost, and interest charges, are both allowable expenses against tax. Overseas investors are allowed only to remit 50% of each year's pre-tax, but after interest, *accounting profits* back to the parent. All blocked funds earn 4% tax-free in a special government account and can only be repatriated at the end of the project's life. The project is not expected to attract any German tax on the remitted cash flow.
	The current spot EUR/USD exchange rate is €0.70 = US$1. The dollar is expected to depreciate against the euro by 2% per year, for the foreseeable future.

Calculations:

1. *Annual interest of US$ loan*

   US$4m $\times$ 0.08 = US$0.32 million

2. *Annual depreciation on the investment*

   US$12m $\div$ 3 years = US$4 million per year

▶

3. Accounting profit

	($m)
Annual operating cash flow	+8.0
less depreciation	−4.0
less interest on US$ loan	−0.32
Accounting profit	+3.68

4. Annual tax charge
$3.68m × 0.40 = $1.47 million

5. Annual remittable cash flow
$3.68m × 0.50 = $1.84 million

6. Project's remittable cash flows to parent

		(US$m)	
Year	1	2	3
Operating cash flow	+8	+8	+8
Tax charge	−1.47	−1.47	−1.47
Interest on US$ loan	−0.32	−0.32	−0.32
US$ loan repayment			−4.0
Blocked funds		+4.37	+8.91
Interest at 4%	___	+0.17	+0.36
Net cash flow	+6.21	+10.75	+11.47
Remittable cash flow	−1.84	−1.84	−11.47
Blocked funds	+4.37	+8.91	___

7. Therefore the 'base-case cash flow' of the project is

Year	($m)
0	−8
1	+1.84
2	+1.84
3	+11.47

8. Base-case discount rate

The 'base-case discount rate' can be calculated via the equity beta found from the following expression:

$$\beta_{assets} = \beta_{equity} \times \frac{V_E}{V_E + V_B(1 - T_C)} + \beta_{debt} \times \frac{V_B(1 - T_C)}{V_E + V_B(1 - T_C)}$$

Assuming (for convenience) that the debt beta is zero, then this can then be rearranged and reduced to:

$$\beta_{equity} = \beta_{assets} \times \frac{V_E + V_B \times (1 - T_C)}{V_E}$$

where:

$$\beta_{assets} = 1.34$$

V_E = €5.6m ('exported' euros: loan plus retained earnings)

V_B = €2.8m (euro worth of the dollar loan)

T = 0.40 (foreign corporate tax rate)

$$\beta_{equity} = 1.34 \times \frac{€5.6m + €2.8m \times (1 - 0.40)}{€5.6} = 1.742$$

and using the CAPM, a euro discount rate can be generated:

$$6\% + (9.3\% - 6\%) \times 1.742 = 11.7\%$$

Using the IRPT, this euro discount rate can be converted into a US$ discount rate:

$$\frac{0.117 - \text{US\$ discount rate}}{1 + \text{US\$ discount rate}} = -0.02 \, (2\% \text{ depreciation in US\$})$$

$$0.117 - \text{US\$ discount rate} = -0.02 \times (1 + \text{US\$ discount rate})$$

$$0.117 - \text{US\$ discount rate} = -0.02 - (0.02 \times \text{US\$ discount rate})$$

$$0.117 + 0.02 = (0.98 \times \text{US\$ discount rate})$$

$$\text{US\$ discount rate} = \frac{0.137}{0.98} = 0.14 \text{ or } 14\%$$

9. Base-case present value

Year	US$m		14% discount rate		Present value cash flow
0	−8	×	1	=	−8.00
1	+1.84	×	0.8772	=	+1.614
2	+1.84	×	0.7695	=	+1.416
3	+11.47	×	0.6750		+7.742

$$+\text{US\$2.772m} \times 0.700 = +€1.940m$$

10. Present value of the financing side-effects: € loan tax shield

€1.5m × 0.07 = €0.105 million per year interest

€0.105m × 0.30 = €0.032 million per year tax relief

€0.032m × $A_{3\,7\%}$

€0.032m × 2.624 = €0.084 million present value tax relief on the €1.5m loan

► *11. Adjusted present value*

	(€m)
Base-case present value	+1.940
Present value of € loan tax shield	+0.084
	+ €2.024m

This analysis also indicates acceptance: the project is expected to have a positive APV of €2 024 000 at Year 3:

APV	£+0.35m

TRANSLATION RISK

Translation risk can be defined as the risk a company is exposed to through movements in exchange rates when it holds medium- to long-term assets and liabilities in a foreign currency. The concept specifically refers to the fact that, with such assets and liabilities, at each year-end their values have to be *translated* into home currency terms for inclusion in the parent company's balance sheet. Example 7 illustrates the problems that might arise.

EXAMPLE 7

A Swiss company undertakes a project in Saudi Arabia, costing 25 million Saudi riyal (SR). It is financed with a CHF5.875m loan. The CHF/SAR spot exchange rate is CHF0.2350. The parent company's opening balance sheet will show:

Balance sheet

Loan liability: CHF5.875m	Saudi assets: CHF5.875m

Suppose 12 months go by and the CHF/SAR spot exchange rate has now moved to CHF0.2200. The Swiss company's balance sheet now shows up a foreign exchange loss:[3]

balance sheet (CHF)

CHF loan liability: CHF5.875m	Saudi assets: CHF5.5m

Foreign exchange loss: CHF375 000 (i.e. SR25m × 0.2200 = CHF5.5m). The reason for the loss is that the SR25 million worth of Saudi Arabian assets are now only worth CHF5.5 million in terms of Swiss francs, because the Saudi riyal has depreciated against the Swiss franc.[4]

Overcoming the firm's exposure to translation risk is quite simple – if it is possible. The solution is to finance the project through a Saudi riyal loan rather than a Swiss franc loan. In such circumstances, the Swiss company is protected against foreign exchange risk through the *matching principle*: the foreign currency asset is *matched* with a foreign currency liability. Therefore a fall in the value of one – through a movement in the exchange rate – will be countered (or matched) through a corresponding fall in the other. Example 8 illustrates the situation.

EXAMPLE 8

Using the data from Example 7, if the Swiss company financed the project with a SR25 million loan, then the opening Swiss balance sheet would show:

Swiss company balance sheet (CHF)

Saudi riyal loan liability: CHF5.875m   Saudi assets: CHF5.875m

If, 12 months later when the CHF/SAR spot exchange rate has moved to CHF0.2200, the balance sheet now becomes:

Swiss company balance sheet (CHF)

Saudi riyal loan liability: CHF5.5m   Saudi assets: CHF5.5m

Although the Swiss franc value of the Saudi assets has declined – because of the depreciation in the Saudi riyal – this decline has been matched by the Swiss franc worth of the Saudi riyal loan. As a result there is no net foreign exchange loss.

The difficulty with the solution to the problem of translation risk as advocated in Example 8 is that such a financing method is usually unavailable or inadvisable. For example, a foreign government may insist that a minimum proportion of a project's outlay is financed directly by the parent company's currency. Even where such a requirement is not legally stipulated, it may not be advisable, from a public relations viewpoint, for the parent not to put *any* of its 'own' money into the project.

Indeed, there is a third reason why 100% foreign currency financing might not be possible. Quite simply the host country's capital market may not be sufficiently developed to provide the financing levels required.

Given, therefore, that it is not always realistic to suppose that 100% foreign currency financing is possible, the standard financing advice for overseas projects is:

1. *The project's property non-current assets:* finance with a matching foreign currency loan.

2. *The project's non-property non-current assets:* finance via the export of the company's home currency.

3. *The project's 'working capital'/current assets requirements:* finance with a matching foreign currency loan.

This advice means that the international investor firm will be protected from foreign exchange risk as far as *property* non-current assets and *working capital*/current assets are concerned, through the matching principle. But what about the non-property non-current assets?

It is with the non-property non-current assets that the 'law of one price' (referred to earlier, in Chapter 22, in respect of the PPPT) might come to the rescue. The idea here is that non-property non-current assets (such as industrial machinery and equipment) obey, to some extent, the workings of the law of one price because they are capable of being traded internationally. Neither property assets nor working capital are capable of being physically traded internationally,[5] and so do not follow the law and need to be protected against exchange rate risk through matching.

We will use what appears to be a highly specific example to illustrate how the law of one price can give protection against foreign exchange risk. However, the example is only as specific as it appears to ease the explanation. It will tend to hold generally, whatever the circumstances, given that the assets in question can be traded internationally (and that the transportation costs do not form too significant an element in its total value). Example 9 gives the details.

EXAMPLE 9

Suppose that the SR25 million Saudi project referred to in Examples 7 and 8 was composed of the following elements:

Property:	SR5 million
Machinery:	SR17.5 million
Working capital:	SR2.5 million

The suggested financing scheme would be a SR7.5 million loan and SR17.5 million worth of Swiss francs – say, a SR17.5m × 0.2350 = CHF4 112 500 loan.

The fall in the CHF/SAR spot exchange rate from 0.2350 to 0.2200 from one year-end to the next will cause the Swiss franc worth of the Saudi property and working capital assets to decline, but this will be matched by a corresponding decline in the Swiss franc value of the Saudi riyal loan. But in these circumstances what happens as far as the Saudi machinery assets are concerned?

Suppose (for the purpose of easing the explanation) that the machinery in question is manufactured in Switzerland and is normally sold for CHF4 112 500. At an opening CHF/SAR spot exchange rate of 0.2350, this is why it cost SR17.5 million to purchase it for the Saudi project.

After an elapse of 12 months, the machinery still costs CHF4 112 500 but, because the Saudi riyal has depreciated against the Swiss franc, the Saudi riyal cost of the machinery now becomes: CHF4 112 500 ÷ 0.2200 = SR18 693 182 (in other words, approximately SR18.7 million). What is being seen here is the working through of the law of one price: the Swiss franc price of a good ÷ CHF/SAR spot exchange rate = Saudi riyal price of the good.

Therefore (ignoring the problem of depreciation which is just a complication and does not change the basis of the argument), the Swiss parent company would be justified in valuing the machinery in its Saudi project at the end of the first year at SR18.7 million rather than the original value of SR17.5 million, on a 'replacement cost' basis. (And the company's Swiss auditors are likely to accept such an argument.)

As a result, the company's balance sheets would appear as follows:

Year 0 Balance sheet: CHF/SAR: 0.2350

SR7.5m loan	CHF1 762 500	SR5m property:	CHF1 175 000
CHF loan	CHF4 112 500	SR17.5m machinery:	CHF4 112 500
		SR2.5m working capital:	CHF587 500
	CHF5 875 000		CHF5 875 000

▶

▶

Year 1 Balance sheet: CHF/SAR: 0.2200

SR7.5m loan	CHF1 650 000	SR5m property:	CHF1 100 000
CHF loan	CHF4 112 500	SR18.7m machinery:	CHF4 112 500
	_____	SR2.5m working capital:	CHF550 000
	CHF5 762 500		CHF5 762 500

The company has managed to hedge its exposure to foreign exchange translation risk through a combination of the matching principle and the operation of the law of one price.

It is not suggested that the law of one price will work as perfectly in practice as is the case in Example 9. But, given that the Saudi riyal depreciates against Swiss franc and given that industrial machinery is traded internationally, there will be a definite tendency for the Saudi riyal value of the machinery to rise as the value of the riyal declines. Thus, at the very least, companies can expect to get *some* protection (if not perfect protection) against foreign exchange risk through the workings of the law.

In summary, therefore, the general principle behind financing foreign projects is to raise as much finance as possible in the foreign currency so as to get the maximum protection from translation risk through matching. Where 100% foreign currency financing is not possible, then the company should try to ensure that at least those assets which are not going to be responsive to the operation of the law of one price are financed in the overseas currency.

However, it is debatable whether or not translation risk represents a real risk or is simply a 'presentational problem' for the company's financial statements.

ECONOMIC RISK

The previous discussion on translation risk also touches upon another risk of foreign investments, which is termed foreign exchange 'economic risk'. This is the risk of unexpected changes in exchange rates.

For example, an APV investment appraisal evaluation might have been undertaken which had indicated that a project would bring about an *increase* in parent shareholders' wealth. The project then performs perfectly to plan but, because of unexpected and adverse exchange rate movements, in hindsight, it leads to a *reduction* in parent company shareholders' wealth.

The possible presence of this risk causes real difficulties. The first question it raises is whether the risk is systematic or unsystematic. The second is: if it is systematic, how should it be taken into account in the appraisal process? There is, of course, an even more fundamental question here: does this type of risk exist at all? Example 10 illustrates what is behind this latter question.

EXAMPLE 10

Major Technologies plc is a UK company. It is evaluating a manufacturing investment in the USA. The US project costs US$1 million. It has a life of 3 years and results in an annual production output of 1000 tons of irradiated copper. The net after-tax cash flow resulting from the production is expected to be US$0.5 million in *current* terms. This cash amount is expected to increase in line with the average US inflation rate which is expected to remain constant at 4% per year.

The project will be entirely financed with UK pounds and there are no restrictions on net cash flow remittance from the US to the UK parent. A similar-risk UK project would be expected to produce a minimum annual return of 16%.

The current GBP/USD spot exchange rate is 0.6250 and the UK general inflation rate is expected to remain constant at 2% per year.

On the basis of this information, the US dollar discount rate can be estimated via the IRPT. First, though, the annual rate of change in the GBP/USD exchange rate has to be estimated. This can be done through the PPPT:

$$\frac{0.02 - 0.04}{1 + 0.04} = -0.019 \text{ or } 1.9\% \text{ annual rate of depreciation in the US\$}$$

and so, using the IRPT:

$$\frac{0.16 - \text{US\$ discount rate}}{1 + \text{US\$ discount rate}} = -0.019(1.9\% \text{ depreciation in US\$})$$

$$0.16 - \text{US\$ discount rate} = -0.019 \times (1 + \text{US\$ discount rate})$$

$$0.16 - \text{US\$ discount rate} = -0.019 - (0.019 \times \text{US\$ discount rate})$$

$$0.16 + 0.019 = (0.981 \times \text{US\$ discount rate})$$

$$\text{US\$ discount rate} = \frac{0.179}{0.981} = 0.182 \text{ or } 18\% \text{ (approx.)}$$

The project can now be evaluated:

Year	US$m		14% discount rate		Present value cash flow
0	−1.0	×	1	=	−1.000
1	+0.52	×	0.8772	=	+0.460
2	+0.541	×	0.7695	=	+0.416
3	+0.562	×	0.6750	=	+0.379
					+ US$ 0.255m

$$+\text{US\$0.255m} \times 0.625 = +\text{£159 375 NPV}$$

The project is worthwhile and should be accepted.

If Major Technologies then undertakes the project, the GBP/USD exchange rates that they are expecting over the next 3 years can be found from the PPPT:

Spot:	0.6250
Year 1:	$0.6250 \times (1 - 0.019) = 0.6131$
Year 2:	$0.6131 \times (1 - 0.019) = 0.6015$
Year 3:	$0.6015 \times (1 - 0.019) = 0.5901$

Therefore, they are expecting the following sterling cash flow from the project:

Year	US$m	×	GBP/USD	=	£m
0	−1	×	0.6250	=	−0.625
0	+0.52	×	0.6131	=	+0.318
0	+0.541	×	0.6015	=	+0.325
0	+0.562	×	0.5901	=	+0.332

(And this cash flow will, of course, have a +NPV of £ 159 375 when discounted at 16%, ignoring rounding errors.)

However, suppose that US inflation turns out to be higher than expected, say 8% rather than 4%.

$$\frac{0.02 - 0.08}{1 + 0.08} = -0.056 \text{ or } 5.6\% \text{ annual rate of depreciation in the US\$}$$

It means that the future exchange rates will also differ:

Spot:	0.6250
Year 1:	$0.6250 \times (1 - 0.056) = 0.5900$
Year 2:	$0.5900 \times (1 - 0.019) = 0.5570$
Year 3:	$0.5570 \times (1 - 0.019) = 0.5258$

Will the UK parent suffer as a result of this unexpected, adverse movement in the GBP/USD exchange rates? They should not, if the project performs as expected and produces 1000 tons of irradiated copper per year; the reason being that the increased US inflation rate *should* result in increased dollar cash flows from the project which will now inflate up at 8% rather than 4%, leaving an *identical*[6] cash flow in terms of UK pounds:

Year	US$m	×	GBP/USD	=	£m
0	−1	×	0.6250	=	−0.625
0	+0.54	×	0.5900	=	+0.318
0	+0.58	×	0.5570	=	+0.325
0	+0.63	×	0.5258	=	+0.332

Therefore the UK parent – Major Technologies – will receive exactly the same UK pound cash flow, whose NPV will remain at +£159 375.

The problem with Example 10 is that life does not work quite so perfectly. Remember, although the IRPT tends to work well, the PPPT tends to be more approximate because of the imperfections in the workings of the law of one price. Therefore, the foreign exchange rates may not turn out as predicted at an 8% inflation level and, indeed, the project's net after-tax cash flow may not respond, in the perfect way illustrated, to the rise in US inflation. Thus it is fairly safe to conclude that, in the real world, the risk of unexpected exchange rate movements *does* exist for firms in investing overseas.

This then brings us back to the first question posed: is this risk wholly systematic or unsystematic or partly both? The answer is highly uncertain, but probably some of it is capable of being diversified away through international diversification.

The uncertainty arises because economists cannot agree whether individual country financial markets are *segmented* (and so largely *independent* of each other) or *integrated* (and so highly *interconnected*). But, despite this, there is a relatively simple solution (although this is not always possible to apply and it is far from a perfect answer). That solution is to eliminate the risk of unexpected exchange rate movements by using the forward markets to sell forward a project's expected foreign currency net cash flow.

This solution may not be possible to apply in practice because forward markets only extend substantial periods of time forward in the world's *major* currencies. If the project were in Egypt, for example, we would have difficulties trying to apply this solution in relation to Egyptian pound cash flows. Even when suitably extended forward markets do exist (such as with GBP/USD), forward contracts are for *certain* amounts of currency, while the project's cash flow is only *expected*. Thus a perfect hedge against the exchange risk is unlikely to be achieved. Another alternative would be to use options to forward sell the project's expected foreign currency cash flows but, as we know, there may well be a significant cost attached to such a strategy.

Alternatives to the forward sale of currencies also exist through the matching principle. For example an overseas currency loan extending over the life of the project could be raised. This loan could be converted immediately into the company's home currency and the loan capital and interest could be repaid out of the project's net cash flow. Again, this would not give a perfect hedge, but it would provide a significant degree of protection. A further alternative would be to use the overseas project's net cash flow to purchase exportable goods from the host country; thereby converting the project's foreign exchange risk-exposed cash flow into a non-exposed (or less exposed) goods cash flow.

COUNTRY/POLITICAL RISK

The final risk attached to foreign projects is 'country' or 'political' risk. There is an academic debate as to whether or not there is a difference between country risk and political risk but we will treat them as though they are one and the same. This is the risk that, once a project has been undertaken, something of a political or serious economic nature will happen to inhibit the ability of the company to remit the cash flows expected from the project. This may be because of war or revolution, or it may simply be that the host government adversely changes the 'rules of the game' for either political or economic reasons. Whilst there is evidence that there is little systematic, quantitative analysis by companies of this type of risk, simply because it is so unpredictable, it is fair to say that it is generally possible to judge if a partner country is high or low risk. Generally, politically stable countries are likely to be viewed as being of low risk from the viewpoint of FDIs; whilst countries with a more unstable political environment would be viewed as having a higher exposure to political/country risk. There are several sources of commercially available political risk 'league tables', and some references are given in the 'Further reading' section at the end of the chapter. Whilst these rankings are better than nothing, they are bound to remain more or less subjective.

It is unusual for governments to seize the assets of overseas companies, if only because it is likely to be counterproductive in the longer term. Multinational companies exercise considerable power in terms of the control of both production and markets. There are also international bodies that might be expected to exert pressure on countries that act in an unreasonable way. Thus, whilst assets might be lost or destroyed as the result of war or expropriation, the most likely problems concern changes to the rules on the transfer of cash out of the host country.

As far as the risks of restrictions being imposed unexpectedly on net cash flow repatriation, the simple rule is to try and minimize its possible impact by using as many different remittance channels as are available. Thus a project's net cash flows may be remitted back to the parent in the form of dividend payments or interest payments (on inter-company loans). If the FDI project undertakes any process for which the parent has royalty rights, then royalty payments may be another possible channel.

Although an FDI's lower and middle management are drawn from the host country itself, the top management are normally seconded from the parent. The parent might then charge the foreign project for the services of these top management, effectively using the 'management charge' as a further means of remitting back the project's net cash flow.

Finally, if there is any transfer of goods between the parent and the overseas project, then the transfer pricing mechanism can be employed as yet another channel for remitting back the project's net cash flows. This is covered in the next section.

Obviously, national governments are aware of all these different possible channels and so if they really want to restrict the repatriation of a project's net cash flows to a foreign parent company, then they are perfectly capable of doing so. However, sometimes a government might want to be seen to be *doing something* about restricting foreign project cash flows, without wishing to restrict them *absolutely*. Thus they might enforce restrictions on, for example, dividends as they are seen as a politically sensitive area linked directly to profits. At the same time, however, such things as interest and royalty payments may be seen as much more 'legitimate' *business* expenses and so remain unrestricted.

As far as the other elements of country risk are concerned there are two main possible courses of action that can be taken to reduce them. The first would be to tie in host country investors or even the host government, through joint venture investment. This sort of arrangement is likely to discourage any host government from taking such adverse action against the project that the overseas parent pulls out, if this would then cause the project to fail. Such action would not only hurt the foreign parent, but would also hurt host country investors.

The second course of action is insurance. It is possible to insure an overseas project against the most extreme forms of country risk such as expropriation. In such circumstances, the cost of the insurance should be included as part of the overall cost of undertaking the project in any financial appraisal.

SUMMARY

This chapter has provided an overview of a highly complex area which contains many still unresolved difficulties. The main points covered were as follows:

- As far as foreign project appraisal is concerned, there are two equivalent approaches: the project's foreign currency cash flows can be converted to home currency cash flows and a 'home currency' discount rate applied to produce a home currency NPV; alternatively, the project's foreign currency cash flows can be discounted at the 'foreign currency' discount rate to produce a foreign currency NPV. This can then be converted at spot into a home currency NPV.

- A major difference between domestic and foreign project evaluation arises when the latter suffers from cash flow remittance restrictions. In such circumstances the project must be evaluated from the viewpoint of the cash flows that are available to be remitted back to the parent company. In particular, this means including in the project's cash flows any foreign currency financing cash flows.

- Once taxation is brought into consideration, then an APV analysis becomes appropriate. However, such an approach can be complex and a simplified approach can be utilized by modifying APV.

- Foreign project financing can play a significant role in reducing the parent's exposure to translation risk. Here, the standard advice is to finance the project requirement for property and working capital in the foreign currency, while the non-property non-current assets can be financed via the export of the parent company's home currency.

- Economic and country/political risk were examined and ways by which exposure to both may be reduced were discussed.

NOTES

1. There is a 'rounding' error of just 2 cents.
2. Notice the Belgian parent only has to contribute R5 million to the project, in terms of euros.
3. For simplicity, these examples ignore depreciation. The conclusions of the analysis remain unchanged in a more realistic setting
4. The Saudi riyal could equally have *appreciated*, and a foreign exchange *gain* would have been made by the Swiss company.
5. Although it could be argued that some elements of working capital – such as inventories – might be capable of being traded across international boundaries.
6. Given a small amount of rounding error.

FURTHER READING

1. International aspects of investment appraisal and financing decisions are complex and form the subject matter of specialist books. M. Eiteman, A. Stonehill and D. Moffet, *Fundamentals of Multinational Finance*, 3rd ed., Pearson, Prentice Hall 2009; G. Bekaert, R.J. Hodrick, *International Financial Management*, Pearson, Prentice Hall 2009; J. Madura and R. Fox, *International Financial Management*, 3rd ed., Cengage Learning 2014; and M.D. Levi, *International Finance*, 5th ed., Routledge 2009 – provide good coverage.

2. G. Allayanis, J. Ihrig and J.P. Weston, 'Exchange Rate Hedging: Financial versus Operational Strategies', *American Economic Review*, May 2001. This article contains an interesting discussion of how FDI cash flows might best be hedged.

3. Finally, an interesting discussion is put forward in W.P. Chiou, 'Who Benefits from International Portfolio Diversification?', *Journal of International Financial Markets, Institutions and Money*, 18(5) 2008.

QUIZ QUESTIONS

1 What is the PPPT formula?
2 If a project requires a 15% return in Spain and the EUR/USD spot exchange rate is 0.7220 and 0.7580 12-months forward rate, what is the project's US dollar required return?
3 The current EUR/GBP spot rate is 1.2250. The UK pound is expected to depreciate against the euro by 3.5% per year. Estimate the EUR/GBP exchange rate in 3-years' time.
4 The EUR/USD spot rate is 0.7440, the 2-month forward rate is at a premium 0.0030. What is the forward rate?
5 What are the two basic approaches by which a company can evaluate an FDI project?
6 Why should foreign financing flows be included in an FDI project's appraisal?
7 What is the standard advice for financing foreign projects?
8 What possible channels might a company use to remit back a foreign project's cash flows?
9 What is country risk?
10 What is economic risk?
    (See the 'Answers to Quiz Questions' section at the back of the book.)

PROBLEMS

The answers to the following problems are available to students online.

1 Blue Grass Distillery Inc., a North Carolina based manufacturer of rye whiskey, is evaluating its position with respect to the UK market.

The European Union has just announced a 5-year 25% common external tariff on rye whiskey, to protect Scottish and Irish distillers. Blue Grass Distillery Inc. believes that this tariff will reduce the profits on its exports to the UK to negligible levels. The company is therefore considering whether to establish a subsidiary in an EU Development Area in southern England, in order to avoid the tariff; or to pull out of the UK market completely.

If the company immediately stops exporting to the UK market some production could be diverted to the non-EU European market, yielding an annual after-tax net cash flow of US$1.5 million for the foreseeable future. The company is currently working at full capacity and has no plans to expand production in the USA.

The proposed UK subsidiary would cost £15 million to establish, 20% of which would be met by a grant from the European Union. A suitable factory has already been located and production could commence quickly. The company's marketing department forecast possible sales of 20 000 gallons in the first year and 50 000 gallons a year for the following 4 years. Blue Grass Distillery Inc. evaluate all projects on the basis of a 5-year planning horizon.

The rye whiskey would be sold at a price of £300 per gallon in the first year. Subsequently this price is expected to rise in line with the rate of UK inflation. The distilling and bottling costs in the UK have been estimated at £140 per gallon plus £2 million of fixed costs in the first year. These too are expected to rise in line

▶

with inflation. In addition a royalty of US$50 per gallon will be charged by Blue Grass Inc. The realizable value of the factory at the end of 5 years is expected to be £10 million.

It is the company policy of Blue Grass Distillery Inc. to remit to the USA all possible funds from its foreign subsidiaries at the end of each year. Corporate taxes, payable at the end of each year, are levied at a rate of 22% in the USA and 25% in the UK. A bilateral tax agreement exists between the two countries.

The UK government will allow tax relief on the entire £15 million investment, at the rate of 25% per year for 4 years.

Exchange rates USD/GBP: Spot	US$1.5500
12 months forward	$1.4725

The UK pound is expected to depreciate against the US dollar by 5% per year.

UK inflation rate forecasts for the next 5 years have been published by the UK government, as follows:

Year	Inflation (%)
1	4
2	4
3	3
4	3
5	4
6	5

Return on UK government bonds (5-year maturity): 5% per annum. UK market return: 9%. A similar risk project would be expected to produce a 14% return in the USA.

Required:

(a) Evaluate the project using NPV and advise management on the proposal to set up a UK subsidiary.

(b) How would you advise the management of Blue Grass Distillery Inc. about the financing of the UK subsidiary?

2 Polycalc BV is an internationally diversified company, based in Amsterdam. It is presently considering undertaking a capital investment in Australia to manufacture agricultural fertilizers. The project would require immediate capital expenditure of A$15 million plus A$5 million of working capital which would be recovered at the end of the project's 4-year life. It is estimated that an annual revenue of A$18 million would be generated by the project, with annual operating costs of A$5 million. Straight-line depreciation over the life of the project is an allowable expense against company tax in Australia which is charged at a rate of 20%, payable at each year-end without delay. The project can be assumed to have a zero scrap value.

Polycalc BV plans to finance the project with a €5 million 4-year loan at 10%, plus €5 million of internal funds. The proposed financing scheme reflects the belief that the project would have a debt capacity of two-thirds of capital cost. Issue costs on the loan will be 2½% and are tax deductible.

In the eurozone the fertilizer industry has an average equity beta of 1.40 and an average debt:equity gearing ratio of 1:4. Debt capital can be assumed to be virtually risk-free. The current return on ECB bonds is 5% and the average eurozone market return is 11%.

Corporate tax in the Netherlands is at 25% and can be assumed to be payable at each year-end without delay. Because of a double-taxation agreement, Polycalc BV will not have to pay any tax on the project in the Netherlands.

The current EUR/AUD spot rate is 0.6800 and the A$ is expected to depreciate against the euro at an annual rate of 3%.

Required:

(a) Using the adjusted present value technique, advise the management of Polycalc on the project's desirability.

(b) Comment briefly on the company's intended financing plans for the Australian project. Suggest, with reasons, a more sensible alternative.

TABLES

COMPOUNDING AND DISCOUNTING TABLES

TABLE A Compound interest factors $(1 + i)^N$

i	0.04	0.06	0.08	0.10	0.12	0.14	0.16	0.18	0.20
N 1	1.0400	1.0600	1.0800	1.1000	1.1200	1.1400	1.1600	1.1800	1.2000
2	1.0816	1.1236	1.1664	1.2100	1.2544	1.2996	1.3456	1.3924	1.4400
3	1.1249	1.1910	1.2597	1.3310	1.4049	1.4815	1.5609	1.6430	1.7280
4	1.1699	1.2625	1.3605	1.4641	1.5735	1.6890	1.8106	1.9338	2.0736
5	1.2167	1.3382	1.4693	1.6105	1.7623	1.9254	2.1003	2.2878	2.4883
6	1.2653	1.4185	1.5869	1.7716	1.9738	2.1950	2.4364	2.6996	2.9860
7	1.3159	1.5036	1.7138	1.9487	2.2107	2.5023	2.8262	3.1855	3.5832
8	1.3686	1.5939	1.8509	2.1436	2.4760	2.8526	3.2784	3.7589	4.2998
9	1.4233	1.6895	1.9990	2.3580	2.7731	3.2519	3.8030	4.4335	5.1598
10	1.4802	1.7909	2.1589	2.5937	3.1058	3.7072	4.4114	5.2338	6.1917
11	1.5395	1.8983	2.3316	2.8531	3.4785	4.2262	5.1173	6.1759	7.4301
12	1.6010	2.0122	2.5182	3.1384	3.8960	4.8179	5.9360	7.2876	8.9161
13	1.6651	2.1329	2.7196	3.4523	4.3635	5.4924	6.8858	8.5994	10.6993
14	1.7317	2.2609	2.9372	3.7975	4.8871	6.2613	7.9875	10.1472	12.8392
15	1.8009	2.3966	3.1722	4.1773	5.4736	7.1379	9.2655	11.9737	15.4070

TABLE B Discounting factors $(1 + i)^{-N}$

i	0.04	0.06	0.08	0.10	0.12	0.14	0.16	0.18	0.20
N 1	0.9615	0.9434	0.9259	0.9091	0.8929	0.8772	0.8621	0.8475	0.8333
2	0.9246	0.8900	0.8573	0.8264	0.7972	0.7695	0.7432	0.7182	0.6944
3	0.8890	0.8396	0.7938	0.7513	0.7118	0.6750	0.6407	0.6086	0.5787
4	0.8548	0.7921	0.7350	0.6830	0.6355	0.5921	0.5523	0.5158	0.4823
5	0.8219	0.7473	0.6806	0.6209	0.5674	0.5194	0.4761	0.4371	0.4019
6	0.7903	0.7050	0.6302	0.5645	0.5066	0.4556	0.4014	0.3704	0.3349
7	0.7599	0.6651	0.5835	0.5132	0.4532	0.3996	0.3538	0.3139	0.2791
8	0.7307	0.6274	0.5403	0.4665	0.4039	0.3506	0.3050	0.2660	0.2326
9	0.7026	0.5919	0.5002	0.4241	0.3606	0.3075	0.2630	0.2255	0.1938
10	0.6756	0.5584	0.4632	0.3855	0.3220	0.2697	0.2267	0.1911	0.1615
11	0.6496	0.5268	0.4289	0.3505	0.2875	0.2366	0.1954	0.1619	0.1346
12	0.6246	0.4970	0.3971	0.3186	0.2567	0.2076	0.1685	0.1372	0.1122
13	0.6006	0.4686	0.3677	0.2897	0.2292	0.1821	0.1452	0.1163	0.0935
14	0.5775	0.4423	0.3405	0.2633	0.2046	0.1597	0.1252	0.0985	0.0779
15	0.5553	0.4173	0.3152	0.2394	0.1827	0.1401	0.1079	0.0835	0.0649

TABLE C Annuity discounting factors $A_{N\neg i}$

i	0.04	0.06	0.08	0.10	0.12	0.14	0.16	0.18	0.20
N 1	0.9615	0.9434	0.9259	0.9091	0.8929	0.8772	0.8621	0.8475	0.8333
2	1.8861	1.8334	1.7833	1.7355	1.6901	1.6467	1.6052	1.5656	1.5278
3	2.7751	2.6730	2.5771	2.4869	2.4018	2.3216	2.2459	2.1743	2.1065
4	3.6299	3.,4651	3.3121	3.1699	3.0373	2.9137	2.7982	2.6901	2.5887
5	4.4518	4.2124	3.9927	3.7908	3.6048	3.4331	3.2743	3.1272	2.9906
6	5.2421	4.9173	4.6229	4.3553	4.1114	3.8887	3.6847	3.4976	3.3255
7	6.0021	5.5824	5.2064	4.8684	4.5638	4.2883	4.0386	3.8115	3.6046
8	6.7327	6.2098	5.7466	5.3349	4.9676	4.6389	4.3436	4.0776	3.8372
9	7.4353	6.8017	6.2469	5.7590	5.3282	4.9464	4.6065	4.3030	4.0310
10	8.1109	7.3601	6.7101	6.1446	5.6502	5.2161	4.8332	4.4941	4.1925
11	8.7605	7.8869	7.1390	6.4951	5.9377	5.4527	5.0286	4.6560	4.3271
12	9.3851	8.3838	7.5361	6.8137	6.1944	5.6603	5.1971	4.7932	4.4392
13	9.9856	8.8527	7.9038	7.1034	6.4235	5.8424	5.3423	4.9095	4.5327
14	10.5631	9.2950	8.2442	7.3667	6.6282	6.0021	5.4675	5.0081	4.6106
15	11.1184	9.7122	8.5595	7.6061	6.8109	6.1422	5.5755	5.0916	4.6755

TABLE D Annual equivalent factors $A^{-1}_{N\neg i}$

i	0.04	0.06	0.08	0.10	0.12	0.14	0.16	0.18	0.20
N 1	1.0400	1.0600	1.0800	1.1000	1.1200	1.1400	1.1600	1.1800	1.2000
2	0.5302	0.5454	0.5608	0.5762	0.5917	0.6073	0.6230	0.6387	0.6545
3	0.3603	0.3741	0.3880	0.4021	0.4163	0.4307	0.4453	0.4599	0.4747
4	0.2755	0.2886	0.3019	0.3155	0.3292	0.3432	0.3574	0.3717	0.3863
5	0.2446	0.2374	0.2505	0.2638	0.2774	0.2913	0.3054	0.3198	0.3344
6	0.1908	0.2034	0.2163	0.2296	0.2432	0.2572	0.2714	0.2859	0.3007
7	0.1666	0.1791	0.1921	0.2054	0.2191	0.2332	0.2476	0.2624	0.2774
8	0.1485	0.1610	0.1740	0.1874	0.2013	0.2156	0.2302	0.2452	0.2606
9	0.1345	0.1470	0.1601	0.1736	0.1877	0.2022	0.2171	0.2324	0.2481
10	0.1233	0.1359	0.1490	0.1627	0.1770	0.1917	0.2069	0.2225	0.2385
11	0.1141	0.1268	0.1401	0.1540	0.1684	0.1834	0.1989	0.2148	0.2311
12	0.1066	0.1193	0.1327	0.1468	0.1614	0.1767	0.1924	0.2086	0.2253
13	0.1001	0.1130	0.1265	0.1408	0.1557	0.1712	0.1872	0.2037	0.2206
14	0.0947	0.1076	0.1213	0.1357	0.1509	0.1666	0.1829	0.1997	0.2169
15	0.0899	0.1030	0.1168	0.1315	0.1468	0.1628	0.1794	0.1964	0.2139

AREA UNDER THE NORMAL CURVE

TABLE E Areas under the normal distribution

z	0.00	0.01	0.02	0.03	0.04	0.05	0.06	0.07	0.08	0.09
0.0	.0000	.0040	.0080	.0120	.0160	.0199	.0239	.0279	.0319	.0359
0.1	.0398	.0438	.0478	.0517	.0557	.0596	.0636	.0675	.0714	.0753
0.2	.0793	.0832	.0871	.0910	.0948	.0987	.1026	.1064	.1103	.1141
0.3	.1179	.1217	.1255	.1293	.1331	.1368	.1406	.1443	.1480	.1517
0.4	.1554	.1591	.1628	.1664	.1700	.1736	.1772	.1808	.1844	.1879
0.5	.1915	.1950	.1985	.2019	.2054	.2088	.2123	.2157	.2190	.2224
0.6	.2257	.2291	.2324	.2357	.2389	.2422	.2454	.2486	.2517	.2549
0.7	.2580	.2611	.2642	.2673	.2704	.2734	.2764	.2794	.2823	.2852
0.8	.2881	.2910	.2939	.2967	.2995	.3023	.3051	.3078	.3106	.3133
0.9	.3159	.3186	.3212	.3238	.3264	.3289	.3315	.3340	.3365	.3389
1.0	.3413	.3438	.3461	.3485	.3508	.3531	.3554	.3577	.3599	.3621
1.1	.3643	.3665	.3686	.3708	.3729	.3749	.3770	.3790	.3810	.3830
1.2	.3849	.3869	.3888	.3907	.3925	.3944	.3962	.3980	.3997	.4015
1.3	.4032	.4049	.4066	.4082	.4099	.4115	.4131	.4147	.4162	.4177
1.4	.4192	.4207	.4222	.4236	.4251	.4265	.4279	.4292	.4306	.4319
1.5	.4332	.4345	.4357	.4370	.4382	.4394	.4406	.4418	.4429	.4441
1.6	.4452	.4463	.4474	.4484	.4495	.4505	.4515	.4525	.4535	.4545
1.7	.4554	.4564	.4573	.4582	.4591	.4599	.4608	.4616	.4625	.4633
1.8	.4641	.4649	.4656	.4664	.4671	.4678	.4686	.4693	.4699	.4706
1.9	.4713	.4719	.4726	.4732	.4738	.4744	.4750	.4756	.4761	.4767
2.0	.4773	.4778	.4783	.4788	.4793	.4798	.4803	.4808	.4812	.4817
2.1	.4821	.4826	.4830	.4834	.4838	.4842	.4846	.4850	.4854	.4857
2.2	.4861	.4864	.4868	.4871	.4875	.4878	.4881	.4884	.4887	.4890
2.3	.4893	.4896	.4898	.4901	.4904	.4906	.4909	.4911	.4913	.4916
2.4	.4918	.4920	.4922	.4925	.4927	.4929	.4931	.4932	.4934	.4936
2.5	.4938	.4940	.4941	.4943	.4945	.4946	.4948	.4949	.4951	.4952
2.6	.4953	.4955	.4956	.4957	.4959	.4960	.4961	.4962	.4963	.4964
2.7	.4965	.4966	.4967	.4968	.4969	.4970	.4971	.4972	.4973	.4974
2.8	.4974	.4975	.4976	.4977	.4977	.4978	.4979	.4979	.4980	.4981
2.9	.4981	.4982	.4982	.4982	.4984	.4984	.4985	.4985	.4986	.4986
3.0	.4987	.4987	.4987	.4988	.4988	.4989	.4989	.4989	.4990	.4990

NATURAL LOGARITHMS

TABLE F

N	0	1	2	3	4	5	6	7	8	9
1.0	0.0000	.0099	.0198	.0295	.0392	.0487	.0582	.0676	.0769	.0861
.1	.0953	.1043	.1133	.1222	.1310	.1397	.1484	.1570	.1655	.1739
.2	.1823	.1906	.1988	.2070	.2151	.2231	.2311	.2390	.2468	.2546
.3	.2623	.2700	.2776	.2851	.2926	.3001	.3074	.3148	.3220	.3293
.4	.3364	.3435	.3506	.3576	.3646	.3715	.3784	.3852	.3920	.3987
.5	.4054	.4121	.4187	.4252	.4317	.4382	.4446	.4510	.4574	.4637
.6	.4700	.4762	.4824	.4885	.4947	.5007	.5068	.5128	.5187	.5247
.7	.5306	.5364	.5423	.5481	.5538	.5596	.5653	.5709	.5766	.5822
.8	.5877	.5933	.5988	.6043	.6097	.6151	.6205	.6259	.6312	.6365
.9	.6418	.6471	.6523	.6575	.6626	.6678	.6729	.6780	.6831	.6881
2.0	0.6931	.6981	.7031	.7080	.7129	.7178	.7227	.7275	.7323	.7371
.1	.7419	.7466	.7514	.7561	.7608	.7654	.7701	.7747	.7793	.7839
.2	.7884	.7929	.7975	.8020	.8064	.8109	.8153	.8197	.8241	.8285
.3	.8329	.8372	.8415	.8458	.8501	.8542	.8586	.8628	.8671	.8712
.4	.8754	.8796	.8837	.8878	.8920	.8960	.9001	.9042	.9082	.9122
.5	.9162	.9202	.9242	.9282	.9321	.9360	.9400	.0439	.9477	.9516
.6	.9555	.9593	.9631	.9669	.9707	.9745	.9783	.9820	.9858	.9895
.7	.9932	.9969	.0006[a]	.0043[a]	.0079[a]	.0116[a]	.0152[a]	.0188[a]	.0224[a]	.0260[a]
.8	1.0296	.0331[a]	.0367	.0402	.0438	.0473	.0508	.0543	.0577	.0612
.9	.0647	.0681	.0715	.0750	.0784	.0818	.0851	.0885	.0919	.0952
3.0	1.0986	.1019	.1052	.1085	.1118	.1151	.1184	.1216	.1249	.1281
.1	.1314	.1346	.1378	.1410	.1442	.1474	.1505	.1537	.1568	.1600
.2	.1631	.1662	.1693	.1724	.1755	.1786	.1817	.1847	.1878	.1908
.3	.1939	.1969	.1999	.2029	.2059	.2089	.2119	.2149	.2178	.2208
.4	.2237	.2267	.2296	.2325	.2354	.2383	.2412	.2441	.2470	.2499
.5	.2527	.2556	.2584	.2613	.2641	.2669	.2697	.2725	.2753	.2781
.6	.2809	.2837	.2864	.2892	.2919	.2947	.2974	.3001	.3029	.3056
.7	.3083	.3110	.3137	.3164	.3190	.3217	.3244	.3270	.3297	.3323
.8	.3350	.3376	.3402	.3428	.3454	.3480	.3506	.3532	.3558	.3584
.9	.3609	.3635	.3660	.3686	.3711	.3737	.3762	.3787	.3812	.3837
4.0	1.3862	.3887	.3912	.3937	.3962	.3987	.4011	.4036	.4061	.4085
.1	.4109	.4134	.4158	.4182	.4207	.4231	.4255	.4279	.4303	.4327
.2	.4350	.4374	.4398	.4422	.4445	.4469	.4492	.4516	.4539	.4562
.3	.4586	.4609	.4632	.4655	.4678	.4701	.4724	.4747	.4770	.4793
.4	.4816	.4838	.4861	.4884	.4906	.4929	.4951	.4973	.4996	.5018
.5	.5040	.5063	.5085	.5107	.5129	.5151	.5173	.5195	.5217	.5238
.6	.5260	.5282	.5303	.5325	.5347	.5368	.5390	.5411	.5433	.5454
.7	.5475	.5496	.5518	.5539	.5560	.5581	.5602	.5623	.5644	.5665
.8	.5686	.5707	.5727	.5748	.5769	.5789	.5810	.5830	.5851	.5871
.9	.5892	.5912	.5933	.5953	.5973	.5993	.6014	.6034	.6054	.6074

a. Add 1.0 to indicated figure.

ANSWERS TO QUIZ QUESTIONS

Chapter 1

1. The process by which the company seeks out alternative courses of action, alternative investments, etc.

2. The assumed objective of financial decision-making is maximization of shareholder wealth. While recognizing that this is a simplification of the real world, it is reasonable to accept that this should be the main objective, other things being equal.

3. It is a *reporting* concept, not a decision-making concept. Its purpose is to report on the success or failure of decisions taken. It has only a secondary role in the decision-making process itself. Accounting profit is also based on historic cost whereas financial management is concerned with value. The two things are very different. Finally, profit as reported is subject to the judgement of the accountant and cannot be viewed as entirely reliable.

4. On the basis of the expected flow of dividends the shares will generate in the future.

Chapter 2

1. The problem is one of control. How does the principal control the agent to ensure that the agent acts in the principal's best interests?

2. Fiduciary responsibilities; independent external audit; stock exchange rules and regulations; legal restrictions: and corporate governance regulations and practice.

3. Reward managerial ability, not luck; rewards should have a significant impact on managerial remuneration; reward system should work two ways; concept of risk should be taken into account; the shareholders' time horizon should be taken into account; scheme should be simple, inexpensive and difficult to manipulate.

Chapter 3

1. Stage one: The best of the alternative projects has the shortest payback. Stage two: Accept the best project as long as its payback period satisfies the decision criterion.

2. Working capital should be excluded from the analysis. Project W net cash flow:

    0 − 11 000
    1 + 4 000   Payback = 2.75 years
    2 + 4 000
    3 + 4 000
    4 + 3 000
    5 + 3 000

3. (a) Quick and simple to calculate.

    (b) Thought to automatically select less risky projects in mutually exclusive decision situations.

    (c) Saves management the trouble of having to estimate project cash flows beyond the maximum payback time period.

    (d) Convenient method to use in capital rationing.

4. The payback criterion is reduced until total capital expenditure equates with the amount of finance available.

5. Management's experience of successful projects within the firm.

   (a) Industry practice.

   (b) Reflects the limit of management's forecasting skills. However, none of these can be seen as being really objective.

6. The payback decision rule, adjusted to take account of the time value of money.

7. Ignores cash flows outside the payback time period. (The fact that 'normal' payback ignores the time value of money is equally important but this criticism can, of course, be easily overcome through the use of discounted payback.)

8. Money has a time value because it can earn a rate of interest/a rate of return. This has nothing to do with inflation although that might have an effect on the levels of return expected.

9. The question does not specify which ROCE to calculate, so both are given:

Profit:	=	£2 000	Year 1
	=	£2 000	Year 2
	=	£2 000	Year 3
	=	£1 000	Year 4
	=	0	Year 5
Total profit	=	£7 000	÷ 5 = £1 400
			Average annual profit

   Average capital employed:

   $$\frac{£11\,000 - £1\,000}{2} + £1\,000 + £4\,000 = £10\,000$$

   Return on *initial* capital employed = £1400 + £15 000 = 9.33%
   Return on *average* capital employed = £1400 ÷ £10 000 = 14%

10. (a) Evaluates via a percentage rate of return.

    (b) Evaluates on the basis of profitability.

    (c) Appears logical to evaluate projects on the same basis as management have their own performance evaluated by shareholders.

11. (a) Ignores the time value of money.

    (b) Evaluates on the basis of profit, not cash flow.

Chapter 4

1. This is an example of the economic concept of diminishing marginal utility. Each additional €1 of t_0 consumption forgone, through investment, is likely to be of increasing value in terms of consumption benefits forgone. Each additional €1 of future consumption gained is likely to be of decreasing value. Hence, the time value of money rises.

2. The complete range of maximum consumption combinations that the firm owner can obtain at t_0 and t_1.

3. The marginal return on the investment opportunity at any particular point.

4. A curve of constant utility. All combinations of consumption at t_0 and t_1 that lie along a single indifference curve would provide the same level of utility or satisfaction.

5. It invests until the return on the marginal investment equates with the owner's marginal time value of money.

6. Lending at t_0 would reduce the amount of money available for consumption at t_0 and increase the amount available at t_1, hence the move would be up the financial investment line.

7. The firm should continue to invest in projects as long as the marginal rate of return is not less than the market rate of interest. This rule is, of course, obvious. There would be little point in investing money in a project that gave a lower return than could be obtained by lending the money on the capital market.

    The cash (dividend) distribution to shareholders in t_0 and t_1 that arises out of the firm's investment decision can then be redistributed by shareholders, using the capital markets, to suit their own set of indifference curves.

8. A risky investment is one where the outcome is uncertain.

9. Ensure that any project earns at least the capital market rate of return that is available for investments of equivalent risk to the project.

10. (a) Single time horizon.

     (b) Infinitely divisible projects.

     (c) All independent projects.

     (d) Rational investors.

11. Investors dislike risk: they are said to be risk-averse. Hence they require a reward for taking on a risk, which is the expectation (but, of course, not the certainty) of a higher return.

12. In these circumstances, the market rate of return offers you greater compensation than you require to forgo current consumption. Therefore you would want to lend money.

Chapter 5

1. | | | | | | |
    |---|---|---|---|---|---|
    | 0 | $-£1\ 000$ | $\times$ | 1 | $=$ | $-\quad£1\ 000$ |
    | 1 | $+\quad£500$ | $\times$ | 0.8772 | $=$ | $+\quad£438.60$ |
    | 2 | $+\quad£600$ | $\times$ | 0.7695 | $=$ | $+\quad£461.70$ |
    | 3 | $+\quad£400$ | $\times$ | 0.6750 | $=$ | $+\quad\underline{£270}$ |
    | | | | | | $+\quad£170.30$ NPV |

2. There are several interpretations:

    (a) It produces a return > 10%.

    (b) It produces €120 more (in t_0 terms) than a €1000 capital market investment of similar risk.

    (c) The project would produce a sufficient cash flow to repay its outlay, pay its financing charges *and* provide an additional €120 in t_0 terms.

    (d) If accepted, shareholder wealth would increase by €120.

3. At 4% discount rate: NPV $= +\$147.48$

    At 20% discount rate: NPV $= -\$9.28$

$$\text{Therefore IRR} = 4\% + \left[\frac{147.48}{147.48 - (-9.28)} \times (20\% - 4\%) \right] = 19.05\% \text{ approx.}$$

4.

Year	Cash flow.		Discount factor		
0	−$500	×	1	=	−$500
1	+$200	×	0.9091	=	$182
2	+$300	×	0.8264	=	$248
3	+$200	×	0.7513	=	$150

$$-\$500 + \$182 + \$248 = -\$70 \div \$150 = 0.47$$

Therefore payback is 2.47 years approx.

5. The return available elsewhere on the capital market on a similar risk investment.

6. For the same project they should be identical. In both cases they are the opportunity cost return referred to in the answer to question 5.

7. $-\text{CHF}1000 + \text{CHF}350A_{4:0:10} = \text{NPV}$
   $-\text{CHF}1000 + (\text{CHF}350 \times 3.1699) = +\text{CHF}109.47 \text{ NPV}$

8. (a) Annuity due.

   (b) Immediate annuity.

   (c) Deferred annuity.

9. Given that the PV of a perpetuity is:

$$\frac{€100}{€1000} = 0.10 \text{ or } 10\%$$

Therefore 10% is the project's IRR:

$$-€1000 + \frac{€100}{0.10} = 0 \text{ NPV}$$

10. $-¥1000 + ¥200A_{20.16\%} + [¥500A_{30.16\%} \times (1 + 0.16)^{-2}] = \text{NPV}$

$$-1000 + (200 \times 1.6052) + (500 \times 2.2459 \times 0.7432) = +¥155.62 \text{ NPV}$$

Chapter 6

1. The NPV rule is to accept whichever project has the largest positive NPV. Differences in magnitude, duration and risk can be ignored. Hence Project A should be accepted.

2. The assumptions made are:

   (a) There is a perfect capital market so that the firm can finance the large project just as easily as it can finance the small project.

   (b) The projects represent independent decisions in that they are not part of a continuous replacement chain.

   (c) The discount rates used do correctly reflect the risk of each project.

3. NPV and IRR both make assumptions about the rate of return at which project-generated cash flows are reinvested. NPV assumes that the rate is the market discount rate, while IRR assumes that it is equal to the IRR of the project generating those cash flows. Given a perfect capital market, the NPV method is making the correct assumption.

4. Non-conventional cash flows, where there is more than one change in sign. The problem can be avoided by using the 'extended yield technique' or the 'modified IRR'.

5. Using the extended yield technique (€000s):
Year 3: $-20 (1 + 0.10)^{-3} = -15.02$ at Year 0
Therefore the revised cash flow is:

€000s	
0	−115.02
1	+60
2	+80

At a 4% discount rate: +€16.64 NPV
At a 20% discount rate: −€9.46 NPV

$$\text{therefore: IRR} = 4\% \left[\frac{16.64}{16.64 - (-9.46)} \times (20\% - 4\%) \right] = 14.2\%$$

Given that the project's IRR is 14.2% and the minimum acceptable IRR is 10%, it should be accepted.

7. If the IRR of the differential cash flow is greater than the hurdle rate, then accept the project with the smallest IRR.
If the IRR of the differential cash flow is less than the hurdle rate, then accept the project with the largest IRR.

8.

		(£)
1	$+ 40 (1.10)^2$ =	+60.5
2	$+ 80 (1.10)^1$ =	+88
3	$- 30$ =	−30
Year 3 Terminal value		+118.50

Modified cash flow of the project:	Year	(£)
	0	−80
	3	+118.50

Estimating the IRR using linear interpolation:

NPV at 5% = +22.36
NPV at 20% = −11.42

$$\text{IRR} = 5\% + \left[\frac{22.36}{22.36 - (-11.42)} \times (20\% - 5\%) \right] = 14.9\%$$

Chapter 7

1. $\frac{(1.13)}{(1.04)} - 1 = 0.086$ or 8.6%

2. Either: (a) Project money cash flows discounted at the market discount rate to NPV; or (b) Project money cash flows discounted at the general rate of inflation and then at the real discount rate to NPV.

3. The money cash flow, deflated (discounted) by the general rate of inflation.
1.155.

4. $\dfrac{1.155}{1.05} - 1 = 0.10$ real discount rate

   (a) €10 000 $(1.05)^2$ = €11 025
   (b) €10 000
   (c) €11 025 × $(1.155)^{-2}$ = €11 025 × $(1.10)^{-2}$ × $(1.05)^{-2}$ = €8263.73
   (d) €10 000 × $(1.155)^{-2}$ = €10 000 × $(1.10)^{-2}$ × $(1.05)^{-2}$ = €7495.45

5. Historic cost: £60 000, irrelevant, sunk cost.
   Written-down book value: £10 000, irrelevant non-economic figure.
   Scrap now: £3000.
   Rent and then scrap: £2500 + £800 = £3300.
   Therefore, if the machine is used to undertake the project, the best opportunity forgone is the 'rent and then scrap' alternative. So this is the opportunity cost of using the machine on the project: –£3300.

6. Discount the after-tax cash flows by the after-tax discount rate.

7. They are non-incremental.

8. Market price of factory space: €2 per metre (external opportunity cost). Contribution €15 per m² (internal opportunity cost).

   Cost to project: 150m² × (€15 + €2) = €2550.

Chapter 8

1. Hard and soft capital rationing.

2. The firm cannot necessarily accept a project just because it has a positive NPV, nor can it necessarily reject a project just because it has a negative NPV. Hence the standard NPV decision rule breaks down. In theory, capital rationing should not exist because we assume that cash will be available for investments at an appropriate rate of return. In another sense it causes no problem for NPV because we could assume that the appropriate discount rate is the return on the alternative investments (i.e. opportunity cost of capital).

3. The benefit–cost ratios are:

A:	+60	÷	100	=	+0.60 (1)
B:	+90	÷	200	=	+0.45 (3)
C:	+20	÷	40	=	+0.50 (2)
D:	−10	÷	100	=	−0.10 (−)

200	available		
−100	invest in A, producing	:	+60 NPV
100			
− 40	invest in C, producing	:	+20 NPV
60			
− 60	invest in 30% B, producing	:	+27 NPV
0			+107 Total NPV

4. The benefit–cost ratios are:

A: +60   ÷   50   =   +1.200   (1)
B: +90   ÷   200   =   +0.450   (2)
C: +20   ÷   150   =   +0.133   (3)
D: −10   ÷   —   =   —

    240   available
    −50   invest in A, producing   :   +60 NPV
    190
    −190   invest in 95% of B, producing   :   +85.5 NPV
     0   +145.5 Total NPV

As D has a cost–benefit ratio of: $-10 \div 20 = -0.50$ and B, the marginal project, has a benefit–cost ratio of $+0.45$, further investment is not worthwhile.

5. Benefit–cost ratios:

A: 40   ÷   100   =   0.40   (1)
*B: 30   ÷   100   =   0.30   (2)
*C: 50   ÷   200   =   0.25   (3)
D: 10   ÷   100   =   0.10   (4)
E: 4   ÷   50   =   0.08   (5)

    300   available
    −100   invest in A, producing   :   +40   NPV
    200
    −100   invest in B, producing   :   +30   NPV
    100
    −100   invest in D, producing   :   +10   NPV
     0   +80   Total NPV

alternatively:

    300   available
    −100   invest in A, producing   +40   NPV
    200
    −200   invest in C, producing   +50   NPV
     0   +90   Total NPV

Therefore, the best alternative is to undertake Projects A and C.

6. $40a$ − $20b$ + $50c$ Max.
      $100a$ + $150b$ + $200c$ ≤   190
      $200a$ + $120c$ ≤ $110 + 70b$
                           $30c$ ≤ $50a + 70b$
                          a, b, c ≤   1
                          a, b, c ≥   0

7.

Dual values	+	10% discount factor	=	Total opportunity	Cost of cash
1.86	+	1.0000	=	2.8600	t_0
0.73	+	0.9091	=	1.6391	t_1
0.64	+	0.8264	=	1.4664	t_2
1.21	+	0.7513	=	1.9613	t_3

Gain from an extra £1 at t_1:

$$£1 \times 1.6391 = £1.6391$$

Loss from repayment of £1, plus interest (i) at t_2

$$£(1 + i) \times 1.4664 = £1.4664 + 1.4664i$$

The maximum interest rate would occur at the point where the gain equals the loss:

$$1.6391 = 1.4664 + 1.4664i$$

$$1.6391 - 1.4664 = 1.4664i$$

$$\frac{1.6391 - 1.4664}{1.4664} = i = 0.118 \text{ or } 11.8\% \text{ max.}$$

8. NPV:

−100	×	1	=	− 100.00
+ 40	×	0.9091	=	+ 36.36
+ 90	×	0.8264	=	+ 74.38
				+ 10.74 NPV

Internal opportunity cost:

−100	×	1.86	=	−186.00
+40	×	0.73	=	+29.20
+90	×	0.64	=	+57.60
				−99.20

Total opportunity cost:

+10.74   NPV
−99.20   Internal opportunity cost
−88.46   Net total opportunity cost
As this net figure is negative, the additional project will not be a worthwhile investment, so reject.

Chapter 9

1. Success: $-€1000 + €500\, A_{3.10\%} = +€243$ NPV
   Failure: $-€1000 + €350\, A_{3.10\%} = -€130$ NPV

State	Probability		NPV		
I	0.45	×	+€243	=	+€109
II	0.55	×	−€130	=	−€72
					+€37 ENPV

2. | Survey indicates | Action | Probability | | Outcome | | |
   |---|---|---|---|---|---|---|
   | State I | Accept | 0.45 | × | +€243 NPV | = | +€109 |
   | State II | Reject | 0.55 | × | 0 NPV | = | 0 |
   | | | | | | | +€109 ENPV |

   ENPV with survey   + €109
   ENPV without survey   + €37
   Max. worth of survey   €109 − €37 = + €72

3. | Survey indicates | Probability | | | State |
   |---|---|---|---|---|
   | State I correctly | 0.45 × 0.75 | = | 0.3375 | A |
   | State I incorrectly | 0.45 × 0.25 | = | 0.1125 | B |
   | State II correctly | 0.55 × 0.75 | = | 0.4125 | C |
   | State II incorrectly | 0.55 × 0.25 | = | 0.1375 | D |

State	Action	Probability		Outcome		
A	Accept	0.3375	×	+€243 NPV	=	+€82
B	Accept	0.1125	×	−€72 NPV	=	−€8
C	Reject	0.4125	×	0 NPV	=	0
D	Reject	0.1375	×	−€243 NPV	=	−€33
				ENPV		+€41

   ENPV with survey   +€41
   ENPV without survey   +€37
   Max. worth of survey   + €4

4. | State | Probability | | NPV | | |
   |---|---|---|---|---|---|
   | I | 0.3 | × | +$100 | = | +$30 |
   | II | 0.5 | × | +$50 | = | +$25 |
   | III | 0.2 | × | −$300 | = | −$60 |
   | | | | ENPV | | −$5 |

   Therefore, without the survey we would *not* accept the project and so incur a zero NPV.

Survey indicates	Action	Probability		Outcome		
State I	Accept	0.3	×	+$100	=	+$30
State II	Accept	0.5	×	+$50	=	+$25
State III	Reject	0.2	×	+0	=	0
				ENPV		+$55

ENPV with survey   +$55
ENPV without survey   0
Max. worth of survey   +$55

5. If the machine is bought and, at the end of Year 1, the decision is taken not to abandon the project, then the outcome will be:

State	Year 1	Year 2	NPV	Decision
I	−10 000	+10 000	+2 260	Don't abandon
II	− 6 000	+ 6 000	−4 244	Abandon
III	− 4 000	+ 4 000	−7 496	Abandon

The investment decision is therefore (R000s):

State	Year 0	Year 1	Year 2	NPV		Probability		
I	−14	+10	+10	+2.26	×	0.70	=	+1.58
II	−14	+ 6 + 6 }		−3.56	×	0.10	=	−0.36
III	−14	+ 4 + 6 }		−5.30	×	0.20	=	−1.06
						ENPV		+0.16 or R160

The complete decision is that the company should purchase the machine but, if either states II or III occur, then the machine should be sold off at the end of the first year.

6. $-£1000 + £280\,A_{5.10\%} = +£61.42$ NPV

$Life = x$ at 5 year life: $+£61.42$ NPV
           at 4 year life:
$-£1000 + £280A_{4.10\%} = -£112.40$ NPV

Using linear interpolation:

$$x = 4 + \left[\frac{112.40}{61.42 + 112.40} \times (5 - 1) \right] = 4.65 \text{ years}$$

Thus the life of the project can be reduced by up to 0.35 of a year (or *4.2* months) before the original decision advice is incorrect. This represents a maximum change of $0.35 \div 5 = 0.07$ or 7%.
Net cash flow $= x$

$$-£1000 + xA_{5.10\%} = 0\text{NPV}$$

$$x = £1000 \div A_{5.10\%} = £264$$

Thus the annual net cash flow can fall by up to: $£280 - £264 = £16$ per year, or $£16 \div £280 = 5.7\%$ before the original decision advice is incorrect.

Chapter 10

1. (a) How to measure the project's risk.

   (b) How to find the return available on the capital market for that level of risk.

2. Transitivity means that choice between alternatives is consistent: if X is preferred to Y and Y is preferred to Z then X must be preferred to Z if the choice is to exhibit transitivity.

3. It is the guaranteed outcome that is regarded as being of equal value to the expected value of an uncertain investment. The guaranteed outcome will be smaller in cash terms than the equivalent uncertain outcome with the same perceived value so long as the investor is risk-averse.

4. $U(+€10\,000) = 1$
   $U(-€5000) = 0$
   $U(C - E) = pU(+€10\,000) + (1 - p)\,U(-€5000)$
   $U(€3500) = (0.60 \times 1) + (0.40 \times 0) = 0.60$

5. Risk aversion.

6. Linear. However, it is likely that any individual will be risk-averse.

7. Certainty-equivalent < expected outcome.

8. $$\frac{(\text{Selling price} - \text{Purchase price}) + \text{Dividends received}}{\text{Purchase price}} = \text{Return}$$

9.

State of world	Probability		Return		
I	0.20	$\times$	+40%	=	+ 8%
II	0.60	$\times$	+15%	=	+ 9%
III	0.20	$\times$	−10%	=	<u>− 2%</u>
					+15% = $E(r)$

$(Return)^2$		Probability		
$(40\%)^2$	$\times$	0.20	=	320
$(15\%)^2$	$\times$	0.60	=	135
$(-10\%)^2$	$\times$	0.20	=	<u>20</u>
				475 = $E(r^2)$

$$\sigma^2 = E(r)^2 - E(r)^2 = 475 - (15\%)^2 = 475 - 225 = 250$$

$$\sigma = \sqrt{\sigma^2} = \sqrt{250} = 15{:}81\%$$

Solution: Expected return:	15%
Risk (standard deviation):	15.81%

10. Downside risk is concerned with the possibility that an investment might do worse than expected.

11. In this situation the variance or standard deviation of the returns are not adequate descriptors of risk. An investment with a lower variance might also be the investment that bears the greater chance of a loss.

Chapter 11

1. The correlation coefficient. The further away it is from +1, the greater the degree of risk-reduction effect.

2. $\sigma_p = \sqrt{[x^2\sigma^2_A + (1 - x)^2\sigma^2_B + 2x(1 - x)Cov(r_A, r_B)]}$,

    or

    $\sigma_p = \sqrt{[x^2\sigma^2_A + (1 - x)^2\sigma^2_B + 2x(1 - x)\sigma_A\sigma_B\rho_{A,B}]}$

3.

A:	0.3	×	28%	=	8.4%	B:	0.3	×	35%	=	10.5%
	0.4	×	18%	=	7.2%		0.4	×	15%	=	6%
	0.3	×	6%	=	1.8%		0.3	×	20%	=	6%
			$E(r_A)$	=	17.4%				$E(r_B)$	=	22.5%

(28% − 17.4%)	×	(35% − 22.5%)	×	0.3	=	+39.75
(18% − 17.4%)	×	(15% − 22.5%)	×	0.4	=	−1.80
(6% − 17.4%)	×	(20% − 22.5%)	×	0.3	=	+8.55
				$Cov(r_A, r_B)$		+46.50

A:	0.3	×	$(28\%)^2$	=	235.2	B:	0.3	×	$(35\%)^2$	=	367.5
	0.4	×	$(18\%)^2$	=	129.6		0.4	×	$(15\%)^2$	=	90.0
	0.3	×	$(6\%)^2$	=	10.8		0.3	×	$(20\%)^2$	=	120.0
			$E(r^2_A)$	=	375.6		$E(r^2_B)$			=	577.5

$$\sigma_A = \sqrt{[E(r^2_A) - E(r_A)^2]} \qquad \sigma_B = \sqrt{[E(r^2_B) - E(r_B)^2]}$$

$$\sigma_A = \sqrt{(375.6 - 17.4^2)} = 8.5\% \qquad \sigma_B = \sqrt{(5775 - 22.5^2)} = 8.4\%$$

$$\rho_{A,B} = \frac{Cov(r_A, r_B)}{\sigma_A \times \sigma_B} = \frac{46.50}{8.5 \times 8.4} = 0.65$$

4. $E(r_p) = xE(r_A) + (1 - x)E(r_B)$

$$20\% = x \times 17.4\% + (1 - x)\,22.5\%$$

$$20 = 17.4x + 22.5 - 22.5x$$

$$20 - 22.5 = 17.4x - 22.5x$$

$$-2.5 = -5.1x$$

$$x = -2.5/-5.1 = 0.49$$

$$1 - x = 1 - 0.49 = 0.51$$

Therefore invest 49% of the funds in investment A, and the remaining 51% in B.

$$20\% = (0.49 \times 17.4\%) + (0.51 \times 22.5\%):$$

5.

$$E(r_i) = \sum_{i=1}^{N} X_i \rho_i$$

$$\sigma_p = \sqrt{\sum_{i=1}^{N} \sum_{j=1}^{N} X_i X_j \sigma_i \sigma_j \rho_{ij}}$$

6. A portfolio which lies along the capital market line (CML). It provides either (a) the maximum level of expected return for a given level of risk; or (b) the minimum level of risk for a given level of return.

7.

$$E(r_j) = r_F + \lambda \sigma_j \text{ or } E(r_j) = r_F + \frac{E(r_M - r_F)}{\sigma_M} \sigma_j$$

8. An efficient portfolio consists of investing in the market portfolio and government bonds (or borrowing at the risk-free interest rate). Thus, using:

$$E(r_p) = xE(r_M) + (1 - x)r_F$$

$$15\% = x \times 16\% + (1 - x)\ 10\%$$

$$15 = 16x + 10 - 10x$$

$$15 - 10 = 16x - 10x$$

$$\frac{5}{6} = x = 83.3\%$$

Therefore 83.3 % % of the funds should be placed in the market portfolio and the balance, 16.7%, should be invested in government bonds. The resulting portfolio's risk can be calculated from:

$$E(r_p) = r_F + \frac{E(r_M) - r_F}{\sigma_M} \sigma_p$$

$$15\% = 10\% = \frac{16\% - 10\%}{3\%} \sigma_p$$

$$\frac{15\% - 10\%}{2\%} = \sigma_p = 2.5\%$$

9.

$$
\begin{aligned}
20\% &= x\ 16\% + (1 - x)\ 10\% \\
20 &= 16x + 10 - 10x \\
20 - 10 &= 16x - 10x \\
10 &= 6x \\
\frac{10}{6} &= x = 1.66
\end{aligned}
$$

Therefore borrow 66.7% of own personal funds at the risk-free interest rate of 10%:

$$\text{Borrow } €1000 \times 0.67 = €667$$

Invest your own funds (€1000), plus the borrowed funds (£667) in the market portfolio. Risk of the portfolio would be:

$$20\% = 10\% + \frac{16\% - 10\%}{3\%} \, \sigma_p$$

$$\frac{20\% - 10\%}{2\%} = \sigma_p = 5\%$$

10. The market portfolio is the ultimate diversified portfolio and so contains *only* non-diversifiable risk. It consists of shares in *all* companies quoted on the stock exchange, held in proportion to the companies' total market values.

Chapter 12

1. $r_A = r_F + [E(r_M) - r_F] \, \beta_A$

2. The systematic risk of an investment, relative to the risk of the market portfolio.

3. Unsystematic risk is that part of an investment's total risk that can be diversified away. The sources of unsystematic risk are those factors that are specific to the investment, such as its management's ability and the quality of its research and development activities.

4. There are three principal factors:

   (a) The sensitivity of the firm's revenues to the level of economic activity in the economy.

   (b) The proportion of fixed to variable costs.

   (c) The amount of debt finance (gearing).

5. $20\% \times 0.6 = 12\%$ = systematic risk
   $\underline{8\%}$ = unsystematic risk
   20% = total risk

$$\beta_B = \frac{20\% \times 0.6}{10\%} = \frac{12\%}{10\%} = 1.20$$

6. $\beta_C = Cov(r_C, r_M) \div \sigma^2_M = 73.5 \div [7\% \times 7\%] = 73.5 \div 49 = 1.5$.

7. $\beta_{company+project} = (1.20 \times 0.90) + (1.70 \times 0.10) = 1.25$.

8. If a share is overvalued, it is giving an expected return of less than it should. Hence, it would lie below the CAPM.

9. The CAPM is a single-factor model: expected return is determined by a single factor – systematic risk or beta. The arbitrage pricing model is a multi-factor model: expected return is determined by more than a single factor.

10. $E(r_{project}) = 8\% + (12\% - 8\%) \times 1.75 = 15\%$

$$= -100.00$$

$$+ 60(1.15)^{-1} = + \quad 52.18$$

$$+ 50(1.15)^{-2} = + \quad \underline{37.80}$$

$$- \quad 10.02 \text{ NPV}$$

The project has a negative NPV when discounted at 15%. Thus it produces a return of less than 15%. As the CAPM indicates that the minimum return from an investment with this level of systematic risk (estimated by the beta value of the industry group into which the project can be classified) is 15%, the project should be rejected.

Chapter 13

1. An option to sell shares that can only be exercised on the expiry date.
2. An option to buy shares that can be exercised at any time up to the expiry date.
3. At expiry.
4. Use a straddle. Simultaneously buy both call options and put options at the same exercise price and expiry date.
5. The effect is the same as if the underlying shares had been bought: if the share price goes up, you gain; if the share price falls you make a loss. However, buying a call and selling a put is significantly cheaper than buying the underlying shares instead.
6. The intrinsic value of the option and the time value of the option.
7. The Black and Scholes model is a function of:

    (a) The current share price.
    (b) The future exercise price.
    (c) The risk-free rate of interest.
    (d) The time to expiry.
    (e) The volatility of the market price of the underlying shares.

8. Shares, risk-free bonds, call options on the shares and put options on the shares. The fundamental equality relationship is:

$$S + P = B + C$$

9. $S - X(1 + r_f)^{-T} = C - P$ or $S - Xe^{-r_{FT}} = C - P$
10. Delta risk is the hedge ratio of the option. It measures the sensitivity in the value of the option to changes in the value of the shares. It is given by $N(d_1)$. The greater the delta risk, the greater the sensitivity of the option's value to changes in the underlying share price, and vice versa.

Chapter 14

1. 8% ÷ 4 = 2% per 3 months. €1 million × 0.02 = €20 000.
2. Borrow €5 million now for 5 months and place the money on deposit for the next 2 months until it is required.
3. You would receive compensation equal to:

$$€10m × 6/12 × (0.07 - 0.065) = €25 000$$

4. FRAs provide a hedge against adverse and favourable interest rate movements. IRGs provide a hedge against adverse movements, but allow advantage to be taken of a favourable movement in interest rates.

5. You require a short hedge: you would sell futures.

6. Futures are priced on an indexed basis and so this implies: $100 - 92.75 = 7.25\%$.

7. It is the risk that the futures price will not move precisely in line with interest rate movements.

8. Because of basis risk and because only *whole* contracts can be traded.

9. No. For there to be an advantage to an interest rate swap there must be a quality spread differential. Here, the QSD is zero. Fixed interest: $9.75\% - 8\% = 1.75\%$; LIBOR $+ 2.75\% - 1\% = 1.75\%$; QSD $= 1.75\% - 1.75\% = 0$.

Chapter 15

1. (a) Weak efficiency.

   (b) Semi-strong efficiency.

   (c) Strong efficiency.

2. (a) Share prices will reflect management decisions as long as they are communicated to the stock market.

   (b) Shares are never overvalued or undervalued from the point of view of the timing of capital raising.

   (c) A takeover of a quoted company is unlikely to represent a positive NPV investment.

3. With weak efficiency, technical analysis is worthless; with semi-strong efficiency, so too is fundamental analysis; and with strong efficiency investors cannot even expect to gain from inside information.

4. Share prices react to the disclosure of new, relevant information. New information arises at random intervals of time and can be randomly either good or bad. Hence share price movements themselves occur at random.

5. A technical analyst tries to identify patterns that recur in past share price movements. Then, if one of those patterns is observed starting to develop, the technical analyst hopes that this will provide an ability to predict the future share price movement as the pattern develops more fully.

6. Upward sloping. See Fig. 15.4 in the text.

7. This states that the shape of the yield curve is determined by expected future interest rates.

8. This states that the normal yield curve is upward sloping because investors prefer short-term bonds – they have a preference for liquidity. Thus they are willing to accept a low interest rate on short-term bonds, but have to be offered a higher interest rate to attract them to the less-preferred long-term bonds.

9. According to the Fisher Effect, market interest rates are determined by inflation rates. Thus if the market expects future interest rates to be lower – based on the pure expectations hypothesis and a falling yield curve – this implies that inflation rates are also expected to fall in future.

10. Suppose you invest €100 in a 2-year bond. At the end of 2 years you will have: $€100 \times (1.065)^2 = €113.42$. If you invest €100 in a 1-year bond, at the end of 1 year you will have: $€100 \times (1.05) = €105$. This implies that the market expects the yield on 1-year bonds next year to be: $(€113.42 \div €105) - 1 = 0.08$ or 8%, so that $€105 \times (1.08) = €113.42$ (approx.).

Chapter 16

1. $P_E = €1.47 - 13c = €1.34$ ex div

   $11.25c \times (1 + g)^3 = 13c$

   $$g = (13c \div 11.25c)^{1/3} - 1 = 0.049$$

   $$K_E = \frac{13c \times (1 + 0.049)}{130c} + 0.049 = 0.154 \text{ or } 15.4\%$$

2. (a) Both r and b remain constant values.

    (b) All-equity financed company.

    (c) All projects financed out of retained earnings.

3. $P_B = €128 - €15 = €113$ ex int

    $+€113 - €15 \times (1 - 0.33)A_{4:\ K_{DAT}} + €110(1 + K_{DAT})^{-4} = 0NPV$

    At 5%, NPV $= -€12.07$

    At 15%, NPV $= +€22.28$

    $$K_D = 5\% + \left[\frac{12.07}{22.28 + 12.07} \times (15\% - 5\%) \right] = 8.5\%$$

    $$V_B = €12m \times 1.13 = €13.56 \text{ million.}$$

4. $\left. \begin{array}{l} 12(1 - 0.35)A_{3-0.085} + 100(1.085)^{-3} \\ (7.8 \times 2.5540) + (100 \times 0.7216) \end{array} \right\} = £92.08 = P_B$

    $£10m \times 0.9208 = £9.208m = V_B$

5. Given note 19 and the fact that:

    $$P_B = €118 - €18 = €100 \text{ ex int}$$

    and the debt is redeemable at par then the coupon rate equals K_D and so:

    $$K_{DAT} = 18\% \times (1 - 0.35) = 11.7\%$$

6. $R87 = R100 \times (1 + K_D)^{-3}$

    $\dfrac{87}{100} = (1 + K_D)^{-3} = 0.87$

    Using the present value tables:

    $(1 + 0.05)^{-3} = 0.864$

    Therefore the company's cost of debt is approximately 5%.

7. (a) The bonds are issued at par and are redeemable at par and carry a coupon rate reflecting the market interest rate at the time of issue.

    (b) The bonds are issued at a substantial discount on par but are redeemed at par value. They pay zero interest. Thus the investor receives a return purely in the form of a capital gain.

    (c) The conversion ratio is the number of shares into which each unit of convertible debt can be converted.

    (d) The conversion price is effectively the exercise price of the call options on the company's shares which is contained in an issue of convertible debt.

    (e) The conversion premium is the percentage by which the conversion price exceeds the current share price (normally, at the time of issue).

8. Convertibles have advantages from both the investor's and the company's viewpoint. From the investor's viewpoint they offer the security of a fixed rate of interest, plus the possibility of making a significant capital gain on conversion, together with the security of being able to have the debt redeemed if they so wish. From the company's viewpoint convertibles have the twin advantages of paying a lower coupon than straight debt and, with luck, never having to repay the loan (as investors will convert).

9. In 4-years time, the share price is likely to be: €1.65 × $(1.08)_4$ = €2.245. Thus 50 shares will be worth: 50 × €2.245 = €112.25. Therefore we would expect investors to convert. The coupon rate is 5% and so the after-tax interest payments payable by the company are: €5 × (1 − 0.20) = €4. The after-tax cost of the convertible debt is given by the internal rate of return on the following cash flow:

Year:	0	1	→	4	4
	88		(4)		(112.25)

NPV at 4% = −22.49
NPV at 12% = +4.46

$$K_D = 4\% + \left[\frac{-22.49}{-22.49 - 4.46} \times (12\% - 4\%) \right] = 10.7\%$$

10. The minimum value of a convertible is the greater of its value as straight debt and its conversion value.

Chapter 17

1.

$$K_E = \frac{5(1.04)}{83} + 0.07 = 13.4\% \qquad V_E = 24m \times 83p = £19.92 \text{ million}$$

$$K_{D_Q} = \frac{15(1 - 0.35)}{110} = 8.9\% \qquad V_{B_Q} = £24m \times 1.10 = £27.5 \text{ million}$$

$$K_{D_{UQ}} = K_{D_Q} = 8.9\% \text{ (assuming similar risk)}$$

$$P_{B_{UQ}} = \frac{12(1 - 0.35)}{0.089} = £87.64 \qquad \text{therefore:} V_{B_{UQ}} = £10m \times 0.8764 = £8.76$$

$$K_L = 14\%(1 - 0.35) = 9.1\% \qquad V_L = £3 \text{ million}$$

$$V_O = £19.92m + £27.5m + £m = £59.18 \text{ million}$$

$$K_O = \left(13.4\% \times \frac{19.92}{59.18} \right) + \left(8.9\% \times \frac{27.5}{59.18} \right) + \left(8.9\% \times \frac{8.75}{59.18} \right)$$

$$+ \left(91\% \times \frac{3}{59.18} \right) = 10.4\%$$

2. In the medium-to long-term the company will maintain a fixed capital structure and it is the overall return on this mix of capital that projects must be able to generate to allow the company to continue in existence.

3. (a) Project is small relative to the size of the company.
   (b) Project will be financed in such a way as not to change the capital structure.
   (c) Project has the same degree of systematic risk as that of the company's existing cash flows.
   (d) All level-perpetuity cash flows.

4. Its WACC will reflect its *average* level of systematic risk, and not the particular level of systematic risk of any one of its individual business activities. Thus the WACC is an unsuitable NPV discount rate with which to evaluate projects in any one of the company's areas of activity.

5. The CAPM produces an NPV discount rate which is tailor-made to the level of systematic risk of the individual project. The WACC only reflects the company's existing, *average* systematic risk level.

6. Because companies, but not individual investors, can get tax relief on debt interest.

7. Companies should finance themselves almost entirely with debt capital.

8. The gearing or leverage ratio is usually measured as $V_B \div V_E$, although it is sometimes measured, as a percentage, as: $V_B \div V_O$.

Chapter 18

1. Given

$$K_{E_g} = K_{E_{ug}} + (K_{E_{ug}} - KD) \frac{V_B}{V_E} \text{ then}$$

$$20\% = K_{E_{ug}} = (K_{E_{ug}} - 10\%) \frac{1}{4}$$

$$20\% = K_{E_{ug}} + 0.25K_{E_{ug}} - 2.5\%$$

$$20\% + 2.5\% = 1.25K_{E_{ug}}$$

$$\frac{22.5\%}{1.25} = K_{E_{ug}} = 18\%$$

2. Again using the M and M equation:

$$K_{E_g} = 18\% + (18\% - 10\%)\tfrac{3}{5} = 22.8\%$$

In a no-tax world, the gearing ratio does not affect the WACC. So the change in capital structure will leave K_0 unchanged:

$$K_0 = 20\% \times \tfrac{4}{5}\, 10\% \times \tfrac{1}{5} = 18\%$$

$$K_0 = 22.8\% \times \tfrac{5}{8}\, 10\% \times \tfrac{3}{8} = 18\%$$

3. Sell your shares in company A for €100 cash and buy €25 of debt in company B and €75 of company B's equity.

4. In arbitrage it is necessary to show the *pure* gain that can be made with no change in either business or financial risk. Business risk does not cause problems as the two companies involved in the arbitrage would be in the same business risk class (same asset betas). However, if a shareholder in a geared company wished to arbitrage into another company, care must be taken in order to preserve the existing degree of financial risk held. This is maintained by substituting home-made for corporate gearing.

5. Financial risk is borne by the shareholders in a geared company. It arises out of the fact that, because debt interest has to be paid in full before equity dividends can be paid, then shareholders are at risk that the company may have insufficient cash flow to pay dividends because it has all gone out in interest payments. This is financial risk.

6. As $K_D = r_F = 10\%$, then we can assume $\beta_{debt} = 0$

Using CAPM, $20\% = 10\% + (15\% - 10\%) \beta_{equity}$

therefore: $\dfrac{20\% - 10\%}{(15\% - 10\%)} = \beta_{equity} = 2.0$

$\beta_{assets} = 2.0 \times \dfrac{2}{3} + 0 \times \dfrac{1}{3} = 1.33$

7. $\beta_{assets} = \beta_{assets} \times \dfrac{V_0}{V_E} = 1.33 \times \dfrac{7}{5} = 1.87$

8. For two companies to be in the same business risk class, they should have the same asset betas and – in a no-tax world – the same WACC. As the WACCs of the two companies are not the same, we can conclude that they are not in the same business risk class:

$$K_0 = 20\% \times \dfrac{2}{3}\ 10\% \times \dfrac{1}{3} = 16.67\%$$

$$K_0 = 20\% \times \dfrac{5}{7}\ 10\% \times \dfrac{2}{7} = 17.14\%$$

Alternatively, the asset beta of the question 6 company is 1.33. The asset beta of the question 8 company is:

$$\left(2.0 \times \dfrac{5}{7}\right) + \left(0 \times \dfrac{2}{7}\right) = \beta_{assets} = 1.43$$

Chapter 19

1.

Using: $K_{E_g} = K_{E_{ug}} + (K_{E_{ug}} + K_D) \dfrac{V_E(1 - T_C)}{V_E}$

then:

$$25\% = K_{E_{ug}} + (K_{E_{ug}} - 10\%) \dfrac{1(1 - 0.35)}{3}$$

$$25\% = K_{E_{ug}} + 0.217K_E - 2.17\%$$

$$25\% = 2.17 = 1\ 217K_{E_{ug}}$$

$$27.17\% \div 71.217 = K_{E_{ug}} = 22.32\%$$

2.

$$K_{0_g} = K_{E_{ug}}\left(1 - \dfrac{V_B T_C}{V_0}\right) \text{ therefore:}$$

$$K_{0_g} = 22.32\%\left(1 - \dfrac{1 \times 0.35}{1 + 2}\right)$$

$$K_0 = 22.32\% \times 0.8833 = 19.7\%$$

3. $V_{0_g} = V_{E_{ug}} + V_B T_C$, therefore
   $V_{0_g} = €40m + (€10 \times 0.35) = €43.5$ million
   Shareholder wealth would have increased by the value of the tax shield:

   $$V_B T_C = €10m \times 0.35 = €3.5 \text{ million}$$

4.
   $$K_{0_g} = K_{0_{ug}}\left(1 - \frac{V_B T_C}{V_0}\right)$$

5. The tax shield represents the present value of the tax relief on debt interest. It is the source of the increase in shareholders' wealth that arises from increasing the level of gearing.

6. Debt capacity describes an asset's ability to act as security for a loan. Specifically, an asset's percentage debt capacity indicates the size of loan it would act as security for, expressed as a percentage of the asset's worth.

7. Using:
   $$V_{0_g} = V_{E_{ug}} + V_B T_C - E(b/c)$$
   then:
   $$\$40m = V_{E_{ug}} + (\$10m \times 0.40) - (0.05 \times \$1m)$$

   $$\$40m - \$4m + \$0.05m = V_{E_{ug}} = \$36.5 \text{ million}$$

8.
   $$V_{0_g} = V_{0_{ug}} + V_B\left[1 - \frac{(1 - T_C)(1 - T_E)}{1 - T_D}\right]$$

9.
   $$\frac{\text{Long-term debt and short-term debt} - \text{Cash balances}}{\text{Shareholders' funds}}$$

   However, the definitions of debt, etc. are not entirely unproblematic and thought needs to be given to items such as the capitalized value of leases.

10.
    $$\frac{\text{Earnings available for shareholders (after tax and interest)}}{\text{Number of shares in issue}}$$

11. Gearing ratios cannot be viewed as being high or low in absolute terms (within reason), but only in relative terms. Thus whether, at 50%, a company could be considered to have a high or low level of gearing would depend on the gearing ratio of other companies in its industry group.
    This is likely to be related to the business risk of the particular industry, cost structures, etc.

12. Financial risk is all systematic. It is not unsystematic.

13. There are two main factors:

    (a) The revenue sensitivity of the company.
    (b) The proportion of fixed to variable operating costs.

14.
    $$\frac{\text{Revenues} - \text{Variable operating costs}}{\text{Earnings before interest and tax}}$$

15. DOG gives the percentage change in EBIT for every 1% change in revenues.

16. The greater the DOG value, the greater the systematic business risk of a company in comparison with similar companies. Thus the company with a DOG of 2.50 has a greater degree of systematic business risk than a similar company whose DOG value is only 1.50.

Chapter 20

1. Because the project's NPV will add to the market value of the equity.

2. The return required from the project which purely reflects its systematic business risk (i.e. it assumes the project is all-equity financed).

3. What the NPV of the project would be, if it was all-equity financed.

4. An operating lease is essentially a marketing device to encourage sales and can be viewed as an operating cash flow. A financial lease is a particular method of project financing.

5.
$$\beta_{assets} \; 1.45 \times \frac{5}{5 + 2(1 - 0.35)} + 0.25 \times \frac{2(1 - 0.35)}{5 + 2(1 - 0.35)} = 1.20$$

$$\beta_{assets} \qquad 5 + 2(1 - 0.35) \qquad 5 + 2(1 - 0.35)$$

6. The equity beta reflects both the business and financial systematic risk. The asset beta purely reflects the business systematic risk. Therefore the financial systematic risk is reflected in a beta value of: $1.45 - 1.20 = 0.25$.

7. Debt capacity concerns an asset's ability to act as security for a loan.

8. The present value of the tax shield is based on debt capacity. Therefore the present value of the tax shield can be calculated as:

$$R2500 \times 0.10 = R250 \times 0.28 = R70 = \text{Annual tax relief}$$

$$\text{Present value of tax relief: } R70 \times A_{50.10\%} = R265.37$$

Chapter 21

1. The dividend decision could be said to be irrelevant because it does not affect the overall return on the shares, but simply determines how that return is split up between dividend and capital gain.

2. Given the irrelevancy argument of the dividend decision, a company should invest as much of its retained earnings as possible in positive NPV projects. If all earnings cannot be utilized in this way, then the residual should be paid out as a dividend. In this way, shareholder wealth will be maximized.

3. If dividends are to be truly irrelevant, then companies must be indifferent between financing projects with retained earnings and financing via cash raised externally. For this to be the case, the company's capital structure must also be an irrelevant consideration.

4. The bird-in-the-hand argument is that dividends, because they represent a certain current cash flow, are worth more than retained earnings which represent an uncertain future cash flow. Hence dividends are preferred to capital gains.

5. Investors with high marginal rates of personal tax are likely to prefer capital gains to dividends. There are two reasons. The first is that the marginal rate of capital gains tax is likely to be less than the marginal rate of tax on dividends. Second, the investor can control the time at which he takes his capital gains to give the greatest degree of tax efficiency. In contrast dividends must be taken when the company decides to pay them.

6. The clientele effect implies that companies should follow a consistent dividend policy to attract a specific clientele of investors.

7. There are two main classes of evidence. One is that companies seem reluctant to face a situation where they have to reduce dividends from one year to the next. Thus dividend growth lags behind earnings growth. The other evidence suggests that share prices react significantly to unexpected changes in dividends.

8. Given the evidence on signalling, to retain an expected dividend for capital investment purposes might be thought of as unwise. The market might interpret the decision as a signal about an unfavourable financial position.

There is, however, evidence that so long as shareholders are properly prepared by the company, the withholding of a dividend for investment purposes can be seen as a good thing.

Chapter 22

1. EUR/AUD spot: 0.6725 − 0.6735
   plus Premium   0.0010 − 0.0015
   1 month forward   0.6735 − 0.6750

2. Appreciating.

3. €350 000 ÷ 0.6735 = A$519 673

4. A$450 000 × 0.6735 = €303 075

5. Using the EUR/AUD mid rate: 0.6730
   $0.6730 \times (1 - 0.03)^4 \times (1 + 0.10)^2 = 0.7209$

6. $\dfrac{1 + \text{€ yield}}{1 + 0.05} = \dfrac{0.8082}{0.8160}$

   therefore:

$$\frac{1.05 \times 0.8082}{0.8160} - 1 = 4\% \text{ yield on ECB bonds.}$$

7. $$\frac{1 + 0.03}{1 + 0.05} = \frac{\text{Year 1 GBP/USD spot}}{0.6120}$$

$$\frac{1.03 \times 0.6120}{1.05} = 0.6000 \text{ Year 1 GBP/USD spot forecast.}$$

8. $$\frac{1 + 0.02}{1 + 0.01} = \frac{\text{Year 1 EUR/CHF spot}}{0.8240} = 0.8322$$

$$\frac{1 + 0.03}{1 + 0.03} = \frac{\text{Year 2 EUR/CHF spot}}{0.8322} = 0.8322$$

$$\frac{1 + 0.04}{1 + 0.02} = \frac{\text{Year 3 EUR/CHF spot}}{0.8322} = 0.8485$$

Chapter 23

1. (a) Forces of supply and demand for currencies from:

   (i) 'Hot money'.

   (ii) International trade and investment.

2. The IRPT determines forward rates through the workings of 'covered interest arbitrage'. Forward exchange rates will be set so that it is impossible to make a risk-free gain through borrowing money in one currency, at a lower rate of interest, and placing it on deposit in another currency, at a higher rate of interest.

3. Forward rates are determined by the IRPT. Spot exchange rates are determined by supply and demand market forces arising out of economic conditions and speculation. Empirical evidence suggests that forward rates are poor predictors of future spot rates.

4. (a) Forward market hedge:

   Sell C$100 000 3 months forward:
   C$100 000 × 0.6512 = €65 120 receipt in 3-months' time.

   (b) Money market hedge:

   Borrow C$x for 3 months so that: C$x × (1 + 0.01) = C$100 000 at Month 3.

   $$\text{Borrow:} \frac{\text{C\$100 000}}{1 + 0.01} = \text{C\$99 099}$$

   Sell C$99 099 at spot: C$99 099 × 0.6545 = €64 802 receipt now.

   (c) Comparing the hedges:

   €64 802 × (1 + 0.005) = €65 126 at Month 3.
   Therefore the money market hedge is very slightly better.

5. (a) Win contract:

   (i) Sell US$100 000 at spot: US$100 000 × 11.25 = R1 125 000 receipt

   Exercise option: US$100 000 × 10.41 = R1 041 000 receipt.
   Therefore sell at spot and allow the option to lapse.

   (iii) Sell US$100 000 at spot: US$100 000 × 9.25 = R925 000 receipt

   Exercise option: US$100 000 × 10.41 = R1 041 000 receipt.
   Therefore exercise the option.

   (b) Lose the contract:

   (i) Buy US$100 000 at spot: US$100 000 × 11.25 = R1 125 000 cost

   Exercise option: Sell US$100 000 × 10.41 = R1 041 000 receipt.
   Therefore don't buy US dollars at spot instead, simply allow the option to lapse.

   (ii) Buy US$100 000 at spot: US$100 000 × 9.25 = R925 000 cost.

   Exercise option: Sell US$100 000 × 10.41 = R1 041 000 receipt.
   Therefore buy US$100 000 at spot and sell through the exercise of the option to realize a profit of: R116 000.

6. With time-option forward contracts, the deal is done at the worst rate of exchange (from the company's viewpoint):
   5-month forward rate: Sell US dollars at €0.7285 = US$1
   6-month forward rate: Sell US dollars at €0.7298 = US$1
   Therefore the 5–6 month forward contract to sell US dollars will be at an exchange rate of 0.7285.

7. (a) OTC options available in large numbers of currencies, traded currency options available only in major currencies.

   (b) OTC options are available for any reasonable exercise date; traded currency options only 3/6/9 months forward.

   (c) OTC option prices determined by bank. Thus a big company can use its financial strength to strike a better deal.

   (d) A *very* large transaction may be difficult to arrange on a traded currency option exchange.

   (e) OTC currency options are not dependent on the option exchange being open to deal or exercise.

   (f) OTC currency options are available for any amount of currency; traded currencies are only available for specific currency size multiple – the contract size.

8. (a) Target receipt: US$526 000 × 0.7320 = €385 032

   Number of contracts:
   US$526 000 ÷ US$20 000 = 26.3 rounded to 26
   Buy or sell?

   - contract size currency: US$20 000 per contract
   - cash market: sell US$526 000
   - therefore: sell futures.

   Hedge: sell 26 USD/EUR September futures at €73.55

   (b) In August, the company receives US$526 000 which it sells at spot:

   US$526 000 × 0.7228 = €379 246

   Target receipt: €385 032
   Loss on target: €5786

   Close out the futures position: buy 26 USD/EUR September futures at €72.22 Profit or Loss on futures:
   Buy 26 × US$20 000 = US$520 000 × 0.7222 = €375 544 cost
   Sell 26 × US$20 000 = US$520 000 × 0.7355 = €382 460 receipt
   Profit on futures: €6916
   Loss on target: €5786
   Hedge efficiency: 119.5%

9. (a) Forward market hedge

   Buy US$297 500 forward to October, costing:
   US$297 500 × 0.7345 = €218 514 cost payable in October

   (b) Futures market hedge

   Target cost: US$297 500 × 0.7300 = €217 175
   Number of contracts:
   US$297 500 ÷ US$20 000 = 14.875 rounded to 15
   Buy or sell?

   - contract size currency: US$20 000 per contract
   - cash market: buy US$297 500
   - therefore: buy futures.

   Hedge: buy 15 December futures at €73.15

   (c) In October, the company buys US$297 500 at spot which costs:
   US$297 500 × 0.7360 = €218 960

Target cost: €217 175
Loss on target: €1785
Close out the futures position: selling 15 USD/EUR December futures at €73.75 Profit or Loss on futures:
Buy 15 × US$20 000 = US$300 000 × 0.7315 = €219 450 cost
Sell 15 × US$20 000 = US$300 000 × 0.7375 = €221 250 receipt
Profit on futures: €1800
Loss on target: €1785
Hedge efficiency: 100.8% efficiency

Chapter 24

1. $$\frac{\text{Home inflation rate} - \text{Foreign inflation rate}}{1 + \text{Foreign inflation rate}} = \text{\% change in the Foreign currency}$$

If this % change is 'positive' the Foreign currency is appreciating, but, if this % change is 'negative' the Foreign currency is depreciating.

2. $$\frac{1 + \text{Spanish return}}{1 + \text{US return}} = \frac{\text{EUR/USD forward}}{\text{EUR/USD spot}}$$

$$\frac{1 + 0.15}{1 + \text{US return}} = \frac{0.7580}{0.7220}$$

$$\frac{1.15 \times 0.7220}{0.7580} - 1 = 0.095 \text{ or } 9.5\%$$

3. $1.225 \times (1 - 0.035)^3 = 1.1008$

4. $0.7440 + 0.0030 = 0.7470$: 2-month forward rate.

5. (a) Project's foreign currency cash flows are discounted by the foreign currency discount rate to give a foreign currency NPV which is then converted at spot to a home currency NPV, or

    (b) project's foreign currency cash flows are converted into home currency cash flows and then discounted at the home currency discount rate to give a home currency NPV.

6. Because they may well affect the cash flow available to be remitted back to the parent company.

7. Property assets and working capital should be financed in the foreign currency. Non-property non-current assets finance should be financed via the export of the parent company's home currency.

8. (a) Dividends.

    (b) Interest.

    (c) Management charges.

    (d) Royalty payments.

    (e) Transfer prices.

9. The risk that the host government might take action, after the FDI has been made, that adversely affects the financial viability of the investment.

10. Economic risk describes the risk that a company is exposed to from unexpected foreign exchange rate movements and their resulting impact on the worth of a foreign project's cash flows in terms of the parent company's home currency.

REFERENCES FOR
REAL WORLD VIEWS

The following *Real World View* features have been written specifically for this edition of *Corporate Finance*:

Chapter	Real Word View	References
1	The rise of shareholder revolts	
2	The failure of external auditors	
3	The importance of CFOs	Jim Singh, CFO Nestlé, Strategic Finance, September 2011, http://www.imanet.org/PDFs/Public/SF/2011_09/09_2011_sjoblom_kim_revised.pdf; 'The evolving role of today's CFO', *EY*, http://www.ey.com/GL/en/Issues/Managing-finance/The-DNA-of-the-CFO---perspectives-on-the-evolving-role (accessed 6 March 2014); 'Describe your role as a CFO in a single word', *The Finance Director*, http://www.the-financedirector.com/features/feature84387/ (accessed 6 March 2014).
5	Dilemma for pensioners – annuity or lump sum?	K. Peachey, 'Q&A: Pension automatic enrolment', BBC News Business, 8 August 2013, http://www.bbc.co.uk/news/business-19589265 (accessed 6 March 2014); 'Should you take a cash lump sum from your pension?', The Money Advice Service, https://www.moneyadviceservice.org.uk/en/articles/should-you-take-a-pension-tax-free-cash-lump-sum (accessed 6 March 2014).
6	Limitations of the NPV and its practical uses in day-to-day life	J. Fickett, 'Net Present Value Analysis in Practice', *Clear On Money*, 7 December 2011, http://www.clearonmoney.com/dw/doku.php?id=investment:commentary:2011:12:07-net_present_value_analysis_in_practice (accessed 15 May 2014); A. Arya, J.C. Fellingham and J.C. Glover, 'Capital Budgeting: Some Exceptions to the Net Present Value Rule, *Issues in Accounting Education*, Vol. 13, No. 3, August 1998, http://fisher.osu.edu/~young.53/AFG-NPV.pdf (accessed 15 May 2014); 'Net Present Value: Why You Should Use It In Everyday Life, *Darwin's Finance*, 8 March 2009, http://www.darwinsfinance.com/net-present-value-why-you-should-use-it-in-everyday-life/ (accessed 15 May 2014).

8	Interest rates go nuclear	J. Speares, 'Nuclear Overhaul: Darlington's Multimillion-dollar Mock-up', *The Star – Business*, 25 February 2014, http://www.thestar.com/business/2014/02/25/nuclear_overhaul_darlingtons_multimillion_mockup.html (accessed 14 May 2014).
9	When to abandon a project? – fail to plan = plan to fail	R. Syal, 'Abandoned NHS IT System has Cost £10bn so Far', *The Guardian*, 18 September 2013, http://www.theguardian.com/society/2013/sep/18/nhs-records-system-10bn (accessed 16 May 2014); F.M. Muharam and M-A. Tarrazon, 'Dealing with Recession: A Real Option Approach to Evaluation of SMEs', Research paper, 1 December 2010; G.V. Reklaitis and J.C. Zapata, 'New Product Development c Pipeline Management', Purdue University (accessed 16 May 2014).
10	Are you a risk taker?	'New Research Reveals Baby Boomers Taking More Risk, Bringing More Entrepreneurial Spirit to the Workforce than Gen-Y', Monster, 27 February 2013, http://www.about-monster.com/sites/default/files/US_Monster_Millennial_BrandingSurvey_FINAL022113.pdf (accessed 18 March 2014); 'Multi-Generational Worker Attitudes', Monster, D. Schawbel, 14 March 2013, http://www.about-monster.com/sites/default/files/MillennialBrandingMulti-GenerationalWorkerAttitudesWhitePaper.pdf (accessed 18 March 2014).
11	Is diversification the 'best bet'?	J. Yarker, 'Diversification December: The Share Centre's Top Five Funds at End of 2013', *Money Marketing*, 30 January 2014, http://www.moneymarketing.co.uk/news-and-analysis/wraps-and-platforms/diversification-december-the-share-centres-top-five-funds-at-end-of-2013/2005982.article (accessed 18 March 2014); J. Reeves, 'This Shocking Strategy Will Save Your Portfolio – Opinion: Diversification Doesn't Sound Sexy, but it Works', *Market Watch / Wall Street Journal*, 15 January 2014, http://www.marketwatch.com/story/this-shocking-strategy-will-save-your-portfolio-2014-01-15 (accessed 18 March 2014); 'Staying Balanced in Volatile Markets', J.P. Morgan Asset Management https://www.jpmorganfunds.com/cm/Satellite?pagename=jpmfVanityWrapper&UserFriendlyURL=portfoliodiscussions&portfoliodiscussionid=1317247269821 (accessed 18 March 2014).
12	Divided opinion – is the CAPM still relevant today?	J. Mackintosh, 'Searching for a Nobel for Common Sense', *Financial Times*, 21 October 2013; J. Kay, 'Economists: There is no Such Thing as the 'Economic Approach', *Financial Times*, 14 January 2014; A. Lewis, 'Theorist Sheds Light on Practicality', *Money Marketing*, 6 August 2007, http://www.moneymarketing.co.uk/home/theorist-sheds-light-on-practicality/147391.article (accessed 8 April 2014).
15	Increasing capital in Saudi banks	'New Capital Infusion to Give Banks Opportunity to Increase Lending', *Arab News*, 26 March 2014, http://www.arabnews.com/news/545826 (accessed 8 April 2014).

16	Negative yields, the role of rating agencies and lending to countries	E. Sprott and D. Baker, 'NIRP: The Financial System's Death Knell?', Sprott Asset Management LP, https://www.sprott.com/markets-at-a-glance/nirp-the-financial-system%E2%80%99s-death-knell/ (accessed 15 May 2014); J. Archer and O. Mikkelsen, 'Denmark Sets a Negative Rate for First Time', *Reuters*, 5 July 2012, http://uk.reuters.com/article/2012/07/05/denmark-rates-idUKL6E8I5A8520120705 (accessed 10 March 2014); R. Marston, 'What is a Rating Agency?', BBC News, 25 February 2013, http://www.bbc.co.uk/news/10108284 (accessed 6 May 2014); 'Sovereigns Rating List', *Standard & Poor's Ratings Services*, http://www.standardandpoors.com/ratings/sovereigns/ratings-list/en/us/?subSectorCode=39 (accessed 6 May 2014); 'Russia: Moving Away from International Rating Agencies Only Question of Time', RT.com, 14 May 2014, http://rt.com/business/158856-russia-raitings-agency-ministry/ (accessed 15 May 2014).
18	Cost of capital in industry	'Cost of Capital by Sector', NYU, January 2014, http://w4.stern.nyu.edu/~damodar/New_Home_Page/datafile/wacc.htm (accessed 14 May 2014); 'Cost of Capital Study 2012/2013: Managing Uncertainty', KPMG, http://www.kpmg.com/CH/en/Library/Articles-Publications/Documents/Advisory/pub-20131122-cost-of-capital-study-2013-en.pdf (accessed 14 May 2014).
19	The true cost of bankruptcy	A. Jones, 'Lawyers Set to Profit on Lehman', *Wall Street Journal*, April 16 2009, http://www.freep.com/article/20140122/NEWS01/301220086/Judge-Steven-Rhodes-Detroit-Institute-of-Arts-bankruptcy (accessed 14 May 2014); http://www.instantshift.com/2010/02/03/22-largest-bankruptcies-in-world-history/ (accessed 14 May 2014); L. O'Carroll, 'Ireland turns to bankruptcy tourism', *The Guardian*, http://www.theguardian.com/business/2011/feb/18/ireland-property-crash-bankruptcy-tourism (accessed 14 May 2014).
21	Dividends at easyJet and the John Lewis Partnership	G. Ruddick, 'John Lewis Pays Staff More than £200m in Bonuses for First Time', *The Telegraph*, 7 March 2013, http://www.telegraph.co.uk/finance/newsbysector/retailandconsumer/9914686/John-Lewis-pays-staff-more-than-200m-in-bonuses-for-first-time.html (accessed 14 May 2014); John Lewis official website, http://www.johnlewispartnership.co.uk/content/dam/cws/pdfs/our%20responsibilities/our%20employees/Guide_to_Employee_Ownership.pdf (accessed 14 May 2014); N. Thomas, 'easyJet Pays £175m Special Dividend as Profits Rise 51pc', *The Telegraph*, 19 November 2013, http://www.telegraph.co.uk/finance/newsbysector/transport/10458896/easyJet-pays-175m-special-dividend-as-profits-rise-51pc.html (accessed 14 May 2014).
23	Chinese foreign exchange hedging	D. Tsang and B. Robertson, 'Nervous China Factory Owners Hedge on Yuan Foreign Exchange Risk', *South China Morning Post,* 18 March 2014, http://www.scmp.com/business/banking-finance/article/1451135/nervous-china-factory-owners-hedge-yuan-foreign-exchange (accessed 18 March 2014); F. Li, 'Yuan Tumbles to 11-month Low as Band Widening Spurs Volatility', *Bloomberg*, 17 March 2014, http://www.bloomberg.com/news/2014-03-17/yuan-volatility-climbs-to-18-month-high-as-trading-band-doubles.html (accessed 31 March 2014).

24   Opening up the Saudi market   P. Kohli, 'Will the Saudi Market Finally Open to the West?', *Market Watch*, 15 January 2014, http://www.marketwatch.com/story/will-the-saudi-market-finally-open-to-the-west-2014-01-15?pagenumber=1 (accessed 18 March 2014); 'TADAWUL: Shares Worth SR8.7bn Traded', *Arab News*, 24 March 2014, http://www.arabnews.com/news/544881 (accessed 25 March 2014); Tadawul Official Site, http://www.tadawul.com.sa/wps/portal/!ut/p/c1/04_SB8K8xLLM9MSSzPy8xBz9CP0os3g_A-ewIE8TIwP3gDBTA08Tn2Cj4AAvY_dQA_3g1Dz9gmxHRQCHg5RU/ (accessed 26 March 2014).

INDEX